ENEMIES, A LOVE STORY

Enemies, a Love Story

Mizrahi-Arab-Ashkenazi Relations Since the Dawn of Zionism

HILLEL COHEN

Translated by Haim Watzman

The Pennsylvania State University Press
University Park, Pennsylvania

Library of Congress Cataloging-in-Publication Data

Names: Cohen, Hillel author | Watzman, Haim translator
Title: Enemies, a love story : Mizrahi-Arab-Ashkenazi relations since the dawn of Zionism / Hillel Cohen ; translated by Haim Watzman.
Other titles: Śon'im, sipur ahavah. English
Description: University Park, Pennsylvania : The Pennsylvania State University Press, [2025] | Originally published in Hebrew: Tel Aviv: Ivrit Hotsaah la-Or, 2022. | Includes bibliographical references and index.
Identifiers: LCCN 2025039203 | ISBN 9780271099897 hardback | ISBN 9780271099958 paperback
Subjects: LCSH: Mizrahim—Israel | Jews—Israel—Identity | National characteristics, Israeli | Group identity—Israel | Ashkenazim—Israel | Palestinian Arabs—Israel
Classification: LCC DS113.8.S4 C6413 2025
LC record available at https://lccn.loc.gov/2025039203

Printed in the United States of America
Published by The Pennsylvania State University Press, University Park, PA 16802–1003

Originally published in Hebrew as Hillel Cohen, שונאים סיפור אהבה: על מזרחים וערבים (ואשכנזים גם) מראשית הציונות ועד מאורעות תשפ"א (Enemies, a love story: On Mizrahi Jews and Palestinians [and Ashkenazi Jews] from the rise of Zionism to the present) (Tel Aviv: Ivrit Hotsaah la-Or, 2022).

The Pennsylvania State University Press is a member of the Association of University Presses.

It is the policy of The Pennsylvania State University Press to use acid-free paper. Publications on uncoated stock satisfy the minimum requirements of American National Standard for Information Sciences—Permanence of Paper for Printed Library Material, ANSI Z39.48–1992.

To my loved ones

CONTENTS

PREFACE

This book was written in 2021–22 and was published in Hebrew in a different Israel, a pre–October 7 Israel, before the Hamas attack and massacres and before the Israeli counterattack in Gaza. This was an Israel that was more self-confident and less isolated internationally, an Israel that thought the Palestinian problem had disappeared. It was also an Israel that suffered from substantial internal divisions, including the one between Mizrahi Jews—that is, Jews whose origin is the Muslim world—and Ashkenazim, Jews of European origin, a division that is at the center of this book.

This sociopolitical division has manifested itself in recent years, both symbolically and practically, in the political rivalry between Benjamin Netanyahu's supporters and his opponents, a rivalry with strong ethnic dimensions. Mizrahi Jews, primarily though not exclusively from the lower-middle classes, constituted an important component in the camp of Netanyahu's supporters, while secular Ashkenazim of the upper-middle classes formed the backbone of the camp of his opponents. This ethnic division was expressed in the stormy demonstrations against the legal reform initiated by the Netanyahu government sworn in in December 2022, but also in the debate regarding the "Palestinian Question." For many in the Netanyahu camp, the label "Ashkenazi" symbolizes progressive ideas, detachment from the reality of the Middle East, a failure to understand Netanyahu's historical greatness as a leader, and naïve support for a reconciliation with the Palestinians. This image has become so entrenched that even Ashkenazim who are located on the right of the political map, like Major General Gershon HaCohen, operate within its premises. "A country without national pride will have no existence, and the Ashkenazim do not understand this," HaCohen said in a television interview.[1]

In recent years, two opposing concepts of patriotism took shape in Israel, which were reflected in the fight over what the government called judicial reform and the opposition referred to as constitutional revolution. At the height of the struggle between the blocs, dozens of air force pilots announced that they would stop volunteering for reserve service—beyond what they are legally required to do—if the government continued with the reform/revolution.[2] For them, this step was aimed at saving Israeli democracy. For others, it was a move taken by a privileged Ashkenazi stratum, with the aim of overturning a democratic decision by the citizens of Israel, who had elected Netanyahu as prime minister and supported the legal reform moves he led.

Then, in the midst of the crisis, came the Hamas attack of October 7, 2023. Kibbutzim, moshavim and development towns, and army camps were attacked by thousands of Hamas fighters. They killed more than twelve hundred Israeli soldiers and civilians—an unprecedented number in Israel's history—wounded hundreds more, sexually assaulted women and men, and took more than two hundred soldiers and civilians hostage. The tragedy was intensified by the slow reaction of the Israel Defense Forces (IDF), whose fighting units did not reach the many arenas of combat for a long time, and thus many civilians were left exposed and unarmed to confront the attack. On the same day, Israel began its counterattack in the Gaza Strip—in which tens of thousands of Palestinians have been killed, many of them noncombatants—without succeeding, as of this writing in February 2025, in defeating Hamas.

For the Israelis, the attack was an unprecedented trauma, a crisis of enormous magnitude, but also a moment of potential unity. On the day of the event and shortly thereafter, the deep divisions that tore Israeli society—the dispute over the proposed legal reform and the disputes between Right and Left, religious and secular, and Mizrahim and Ashkenazim—were forgotten. The disagreements about the appropriate way to deal with the Palestinians also disappeared almost completely. In the face of the brutal attack by Hamas, the general opinion among Israelis was: we must unite and respond with all our might. The internal Jewish ethnic discourse, which is the focus of this book, went silent. In the words of Education Minister Yoav Kisch, who put forward a bill to establish a "Unity Day," "These haters [Hamas] don't care if you're right-wing or left-wing, if you're secular, ultra-Orthodox, if you're gay, if you're straight. They don't care if you're Ashkenazi, if you're Moroccan. They look at us as one piece, as one unified nation, and we too must see the unifier within ourselves as a part that strengthens us and leads us to meet the challenges before us."[3]

Indeed, many in Israel hoped for unity after a year of demonstrations and counterdemonstrations surrounding the proposed juridical reform and the question of the place of religion in public life in Israel, fully aware of the class and ethnic nature of these disputes. The war made such unity, or at least the appearance of such unity, possible. One moment stands out and has become iconic. On the night of November 26, 2023, thirteen hostages were released from Hamas captivity, almost all of them from kibbutzim. As detailed in the book, there has been tension between the primarily Ashkenazi kibbutzim and the Mizrahi towns surrounding them for many years: disputes over municipal borders, a socioeconomic gap that originates in the kibbutzim's control over the means of production, and deep divergences in worldviews. In recent years, residents in the towns have also organized demonstrations in front of the kibbutzim. Therefore, the initiative of the people of the town of Ofakim and the moshavim to stand along the road with Israeli flags and greeting signs, and to warmly and joyfully welcome the abducted kibbutzniks who returned, was seen as a moment of grace and perhaps a sign of change.

And so the triangle of relations between Mizrahim, Ashkenazim, and Palestinians, which this book deals with, was *seemingly* reshaped following the events of October 7. A united Jewish-Israeli identity had formed in the face of the attack. It was an identity united against the Palestinians, in which the intra-Jewish rift narrowed; the dispute over the possibility of peace with the Palestinians—which was considered part of the Ashkenazi-Mizrahi divide—had become moot and the ethnic intra-Jewish discourse was as good as gone.

This, though, was merely temporary. The welcome reception for the freed kibbutzniks indicated good intentions and a desire for unity, but the war did not erase the old social, cultural, and economic divisions and structures. And so, when the secretary-general of the Kibbutz Movement expressed his excitement at this gesture, he also added—in answer to a question—that the townspeople were not invited to the kibbutz for a barbecue. "The kibbutz yard is the home of the kibbutzniks and not a public space," he said.[4] This was perceived as saying: do not forget the profound differences between our respective communities, between Ashkenazi and Mizrahi cultures.

In the Israeli parliament, the Knesset, ethnic tensions have continued to reverberate. In January 2024, during the same meeting in which "Unity Day" was proposed, a long and difficult exchange took place on the topic of Mizrahi political identity and representation. David Amsalem, a member of the right-wing Likud party who sees himself as a key spokesperson of Mizrahim and Mizrahiness, attacked those who criticized him (on other matters) as racists, sparking an intense debate between himself and other Mizrahi members of the Knesset on the question of whether only right-wingers represent Mizrahiness authentically. This was another sign that ethnic discourse is not disappearing, despite the tragic events of the preceding months and the new desire for Jewish-Israeli unity.

In the last chapter of this book, I discuss the ways in which the Likud acts in order to consolidate the Mizrahi public around Benjamin Netanyahu.

What we can conclude from the Knesset meetings of January 2024 is that despite the prevalent discourse on unity, the events of October 7 did not change this pattern of political conduct, nor did they significantly undermine ethnic and social identities. As this book suggests, the long history of Mizrahi-Palestinian-Ashkenazi relations still has a lot to teach us.

NOTE ON THE TRANSLATION

Translating a book and transmitting ideas from one language to another, and from one world of meaning to another, necessarily means facing gaps that are not only linguistic but also terminological. Haim Watzman, the translator, and I managed to bridge the majority of these gaps using alternative terms, and, when necessary, adding explanations. One concept is unusual in its translational complexity, and this is the concept of "settlement." The word's definition in Hebrew holds different historical meanings and means different things to different groups in Israeli society.

At the beginning of Zionism—that is, from the days of the First Aliyah (a wave of Zionist immigration to Palestine) in 1882 until the occupation of the territories in 1967—the Hebrew terms *hityashvut* and *hitnahalut* were used synonymously and were both translated as "settlement." After the 1967 war, however, a distinction was made between the Hebrew terms *hityashvut* and *hitnahalut*. While the former remained the main term for Jewish settlement pre-1967 and within the pre-1967 borders, the latter was used to distinguish the Jewish localities established in the Occupied Territories. This term was originally used by both the supporters of the settlements in these areas and their opponents, but supporters of the settlements gradually preferred to call their places of residence by the general term *hityashvut* in order not to exclude them from the Israeli consensus. In addition, it should be noted that the settlements in the post-1967 sense were declared illegal by the United Nations, while the settlements within Israel's pre-1967 borders are considered legal. Thus the same concept in English signifies two different phenomena in terms of international politics and Israeli politics alike. It should be noted also that in Arabic two terms are used interchangeably—*must'amara* and *mustawtana*—to refer both to settlements within the recognized borders of Israel and to those in the Occupied Territories (although the PLO distinguishes between them when discussing political arrangements in an official context).

Here, then, a certain responsibility rests on the reader: he or she should pay attention when reading the term not only to the period in question but also to the speaker.

ACKNOWLEDGMENTS

This book was written while in ongoing conversation with many people. Some of these communications were direct and took the form of conversations, correspondence, and sitting together. Others were indirect and came from perusing written sources, including polemics, poetry, and social media posts. I did not read these sources as part of a research project. I took an interest and sometimes participated in long-running exchanges on ethnicity and discrimination, social justice, Mizrahim and Palestinians, political violence, racism on the part of Jews toward other kinds of Jews and toward non-Jews on the left and on the right, and the like. While these conversations do not appear as such in the book, it is through them that I came to understand something of the tensions between different views of Mizrahiness among Mizrahim and others, and I learned about the variety of Mizrahi perceptions of "Arabness." By that term I mean the entire complex of Arab culture, society, and identity in the Israeli-Jewish context.

Several people read parts or all of my manuscript and made helpful comments. Amos Noy, as usual, expanded my horizons—I could write another whole volume on the subject on the basis of his observations. Itamar Tubi Taharlev offered interesting sociological insights. Yifat Mehl drew my attention to awkward and sometimes biased passages. Tamir Karkason offered his thoughts on chapter 1, and Avner Wishnitzer shared the intricacies of his thoughts on the question of modernity. Through the eyes of Efrat Cohen-Bar and Ahikam Baruchi, I was able to get a sense of how the book would be read by interested nonacademic readers. Ron Dudai, as always, got me to see past some of my blind spots—though I'm sure some remain—for which I'm grateful.

It would be impossible for me to list all the people whose ideas and insights helped me think through the Mizrahi-Arab question, and I'm sure that some have slipped my memory. The list that follows is thus necessarily incomplete. In my notes, in accordance with accepted practice, I reference sources that I made direct use of. Here, I make note mostly of those I did not quote from, those that sent me to an interesting source, those who sent me relevant material or spoke to me about the subject, and many others from whom I learned indirectly, without their cognizance, in some cases on Facebook, sometimes by identifying with and accepting their arguments, or by debating them or opposing them in my own thoughts. I want to thank both kinds of sources, and both those I have forgotten and those who come readily to mind: Avi-Ram Tzoreff, Ophir Toubul, Orit Bashkin, Orit Vaknin-Yekutieli, Orly Noy, Iris Hefetz Amsalem, Albert Suissa, Alona Miryam Illouz, Eli Bareket, Amnon Raz-Krakotzkin, Benny Zada, Gadi Algazi, David Amsalem, Hila Shalem Baharad, Haggai Ram, Haya Bambaji-Sasportas, Khen Elmaleh, Yair Wallach, Yali Hashash, Yehouda Shenhav, Yuval Evri, Yonit Palomba-Naaman, Yael Gidanyan, Lihi Yona, Meir Babayof, Meir Buzaglo, Meir Amor, Meirav Aharon Gutman, Moshe (Shiko) Behar, Menashe Anzi, Matanel Buzaglo, Nadav Cohen, Noa Shaindlinger, Natalie Baruch, Netta Hazan, Nissim Mizrachi, Sigal Davidi, Smadar Lavie, Sami Shalom Chetrit, Ido Cohen, Uzi Levia, Ammiel Alcalay, Omri Sheffer Raviv, Amram Ben-Yishai, Zvi Ben-Dor Benite, Racheli Said, Rafael Balulu, Shabtai (Shabi) Amedi, Shoshana Gabay, Shai Orr, Shai Hazkani, Tom Mehager, and Tammy Riklis. Just as all have their own names, so they all have their own faces and opinions. I apologize to those with whom I spoke or whom I read but whose names escaped my memory as I wrote, and to those I have misunderstood. Any errors in this book are mine alone.

I researched and wrote this book without any direct financial support, yet it rests on public funding. As an employee of the Hebrew University, I receive my salary from the public purse, along with the opportunity to take time for writing. I am therefore grateful to the public and its purse.

This is a work both of history and of current events, written by the person I am: a Jew of Jerusalem of Afghan-Polish extraction (that is, neither Ashkenazi nor Mizrahi in the full sense of either term). Furthermore, I speak fluent Arabic and generally feel comfortable in Arab spaces. I was educated in Ashkenazi religious Zionist schools but fled from them. I'm halfway traditional in Jewish observance and switch back and forth among Ashkenazi, Mizrahi, and left-wing discourses. I feel a connection to all these groups but don't belong fully to any one of them. To a certain extent, my fluid attitude toward Mizrahi and Ashkenazi culture, to the Mizrahi struggle for equality, to the Jewish-Arab nexus, to the Palestinian struggle, and to the question of Jewish solidarity—with all the tensions that these attitudes incorporate—is what has motivated my writing of this book and what shapes it. So, while I am not writing about myself, the book does have a dimension of internal, personal investigation.

Like my previous books, this one was written at home, on the living room table and the kitchen table, usually with Efrat around, and our children Aya, Avshalom, and Osnat as well. They know that they can speak to me while I am at my computer, and when I ask for a moment of quiet so that I can concentrate, they generally comply. To all four of them, my thanks and love for their benevolent presence.

Introduction

It was the night marking the end of the weeklong Pesach holiday of the Jewish year 5781, the Gregorian year 2021. As Maghrebi Jewish communities commenced celebrating their Mimouna festival, I opened a new Word file and gave it the title "On Mizrahim and Arabs (and Ashkenazim, Too): The Book." If I could harness my faculties, one line would become two and then three and beyond, pages would accumulate, and one chapter would follow another. It would swell and shrink, undergo cuts and augmentations, get edited and reedited, as manuscripts do. It would no doubt include obscure sentences (may they be clarified) and needless paragraphs (may they be struck out). It would omit events and people (not intentionally; that's the nature of writing), yet it would contain errors and misunderstandings (very few, I hope). There would be important issues that I would neglect to address (you can't include everything), and perhaps incorrect commentary on acts and processes. I could only pray, as did King David, may peace be on him, "Who can be aware of errors? Clear me of unperceived guilt" (Ps. 19:13). That meant taking on a commitment to seek to understand people whose actions are not in line with my own views and to empathize with those I disagree with. The purpose was not to paper over injustices but rather to increase understanding in the world.

These initial lines are being written at a time of political uncertainty in Israel, after the national elections of March 2021 and before the formation of a government. This was the fourth round of elections in just two years. By the time these pages reach the printer, that will be a distant memory. As I write, however, the political system is at the height of an ongoing drama. Will Benjamin Netanyahu be able to form a government, or will the task of doing so be assigned to someone else? Will the system stabilize? Will the new government pursue policies different from those of its predecessor? Whatever the case, the issue of the Mizrahi vote is in the air. On the center-left, the question is voiced in frustration: why can't we get the Mizrahim—Jews whose origins lie in the Islamic world—to vote for us? Alternatively, sometimes, it comes along with the conviction that, time and again, they vote for the parties that want to screw them. On the right, it takes the form of a natural law, a fact that requires no explanation—Mizrahim are right-wingers because they know what's best for the Jewish people, and Binyamin Netanyahu is the leader who best represents them.

The underlying subject of this book is Mizrahi-Arab relations. As such, it addresses voting patterns and political leanings largely when they show something about positions regarding or affecting the Palestinian question. Scholars and political activists—Mizrahim, Ashkenazim, and Palestinians—have for decades been asking what lies behind the Mizrahi penchant for the political Right (with regard, of course, to those Mizrahim who display that preference). They offer a range of answers. Some claim that the Mizrahim harbor anti-Arab sentiments that they brought over from the Arab lands they came from; others point to Mizrahi opposition to Israel's old elites, which are seen as both too liberal and anti-Mizrahi. Another explanation is the Mizrahim's ties to religion and tradition, still another that voting for right-wing parties is a way of expressing love for the Jewish people and the Land of Israel, and yet another is that the Mizrahim do so as a way of shaking off their Arabic heritage, which they see as shameful. Some maintain that it's not their origins that point them to the Right but rather their socioeconomic position. We'll consider the insights of a range of people, the analyses they've written, and the fantasies they have floated over the years.

This most recent election introduced a new factor that complicated the question. The southern wing of the Islamic Movement ran on its own, rather than as part of the United Arab List, as it had in four of the previous five contests. As of this writing, the party is being courted by both the right-wing and centrist camps. Politicians and public figures, among them Mizrahim and right-wingers who have thus far shown no interest in joining up with Arab parties, have begun to talk about the possibility of cooperation. There is nothing wrong with a Jewish-Arab alliance, they say, especially when the Arab party involved is Islamic, not Palestinian nationalist. They cite the common principles that Islam and the traditionalist Right share—family values, conservatism, and respect for religion—and they highlight the pragmatism of the United Arab List.[1] By the time the book goes to press, we may know whether there was something to these political visions.

These thoughts are the product of the present political moment, but the book was not written in the immediate context of the recent rounds of elections. Rather, its backdrop is several brutal acts of violence that took place in recent years in which Mizrahim were involved. These cases brought the Mizrahi-Arab question to the fore. Was it simply a coincidence that Eden Natan-Zada, who shot and killed four people in Shefa-Amr in 2005 as he sought to avert Israel's disengagement from the Gaza Strip, was Mizrahi? That the killers of the boy Mohammed Abu Khdeir in Jerusalem in 2014 were Mizrahim? Was it just by chance that Elor Azaria, a soldier who shot and killed a wounded stabber in Hebron in 2016 was Mizrahi? What about the fact that the arsonists who set fire to the Hand in Hand bilingual Jewish-Arab school in Jerusalem were Mizrahim? Did Yigal Amir's Mizrahi ethnicity play a role in his decision to assassinate Prime Minister Yitzhak Rabin? Ashkenazim, such as Baruch Goldstein, have also murdered Arabs. Was their ethnic affiliation also significant?

These questions have been the subject of animated debate, as have the issues of when it is relevant to cite the ethnicity of a political lawbreaker, at what point ethnic origin fades from the public consciousness, when killing is to be considered unacceptable violence and when it is to be seen as a sacred duty, and who is referencing the ethnic origin of a lawbreaker and to what end. Another point of debate is whether ethnic origin is a central factor in shaping the consciousness of violent extremists, or whether socioeconomic class and attitude toward religion are more influential. Furthermore, some claim that Mizrahim maintain better, more humane, and warmer relations with Arabs, except at moments of crisis. Others stress the attempts by some (fringe) Mizrahi groups to forge a Mizrahi-Palestinian alliance.

This is the field that the present book addresses, but in order to plow it deeply, it offers a journey through the Mizrahi-Arab-Ashkenazi triangle from the dawn of Zionism (actually, a bit before that) to today, a period of more than 150 years. During this time, Jewish-Arab and Mizrahi-Arab relations have metamorphosed considerably and in interesting ways. Before hitching up the plow, I want to present the fundamental questions on which the book is founded and some of its basic assumptions.

QUESTIONS AND ASSUMPTIONS

A fundamental assumption, without which there would be no point in writing this book, is that Mizrahi attitudes toward the Arabs and the Palestinian issue differ from Ashkenazi attitudes. In other words, I presume here that ethnic affiliation shapes political consciousness and the nature of social bonds with Arabs. This assumption is not a sweeping one, however. It does not suggest that this is the central or only variable. Rather, it accepts the common intuition in Israeli society that ethnic origin affects emotional and political positions with regard to Arabs. Other research assumptions are:

1. An ethnic identity's effects are not one-dimensional—rather, it can push an individual in different and even contrary directions. In the case at hand, this means that being Mizrahi can induce anti-Arab sentiments, but it can also imbue a person with a sense of intimacy toward Arabs. These sentiments can coexist in a single individual, who may cycle from one to the other and back again.
2. The way in which an ethnic identity manifests itself in attitudes toward another group is not necessarily fixed and can change over time.
3. This ethnically colored attitude toward the Palestinians and positions on policy affecting them is not only a response to the Palestinians. It also responds to intra-Jewish relations—that is, the interethnic dynamic among Jews. This is a result of the fact that being Mizrahi does not engender a uniform set of values. Rather, it is dynamic and complex—central for some individuals, negligible for others, and most often variable in the presence of the Other. Its substance is shaped and reshaped over time and in response to changes in relations between different groups. It can engender different sets of values, which contest one another in the discourse among activists and thinkers within and outside the Mizrahi group.

WHAT IS A "MIZRAHI ACT"?

A challenge I faced during my research and writing was the question of what events, views, and actions could be termed Mizrahi and thus be included in my story and analysis. Clearly, it would not be reasonable to analyze every act and every pronouncement of every person, of every ethnic origin, in an ethnic context. For example, both Ashkenazim and Mizrahim vote for the Likud under the leadership of Binyamin Netanyahu. Are the Mizrahim casting Mizrahi votes and the Ashkenazim casting nonethnic votes? There is a tendency in Israeli discourse today to view the votes of Mizrahim as ethnic votes, certainly when they vote for the Right. But what justifies this, other than a gut feeling? And why should an Ashkenazi vote for the Likud not be seen as an ethnic vote?

To answer this question, I propose a definition of a "Mizrahi act," one that can also, with the appropriate adjustments, define an "Ashkenazi act," should those ever be studied. In this book, I will take acts and views to be Mizrahi if they meet one of two conditions: (1) The person who performs or affirms them states them to be such; and (2) they are seen, from an external perspective, to derive from Mizrahi ethnicity. The cases of the first instance can be used to study how Mizrahim think of themselves; those of the second instance will be used to understand the general Israeli discourse on the Mizrahi community. The book thus includes, for example, the case of Yona Avrushmi, who cast the grenade that killed peace demonstrator Emil Grunzweig in 1983. Avrushmi declared, in an interview with Sara Leibowitz-Dar, that it had been a "Mizrahi act." Mizrahi activists, among them members of the Black Panthers, met with representatives of the PLO in the 1970s and 1980s and declared explicitly that they did so as Mizrahim. A similar explicit connection is made by those who fill out survey questionnaires about their social and political views on the Arab question and check the Mizrahi box in the ethnic affiliation section. These are all examples of self-definition.

But gaining a deeper understanding of the Mizrahi-Arab-Ashkenazi triangle necessitates the inclusion of acts and statements that are defined as Mizrahi by observers. Here are some examples of such statements: "The fundamental reason [why Arabs were attacked in Netanya], in my opinion, is the especially sharp sensitivity of members of Edot Hamizrah [Mizrahi community] in the area of a woman's honor" (Arab affairs advisor Shmuel Toledano, 1966); "Like the rest of their brethren, they are entirely Arab in their speech, their mores, their commerce, and everything else" (*Hapoel Hatzair*, a socialist Zionist newspaper in Palestine, on Sephardim in Haifa, 1910); "Like glass vessels, which take on the color of the materials within them, so do [the Sephardim] always tilt toward the strongest side" (*Filastin*, a Palestinian Arab newspaper, 1921); Mizrahi Jews "complained bitterly about how they were treated by the Western Jews, and expressed a strong desire to receive our protection" (Fawzi al-Qawuqji, commander of the Rescue Army, 1948). I will analyze all these and many other such cases in their context, as I present a variety of events, on the basis of a wealth of sources, pronouncements, feelings, and actions. I will consider what Mizrahiness—a term that comprehends the ethnic and cultural character and identity of Mizrahim—means to those who act in its name (for the most part with regard to Arabs), and what it constitutes as others see it. I will examine interrelations among Mizrahim, Palestinians, and Ashkenazim from Mizrahi, Palestinian, and Ashkenazi perspectives.

ETHNICITY IN CONTEMPORARY ISRAEL

I now take a small step backward. What I have written above is based on the assumption that ethnic identities remain meaningful in early twenty-first-century Israel. For many, that is an axiom that needs no proof. Many others across the range of the ethnic spectrum, however, claim that these identities are no longer meaningful. Some point to the emergence of a Mizrahi middle class as proof that ethnic origin is no longer relevant; others note that the large number of interethnic marriages shows that these identities are breaking down or becoming more restricted. Furthermore, the salient presence of Mizrahim in Israel's political, economic, and security leadership, they argue, proves that these identities are dissolving.

These are important but not persuasive claims. Israel's political and social milieux clearly display the salient character of ethnic identities for both individuals and the public. This can be seen not only in voting patterns and partisan discourse but also in reality TV shows that explicitly perpetuate ethnic stereotypes, in the underrepresentation of Mizrahim (Mizrahi women in particular) on the Supreme Court and among the ranks of faculty at universities, in measures of education and income, and in ethnic stereotypes in advertising.[2] The discourse about the ethnic question gives a central place to the question of Mizrahi attitudes toward Arabs, and to the role of the Ashkenazim in shaping these attitudes. As these are identities with roots in the past, they demand a historical examination of the reciprocal systems among them, and these processes must be tracked over time.

TERMINOLOGY: SEPHARDIM, EDOT HAMIZRAH, MIZRAHIM

Several terms naming Jews from the Islamic world and their descendants are current in Israeli discourse. The usage of the variants differs over time, and each variant bears explicit and implicit connotations. At the beginning of the period covered in this book, the most common term for Jews of Islamic culture was "Sephardim." This was because descendants of Jews exiled at the end of the fifteenth century from Spain—*Sefarad* in Hebrew—became the leaders of the Jewish communities they settled in, including Palestine. Furthermore, in Palestine they saw themselves as the guardians of all Jews from the Islamic lands—those from Iraq, North Africa, the Persian-Afghan-Bukharan region, and elsewhere. In Palestine under the British Mandate, the common term in Hebrew parlance was *Edot Hamizrah*, the Eastern or Oriental communities. Sometimes the terms were used together in the form "Sephardim and Edot Hamizrah," which was also the name of the "ethnic" slate that won seats in Israel's Constituent Assembly in 1948. The term "Mizrahim" was also used here and there. That term became much more current four decades after Israel's birth, but there are groups and organizations that continue to employ the term "Sephardim." That is the case, for example, with the Shas party, the full name of which is the Worldwide Sephardic Association of Torah Guardians. What is common to all these terms on the factual level is that they all mean "not Ashkenazi." It's important to keep in mind that the emotional and political connotations of each of them have changed over time, as has the definition of what it means to be Ashkenazi and attitudes toward that term.

CONTINUITY FROM THE OTTOMAN PERIOD?

The change in terminology is a subject in and of itself, but substantive social and political changes also, so it seems, undermine this book's underlying claim of continuity from the dawn of institutionalized Zionism to the present day. The counterclaim can be stated in the form of a question: are the identities of the nineteenth-century Sephardim of Jerusalem, Tiberias, and Hebron linked to those of today's Mizrahim robustly enough to warrant treating them as a single group in this book? After all, in the late Ottoman period, the Sephardim of Palestine were the elite of the country's Jewish population in terms of education, status, and economic power. In contrast, the immigrants from the Islamic world who arrived in Israel in the 1950s and 1960s were relegated to the social, economic, and geographical periphery, and some of them remain there today. What is it that conjoins these groups? Furthermore, over this long period, Ottoman rule gave way to British rule, which in turn gave way to the independent Jewish state. And there were also major transformations in the power structure within the Jewish community. Mapai (from 1968 the Labor Party) led the Yishuv (the pre-state Jewish community in Palestine) and then the state for its first three decades, until it was ejected from power in 1977. These changes challenge the logic of presenting interethnic Jewish relations and the relations between Sephardim/Mizrahim and Arabs as a continuum from the start of the Zionist era to today. Moreover, there were significant cultural developments over these years. During the British Mandate, Mizrahi culture was shunted off to the margins, and it remained there for many years after the State of Israel came into being. But in recent years it has become a central component of Israeli culture, if only because of demographic shifts and the increasing political clout of the Mizrahim. What is the point, then, of placing such heterogeneous groups, which operated then and operate now under such different conditions, into a single analytic framework?

These are all pertinent questions, deserving appropriate answers. First, the very nature of the writing of history is to point out changes over time. This means that difference is not a reason to refrain from writing history. On the contrary, the differences stimulate writing that analyzes the processes of change. Nevertheless, there is reason to write history only if it is possible also to show continuity. In the case under study, this means a continuity of identity stretching from the Sephardim of the late Ottoman period and the Mandate and the Mizrahim of the State of Israel. There is certainly such continuity. In fact, as I will show, only a small portion of the Sephardim and Oriental Jews in Palestine prior to the coming of Zionism were members of the elite, and only a fraction of the members of that elite maintained their standing and bequeathed it to their descendants. Indeed, most of the Sephardim and Edot Hamizrah belonged to the lower class, and their socioeconomic peripherality became fixed during the Mandate, as scholars have shown, and as I will show below.[3] In this sense, there is clearly continuity between the lower Sephardi-Mizrahi class before the mass waves of immigration and thereafter.

And there are other manifestations of this continuity of identification. The most fundamental is the persistence of distinct Sephardi and Ashkenazi identities that have faced off against each other throughout this period, even as the power relations between them changed. Also significant is the ongoing discourse about the tension between the ideal of unity of the Jewish people and the existence of rival ethnic communities within it. What is germane to this book is the long-standing discourse about Sephardi-Mizrahi relations with Arabs. Furthermore, as the Zionist movement was founded in Europe, it looked on the Jews of the East as Others, not Europeans. This attitude endures in many ways to this day. The socialist Zionist vanguard of the Second Aliyah, the wave of Zionist immigration from 1904 to 1914, sought to utterly demolish the world of traditional Judaism and create a new, secular, proletarian Jewish nation. In this context, their gaze from the outside on Sephardi and Eastern Jews became an arrogant one. The ethnic discourse of the Zionist labor movement was pressed into a dichotomous template—revolutionary zeal and initiative versus rockbound traditionalism, and activist

Zionism versus indifference to Jewish nationalism. While this attitude has diminished in recent years, it has not entirely disappeared.

Moreover, Mizrahim (or Sephardim) fashioned, from the beginning of the Zionist era, three principal approaches to the Arab question, each growing out of their identity. While the relative weight among them has changed over time, they are all still in play today. The first places Mizrahiness, in particular familiarity with Arab language and culture, at the service of European Zionism, without any manifestation of ambiguity. The second sees Mizrahiness as a possible bridge between Jews and Arabs that can help create understanding between Jews and Palestinians. This approach comes in two versions—a Zionist version that believes that it is possible to mediate between Zionism and the Arabs, and an a-Zionist one that seeks a Mizrahi-Arab alliance based on Jewish-Arab equality while challenging Zionism. The third approach is anti-Arab Mizrahiness. This approach promotes the use of force, on the grounds that Mizrahim are familiar with Arab culture and thus know that peace and mutual trust are impossible. This approach links up with the doctrine of Jewish supremacy. The movement along this range, over the course of more than a century, is one of this book's axes.

ARE THE MIZRAHIM A SINGLE COMMUNITY?

It's an important question. As Mizrahi activists and scholars have shown, Mizrahi identity today is a product of life in the State of Israel. And, as I propose in this book, two melting pots simmered during the country's initial decades. The first was the pot that melded the immigrants from the Islamic world into a Mizrahi community; the second stirred immigrants from Europe into an Ashkenazi community. In the latter case, however, the original distinctions between Lithuanian, Galician, and Polish Jews (to name just a few of the Ashkenazi groups) gradually disappeared, except among the Haredim, the ultra-Orthodox Jews, who managed to stay out of the melting pot. In contrast, Mizrahi identities—such as Persian, Moroccan, and Yemenite—persist in many dimensions of Israeli life, from personal identity to stereotypes in common use in daily life and standup-comedy routines (the stingy Persian, short-tempered Moroccan, pajama-clad Iraqi). The view of the Mizrahim as a single group is thus somewhat oversimplified. In this book I will briefly address the different voting patterns of Israelis of Moroccan and Iraqi origin; I will also note the relatively easy absorption of Iraqi and Syrian immigrants into the security establishment, thanks to the relative similarity of their Arabic dialects to that spoken by Palestinian Arabs. This was an asset that Moroccan and other North African Jews lacked. An in-depth study of differing attitudes toward the Palestinian question (and other issues) among Mizrahi subgroups may well be worth pursuing. My lack of detail on this issue marks a certain weakness of my book. And there are other weaknesses as well, some of them deriving from the limitations of the framework I have chosen and the sources available to me, and others from my own inadequacies.

STRUCTURE

The book runs roughly chronologically, as befits a historical journey. The first chapter examines the Sephardi-Arab-Ashkenazi encounter at the end of the Ottoman period, the time in which both the Zionist movement and the Arab national movement established themselves. This was, in a sense, the golden age of Sephardi-Arab relations: the Ottoman Empire announced its new policy of interreligious equality and Jews of the Middle East integrated into public life, and a few also into the Arab national movement. At the very same time, the nascent European Zionist movement started its activity in Palestine / Eretz Israel, declaring its hope to reestablish the Jewish kingdom there. The chapter explores changes in Jewish-Muslim relations following the rise of Zionism, the variety of Jewish attitudes toward the "Arab question," and the role of culture (European vis-à-vis "Oriental") in shaping these attitudes. In this period, the concept of Sephardi/Mizrahi Jews as a bridge between European Zionism and the Arabs of Palestine was created, together with the notion of difference in Jews' attitudes toward the Arabs of Palestine, Sephardim being more attentive to the Arabs' sentiments of belonging to Palestine.

Chapter 2 moves into the Mandate period, when the labor movement—composed mainly of eastern European pioneers—gained hegemony in the Jewish Yishuv. During this time, social and political fissures appeared along ethnic lines, and a Mizrahi lower class was created. The national tension between the Arabs of Palestine and Zionists was manifested in waves of anti-Zionist violence. As many of the Jewish victims were of Sephardi origin, this phase of the conflict created a new Mizrahi anti-Arab sentiment: "As natives of the Middle East, we know that Arabs understand only power" became a common saying. On the other hand, the Palestinian Arabs felt betrayed by the Mizrahi and Sephardi Jews, who supported Zionism despite what the Arabs perceived as neighborly relations throughout the years. The participation of Mizrahi Jews in the War of 1948—the Palestinian catastrophe (Nakba)—was perceived as evidence of their treacherous nature.

The period between the founding of the state in 1948 and the Six-Day War of 1967, including the years of the mass immigration that followed independence, lies at the center of chapter 3, in which I address absorption policy and the Mizrahi-Arab encounter (in particular in the mixed cities) and the discourse surrounding it. The main question I consider here is whether Mizrahi Jews were indeed more violent toward Arabs than Ashkenazim were. If so, why? And if not, what were the sources of this image circulating in popular media at the time? Interestingly enough, during these years, in which the post-Nakba Palestinian national movement was established (first through Fatah and later through the Palestine Liberation Organization), the idea of an alliance between the victims of Zionism (i.e., Palestinians and Mizrahim) began to take hold in Palestinian circles.

Chapter 4 takes up the decade between 1967 and the political upheaval of 1977, when the right-wing Likud, with notable support from the Mizrahi population, defeated the Labor Party. Its main subject is Mizrahi-Arab relations in the context of Israeli rule over the territories that Israel had occupied in the Six-Day War. What kind of social relations were created between Mizrahim and Palestinians? How did changes in the labor market influence Mizrahi-Ashkenazi-Arab relations? How did Palestinian terror attacks shape Mizrahi views of the Palestinians? What was the influence of the Israeli Black Panthers on Israeli politics and Israeli-Palestinian relations? And how were Mizrahi Jews seen by the Palestinians during these years?

Chapter 5 covers the period from the Likud's rise to power in 1977 to the assassination of Prime Minister Yitzhak Rabin in 1995, years in which Mizrahi political representation made major gains at the expense of established elites. It was during this time that being Mizrahi became, at least among many Likud members, equivalent to being right-wing. However, and paradoxically, these were also the years in which Mizrahim—especially Moroccan politicians—revived the concept of Mizrahim as a bridge to Israeli-Arab peace, though "not from a position of weakness but of strength." These are the years of the Oslo Accords between Israel and the PLO, as well as of the assassination of Prime Minister Rabin at the hands of Yigal Amir, a Yemenite Jew. Should Rabin's assassination be interpreted as a symbol of Mizrahi attitudes toward the idea of peace with the Palestinians, as a result of the assassin's national religious habitat, or as a combination of these two factors? To answer this question, the chapter discusses the attitude of Rabbi Ovadia Yosef, the spiritual leader of the Shas party, toward the Palestinian question.

The book's conclusion looks at the different Mizrahi streams of the present day with regard to the Palestinian question, and asks about the dynamics among three elements that shape Jewish-Israeli attitudes toward Palestinians: the religious dimension—the correlation between the level of religiosity and support for compromise with the Palestinians; the ethnic dimension—Mizrahi vis-à-vis Ashkenazi; and the class dimension—differences between classes in their attitudes. As I suggest, aggressive Mizrahi attitudes—and acts—toward the Palestinians are to be found primarily in the lower classes, and thus can be better understood through a lens of class rather than ethnic politics. This conclusion is supported by the fact that Jewish violence in the West Bank—the Palestinian territory—is by no means characterized by ethnic origin but rather is justified by the religious notion of Jewish supremacy, shared by Mizrahi and Ashkenazi violent settlers alike.

One of the events that form the backdrop of this book is the lynching attack carried out by Mizrahi Jews in Bat Yam in May 2021 on an Arab Israeli citizen passing through the city. This event symbolizes the deep change that the Mizrahi consciousness underwent during the years of Zionism: 113 years earlier, and a few kilometers from the lynching site, it was Zionists from eastern Europe who attacked an Arab passerby in the nearby city of Jaffa, an act of aggression that Mizrahi-Sephardi Jews viewed as cruel and harmful to Jewish-Arab relations in the country. The attack of 1908 is the event that opens the book, which throughout tries to understand the different Mizrahi approaches to the Arab question and the transformations that have taken place over more than a century.

CHAPTER 1

And the Turk Was Then in the Land

In which we will tell of the somewhat violent Arab-Ashkenazi encounter that took place in 1908, and then move backward and forward to learn a bit about everyday Jewish-Muslim life in Palestine prior to Zionism. We will see the friction between Jews and Muslims regarding holy sites, and their common effort to prevent intermarriage between the members of different religious faiths. We will also read what Zionist immigrants from Europe thought of Palestine's inhabitants, both Jewish and Arab, and how the longtime inhabitants looked on the Moskobi ("Moscovite") immigrants. We will inquire into Eliezer Ben-Yehuda's secret plan and ponder the dispute between the hakham bashi—the Ottoman chief rabbi—and David Ben-Gurion on the eve of World War I.

JAFFA 1908: POGROM AGAINST THE JEWS OR ARAB-ASHKENAZI CONFLICT?

On the eve of the Purim holiday, March 16, 1908, a street fight broke out between young Arabs and young Jewish immigrants of the Second Aliyah in Jaffa. In the course of the fight, one of the Jews stabbed an Arab, mortally wounding him. As usual with fights, there are different accounts of how and why it broke out. Some see it as the first example of a Zionist reprisal operation, claiming that it was initiated by Second Aliyah activists in response to previous incidents in which Arab boys had harassed Jewish women. Others maintain that the Arabs started the fight. Whatever the case, the family of the

Arab victim lodged a complaint with the Ottoman police. Policemen were sent out to arrest the assailant and his accomplices. The police also instigated a provocation—a detail of Ottoman soldiers assisting them snuck into the Spector Hotel, where Jewish immigrants were making preparations for a Purim party. The soldiers fired into the air from inside the building. The policemen outside began shouting, "The Jews are shooting!" and charged into the building, where they beat, bayoneted, and otherwise injured thirteen Jews, two of them seriously. Twelve of them were immigrants from Russia. The other one had come from the United States.[1]

The attack on the Jews in the hotel was instigated by the Jaffa *kaymakam* (district officer), Mehmed Asif Bey. He, like the governor of Jerusalem, Akram Bey, viewed Zionist immigration as a danger to the integrity of the Ottoman Empire and a threat to Palestine's fabric of life. In this, they were no different from many other Ottoman officials. Nevertheless, most Ottomans in such positions took no concerted action against the immigrants. The government's attitude toward Zionism zigzagged, and the fact that most of the immigrants were citizens of foreign countries limited what measures could be taken against them. According to treaties with the Western powers—the so-called capitulations—foreign citizens could not be arraigned in Ottoman courts. As a result, the immigrants could flout local laws without being brought to trial. Ottoman governors thus often found themselves in a weak position with regard to Zionists. This was the case in Jaffa in 1908. A diplomatic campaign carried out by the Zionist Executive, involving its offices in Europe and Palestine, the German deputy consul in Palestine, the Russian consul, the *hakham bashi*, officials of Alliance Israélite Universelle, and wealthy Jews convinced the Ottoman government to dismiss the governor of Jaffa, who had ordered the attack on the Jewish hotel. This was a demonstration of just how much power the Zionist movement had accrued even then.

But that is not our focus here. Rather, we are interested in the conduct of Jaffa's Sephardim during the altercation and its aftermath. The evidence is scant, unfortunately, and in the form of hearsay. There is an incidental remark in a letter that Menachem Sheinkin, a Zionist activist, sent to the Zionist office in Vilna: "It is interesting also to note the attitude of the Sephardi Jews to this case," he wrote. "Immediately after the episode, when we had the lower hand, they almost celebrated the defeat of the Russians [Jewish immigrants]. Some of them said to the Arabs, up until now we have lived in peace, but ever since the Moskobim ["Moscovites," meaning the Second Aliyah immigrants, many of whom came from Russia] arrived we have had trouble. From some we could hear that the right thing to do would be to send away all the Russians who have come over the last five years."[2]

Such an attitude might be surprising to the twenty-first-century reader. Jews (Sephardi Jews in particular) demanding the expulsion of other Jews (immigrants from eastern Europe) because of their belligerence toward Arabs? Didn't all Jews advocate the principle that every Jew had a right to settle in the Land of Israel? Was it more important for the long-established Sephardim in Palestine to maintain their good relations with their Arab neighbors than to welcome their Ashkenazi brethren? What about the Mizrahi tradition of love of the Land of Israel and the people of Israel? And there are other questions. Why do books about this period play down this pro-Arab and anti-Zionist Sephardi mindset? Isn't it part of the history of that time? I will offer answers to the first four questions later in this chapter. But let's first consider the latter two.

HISTORY VERSUS THE PAST

When reading a work of history—textbook, nonfiction, or historical novel—it's important to keep in mind the difference between history and the events of the past. While the two are connected, they are completely different. The past is what happened. It cannot be reexperienced. It no longer exists. It is the past—it has passed from the world. History, by contrast, exists. It is what the present says about the past. Another thing—the past does not change, because it no longer exists. What we say about it, however, can change over and over again. That is history.

And, of course, when men and women write books of history, they choose what to include in them and what to leave out. They have any number of considerations—the availability of sources, the questions that interest them, and their political leanings, to name a few. When it comes to writing the history of the Mizrahi-Ashkenazi-Arab triangle, the story of the Sephardim in Jaffa 1908 does not match what Ashkenazim and Mizrahim (in general) want to tell.

ASHKENAZIM AND MIZRAHIM?

Before offering a preliminary answer to the question of what Ashkenazim and Mizrahim want or do not want to tell, I should note that the terms "Mizrahi" and "Ashkenazi" as they are understood today are relatively new terms. They were not in use at the end of the Ottoman period, originating only well into the twentieth century. But the distinction between Jews with origins in the Islamic world (who, as noted, were called Sephardim because Jews of Spanish ancestry generally led their communities) and those who came from

Europe predated Zionism. This distinction was important but hardly black and white. There were Jewish communities in the borderlands between those two worlds, such as the Balkans and Romania, and there was intermarriage between the two groups—indeed, a bit more often in some circles than the common wisdom would have it. Also, Jews moved from one realm to the other. Even more important is the "multifarious and dialogic, contextual, and acquired nature, changing over time and connected to daily practices," of collective identities, as Amos Noy writes. In other words, Sephardi and Ashkenazi and Mizrahi and German and Moroccan and Palestinian and Arab and all other identities emerge from dialogue and contact. That, after all, is the nature of identity. While identities are sometimes of profound significance, they are not rigid.[3]

WHAT DO ASHKENAZIM AND MIZRAHIM SAY ABOUT THEMSELVES AND OTHERS?

Consciousness of belonging to a group emerges from contact with other members of the group and even more so with other groups. Those who seek to bolster a collective identity tell a story about the group and esteem it over other groups. The leaders of the Zionist movement stressed the role of European Jewry in the building of the Jewish national home. As prime minister, David Ben-Gurion said that the Zionist immigration from Europe "contained within it creative forces and powerful drives and the ability to build the Third Temple in all its glory by material and spiritual means." While serving as minister of education, Aharon Yadlin offered his assessment of the history of Zionism: "East European Jewry was that which largely laid the foundation of the national renaissance enterprise; the children of these immigrants, who were born and educated in the land, are those who liberated it, in particular during the War of Independence. And the immigrants of the 1950s from the lands of the East—they are in particular those who renewed the momentum of the settlement of the land and who joined the succession of its defenders." Yadlin said this in the Knesset in 1976 in response to a motion for the agenda protesting the absence of the history of Oriental Jews from textbooks.[4] He stressed the contribution made by the immigrants from the Islamic world, but only as settlers in Israel's periphery, during what he termed Zionism's third stage. Neither he nor Ben-Gurion, the alert reader will note, used the word "Ashkenazim."

The Sephardi-Mizrahi story tends, by contrast, to stress that the Sephardim were connected to Zionism from the start. The book *You Were Born Zionists* by

Itzhak Bezalel, published in 2007, is a classic example of this approach. Bezalel does not disregard the tension between the established Sephardi population and the immigrants from eastern Europe, but he stresses the Zionism of the former and claims that they did not have to undergo reeducation to become Zionists, because they had been born as such. When Israeli historians, especially those of the Hebrew University of Jerusalem and Yad Yitzhak Ben-Zvi, began to investigate the history of the Jews of the Islamic world, they focused on Zionist activism in that area, so as to grant the Jews of these lands a place in the Zionist story.[5] The same was true of writing outside the academy. The book *Kol hator: Tziyonut masortit-sepharadit* (Voice of the dove: Traditional Sephardic Zionism), edited by Ophir Toubul (2021), refers to Sephardi settlement prior to the Zionist waves of immigration and Sephardi forerunners of Zionism. It views Zionism as a whole, and Mizrahi Zionism in particular, as an extension of Mizrahi tradition and all of Jewish tradition.[6] Such books obviously will not mention that Jaffa's Sephardim, like the city's Arabs, thought that the Second Aliyah immigrants were uncouth, wild, and inconsiderate of the locals' customs and mores.

Some would call this repression, but that would be too dramatic a term. It's not an act of actively suppressing something. It's simply refraining from writing about it. Such an act of omission is sometimes the product of a lack of knowledge (not every historian sees every document); sometimes it is a matter of deliberate exclusion (I see a document, but it does not fit into the general picture as I perceive it); and sometimes particular incidents seem unimportant to a writer (so someone said something, big deal). Whatever the reason, events do not enter the pages of history unless someone decides they are important and writes about them. The Sephardi-Arab alliance against the Zionist immigrants, who were overly vulgar for their tastes, happened, but it was not seen in a positive light in Zionist writing, both official and unofficial, both Sephardi and Ashkenazi, so its traces almost entirely disappeared. More recently, some historians have given this alliance a more important place, and I will consider, among other things, how central it was, and what Sephardim, Ashkenazim, and Palestinians thought about it.

THE SEPHARDI-ARAB ALLIANCE IN JAFFA: AN EXCEPTION?

One of the few documents to offer an account of the 1908 incident implies that it was young Sephardim in Jaffa, those of about the same age as the European immigrants, who were particularly infuriated by the newcomers' behavior. But was that true of all Sephardi youth in the city at the time? Or was it a marginal phenomenon? Maybe a handful of Sephardi guys said something among themselves, or in conversations with Arabs, and Sheinkin heard about it and reported it to his colleagues in Vilna. The recipients, sharing the Zionist obsession with keeping every scrap of paper the movement produced or received, filed it away, and the file was later deposited in the Central Zionist Archives in Jerusalem, where, decades later, historians read it. But what, if anything, can be learned from it about the general mood of the Sephardi-Mizrahi public? Presumably, the demand to block Zionist immigration was not supported by the entire established Jewish population in Palestine, both Sephardi and Ashkenazi. From the inception of Zionist immigration, the country's Sephardi and North African (Mughrabi) Jews helped set up the new European immigrants, as I will show below. The Jews of the Islamic world in general saw themselves as tied to the Land of Israel and to the Jewish people as a whole. On the other hand, the Sephardi youths on the streets of Jaffa were clearly not the only ones who found the eastern European immigrants confrontational. The (Sephardi) Jewish representative on Jerusalem's City Council, Haim Valero, condemned their actions and accepted the version of the events provided by Jaffa's governor. Presumably, others like him did the same.[7]

But even eastern European Zionist immigrants were sometimes critical of the vicious behavior of their compatriots. Banker and businessman Zalman David Levontin maintained that the background of the incident was the comportment of members of the militant socialist Poalei Zion party, "who behave toward the Arabs with arrogance and contempt and with hostility and belligerence." But the Zionist critics nevertheless closed ranks with the radicals. The position taken by some Sephardim, according to Sheinkin, was that people looking for a fight had no place in Palestine. They, Sheinkin wrote in his letter, did not see it as a Jewish-Arab quarrel but rather as a conflict between interlopers and the local population. Jews and Arabs lived side by side in serenity. To preserve these good relations, they thought that the correct thing to do was to expel the pugnacious pioneers. "Pioneers" was the term the socialist Zionists used to describe themselves.

LIVING IN PEACE: A COMMON VIEW

The notion that Palestine's established Jewish population and Arabs lived as good neighbors appears repeatedly in memoirs from the Ottoman period, those of both Jews and Arabs, including those who mention altercations between the two communities. The accusation that the Second Aliyah immigrants were responsible for ruining these relations is also a recurrent motif.

Take, for example, Mordechai Elkayam's depiction of relations between the Moroccan Jews and the Arabs of Jaffa. "This harmony," wrote Elkayam, a member of a venerable Moroccan Jewish family in that city, "although there were exceptions, was disrupted by the immigrants from Russia." They were at fault because of the immodest way in which their women dressed, and because their plan, as it was understood by the locals, was to seize control of Palestine.[8]

Palestinian Arabs wrote in the same vein. Their autobiographical literature, works of research by both scholars and laymen, and journalistic commentary for the most part extol the close social relations between Jews and Arabs prior to Zionism. Here are a few examples from what the Jews termed the "four holy cities," in which small communities of Jews lived alongside Arabs. In his book about Tiberias, Issam Sakhnini writes of the neighborliness between Jews and Arabs in that city and their joint business ventures. Shehada al-Rajabi stresses the peaceful lives of Hebron's Jews under Ottoman rule, noting that Jews served as judges in the civil courts and as elected members of the district council. Yasir al-Askari of Safed writes extensively about the just and beneficent Islamic regime and depicts Jews as part of the city's social fabric. He describes how they dressed in Arab garb and spoke the local language, and (like many Jews who came from the Islamic world) nostalgically recalls the prevalent Muslim custom of delivering a feast to Jewish neighbors on the last night of the Pesach holiday, in exchange for which the Jews gave them their leftover matzah. Amin al-Khatib chronicles shared lives in Jerusalem's Old City and describes how Jews and Arabs socialized in coffeehouses. While these works were clearly written against a political background, they must certainly reflect something of life during this period.[9]

SO WAS THERE REALLY HARMONY?

This question must be revisited constantly. That is because it has no unequivocal answer, and because of its prominence in the political discourse, and, most important, because there is a contradictory view according to which Jews lived in constant terror and fear under Islamic rule. Sheinkin's letter offers evidence, from the point of view of the new Zionist immigrants, that (at least some of) the Sephardim had a positive experience of life alongside Arabs, to the extent that they perceived the influx of the Moskobim as upsetting the old and good order. The letter's importance lies in that it was written at the time of the events, and was thus not the result of saccharine nostalgia or biased historical writing. At the same time, it is important to keep in mind that it is one man's interpretation of the events, and that it is but an item of testimony from the past, not a comprehensive survey of all views, events, and experiences.

Sheinkin's letter differs from Elkayam's account. Sheinkin reports on a group that is foreign to him; Elkayam writes of his family and community. Born in Gaza in 1910 to a Mughrabi family who had settled in that city south of Jaffa, Elkayam spoke Arabic and joined the Haganah, the Jewish self-defense force, at a young age. He saw combat in 1948 and then served in a series of positions in the Israeli government and other central institutions. He worked on immigrant absorption for the Jewish Agency and served as a military governor, first in Gaza in 1956 and then in Jericho in 1967. His view of the Ottoman past was based on family memories and documents he collected and lacked a manifestly political agenda. Moreover, in joining the Haganah, he for all intents and purposes joined up with the Moskobim. In other words, there are no grounds for suspecting that he was attempting to paint an idealized picture out of anti-Zionist or anti-Ashkenazi bias.

BIASED HISTORY

Jewish-Arab or Muslim-Jewish relations displayed both harmony and dissonance, mutual aid and riots, neighborliness and alienation, intimacy and hostility, and everything that all of these oppositions imply. It is therefore possible to write history that includes these components in different measures, in keeping with the writer's taste. No human being knows precisely what the measures of good and evil were in the real lives of all the Jews who lived in all the Jewish communities under Islam, from the dawn of that faith until the founding of the Zionist movement and thereafter. Each and every writer, Jew and Arab, inimical to Zionism or enamored of it, thus has the discretion to present these relations as he or she sees fit. There are those who stress the benevolent aspect of Islam and its protection of minorities, while others highlight its stringency and even its cruelty. Both perspectives are true (though a reader might well ponder whether writers who resolutely adhere to just one of them are fully aware of how biased and unreliable that makes them look).

The historian has the option of presenting testimonials of wonderful friendships or documenting acts of killing and violence that undermine such coexistence. Or he may combine them. My decision to open this chapter with Sephardim who opposed the immigration of revolutionary Ashkenazi Zionists is deliberate. I could have chosen to begin with how the Jews of the East yearned for the Land of Israel, or with the friendly meetings between Ottoman Judaism's religious leader, the hakham bashi, and his Muslim counterpart, the mufti, or with Arab aggression against Palestine's Jews, or with Ashkenazi-Sephardi cooperation in fostering the Jewish return to Zion, all of which the reader will find as this book goes on. But I chose a violent incident that involved intra-Jewish discord. Why? Because it happened, and disregarding it distorts the general picture. Furthermore, it has the potential to cast new light on an ambiguity that persists in Mizrahi-Arab relations to this day. Also, I want to bring home that what seems obvious today did not seem obvious then, and that what the current generation sees as eternal truths are actually perceptions shaped by historical processes that can be traced. And that is what I will do. To that end, I want to examine two more commonly used terms.

TERMS: JEWISH-ARAB RELATIONS AND MUSLIM-JEWISH RELATIONS

"Jewish-Arab relations" became a thing in the era of the national awakening in the Middle East—namely, at the end of the nineteenth century. Prior to the age of nationalism, there was no such thing as Jewish-Arab relations. The salient mark of identity was religious affiliation, and the political order was also based on religious frameworks. In lands under Muslim rule, Muslims enjoyed a legal status superior to that of Christians and Jews, and the principal division was between Muslims and everyone else. To put it another way, Muslims stood at the apex of a triangle, with Jews and Christians below them. Jews and Christians were dubbed *ahl al-kitab*, adherents of the religions of the books, the Hebrew Bible and the New Testament. They followed revealed religions, but these religions were obsolete. As such, their legal status was that of *ahl al-dhimma*, protected communities. Muslim religious law, the sharia, required that they obey the government. They were subject to a special tax and by law could not hold high positions. A variety of other restrictions were also placed on Jews and Christians, among them prohibitions against building places of worship, bearing arms, and riding horses. They were required to accept this inferior status. In exchange, the Muslim ruler granted his protection. They were permitted to perform their religious rites, and no one was allowed to harm them or their property. These are the strictures imposed by Muslim law, which was, for centuries (in the Ottoman Empire, until the mid-nineteenth century), the law of the land. But these rules were not always enforced. In fact, Jews sometimes reached high governmental and official positions and usually were not prevented from building synagogues. On the other side, Muslim rulers did not always protect the lives and property of the religious minorities. In any case, the political structure described here makes it clear that the term "Jewish-Arab relations" cannot be applied to the pre-national era. The idea that Muslims and Christians were Arabs and on one side of the hyphen while Jews were on the other simply did not exist. Furthermore, the very word "Arab" had a different meaning then. It was for the most part used to refer to nomads whose origin lay in the Arabian Peninsula and who retained tribal affiliations—that is, what we today call "Bedouin" or "settled Bedouin." The term "Arab" was not yet used to label a nation.

THE TERMS "JEW" AND "JEWISH"

The terms "Jew" and "Jewish" also meant something different in the Middle East before the national era. This was the case more from the point of view of outsiders than from that of the Jews themselves, but it was nevertheless different. In Ottoman writing, the term "Jew" was reserved for the Sephardim. The widely read Hebrew newspaper *Hatzfirah*, published in Poland, commented on this sadly in 1894: "It is taken for granted that there are no Jews in Jerusalem except for the Sephardim. In the *seraya* [government building] there is a *Sefer Hanufus la-Yahud* [population registry of Jews], but the *Yahud* there are only Sephardim. True, there is another *sefer nufus* in Jerusalem for Israelites, but its name is *Sefer Nufus al-Shiknaz*—that is, for Ashkenazim. While the government sees them as 'a sort' of Jew, they are not 'actually' Jews but rather some strange creature among the Jewish people, as we see the Samaritans from Nablus."[10] These delineations also changed over time, of course, and it is clear that the general Jewish perception was that Ashkenazim were also Jews.

OVERVIEW OF INTERCOMMUNAL RELATIONS

The control of Jewish communal institutions in Jerusalem and Palestine as a whole lay for generations in the hands of the Sephardi public, which constituted a majority of the Jewish populace. That was the case until the second half of the nineteenth century, when European Jewish immigration overtook that from the Mediterranean region. When the different communities encountered each other in Palestine, Eliav writes, "Both sides saw the other as coming from a foreign and strange world. . . . Undoubtedly at first what separated them was much greater than what they shared, and the differences between communities lay at the root of most conflicts and struggles . . . but the need to live together mitigated the disparities and created, over time, a foundation for cooperation, adaptation to coexistence, based on tolerance, mutual concessions, intercommunal contact, and appreciation of the other until, in the end, a Jewish Yishuv took form in Palestine, despite the persistence of ethnic differences."[11] This is the harmonizing approach to the writing of Jewish history. Other writers stress the tensions between Jewish ethnic groups and the arrogance displayed by the Sephardi elites at the end of the Ottoman period. Like other elites, the Sephardim did not happily give up their superior position.

The initial cooperation between the Sephardim (comprising all its subcommunities) and the Ashkenazim (ditto), in Jerusalem and in Palestine as a whole, was based on religion, not nationhood. When the winds of nationalism began to blow in Europe and the Middle East in the last quarter of the nineteenth century, buffeting their Jewish communities as well, it raised the question of how the Jews fit into the new world order. Were they part of the emerging nations or a separate and distinct group? To put it another way, in more essentialist terms, was Judaism a religion, in which case its believers could be members of other nations? Or were the Jews a nation unto themselves, in which case they necessarily stood apart from other nations? This is not the place to delve into the arguments made on both sides. For our purposes it is enough to state the important fact that many Jews of the time—in both the East and the West—were inclined to see Judaism as a religion only. For them, the term "the Jewish people" did not mark them as a nation in the modern sense of the term. In part, this was because they aspired to integrate into the countries in which they lived.

THE MIDDLE EAST: CHANGING IDENTITIES AND ASPIRATIONS TO EQUALITY

In the Middle East, the theorists of Arab nationalism sought, in the mid-nineteenth century, to set in motion a profound metamorphosis in the way people in the region thought about their identities. Most centrally, they wanted to diminish the importance of religious affiliation as a collective identity and the central focus of loyalty and to replace it with the nation. They defined national affiliation as cultural collectivity, principally on the basis of the Arabic language, and on geography—living in Arab lands. In other words, the early Arab national movement advocated a separation of church and state, to the point of equality between members of different religions. The national idea, formulated in the spirit of liberal republicanism, attracted many in the Arab world, people from different areas and of different religions—modernists and Islamists, Jews swept up by the spirit of the times and Christians educated in church schools, along with other members of the public. The influential anthem "Balad al-Arab Awtani" (All the Arab lands are my homeland), written by Fakhri al-Baroudi (born in Damascus in 1887), exemplifies this sensibility, presenting the greater Arab homeland as a single entity belonging to all speakers of Arabic:

My homeland is the land of the Arabs,
From Damascus to Baghdad,
And from Najd to Yemen and to Egypt and Tetouan
No border will divide us
And no religion will make distinctions among us
The Arabic language connects us.[12]

This is the concept of Arab nationalism that took form on the eve of World War I, and it invited Muslims, Jews, and Christians, at least on the declaratory level, to take part in it. Like all phenomena, this concept did not emerge from nowhere but had earlier roots. In fact, the idea of religious equality had appeared in the Ottoman Empire prior to the rise of Arab nationalism, in part because of pressure from Europe. The era of imperial reform of 1839–76, known as the Tanzimat, produced constitutional changes that included the end of protected status for Jews and Christians, raising them to the status of Ottoman citizens alongside Muslims, marked and implemented by a decree of the sultan in 1856. It continued with the Ottoman Nationality Law of 1869 and the new law of equality, incorporated into the constitution of 1876.[13] But this idea of equality did not galvanize the masses, in the Middle East or elsewhere. In Europe, legislation of this type produced violent reactions—the rise of a new form of antisemitism. In Greater Syria, it led to interreligious riots. In any case, the constitution was revoked in 1878, nullifying the laws. The Ottoman elite continued, however, to promote the unity of the empire and its inhabitants, and the idea was taken up by large segments of the public, with varying intensities, until the collapse of the Ottoman state.

In the decades prior to World War I, the empire saw ups and downs in its internal administration, as its weakness in comparison with the Western powers became ever more apparent. The Arab provinces also underwent political, economic, and social changes as the region became integrated into the world economy. The Arab cultural awakening, the Nahda, gained strength, and with it national ideas. In the meantime, another national idea began to affect the region—the immigration of Zionist Jews, pushed out of Europe by the rising antisemitism, a product of struggles over the boundaries of nationalities there. These Jews were drawn to Palestine because it was the historic homeland of the Jews imprinted in their consciousness. These Jews had no interest in integrating into the Arab region. Rather, they wanted to create a separate Jewish nationalism. They were the Moskobim, some of whom we met in the altercation in Jaffa.

At the height of these changes, and as part of the hopes for repairing and strengthening the Ottoman Empire, the Young Turks rebelled in 1908 under the slogan "Freedom, Equality, Brotherhood, and Justice." The principle of equality under a constitution was revived, and Christians and Jews were permitted to bear arms (soon afterward they were also required to perform military service). Another real change came in the unique context of Jerusalem: the centuries-old prohibition against Jews entering the Temple Mount was revoked. The city's rabbis were apprehensive. The Hebrew weekly *Mahzikei Hadat*, which was published in Lvov but whose correspondents in Jerusalem sought to bolster religious law, bewailed the "insolence of the young people of Jerusalem" who hoped that they could, with the proclamation of the constitution of 1908, "introduce free living in the holy city," as they had "desecrated the Sabbath in public and walked on the Temple Mount etc."[14] As the Ottoman regime saw it, however, allowing Jewish entry to the Temple Mount was an unprecedented step toward equality and the elimination of barriers between religions that is hard to imagine happening today.

THE DREAM OF EQUALITY, AND ITS CHALLENGES

The Ottoman grant of safe haven to Jewish refugees expelled from Spain in 1492 was a cornerstone of the Sephardi communal memory in the empire. Now, a few hundred years later, they were being offered equality as well. No wonder, then, that the Jewish community in Jerusalem, and Jews throughout the realm, fervently celebrated the 1908 revolution. The Hebrew newspaper *Hashkafah* offered an account of the celebrations:

> At seven o'clock some 40,000 people gathered, Ishmaelites [Muslims], Jews, Christians, in the army palace and on the streets before the army palace, and his honor the minister pasha and his army received the visitors with a salutation of welcome, with very beautiful countenances.... And also many of our Sephardi compatriots walked in a large assembly and before them a beautiful and elegant ornate curtain with silver and golden pomegranates on it like a beautiful wedding canopy, and behind them young men going out with swords [fencing foils] and lances and rifle barrels. And the rifle barrels proclaimed their strong

voices. And when the Jewish assembly had passed with the curtain before the men of the army, all the men of the army and the officials and the ministers raised their weapons and swords in their honor.[15]

This was not a passing enthusiasm. The change was profound, both in its political import and in its impact on the identities of Ottoman subjects in Palestine. But it did not come as a shock; people were already emotionally prepared for it. Michelle Campos called her book on this period *Ottoman Brothers: Muslims, Christians, and Jews in Early Twentieth-Century Palestine*. The new Arabic-language press stressed the concept of Ottoman brotherhood.

But a close reading of *Hashkafah*'s account of the celebrations reveals, if only in hindsight, the seeds of the crisis to follow. "And afterward a very great throng walked to the City Garden and there they made speeches in the Hebrew language . . . and a great throng of the members of our nation walked through the markets and streets and in all the Jewish neighborhoods and sang songs in Hebrew. And the flags of our exalted government, and flags of Zion bearing the Star of David before them."[16] The two flags waved side by side. But what did the imperial flag symbolize? And what did the Zionist flag symbolize? Was there a contradiction between them? Was it possible to combine fealty to Ottoman brotherhood and allegiance to the Zionist idea? The same question can be asked from the Jewish direction. Could living as equals in the empire fulfill Jewish aspirations, or was it necessary to work toward Jewish sovereignty in Palestine, for Jewish rule, which would necessarily also mean rule over non-Jews? Was that realistic? Was it proper? This was a dilemma faced by both the Jews of the Ottoman Empire as a whole and the Jews of Palestine in particular.[17] As with every dilemma, there were those who had an immediate answer. One of the leading Sephardim in Jaffa, reported *Hapoel Hatzair*, seized the Zionist flag from a Jew who was waving it, furled it, and let it fall to the side. The writer, Yosef Aharonovich, one of the leaders of the Hapoel Hatzair movement, stated his own opinion: "A desecration of the flag—it says something about the quality of the desecrator, and in this case also about the cowardice of a rabbit, or simply slavish Sephardi submissiveness."[18] Here was another juxtaposition between staunch Zionists and Sephardim from the pioneering-Moskobi point of view. The former depicted themselves as proud members of the Jewish nation, while viewing the others as Jews lacking in national consciousness who sought appeasement and cooperation with the Arabs. It's important to note that, as the Moskobim saw it, the man who had cast the flag aside had done so not as a personal act but as an emissary of his entire community.

WHAT DID PALESTINE'S ARABS WANT?

The intra-Jewish dispute took place within a minority. The Jews constituted at that time about 10 percent of the population of the area that was called Palestine in Arabic and the Land of Israel in Hebrew. The Arab majority faced a somewhat different dilemma: to what extent should they stress their national aspirations, and to what extent should they blend into the atmosphere of Ottoman fraternity? The range of opinions on this question grew out of different analyses of the political changes in progress, and out of the differing emotions that they engendered. That's how things work. Nationalism begins with the feeling that "we don't want to be ruled by foreigners and we don't want foreigners to rule our land." The feelings motivate intellectuals, who put the turmoil in their souls into words in the form of ideas that they disseminate in speeches and writings. If many others start to feel the same emotion, among them people of action, they move on to the next stage—forming organizations, founding newspapers, and setting up armed underground cells if that becomes necessary. Alongside this political and sometimes armed action, the theorists and activists continue to formulate and consolidate a national ideology. Actions and words influence each other and the emotions of a broader public. Certain emotions are augmented, while others are marginalized. These are the principal stages of the rise of national movements. They can be discerned both in Zionism, the Jewish national movement, and in the Palestinian national movement.

Some of the Arabs of Palestine—certainly the Muslims prior to the reforms—were contented under Ottoman rule. They did not see it as a foreign or occupation regime. They shared a set of values with other Ottoman subjects and with the government and could enjoy the empire's benefits and live as part of it. The rise of the Arab national movement is evidence that there was, nevertheless, a measure of unease, and that this unease grew as the Ottomans increasingly stressed the empire's Turkish character. An interesting testimony of the mood in the 1880s can be found in the words of a Jew who had been born to a family of the Old Yishuv (the Jewish community that preceded the Zionist immigration) but who grew up in Zionist circles. It may be the first text we have that includes a detailed examination, from a Jewish point of view, of the social conditions of the Arabs of Palestine and the existence among them of something like national feelings. The context of the letter is a land dispute between the Jewish residents of Petah Tikva, a settlement founded by members of the Old Yishuv, and the surrounding Arab villages. Its author, Eliezer Rokach (1854–1914), wanted to explain the case to Yehuda Leib (Leon) Pinsker, a Hovevei Zion leader. But before going into that, he provided Pinsker, who was unacquainted with conditions in Palestine, with some political and social background:

> Anyone who knows the state of the government of Togarmah, and especially its attitude to the district of Peleshet (and the other districts of Arab origin where the Arabic language is used), knows that the ties that connect these districts to the Togarmah kingdom have always been loose, namely, because the Arabs think of themselves as the pillars of the Islamic faith. . . . And one who knows the nature of the local people here knows that they have no great love or fondness for the Togarmahs, and chafe much when the government appoints Togarmahs as officials, not one of their own.[19]

Togarmah appears in the biblical book of Genesis (10:1–2) as a son of Yefet, son of Noah. In Jewish tradition he is identified as the forefather of the Turkish tribes. The name was thus applied to the Ottoman Empire. But this terminology is not what is important. The letter shows that Rokach had a sharp eye for developments that were just beginning to emerge. He discerned the Arab collective sensibility that saw itself as something different from and superior to the Ottomans and sought some measure of self-rule. In other words, he identified the budding of what would some years later become Arab nationalism. Furthermore, he recognized the local, Palestinian dimension of this phenomenon, the specific national feeling of the Arabs of Palestine. "Here in Peleshet [Philistia, Palestine] as a whole and in Jerusalem in particular," he wrote, "there are two families descended from the Prophet's loins, the Husayni, whose ancestry is known to all Muslims, and the Khalidis. . . . All the inhabitants of this place revere them and hold them sacred, as being of great honor and exaltedness." To put it another way, the Arabs of Palestine accepted the authority of these two families of distinguished descent, the Khalidis and the Husaynis, and viewed Jerusalem, not Istanbul or Damascus, as their religious and political center.

This is very interesting. Rokach did not write these words after encountering the institutionalized Arab Nationalist Movement but before it was even founded. He was not part of a political debate about how far back Palestinian nationalism can be traced, because that debate had not even begun. He was not deliberating with academic researchers about the inception of nationalism in the Fertile Crescent, because he was not a scholar. He described in real time developments he detected in the majority culture within which he lived. It may well be that he was the first to put such things down on paper—I, at least, have not encountered any earlier document of the sort. And there's another point. He wrote about feelings. The Arabs did not feel love and fondness for the Ottomans. They did not want to be ruled by officials from elsewhere. That, as I have noted, is the foundation of nationalism. That was how the Arabs of the Land of Israel—that is, Peleshet, that is, Palestine—felt after the Ottomans began to act like foreigners, and that was how Arabs in the empire's other provinces also felt.

Rokach also noted the measures the Ottomans took to avert the growth of Arab national sentiments. They bolstered Ottoman nationalism while making all their subjects Ottoman citizens and granting them a measure of autonomy. The empire took it upon itself "to install commissioners and officials, policemen and judges in Peleshet—and in the rest of the said districts—but to choose them from among the people living there, that is, from among the Arabs." That is the beginning of intentional self-rule. Before this, members of highly placed local families served in senior positions, especially religious positions, and there had also been Arabs who thought they ranked higher than the Turks in the Islamic context. But in the age of nationalism, these feelings were translated into concrete, protonational political demands—the appointment of Arabs, not Turks, as district governors. At that time, the Arabs of Palestine did not demand more than this. For them, the primate city was Jerusalem, and the senior members of the families descended from the Prophet—the Husaynis and Khalidis—were the "natural" leadership. We now know that, soon after Rokach wrote his letter, these two families would emerge as the national and intellectual leadership. We will encounter them over the decades that followed.

Among the scholars who study the Arab Nationalist Movement, there are those who stress the role played by Christians in establishing and strengthening it. They attribute this to the desire of this minority to achieve equal standing with the majority community. The importance of Christians in the process should not be minimized, but, from the point of view of the people of the time, the Muslims constituted the numerical majority in the emerging nation, and Islam was one of the axes around which the nation consolidated. At least Rokach saw it that way, and he wrote of it to Pinsker.

PINSKER, ZIONISM, AND MOROCCANS

Yehuda Leib Pinsker was sixty-five years old when he received Rokach's letter. He was a Russian Jew, a physician, a thinker, a journalist, and a leader of Hovevei Zion. By the time he began corresponding with Rokach and other Jewish settlers in Palestine, his consciousness had made any number of sharp turns. As one might expect, the changes he underwent reflect the process by which the Zionist idea emerged among Jewish activists. At the beginning of his public career, Pinsker advocated Jewish integration into Russian life. When the relatively liberal Czar Alexander II assumed the throne, in 1855, he believed that would be possible. So he called on Jews to learn Russian and assimilate as much as possible into the larger society around them, while maintaining their Jewish identity. The Odessa pogrom of 1871 led Pinsker to begin to doubt that position. The wave of pogroms that followed a decade later impelled him to the conclusion that Jewish integration in Russia was impossible. The pain and shock he experienced prompted him to write *Auto-Emancipation*, a pamphlet that changed the way many Jews of his generation thought and became a milestone in the history of the Zionist movement. He argued that antisemitism was a natural force that could not be battled. "Antisemitism seems as if it will never die. He must be blind indeed who will assert that the Jews are not the chosen people, the people chosen for universal hatred. No matter how much the nations are at variance in their relations with one another, however diverse their instincts and aims, they join hands in their hatred of the Jews," he wrote. Pinsker claimed that emancipation—the granting of equal rights by several European countries—was merely a form of alms that these nations "willingly or unwillingly flung to the poor, humble beggars whom no one cares to shelter." He presumed that the Jews of Europe would remain eternal foreigners, no matter what constitutional changes were made. "To the living, the Jew is a corpse," he declared, "to the native a foreigner, to the homesteader a vagrant, to the proprietary a beggar, to the poor an exploiter and a millionaire, to the patriot a man without a country, for all a hated rival."[20]

On the basis of this insight, Pinsker proposed practical measures. On the spiritual level, he called for a rehabilitation of the Jewish sense of honor. On the political level, he called for the unification of the Jewish people and the establishment of a national home. The national home did not have to be in the Land of Israel, he maintained. "We must, above all, not dream of restoring ancient Judea," he declared. "The goal of our present endeavors must be not the 'Holy Land,' but a land of our own." The lives of millions of Jews hung in the balance—it was not the time to insist on a particular land of refuge.

He then proceeded to evaluate which Jews needed refuge most desperately. According to his analysis, when Jews came to be a large proportion of the population of a given country, the danger to their lives increased. "There is a certain point of saturation beyond which their numbers may not increase, if the Jews are not willing to be exposed to the dangers of persecution as in Russia, Romania, Morocco and elsewhere," he maintained. "It is this surplus which, a burden to itself and to others, conjures up the evil fate of the entire people. It is now high time to create a refuge for this surplus."[21]

Pinsker did not cite the Jews of Morocco as a mere random example. They were the largest Jewish community in the Islamic world. The Zionist movement aspired to be the national movement of all Jews, wherever they were. As such, some Zionist thinkers from the beginning took into account the Jews of the Islamic lands. True, the Zionists hoped to establish in Palestine a European outpost within the barbaric East, as Theodor Herzl put it. Their encounter with the Jews of that region was thus not at all simple. But Zionism's overall worldview took all Jews into account. The prevailing Zionist view can be put this way: facing off against the gentiles, we are (generally) a single nation; among us, the Jews of Europe are superior to the Jews of the Islamic world.

The "Storms in the South" pogroms of 1881–82 were the central impetus for the establishment, from the grass roots, of a loose network of Hovevei Zion groups in the towns and cities of eastern Europe. After the publication of his pamphlet, some of the leading figures of these groups invited Pinsker to help unite them into a single organization and to serve as its chairman. It was then that Pinsker began to advocate the idea of a return to Zion as the preferred solution to the Jewish predicament. He received Rokach's report on the Palestinian Arabs' attitudes toward the Ottoman regime in this capacity.

So at just the time when Hovevei Zion was taking its first steps in Palestine, the Arabs who lived there had begun to hope for, and to receive, a measure of self-rule. Neither group was then challenging the empire's legitimacy. The Zionists obtained some autonomy as well—their own flag and schools, for example—and the Arabs received senior administrative positions. This marked out the line for further confrontation. Arab national aspirations inevitably included opposition to Zionism. Not unreserved opposition, not all Arabs, and not all the time, but the Zionist waves of immigration aroused anxiety and resentment because they presented a danger that foreigners would take over Arabs' land.

THE CLASH OF NATIONS PRIOR TO NATIONALISM

Contemporaries predicted the clash between the two national movements, Jewish and Arab, even before these movements had fully consolidated, and before what came to be called simply "the Conflict" had taken shape. The Arab leadership in Palestine and the Ottoman authorities opposed Hovevei Zion immigration from the start. Indeed, the Ottomans imposed restrictions on Jewish immigration as early as 1882, as the Hebrew press at the time reported.[22] Not long after the Zionist movement officially came into being at the First Zionist Congress of 1897, Yusuf Zia Khalidi, a former mayor of Jerusalem and member of the Ottoman parliament, wrote to Theodor Herzl, the movement's president, in an attempt to dissuade him from the idea of establishing a Jewish state in Palestine. He began by acknowledging that "historically it is your country."

> And how wonderful it could be if the Jews, who are so able, were again to constitute an independent, respected, happy nation that could benefit wretched humanity on the moral level, as it did in the distant past. Unfortunately, the fate of nations is not determined by abstract views, as pure and as noble as they might be. They must take into account reality, the facts as they are, and the force, yes, the brutal force of circumstances. And the reality is that Palestine is today an integral part of the Ottoman Empire and, even worse, is populated by non-Jews. . . . While I most esteem Dr. Herzl as a man and an author, it would be folly for him to think that at some time they may seize control of Palestine, even if it were possible to obtain the consent of His Highness the Sultan. I therefore see in this movement a great danger to the Jews in Turkey and, especially, in Palestine. . . . Seek another place for the wretched Jewish people. There are empty territories on the globe. That will be the solution to the Jewish question. Also, the Prophet of Islam invited the Jews to recognize his divine mission [and they rejected it], and yet the Jews live freely and in honor in Palestine, but on condition that they entertain no thought other than to be, like us, loyal Ottoman subjects.[23]

Khalidi wrote as a representative of a public loyal to the empire, but also as a man of Jerusalem representing the inhabitants of Palestine. Herzl was not persuaded. In his reply, he assured Khalidi that the Jewish return to Zion would benefit all its inhabitants,[24] a Zionist claim that continues to be made to this day. Other voices warned of the coming clash, continuing after Herzl's death. In 1905, Naguib Azouri, a Syrian Christian and former Ottoman official, forecast the region's future. Azouri was living in exile in Paris at the time and wrote in French, leading scholars to wonder whom he intended as his audience. "Two extremely important phenomena of the same nature but opposed, which have still not drawn anyone's attention, are emerging at this moment in Asiatic Turkey," he wrote. "They are the awakening of the Arab nation and the latent effort of the Jews to reconstitute, on a very large scale, the ancient kingdom of Israel. Both these movements are destined to fight each other continually until one of them wins."[25]

Arabs were not the only ones to warn that confrontation was inevitable. Abraham Shalom Yahuda, a scholar living in Jerusalem, brought the subject to Herzl's attention and implored him to find a way to reach the hearts of Palestine's Arabs. Yahuda, a Jerusalem native, was an expert in the Arabic language, thanks both to his studies and to his Iraqi roots on his father's side. He published his first monograph, *Arab Antiquities*, in 1893, when he was sixteen years old. He met Herzl for the first time three years later, when he was a student and attended a lecture the prophet of the Jewish state gave at a Jewish workers' club in London. A year later, he attended the First Zionist Congress as a representative of the Jewish youth of Frankfurt (he was then studying in Germany and was active in Zionist groups there). In both cases, he told Herzl that it was not enough to engage in diplomacy with foreign leaders, including the sultan. It was vital, he said, to start speaking to the Arabs of Palestine, so as to mitigate hostility toward Zionism. Herzl did not take up the challenge. Fifty years later, in 1949, Yahuda published an account of these meetings in *Hed Hamizrah*. He cited them in support of his claim that the Sephardim had been excluded from Zionist activity even though they could have turned Jewish-Arab relations in a less bloody direction and reduced hostility to Zionism.[26]

HOSTILITY TO ZIONISM OR JEW HATRED?

Khalidi, quoted above, is an example of a firm opponent of Zionism who viewed Judaism and the Jews in a positive light. He empathized with Jewish suffering, recognized the existence of a Jewish people and its national rights, and acknowledged the Jews' historical connection to the Land of Israel. Today, these views are almost entirely nonexistent in Palestinian political and historical discourse. Nevertheless, he opposed Zionism resolutely because he understood it to be a national movement that aimed to establish a political entity in Palestine that would necessarily be detrimental to its inhabitants, including its Jewish inhabitants. When he spoke well of the Jews of Jerusalem, he was not simply paying lip service. Two decades earlier, in 1875, when the British Sephardi Jewish philanthropist Moses Montefiore visited the city for the seventh and final time, Khalidi sent him a letter supporting his work on behalf of Jerusalem's Jews. He also reminded the philanthropist of the need to beware of flatterers and swindlers looking out only for themselves. He proposed that Montefiore establish boarding schools in which poor Jewish children could study European languages and useful trades, so that they could take part productively in the economy. "I hope that you will attend to these words, which emerge from a man who loves all who are created in God's image," he concluded. He left no room for doubt that he harbored no resentment against Jews simply because they were Jews, despite his opposition to turning Palestine into a Jewish land.[27]

ZIONISM IS NOT JUDAISM

The distinction was a central one in the Palestinian political lexicon in its early days. Official Palestinian spokespersons continue to adhere to it today. During the Ottoman and Mandate periods, it came fairly naturally. The overlap between Jews and Zionists was still limited. But it was maintained in the constitutive documents of the post-1948 Palestinian national movement. Among these documents are the PLO Covenant of 1968. According to Article 20 of that document, Judaism is a divine religion; Zionism, by contrast, according to Article 22, is an aggressive, racist, fascist, Nazi movement. The rival Palestinian mass movement, Hamas, treats Zionism and Judaism differently in the covenant it issued upon its founding in 1988. Article 31 of that covenant addresses the right of Jews to live securely and in peace under Islam, even as Hamas presents itself as the spearhead of the struggle against Zionism (Article 32). The Hamas Covenant only partially distinguishes Judaism from Zionism, as it also contains antisemitic imagery. The so-called new charter that Hamas issued in 2017 further emphasizes the difference, however: "Hamas affirms that its conflict is with the Zionist project, not with the Jews because of their religion. Hamas does not wage a struggle against the Jews because they are Jewish but wages a struggle against the Zionists who occupy Palestine" (Article 16). A similar distinction can be found in the writings of the Popular Front for the Liberation of Palestine, the leading faction in the Marxist stream of Palestinian politics.[28]

POLITICAL VERSUS POPULAR DISCOURSE

The fine points of the political lexicon are not necessarily reflected in everyday speech. I recall a demonstration staged by the Arab Students Committee at the Hebrew University of Jerusalem during the First Intifada. At one point the protesters chanted, "'almakhshuf wa'almakhsuf, Yahudi ma bidna nshuf" (We say it straight out, straight out, we don't want to see Jews). The novelist Emile Habibi, who was present at the event, silenced the demonstrators. "Say: We don't want to see Zionists," he corrected them. "We have no problem with Jews." The demonstrators acquiesced, but in everyday Palestinian conversation one can hear "Aju al-yahud" (the Jews are coming) when a military force arrives to demolish a house or carry out some other action. More important, the murders committed by Palestinians in 1929 (and not just then) show that in such bloody moments, the assailants make no real distinction between Jews and Zionists. Perhaps they assume that all Jews support Zionism in some way in their hearts, or perhaps they are influenced by anti-Jewish sentiments that can be found in Muslim sacred scriptures.

In any case, there are several reasons why the distinction between Zionists and Jews is maintained in the Palestinian political lexicon. On the political and diplomatic level, it is a response to accusations of antisemitism, which is unacceptable in Western discourse today. Antisemitism was also forbidden by Ottoman law. We have nothing against Jews, the Palestinians claim. We are only invoking our right to self-defense against a foreign invader. On the level of Israeli-Palestinian relations, the distinction is a tool for forging alliances with Jews who are anti-Zionist or a-Zionist. With regard to the State of Israel and the Zionist movement, the claim to observe the distinction is a way of saying: You do not represent the Jewish people as a whole, only a part of it, despite your pretense of representing all the world's Jews.

The distinction between Jews and Zionists is also grounded in reality. There are non-Jews (Christians, Druze), who declare themselves Zionists. And there are Jews who are not Zionists. For them, too, the distinction is important.

In Palestinian discourse on non-Zionist Jews, a place of honor is reserved for Jews from the Islamic world. Over the years, Palestinian figures have stated again and again their belief that they could find among the Sephardim and Edot Hamizrah allies in their struggle against Zionism. Why? Because it was not the Jews of the East who brought about the change in relations between Jews and Arabs. It was the Moskobim. And in the incident in Jaffa in 1908, for example, the position expressed by young Sephardim reflected assumptions similar to those that the PLO and Hamas would later voice.

SIMILAR POSITIONS?

That claim should be scrutinized. Here are the points of resemblance: both parties (1) differentiated between Jews and Zionists; (2) did not recognize the Zionist movement as the representative of all Jews; (3) did not view the Jewish religion as the source of the demand for sovereignty in Palestine; (4) accepted that it was possible for Jews to live in Muslim or Arab lands under Arab/Muslim rule; (5) believed that Zionist aggression was to blame for the outbreak of conflict between Jews and Arabs in Palestine; (6) proposed that the solution was expelling the Zionist invaders from Palestine.

What were the differences? They lay not in analysis of the situation but in the actions taken. Palestinians battle Zionism in part with armed struggle. The Sephardim opposed the immigration of revolutionary Zionists by muttering under their breaths. That is, of course, a very important difference, perhaps the most important. Also, Palestinian opposition to Zionism persists today. On the Sephardi side, the situation changed over the years, as we will see.

THE SEPHARDIM WERE NOT ALONE

Jewish opposition to Zionism was not a Sephardi invention. Broad swathes of the Jewish public opposed Zionism from its inception, for a wide range of reasons. Jews who sought to assimilate into majority societies in Europe and the East feared that the spread of Zionism would undermine their position in their countries of residence. Haredi Jews rejected it because it sought to replace messianic redemption with redemption by human agency. There were Jews who maintained that Judaism was a religious, not a national, identity. And there were those who maintained that the great socialist revolution would solve the Jewish Question just as it would solve all other national issues.[29] Sephardi opposition to Zionism—we will soon encounter many pro-Zionist Sephardim—grew out of their Ottoman identity, their interest in bolstering their standing as loyal citizens, and their desire to maintain their good relations with Palestine's Arabs. As their opposition was a product of being native Palestinians and part of the local culture, their positions were similar to those of the Arabs.

THE COUNTERREACTION AND THE FIGURE OF THE TREACHEROUS SEPHARDI

The Sephardi reaction was a cause for concern among the immigrants from Europe. They feared not only the Sephardi opponents of Zionism but also those who supported it but suggested that the Zionist activists change their tactics and adapt to some extent to their surroundings. This was the approach taken by a broad circle of educated Sephardim native to Palestine who aligned with the Zionist movement in the belief that Zionist immigration and settlement could continue without arousing Arab animosity. For example, Shimon Moyal proposed founding an Arabic-language newspaper, which he believed could stimulate dialogue with Palestine's Arabs (1911). Nissim Malul, a journalist and political activist, considered establishing an organization of Jewish teachers of Arabic (1913). The responses to their proposals indicate how they were perceived by the Moskobim. "They are alien to our lives in general," said Meir Meirovitz of these Sephardi intellectuals. They are "assimilationists," maintained the writer and activist Avraham Ludvipol, adding that "if you pound the Sephardi Jew in a mortar an Arab will remain." Y. K. Silman, a friend of the author Yosef Haim Brenner, noted the number of intermarriages between Sephardim and Arabs. "They are closer to the Arabs than to the Ashkenazim," he concluded. Yaacov Rabinovich summed it up: "They can be dangerous for us, especially if the natives of the country receive any sort of rights."[30] And note that these intellectuals, part of the circle connected to the Sephardi-Zionist newspaper *Haherut,* did not oppose the Zionist idea. Instead, they sought to moderate the pioneer-socialist attitude of blindness toward the country's Arabs, saturated as it was with a sense of superiority.[31] They seem to have aspired more to equality and cooperation with the Arabs than to control and to the establishment of a Jewish state, even as among the European Zionists the aspiration to found a Jewish nation-state increased.

In other words, from the point of view of the European Zionists, the entire Sephardi community, not just a handful of young Sephardim in Jaffa, were socially and politically akin to the Arabs. We will encounter the Sephardi intellectuals and *Haherut* further on.

WERE THE SEPHARDIM AND THE ARABS REALLY ALIKE?

It's now time to return to the question of the relations between the local Jews (largely, but not only, Sephardim and Jews from the Muslim East and Maghreb) and the Muslims (and Arabs in general) during the Ottoman period. In his book *Lives in Common: Arabs and Jews in Jerusalem, Jaffa, and Hebron,* Menachem Klein writes, "There was no mental barrier dividing the Muslim and Jewish regions. The linguistic and cultural walls were low, and the person who entered the physical or linguistic space of the Other was not overcome by a sense of being foreign."[32] That sense of foreignness is indeed one of the important measures of the relationship between identities—where a person feels comfortable, where less comfortable, where undesirable. With what people do they feel at ease sitting, laughing, smoking, and drinking, and from whom do they maintain a distance? Many of the Jews with roots in the Islamic world, and the Sephardim who had lived in Palestine for generations, felt at ease in Arab cafés and marketplaces. They did not frequent these locations as tourists or marvel at their exoticism, nor were they weighed down by fear when they went there. Does that mean that there were no moments of anxiety or strife? Not necessarily. It is difficult, of course, to know just how often that happened.

RAMADAN NIGHTS AS TIMES OF DREAD

Rabbi Yaakov Shaul Elyashar, known as the Yisa Berakhah (1817–1906), served as Jerusalem's chief rabbi (bearing the titles hakham bashi and *rishon letziyon*) and president of its Jewish religious court (*av beit din*) from 1893 until his death. A succinct letter he sent to the Ottoman governor of Jerusalem is preserved in the National Library of Israel in Jerusalem:

> As is known to you, your honors, the members of the Jewish community [*al-ta'ifa al-Musawiya*—the community of Moses] are complaining about bad behavior of Muslim youths and boys during Ramadan, especially at night. They assail whomever they encounter—not only that, but they also beat or curse or attack them. And as we know of your honors' love of justice and ambition to provide security for all the subjects of our lord and highest majesty the great sultan, may God support and sustain him, we [request] that you issue a directive to the police and the guardians of the city and urge them to maintain the public peace in accordance with the law. And we, for our part, wish your honors ascent and progress, amen. And in any case all is in the hands of the governor, my lord.[33]

The letter is undated, and the name of its writer does not appear on it. The addressee is indicated only by his titles and position, the governor of Jerusalem (*mutassarif al-Quds al-sharif*). So there is no internal evidence as to when it was written. But its substance is clear.

What is clear? First and most important, it is clear that Arab youths harassed Jews in Jerusalem on the nights of Ramadan. (That it is clear depends, of course, on the credibility we assign to the document and its author. There is no reason to doubt either.) It is also implied that this behavior was a violation of the will of the Ottoman authorities—or at least so the rishon letziyon hoped. It may be something like the contemporary Israeli phenomenon of young men harassing Arabs on the night of Yom Kippur, which, while in violation of the law, barely encounters a response from law enforcement authorities.[34] In any case, we are left with a number of questions. To what extent did these Ramadan assaults color relations between the two communities on the whole? Did both sides view them as the actions of a handful of young people that had no real significance? Did they make Jews feel less safe in general? Were they an unofficial means of ensuring that Jews would feel inferior? We have an answer to one question. The case that the hakham bashi referred to was not an exception.

DOCUMENTARY EVIDENCE

The Hebrew press during the last quarter of the nineteenth century reported again and again about the harassment of Jews during Ramadan, the holy month in which Muslims fast during daylight hours and feast after sundown. "During this moon, Ramadan, they fast for thirty days, and all those who have no fixed business reverse the order of night and day, and all night they roam the streets and revel and make merry, and during the day, when their hunger irks them, they take out their fury on any Jew, who is designated for blows," wrote a correspondent for *Hatzfirah* from Jerusalem in the issue of October 31, 1877. "And if a Jewish person gets up the courage to respond to his [Muslim] abuser, then the fanatics will quickly swarm around him like bees and beat him brutally."[35] The newspaper remarked that the pasha (governor) of Jerusalem announced that he would act with an iron fist against those who attacked Jews, but the correspondent was skeptical. Such reports appeared from time to time in later years as well. For example, in 1889 *Hatzfirah* reported:

> These days are those of the Remetz [Ramadan] holiday of the Mohammadans, and their notorious wild young men have made a habit every year when these days come . . . to beat with an evil fist and to [cast] dust and stones on the Jews, to break their windowpanes and so on, and no one makes any response. And so it was last week when some of our brothers were beaten by those unruly youths, and they went to complain to the pasha of our city, and he raged at the chief of police and ordered him sternly that there should be no other such thing. And a government notice was put up on all the streets [warning] that anyone who raised his hand on his fellow would be punished severely.[36]

And in 1893, the year in which the Yisa Berakhah was invested as rishon letziyon:

> The firing of every cannon on the city wall [marking the beginning and end of the fast on each day of Ramadan] reminds us of the Muslim fast of the month of Ramadan on each day of [the Hebrew month of] Nisan. And this is added to our woes, because the Ishmaelites [Muslims] will not allow us to walk the streets without raining on us vigorous blows. Woe to the man assaulted by these wild men at night at the time they sit down to eat after fasting all day . . . they do not spare the old and have no mercy on the young. They mistreat and abuse us.[37]

Similar reports on other Jewish communities throughout the Muslim world appeared during these years in the Hebrew press.

ON RAMADAN, VIOLENCE, AND MINORITIES

I am writing this chapter in the midst of Ramadan of the year 1442 since the Hijrah in Jerusalem. It's the Hebrew month of Iyar in the year 5781, April 2021 in the Gregorian calendar. A few days ago, a fight broke out between two Palestinian families in Wadi Joz, a Jerusalem neighborhood. A girl was killed by a stray bullet and four other people were wounded.[38] During Ramadan, the number of violent incidents within Palestinian society in the West Bank increases.[39] This year, it's also been a week of violence between members of different religions, or nations, in Jerusalem, Jaffa, and elsewhere. Arabs against Jews. Jews against Arabs. There has also been violence against women this month, unconnected to religious or national affiliation. In other words, violence in general, including that of Muslims during Ramadan, is not only anti-Jewish or interreligious. But when violence breaks out between members of different religious or national groups, it is perceived entirely differently from violence of other types.

Here's an example from Jaffa in 1909. The report is from the Yiddish newspaper *Der Yud*, which quoted an Egyptian newspaper:

> Moroccan Muslims are concealed and hiding out in Jaffa, armed with all kinds of swords and bayonets and innumerable pistols. . . . When they see that the government is preoccupied, and there is no higher oversight in the city, they burst out and commit murders. . . . They will strike out on one of the coming nights, to murder, according to their

> oath, 300 people at once. An arousal against the Jews [can be felt]. The Arabs are murmuring and there are provocateurs who are disseminating among the Arabs false rumors about the Jews laboring to take over the country and expel the Arabs from it or to make them slaves.[40]

On the face of it, this sounds like anti-Jewish activity of the purest sort. News items about robberies committed against Jews can also be understood in this way. But a more comprehensive examination of the phenomenon, and perusal of the Arabic press, paints an entirely different picture. *Filastin* repeatedly highlighted the violent behavior of Muslim immigrants from Morocco, Afghanistan, and other countries. Some of these immigrants came to Palestine as seasonal orange pickers and packers, working mostly for Arab fruit growers. They remained in the country after the harvest and began to demand protection money from the owners of citrus groves. Their criminal activity posed a threat to economic life in the port city. *Filastin* warned:

> In Jaffa there is a large group of Moroccans and a similar one of Afghans who vie to guard the orange groves each year during this season [the article was written in October, the orange-picking season]. Bloody confrontations between the two groups happened frequently, and the damage they caused fell largely on the landowners [the growers]. This year a third group appeared, from among marginal elements in the city, and [the three groups] divided up areas of influence, one for the Afghans, one for the Moroccans, and one for the natives of the city. . . . The consequences of this agreement are already evident. The leader of each group goes to the landowners in his zone and demands that they promise to receive security services in their groves. If they grasp for excuses or refuse, their trees get cut down and everything on their land is stolen and the cuttings are uprooted and the oranges are stolen, and they have no way of being saved from their plight except going submissively to the head of the gang and asking for protection.[41]

The newspaper demanded time and again that the government impose law and order. It called on the police commander and the district governor to address the problem, and covered violent incidents—including, but not only, against Jews—and demanded the deportation of the illegal Moroccan immigrants. This was a very real problem for all of Jaffa's inhabitants, not a specifically Jewish or Zionist story, and that was also the case in many instances of violence at times when the central government was weak.[42] Nor were Ramadan attacks necessarily directed at Jews, although they were among its principal victims. This was the reason for the Yisa Berakhah's letter.

A FITTING SEPHARDI RESPONSE

Communication between public figures is one way of coping with violence and humiliation. Ovadiah Camhi, born in Hebron in 1888, was a journalist, banker, public activist, translator of French works into Hebrew, and a poet. He recounted, in a boyish and spontaneous way, his own experience of the humiliation of Jews in a poem from his book *Hebron During My Boyhood*:

> *I am so bitter, bitter*
> *To see how the ruffians*
> *From among the Arabs of Hebron*
> *Pulled as one pulls a rope*
> *From above to below*
> *On the street, where all could see*
> *The hairs of your sidelocks!*
> *And so recall, abject Talmudists*
> *How a ruddy boy of younger years*
> *Overcome at once by a drive for revenge*
> *Broke the wall that circles you*
> *And turning harshly to the stoutest of the attackers*
> *Resolutely slapped him on the face.*[43]

This is the image of the self-respecting Sephardi defending his humbled Ashkenazi brothers.

ANOTHER WAY OF COPING

Another way of coping with Arab violence emerged at this time, when the first new Jewish agricultural settlements were being founded. It was to use Jewish guards—including so-called Arab Jews—to protect these communities and their lands. Ehud Ben-Ezer wrote about his grandfather, Yehuda Raab, one of the first settlers in Petah Tikvah and the first Jew to guard the settlement. One day, Ben-Ezer relates, Raab saw a magnificent rider on horseback galloping past the settlement, then vanishing into the distance.

The next day Yehuda Raab returned, mounted on his horse, from guarding the fields. His eyes were so heavy with sleep that he could barely keep them open. Suddenly he made out blurrily, against the rising sun, a sight that seemed at first like a desert mirage. The strange Bedouin horseman was galloping again, from the east, from the direction of the [Arab] village of Faja, toward the Jewish village.

Yehuda turned his horse toward the stranger. He again intended to invite him to meet and get acquainted, as the etiquette of the East toward guests required. . . . Yehuda leveled his gaze at him, examined him well as if again seeking to assess him. Suddenly the stranger cried: "*Ana Israeli*!" Yehuda was astounded, and the Bedouin, seeking to prove what he said, directed his eyes to the blue winter skies of the Petah Tikva Valley and recited: "*Shema Yisrael Adonai Eloheinu Adonai Ehad*."[44]

Moshe Smilansky was a pioneer of the First Aliyah, the first wave of Zionist immigration, which founded the farming villages called the moshavot. One of the First Aliyah's signature authors, he described Daud Abu Yussef—the Jewish Bedouin guard whom Raab encountered—as the scion of the Jewish tribes of pastoralists from the Arabian Peninsula who arrived at Petah Tikva in a storm and vanished in a storm. Yehuda Raab related how Abu Yussef taught him the finest details of how to comport oneself in the East—how to ride a horse and use a sword, when to speak and when to remain silent, under what circumstances to be stern and when to be forbearing. In other words, how to turn into a son of the land, a native, a local. Another Petah Tikva guard was Maimon Zarmati, a member of Jaffa's Moroccan Jewish community.

Abu Yussef did not come or vanish in a storm, remarks Liora Halperin, who has written about both these figures. He was a Jew from Baghdad who did business all over the Middle East. He spent some time in Petah Tikva and then carried on with his trade with Baghdad, Damascus, Jerusalem, and Jaffa. Zarmati was also an urban Jew. The guards were depicted as figures of primal grandeur so they could play the role assigned them by Smilansky and his associates in the history. Their goal was to create a bond between the newly arrived Ashkenazi immigrants and the soil of their ancient homeland by means of local Jews.[45]

Shlomo Abbo, known as Shlomo al-Khayyal, the horseman, came from a family with a long history in Safed and Tiberias. He was also one of the first

Jewish guards, patrolling the lands purchased by the Jewish Colonization Association at Sejera in the Galilee, where he was wounded in a skirmish.[46] Yehuda Antebi, born in Safed in 1878 to a well-known family with branches in Aleppo, Damascus, and Egypt, served as a teacher of Hebrew and Arabic in Rosh Pina and Yavne'el, two other moshavot in the Galilee. At first, the farmers of Rosh Pina, immigrants from Romania, refused "to accept and house among them a teacher of the *Frenk* [Sephardi] community," Antebi wrote in his memoir. He was often the butt of derogatory comments, but in time he won the farmers' esteem and served as a mediator in disputes between the inhabitants of the moshava and the Arabs living in its vicinity.[47] In addition to guarding and arranging conflict-resolution (*sulha*) ceremonies, Eastern Jews served the Zionist immigrants as middlemen in land purchases, as we will see below. Their role as guards diminished when the Moskobim founded Bar-Giora and then Hashomer, Jewish irregular militias made up of Second Aliyah immigrants. The members of these organizations learned Arabic and horseback riding, as well as how to wield swords and use firearms. They also saw themselves as experts in conducting relations with Palestine's Arabs.

Outside observers, including members of the labor movement (the general term for the parties, organizations, and institutions that advocated socialist Zionism and a return to working the land and manual labor), remarked on the two contradictory attitudes of Hashomer's members. Some of them sought to establish benevolent relations with the Palestinian Arabs, displaying physical prowess only as a way of shattering the Arab stereotype of the Jew as a person who could not defend himself, while others displayed "a lust for power, the lash, Ishmaelite garb, a 'number five' rifle, a noble horse, speaking in Arabic, and telling tall tales. This produced most of the conflicts between Hashomer and its [Arab] neighbors."[48] This was the fundamental difference between the conduct of the Moskobim and that of the local Jews—the former sought power, the latter, compromise. Perhaps this was the difference between those who saw themselves as the future rulers of the land and those who conceived of themselves as a prudent minority or mere neighbors.

YITZHAK THE YEMENITE

Only a handful of members of the Old Yishuv joined Hashomer. One of them was Yitzhak Nadav (originally Nadaf), whose father had come to Palestine from Yemen in 1881 and whose mother had come from Algeria. His family lived in Jerusalem's Mishkenot neighborhood, built in 1875 outside the Old City walls as the first part of what came to be called Nahla'ot. Its Old Yishuv inhabitants were joined by a group of Moskobim under the leadership of Boris Schatz, the founder of the Bezalel Academy of Arts and Design, who wanted to learn masonry from Yemenite stoneworkers. As a boy, Nadav was fascinated by the Moskobim. "I'd often sneak into their common room and visit it secretly. More than once I emerged full of astonishment and wonder," he related. "My heart was full of envy for this crew, and more than once I saw Jews of the halukah [Jews of the Old Yishuv who lived on charitable donations from overseas] who were prepared to spit in their faces because of their strange practices and arrogance. . . . The Arabs called them Moskobim. I understood that very well and I craved to be called by that name." The Moskobim, however, did not forge social relations with the Yemenites and treated them with disregard. Here, again, there was mutual alienation.

The barrier was broken by Yitzhak Ben-Zvi, one of Hashomer's founders. He noticed the curious boy and invited him to join the group. When he turned sixteen, in 1906, Nadav signed up as a member of the socialist Poalei Zion party. His new comrades took him to a barber. "I cut off my handsome curled sidelocks, and when we reached Lifta [the moment they left Jerusalem], I shed my garb of the Yemenite exile and dressed in European clothes—trousers, a shirt, and so on," he recalled.[49] This marked the completion of his conversion from an old to a new Jew. It was also a symbol of the boundaries of the collective marked out by the Moskobim, for whom "our people" were only those who cast aside the traditions of their forebears.

Nadaf became Nadav and joined the first Zionist guard militia in Palestine, Bar Giora, which became the nucleus of Hashomer, which was founded in 1909. He moved between the moshavot in the Galilee, Jezreel Valley, Judea (the southern coastal plain, around Jaffa), and the Negev. His knowledge of Arabic helped him in his contacts with the Arab laborers and sentries at the moshavot he guarded. He adopted his comrades' positions on the issues central to the Zionist labor movement at the time—the conquest of labor, by means of Jews replacing Arab farm laborers, and the conquest of guarding, by means of replacing Arab guards with Jewish ones. In this he differed from the Sephardim who wrote for *Haherut*, who opposed actions that unnecessarily impinged on Palestine's Arabs. When the inhabitants of Kfar Tavor asked Bar Giora, in the summer of 1908, to take over the protection of their moshava, the members of the group made a condition, not just about guarding but also about farmwork. "Not a single Arab should remain," the militia directed, according to Nadav, "and we will provide the manpower for work." Nadav also noted, perhaps in an effort to display sensitivity to the plight of the Arab workers, that the condition was made "despite the fact that the families of the Arabs who worked for every one of the farmers each numbered some twelve souls." As a member of a closed and elitist collective, he did not protest, and the Arab families lost their livelihoods.

The members of Bar Giora racked up achievements in their efforts against theft in the moshava, and also engaged in physical altercations with local Arabs, Nadav related. This, he said, "enhanced the prestige of the [Bar Giora] guards and filled them with national pride. It lifted the self-confidence of the moshava's inhabitants, who realized that . . . the groveling and flattery they had engaged in thus far was now a thing of the past. Only force can restore a person's honor and maintain his [human] image. 'With fire and blood Judea fell—with fire and blood Judea will rise'—that was the slogan emblazoned on our banner."[50]

The Moskobim sensed what the anticolonial thinker Frantz Fanon would articulate fifty years later—that the use of force by an oppressed people frees them from their inferiority complex and restores their self-respect and identity. But there may be other ways of achieving that result. And there is another problem with that approach—the use of violence might become a habit detrimental to the humanity of those who use it.

We'll now turn a few years back from the Moskobim and the Yemenite who joined them galloping through the fields of the moshavot. We'll go deep into Jerusalem and its hakham bashi, who employed the traditional "exilic" ways of coping with violence against Jews—cajolery and dialogue.

THE HAKHAM BASHI AND THE MILLETS

The Yisa Berakhah wrote his letter of complaint about violence against Jews during Ramadan to the governor of Jerusalem in his capacity as hakham bashi of Jerusalem. That was an official title. The Ottomans organized each non-Muslim community as an ethnoreligious framework, or, in Turkish, *millet*. The head of each millet represented its members before the authorities. The communities that the empire recognized were the Greek Orthodox, Armenian, and Jewish communities, with the Melkites (Greek Catholics) added at the end of the nineteenth century. The heads of these millets, the patriarchs of these churches and the Jewish hakham bashi, had official duties and powers. Through them, their communities paid the collective taxes imposed on them, and they headed their communities' internal judicial system, consisting of church and rabbinic courts. These courts heard cases relating to family affairs and personal status, a system that has been preserved in some

Middle Eastern countries, Israel included, to this day. The hakham bashi also oversaw Jewish ritual slaughter and burial, and sent emissaries to Jewish communities in other lands to collect donations to support the Jews of Jerusalem. He also distributed these funds.

The hakham bashi's role was institutionalized in the mid-nineteenth century, alongside the empire's Tanzimat reforms. The first hakham bashi of the entire empire, Hakham Avraham Halevi, was appointed in Constantinople in 1835. There are different understandings today of just what powers he had, formally and in practice, over the chief rabbis of the empire's provinces. In any case, the appointment of these regional holders of the title of hakham bashi required his formal approval. The first hakham bashi of Jerusalem, Avraham Haim Gagin, was installed in 1841, soon after the Ottomans reestablished full control of the city (after about a decade when Palestine was under the control of the governor of Egypt, Muhammad Ali).[51] This was a period of far-reaching changes in the Jewish community of Jerusalem and Palestine as a whole, leading to disputes between families and subgroups within the Sephardi community in Jerusalem and the Jewish community more broadly. One important point of conflict was economic. The Ashkenazi, Mughrabi, and Edot Hamizrah communities accused the Sephardim, who controlled most of the donation money and also the funds earned from their control of ritual slaughter, an important source of income, of not giving them their fair share. All three of these groups took action to shake off the authority of the Sephardi leadership.[52] On top of this came conflicts over the work of overseas philanthropists who were endeavoring to change the educational system and employment profile of the Jewish community in Palestine. One of these was Alliance Israélite Universelle, a Paris-based organization that established French-language schools and other institutions to provide Jewish communities in the Middle East with modern education and instill French culture. Alliance opened its first school in Palestine, Mikveh Israel, in 1870, and in 1882 it opened a school in Jerusalem. That was a portentous year of change, the one in which Hovevei Zion groups in eastern Europe began to make plans to settle in Palestine, setting off Arab opposition to Jewish immigration.

It is not clear what Sephardi religious leaders thought about Zionist activity. The hakham bashi of Constantinople, Rabbi Moshe Halevi, voiced disapproval in a letter he sent to the Yisa Berakhah in 1895. He reported an imperial directive not to subscribe to *Hatzfirah*, which was publishing "innumerable articles on 'Zionism' . . . and a cord of suspicion stretches over us, and I do not know how this evil and bitter matter will end." Was the evil matter

Zionism, or was it the suspicion of the authorities? There is no way of knowing. "We, the Children of Israel, should not [be involved] in great things and what is beyond," he concluded.[53] The aversion to Zionism contained in those words derives from a viewpoint with roots both in Jewish tradition and in Ottoman reality, according to which Jews should not act against the wishes of the state because doing so might hurt Jewish communities. Best, in this view, to leave political and national matters to heaven. That might be what the expression "great things and what is beyond" refers to. The phrase comes from Psalm 131: "O Lord, my heart is not proud nor my look haughty; I do not aspire to great things or to what is beyond me; but I have taught myself to be contented like a weaned child with its mother; like a weaned child am I in my mind. O Israel, wait for the LORD now and forever" (Jewish Publication Society, new JPS translation). In the contemporary context, it would seem that Rabbi Halevi meant that the political maneuvers of the Zionist movement were an attempt to do great things, but in the negative sense of acting arrogantly. The correct attitude, the one to aspire to according to the psalmist, was to be contented, like a baby dependent on its mother. The Jews should await God's salvation just as a baby puts its trust in its mother, and not pursue political nationalism like the world's other nations.

Note that the need to warn against even a symbolic connection to the Zionist movement, in the form of a subscription to a newspaper, attests to the movement's appeal and the danger presented by affiliating with it. This tension led Jerusalem's Sephardi rabbis to maintain a distance from Theodor Herzl when he visited the city three years later.[54] But despite the hakham bashi's reservations about Zionism, a paramount Zionist spokesman, Eliezer Ben-Yehuda, underlined the national aspect of the hakham bashi's position, seeing in it "a dimension of leadership, prestige, honor, and even governing authority, what was in his opinion the position closest to that of the president of the nation," as David Lavie argues. Ben-Yehuda, Lavie writes, sought national symbols for the emerging national community in Palestine and beyond.[55]

The view that the rishon letziyon—that is, the hakham bashi of Jerusalem—was a communal leader, in fact part of the national leadership, reappeared many decades later. "As Mizrahi rabbis, like Rabbi Ovadia [Yosef], see it," writes sociologist Nissim Leon, "the institution of the rishon letziyon is not perceived as just another rabbinic institution but rather as one of the most important rabbinic institutions. . . . They continued to see the institution of rishon letziyon as an anchor of identity, a continuous history that could be connected so as to construct an axis of local rabbinical authority, one that is manifestly of the Land of Israel and which predates Zionism." Leon adds that this is what lies behind the instruction, in the schools sponsored by the Shas party, which Rabbi Yosef founded, in the history of the Sephardi rabbinate in Palestine.[56] But the Yisa Berakhah knew nothing of this at the end of the nineteenth century. He was concerned about the effect that Zionism, including Ben-Yehuda's activity, was having on Jewish-Arab relations in Palestine.

BEN-YEHUDA, THE HAKHAM BASHI, AND THE MUFTI

Ben-Yehuda's attitude toward the office of hakham bashi did not necessarily say anything about the nature of his actual relations with the holder of that office. On the Hannukah holiday in December 1893, the Yisa Berakhah and Rabbi Shmuel Salant, the chief rabbi of Jerusalem's Ashkenazi community, issued a herem, a rabbinic interdict, on Ben-Yehuda. They conducted the requisite ceremony, reported *Hamagid*, including black candles, the blowing of a shofar (ram's horn), and a public declaration.[57] The immediate cause was the publication, in Ben-Yehuda's newspaper *Hatzvi*, of an article on Hannukah by his father-in-law, Shlomo Jonas. Jonas recounted the heroism and victories of the Hasmoneans, and concluded his piece with the words "We shall act with valor and stride forward." Jerusalem activists who were hostile to Ben-Yehuda translated the article into Arabic and sent it to the governor. They claimed that the final words were a call to emulate the acts of the Hasmoneans—namely, to rebel against the sultan. In support of their charge, they spread rumors that Ben-Yehuda commanded a force of "5,000 young men who have resolved to carry out an armed conquest of Mt. Moriah [the Temple Mount], to break into the site of the Temple, to destroy during the days of Hannukah the 'Mosque of Omar' [Al-Aqsa], and that they have spoken with the English, who have agreed to send ten warships to Jaffa for them." *Hatzfirah* reported the accusations and rumors and could not hold itself back from pointing out the irony that Ben-Yehuda's advocacy of Sephardi-Ashkenazi unity had achieved its goal—by uniting the leading rabbis of both communities against him.[58] In fact, the two rabbis were acting out of fear of the authorities and concern for the fate of their communities. The activism of the Zionist immigrants was too dangerous, as they saw it. Their actions were being monitored not only by the government in Constantinople but also by the Arabs of Palestine, foremost among them the mufti of Jerusalem, Mohammed Tahir al-Husayni.[59] Al-Husayni was motivated by religious sentiments (especially in the local Jerusalem context), as Eliezer Rokach had discerned some years before. It was on this basis that the mufti demanded that action be taken against Ben-Yehuda. This was precisely why Ben-Yehuda's Jewish opponents had flagged the danger the Zionists posed to Al-Aqsa. They knew that the Muslim shrines on the Temple Mount were a focus of Muslim identity and feeling in Palestine. In the 1990s, Sheikh Raed Salah coined the slogan "Al-Aqsa is in danger." Hajj Amin al-Husayni, Mohammed Tahir's son and successor as mufti of Jerusalem, voiced the same concern in 1920, just as his father had done thirty years earlier.

To help explain the picture in Ottoman Jerusalem at this time, it's worth mentioning that, just three weeks earlier, the mufti had taken part in the celebrations surrounding the investiture of the Yisa Berakhah. *Hatzfirah* recounted the scene:

> Invited to the honored rabbi's house that day were the dignitaries of the Sephardi and Ashkenazi communities. The dignitaries came, and our honored rabbi donned a mantle embroidered in silver on his shoulders and throat and chest and a miter with a silver ribbon, which were brought from Istanbul, and the honored rabbi made the *sheheheyanu* blessing [thanking God for allowing him to live to reach this event], and all the assembled blessed him with good fortune and a long life on the rabbinical cathedra, and the procession began. At the head walked the leaders of the Sephardim and Ashkenazim, and then the sextons, and after them the sexton of the [Sephardi] community bore the firman [royal order] in a silken pouch on a silver tray, and after him came the kaymakam effendi official dressed in his official uniform, with a sword on his thigh in a golden belt, and after him our honored chief rabbi, a splendid figure.... And waiting in honor of the rabbi in the chamber of the district administration were his honor the pasha, his honor the mufti effendi, the qadi effendi, his honor the *muhasabji muhasabji* [financial officer of the district administration], his honor Mayor Salim [al-Husayni] effendi . . . and other dignitaries, officials of the authority . . . and the entire assembly stood up, and pasha effendi read out the firman that His Majesty signed with his own hands. And when he had finished reading his honor the pasha wished all those standing and his honor our rabbi good fortune. Then his honor our rabbi recited in Arabic a fine prayer for the peace of our merciful king His Majesty the Sultan, and all the assembled shouted amen with all their might.[60]

On the public, ceremonial level, the head of the Jewish community merited all honor, both from the sultan and his court and from the local Jerusalem Muslim leadership. That pertained as long as the rabbi and his community accepted the rules of the place and the regime. In Islamic terms, this meant as long as they accepted the rules stating that the Jews were subject to the Islamic regime and refrained from seeking sovereignty. In the terms of the Ottoman nationalism that replaced Islamic terminology, it meant that they had to accept the principle of interreligious equality and brotherhood under the empire's sovereignty. But if their goal was to seize control of Palestine, then the government and the public, on the grounds of Ottoman, Arab, and religious identity, would fight them with all their might. The overarching Ottoman spirit that prevailed at the time meant that it was not only the mufti who was taken aback by the (false) report of Ben-Yehuda's plans but the hakham bashi as well. The mufti thus resolved that Ben-Yehuda should be excommunicated. It may well be that the hakham bashi not only feared provoking the gentiles but also felt a part of the sense of shared Ottoman identity and destiny that the regime was promoting at the time.

Ben-Yehuda and his father-in-law were acquitted two months after they were arrested, having proved to the court that the charges against them were unsubstantiated.[61] Immediately thereafter, the hakham bashi declared that the ban against them had been removed. For Ben-Yehuda, it took another fifteen years and the Young Turk Revolution to get over his trauma and to address the event in *Hatzvi*. He referred sarcastically to the charge that Jonas had fomented rebellion against the Turks so as to expedite the redemption of the Jewish people. "My late father-in-law, who was not at all a Zionist in his heart, and did not believe in the redemption, and denied that a messiah would come to the Jewish people, any sort of messiah, not miraculous and not natural. . . . He, who feared the coming of the messiah, because he stood in awe of the rule of the rabbis and of the yoke of the *Shulkhan Arukh* [code of Jewish law] . . . he, who always laughed at the Zionists and their actions, because he did not believe that there really was a Jewish people, because he said that the Jews were not truly capable of national action . . . he called on Israel to rebel, to rebel against the sultan and conquer the Land of Israel?!"[62] (Take note of what kinds of strange people could be found in Jerusalem at the time—those who did not believe in the messiah or in Jewish nationalism. But they were a small minority. The majority believed in either one of those principles or both of them.)

Ben-Yehuda himself, by the way, really did believe that the Jews had to seize control of Palestine, if only by means of money and subterfuge. In 1882 he wrote to Peretz Smolenskin, then in Vienna, "What we need to do now is to reach our full strength to conquer the land, little by little and surreptitiously. Every expanse of land that we remove from the hands of the non-Jew, whether good or bad, whether large or small, will bring us a little closer to the ultimate goal. . . . But we can only do all this covertly, silently. We will not blow rams' horns, nor will we sound trumpet blasts, we will not organize conferences that will enable the Arabs to know about what we want." As with Pinsker, Ben-Yehuda's vision encompassed the entire Jewish people, in the East and in the West. "If we succeed in buying land," he wrote, "then we'll easily find people who will come from the lands of our dispersion, whether from Russia, Romania, Bulgaria, or from Morocco and Tunis and all other countries."[63]

It turns out, then, that the rumors about what Ben-Yehuda aspired to were not entirely baseless, and that may be what triggered the concern voiced by the hakham bashi of Jerusalem. His counterparts in other parts of Palestine, far from Jerusalem, were more concerned with local issues.

FAR FROM THE CENTER: THE STRUGGLE AGAINST THE CONVERSION OF SEPHARDI WOMEN TO ISLAM

The hakham bashi of Jerusalem, as a person of consequence and a symbol, was involved in the power struggles that shaped the rich and complex relations between the Sephardi community, the Ottoman government, Zionists, the local Arab community, and the Ashkenazi community in Jerusalem at the end of the nineteenth century. The other Ottoman administrative districts in Palestine all had their own hakham bashi, but these men were active largely at the local level. Here is a brief account of the work of Rabbi Makhlouf Eldaoudi, the hakham bashi of Acre, Haifa, Safed, and Tiberias from 1889 until his death in 1909, in the area of Jewish-Muslim relations. Rabbi Makhlouf was born in Marrakesh in Morocco in 1825; his family moved to Palestine when he was a small child. At the age of eighteen, he married Rachel, from the well-known Abbo family in Safed, and served as the rabbi of communities in the Galilee. He was appointed to the post of hakham bashi when he was seventy-five years old, by official order of the sultan and with the consent of Rishon Letziyon Elyashar. This was an indication that Jerusalem's influence extended beyond the borders of the Jerusalem district. The rabbi's son, Salim Eldaoudi, assisted him in his work and accompanied him to many meetings. The memoir written by the younger Eldaoudi is our principal source of knowledge about the rabbi.[64]

One of the challenges that Hakham Eldaoudi had to deal with was the desire of Jews—especially Jewish women—to convert to Islam. This was not a rare phenomenon, the extent of which is difficult to estimate. In his memoir, Salim Eldaoudi tells the story of two young women from Haifa, one from a well-off Sephardi family and the other a Moroccan Jewish woman who worked as a maid in her house, who went to the home of the mufti of Acre to convert to Islam. Representatives of the Jewish community in Haifa traveled to Acre to plead with the rabbi to do all he could to prevent the apostasy. They feared that if the women carried out their intention, it would set off a wave of conversions in their own community. The mufti himself notified Hakham Eldaoudi that the women had come to him, because Ottoman law required the presence of the hakham bashi when Jews converted to Islam.

The rabbi immediately took measures to counter the women. He knew that registry officials had the discretion to deny conversions to Islam if they were not convinced that supplicants had acted of their own free will. He therefore contacted a local dignitary he knew to inquire about what payment the officials would require to reject the applicants. On top of this, he asked the mufti to postpone the conversion for a week (and then for another week) to give him time to have heart-to-heart talks with the women, who were staying at the mufti's home, in an effort to deter them from their plan. The sheikh, mufti, and registrars all agreed to cooperate, some because of the money they received and some because of their personal relationship with the hakham bashi. The rabbi and his son spoke with the young women several times, trying to understand what had caused them to want to convert. Since they presumed that the reason was that they wanted to marry, the two men proposed Jewish husbands to them. Salim relates in his book that, on his father's instructions, he told the better-off Sephardi woman that he was interested in marrying her himself. She realized that his intention was to change her mind, so she rejected his offer. But in the end, the two women gave in. They moved from the mufti's residence to the rabbi's home, and he indeed found matches for both of them.

What insights can we gain from this story about Sephardi-Arab relations?

OF STORIES AND INSIGHTS

The question of how to reach conclusions on the basis of "small" events is a big subject in the writing of history. Sephardi youths may or may not have said something following the fight between the Moskobim and the Arabs; Arab youths harassed Jews during Ramadan; two young Jewish women fled from Haifa to Acre in the hope of converting to Islam. What can be done with these stories? In all these cases, not even the names of those involved appear in the contemporary accounts. What use can such trivial events be to the writing of history? History is about great events—Admiral Nelson and the Battle of Trafalgar, Herzl covering the Dreyfus trial, Sultan Abdul Hamid II suspending the constitution, the Zionist Congress deliberating on the possibility of establishing a Jewish state in east Africa.

Which takes us back to the question of what the writing of history actually is. There are in fact different kinds of historical writing. There is world history and national history and social and personal history, to cite one of many ways of dividing up the field, and these different levels of writing are connected. Global phenomena affect nations, and individuals are affected by and influence national movements. One of the matters that interest us here is the way in which larger categories—religion, nationality, class, gender—are expressed in the lives of individuals, and vice versa. And we know that conversations between people and the mutterings of youths do not take place in a vacuum. They express emotions, grow out of identities, reinforce or lessen the boundaries of identities, and are the outward manifestations of an individual's experience and consciousness. These are the things that we want to investigate.

So what do we learn here? First, the very desire of these young women to become Muslims indicates that Islam was not perceived by all Jews as something repulsive. Furthermore, the concern by the leaders of the Haifa community that the women's action could lead to a wave of Jewish conversions indicates that Islam (or young Muslim men) had real drawing power. No less significant is the willingness of Muslim clerics and officials to help the rabbi prevent the conversions. They did not see the conversion of Jewish women to Islam as a great precept of their religion, despite the ethos of the *da'wah* calling on people to embrace Islam. This is one of many examples of the difference between the official principles of a religion and the actual behavior of members of that religion, including religious leaders. There may also be something about female sisterhood going on in this story. The mufti's mother herself, according to Salim Eldaoudi's book, took part in dissuading the young women from conversion, warning them that, after a brief period of infatuation, their husbands would begin to insult them, call them unfaithful Jewesses, and even beat them.

The claim that Jewish (or formerly Jewish) women are beaten by their Muslim husbands or partners is commonly heard today as well. Without closely scrutinizing the claim, there is no way of knowing whether Muslim men indeed are more violent toward Jewish women than Jewish men are. It could be that the charge was made then and is made now to deter Jewish women from intermarrying with Muslim men. But warnings of this sort do not always work as planned. Small numbers of Jewish women (especially Mizrahi women) nevertheless married Arabs, both during the Mandate years and later in the State of Israel. The efforts of religious leaders and lay activists on both sides never succeeded in putting a complete end to the practice. In a certain sense, the fight against intermarriage is an area of Jewish-Muslim cooperation, growing out of a common belief in the primary importance of protecting family and religious affiliations from the grip of romantic love. Like Acre's chief rabbi and mufti, the mukhtar (communal leader) of the Kerem Hateimanim neighborhood in Tel Aviv, Nahum Levi, recounted that he worked together with his neighbor, the Muslim qadi, to dissuade Jewish women in the area from converting to Islam in order to marry.[65]

That this phenomenon can be found both when Jews lived as a minority under Muslim rule and now that they live as a majority, under Jewish sovereignty, indicates that intimate relations with Arabs, including conversion to Islam, are not only the product of a desire to affiliate with the stronger group. But what, then, causes women (mostly) to convert in order to marry, then and now, to the extent that it happens? Does the culture that Arabs and Mizrahi Jews share mean that, among Mizrahim, love and physical attraction more easily overcome national and religious barriers? Or is it that the two groups tend to be on the same rung of the socioeconomic ladder? There is evidence that it is easier for Mizrahi women than it is for their Ashkenazi counterparts to integrate into Arab communities.[66] But such questions require comprehensive research that lies outside the purview of this book. In any case, the desire to prevent such relations persists, as evidenced by Rabbi Mordechai Eliyahu.

RABBI ELIYAHU AND YITZHAK NAVON ON INTERMARRIAGE

In 1984, soon after the end of his term as Israel's president, Yitzhak Navon was appointed minister of education. The rishon letziyon—Sephardi chief rabbi—at the time was Rabbi Mordechai Eliyahu, who had been born in Jerusalem's Old City. Navon also came from a venerable Jerusalem family, with both Sephardi and Mughrabi ancestry. As president, he promoted encounters between Jewish and Arab schoolchildren. The following story is told in the name of Rabbi Shmuel Eliyahu, Rabbi Mordechai's son:

> Once there was a school program to bring Jewish and goyim [non-Jews] together. The minister of education then was Yitzhak Navon and Rabbi [Eliyahu], my father, was chief rabbi. The rabbi told him [Navon] that this was absolutely forbidden. Yitzhak Navon asked him, did both of us not grow up in the Old City, and did we not have good, neighborly relations with Arabs? The rabbi said: there were relations of respect, but never did a Jew eat in the home of an Arab. He would not marry his daughter. Not learn with her and not play with her. They stayed to themselves and we stayed to ourselves. If there was, God forbid, such a connection, both the goyim and the Jews saw it as a catastrophe. This [cabinet] minister saw himself as wise and thought that he knew what was best for the Jewish people and what would bring peace between Jews and their Arab neighbors and made such meetings to increase "peace, love, and brotherhood." Immediately after these meetings the First Intifada began, and after it came the "peace agreement" of Oslo. Which since it broke out it is impossible to walk around Gaza or Nablus. After the peace broke out, when you walk around Jerusalem you need to pray not to be hurt. And it all began with those meetings.[67]

That there was a causal connection between the encounters and the Intifada seems open to question. What is important for the current discussion is the constant fear of interreligious marriage, of allowing Jews, Muslims, and Christians to spend time together, and how this fear affects relations between the groups.

THE CLASS QUESTION

The two girls who ran away from home so as to convert to Islam were from different social backgrounds. One was a well-off Sephardi girl who knew French and who was described as beautiful; the other was a Moroccan girl who worked in the first one's house as a maid. She spoke Arabic and her looks did not impress the rabbi. The two girls spoke Ladino to each other.[68] Arabic speakers were more immersed in the local Arab culture and more involved with Arabs in their day-to-day lives. These were the people, more than any others, whom the Zionists accused of assimilation and a lack of national consciousness. So it was in Jaffa, so it was in Jerusalem, and so it was in Haifa, where the girls lived. These "assimilationists" (or those who lived peacefully with the Arabs) came from all social strata, from the poorest, from the commercial class, and from the Sephardi literary elite.

The social gaps in mid-nineteenth-century Jewish society in Palestine were magnified by a unique factor: the Jews who were then settling in the country came mostly from the two ends of the socioeconomic spectrum—elites and public figures, on the one hand, and the destitute, on the other. This entrenched a society with ingrained disparities. In the 1850s, the leaders of the Sephardi communities warned, "Regrettably, ships are coming in from the east and from the west [carrying immigrants] from Syria and the Arab countries and Turkey, all of them poor and naked and indigent."[69] These immigrants wanted to join the Jewish community of the Land of Israel and believed that if they could not find work, they would be able to live off the public purse, because they were maintaining the Jewish connection to the Holy Land. The leaders of the Sephardi community were alarmed. The flow of poor Jews into Palestine meant lower subsidies for all the families that lived off community funds. Their critics charged that their real interest was to maintain their own public funding. In any case, the continuation of unregulated immigration led to the creation, a century before the State of Israel was founded, of an underclass made up mostly of Jews from the Islamic world. The warning voiced by the Sephardi leaders was an early example of the claim that immigrants should be classified according to their ability to support themselves and the extent to which they would be a burden on the public purse. This was the idea of selective immigration that was also discussed by David Ben-Gurion and other Israeli leaders during the Jewish state's early years. They did not invent it.

NOT JUST THE SEPHARDI INDIGENT

"And here the hour has arrived and Ashkenazim are seen and more than is proper. New Ashkenazim are walking around all the streets and they and their possessions are filling every hole in Jaffa. Who are they? *Poylishe*—refugees from the pogroms in Russia and Romania, who could not afford to go to America and came here. For what? They have heard a rumor that 'colonies' are to be built in the Land of Israel by organizations and philanthropists—and these wretched people preceded them and came to settle." So Simha Ben Zion, the father of the artist Nahum Gutman, described the people of the First Aliyah. He did not write of them from personal experience of their arrival—he himself came during the Second Aliyah—but as a writer. "And all of Jaffa teems with these," he continued. "Hungry and idle people debate colonization on the streets . . . and the shores have already been closed to this immigration of abject penury."[70] The Sephardi notables looked down on the Ashkenazi immigrants; Hovevei Zion associations tried to limit immigration from eastern Europe by setting economic standards. Immigration restrictions—selection—seemed imperative to many.[71]

THE MOSKOBIM AND THE SENSE OF SUPERIORITY

This was the situation prior to the immigration of the socialist Moskobim, who made up the core of the Second Aliyah. Infused with revolutionary fervor, they wanted to change the world. They believed that they alone held the key to the redemption of the Jewish people from the humiliation of the Exile, from living as parasites off the labor of others, and from the sword that the gentiles wielded against them. They viewed their parents as part of a generation whose time had passed, and their initial rebellion was against them. In Europe, before they came to Palestine, they saw Jews who were assimilating into the cultures of the countries in which they lived as a threat to Jewish nationhood. When they settled in Palestine, they brought with them an emotional worldview shaped by pogroms, the barricades of the socialist struggle, and their confrontations with Jews devoid of national consciousness. They sought to put their principles into operation in Palestine. They wanted to shake up the traditional outlook of the country's Jews and to impel them to accept the authority of socialist Zionism. The Sephardi bourgeoisie might have been amenable to new initiatives and modernization, but in the view of the Moskobim, they sought to maintain the old Oriental world. The educated Sephardim who adopted the ideas of the European Enlightenment (sometimes in their Ottoman incarnation) were, as far as the Second Aliyah pioneers were concerned, Levantines in the negative sense of the word—they were people who had exchanged their traditional Oriental garb for European suits, lost their traditional culture, but failed to become Europeans.

Here is a portrait of the Jewish community in Haifa that appeared in *Hapoel Hatzair*, a periodical put out by the socialists. "We can easily comprehend the picture of Sephardi public life," one of the publication's senior writers declared. "In a single word: zilch! And the masses, far more ignorant than in Jaffa and Jerusalem, appalling in their excessive Arabization, remain abandoned, without any leaders and without public officials." But it was not just the ignorant masses who bore the defect of Arabization. So did the graduates of the Alliance Israélite high school. "Like the rest of their brethren, they are entirely Arab in their speech, their mores, their commerce, and everything else," he maintained. "They are as distant from a knowledge of Hebrew and of Hebrew studies as they are from general knowledge." In sum, he wrote, "It would be impossible to describe a greater distance than that between the Sephardim in Haifa and the new Ashkenazi element. . . . They largely view the new Ashkenazim, who are, after all, the great majority of the Ashkenazim, as 'Moskobim,' while they refer to themselves as *wlad al-'Arab* [children of Arabia]. . . . You must admit that in much they may well be closer to the local Arabs than to us."[72]

CLOSENESS

The question of just how close Mizrahim and Arabs were to each other is an essential one for the subject of this book. It requires distinguishing between different types of propinquity. One sort is cultural affinity—namely, affiliation with the same culture in terms of family structure, cuisine, musical taste, the use of language, attitudes toward sacred scriptures, and all that comes with these things. This sort of closeness is a cultural and sociological fact. But it does not necessarily produce political partnership (in some cases it can actually exacerbate tensions and competition). Another sort of closeness is the social kind—the existence of common social circles whose members want to maintain them. Beyond these, there is emotional closeness, when social contact gives rise to affection that is not impinged on by disparities of religion or nation. Another possible axis of closeness is political—there may be a political alliance between religiously or nationally disparate groups or people, or a desire to create such an alliance. Let's try to track these different types over time. One thing that needs to be kept in mind, though, is that the historical record is relatively rich when it comes to documenting the political dimension, whereas emotional ties rarely produce documents. The former will thus get more attention.

In Haifa, the affinities were cultural and linguistic, and there were also common social circles. When it comes to politics, the situation is more complex. We will soon encounter Sephardi and Mughrabi Jews who moved toward Zionism and fought for it, others who disregarded it, and still others who opposed it. The members of the Hapoel Hatzair faction who saw the members of these communities as ignoramuses and nonentities hardly ever made such distinctions. As far as they were concerned, a Sephardi Jew who did not join the socialist ranks was inferior, an "Arab." The discourse about the inferiority of Sephardi and Mizrahi youth would continue during the Mandate and loom even larger during the waves of mass immigration during Israel's early years.

MIZRAHIM AS ARABS

Likening Mizrahim to Arabs served as a tool for asserting Ashkenazi superiority. The report from Haifa was a relatively early example of this. The implicit assumption was that Arabs and their culture were inferior to European culture. In this case, the comparison was made by a publication put out by a political party. The same view was voiced in 1984 by a former chief of staff of the Israel Defense Forces (IDF), Knesset member Motta Gur, of the Labor Party. He was responding to right-wing demonstrators who disrupted one of his party's election rallies. From the podium he declared that his party would fuck the right-wing Mizrahi demonstrators just as it had fucked the Arabs. "Just as with them their screams didn't help and we fucked them, your screams won't help, either, and we'll fuck you."[73] In 2020 it was the director-general of the Kibbutz Movement, Nir Meir, who compared (with some disclaimers, of course) the Hamas rocket attacks on the kibbutzim on the perimeter of the Gaza Strip to the demands of the Free the Asi protest campaign. The protesters, many of them from the nearby town of Beit She'an, demanded that the Asi stream, on the banks of which a kibbutz, Nir David, stood, should be open to the public. Meir depicted both the town's inhabitants, most of them Mizrahim, and the people of the Gaza Strip as primitives who were jealous of the success of others—in this case, the kibbutz and its members.[74] Here is an example of the continuity of fraught Ashkenazi–Edot Hamizrah relations extending from the beginning of the twentieth century to this day. It reinforces the view of the historical continuity of Ashkenazi arrogance toward the Mizrahim. Consistently, over this period, Ashkenazim have identified Mizrahim as fundamentally Arab and have condemned them for this. And there are other lines of continuity that we will encounter in subsequent chapters.

THE GENERATIONAL DIFFERENCE

As we note the continuity in this sense of Ashkenazi superiority, it is also important to pay attention to the difference. At the beginning of the twentieth century, the Moskobim were just at the beginning of their process of building up their economic and political power, and the struggle for dominance between the different currents in the emerging Yishuv had not yet been decided (of course, struggles that have already been decided can flare up anew). Condescension toward other groups in a state of relative equality is not the same as accusations, or a sense of superiority, when the power disparities are salient and when one side can substantively determine the fate of the other group, as would be the case two decades later. While we are now examining the roots of the European Zionist sense of superiority, it's important to keep in mind that there was also a Sephardi sense of superiority, and, as we proceed, we will see who had the upper hand and when. In doing so, it's crucial to remember that the sense of superiority is not the most significant variable. Rather, it is the power relationships and the modes of action of the different players when they had power that is critical. The question is thus how the Ashkenazim acted when they sought to achieve hegemony, and how they acted when they gained it. Also, how Mizrahim acted then and act now to challenge that hegemony, and what arrangement they think should rightly come into being when the old hegemony is dismantled.

One more historical remark: the expression "Awlad Arab," or alternately "Arab Jews," was used by writers in *Hapoel Hatzair* as a mark of Mizrahi inferiority. More recently, starting at the end of the twentieth century, a few Mizrahi intellectuals have sought to revive this Arab-Jewish identity as an act of reclaiming—that is, declaring their pride in—Arab and Mizrahi culture. It resonates with the original term despite the fact that the necessary conditions for its existence—interreligious political equality and involvement in Arab culture and life—do not exist today (I have written at length about this elsewhere).[75]

A WORD ABOUT ALLIANCE

Some of these Arab-Jews (the concept was a valid one then) in Haifa had attended the city's Alliance Israélite Universelle school. The organization had been founded in France in 1860 with the goal of defending persecuted Jews all over the world. The immediate impetus was the Damascus blood libel twenty years earlier and a series of other antisemitic incidents. These French Jews were aware that the great powers within whose borders they lived wielded influence over countries in Asia and Africa. They were also cognizant of their own power, as some of them had attained key posts in their home countries, even as they continued to advocate Jewish solidarity. Alliance's first president was Adolphe Crémieux, a French Jew who had been involved in the fight against the Damascus blood libel (1840) and who was appointed France's minister of justice in 1848. Alliance did impressive work to save Jewish communities all over the world (including providing assistance to Jews to enable them to leave the eastern European killing fields). But at the same time it founded a network of schools in North Africa and the Middle East that changed the face of Jewish education in these communities. (This sometimes involved disputes with the local religious leadership.) Alliance opened its school in Haifa in 1884, two years after its school in Jerusalem opened its doors, and enrolled both boys and girls. The Moskobim vilified these schools and their students, in no small part on matters of principle. Michael Abitbol, a historian of North African Jewry, sums up the debate: "Alliance was not simply a philanthropic institution. Its activity was founded on an idea that constituted an ideological and practical alternative to the Zionist idea. Instead of the Land of Israel, Alliance placed France at the center, and disseminated its culture and values." Furthermore, "Alliance Israélite Universelle believed that the Jewish Question could be solved within the countries the Jews lived in . . . by means of their social and cultural integration and their integration into the economies of the countries in which they lived."[76]

This integrationist approach stood in opposition to the position of Zionists everywhere, and certainly in the Land of Israel, in which the labor movement promoted Jewish isolation from Palestinian Arabs much more vehemently than the settlers of the First Aliyah had done. Alliance's students, by contrast, saw themselves as part of the social fabric of their cities. The same was true of the schools themselves, which were open not just to Jews but to all the country's inhabitants. Indeed, a number of leading Muslim families, among them the Khalidi and Husayni families already mentioned, sent their sons to be educated at Alliance schools. This trend grew stronger under the growing influence of the ideas of integration and fraternity that came to the fore following the Young Turk Revolution of 1908.[77] The self-styled new Ashkenazim had a different approach, one of separation.

THE NATIONAL SEPARATION PROJECT

This separation approach was a point of contention between Jews born and bred in Palestine (especially, but not only, the Sephardim) and the Moskobim. Even though their relations with the Arabs were not always ideal, despite the harassment on Ramadan nights, and despite intercommunal rivalry, the Jewish natives viewed themselves as part of the same broad local Ottoman milieu. This was true of both the lower strata and the elites who walked the path of Ottoman modernization. Their political imagination did not conjure up a Jewish state based on immigration from eastern Europe but rather a multireligious society rooted in the local space. The Moskobim, by contrast, aspired to detach the Jews from the Arabs. This was absolutely clear to the

Arabs as well. The Arabic newspaper *Filastin* recounted, in 1914, the developments set in motion since the arrival of members of the Second Aliyah. The Jews, who had in the past been considered "a patriotic, Ottoman race, a brother, beloved and honored among all its fellow Ottoman races," had changed "since the arrival of the Zionist adversaries, those who were German revolutionaries, those who were Russian anarchists," who bellowed and called out, "Beware, Jews, of mixing with the local inhabitants, lest you lose your national consciousness." The new Jews also spread the claim that "they are a 'nation,' not just a 'religion,' and that they are trying to lease the land so that they can have self-rule, in a self-ruled land, and not be part of a simple race in a multiracial land. Indeed, they first of all began to build private suburbs for themselves, and afterward began to draw to them the members of their nation, sifting them out from among the Muslims and Christians, just like a farmer sifts out the seeds. And then they boycotted the Arabic language, to the point where you do not hear its ring in their marketplaces and in their conversation, and then they authored textbooks in their schools in their own non-living language."[78]

The text above is an English translation made not from the Arabic original but from a Hebrew translation by Nissim Malul for the Palestine Office of the Zionist Executive. The article precisely and incisively diagnoses the separation process. On the level of identity, it privileges Judaism's national dimension over its religious dimension, which leads to the demand for self-determination. On the political level, it aspires to self-determination while rejecting cooperative political models. On the practical level, it purchases land and builds settlements solely for Jews. On the social level, it invites Jews living among Arabs to shed their Arab character and become part of a separate Jewish society.

THE CHAIN OF ORIENTALIZATION

Zionism proposed to the Sephardim that they make a break with their hoary identities and accept the yoke of the organized European Zionist movement, which meant looking down on Arabs. As sociologist Aziza Khazzoom puts it, they were to join "the great chain of Orientalization" by directing an aloof gaze toward the Orient. In her view, the chain originated in the superiority that central European Christians felt toward the Orient, including toward the Jews who lived among them, whom they perceived as an Oriental vestige. When the Jews of central Europe began to Westernize, they adopted this sense of superiority and directed it at the Jews of eastern Europe (*Ostjuden*). When the *Ostjuden*—the Moskobim—settled in Palestine, they began to see themselves as Europeans and adopted a condescending attitude toward the Jews of the Islamic world, toward the Ashkenazi Old Yishuv, who had not undergone the process of European acculturation, and toward the Arabs.[79] Now it was time for the Jews of the East to join them, and to adopt a position of cultural superiority over the Arabs. The assumption was that simply by virtue of being Jews, the Sephardim could move into the "advanced" camp.

For the members of the Sephardi elite in Palestine, this was a transformation of the highest order. Until the middle of the nineteenth century, they had seen themselves as manifestly superior to the Ashkenazim. Beyond heading the ethnic group that comprised the majority of the Jews in the country, these Sephardi leaders held the political and economic power. At the same time, they felt an affinity with their class counterparts among Muslims and Christians. The relative size and status of the Sephardi community began to decline as immigration from Europe picked up, and as European Jewish actors gained influence in Jerusalem's economy.[80] The Zionist waves of immigration accelerated this process.

A BIRD'S-EYE VIEW

The change in the balance of power between Ashkenazim and Sephardim in Jerusalem, to the detriment of the latter, mirrored a global phenomenon, as Europe gained technological, economic, and military dominance over the rest of the world, including the Muslim world. As the European powers grew stronger, European Jews also gained influence within the Jewish arena, and that sense of power brought with it a sense of superiority toward the Jews of the East (though it was combined with a sense of solidarity, as shown by the work of Alliance Israélite Universelle).

But an opposite process took place in Europe as well. As nationalism gained force in Europe, it led to the exclusion and rejection of Jews. As a result, some Jews felt they need a nationalism of their own, Zionism, which slowly threaded its way into the ideological fabric of Jewish communities in Europe. Zionism was a modern movement, acting in a new reality to achieve political goals formulated in modernistic language. As such, it served its activists of all stripes—liberal, socialist, and otherwise—as a central path toward becoming part of modernism and the new age. At the same time, its leaders, who felt a duty to the nation, could not disregard the "backward" parts of the nation—namely, the Mizrahim, who looked like Arabs, and the Haredim, who maintained premodern customs. It wanted to Westernize and secularize these groups.

As the Zionist movement grew stronger and everything Arab came to be seen as a mark of degeneration, the invitation to give up Arab and Mizrahi identities and to look down on the Arabs of Palestine grew increasingly attractive. It was not, however, necessary to join the Zionist movement in order to adopt the modernist view or to see the East as benighted—that was also the view of a part of the Arab elite. For these Arabs as well, Europe represented initiative, progress, and the power to shape the course of history. So Arab effendis marveled at the Zionist moshavot, as Eli Osherov has shown, and disparaged the Arab fellahs.[81]

WESTERN SUPERIORITY: A PALESTINIAN ARAB PERSPECTIVE

Filastin, like the Hebrew newspapers *Hapoel Hatzair* and *Haherut*, also took up the issue of the East's inferiority. It was a recurring theme, addressed both directly and metaphorically. An article from October 1912 was written in the form of a conversation between stalks of grain in a field. One bemoaned growing in a field in a country settled by Orientals who did not properly care for their land or understand agriculture. As a result, it yielded little grain. A second stalk said that God had sent the prophets to the inhabitants of this land precisely because they most needed guidance. A third spoke of the state of Palestine's schools—they were empty of students, and the only thing they taught was sycophancy and selfishness from teachers devoid of repute. Any comparison with the West underscored the weakness of the East in general and of Palestine in particular, the grain stalks agreed. Like many who lived under Western colonialism, they reached the conclusion that the country needed modern methods of instruction and new ways of doing things. It was necessary to learn from the West.[82]

The members of the local Arab elites had social relations with members of the First Aliyah. They invited one another into their homes, to their weddings, and to cultural events.[83] They also had contacts with the leading lights of the Sephardi community, those people who were in a complicated relationship with the institutionalized Zionist movement. This latter group supported Jewish immigration to Palestine but took exception to the conduct of the Moskobim; they saw themselves as part of the Ottoman Empire but also as part of the Jewish renewal. They instituted Hebrew language instruction in Sephardi schools but stressed the great importance of teaching Arabic as well. Some of them worked actively with official Zionist institutions, mainly by serving as mediators between these bodies, on the one hand, and the Arab population and Ottoman leadership, on the other. Years earlier, when the

First Aliyah began, the old Sephardi families had taken in the immigrants and helped them take their first steps in Palestine—including the purchase of land.

THE SEPHARDI ELITE AND ZIONIST INSTITUTIONS

Panicked Jews began emigrating from eastern Europe in the 1880s in the wake of the pogroms. An absolute majority of them set their sights on North America, but some chose Palestine. These were largely members of Hovevei Zion and other such associations that had emerged in different cities. Representatives of these different associations convened in Katowice (then in Germany, now in Poland) in 1884 and set up an umbrella organization to unite their political and practical efforts. The conference decided to send a delegation to Palestine to study the condition of the moshavot that had already been established and to formulate plans for further settlement. The task was undertaken by Kalonymus Wissotzky, a tea merchant and one of the leaders of the movement. During Wissotzky's visit to Jewish points of settlement, the newspaper *Havatzelet* wrote, "he made an acquaintance with the wolves in sheep's clothing and ejected them [to keep them from] insinuating themselves into the lands of the real Hovevei Zion, and not only that but endeavored and sought and found a man more precious than a thousand, the honorable man of wealth, possessor of precious talents, his excellency, our teacher and rabbi Avraham Moyal, may his candle shine, and placed him at the head of all the Yishuv's affairs, and to oversee the moshavot in particular."[84]

The writer signed himself "E. R." He was Eliezer Rokach, whom we've met before. Rokach was also a member of Hovevei Zion and served as its representative in Palestine.[85] In addition to the assistance they provided to the existing moshavot, Moyal and Rokach searched for land that could be purchased for the establishment of new moshavot and helped Jews settle in Arab cities such as Lod, Nablus, and Gaza.

Wissotzky's choice of Moyal was a pragmatic one. On his way to Palestine, he had written those who had sent him that "we must try with all our might to win the hearts of our Sephardi brethren, who are well known here, and who have a hand in all arms of the government, and the government is sure of their loyalty and sincerity, and only at their hands may a person be saved." Wissotzky also tried to persuade the leaders of Hovevei Zion not to stop with the employment of Moyal but to make an effort also to bring "the best of our brothers the Sephardim" into the workings of the movement. But this proposal of his was not brought up for discussion. Menashe Mani, who was born in Hebron in 1889 to a long line of rabbis and kabbalists from Baghdad and became a banker and lay historian, saw this disregard as the beginning of the alienation between the Zionist movement and the Sephardi public.[86] Moyal died not long after taking up his position with Hovevei Zion, but he was hardly the only, and not even the first, member of the Sephardi elite in Jaffa to help Ashkenazi settlers buy land. He was preceded by Haim Amzaleg, a banker and the deputy British consul in the city, who helped the settlers who established the moshava Petah Tikva to purchase land of the Arab village of Mulabes, and the settlers of Rishon Lezion to purchase land from the village of ʿUyūn Qārā.[87] Aharon Chelouche, the head of the Jaffa Chelouche family, also helped purchase land at the beginning of the Zionist influx.[88]

A generation later, another member of Avraham Moyal's family, Shimon Moyal, belonged to the circle of some twenty Sephardi writers who published their work in *Haherut*. They produced hundreds of pieces on the Arab problem—in quite a different environment, that which followed the Young Turk Revolution.

THE SEPHARDI ELITE AS A DEFENSE FORCE

The initial enthusiasm about the Young Turk Revolution, and the feeling of brotherhood among the adherents of all religions that came with it, did not last long. The freedom of expression guaranteed by the constitution allowed Palestine's Arabs to voice their opposition to Zionism openly and clearly. Zionism, as both an ideology and a practice, privileged Jews over other people and was thus seen as harmful, not only by explicit and implicit antisemites but also by Arabs who advocated civil intercommunal equality. The most notable Arabic-language newspapers founded in Palestine in the wake of the revolution, such as Haifa's *Al-Karmel*, founded in 1908 and edited by Najib Nassar, Jaffa's *Filastin*, which began to appear in 1911, and Jerusalem's *Al-Munadi*, devoted much space to the struggle against Zionism and the sale of land to the movement. They called on the government to keep a closer watch over what the Zionists were doing. The Palestinian Arab representatives in the Ottoman parliament demanded an end to Jewish immigration. Tension between Jews and Arabs increased, and the people who felt the change most acutely seemed to be the veteran, Arabic-speaking Sephardim, who changed the way they wrote about the Arabs in Palestine. Yosef Meyuhas is a good example. He was born in 1868 in Kfar Hashiloach, the Arab village of Silwan, just outside the walls of Jerusalem's Old City. Meyuhas wrote many books on Arab culture and served as a member of the National Council (Hava'ad Hale'umi), the executive of the Jewish community in Palestine. In 1896 he wrote, "The Arabs have long been our loyal brothers. . . . [The Arab] has shared his beautiful language with us, has taught us his good values, has endowed us with his pleasant proverbs, and has showered us with his sublime spirit."[89] Avraham Elmalih wrote retrospectively about the period following the revolution that "among our adversaries, newspapers of greater or lesser importance stood in the first ranks, and the hostility was not spontaneous, from time to time, but rather fixed, ongoing, systematized, and practiced with very, very fierce military tactics." In contrast with the claim that Arab writers took pains to distinguish between Jews and Zionists, Elmalih argued that this was only a stratagem to evade being put on trial for fomenting interreligious conflict:

> Amid all the invective of all the hostile newspapers you will almost never find the term "Jew." They would not, God forbid, stir up the coarse masses with defamatory rhetoric, all sorts of incitement . . . except against the Zionists, the "Zionist nation." With this stratagem they avoid prosecution . . . and having found that stratagem, the way was clear before them. There are no longer any impediments, nothing to prevent them, no qualms. Everything was permitted. They could fabricate all sorts of lies about the Zionists, make the most horrible threats, ascribe to them the most horrible abominations, and there was no way they could be brought to justice.[90]

Both the Sephardim and *Filastin*'s writers took note of the deteriorating relations between Jews and Arabs. It was a change for the worse that could hardly be ignored. But each side, as usual, attributed the change to the conduct of the other side. The Sephardim associated with *Haherut* came to the defense of the slandered Zionist movement, proposing to publish a pro-Zionist newspaper in Arabic. This led to an intra-Zionist polemic in which they were accused of assimilation, and the idea was shelved. Some of them also came to Zionism's defense at public events—one example being Shlomo Buzaglo of Haifa.

BUZAGLO VERSUS NASSAR—HAIFA, 1911

Shlomo Buzaglo came from a Mughrabi family in Haifa and taught at the Alliance school in that city. Najib Nassar was a Christian of the same city, the editor of *Al-Karmel*, and a fervent anti-Zionist. The two men encountered each other at Jarina Square during a rally in support of the Ottoman Empire in the crisis over Cretan political representation. Following speeches by four Muslims, Nassar rose to speak as well. Buzaglo interrupted his speech, calling out, "Get off this Ottoman platform! Down, you are sowing discord among the peoples! We need unity here in Turkey! Get down!" Debates broke out within the audience over who was right. Was Nassar indeed sowing discord with his attacks on Zionism, or was it the Zionists who were doing damage to the empire's integrity? Nassar quickly declared that Buzaglo had slandered the empire's honor. His associates echoed the message and many began pursuing Buzaglo, shouting, "Catch the Jew! Kill him! Smash his head in!" Buzaglo managed to escape with help from an Ottoman police detail. Afterward, he sent the British consul—he was also a British subject—a request for help in filing a lawsuit against Nassar.[91]

Buzaglo defended Zionism on the streets of Haifa, setting himself apart from the young Sephardim in Jaffa who made fun of the Moskobim's woes in 1908. On the other hand, like those young Sephardim, he saw the Ottoman order as positive, and considered the local Arab culture his culture. For that reason, the Moskobim looked down on and scorned him. Even so, no small number of educated Sephardim sought a way into the Zionist institutions, which were growing stronger.

MOYAL AND ARAB CULTURE

The World Zionist Organization set up its Palestine Office in 1908, under the direction of Arthur Ruppin, to coordinate Zionist activity in the country. Ruppin brought in Sephardi intellectuals who, among other things, translated articles from the Arabic press. Sometimes they published their translations and wrote about their views on the Arab problem in the pages of *Haherut*, which became their unofficial mouthpiece. Their goal was to rouse public opinion in the Yishuv to work to improve Jewish-Arab relations, and they wanted to demonstrate that good relations between the two communities were essential. Shimon Moyal was the most prominent spokesman for this approach.[92] He maintained that the future of the Jews in Palestine lay in aligning with the Arabs and not the West. It seems that he felt closer to the Arabs and their identity than many of his Sephardi associates did.

In February 1912, Moyal published in *Haherut* a letter he had sent to rabbis, the boards of the moshavot in the Galilee and Judea, the leaders of public institutions, and a range of authors and functionaries. In it, he called for a meeting to discuss relations with Palestine's Arabs and laid out his views. He reiterated his call not to neglect the issue, while stressing the commonalities

Jews and Arabs shared: "Palestine is inhabited largely by the Muslim Arab nation, our primordial relatives. This affable and well-bred nation does not hate the Jewish soul and race, which has no remedy, like the antisemitic hatred of Europe. . . . Such hatred will eventually be displaced from people's hearts by the tolerance for other opinions that has come in the wake of the development of the mind and in particular by living together and by conclusion of a defense pact with it against the common hatred of the children of Shem [the Semites]." This was the conclusion reached by "an Arab writer, who has spent more than a quarter century of his years in Arabic literature and the Arabic press."

Moyal reminded his readers of how he had endeavored to rouse the public opinion of the Hebrews (Jews) to give its attention to relations with the Arabs, "but our brethren," he wrote, "did not listen to me and based themselves on their European experiences, or on other presumptions that were completely inappropriate to the conditions we lived in, until evil grew." Then he presented the best away to proceed and offered his vision of the two peoples' common future: "To explain to the Arabs that our, the Hebrew nation's, aspirations do not contradict their own aspirations, and that we have qualities that are needed for working intensively and with devotion for our common homeland and for enhancing the estimation of the Ottoman nation, under whose protection our banner waves, at the same time that we desire to be a distinctive Jewish people that fosters its own language, character, past, future, and customs." In other words, Palestine was a common homeland in which there was room for a shared life and development that would benefit all sides—without either group's having to sacrifice its unique identity or national character.[93]

There were Zionist activists who advocated Jewish-Arab cooperation. Others aspired to a discrete Jewish society. Some believed that Palestine was the homeland of two nations; others, apparently more numerous, maintained that it was exclusively the homeland of the Jews. The prevalent Arab construal was that Jews were coming to Palestine expressly to hem in the Arabs and, if possible, to expel them. For example, Mustafa Effendi Tamer, a Jerusalem teacher, denounced the Arabs who were selling land to Jews. "You are selling the possessions of your forefathers and grandfathers for a minuscule sum to people who will have no mercy on you, to those who are working to expel you and to obliterate all memory of you from the places where you live and to scatter you among the nations."[94] This was not the only possible way for the Arabs of Palestine to understand what they saw happening around them, but it was a reasonable interpretation. When other Jews attacked Moyal and his associates and took no cognizance of their positions, it simply confirmed to Arabs that the central stream of Zionism had rejected the path of cooperation and equality.

THE ZIONIST HAKHAM BASHI

The tension between their views and those of the Zionist mainstream did not deter the Sephardim from working within Zionism's institutions. Some hoped to change the movement from within; others sought a livelihood. And the Zionist movement needed them as intercessors with the Turkish authorities and as bridges to the Arab population. This prompted a request, accepted by the Ottoman authorities, to create a new position: a hakham bashi for Jaffa and the moshavot. In August 1911, a forum authorized to choose the person to fill the post, made up of representatives of the Jewish communities of Jaffa and the Jewish settlements in its environs, convened. It elected Rabbi Ben-Zion Meir Hai Uziel by a vote of fifty-two to twelve. Soon thereafter, the conditions of his employment were finalized, with the cost of his salary being split between the moshavot and the committee that administered the affairs of Jaffa's Jews. Rabbi Uziel moved from Jerusalem to Jaffa and worked alongside Rabbi Avraham Yitzchak HaCohen Kook, who had served as the spiritual leader of Jaffa's Ashkenazi community since 1904.[95]

Rabbi Uziel was thirty-one years old when he took up his position, some fifteen years younger than Rabbi Kook, but he had experience as a rabbi and public figure. He was the scion of a rabbinic family and a graduate of the Doresh Zion Talmud Torah (religious school), which had been set up to serve both Ashkenazi and Sephardi boys but was boycotted by the Ashkenazim because it taught Arabic and arithmetic. As a young man, he served under the Yisa Berakhah and taught at the Tiferet Yerushalayim yeshiva (seminary). Prior to his appointment as hakham bashi, he had represented the Jewish public before the Ottoman authorities in Jerusalem. After taking up his new position, he maintained regular contact with Arthur Ruppin of the Palestine Office. He served as the representative of the Jews of Jaffa and its periphery until the end of World War I. The Jews of Jerusalem could not agree on who would serve as their hakham bashi, so Rabbi Uziel became by default the most senior official representative of Palestine's Jews, accepted by both the Zionist settlers and the Old Yishuv. He took part in official ceremonies in the Jaffa district and as a member of Jaffa's City Council. He voiced support for the Ottoman Empire, as did other Jews of all streams and ethnic groups.

A wave of Arab attacks fell on the moshavot of Judea and the Galilee during the second half of 1913. The Palestine Office charged Rabbi Uziel with appealing to the hakham bashi of Istanbul, Rabbi Haim Nahum, to use his connections with the government to bolster the security of the Jewish settlements. In his missive to Rabbi Nahum, Rabbi Uziel wrote that "recently there have been frequent cases of murder in the moshavot of Judea and the Galilee, one after the other. . . . There have been six murders thus far in Palestine, not including cases of assaults along the roads, beatings, robberies, and a case of rape. . . . These frequent incidents, which began only recently, demonstrate on the one hand the impunity of those who take no account of the government's authority. . . . We cannot remain silent in the presence of our brothers' blood and the theft of their property." He asked his superior, "as a faithful shepherd to stand up at this hour to protect his flock, and to inform the central government of all these events and to obtain in this way a firm order to seek out the criminals and punish them fittingly for their past transgressions and to use all necessary means to protect [the settlements] in the future."[96]

RABBI NAHUM, CHIEF OF THE RABBIS OF THE GREAT TURKISH KINGDOM

This was how Rabbi Uziel addressed Rabbi Nahum in the letter quoted above. The latter used his influence in the corridors of power, as he had done at other opportunities, and the Ottomans steadfastly promised him that they would take action to prevent further attacks. But Rabbi Nahum's relationship with the Zionist movement was complicated. During a visit to Palestine a few years earlier, in 1911, he had been given a very impressive welcome. "There was a great and wonderful festival for the Jewish inhabitants of Jerusalem on Sunday, 5 Sivan, a festival that will remain inscribed in golden letters in the chronicles of the Hebrew communities of Jaffa and Jerusalem," *Haherut* reported, "for on this day the two communities had the privilege of receiving the beloved and wise face of the great Rabbi Haim Nahum, the beloved chief of the rabbis of Turkey and his famed entourage. . . . At the break of dawn all of Hebrew Jaffa awoke and donned their holiday garments to receive the presence of this august guest and his respected entourage." From Jaffa, the rabbi and his party took the train to Jerusalem.

"And here I must declare," the newspaper's correspondent continued, "that the magnificent reception that Jerusalem prepared for the chief of the rabbis of Turkey had never been held in Jerusalem even for kings. We still remember the visit of the German kaiser himself. . . . At those receptions there were cavalry, more soldiers, more flags, but never was a person received in Jerusalem with such great enthusiasm, by such a great multitude, with such great adulation, as his honor the great Rabbi Haim Nahum." One of the speakers at the reception was the Hebrew educator and Yishuv leader David Yellin. "For the first time," he declared, "we see in Turkey that the hakham bashi, not an emissary, will take up the mission that our teacher Moses gave to the man who commands the community, 'who shall go out before them and come in before them, and who shall take them out and bring them in, so that the Lord's community may not be like sheep that have no shepherd.'"[97]

THE ONE WHO WAS NOT PLEASED: DAVID BEN-GURION

The fervor of the great majority of the Jewish communities in Palestine irked David Ben-Gurion. Four years after settling in Palestine, he devoted an article (one of his first) to the hakham bashi's visit to the country. It was published in the first issue of *Haahdut*, "the newspaper for the affairs of workers and the nation's masses in Palestine." It was the newspaper of the Poalei Zion party, the party that would, twenty years later, merge with Hapoel Hatzair to form the Workers of the Land of Israel Party, best known by its Hebrew acronym, Mapai, which became the hegemonic party in the Yishuv and the State of Israel up until 1977. Ben-Gurion objected to the fact that

> in all the speeches of the meeting the same opinion was heard, that the hakham bashi is not only the religious leader, but also the national emissary of the Jews of Turkey, who sees to all the nation's needs, and whose influence is decisive in all public matters. . . . Also in the press, whether in the Land of Israel or outside it, the same national stature and political importance is assigned to the hakham bashi for the development of Turkish Jewry as a whole and that of the Land of Israel in particular. Is the standing of the hakham bashi indeed so great these days? Is he indeed competent to perform this national role, in terms of his position and personality?

Ben-Gurion did not leave the question unanswered. "The capabilities of religious sages have no relevance outside the field of religion," he declared. He added that the reason was not only the separation between church and state mandated by the Ottoman constitution, but also Rabbi Nahum's personality. "Could it be that Rabbi Haim Nahum's influence as an excellent personality, of great determination and broad views, [has given him this power,] and as such he has acted to bolster the position of Turkish Jewry within and without? . . . But what did the hakham bashi do during the two years he has held his position? Zero."[98]

The debate was not just about religion and state relations in Jewish nationhood. On either side stood a view of the organization of the Jewish people, the place of tradition, relations between East and West, and two conceptions of Jewish nationalism. Rabbi Nahum had attended the Alliance school in Istanbul, and the tension between the city's Zionists and Alliance Israélite Universelle was at its height. The major issue was the extent to which the Jews should integrate into the Ottoman majority community and to what extent they should keep themselves separate. On the personal level, Rabbi Nahum confronted the dilemma faced by Jews of the Islamic world during the age of nationalism. On the one hand, he felt that Zionist activity was undermining Jewish relations with the majority communities in these lands, so he opposed it. On the other hand, he could not disregard the attacks on the Jewish settlements, and he exerted all his abilities to intercede with the Ottoman government to keep Jews safe.[99]

RABBI UZIEL

Unlike Rabbi Nahum, who in Turkish intra-Jewish politics was seen as close to Alliance circles but not to Zionist circles, Rabbi Uziel was part of the Zionist system then emerging in Palestine. It was the Zionists who paid his salary, even though he had been appointed by the Ottoman government and held an imperial position.

As an official representative of the Jews in Palestine, Zionist and otherwise, Uziel collected donations to be used to purchase a plane for the Ottoman air force, as a gift from the Jews of Palestine for the sultan's birthday.[100] As an Ottoman government appointee, he petitioned the authorities to improve the security of the moshavot. In his speeches, he pointed to the positive attitude the Jews had displayed toward the Ottoman regime ever since the Spanish expulsion. Following the Young Turk Revolution, he had to navigate the stormy waters of Ottoman politics.

INTERNAL OTTOMAN POLITICS: THE END

The Young Turk Revolution was followed by years of upheaval in the empire, both within and without. In hindsight, we know that this was the turmoil of the empire's collapse. But no one knew that then. Some ten months after the revolution, in the spring of 1909, Sultan Abdul Hamid II tried to retake power in a military coup. He failed and was deposed and replaced by his brother Mehmed V, who served as a symbolic monarch with few prerogatives. The Committee of Union and Progress, the most important Young Turk forum, was taken aback by the awakening of an opposition and tightened its grip on power, one aspect of which was the imposition of partial military rule and limitations on the right to strike. In the midst of this unrest, in September 1911, Italy launched an offensive against Ottoman territories in North Africa, which demanded great imperial energies and resources and increased the tension between the empire's Christians and Muslims. In the summer of 1912, the Turkish opposition managed to seize power for a few months, but in January 1913 the Committee of Union and Progress returned to power when a military force acting in its name broke into the office of the grand vizier (prime minister) and forced him to resign. The First Balkan War, launched by Orthodox Christian peoples (Serbia, Montenegro, Greece, and Bulgaria) against the empire, was already raging. Despite the self-assurance evinced by army commanders and many members of the Turkish and Arab public, the Ottoman army was defeated, and the empire lost nearly all its European territory.[101]

But it was not just the Christian areas of the shrinking empire that wanted out. The allegiance of the inhabitants of the Arab provinces was also declining. As the Committee of Union and Progress tightened its hold and sought to enforce Turkish political and cultural hegemony throughout the empire, Arab opposition grew. Avraham Elmalih followed this process and in May 1912 wrote that the Arabs had, during the initial months after the Young Turk Revolution and the restoration of the constitution, supported the Young Turks almost unanimously. But the Arab mood had now turned in the opposite direction. "Never before in [Greater] Syria has hatred and rancor, disgust and contempt for Union and Progress been expressed so forcefully. Anyone who has not read [the Arab] press during this time has never read such vituperation and invective." He explained that the Turkish attempt to "Turkify" the peoples the empire ruled had produced an Arab reaction aimed at "preserving their spiritual assets, their national distinction, and their ancient culture." Contemporary scholarship also views the Turkification campaign as one of the important catalysts for the intensification of Arab national sentiment prior to World War I. Elmalih evinced understanding for Arab nationalism. What bothered him, as we have seen, was the accusation that the Jews and Zionism had pushed the Ottoman government's anti-Arab policies.[102]

That same spring of 1912, Sharif Ja'far, a descendant of the Prophet Mohammad, arrived in Palestine in an effort to bolster declining Arab support for the ruling party. The Young Turks hoped that he could speak to the hearts of the country's Muslims. Local government officials welcomed him with impressive ceremony. The leaders of the different faiths accompanied him to the train station when he set out from Jaffa to Jerusalem and back. Rabbi Uziel was among those who greeted him. He voiced his hope that the political turbulence would lead to an awakening and closer relationships among all the Ottoman peoples. As part of this hope, he laid out his historical and religious views:

> All our brothers, the Semitic Ottomans, should know that it is impossible for a Jew faithful to his law and his religion to harbor in his heart any feeling of hostility and animosity to the children of the caliphs and the descendants of the Ottoman sultans, who opened their arms to save his forefathers from murder and robbery, from fear and persecution. And anyone who casts any suspicion and doubt on the Jews' loyalty to our government—such a person commits an unforgivable sin against the truth. . . . We hold within our hearts love and fondness for the descendants of the just and merciful King Bayezid II [the Ottoman sultan at the time of the Spanish expulsion], who in his mercy and great benevolence showed charity to our persecuted forefathers, and opened the gates of his country to them.[103]

Rabbi Uziel was not just paying lip service to the authorities. He voiced how Jews really understood and experienced their history. The same was true of Shimon Moyal, who wrote about "the Muslim Arab nation, our ancient kin, a beloved nation of distinguished pedigree." He spoke in the context of life with Muslims, not theoretical investigation. These people were aware of Arab opposition to Zionism and tried, in their own way, to fight it. But their goal was not to defeat Arab nationalism in Palestine; it was, rather, to forge cooperation. In this, they differed from most of the immigrants from Europe.

In 1939, a quarter century after that speech, Rabbi Ben-Zion Meir Hai Uziel was appointed rishon letziyon, a post he held (under the title of chief rabbi following the establishment of the State of Israel) until his death in 1953. At the end of the Arab-Israeli War of 1948, Rabbi Uziel refused an offer from the custodian of absentee properties of the home of a wealthy Palestinian in Jerusalem's Talbiya neighborhood, at a time when public figures—among them judges, government officials, and senior academics—were accepting such offers. The reason he was quoted as giving was "And what will the gentiles say?"[104] But presumably his close relations with Arabs and his grasp of the way Jews and Arabs should treat each other also stood behind his exceptional decision.

Nevertheless, Uziel's refusal should be seen more in personal than public context. When land belonging to Palestinian refugees was assigned to Jewish settlements after the war, it prompted deliberations over a matter of halacha—Jewish religious law. The question was whether the crops grown on these lands required tithing, a religious requirement that applies to Jewish-owned soil in the Land of Israel. If the custodian represented the original owners of the fields, the land belonged to non-Jews, and therefore the crops were partially exempt from the laws of tithing. But if the custodian represented the state, these properties were considered to be Jewish land. Rabbi Uziel's answer to this question was concise: "The question of the return of the Arab refugees will certainly come up for discussion before the United Nations. I believe that it will never happen. God's mighty and invisible hand expelled them from the land, and will prevent their return."[105] That being the case, the farmers had to tithe their crops, as they would on Jewish-owned land. Human sympathy for the Arabs of Palestine and a sense of discomfort at their having been expelled or compelled to flee their homes are personal matters, but Rabbi Uziel interpreted the larger historical event as God's will.

We have jumped thirty years ahead here, to the time after the establishment of the State of Israel. But Ottoman rule over Palestine ended in the wake of a horrible war, World War I, which opened a new age in Palestine and in Mizrahi-Arab-Ashkenazi relations—the era of the British Mandate. It is to the events of that time that we now turn.

CHAPTER 2

Under the Union Jack

Classes Solidify

In which we will meet Jews who immigrated from Casablanca to Jerusalem but could not find a place for themselves there, and Arab politicians who tried to enlist the Old Yishuv, both Ashkenazim and Sephardim, in their cause. Also Yemenite, Moroccan, and Afghan Jews who joined Etzel, the Revisionist Zionist right-wing nationalist underground, and planted bombs in Arab marketplaces. We'll encounter Palestinian Arab rebels who showed their respect for lost young Sephardim, and also members of Histadrut, the Yishuv's Zionist labor union, who beat up Yemenite Jews. In the process, we'll follow the emerging rift between Edot Hamizrah Jews and the labor movement, and see what Palestinians thought about the role of the Mizrahim in the events of the Nakba that ended the era.

A ship bearing 126 Jews sailed from Casablanca to Palestine in the summer of 1919. It docked first in Marseille and then continued its journey via Alexandria to Jaffa, from which the ship departed for its final destination, Beirut. From Jaffa, the Jewish passengers headed to Jerusalem. At the time, the city was under military rule, imposed following the capture of the city in December 1917 by British forces under General Edmund Allenby. The regime was not harsh. One of its objectives was to help the Zionist movement establish a Jewish national home, in keeping with the Balfour Declaration. Along with the Zionist Commission, the supreme official body representing the Zionist movement in Palestine, the military regime worked to rebuild the war-damaged city. By the summer of 1919, Jerusalem was in much better shape than it had been a year earlier.

The Moroccan immigrants arrived in the city with no possessions and no money. They could not find work. *Haaretz* described them as young and healthy Jews who, although lacking skills, had come to live and work in the Land of Israel after hearing the good tidings of the Balfour Declaration and the conquest of Palestine by the British. But jobs were scarce. They appealed to the Zionist Commission for help; they applied to the municipal employment office for jobs; they sought assistance from the British military government. *Haaretz* wrote about them again, reporting that "Moroccan Jews idly walk the streets of Jerusalem" and that no solution to their plight had been found. Military governor Ronald Storrs asked the Zionist Commission to help him understand their situation. "The statements which they made in their various letters are in several instances quite fantastic," the Zionist Commission informed Storrs, "such as when they say the Zionist Organization conducted a propaganda [campaign] in Morocco, urging them to leave the country and promising them every kind of aid while settling in Palestine. What the Zionist Organization had done is to issue a stronger prohibition for any Jew to leave his home and come to Palestine at the present time." But what happened in practice? "Irresponsible individuals stated in the synagogue in Qasablanca [*sic*] that Palestine has emptied out [of Arabs] and was only waiting for the Jews to return," the commission charged. "Simpleminded hearers acted on these words. They broke up their homes and came to Palestine, with the result that they have incurred every kind of trouble."[1]

THE LAND HAD EMPTIED AND AWAITED THE JEWS

The extent to which the early Zionists were aware of the existence of Arabs in Palestine, and what was meant by those who declared "a land without a people for a people without a land," has been debated for decades. In fact, the Jews who came to Palestine were not able, and did not seek, to disregard the Arab presence and Arab opposition to Zionism. We saw examples of this resistance in the previous chapter. The question facing the settlers was not whether there were Arabs in the area but how to cope with them (much has been written about this as well). They had a wide range of approaches that can be analyzed along different lines—practical versus utopian, morality-based versus interest-based, conciliatory versus tough. At the far ends were the dream of creating a common Jewish-Arab nation versus evicting the Arabs from the country, what came to be called "transfer."

Academic studies of the transfer idea in Zionist thought propose that it originated in the idea of the modern nation-state, which became widely current toward the end of the nineteenth century. The advocates of nation-states sought to establish monoethnic entities.[2] But that was not the way of thinking that led the poor Jews of Casablanca to believe that Palestine was emptying for them. It was an idea that came from Jewish tradition. The vision of the Holy Land emptying of foreigners in advance of the return of the Children of Israel can be found in the Hebrew Bible and Jewish piyyut (liturgical poetry). It entered the Jewish collective consciousness as part of the doctrine of redemption.

First came the Five Books of Moses. Jews who attend synagogue and hear the Torah read in public there know very well what it says. When the Children of Israel fled their Egyptian bondage and headed to the Land of Israel, the vision they had was not of being good neighbors of the inhabitants there, or of joining the federation of the seven nations that dwelt in Canaan, or of the creation of a state of all its citizens. The commandment they received was: "In the towns of the latter peoples, however, which the Lord your God is giving you as a heritage, you shall not let a soul remain alive" (Deut. 20:16).[3] The ideal was: "When the Lord your God brings you into the land that He swore to your fathers, Abraham, Isaac, and Jacob, to assign to you—great and flourishing cities that you did not build, houses full of all good things that you did not fill, hewn cisterns that you did not hew, vineyards and olive groves that you did not plant—and you [will] eat your fill" (Deut. 6:10). In other words, this was a vision of waging a war of obliteration in order to seize all the goods the land had to offer, and it was understood as a promise not just to the Israelites who left Egypt but as a prophecy of the future. The Jewish people's exile was, over the generations, seen as a temporary state, punishment for the sins of the past ("because of our sins we were exiled from our land," according to the liturgy), but not an annulment of the covenant between God and his people: "Yet, even then, when they are in the land of their enemies, I will not reject them or spurn them so as to destroy them, annulling My covenant with them: for I the Lord am their God" (Lev. 26:44). The redemption is guaranteed; even if it takes a long time, it will come, and when it does, the Jews will return to the Land of Israel and the Davidic monarchy will be restored. There are different answers to the question of what will happen to the other nations at the time of redemption—according to some, they will be destroyed; according to others, they will accept the supremacy of the Jewish God. But their expulsion from the land, especially if they do not recognize the God of Israel, is prominent in piyyutim written in the Islamic world from its inception up through the twentieth century. Some Jews saw Zionism as a sign that the redemption was beginning.

SOME EXAMPLES, FOR THE INTERESTED

I have written elsewhere about the prophecies of vengeance against the Muslims, including their expulsion from the Land of Israel, that appear in Jewish piyyutim.[4] Here, I will offer just a few examples for purposes of illustration. First, a reminder. Ishmael (Yishmael in Hebrew, Ismail in Arabic), was the son Abraham (Avraham, Ibrahim) fathered when, at his barren wife Sarah's request, he took her slave-woman, Hagar, as a wife. He is counted, by both Jews and Muslims, as the forefather of the Arabs. Sarah later had a son with Abraham, Isaac (Yitzhak), from whom the Jews trace their (literal or mythic) descent. Isaac and Ishmael thus became rivals for the inheritance of their father, Abraham—namely, his material possessions but also, even more so, the divine favor he had enjoyed. As part of this contention, Sarah, Abraham's wife, enjoined him: "Cast out that slave-woman and her son, for the son of that slave shall not share in the inheritance with my son Isaac." Read that verse carefully: Hagar, the slave-woman with whom Abraham had fathered Ishmael, did not think that she and her son should be the only heirs. She and Ishmael saw themselves as coequal heirs of Abraham and his heritage. Sarah, on the other hand, wanted exclusivity for her son, Isaac, without sharing it with the son of the slave-woman. The term "son of the slave-woman" (*ben haamah* in Hebrew) thus became a common epithet for Muslims, one that implied a desire for separation that grew out of a sense of hereditary Jewish spiritual superiority. The expulsion of the descendants of the slave-woman from the Holy Land was seen by Jews as the proper and necessary end not only of the earthly struggle between Jews and Muslims but also of the struggle in heaven between the guardian angels of Ishmael and Israel (Jacob, Isaac's son and heir).

This view can be seen in many piyyutim written from the dawn of Islam to this day. Here are a few brief examples from the modern age. The greatest halachic authority in Baghdad in his generation, Rabbi Yosef Hayyim, known as the Ben Ish Hai (1835–1909), was not only a scholar and merchant but also a poet who composed piyyutim. Like many Jews throughout the Exile, he beseeched the matriarch Rachel, Jacob's wife, to intercede with God on behalf of the Children of Israel to hasten the redemption. In his piyyut "Pardon Us by the Merits of Rachel Our Mother," he wrote, "And quickly build a canopy / From the ash heap raise the pauper / To God in Zion / Quickly show our eyes // Expel the servant and slave-woman / And create wrathful annihilation / Wed your innocent dove / Shine your mercy upon us."[5] The components of the redemption are the construction of the canopy, symbolizing the Temple; raising the Jewish people from the ash heap of the Exile;

the expulsion of the Muslim children of the slave-woman; the obliteration of the enemies; and the wedding, meaning the reconnection, of the Jewish people (the dove) with God.

And here is an example better known to those who attend synagogue. It is a popular piyyut sung on a variety of occasions that contrasts Israel and Ishmael: "A day of light for Israel / An accursed day for Ishmael // A day of blessing for Israel / A day of bewilderment for Ishmael // A day of redemption for Israel / A day of exile for Ishmael." The Hebrew lines form an alphabetical acrostic.[6] Israel's redemption depends on and emerges from the exile of Ishmael. A piyyut beloved of Afghan Jews, "El Ram Hasin Yah" (author and date of composition unknown), is a bit more diplomatic: "Strengthen the son of David / And judge forever // Every enemy destroy / Expel from the city of God."[7] Note that in this case the call is for the destruction and deportation of enemies, not necessarily all the children of Ishmael or the gentile nations.

THE DEBATE OVER WORDING

The piyyut "A Day of Light for Israel / An Accursed Day for Ishmael" ends with the lines "A day of peace for Israel / A day of conflagration [*shoah*] for Ishmael // A day of salvation for Israel / A day of defeat for Ishmael." In its popular form, there are other wordings. The version I present here comes from the prayer book for the Sukkot festival based on the rulings of the rishon letziyon, Rabbi Mordechai Eliyahu. People in a number of yeshivot and synagogues felt uncomfortable with the words that entreat for a shoah—the modern Hebrew term for the Holocaust—against Muslims. A few years ago, one of the great Torah scholars of our generation, Rabbi Meir Mazuz, head of the Kisse Rahamim yeshiva, was asked whether it was appropriate to sing this piyyut. He replied, "We sing [it] with a small emendation: 'An accursed day for their enemies,' instead of Ishmael. To include also other nations and to exclude the righteous members of [foreign] nations (also from Ishmael, there is such a thing)."[8]

The distinction between wishing for the annihilation of all the children of Ishmael and wishing for the annihilation solely of all the Jewish people's enemies is significant, and it's worthy of mention because of Rabbi Mazuz's position on the extreme right of the political spectrum. It's also important to note that his father, Rabbi Matzliah Mazuz, who founded the Kisse Rahamim yeshiva in Tunis, was murdered by a Muslim assailant in 1971 in the city of his birth on his way back from morning prayers. Following the murder, his children immigrated to Israel and Kisse Rahamim moved from Tunis to Bnei

Brak, a suburb of Tel Aviv that is one of Israel's main centers of Haredi life and learning.

Now let us return to the piyyutim of expulsion.

THE NAKBA IN PIYYUTIM

In the mid-twentieth century, the prophecy of expulsion continued to be a trope in the work of some authors of piyyutim, even as Arabs were in fact being expelled from the State of Israel. At the height of the Arab-Israeli War of 1948, Rabbi Meir Abuhatzeira, known as the Baba Meir (1917–1973), composed the well-known and much sung piyyut "The One on High Razes Forests" (*Yahid Ram Yaarot Hosef*), which includes the lines "He who founded the earth on naught / Please expel the son of the slave-woman / Raise up the banner of Israel." The phrase "He who founded the earth on naught" is an epithet for God, to whom the poet appeals; as in previous generations, he prays for the expulsion of the slave-woman's descendants. In case that is not clear, Avraham Yagel glosses: "Expel the Ishmaelites from the Holy Land."[9] Baba Sali, Baba Meir's father, reportedly said of this piyyut, "My son's prayer made a great impression in heaven." In other words, the prayer helped uproot the Palestinian Arabs in the 1948 war.[10]

WHICH RECALLS WHAT JAMAL ZAHALKA SAID

Jamal Zahalka served as leader of, and Knesset member for, Balad (National Democratic Alliance), a political party that advocates the national rights of Palestinian citizens of Israel. In the film *Ashkenaz*, directed by Rachel Leah Jones (2007), he voices a claim that has become a cliché among the Mizrahi Left:

> The Ashkenazim took Palestine from us. Not the Mizrahim. It wasn't those who say death to the Arabs who took the country from us. [It was] those who said we have brought peace upon you [*hevenu shalom sleikhem,* which is also the title of a song that became popular in the Yishuv in the late 1930s]. [In] every Arab village they came and conquered, they sang to us we have brought peace upon you. What peace, what a joke. That's what infuriates me. We brought peace upon you. What a lie. Those who shout death to the Arabs don't do that. But those who shout we have brought peace upon you . . . they demolish the homes and expel the people, take the lands, and on top of that come and piss on us from above in the name of socialism, in the name of values, and in the name of universalism.

He spoke in much the same vein in a Knesset debate in 2015.[11]

Zahalka's assignment of responsibility is a little coarse, and it has certainly not remained unchanged from the Mandate era to the present day. In the years following that interview, there were Mizrahim who shouted "death to the Arabs" and who put that call into practice. There is, however, a kernel of historical truth in what he said. The expulsion of the Arabs in 1948 was led by the Ashkenazi leadership. Nevertheless, those who actually carried it out were members of all Jewish ethnicities. So what is the origin of the impression that the Mizrahim were not involved in the Palestinians' catastrophe? The Haifa Mizrahim who saw themselves as *awlad Arab*, "sons of the Arabs," the young Sephardim of Jaffa who thought the Zionists were stirring up animosity, and others like them created that impression, as did a number of events that took place during the Mandate period that we will touch on later. Most important was the Palestinian desire to believe in a Mizrahi-Arab alliance. We will address that as well in the chapters to come.

PIYYUT VERSUS REALITY

If the expulsion of the Arabs was fundamental in traditional Jewish consciousness as reflected in piyyutim, why did Sephardim in Palestine at the end of the Ottoman period—in part, of course—align more with the Arabs than with the Moskobim? Why did some of them think that they would be better off living alongside their Arab neighbors, and thus oppose the immigration of socialist Zionists from eastern Europe?

The answer is that both the holy scriptures and human consciousness make generalizations about the "Other" but at the same time are flexible and diverse. This means that the fact that the idea was present in the canonical books did not directly affect life as it was lived. The corollary is that the fact that expulsion was part of their consciousness could be expressed in a variety of ways and take on different interpretations. The uprooting of the gentile nations could be taken as a real halachic injunction, or, alternately, it could be regarded one of those theoretical laws that, in halachic parlance, Jews are not enjoined to act on. Some might suggest that other approaches that appear in the Hebrew Bible should be emphasized, while others deny the relevance of biblical injunctions to current politics. One can interpret the texts to mean that the expulsion is the prerogative of the Messiah rather than a task assigned to the current generation, and one can reject the idea of expulsion on humanitarian grounds. None of this makes the injunction any less important a part of Jewish consciousness, and thus of Jewish political imagination, but it explains the mismatch between consciousness and action. The complexity of the connection between scripture and political life can be seen among those who chant the piyyutim themselves. For example, a Jew of the Ottoman Empire could read the line of the poet Rabbi Israel Najara (born in Damascus in 1555, died in Gaza in 1625)—"The sons of Kedar and Ishmael into the flame—bring them,"[12] ostensibly a desire to see God burn Muslims at the stake—while at the same time voicing gratitude to the Ottoman rulers who took in the exiles from Spain. (The Jewish chroniclers Rabbi Elijah Capsali and Rabbi Yosef Sambari are prominent examples of writers who highlighted the benevolence of the Ottoman dynasty.)[13] The bitter fate that the piyyut authors wished on the Muslims was directed, so it seems, at the Muslim as a mythical character, not necessarily at the rulers of their country and not the Jews' Muslim neighbors—at least not until the age of nationalism.

DON'T GET IT WRONG—IT'S NOT JUST A MIZRAHI ATTITUDE

The idea of expelling the gentiles so as to inherit the Holy Land did not pass from the Bible only to Jewish communities in the Islamic world. The greatest commentator on the Talmud, Rashi (Rabbi Shlomo Yitzchaki, France, eleventh century), explained in one of his glosses on the Gittin tractate (page 8b) that the essence of the precept of settling the Land of Israel is "to expel *kutim* [gentiles] and settle [the people of] Israel there." The issue was debated in the 1940s and 1950s by religious Zionists as well.[14]

PUTTING THE CART BEFORE THE HORSE: HALACHA, TRADITION, AND POLITICAL SOLUTIONS

Jakob Thon, one of the leaders of the Jewish National Council, was associated with Brit Shalom, a group of Yishuv intellectuals who promoted Jewish-Arab coexistence. At the end of 1942, Thon sent Rabbi Uziel a political program for Jewish-Arab relations, drafted by members of Kedma-Mizraha, a group of moderate Zionists. The core of the proposal was the establishment of two national autonomies in Palestine, one Arab and one Jewish, with equal rights. Rabbi Uziel was involved in Kedma-Mizraha. He attended its meetings together with activists and officials from a wide swathe of Yishuv society—rightists and leftists, city dwellers and kibbutzniks, Edot Hamizrah and Ashkenazim with a long history in Palestine, and Jews who had arrived in the successive waves of Zionist immigration.[15] He had been acquainted with Thon for some thirty years—Thon had been a top figure in the Palestine

Office when Uziel was invested as hakham bashi of Jaffa in 1911. Now, in 1942, he held the title of rishon letziyon, the chief rabbi of the Jews of Palestine. His response to Thon is interesting.

> The conclusions of our friend Dr. Y. Thon for a regime of two parallel national autonomies seems appropriate and acceptable for the following reasons: While the proposal does not mention the demand for a Jewish state, it nevertheless includes no disavowal, even the slightest, of the Land of Israel as the heritage of our forefathers and of the hoped-for kingship of the House of David; rather, this proposal is taken from the existing reality and from adapting to it at this time, because this reality cannot be disregarded, that we dwell as neighbors of the Arab nation, which is populous and settled on large tracts of land for centuries, and the standards of justice and logic require granting them free autonomy to manage their own affairs and in complete and sincere cooperation in the administration of the state, which is common to and inclusive of all its inhabitants.

And Rabbi Uziel noted in his own hand on the printed copy of the proposal, to which he added the seal of the Chief Rabbinate, "As thus the Torah has commanded 'When a stranger resides with you in your land, you shall not wrong him [Lev. 19:34].'"[16]

The rabbi also addressed the importance of Jewish immigration and settlement throughout the land, stressing the principle that the compact needed "to protect all the land and its inhabitants in justice and forthrightness and without any sort of prejudice and without discriminating against the rights of either of the two national autonomies."[17]

So what do we have here? Uziel was the chief rabbi, from a family with deep roots in Land of Israel, who had headed the religious Zionist Mizrahi movement, who knew that Arabs had inhabited Palestine for centuries (the Zionist claim that the country's Arabs had only recently come into the country had not yet taken root). Furthermore, he recognized that the Arabs had national rights in the country and advocated equality between the two peoples—and all this was a product of his religious consciousness. He did not claim that the Arabs needed to be expelled or that they had to be subordinated to the Jews. On the contrary, as he saw it, there was no halachic reason not to reach a political arrangement that would allow both peoples to live all over the country with equal national and civil rights. He was even willing to set aside the demand for a Jewish state, on the condition that there be no concession on the declarative (and emotional) standing of the vision of a future Jewish return to Zion and the renewal of the Davidic monarchy.

Rabbi Uziel's position resonated with the decision of one of his successors as rishon letziyon, Rabbi Ovadia Yosef, in the context of the Oslo Accords (1993), which we will consider in chapter 5. But now it's time for us to return to the streets of Jerusalem in 1919, where dozens of Moroccans remained homeless after discovering that the tidings that the Arabs had left the country and their homes for the Jews had been a baseless rumor. It's time to examine how Mizrahi-Ashkenazi and Mizrahi-Arab relations developed during the early years of the British Mandate.

THE DESIRABLE AND THE LESS DESIRABLE

The Zionist Commission decided to send the unemployed Moroccans back to Morocco.[18] It was not (just) that they were Moroccans. They were not the type of productive Jew that Zionist activists fantasized about. Selection, in fact, was also practiced on Ashkenazim. Chaim Weizmann, the chairman of the Zionist Commission, said that he did not want Palestine to turn into another Nalewki (the Jewish street in Warsaw).[19] And the diatribes against the "halukah Jews" continued. Ze'ev Jabotinsky expressed some satisfaction, albeit in a private letter to his wife, Joanna, at the death of many members of Jerusalem's Old Yishuv during the war. "The pioneer men and women made an excellent impression, but Jerusalem is in a very bad state," he wrote. "*Even though about half of the halukah people luckily died out before the English arrived*, the half that remains is more than enough. They beg for money, refuse to work, get into fights with each other, write denunciations [to the authorities], and their honorable women and girls frequently engage in an easy livelihood [prostitution]. It's all painful and depressing. The Zionist Commission will need to think about serious and severe actions that the English are ashamed to impose."[20]

THE BALFOUR DECLARATION AND THE MARGINAL MIZRAHI OPPOSITION

The British might have been reluctant to intervene in the internal affairs of Jerusalem's Jewish community, but they were less irresolute in seeking to reshape the entire Middle East—its countries, communities, borders, and resources. They concluded alliances, issued (sometimes contradictory) promises, and drew maps based on their own political, economic, and religious interests. The Balfour Declaration's commitment to establishing "in Palestine a national home for the Jewish people" may have been less than what the Zionists wanted, which was for all of Palestine to be the Jewish national home, but it was a big step forward for them.

As such, most of Palestine's Jews, and most of the world's Jews, celebrated the declaration. But a few, including some Sephardim, disparaged it. They criticized not only the pointless celebrations, which alienated the country's Arabs, but also the Zionist policy of looking to the West, to England, while turning its back on the country's Arabs. Hayyim Ben-Kiki, scion of a rabbinic family from Tiberias, claimed that even before the war Zionism had done damage to Jewish-Arab relations, and that "the Sephardi Yishuv, which came from the lands of the East to an Eastern land, whose soul has been interwoven and tied up with the Arab people for many generations, sensed that something unpleasant was happening here, that this entire movement was not acting properly."[21]

Ben-Kiki proposed to the Zionists that they undergo a profound metamorphosis. They should divest themselves of their sense of Western superiority and instead "go with the spirit of the country." He knew that this ran counter to the movement's internal logic and to its self-image as an outpost of Europe in the East, and that it also went against the interests of the Moskobim, Ostjuden who wanted to re-create themselves in Palestine. But he tried nevertheless. His associate Yosef Haim Castel, who came from a family that lived in Hebron and Jerusalem and who worked in the Zionist Executive's press department, had a less culturally revolutionary proposal, though it was still politically radical. In a memorandum he wrote to Weizmann, Castel argued that it was not yet too late to reach an understanding with Palestine's Arabs, and that the way to achieve this was to ask Britain to rewrite the Balfour Declaration such that it would recognize Palestinian nationality and portray the country as the national home of two peoples. He received no reply.[22]

These voices were marginal among the Jews of the East, but Palestine's Arabs heard them. They took note that the Sephardim were being shunted off to the margins and sensed that these Jews were also Zionism's victims.

THE ALLIANCE OF THE DISPOSSESSED

The ejection of Sephardim and Edot Hamizrah from leadership positions was a long process. The immigration from eastern Europe prior to World War I turned the Sephardim from a majority into a minority, and the war buttressed the political power of the Zionist institutions, as they took charge of the aid committee that helped the Yishuv survive. The Old Ashkenazi Yishuv, in all its shades, along with the Sephardi, Mughrabi, and other Eastern communities, had no choice but to place themselves, at least partially, under the Zionist committees and to subject themselves to their authority.[23] The collapse of the Ottoman Empire, the Balfour Declaration, and international recognition of the Zionist Commission as the representative of the Jews of Palestine cemented the leadership of the top figures in the Zionist movement, both in Palestine and overseas.[24] Following a not very long period in which they found themselves achieving nearly equal rights with the rest of the country's Arabs, Palestine's native Jews now found themselves inferior to the Jews who had arrived from Europe. The Arabs found themselves in the same position.

The Arabs of Palestine voiced their opposition to the Zionist takeover not only in political theater but also with more or less organized physical attacks on Jews. Castel's proposal to change the wording of the Balfour Declaration and Hayyim Ben-Kiki's desire to treat the country's Arabs as equals were written in the wake of the bloody events of May 1921, in which dozens of Jews were killed by Arabs. The Palestinian leadership, which had just begun to institutionalize, acted largely at the diplomatic level. In the summer of 1921, the Arab Executive Committee sent a delegation to London in an attempt to deter the British from implementing the Balfour Declaration. The delegation was headed by Musa Kazim al-Husayni, the chairman of the Arab Executive Committee, the body that represented Palestine's Arabs. Al-Husayni served as mayor of Jerusalem until 1920, when he was dismissed by the British because of a speech he made prior to an Arab attack on Jerusalem's Jews in April. He had previously served in senior positions in the Ottoman administration, including as district officer (kaymakam) in Jaffa and Safed. He believed, or at least hoped, and in any case claimed, that as chairman of the Arab Executive he represented all of the country's longtime inhabitants, not just Muslims and Christians but also Jews. He also claimed that the Old Yishuv had donated money to support the delegation's journey.[25]

MUSA KAZIM AS A FUNDRAISER

Hapoel Hatzair covered the Arab delegation's fundraising campaign in the Galilee, which was run by Musa Kazim al-Husayni. "Here the nobleman of Jerusalem has arrived in Safed—the seat of his government of old as the Turkish kaymakam," it reported sarcastically. Al-Husayni held a public meeting attended by Muslims from Safed's poor neighborhoods. They chanted nationalist slogans but had no money to give. Neither were the city's merchants in a hurry to open their wallets. "The merchant from the Arab market gazed suspiciously at the guest from the time of the Turks and carefully tightened his sash," the report went on. "The sharp city man is in no hurry to place his money in the hands of the members of the delegation." Al-Husayni had a problem. What would he do?

> And here Musa Kazim was helped by a wonderful idea. As one who had been kaymakam in a city in which Jews dwell, he knew from experience "that to give money—is the Jew's forte." The Jew who is entreated gives even to his nemesis, to the one who sheds his blood, who hacks his young ones to pieces. All that is needed is to "sweeten" his agony, to mislead him, to talk sweetly so as to blind him—so the guest from Jerusalem spoke to two Safed Jews who came to visit him as people who had known him since back then, suggesting that the Orthodox [Jews] and the Sephardi community support their delegation—the effendi delegation from Haifa—with a sum of 500 Egyptian pounds. "After all, it is for your own good. We work hard to protect you, and the Zionists as well, from the Communist pioneers, who made the riots against you and us in Jaffa and shed the blood of our children and yours"—this is how the Jerusalem politician wheedled them and added that . . . the Jews may add one of themselves to the effendi delegation to overseas.[26]

Al-Husayni referred to Communists because the riots of 1921 in Jaffa began with a clash among Jews, between two ideological groups holding May 1 demonstrations. The first was Ahdut Haavodah, one of the leading socialist Zionist factions; the second, the Communist Party. The suggestion that Arabs could protect Zionists from the Communists was just rhetoric. The Palestinian offer to include Jews in Palestinian representative bodies by bringing in members of the Old Yishuv remained on the table over the years. In 1921 no Jews took up the offer, but when the Palestinian Authority was established in 1994 in the West Bank and Gaza Strip, its president, Yasser Arafat, named Rabbi Moshe Hirsch, of the extreme anti-Zionist Haredi faction Neturei Karta, his cabinet minister for Jewish affairs. The attempt to maintain the alliance of the dispossessed continued.

THE SEPHARDI COMMITTEES: WE ARE ZIONISTS!

After the Palestinian delegation arrived in England, its members declared that they also represented Palestine's longtime Jewish inhabitants. The Zionist movement was incensed. So were the Sephardim, on the whole. Sephardi, Mizrahi, and Mughrabi communities throughout Palestine placed notices in the press and sent telegrams in which they asserted that they supported the Balfour Declaration and accepted the authority of the Zionist Executive. *Filastin* expressed its disappointment. "These are the Jews we called 'our brothers,' with rights and duties equal to ours, and whom our delegation to England sought to make partners in the national government and parliament and to live with them in peace," its editors admonished. They read the Jews' telegrams and realized that the Sephardim were rejecting their outstretched hand. "It reinforces our understanding that every Jew is a Zionist," the editors concluded. They also offered a diagnosis of the Sephardim: "Like glass vessels, which take on the color of the materials within them, so do [the Sephardim] always tilt toward the strongest side."[27]

YOU'RE ZIONISTS?

The question of whether Edot Hamizrah Jews were Zionists was in the air already in the Ottoman period; it remained there during the Mandate period and is still there, though in a different way today. One view maintains that the Sephardim and Edot Hamizrah were not involved in the Zionist enterprise, whether because they had reservations about Zionist institutions, or because they inclined toward being passive, or because of their close relations with the Arabs. Another perspective sees the Jews of the Islamic world, Palestine included, as part of the Zionist movement from its inception and maintains that the pre-Zionist waves of Sephardi immigration laid the foundation for the Jewish national home. Every so often this debate erupts.

One of the most powerful such eruptions occurred during the preparation of *Pillar of Fire*, a documentary television series on the history of Zionism produced by the Israeli Broadcasting Authority that was aired in 1981. It was one of the flagship productions of what was then Israel's only television station. When the broadcast began, the poet Dahlia Ravikovitch wrote in *Maariv* about "the elation and pride that accompanied the screening of the series," and the Israeli Broadcasting Authority's top management declared that it would be shown again and again in future generations. But prior to the broadcast, a nonprofit organization called Tzalash (the name was an acronym for Zionists for Equality), led by Vicki Shiran, petitioned Israel's Supreme Court to prevent it on the grounds that the program engaged in unacceptable discrimination. Zionist activity in Islamic countries went almost unmentioned, she argued, as did the Mizrahi role in the establishment of the state. The petition was rejected on the grounds that it violated freedom of speech; the justices ruled that it was not their job to make judgments about cultural and educational questions. However, Justice Miriam Ben-Porat added an obiter dictum in her concurring opinion. "The claim in the petition that the injured group is 'the Jews of the East' can be taken as outrageous," she wrote. "Jews can live in the East or the West, but Judaism is a specific concept that encompasses the world. The 'Jews of the East,' like 'Ashkenazi Jews,' are but limbs of the same body, which must be defended against harmful division, reeking of disunity."[28]

The creator of the series, Yigal Lossin, never argued, as Justice Ben-Porat did, that there was no reason to make a point of including all parts of the Jewish people in the story simply because they were a single nation. He instead offered his own view of Zionist history. "How many Edot Hamizrah Jews were at Herzl's Zionist Congress? Maybe one, and he wasn't important," he declared. "Zionism arose to solve the problem of European Jews." And when he was asked about Sephardi entrepreneurial families, he replied, "The question is not whether you are wealthy but rather if you are active. They had no Ben-Gurion or Moshe Sharett among them. Among [the Jewish fighters hanged by the British] there were a few from Edot Hamizrah, so in the *Pillar of Fire* book I included their photographs." He saw no reason to tell the story of people who just "lived and went to synagogue," he said. "I'm sorry, that's not the story."[29]

At the dawn of Zionist activity in Palestine, these questions were not a matter of historical dispute but very contemporary and very political matters. The Moskobim, as already noted, maintained that the Sephardim were a-national and were more aligned with the Arabs than with them, and the Arabs voiced hope that the Moskobim were right about that. Sephardi thinkers were of two minds. They sought a place for themselves under the new circumstances. One of them was Avraham Elmalih, whose work on the origins of Arab nationalism I cited in the previous chapter. Following the British conquest, Elmalih served as a Zionist Executive liaison with the Jewish communities in Syria and Lebanon. One of his duties was coaching the governing boards of these communities in advance of their testimony before the King-Crane Commission, an American delegation sent in advance of the Paris Peace Conference of 1919 to inquire into the disposal of the territories of the former Ottoman Empire. Elmalih induced them—in some cases in a reversal of their original positions—to support the establishment of a Jewish national home in Palestine and Jewish immigration.[30] As the head of the Zionist Commission's press bureau, Elmalih was an example of a Sephardi Jew of Palestine who found a place for himself in Zionist officialdom and placed his connections and talents at the movement's service. But he felt that he was exceptional in this regard.

ELMALIH: THE SPIRITUAL POVERTY OF THE SEPHARDIM

With great animation, Elmalih described, in 1919, the major changes that had taken place in Palestine since the end of the war. "The iron walls within which we have been confined for centuries have been demolished, the steel chains that have bound us for ages have been severed, the land has been liberated from its previous cruel masters who strangled our spirits, and new channels have been opened before us by the new government and the declaration of its emissary Balfour." It was certainly the case that it took only a few months for many of Palestine's Jews to forget their oath of loyalty to the Ottoman Empire, which most of them had sworn in utter sincerity. They quickly declared their fealty to the new British regime. In part, this was because of their suffering during the war, the iron fist of the Turkish military regime, and the hope ignited in them by the Balfour Declaration.

Elmalih was concerned about the breach between the Sephardi public and the Zionist movement. "There is but one corner of the globe where everything is as it always was; there is a single community in our world whose life has undergone no apparent change, and this corner is the Land of Israel, and the community is its Sephardi community."

> Why should we conceal the truth? At a time when a new life is taking form around us; at a time when borders are being drawn and a range of parties are coming into being . . . Sephardi Jewry in the Land of Israel remains ossified . . . like a person standing on the sidelines, taking no interest in what is occurring, as if it has no obligation to take part in its construction. No new national enterprise has been founded at the initiative of Sephardi Jewry; there has been no awakening coming from deep within the heart, nor caused by outside inducement, we have not seen [anything of the sort] from the day of the country's liberation to this day. . . . Who is responsible for this indifference?[31]

Elmalih, like Lossin sixty years later, maintained that the Sephardi community in Palestine was apathetic and frozen in time. It was a corollary of what historians have termed "the theory of the Sephardi decline." The waning of the Ottoman Empire, and of the Muslim world as a whole, meant that the mental faculties of the Jews of these areas weakened as well. The result was that "the greatest historic moment in the annals of the world, which overturned the map of the globe from bottom to top, and of course our historic land with it—has all the more put on display our spiritual poverty and our incapacity to understand the great revelation and to adapt our deeds to these great events."[32] Elmalih's account is quite different from that presented many decades later by Mizrahim about their community's attitude toward Zionism.

This raises two questions. The first one is factual. Were the Sephardim and Edot Hamizrah indeed alienated from the Zionist national revival movement? If the answer is no, we would want to know who spread the story that they were, and why. If the answer is yes, two further questions need to be answered. First, why did the Sephardim not jump to take part in it, all together? Second, was this necessarily a shortcoming, as Elmalih maintained? Or did his self-criticism have its roots in a sense of inferiority arising from an internalization of the claim that the West was superior? There's another question to attend to as well—was it connected to the Arab question? I'll begin with this last point, which is the focal point of our inquiry.

THE CONNECTION TO THE ARAB QUESTION

It is difficult to quantify the extent to which the issue of relations with the Arabs was central to the experience of the Jews of the East. Apparently, up until the disturbances of 1929, it bore some weight. Edot Hamizrah Jews were not drawn to the Haganah self-defense organization when it was established and were in no hurry to join it even after it became independent of the Histadrut—that is, of the labor movement of which they felt no part. When a branch of the Haganah was opened in Haifa in 1922, it was commanded by Yaacov Pat. Under Pat, young Sephardim in Haifa (who, recall, called themselves *yahud awlad Arab*, Jewish Arabs) were not interested in taking part in underground activity. The man in charge of the Haganah's stash of weapons in Haifa, Yekutiel Shevah, related:

> In Haifa there were in 1929 some 450 members of the Haganah. The members of the Haganah came primarily from the factories. No one came to us from the wealthy. They'd come to training after work hours. The training was very tough. . . . Among the members of the Haganah there were only young men from the Ashkenazi community. There were no members of the Sephardi community in the Haganah organization. The Sephardim did not mix with the Ashkenazim. The

> European young men in their shorts were foreign to them. They lived in *hamulot* [extended families], with Arab culture, with Arab dress and the Arabic language. They did not contribute to our funds. They always claimed that we brought troubles on them. Because they lived well with the Arabs. They ate the same things the Arabs ate. After six in the evening you wouldn't see a soul from among them. Until six their cafes were full. We, after work, dressed in their costume and went to them and saw how they lived.[33]

THE HEART OF THE MATTER

Relations with the Arabs were only one of the reasons why the Sephardim, Mughrabim, and Edot Hamizrah as a rule refrained from any significant involvement in Zionist frameworks. Their disaffection seems to have been more a matter of social and cultural mores than of politics. It's important to be precise—they were alienated not from the idea of the Jewish return to Zion (after all, they had returned) but rather from institutionalized Zionism. And that is easy to understand. To get involved, the Mizrahim would have had to become something they were not. They would have had to give up their identity, to break with the traditions of previous generations. As the immigrants from eastern Europe saw it, this was a reasonable demand. They themselves had set aside their previous lives and abandoned the tradition of their forefathers. They were also in the process of giving up the language they had grown up with, adopting a new way of dressing, and creating a new kind of social life. Moreover, for the Moskobim, who looked down on Eastern culture, making such a demand of young Mizrahim was doubly reasonable. But the great majority of Mizrahim saw things differently. They were deeply embedded in their culture and connected to it, and did not necessarily see it as in any way flawed (although there were those who felt it was inferior). They were in no hurry to demolish their old world down to its foundations. That can be termed conservative, or perhaps traditional, but principally they were motivated by a desire to maintain their personal and communal identity.

AND THAT'S WHAT BOTHERED THE ASHKENAZIM—JABOTINSKY REDUX

Ze'ev Jabotinsky, who in a private letter regretted that half of Jerusalem's Old Yishuv Jews managed to survive World War I, offered his opinion of the Jews of the East in a published article. "To the extent that our uneducated masses have ancient spiritual traditions and laws that evoke 'the East,' they need to be weaned away from them," he maintained. He wanted to expunge Mizrahiness entirely: "We are going to the Land of Israel, first, for our national well-being, and second, as [Zionist ideologue Max] Nordau said, to 'extend Europe's borders to the Euphrates.' In other words, Palestine is to be swept thoroughly clean of Judaism, whether of the past or of the future, of all traces of its Eastern soul." In the meantime, until that task was accomplished, "We recommend that gesture that each of us does without thinking when he passes, in an overcoat, through the narrow 'Eastern' streets of Istanbul, Cairo, or Jerusalem: roll up the coat so that it not be covered by dust in any way, and to look where you place your feet. Not because we are Jews, and not even because we are from Europe. Simply because we are cultured human beings."[34]

There were Sephardim who took up the idea of sweeping away the Mizrahi soul, or who were beguiled by what the Zionists were doing and sought to join them, or who were captivated by the ideas of the labor movement—for example, Yitzhak Nadav, who joined Hashomer; Aharon Chelouche of Jaffa, who titled his memoir *From Galabiyah to Pioneer Hat*, to mark the change he underwent from traditional dress and way of life to a Zionist one; and Yehuda Burla and David Avishar, who joined the labor movement. In 1921 Burla wrote to his friend Avishar, "And among you, our Sephardim . . . there is not a community, a group, just ridiculous bragging about lineage. We need to wait until the stream of those welcome pioneer boys cleans out the streets of Jerusalem as well."[35]

And there were, of course, others, some of whom we will meet. But the majority did not want to be weaned away from the East. They trod there in comfort, or as hard workers, not as strangers and not as fastidious Westerners trying not to be contaminated by the East. For them, it was home.

DISCRIMINATION IN ABSORPTION OR A LACK OF VALUES

The East was also home—culturally, at least—to Jewish immigrants from the Islamic world who came to Palestine after the British conquest. They hoped that it would become a real home for them. It wasn't simple. In the few years since the end of the war, the flow of immigration increased, and the rift between those who came from the Islamic world and those who came from Europe widened. In March 1923, members of the Mizrahi-Zionist organization Histadrut Halutzei Hamizrah (Association of Pioneers of the East) wrote to the Zionist Executive about the botched absorption of immigrants from the Islamic lands. Halutzei Hamizrah was one of the first Sephardi organizations to appear after the British conquest of Jerusalem; David Avishar, active in the labor movement, was one of its most prominent activists.[36] Yosef Sprinzak, then one of the leaders of the Hapoel Hatzair party and later speaker of the Knesset, sent them a reply. He maintained that all immigrants received the same assistance when they arrived. At the same time, he understood that "the personal feelings of the immigrants from the lands of the East are sometimes very acute and give cause for anger." He explained why. "It doesn't depend on the adequate or inadequate care taken by the different institutions," he contended, "but rather on the intellectual and psychological preparation of these immigrants prior to their arrival." The immigrants from Europe, he went on, were "infused with pioneering national consciousness. . . . The situation is different with regard to the Jews of the East. Their knowledge about the situation that awaits them in Palestine is very superficial, and frequently their imagination takes the place of reality."[37] For Sprinzak, it should be kept in mind, pioneering national consciousness was equivalent to socialist Zionist consciousness. And, indeed, the immigrants from the Islamic world and Mizrahi workers native to the country were not organized in socialist frameworks but rather in families and communities. This was one of the reasons why they were hurt by socialist Zionism.

THE CONQUEST OF LABOR—FROM THE MIZRAHIM

One of the important principles of the labor movement in Palestine was formulated by Tzvi Rosenstein (Even-Shoshan), a veteran Histadrut leader who had arrived in Palestine as part of the Third Aliyah. "The labor movement in Palestine was not created by workers who were born in the country," he observed. "It was not native-born people, of the Old Yishuv in Jerusalem, Tiberias, and Safed who fashioned it, but rather people born in the towns of Russia, Poland, and Lithuania. And its growth comes not from forces in the country, but rather from the waves of pioneering youth immigrating from elsewhere. This growth is at the top of the concerns of the labor movement of the Land of Israel; it is its most pressing issue."[38] Rosenstein was not writing critically. As a senior figure in the movement, he took it upon himself to write its history. The quoted statement comes from the first of that work's three volumes.

In and between these lines you can make out a fundamental fact: the labor movement's main interest was pioneering immigrants and the unorganized workers who joined them—whom the Histadrut wanted to organize. They were its central concern. But that position caused collateral damage—many

Sephardi workers were pushed out of their jobs. In the Jordan Valley, for example, where a number of pioneering settlements were established, the Histadrut gave priority in job placement to the European settlers over the Old Yishuv Jews of Tiberias. "Among these comrades an impression is forming that they are discriminated against because they are Sephardim," a member of the Tiberias Workers Council warned (to no avail), "and there are those who have an interest in putting that idea into their heads."[39]

At the beginning of 1928, a debate broke out in the pages of *Doar Hayom*. It was set off by an advertisement placed by the World Sephardi Federation regarding its establishment of an employment office in Palestine for Yemenite and Edot Hamizrah Jews. According to the notice, the new agency had been assigned two projects by the government: the paving of a road at the Mamilla intersection in Jerusalem, and excavating and laying concrete on the Jerusalem-Jericho road. The notice prompted a quick response from the Jerusalem Workers Council, an arm of the Histadrut, in the form of a letter to the editor. The council claimed that the two contractors who had won the tenders for the projects were Sephardim with close ties to the federation, and charged that the contractors had submitted bids so low that they would not be able to pay their workers a fair wage.[40] Ostensibly, this was an allegation of administrative malfeasance. But the Workers Council's charge was less than persuasive. The Histadrut's construction company was, at that time, on the verge of bankruptcy because of the low bids it made for tenders in Jerusalem and the high salaries it paid to its own officials.[41] In any case, the Workers Council asserted, there was no reason to set up another employment agency—the Histadrut's was open to all.

Nahman Tzarum, a Yemenite Jewish social activist, responded in turn in the newspaper's pages. First, he countered, Mizrahim did not view the Workers Council as having a monopoly on public-works contracts in Jerusalem or on the employment of laborers for these projects. Second, the reason Edot Hamizrah needed its own employment office was that there was no impartial agency that handed out jobs to workers according to need and in an egalitarian way. Third, hundreds of members of Edot Hamizrah had registered with the Workers Council but did not receive jobs. Fourth, the advocates of organized labor in fact actively took away the jobs of Mizrahi workers who were not union members. In short, unorganized Mizrahi workers who were hired on an individual basis were being robbed of their livelihoods, while those who were registered via the Histadrut did not receive their fair share of workdays. Therefore, an independent employment agency was necessary. Tzarum drew up a list of the principal construction projects that the Jerusalem Workers Council had won contracts to build, using its members as laborers—the Gymnasium high school in Rehavia, the (Sephardi!) synagogue in Bayit Vegan, the Bayit Vegan road, water reservoirs in Atarot and Kiryat Anavim, the teachers' college in Beit Hakerem. He asked for an accounting of how many Edot Hamizrah laborers who were registered with the Histadrut were employed at these sites. He received no response to his challenge.[42]

IMMIGRATION AND SETTLEMENT

The World Sephardi Federation was established "with the goal of uniting the members of Edot Hamizrah into a single entity in order to draw them closer to the idea of the [Jewish national] revival and to make them active partners in the building of our National Home." But along with uniting Edot Hamizrah and Sephardim into a single organization that would take part in the building of the nation as a whole, they had no little criticism of the Zionist project. The federation's leaders argued that, even though they were helping raise money for Zionist institutions from wealthy Jews in the Islamic world, the Jews of these countries were not receiving funds from these bodies. The leaders were encouraging Jews from the Islamic lands to immigrate to Palestine, but Zionist funding bodies were not providing money for the settlement of these Mizrahi immigrants. Indeed, the national institutions employed virtually no Mizrahim. In other words, Sephardi money was going into projects that Sephardim were not benefiting from. The federation's leaders sent these complaints to the Zionist Executive in London, asking it to ensure that the Zionist institutions in Palestine allocate their funds fairly and equally.[43]

The relations between the World Sephardi Federation and the Zionist Executive were a subject of much contention in 1928 and 1929.[44] The Zionist Executive tried to mend the breach at a meeting with representatives of the federation in the summer of 1928. Two issues were on the agenda: Sephardi involvement in Zionist activity, and fundraising. Menachem Ussishkin, president of the Zionist land-purchasing agency, the Jewish National Fund (Keren Kayemet Leyisrael), offered his perspective. "What is the only deficiency that could be seen in the Sephardi community until recent times?" he asked. He answered the question himself: "It is indifference to public life as a whole, the life of the nation." Then he turned to fundraising: "How is it that you Sephardim are still raising money [independently]? . . . I presume that, while the Sephardi speaker is talking about the essential need for money, they [the donors] pose him the question: What do you need money for? Don't

Keren Hayesod [a Zionist fundraising organization] and Keren Kayemet see to all Sephardi affairs? And then the Sephardi speaker replies: they don't give anything to the Sephardim, or give only a little."[45]

The Sephardi representatives at the meeting stuck to their guns. Funds were indeed not allocated fairly. This was the reason for the marginal Sephardi involvement in Zionist activities, one of them—Meir Laniado, an attorney—maintained. "Over the next twenty years, Keren Kayemet will buy another 400,000 dunams of land, will build another fifty settlements, and will create ten more Kupat Holim [the Histadrut medical services and insurance organization] centers. Another ten Histadrut buildings will be built, and I am dubious as to whether over these twenty years one or two settlements will be built for Sephardim," he declared. "And I must say openly: a National Home either has to be for all of us, or it will not be at all."[46]

EITHER THERE'S CAKE FOR EVERYONE OR THERE WON'T BE CAKE

Forty years later, Saadia Marciano, a member of the Mizrahi protest movement the Black Panthers, spoke in much the same way. Either there's cake for everyone, he said, or there won't be any cake. Now, fifty years after *that*, Mizrahi activists are voicing the same principle.[47]

In Zionism's internal debate, "everyone" means the Jews. Very few Jews maintain that the word "everyone" includes the Palestinians. At the beginning of the 1920s, that position was not as rare, although it was on the decline. Consider the following text written by Eliyahu Sasson, who was born in Syria and settled in Jerusalem in 1927. He later worked in the Jewish Agency's Political Department and subsequently served as a member of the Israeli cabinet. In 1928, however, Sasson's livelihood came from commerce, and he devoted much time to journalism and public activism. The passage comes from an op-ed he published in the Lebanese Jewish newspaper *Al-'Alam al-Isra'ili* (The Jewish / Israeli world), under the headline "Between Sephardim and Ashkenazim."

> The readers of this newspaper are aware of the weighty mission that lies on the shoulders of the Arabic-speaking Sephardi Jews, in the framework of the national revival, and they are also aware that the territory of Palestine will not achieve independence and freedom and self-rule unless all its communities unite, Jews, Muslims, and Christians, and all do their utmost to obtain the rights of the country's [inhabitants] and their liberation. . . . The Sephardim among us are also aware that

> none of these communities can be done without because one completes the other, and because all separation or conflict between them will lead to the subjugation of Palestine and the perpetuation of foreign rule over it.
>
> For ten years [since the Balfour Declaration], the Ashkenazi still places his hope in Europe, seeking its support, and Europe fills him with vain hopes and promises, while the Sephardi watches these acts with an aching heart, and his heart burns. He tries to call out to his brother and to explain to him his mistake, but he does not listen. . . . All of our politics are in the hands of the Ashkenazim, from the senior administrator to the lowest clerk, all are foreign to this area, far from its moral conceptions, its customs, from the spirit that imbues it, and from its language. The greatest problem is that the nation's funds are in the hands of the Ashkenazim and they spend the money as they wish and no one can supervise them. . . . It is difficult to presume that their efforts will end in success if they do not work together with us to reach a mutual understanding with the Muslims and Christians and obtain their trust and support on our national issue, instead of reaching an understanding with [British prime minister Stanley] Baldwin and [German foreign minister Gustav] Stresemann and [Benito] Mussolini.[48]

Sasson's op-ed contains the central components of the view that prevailed in Sephardi political circles since the beginning of Zionist activity in the Land of Israel with regard to Jewish-Arab relations. Yosef Eliyahu Chelouche (son of Aharon), Hayyim Ben-Kiki, and Eliyahu Elyashar (grandson of the Yisa Berakhah) were among its most notable spokesmen, as were the members of Hamagen, an association of Sephardi intellectuals who defended the Zionist cause in the Arabic and Turkish press during the latter years of the Ottoman Empire. They believed that an understanding could be reached with the Arabs on the basis of the principle of a common homeland, if the Zionists would only give the Sephardim the authority to represent the Yishuv in its contacts with the Palestinian Arabs. They also demanded that the Zionists operate within and for the larger region, without seeking outside assistance from Europe. As for Sephardi-Ashkenazi relations, they were critical of the fact that Sephardim were kept out of positions of influence, and angry about Ashkenazi control of the national funding bodies.

The Arab affairs expert for the Histadrut daily, *Davar*, the Polish-born Michael Assaf, quickly responded to Sasson's piece, which he called "*dilatoriyah* [defamation] of the Sephardi type." Beyond dismissing the claim that it was possible to reach an agreement with the Arabs, Assaf criticized Sasson's antinational position, and especially his claim that the Ashkenazim were responsible for the tense relations between Jews and Arabs.[49]

In the meantime, tensions rose over the holy site that the Jews called the Temple Mount and the Muslims Al-Haram al-Sharif (I use these names interchangeably in this book, according to what makes sense in context).

INTERIM CONCLUSIONS

The vision of a common homeland that attracted Jews and Arabs at the end of the Ottoman period, and their sense of sharing a common (if limited) identity, dissipated after the British conquest, leaving only a handful of advocates. Most of the established Jews, the Sephardim included, took note of the advantages that the new British order promised the Jews and warmly welcomed it and the Balfour Declaration. The Palestinian Arabs launched a struggle against it. They tried to enlist the Jews of the Old Yishuv in a common struggle but got no response. One important reason for this was that the alternative the Arabs were proposing included establishing the status of the Jews as a minority, even if they would be a minority with guaranteed rights. In the meantime, the Sephardi intellectuals, including those who had previously advocated cooperation, found themselves involved in other struggles. The most important of these were the battle for equal rights within the Jewish community and proper representation for Edot Hamizrah in Zionism's institutions.

The members of Edot Hamizrah, only a few of whom fully joined a Zionist framework and adopted the movement's views, found that they had the status of outsiders. They were no longer Arab Jews but, as far as the official bodies were concerned, neither were they full-fledged Zionists. On the social level, the Mizrahi underclass, comprising both Mizrahim and Mughrabim who had long been in the country, along with immigrants who arrived after the British conquest, grew larger. This group had no political affiliation, and few of its laborers belonged to the Histadrut. Poor Mizrahi neighborhoods emerged in the large cities—in Jerusalem, Nahla'ot; in Tel Aviv, the neighborhoods bordering Jaffa (Kerem Hateimanim, Shekhunat Hakartonim, Manshiya); in Haifa, Ard al-Yahud—and in smaller cities such as Tiberias and Safed.

As this was happening, tensions surrounding Al-Haram al-Sharif and Al-Aqsa Mosque intensified. (I am writing this on May 10, 2021, which in the Hebrew calendar is 28 Iyar 5781, Jerusalem Day, commemorating the unification of Jerusalem under Israeli rule in 1967. Palestinians and security forces are clashing around Al-Aqsa. It's 10:20 P.M., and there are reports that dozens of Palestinians have been wounded. Others were wounded during the previous forty-eight hours. The security forces have arrested large numbers of Palestinians. Some of them were protesting the eviction, at the demand of Jewish settler organizations, of the Palestinian families living in the East Jerusalem neighborhood variously called Sheikh Jarrah, Um Haroun, and Shimon Hatzadik. Jews who had lived and owned homes there during the Mandate period fled during the 1948 war, when the neighborhood came under Jordanian rule. No one has been killed so far. Earlier this evening, Hamas launched a barrage of rockets from the Gaza Strip toward Jerusalem. In response, the Israeli army has launched Operation Guardian of the Walls, Shomer Hahomot in Hebrew. During the operation, Jews and Arabs have clashed and rioted in Jaffa, Acre, Ramla, Bat Yam, and elsewhere.)

THE ROAD TO THE 1929 RIOTS

The tension was set off when Jews put up a divider to separate men and women worshipping at the Western Wall. The spot, barely more than an alley, below the Temple Mount had long been a site of Jewish prayer, but it was also part of a Muslim waqf (holy endowment). The occasion was Yom Kippur, the holiest day on the Jewish calendar, in September 1928. From the Muslim point of view, the installation of this divider violated the status quo that had long prevailed at the site and marked another stage in what Muslims saw as the Jewish attempt to seize control of the entire holy site and build their Third Temple in place of the Muslim shrines in the compound above the wall. The Zionist leadership denied having any such intention, but it carried on with its efforts to purchase property adjacent to the Western Wall so that the area for prayer could be expanded. In an interview with *Doar Hayom*, Rabbi Kook demanded the evacuation of the entire neighborhood adjacent to the wall, known as the Mughrabi Quarter, because it was inhabited by Muslims from North Africa.

In the summer of 1929, fights increasingly broke out between Arabs and Jews in Jerusalem and elsewhere. I detailed the events that led to that summer's deadly riots in my book *Year Zero of the Arab-Israeli Conflict: 1929*. Here, I will note only that the background to the riots was the general Arab fear that the Jews were trying to seize control of Palestine with British backing, and that together they would demolish the Islamic holy sites in Jerusalem. These fears were deliberately fanned by Mufti Hajj Amin al-Husayni and his supporters.[50] The question before us here is whether there was a Jewish ethnic dimension to these events.

ETHNIC DIMENSION NO. 1: VICTIMS

About half the Jews killed in the bloody riots of 1929 were members of Edot Hamizrah. The Palestinian version of the events maintains that Jews native to Palestine, as opposed to Zionists and Moskobim, were not hurt. In fact, the focal points of the massacre were Old Yishuv communities in Hebron, Safed, and Jerusalem.

The first Jew was killed a few days before the "official" start of the riots on Friday, August 23. His name was Avraham Mizrahi, and he was wounded in a fight between Arabs and Kurdish Jews who trespassed on a vegetable garden owned by Arabs near the Jewish Bukharan neighborhood in Jerusalem. He died of his injuries the following Wednesday. The journalists who covered the vegetable garden incident in the Hebrew press offered different versions of the events. Some treated it as an Arab attack on Jews, disregarding the sequence of events leading up to it. This was the approach taken by *Doar Hayom,* which also refrained to mention the ethnicity of the Jews involved. *Davar,* for its part, did not omit the fact that the Jews involved belonged to the Kurdish community.[51]

ETHNIC DIMENSION NO. 2: THE ASSAILANTS

The first Arab killed in 1929, at the very start of the disturbances, was Burhan Dahudi al-Dajjani. He was lynched by residents of the Bukharan neighborhood. Four people were tried for his murder and were acquitted. All were Edot Hamizrah, as *Doar Hayom* reported.[52] Dajjani was attacked by a large gang of Jews in the area of Hashabbat Square, situated between the Bukharan and Mea Shearim neighborhoods, not far from where Avraham Mizrahi was murdered. The prosecution did not succeed in proving that the accused had committed the murder.

Ashkenazi members of the Haganah were also involved in killing innocent Arabs during the riots, on a larger scale, but their ethnic origin was not noted by the press.[53]

ETHNIC DIMENSION NO. 3: HISTAARVUT

On the eve of the riots, Aharon Haim Cohen, a Jerusalem Jew of Persian ethnicity, was enlisted by Yitzhak Ben-Zvi to collect intelligence among the Arabs. "About two weeks before the 1929 riots we were notified of a 'state of readiness,'" he later related to the Haganah Historical Archives. "I was called before the National Council to Yitzhak Ben-Zvi, and they told me that I was to leave my work and to start working in espionage. I was then sixteen or seventeen years old. I worked as a typesetter for a print shop and lived in Musrara, an area that was half-Jewish and half-Arab. I obtained a *kombaz* (robe), *kaffiyeh* (headdress), and *agal* (headband), dressed as an Arab, and went to the Old City."[54] He was later sent to the Jewish community in Hebron. At the time of his enlistment, Cohen belonged to a commune of the Working Youth and was one of the founders of that movement's Jerusalem branch. Years later, his son Doron asked himself, "What was it that drew him to the world of the young pioneers, most of whom were from eastern Europe and who were entirely foreign to his world?" Why did he prefer a way of life that was so different from that in which he had been educated? He found no answer to these questions.[55] Cohen continued to work for the Haganah, the Jewish Agency, and the Histadrut, until his death at a relatively young age in 1962.

Histaarvut—that is, Jews disguising themselves as Arabs—and service in the security forces in general, would, in the years that followed, become an important way for Mizrahim to make their way into Zionist and then state institutions. It was a relatively accessible means of social mobility.

ETHNIC DIMENSION NO. 4: SURVIVORS

During the riots, many Jews were saved by Arabs, and there were cases in which Arabs were saved by Jews. For the most part, this involved people who had a previous acquaintance. One such case involved elderly Moroccan Jews who lived near the Mughrabi neighborhood in Jerusalem's Old City. Rabbi Mordechai Avraham Weingarten, the chairman of the committee that represented the Old City's Jews, related that "several Jews aged 100 to 105 congregated in the Mughrabi courtyard. They remained there with very little food, and Arab neighbors provided them sustenance via the roofs, alerting them to the fact that they were in danger of being killed. For that reason, the Arab neighbors had to get them out of there. But the old men would not agree to leave, and the rescuers arranged for them a protective wall next to the gate in the courtyard."[56]

LONG-RANGE IMPLICATIONS

These manifestations of affinity and friendship could not, however, overcome the general picture. Members of the Old Yishuv, both Ashkenazim and Sephardim, were assaulted and murdered, including some who thought of themselves as Arab Jews. *Haaretz* thought it only proper to mention this in its coverage of the riots in Acre: "It should be noted that they attacked the house of Tzuri, the mukhtar of the Jewish community, who has always had peaceful and friendly relations with the Arabs. His family speaks Arabic at home, some of his children attend Arab schools, and when the Arabs collect donations for a cultural or philanthropic project they do not forget to solicit him—yet they displayed no gratitude and his family was but a step away from death."[57] In Hebron and Safed, the members of such families were also killed, sometimes as they shouted the names of the murderers, whom they knew.

The 1929 riots were thus a turning point in Jewish-Arab relations as a whole, and necessarily a breaking point in Mizrahi-Arab relations. Arab Jews were killed in the bloodbath, thus dooming the Arab Jew as a political concept.[58] This had cultural, political, and organizational consequences. For example, on the cultural level, the periodical *Mizrah Umaarav,* edited by Avraham Elmalih, changed its tune on the subject of Palestine's Arabs. It no longer evinced a sense of closeness; rather, it stressed distance and terror. Its first issue for the Hebrew year 5690—which began in October 1929—gave prominence to disturbing photographs of Jews who were killed or wounded by Arabs in the previous summer. Elmalih's foreword recounted the series of events and issues that led to the riots, and offered no criticism of any part of the Yishuv. The erstwhile Sephardi allegation that the conduct of the Ashkenazi Zionists had exacerbated the conflict was gone. Elmalih's take on the riots took the classical Zionist form: "We will intensify the pioneering spirit in our camp, we will turn primeval wastelands into fertile settlements, our endeavors will expand everywhere we dwell for the redemption of the soil and everlasting construction. The casualties and adversities that came upon us abruptly in the month of Av 5689 [August 1929] will further fortify our hands, and embolden us in confidence and security to broaden our Hebrew settlements, enlarge our population, and create a Hebrew majority in the free Land of Israel."[59]

The Jews learned two major lessons from the 1929 riots. First, when a deadly confrontation is in progress, Arabs make no distinction between one Jew and another. Second, as there had been fewer Jewish casualties where there was an organized Jewish defense, an organized Jewish defense force was essential. And they also learned that when knives flash and the wounded cry out and blood is spilled, there is no room for arguing fine points, for discussion of political disagreements, for "we could have acted otherwise." This was true for Jews in 1929 and thereafter, but not only for Jews.

JERUSALEM'S MOROCCAN JEWS WERE AN EXCEPTION

A small group of Moroccan Jews in Jerusalem, perhaps those whose elderly were saved by their Arab neighbors, acted differently. About a month after the bloodshed, the Palestinian Arab leadership tried to regain the support of the Jews of the Old Yishuv. They sent out a document to the old Jewish communities in Jerusalem, which they asked them to sign. "We, the native-born of Palestine, oppose the Zionist aspirations in the country, which bring destruction and devastation on all the country's inhabitants. We declare our solidarity with Arab aspirations and we justify their recent actions. We have no confidence in the Zionists and their actions that bring only evil on the land." The letter was written in Arabic. The Palestinians asked the mukhtar of the Mughrabi Jews of the Old City, Avraham Touati, to have it signed by the members of his community. He refused and reported the incident to the Jewish Community Council of Jerusalem, to the Zionist Executive, and to Yitzhak Ben-Zvi of the National Council. In the meantime, he reported, a member of the community, Shimon Yifrah, had begun collecting signatures in the community. More than thirty people had already signed. The Community Council turned to Avraham Elmalih, who at the time headed the Mughrabi Community Committee, asking him to try to persuade Yifrah to give them the letter. They also sent people to find him.[60]

AND WE JUSTIFY THEIR RECENT ACTIONS

The Zionist archives don't have the original Arabic document, nor have I been able to find it in the files of the Arab Executive Committee. The wording I quoted above is an English translation of a Hebrew text that comes thirdhand from the transcript of a telephone conversation. It is hard to believe that Jews would knowingly sign a document that affirmed that the Arab massacre of other Jews was justifiable. There are three possibilities: (1) the wording provided in the telephone call was not accurate; (2) those who signed it did not know precisely what the document said; (3) less reasonably, Jews signed it fully cognizant of what it said.

Whatever the case, the signed declaration apparently never made it back to the Arab body that issued it. This we can discern from the fact that it was never publicized. Major political changes followed the bloodshed.

THE ESTABLISHMENT OF MAPAI AND THE INSTITUTIONALIZATION OF LABOR MOVEMENT HEGEMONY

The 1929 riots provided the impetus for completing the negotiations to unite the Yishuv's two major labor parties. Ahdut Haavodah (which itself had been formed previously from a merger of the Poalei Zion party and the Independents led by Berl Katznelson) fused with Hapoel Hatzair. Tom Segev describes the occasion: "The denouement finally came in January 1930, in Tel Aviv's Beit Ha'am hall, festooned with the red banners of socialism and the blue-and-white flags of Zionism, as well as portraits of the movement's spiritual progenitors, among them Karl Marx and Joseph Trumpeldor. At the end of three days of speeches, Ben-Gurion announced the new party's name: the Palestinian Workers' Party, soon known by its Hebrew acronym, Mapai. And he led the crowd in singing the anthem of the first immigrants of the Second Aliyah, 'God Will Build the Galilee.'"[61]

The new party, led by David Ben-Gurion, proved to be greater than the sum of its parts. It became the dominant and unrivaled political force in the Yishuv. Its control of the Yishuv's institutions enhanced its power in the World Zionist Organization and the Jewish Agency, and in 1935 Ben-Gurion was elected the chairman of the Jewish Agency Executive, establishing Mapai hegemony in the Zionist movement both in Palestine and worldwide.[62]

REMINDER: SLOW PROCESS AND SELF-IMAGE

Mapai became the broad political framework that encompassed the great majority of the Moskobim and their political parties. The label "Moskobim" was an expression of the distance that separated them from the longtime Jewish inhabitants of Palestine. The process had begun, it will be recalled, a quarter century before, at the beginning of the Second Aliyah in 1904. The immigrants of this wave did not come to Palestine in order to integrate into its society but rather came to reshape it. They aspired to change the face of the country and its society and saw themselves as the pillar of fire leading the camp. They looked on the people of Palestine—farmers, Sephardim, Arabs, the Old Ashkenazi Yishuv—with more than a tad of condescension. This led to tension between them and other social groups. But the sense of superiority was only one component of the culture they created. Other important components were their desire to change society from its very foundations, their sense of being elected to make this change, and their readiness for self-sacrifice.

And there was another important experience that was part of this process: loneliness. Berl Katznelson described the Hebrew worker as "alone in the simplest sense of the word":

> Alone as an individual, alone in his pain, feeling orphaned day and night as he waited for work in the moshavah's "labor market," when he knocked on the gate of an orange grove that had been closed in his face, as he weltered in a miserable and filthy "hotel," when he sought

> to buy [provisions] from a shopkeeper on credit, when he ate at a [workers'] restaurant [because he had no home to eat in]. It was the tragic loneliness of a person who seemed to others—and sometimes to himself—to be expendable in this world. It was the tragic loneliness of a man who did not know that there was a point to his life and that he had a role.[63]

This loneliness was what impelled the Moskobi immigrants to organize themselves into political parties, and it gave the parties their strength. It's important to understand this if one wants to grasp the power of labor parties at the time.

> The parties were thus the only motivating, directing, and guiding force in the lives of the workers. They did not limit themselves just to political and cultural affairs, as they do today, but rather saw to the entire set of the worker's vital needs: they searched for jobs and handed them out, arranged kitchens and made the arrangements for the new immigrant. . . . The party was then everything to the worker. It took him out of his social isolation, gave reason to his suffering, it served as a source of encouragement. The worker began to feel that he was not alone in battle.[64]

This is an important key to understanding the gap between the experience of the European immigrants and those of the Islamic world and the difference in the nature of their political organization. The passage above does not describe the lives of the latter. Whether they were recent immigrants or born in Palestine, the fundamental experience of Jews from Muslim countries was not loneliness. They belonged to families and communities. As such, they did not need political parties, and the parties (as social and cultural bodies) were not meant for them. With the exception of a minority that became enamored of the pioneering movements, those movements remained alien. In the words of the father of Israeli sociology, Shmuel Noah Eisenstadt, "The immigration of the Jews of the East to Palestine did not generate a break from their traditional social and cultural structure. They came to the country with the hope that they could live better and more secure lives in accordance with their own ways. . . . They were not prepared to consciously change their economic and employment structure, the fundamental principles of their social and cultural life, and their Jewish consciousness."[65] One reason was structural and prosaic—the immigrants from the Islamic world arrived as families, rather than as lonely young adults. When they arrived in Palestine, they were not alone—they felt comfortable in their families and communities. The immigrants from eastern and central Europe were in an entirely different position, and this, it seems, had a very real effect on how they organized. They needed parties and movements that could serve as surrogate families and as communities. Indeed, many of them had already been organized, before they arrived, in frameworks that prepared them for settlement. The Mizrahim maintained their family and communal ties.

But the differences in political behavior between Mizrahi and European immigrants also had deeper causes, lying in the different circumstances the two groups had faced in their countries of origin. The Zionist immigrants from Europe came from a region in which national ideas were at the forefront and in which liberal and socialist ideas flourished. Furthermore, they arrived after ideas of secularism had inundated European society, Jewish society included, for generations. Because of antisemitism, they felt that they had no place in Europe, but the idea of the national home was not aimed, in their view, at maintaining Jewish particularism. Rather, they saw it as a way for Jews to join the family of nations on the basis of the ideas of the Enlightenment. The collective they sought to establish was meant for people like them, those who had chosen to abandon their old Jewish community life and head down the path of modern nationalism. The conditions of life and the struggle to achieve Zionism's goals, before immigration to Palestine and especially afterward, required them to be prepared for self-sacrifice. That in turn granted meaning to their lives. It was based on a potent drive for revolutionary change and the creation of new institutions. It was a world entirely different from that of the Jews of the Islamic world, and this, too, played a role in the two groups' mutual alienation.[66]

THIS SHOULD BE STRESSED

In other words, two different ways of life encountered each other in Palestine. They were two parallel cultures—a traditional family culture facing off against an activist revolutionary culture. Neither side was interested in a melting pot. In a certain sense, each side looked down on the other. The Mizrahim thought that the Moskobim were foreign and strange, people who had cast off the traditions of their forefathers, lacking in values. As far as the Moskobim were concerned, the Mizrahim were a backward society and were playing no part in the urgent task of the time. But the Moskobim, who headed the Mapai party and the Jewish Agency, soon gained political power in the Yishuv's institutions and came to officially represent it in the eyes of the British authorities. Their institutions, most significantly the Histadrut, assumed a decisive role in the labor market. When this happened, their sense of superiority had an effect on the daily lives of all of Palestine's inhabitants. The Moskobim determined who had jobs and who did not, who would have to languish in illness and who received medical treatment. As their control of the political system and the funds reaching the Yishuv increased, so did their interest in maintaining power. This was the beginning of discrimination, not official or glaring, toward groups that did not belong to the labor movement.

They did not lack good justifications. The Moskobim were the ones who had set up the central institutions and, ostensibly, they invited the entire public to join. But even the leaders of the socialist camp sensed that their claim to being the vanguard of the Jewish people as a whole, and the representatives of the working class in particular, was largely empty rhetoric. One of their leaders, Haim Arlosoroff, wrote in the mid-1920s that "the organized workers movement in the Land of Israel is not a proletarian movement. The Histadrut is the settlement aristocracy. If there is a proletariat that sees itself as devoid of public influence, it is the Eastern communities and Mea Shearim [the Haredim]."[67] Berl Katznelson spoke in a similar spirit at Mapai's convention in 1932. "The fact that the labor movement in this country has remained a foreign body in the Eastern communities is a bad sign for it," he said. "If we do not do everything to attract those parts, it is preening to call ourselves a pioneering movement; we are in that case an aristocratic workers movement."[68]

SOCIALIST ARISTOCRATS

The feeling of superiority derived at that time from the Moskobim's willingness for self-sacrifice, some more so and some less. They constituted an elite serving the nation, which made them different from European aristocracies. Some brief background is necessary. The actual work of uniting Jewish forces in order to establish a Jewish national home in Palestine was accomplished by Jews from Europe (even if thinking along these lines could be found in different parts of the diaspora). Most of the immigration to Palestine, from the dawn of Zionism, consisted of Jews from Europe, who needed a refuge more than Jews from other places did. And, of course, until the Holocaust, the Ashkenazim constituted a massive majority of the world's Jews (some 90 percent). During the Mandate period, the Ashkenazim constituted a majority of the country's Jews, and that majority was constantly growing (59 percent in

1918, 75 percent toward the end of the Mandate).[69] That is a birds-eye view of the picture. Closer up, among the immigrants from Europe, members of the labor movement were the most influential, because they arrived imbued with a desire to work for change. They wanted to change themselves, to become workers, settlers, and soldiers, and they wanted to change the entire Jewish people. They were more organized, more determined than other Jews, and they had an overarching concept, an action plan for reshaping the entire world. Most important, again, was their preparedness for self-sacrifice. They were the ones who crafted the local forms of settlement—the moshavim and kibbutzim. They organized the Jewish defense force, the Haganah. They founded the labor union and created marketing networks like the Mashbir general store and the Tnuva dairy, which bought milk from the kibbutzim and moshavim, processed it, and distributed it to stores and consumers. They founded the Kupat Holim health insurance and medical services organization, the credit system that served farming settlements, and the infrastructure of the Yishuv political system. They worked intently to shape a Hebrew cultural revival and laid out the country's borders by establishing settlements on its periphery. In accomplishing all this with funds donated by Jews all over the world, most of whom were not labor Zionists or even Zionists at all, they bolstered their sense of superiority over anyone who did not belong to their political camp. When they invited others to join them, they did so half-heartedly, fearing that newcomers would sully the purity of their cause. But the bottom line was that it was the Moskobim who drove the Zionist movement forward. It is hard to imagine how a Jewish state could have come into being without them, and, if it had, what its borders would have been, what sort of social and economic character it would have had, and what its attitude would have been toward the Middle East at large and the Palestinian Arabs in particular.

THE ENTIRE JEWISH PEOPLE'S MONEY

The upshot is that, from today's vantage point, the world of the pioneers exhibits two faces (at least). The one stressed by the pioneers and their descendants is one of commitment and hard work. That self-image prevails to this day—for example, in the context of the battle over the Asi stream, on the banks of which the kibbutz Nir David was built. The kibbutz claims that its long heritage of pioneering labor gives it the right to keep its stretch of the stream private, while outsiders, in particular the mostly Mizrahi inhabitants of the nearby city of Beit She'an, demand that it be open to the public. The second face, which only rarely shows itself in the discourse of the labor movement, emphasizes the financial support the pioneers received from the larger Jewish world, Mizrahi Jews included. "The Hebrew Yishuv in the Land of Israel does not maintain itself from regular local production, but rather from the import of capital," Arlosoroff declared. In other words, the Yishuv did not support itself. It lived off foreign donations. "This entering capital, national and private," Arlosoroff explained, "constitutes for us the process of the apportionment of output." What he meant was that the socioeconomic issue was not how to allocate profits from labor, which was the focus of the socialist struggle in other societies. Instead, it was how to distribute the capital that came to Palestine from outside sources. Some of that capital was invested in the purchase of land and the construction of buildings, and did not immediately help boost production. But it flowed "through the pipes of the [World] Zionist Organization to the labor settlements, office workers, the American Zion Commonwealth, etc., and a large mass of others who subsist here thanks to the circulation of these sums, from the commerce and credit connected to them, etc."[70] In other words, it was national capital, not only the labor force of the kibbutz and moshav settlers, that enabled development. The same was true of the dairy industry, intensive agriculture, and later the fish-farming industry, which were largely funded by donations from diaspora Jews. To this extent, the growth rate of many economic sectors, and the financing available to them, resulted not just from the hard work and self-sacrifice of the pioneers. It was also thanks to the fact that they had close ties with Zionist institutions.

The 1929 riots broke out in the midst of a wave of immigration known as the Fourth Aliyah (1924–31). Two years after it ended, the Fifth Aliyah began. Both of these waves deepened ethnic social stratification.

THE FOURTH AND FIFTH ALIYOT

The Fourth Aliyah, which peaked in 1924–25, consisted mostly of Polish Jews fleeing an economic crisis and burgeoning antisemitism. Tens of thousands of Jews left Poland, but the United States toughened its immigration policy, which diverted some of the emigrants to Palestine. Many of them were from the middle class and settled in the city. Some of the immigrants arrived bereft of possessions and money. Many of them arrived as family units, in notable contrast with the pioneers of the Second and Third Aliyot. At the end of the Fourth Aliyah there were 175,000 Jews in Palestine, constituting about 17 percent of the country's population. The Fifth Aliyah began in 1932 and surged after Hitler came to power. When the Arab Revolt began in 1936, the Jewish population had reached about 400,000, some 31 percent of the country's total.

"This third [of the population] was cultured, advanced, and of greater economic potential than all the rest of the country's inhabitants," the *Haganah History Book* states.[71] This growth, which brought with it also a wave of land purchases, reinforced the fears of Palestine's Arabs and was one of the major causes of the outbreak of the Arab uprising, which lasted until 1939.

Two points are important here. First, these two aliyot included a large percentage of white-collar professionals and people with money to invest. They created a middle class, a nonsocialist, free-market-advocating urban bourgeoisie that was, significantly, entirely distinct from the image of the barefoot pioneer seeking work picking oranges or paving roads. In the words of Alex Bein, a historian and the national archivist, who himself immigrated during the Fifth Aliyah, "During the years in which the Fifth Aliyah streamed into the country—and especially under the influence of the immigrants from Germany and central Europe and the considerable capital that they brought with them—the enterprise of Jewish construction in Palestine expanded and renewed to an extent without precedent in the previous period."[72]

THE GAPS

It was not only the Zionist enterprise that expanded. So did the socioeconomic disparities in the Yishuv. This was neither deliberate nor surprising. It is what happens when people with capital and people with nothing arrive in the same place, even if the elite defines itself as socialist. Indeed, the surge in development that characterized the years of the Fifth Aliyah came along with a growth in poverty among large swathes of the population.[73] In Tel Aviv, a real underclass developed. In that city alone, during the first half of the 1930s, about three thousand families (including many thousands of children) needed social assistance. The needy families came from both Europe and the Islamic world. Immigrants who belonged to the Histadrut received assistance from labor organizations, while those from Germany had a social bureau of their own. During the years that followed, most of the Ashkenazim, or their children, including those immigrants who were not seen as productive, were integrated into the labor market and the Yishuv institutions. Immigrants from the East received much more limited assistance. Their ties with officials of the Histadrut and other bodies were tenuous, meaning that they had a lower level of access to the labor market. These immigrants had more children, making it more difficult for parents to provide for their economic and educational needs. The social assistance provided by the national institutions, as compassionate as it may have been, could not meet the demand.

The sense of social and cultural superiority and the doctrine of the melting pot (which expected that everyone would unite under the European Zionist banner, even if this was not stated in so many words) made the Europeans more judgmental about immigrants from the Islamic world and made it harder to put in place an appropriate assistance system. For example, the fact that many of the Mizrahim found housing in neighborhoods adjacent to Jaffa and maintained frequent contact with that city's Arabs reinforced the perception that they were culturally inferior and morally weak. We will soon see how, during these years, the social label attached to the Mizrahim grew ever more negative—and received a scientific imprimatur.

MIZRAHI POVERTY AND ASHKENAZI POVERTY: A THOUGHT

First, three facts: (1) during the Mandate period, poor Jewish families from both the Islamic world and Europe arrived in Palestine; (2) there were poor neighborhoods during the Mandate, as there are in contemporary Israel; (3) these poor neighborhoods were and have remained conspicuously Mizrahi (and Arab); then and now, there were no poor Asheknazi neighborhoods (except, perhaps, for Haredi neighborhoods). We need to think about what might be the reasons for this, to see what explanations have been offered and consider others that might seem reasonable.

One explanation attributes this situation to ethnic character traits and the different cultural levels of the immigrants. The Mizrahim, it is said, are lazy, primitive, and deficient in concern for their children and their education. These are character traits similar to those attributed to the Arabs. Mizrahi children thus grow up to be listless, lacking interest in national values and a modern way of life, without any drive to improve themselves and devoid of any interest in the nation's destiny and the generations' missions. In any case, they will not start down a path that would extricate them from a life of poverty and deprivation. Poor Ashkenazim, by contrast, have grit and willpower, invest in their children's education (and have fewer children), see themselves as part of the historical process of the Jewish people's return to its land, and thus affiliate themselves with national institutions and pull themselves up by the straps of their sandals out of the cycle of poverty.

Another explanation places at the center not the character traits (real or imagined) of poor Mizrahim and Ashkenazim but rather the circumstances they encountered in Palestine or Israel. For example, the social-assistance system was better at providing for the needs of European immigrants, as attested by contemporary critiques both by the needy and by professionals.[74]

Why? One possible explanation is that the people who held the public purse—the great majority of whom were Ashkenazi functionaries and activists—instituted ways of operation that fit well into the social structures they knew. And perhaps they also acted in accordance with the Jewish precept that "the poor of your own city come first" and consciously or unconsciously gave preference to immigrants from their own cities. The cultural affinity between established and new European immigrants made it easier for the Ashkenazi underclass in other ways as well. For example, it was easier for them than it was for Mizrahim to integrate into the hegemonic Hebrew culture then in formation, which was fashioned in the spirit of eastern and central European national cultures. Even more important, they did not disdain their culture and their abilities. The result was a milieu in which Ashkenazi children, poor ones included, lived within a supportive community and saw around them people similar to their parents in leadership positions and prestigious professions. In contrast, Mizrahi children were situated at the margins of this community and were presumed from the start to be inferior.

Which explanation is more convincing? Each of them seems to offer a way of understanding certain cases. There were some cases in which family neglect pushed the second generation of Mizrahim into poverty or to the social margins, while there were other cases in which they were tracked in that direction by the establishment. But if we reject the presumption that there are inborn disparities in ability between Mizrahi and Ashkenazi children and focus on indigent members of both communities, it is reasonable to claim that the social-assistance system that took form in Palestine during the Yishuv period, and during the period of mass immigration after the establishment of the state, made it easier for European immigrants to rise out of poverty and offered them an easier path into the middle class. At the same time, this system perpetuated the marginality of Edot Hamizrah. This was seen by the members of that community in real time.

NO PERSON FOUGHT HIS FELLOW

In October 1937, "hundreds of members of Edot Hamizrah as a whole and those born in the country in particular" sent a memorandum to the Jewish Agency.

> Our situation today is terrible. . . . From the day the labor unions were founded, we have had no livelihoods; they have taken over the labor markets and all that is left us is hunger. If we apply to some institution

> to request work, they tell us that we need to see to the needs of the new ones who are coming . . . and in all the occupations it's all yours, big and small institutions, it's all yours like the [Jewish] Agency, Keren Kayemet, Keren Hayesod, the municipal committee, the community committee, the Assembly of Representatives, the banks, the government, it's all yours, and what will [become of] the members of Edot Hamizrah? We'll die so that you can bring others in our place, or will we rise and fight, each man against his brother and his fellow? Absolutely not.[75]

The writers went on to make a list of demands—welfare payments, exemptions from school tuition for poor families, free medical care for the needy, and a Histadrut that operated equitably. "You sit on your chairs and you don't know what's going on in the country," they concluded. "There is no one looking after the suffering Mizrahi people."

Their basic claim had already been voiced a decade earlier. The Histadrut and Workers Councils served the socialist eastern European immigrants and helped them control the labor market and push out the members of long-established ethnic communities, what we have called "the conquest of labor from the Mizrahim." To be precise: the authors of the memorandum had no problem with organized labor itself. They protested organized labor that excluded part of the public. Note also the possibilities offered by the writers—they could either die or fight. Their immediate rejection of the option of starting a civil war underlines, rather than mitigates, their instinctive urge to fight.

AWARENESS OF THE DISPARITIES

Cognizant of the growing disparities, and of the fact that half of Jerusalem's Jews were Mizrahim, the Jerusalem Workers Council established, in 1937, a department to serve the city's Edot Hamizrah inhabitants. Rami Adut, who has investigated the allocation of jobs by ethnicity in Jerusalem, notes that the council was meant primarily to address cultural issues but did not refrain from addressing the provision of work.[76] Unemployment was the principal problem, but there were secondary ones as well, such as wage discrimination. At a meeting of Mapai's Central Committee that addressed the issue, one of the speakers asserted, "It levies a heavy toll on our movement, spiritually and morally. . . . Our ambition is to organize everyone in the Histadrut, the new wave of immigration, Edot Hamizrah. . . . If we were on good terms with the public, if the standard of living and the way of living were otherwise, and if there was mutual assistance among us, if we helped that public, [things would be different]. . . . [But] our comrades relate to any talk about it with derision and distrust." He meant talk about equality without any real intention of carrying it out.[77]

A short time before that, Ya'akov Chechik (later Nitzani), who was born in Bulgaria to a Sephardi family and had been a Zionist activist in the country of his birth, was assigned to take charge of Edot Hamizrah in the Histadrut. He set out on a tour of neighborhoods and settlements inhabited by Sephardim and Jews from the Islamic world, and then submitted a report to the Histadrut's Executive Committee. "There is severe overcrowding, and the neglect is even greater," he wrote in the chapter devoted to the neighborhoods of south Tel Aviv. "The cafés of various types have an influence that is devastating this Aliyah. It was from these cafés that, last summer, the demonstration of the unemployed set out for the municipal building. Many surprises, unpleasant ones, can come out of these neighborhoods. These masses are [easy] prey for exploitive party agents, members of Betar [the right-wing nationalist Revisionist Zionist movement] and Hamizrahi [the religious Zionist party]. Only the Histadrut lacks almost any foothold. I have learned that work of some sort was done here, but then abandoned."[78] Even following his report, and despite his diagnosis of the political danger that the neglect of these neighborhoods was producing, there was no real change.

The discussion of this issue began on the eve of the Arab Revolt and continued after it began, causing an economic collapse among the Mizrahi lower classes.

That was when Mizrahi-Arab relations deteriorated further.

THE REVOLT BREAKS OUT: THE MIZRAHI MOMENT

The Fifth Aliyah, as we have seen, bolstered the Yishuv economy while widening disparities within it. But it also affected Jewish-Arab relations. This wave of immigration was quantitatively unprecedented, boosting Palestine's Jewish population from 220,000 to 400,000 and making the Jews a third of the country's population. The purchase of land from Arabs and the construction of Jewish settlements all over Palestine accelerated. For the Jews of central Europe, immigration to Palestine had been a way of saving themselves. But the Arabs experienced their arrival as a decisive step toward Arab expulsion from Palestine. This was the background to the outbreak of the Arab Revolt of 1936–39.

The historical literature conventionally dates the start of the revolt to an attack on two Jews, Israel Hazan and Zvi Danenberg, on the Tulkarm road. An armed Arab detachment, apparently disciples of sheikh Izz ad-Din al-Qassam, set up an improvised roadblock, where they collected money to buy weapons and ammunition. Arab travelers were told to pay up and did so. When a Jewish vehicle stopped at the roadblock, the Arab militants shot its passengers. Danenberg died of his wounds a few days later. Hazan, a chicken trader from Salonika who had immigrated just a year and a half before, was killed on the spot. Hazan was buried on the Friday following the murder, April 17, 1936, in Tel Aviv. The funeral procession turned into a furious demonstration; at its fringes, over the course of several hours, bands of Jewish youths beat up passing Arabs. "The Hebrew city has a right to be enraged when it is taking a murdered citizen to the cemetery," *Davar* declared in an editorial. "[But] woe to the great Hebrew city if every punk does whatever comes to his idiotic mind in its streets."[79] According to the *Haganah History Book*, "Two things caused [the Jewish rampage]: the fact that the funeral was in Tel Aviv, the country's largest city, and the participation of unorganized [not members of the Histadrut or other labor institutions] hot-blooded members of Edot Hamizrah." According to Berl Katznelson, "Had we ourselves known how to manage Hazan's funeral, we would not have had to manage other funerals."[80]

Here's the point worthy of note in the long view: in 1908, the Sephardim sought to calm down the Moskobim who were setting off altercations in Jaffa. In 1936, it was the Mizrahim who were sparking the clashes. Likewise, in 1908 the Sephardim accused the Moskobim of impairing relations with the Arabs; now the Moskobim were blaming the Mizrahim. The Mizrahi dream of a common homeland, and of the Sephardim's serving as a bridge between the Zionist movement and the Arab world, had not been adopted by the Zionists, but it was also abandoned by the Mizrahi masses, at least in times of pain and grief.

THE HAZAN FAMILY: LOOKING FORWARD

Hazan's eldest son, Avraham, returned to Salonika after the murder and joined his mother, Benvenida, who was still living there. Both were murdered in the Holocaust. Eliezer Hazan, Israel Hazan's grandson by a different son, was an Israeli air force pilot who was killed in a training accident in 1953.[81] But in 1936 the Holocaust was but a nightmare in the minds of Jews, and the Israeli air force but a dream.

A NEW PARADIGM: MIZRAHIM VERSUS MAPAI AND THE ARABS

That Saturday, April 18, the Association of Polish Immigrants held a meeting that focused on the plight of Poland's Jews. Members of Betar broke up the meeting. According to *Davar*, the Histadrut daily, "The arrogance of this mob of the lowest dregs of the Revisionist goblet, notoriously wild adolescents, most members of Edot Hamizrah, who call themselves the 'Youth of the Revolt'—such was the scene on the Tel Aviv street on Friday night and the next day, all of Saturday. These mindless boys booed and sang 'Hatikvah' until their throats were sore, with the refrain 'With blood and fire Judea fell and with blood and fire Judea will rise.'"[82]

After breaking up the meeting, *Davar* reported, these same young people beat up Arabs all over the city. These incidents were the first indications of the link between the Jewish underclass and militant nationalism. Now, after being accused of lacking national feeling, indigent Mizrahim put their nationalist feelings on display, if not in the way that the Yishuv leadership thought proper. At these demonstrations, anti-Arab feelings melded with intense hatred of Mapai. In the decades that followed, there would be many more examples. The anti-Arab slogans of these Mizrahi youths can be understood as an indication that they were decoupling themselves from their Arab background and shaping their own Mizrahi brand of nationalism.

In its coverage of attacks on Arabs and the burning of their homes when the Arab Revolt began, the Arabic press distinguished between two kinds of Jewish assailants—those it labeled members of Zionist youth movements, whom it called "Scouts," and Yemenites from the Hakerem neighborhood in Tel Aviv, which lay on the border between the Arab and Jewish areas.[83] But the Hebrew press outdid the Arabic press in instituting the practice of mentioning ethnic affiliations in cases of violence—except when the person involved was Ashkenazi. That is, the ethnicity of non-Mizrahi youth—in other words, Ashkenazim—who took part in violent acts was never cited. Take, for example, Abba Ahimeir and Benzion Mileikowsky (Netanyahu, the father of Israeli prime minister Binyamin Netanyahu), who broke up conferences and meetings at Hebrew University and elsewhere; members of youth movements who kicked over the boxes of Arab fellah women selling their wares; and Haganah members who killed innocent people as acts of revenge. To be clear, their acts were often reported in the press, sometimes in a positive and sometimes in a negative light. But the perpetrators were never labeled "Ashkenazi." When the perpetrators of violence were Mizrahim, their ethnic affiliation was noted. That's how it was in 1929, that's how it was during the Arab Revolt, and that's how it was until the mid-1980s, as I will show further on. At the same time, the term "Moskobim" fell out of use.

THE MIZRAHIM EVACUATE, THE MIZRAHIM AVENGE

During the first months of the revolt, in the spring and summer of 1936, Mizrahim were among the principal victims of Arab violence. Most of the Jews who lived in Arab and mixed areas, such as Jerusalem's Old City, Ard al-Yahud in Haifa, and the neighborhoods on the border between Tel Aviv and Jaffa, were Mizrahim. They had to leave their homes and became refugees. But unlike in earlier periods, this time the Mizrahim did not stand by impassively. The ongoing harm done to the Edot Hamizrah communities in general and to the Yishuv as a whole roused many of them to action. Their lack of confidence in the labor movement leadership, already, as we have seen, deeply rooted among them, meant that they lacked a political home. Many of them found an alternative in Etzel, the Revisionist Zionist force loyal to Ze'ev Jabotinsky that reorganized about a year and a half into the revolt. Etzel's two major principles galvanized the Mizrahim: separation from the Histadrut and the Zionist Executive, which had been snubbing the Mizrahim for nearly two decades; and its doctrine of avenging Arab attacks irrespective of the policy of restraint advocated by the Jewish Agency—the executive body of the state-in-the-making, headed by Ben-Gurion—and the Haganah.[84]

Jabotinsky, as we have seen, condescended to Mizrahi culture no less than Mapai's leaders did, but this did not blunt his movement's attraction for many members of Edot Hamizrah. Two possible explanations can be offered: first, Jabotinsky's scorn for Mizrahi culture had no real impact on their lives, which was not the case with the Histadrut; furthermore, he did not voice it very often. Second, he nevertheless advocated the allocation of more resources to the Jewish immigrants from the Islamic world. Whatever the case, the central appeal of Etzel for the Mizrahim seems to have been its refusal to abide by the Yishuv leadership's policy of self-restraint.

THE PALESTINIAN ARABIC PRESS

Despite fundamental change in Jewish-Arab relations and the burgeoning violence, some Palestinian Arabs held the misconception that Mizrahi-Arab cooperation was possible. It was as if the talk of brotherhood was what was important, while Arab attacks on Jews (including Mizrahim) should have no impact. In November 1936, during a lull in the revolt, the British government appointed the Peel Commission to study the conflict in Palestine and propose a solution. The Arabic-language weekly *Mir'at al-Sharq* wrote that "some of the Jewish natives [as opposed to the Zionist immigrants] are interested in meeting with the Arab Higher Committee [the leadership body headed by the mufti] to discuss the general situation . . . because they, as we have understood, are not interested in recognizing the Balfour Declaration." The Jews of the Old Yishuv, meaning the Mizrahim and ultra-Orthodox, it asserted, wanted to tell the Palestinian Arab leadership that they were also victims of Zionism. They had lived in peace and security with the Arabs without demanding a national home or a Jewish state on both sides of the Jordan, the newspaper explained, and had functioned as an indispensable part of Palestine's population. The Balfour Declaration and Jewish immigration, according to *Mir'at al-Sharq*, had hurt the economic and social standing of the native Edot Hamizrah residents. These people had come to the realization that they would be better off putting their fate in the hands of the Palestinian Arab nationalist movement.[85]

THE DOCTRINE OF SELF-RESTRAINT

But many members of Edot Hamizrah were in a different political place entirely, opposing the official Yishuv policy of self-restraint, called the havlagah doctrine in Hebrew. The policy mandated that innocent Arab civilians should not be hurt, for three reasons. First, killing the innocent was a violation of Jewish morals; second, terrorist attacks would be detrimental to the Yishuv's relations with the British; and third, Jewish terror would cause an escalation in Arab attacks and in the end redound to the disadvantage of the Jews. Etzel countered all three of these claims. First, it argued, Jewish morality sometimes requires targeting the innocent, examples being the Torah's injunctions to wipe out all members of the Amalekite and Canaanite nations; second, the havlagah policy painted the Jews, in British eyes, as a dishonorable nation, and as such would lead the British to disregard its demands; third, the Arabs would carry on attacking Jews in any case, because they opposed the Jewish presence in Palestine.[86]

The labor movement brandished its moral stance. It was at this time that the imperative to maintain a "purity of arms" was first proclaimed, the term apparently coined by Berl Katznelson. The concept was meant to highlight the difference between the loftiness of Jewish culture as compared to Arab culture. A beloved children's poet, Anda Pinkerfeld, who was thirty-four years old when the Arab Revolt broke out, responded with a poem:

Exult, Arab woman, exult and sing
Over the blood of a child so tender

but four springs old,
your sons, your heroes wounded her.
Exult that a mother hovers
between life and death
your sons, your heroes, struck her . . .

Exult and sing
You know, after all,
that no avenger will arise from his victim
who will pay for blood with blood
harvest with harvest
you know, after all, that
we are not brutish people . . .

We, after all, have known how to love a girl
but four springs old
we have known the purity and innocence of her eyes
that beget faith in the human.
So how could we strike such a girl
even if she was born of our killers?[87]

Pinkerfeld was a loyal member of Hashomer Hatzair, the Marxist-Zionist youth movement that advocated Jewish-Arab coexistence alongside heroic Jewish self-defense and settlement. Her life was the quintessence of socialist pioneering principles. Born in Polish Galicia to a family that had assimilated into the society around it, she attended a Christian school. But she switched to a Jewish high school after a pogrom in Lvov. She immigrated to mandate Palestine in 1920 as part of the Third Aliyah, drained swamps in the Jezreel Valley, and contracted malaria. She settled at Kibbutz Kiryat Anavim, just outside Jerusalem, later moving to Tel Aviv. In 1928 she began writing Hebrew poetry, at the encouragement of Uri Zvi Greenberg, one of modern Hebrew's most powerful poets and a radical nationalist closely associated with Jabotinsky and messianic Revisionist Zionism.

There is some irony in the fact that Etzel decided to defy the havlagah policy after an Arab attack on members of Pinkerfeld's kibbutz, Kiryat Anavim.

KIRYAT ANAVIM AND THE BREAK WITH SELF-RESTRAINT

Five members of Kibbutz Kiryat Anavim were killed by Arab assailants on November 9, 1937, not far from the kibbutz. The Jewish Agency called for restraint and reiterated its importance. Etzel carried out its first reprisal operation two days later. Yaakov Eliav and Eliyahu Duek, "the Edot Hamizrah son of a rabbi and yeshiva head," threw a bomb at Arabs sitting at a bus stop by Jerusalem's Old City at the end of Jaffa Road. Two of the Arabs were killed and five were wounded. To carry out the attack, Duek dressed himself as a yeshiva student.[88] Five days later, on a day that entered Etzel and Yishuv history as Black Sunday, the militia carried out a wave of parallel attacks against Arabs in different parts of Jerusalem, killing ten of them. Jabotinsky approved the attacks, after initially taking the position that innocent people should not be harmed. ("I see no utility in murdering an Arab who is riding a donkey to Tel Aviv to sell his vegetables. I see no heroism in it," he had asserted.)[89] Most of the attacks were carried out with firearms, though sometimes improvised bombs were used. As the revolt continued, Etzel started secreting large bombs in marketplaces. Mizrahim *mistaarvim*—Mizrahim disguised as Arabs—played a central role.

ETZEL'S MISTAARVIM

The year 1938 was the acme of the Arab Revolt. That spring, the Arab armed bands (*al-fasa'il*) multiplied, grew stronger, and carried out more frequent attacks. The number of Jewish victims rose, and with it the Jewish urge to respond. On April 21, Shlomo Ben-Yosef set out with two comrades to avenge the murder of four Jews on the road linking Haifa to Safed. They ambushed an Arab bus on the Tiberias-Safed road, attacking it with gunfire and a grenade (which failed to explode; none of the passengers were hurt). They were captured by a Jewish policeman and brought to trial. Ben-Yosef alone was convicted and sentenced to death. (One of his accomplices was declared unfit to stand trial, and the second, because of his young age, was sentenced to life imprisonment.) Angry Jewish demonstrations broke out all over the country, but they made no difference. Ben-Yosef was hanged on June 29, 1938.

While he was still incarcerated, Etzel embarked on a series of shooting and bombing attacks in marketplaces all over Palestine. They were carried out in a more professional way, most of them by Edot Hamizrah Etzel activists, who could easily pass as Arabs.[90]

These operations multiplied after Ben-Yosef's execution. Yaakov (Sika) Aharoni, a Jerusalem native of Persian origin, was one of the leaders. He laid two bombs in Haifa's open-air market, one on July 6 and one on July 25, killing about seventy Arabs. He carried out a third bombing on February 27, 1939. Aharon Cohen, a Yemenite from Jerusalem, placed a bomb at the clock tower in Jaffa in August 1938; twenty-four were killed. Yaakov Raz, born in Afghanistan, did the same in Jerusalem's Old City. He was identified by some of the local inhabitants, who attacked and wounded him with their knives. When British interrogators arrived at his hospital bed, he killed himself so that he would not, under questioning, provide information about his partners. Rachel Habshush, eighteen years old and of mixed Yemenite-Moroccan origin, took part in laying a bomb in the Rex Cinema in Jerusalem, and was apprehended when she attempted to secrete another one in the visitors' area of the prison in the city's Russian Compound. For many, she became an exemplar of female (and Mizrahi) heroism. And there were other such attacks that received less attention.[91]

YEHUDA LEIB MAGNES'S CRITIQUE OF TERROR AND THE MIZRAHIM

Senior figures in the Yishuv condemned Etzel's refusal to obey the havlagah in the most severe terms. Rabbis and functionaries, settlers and authors, "figures from all corners of the Yishuv, from all camps and circles," issued a public declaration headlined "Thou Shalt Not Murder."[92] Rabbi Binyamin (the pseudonym of Yehoshua Radler-Feldman) and Yaacov Peterzil edited a book titled *Against Terror* that included dozens of short pieces condemning the murder of innocent people. One of the writers was Rabbi Yehuda Leib Magnes, the president of the Hebrew University of Jerusalem, who penned a dialogue between himself and two Mizrahi youths.

> On that day I traveled with two young men from Edot Hamizrah in the Holy City. On that day the despicable Yemenite girl [Habshush] placed her basket at the gate of the prison.
>
> "She is a hero! What they doing to us in Tiberias—killing babies in the arms of their mothers—we are allowed to do to them."
>
> "No, it is forbidden to us and to them, and if they cast off the yoke of their law, we are forbidden to violate the law of Moses. It is written: 'Thou shalt not murder.'"
>
> "An eye for an eye is also written. And just as they are Asian, so we are Asian. And what is permissible for those Asians is permissible for our Asians."

The conversation between Magnes and the two Mizrahi youths continued. Magnes failed to persuade them that Habshush's act was a violation of tradition and morality, and that it was ineffective. They were unable to persuade him that it was the right thing to do. The conversation left him crestfallen. "And the Chosen People in Palestine are slowly approaching the brutal primitivism of the desert," he concluded.[93]

OUR ASIANS

According to Magnes, the fact that they were Asian—that is, Mizrahim—was the justification that the advocates of terror offered in support of their position. It was not the fact that they lived in the Middle East, "a tough neighborhood," that vindicated acts of terror, but their own Mizrahi character. This is an important point, because it proposes a Middle Eastern alternative, in terms of both attitude and action, to the European hegemony of the Yishuv and its liberal self-image. Another contributor to *Against Terror*, Hannah Thon, a social worker and activist born in Germany in 1886, offered an outside but complex view of the Mizrahiness of the supporters of terror. It was a fact, she maintained, that in certain circles among the Ashkenazim, as among the Mizrahim, there were manifestations of brutality toward Arabs. But, she argued, among the Mizrahim this was not the result of careful consideration or a clear political and national ideology. Rather, it was a primitive and ignorant form of hatred. Their approach reminded her of the "blind hatred of Jews by Hitler's people," she wrote, notably offering a European analogy (this was shortly before the Holocaust began). She did not, however, see the "instinct of hate and destruction" as a fundamental component of their characters. It was, rather, the result of many years of neglect by the Yishuv's institutions. "We exiled these families in a ghetto that erased from their hearts the culture that they brought from the countries they had lived in in the East," she charged, "and we have not yet brought them into the new cultural covenant and we have not yet made them partners in the Yishuv's responsibilities."[94] This is an important argument, but it comes close to ignoring that Mizrahim—our Asians—were not the only ones involved in indiscriminate killing. Ashkenazim, both those born in Palestine and those who immigrated from Europe, engaged in murder and terrorism as well.

OUR EUROPEANS

The opponents of terror stressed the role of Etzel—and Edot Hamizrah—in these acts not only as a matter of social analysis but also for political reasons having to do with their view of European moral superiority. Ashkenazi Haganah operatives also carried out reprisals against innocent Arabs, before and during the revolt. They did not, however, do this by secreting bombs in marketplaces; rather, they attacked passersby and killed indiscriminately in strikes against tent encampments and villages. Among the perpetrators were senior Haganah commanders who later became senior figures in the Israel Defense Forces. One of many examples was a retaliation operation carried out by the future commander of the elite Palmach strike force, Yigal Allon, along with his comrades Nahum Shadmi, David Shaltiel, Shlomo Shamir, and others. (Shadmi would, after independence, serve as president of the Military Court of Appeals; his son Yisca commanded the soldiers who carried out the Kafr Qasim massacre in 1956. Shaltiel was the IDF commander of Jerusalem in 1948. Shamir served later as an IDF general and commander of the navy and air force.) In response to the murder of the Jewish policeman Binyamin Krishon near the village of Lubya (near today's Golani Junction) in the summer of 1939, a Haganah detachment infiltrated the village, entered a house where a family was mourning, and, while the dead man lay covered before them, killed several of those present with gunshots and grenades. The *Haganah History Book* offers several other examples from different periods.[95] Even if there were some who severely criticized such actions and tried to prevent attacks on the innocent, no one linked the murderous impulses of the perpetrators to their Ashkenazi ethnicity.

That's how labeling works.

THAT'S HOW THE DIVISION OF LABOR WORKS

A few days after the raid on Lubya, Berl Katznelson published a condemnation in *Davar*. "A new crime occurred in the village of Lubya, a horrifying crime that indicates that its perpetrators have lost what remained of their powers of discernment and that the last spark of human feeling has escaped them. The gunshots that murdered old men and women, and which spilled the blood of a baby and a dying elderly man, show that we have been cast onto a dark slope that slides into an abyss." This was not all. "This abhorrent act," Katznelson wrote, "will doom its destructive perpetrators, whoever they are, to ignominy." It was an unambiguous condemnation—but it did not label the culprits ethnically.

The Palmach men who carried out the killing were insulted. They wanted to go straight to Katznelson's office and explain the operation and its purpose to him. But "Haganah commanders said that there was no point to such a meeting," Shadmi recounted, "and that we should accept the division of labor according to which Berl writes in the newspaper, while our assignment is to operate in the field."[96]

KARL FRANKENSTEIN AND THE LABELING OF MIZRAHIM

The mainstream media's deliberate linking of Mizrahim with terrorism and violence was part of a larger analysis of Mizrahi youth proposed by Ashkenazi educators. One of them was Karl Frankenstein, who in 1938 was a young man, thirty-three years old. He had settled in Palestine just three years earlier after studying social work and then earning a doctorate in psychology in Berlin, where he was active in Zionist organizations. He was concerned about social issues in the Yishuv, in particular the disparity between primitive (as he saw it) Mizrahim and European Jews. He carried out a study of Edot Hamizrah in Jerusalem and reported his findings in *Davar*:

> These ethnic groups also constitute the majority of the primitive strata of the Yishuv, and anyone who examines the lives of these masses will see a serious omen. As long as they live among us as foreign bodies who have not been assimilated, they menace the country's economic and social structure. From an economic point of view they are an unproductive element, because they have not learned to broaden the scope of their needs and cannot be accounted consumers. From a political point of view they are a wasteland, so long as they have not been connected to the unified front of the Jewish people. From a social point of view they are a burden because they are liable to leave the country, so long as they remain distant and in uncomprehending alienness to the modern civilization and the social ideals of the new Land of Israel.... The primitive youth who have not been assimilated into the new society are doomed to a life of constant tension, which is the product of the contradiction between their social and intellectual capacities and the new Land of Israel.[97]

In Frankenstein's view, the principal problem with the Mizrahim was their lack of openness to other cultures, and the fact that their world was founded on a single dichotomy—Jew versus non-Jew. "The meager remnants of messianic consciousness are sufficient to imbue Jewish values with inflated merit over all others. But, as this inflated consciousness of self-esteem is no longer borne by religion, and other values do not support it, it lacks content and is dangerous: they pay no regard to foreign resources, and they do not revitalize their own values by means of self-examination and [addressing] problems. The result is—witlessness and spiritual paralysis."[98]

On the practical level, Frankenstein proposed the enactment of a compulsory education law funded by a tax on the public. In the meantime, until the law was implemented, it was necessary to train teachers who could work with diverse populations. This wasn't a bad suggestion. But what led it in the wrong direction was its basic assumptions about the backwardness of the Mizrahim as a whole. This affected teachers who followed Frankenstein's teachings after the establishment of the state, and thus their students as well. (Frankenstein headed the Hebrew University's School of Education and was awarded an Israel Prize, the country's highest civilian honor, in 1965.) In his view, the Mizrahim were degenerate, of low intelligence, and incapable of recognizing that other people had distinct personalities. He proposed "to change the ethnic character" of the immigrants from the Islamic world.

Mizrahi activists would later point to the oppressive aspect of his teachings. "Because I believed in the sincerity of Frankenstein's intentions, as imparted by my teachers," Henriette Dahan Kalev, a political scientist, wrote years later, "I contended actively with self-repression. . . . I understood that I could not reach, through abstraction, to a recognition of the alien other as the possessor of an ego. . . . Over the years I learned that this polemic had been transformed into a massive apparatus of exclusion, which winnowed out all among us who failed the test of becoming Ashkenazi. . . . They spoiled the meal while I was still gazing at it with wide open eyes."[99] This was why Mizrahi activists protested at a conference held in Frankenstein's memory at the Hebrew University School of Education in 1997.[100]

IN THE MEANTIME, IN IRAQ

In the midst of the Arab Revolt and Jewish terrorist attacks, leading Jews in Baghdad published an unequivocal statement of support for the Arabs of Palestine. They also sent it to the British Colonial Office, with a copy to the League of Nations, signed by thirty-three community leaders, among them rabbis, physicians, lawyers, and public functionaries. Its language was simple: "The Jews of Iraq protest the Zionist policy and support their brothers, the Arabs of Palestine, and beseech you to treat them justly and reinstate peace and tranquility to the Arab lands." Some think that the community leaders were pressured to put out the statement. That same summer of 1938, a bomb had been thrown at the Laura Kadoorie Club, which served Baghdadi Jewish high society, and injured two children. It may well be that this incident spurred the dispatch of the letter, but the position it took had been that of the Iraqi Jewish leadership before the attack as well.[101]

ANTI-ZIONISM AND A WARM JEWISH HEART

Note that the anti-Zionism of the Baghdad community was bound up with a sense of Jewish solidarity. When Zionist institutions wanted to expand investments in Palestine because of the Fifth Aliyah and sought the assistance of the Baghdad Jewish elite, an Iraqi Zionist activist advised:

> Regarding the participation of Baghdad's Jews in the project of settling German Jews in the Land of Israel, we propose that the committee in London apply directly to the people whose names appear on the attached list and ask them to participate together in arranging a fund-raising effort. These people, while refraining from all Zionist activity, have warm feelings for all that is happening with our Jewish brethren and they have influence over the well-off Jews. It would be best if the letter were put in general Jewish (not just Zionist) terms and stressed the unity of the nation and the responsibility that every Jew has to come to the aid of his Jewish brothers. . . . We hope that the project will end with some success, especially if the operation here does not take on a visibly Zionist character.[102]

THE AMAZING STORY OF THE ABDUCTED JEWS

Something of Arab-Mizrahi solidarity remained among the Palestinian Arab rebels as well. Two young Jews appeared at Afula's central synagogue on Friday, December 23, 1938, at 4:00 A.M., exhausted and staggering. Their names were Shabtai Akrish and Albert Tayyar. They were able to identify the building because of the Hannukah menorah that lit its roof. They had spent three weeks as the prisoners of a band of rebels commanded by Yusuf Abu Durra, one of the Arab Revolt's boldest and most violent commanders. His men had captured Akrish and Tayyar at the beginning of the month when they got lost walking from Kibbutz Mishmar Ha'emek to Kfar Baruch. They were brought to the local headquarters, put in a dungeon, and interrogated on suspicion of involvement in throwing bombs in the Haifa marketplace. They denied any connection to the attacks and managed to prove their innocence. Abu Durra sentenced them to two additional weeks in captivity. Before releasing them, he composed a statement and asked them to have it printed in the Hebrew press.

> In the name of Allah the most beneficent, the most merciful. Allah is greatest. The high command of the rebel forces in Palestine. . . . Justice is the foundation of government.

> On the fifteenth of the month of Shawwal of the year 1357 a battle broke out between the mujahideen [holy warriors] and the army of the government which lasted from five to ten in the evening according to the Arab clock. Many in the army fell. The confrontation was in the village of Abu Shusha [west of Mishmar Ha'emek], and when it was over the mujahideen captured two Jews, one by the name of Ibrahim Tayyar and the second Shabtai Akrish. They were taken to headquarters, where Commander Yusuf Abu Durra commanded that they be treated gently and that all their needs be provided, such as food and drink and an appropriate place to live and physical rest during the time of their stay. They remained for twenty days and in the meantime their parents offered Commander Yusuf 2,500 Palestinian pounds as ransom. But it did not occur to the commander to accept this sum. Rather, after twenty days he ordered that they be released and that they be given clothing and expenses so that they could travel. This is how the mujahideen behave and this is the way that their honor and conscience and strength require them to act. They are the masters of justice and masters of the land and cannot be defeated. And all their endeavors are successful despite the additional English forces and their Jewish friends. Because Allah helps those who believe in him.[103]

A report of the Haganah's intelligence branch put the reason for the release into its own words: "The Tayyar family is a well-known Sephardi family. By various means they contacted on the one hand Sabri al-Madi [a rebel leader in the Haifa area], and the heads of the terror in Syria, and managed to obtain their release. The family claims that it paid no money, although there were negotiations about that. The two young men are of a bad type, the scum of Sephardi youth, so no importance should be attached to their stories. We surmise that one of the reasons they were not killed is that on top of everything there was no one to kill."[104]

As the author of the report saw it, Sephardim who maintained their connection to Arab society were "scum," people who were not even worth a bullet. For Abu Durra, such people were potential allies, and definitely not the manifest enemies of the Arabs of Palestine. At the core of the wave of terror—in which, on the Jewish side, Mizrahim played a significant role—something still remained of the view that Mizrahim and Arabs refused to be enemies.

THE COMMUNIST PARTY

The Palestine Communist Party (PCP) was founded by Jews, most of whom came to Palestine from eastern Europe already imbued with Communist ideology. At first, the party's spoken language was Yiddish. It held its first congress in September 1922. The participants evinced different approaches to the question of whether Zionism necessarily contradicted the socialist revolution. At a conference in 1923, the view that the Arab Nationalist Movement was a positive force in the struggle against British imperialism took center stage. Zionism, by contrast, was held to be a bourgeois Jewish movement umbilically tied to imperialism. This position made it possible for the party to join the Comintern, the union of Communist parties led by the Soviet Union. But it brought about the exit of many members of the party who felt connected to Zionism. The party accepted its first Arab member, Muhammad Najati Sidqi, in 1925. In the years that followed, the party made considerable efforts to enlist the Arab masses, but with extremely limited success. After the riots of 1929, the Comintern ordered the PCP to speed up its Arabization efforts. Two Jews, Simha Tzabari, the daughter of Yemenite parents, born in Jaffa, and Meir Slonim, born in Hebron to a Habad Hasidic family, and several Arab activists, among them Radwan al-Hilu ("Musa"), were sent to study at the Communist University of the Toilers of the East in Moscow, a training school for Communist leaders from all over the world. As far as the Comintern was concerned, local Jews, being natives of Palestine and not immigrants, were considered "good-enough Arabs" to be involved in the Arabization project.[105] When they returned to Palestine, "Musa" was named chairman of the party's Central Committee. Slonim and Tzabari served alongside him, and Tzabari became his romantic partner. During the Arab Revolt, sharp differences arose among the Jewish members of the party over the justice of the armed Arab struggle. Tzabari headed the camp that supported maintaining contacts with "terrorist groups of a revolutionary character."[106] Both mistaarvim in the service of Etzel and Communists (that is, at least one) who supported the Arab Revolt thus emerged from the same Mizrahi neighborhoods on the Tel Aviv–Jaffa border.

A PALESTINIAN VIEW

Ahmad Shukeiri, who would found the Palestine Liberation Organization (PLO) in 1964 and head it for three and a half years, wrote of his sense of Mizrahi-Arab affinity in his memoir. During the Arab Revolt, he was a young and energetic attorney, active in the pan-Arab Istiqlal (Independence) Party.

Like other Palestinian Arab activists, he was compelled to flee Palestine to avoid arrest. In 1940, upon the death of his father, Sheih As'ad Shukeiri (an opponent of Hajj Amin al-Husayni who had political ties with people in the Yishuv), the British allowed Shukeiri to return to his home in Acre and reopen his legal office. This happened during World War II, and in his memoir Shukeiri describes the enthusiasm he felt as the Wehrmacht under Erwin Rommel's command advanced toward Egypt. He hoped that the Nazis would clean up Palestine as well. The Jews, he recalls, were terrified at the prospect of a German victory. Once, in connection with his work, he visited the court in Tiberias. "In Tiberias there was a large Jewish community, some of them longtime residents and some new immigrants," he recalls. "I was invited to a meal by a Galilean Christian dignitary, Shehade al-Khouri, at a restaurant by the Sea of Galilee, which was owned by one of the Jewish old-timers." He then relates a conversation he had with the owner, whose name was Cohen:

> I noticed that Cohen's eyes were full of tears as he placed and cleared our dishes. I said to him: *Kheir Inshallah* [I hope you are feeling well], why are you weeping, Cohen?
>
> He replied: I weep for myself.
>
> I asked: Why? What happened?
>
> He replied: I, sir, am not a Zionist. I am an Arab Jew and my family has lived in Tiberias for 400 years, and before that in Damascus for 300 years—he choked back a sob and ceased to talk.
>
> I said to him: And what about that? Speak, O Cohen.
>
> He said: The Germans are already close to Palestine and our brothers the Muslims in Tiberias have already "agreed among themselves" about us.
>
> I asked him: What do you mean agreed?
>
> He said: They met this week and agreed that they will kill us when Rommel arrives. And they divided our homes and property among them. This restaurant that I built with the blood of my heart they assigned to the al-Tabari family [the family of the mufti of Tiberias, thus the family of the local leadership].
>
> I said: Do not believe this talk. The Tabari family will not harm you and they do not covet the restaurant or intend to do you evil.
>
> He said: I swear to God! By the lives of Moses and Mohammad, that is true.
>
> I asked: What do you wish me to do?

> He said: Sir, kill the Zionists and take their homes and property, but leave us, the Arab Jews, alone. We are under your protection. We are Arabs. We are Arabs. We are just like you.[107]

Shukeiri goes on to recount that following the meal he went with Cohen to the Tabari family home. They all drank coffee, and he asked the family to treat the city's Jews, especially the long-established ones, as neighbors worthy of protection, and to refrain from harming them or their property. The Tabari family pledged to do so and Cohen emerged from the encounter voicing immense gratitude to Shukeiri.

That's what Shukeiri says in his memoir. How much of this story is fact and how much is fiction is hard to say, but the message he seeks to convey is clear, and we can understand on what foundation it is built. Later in the book, he relates what happened to Tabari and Cohen in the 1948 war, the Nakba. But first a few words on the Mizrahim as that war approached.

THE MIZRAHIM BEFORE THE WAR

Alongside the Mizrahim who joined Etzel, and those who supported it from outside, and the Mizrahim who carried on with their work and daily affairs, and those who fraternized with Arabs, and those pushed to the social margins, there were also those who were active in the Yishuv's mainstream institutions, as laborers, teachers of Arabic, or members of the Haganah. For them also, the encounter with the Ashkenazi-socialist world was not easy.

During World War II, Palestine served as a logistical center for the Allies. Large numbers of workers were hired to build army camps all over the country. The Histadrut recruited from among its members large groups of workers. In the summer of 1941, at one work camp in the Negev, Yemenite workers worked alongside Ashkenazi members of the Histadrut. Here's what the Yemenite workers said:

> One evening last week the watch of one of the Ashkenazi workers who lived in the Yemenite tent was stolen. In that same tent a number of items and clothing were stolen also from the Yemenites. What did the people in charge and the guards do? To evade the responsibility that lay on their shoulders they found an easy victim: they shunted the blame off on the Yemenites and accused them of stealing the items. Honest working men suddenly became thieves and criminals.

> And how did they treat the supposedly "guilty" Yemenites? Simply, according to the barbaric rules that are practiced in our times. At first, they removed them from work in the middle of the day, then went into their tent and then suddenly . . . carried out a meticulous search of their suitcases and the pockets in their clothes and found a bit of money. It was money the Yemenites had earned as payment for their work. . . . Then they took them to the administration cabin, and the Jewish guard Motkin "had the honor" of thrashing them with his crop and his boots. Motkin the guard took out all his wrath on weak and defenseless men, and while the crop rose and fell on the Yemenites' flesh, and while the ringing of the slaps on their faces could be heard a long way away, and the kicks of his boots threw them from side to side, the representative of the workers committee, Comrade Yeruham Meshel, stood and watched and enjoyed it, and as he did, he cursed "the Yemenite thieves."[108]

Yeruham Meshel would later serve as Histadrut secretary-general. I have not found any account of this incident from his side. Being beaten with a crop evoked memories of the history of the Yemenites in Palestine. In 1913, a Rehovot farmer, Yonatan Makov, came upon two Yemenite women who were cutting dry branches from the grape vines in his vineyard. He tied them to a donkey's tail and dragged them down the moshava's main road and beat them. Then the moshava workers of the labor movement rose up to defend the Yemenites, setting off a long process of self-examination about the estrangement of the pioneers of the Left from the Yemenites that continues to this day. The pioneers called a joint meeting of the Ashkenazi and Yemenite workers. "The assembly ended at a late hour with a sense of elation, if not on the part of the Yemenites, at least on the part of the Ashkenazim. Neither was there any lack of endless dancing," *Hapoël Hatzair* reported somewhat self-consciously.[109] One of Israel's leading lyricists, Dan Almagor, wrote a song, "Dry Branches," about the incident.

Thirty years later, it was Histadrut workers who abetted and encouraged the flogging of Yemenites suspected of theft. No songs were written about that.

WHAT DOES THE CASE TEACH US?

The flogging of the workers certainly did not reflect how Ashkenazi workers on the whole felt about Yemenite workers on the whole, or tell us much about the institutional treatment of Mizrahim. Nor is the incident in Rehovot typical of the behavior of all the First Aliyah farmers of the moshavot. But it is important to know about such exceptional cases because they mark out the range of possibilities, behaviors, and feelings (and things were worse than we thought). Also, the fact that there were no cases of Yemenites abusing Ashkenazim teaches us something about the classes and hierarchies of those years, and about connections and alienation. There was also sometimes alienation in encounters between Ashkenazi members of the Palmach and the mistaarvim units that operated within that organization.

ARABIC TEACHERS AND PALMACH MISTAARVIM

A distinct group of Mizrahim who became part and parcel of the labor movement were Arabic speakers who turned their knowledge of the language into a profession. They served as teachers of Arabic, intelligence personnel, or mistaarvim. Unlike those who enlisted in Etzel, these Mizrahim worked in the Zionist mainstream, in a largely Ashkenazi environment. When the Jewish Agency launched its Arabic instruction program in the kibbutzim, *Davar*'s Arabist, Michael Assaf, crowed that "eighty percent of the teachers are Baghdad born! I believe that, of all the large and important Eastern Diaspora communities, that of Baghdad has thus far little played a direct and systematic role in the project of our adaptation to Palestine." Now a way had been found to make them partners in that process.[110]

The Palmach also set up a mistaarvim unit, called Hashahar, or the Arab Platoon, which operated from 1943 to 1950. In contrast with most Mizrahim, who were expected to integrate and shed the Arab side of their personalities, the mistaarvim had to do the opposite. They were to maintain their Arab identities and even take them to extremes, at least while they were behind enemy lines. For some, this came naturally. For example, David Shemesh, who was born in Baghdad and came to Palestine illegally in 1946, joined his brothers, who were then living at Kibbutz Beit Hashita.

WAIT A MINUTE, IRAQIS AT A KIBBUTZ?

There were also Syrians and North Africans and others at kibbutzim. What I noted above about immigrants from eastern Europe holds true also for those from the Middle East and North Africa: those who underwent Zionist youth movement training in their home countries and immigrated without families found themselves homes in organized frameworks, including those of the labor movement. This includes those who came as minors via Youth Aliyah

(Aliyat Hanoar), an organization set up initially to rescue Jewish children from the Nazis. These young people reached the labor settlements as individuals and as members of organized groups. The Ashkenazi aversion was more to Mizrahiness than to the Mizrahim themselves, and the principle of the ingathering of the exiles and national unity sometimes helped them surmount their distaste for Mizrahim. And Jewish solidarity was a factor, as evidenced by Operation 1,000, which brought Jewish children from Syria to Palestine.

OPERATION 1,000, 1945–1946

The operation to bring children from Syria and Lebanon to Palestine began in 1945 and shows the ambivalence of the Yishuv's attitude toward Jews from the Islamic world. On the one hand, their inferiority was stressed. "First we must carry out a humane educational action, to turn them into human beings, to bring them to become familiar with primary concepts," said Enzo Sereni, a socialist Zionist activist, after his visit to the Jewish community of Baghdad in 1942. On the other hand was a sense of Zionist duty (as Yani Avidov put it to Shaul Avigur—both men were leading figures in the Mossad Lealiyah Bet, a branch of the Haganah that smuggled Jews into Palestine despite British restrictions: "Each time, I remember something I heard you say . . . enthralling and wonderful words in their substance and their historical and national purpose: 'the liquidation of the Exile'").[111]

The operation involved Zionist activists from Syria who had already settled in kibbutzim in Palestine, among them Eliyahu Cohen and a married couple, Shoshana and Menahem Luzia. The Mossad Lealiyah Bet took care of the operational side—organizing the boys and girls in Syrian cities and spiriting them over the border—while Youth Aliyah saw to their absorption in the Yishuv. The emphasis was on teenagers, because "the adults in these countries have largely reconciled themselves with their situation, and it will be difficult to wean them away from the life habits of generations. . . . We did not want to accept as fact that the young generation would also accept the degeneration that threatens it," explained the Mossad Lealiyah Bet's chief of illegal immigration from the Islamic world, Munia Mardur. Rachel Yanait Ben-Zvi, one of the labor movement's leading women, was involved in the track for girls. The training farm for women that she had funded in Jerusalem had largely emptied of students during the world war, and Aliyat Hanoar allocated special legal immigration certificates for girls, who were sent to such programs.[112] "They were good girls, imbued with the innocence of childhood," said Ada Fishman, one of the leaders of Hapoel Hatzair and one of the founders of

Ayanot, an agricultural school that took in dozens of girls. Nevertheless, they did not meet the severe demands required of socialist pioneer women. "They viewed labor as dishonorable," Fishman wrote. "A sort of Oriental lassitude runs through all their limbs." Their spoken language was Arabic, "and they could not be weaned away from it, even at Ayanot." This despite the fines imposed for each conversation in Arabic, as related years later by one of the girls, Yvette (Havva) Kabani. Nevertheless, Fishman wrote, the girls formed a connection with the country and wanted their parents to join them.[113]

BACK TO SHEMESH THE MISTAAREV

Neither was David Shemesh weaned away from speaking Arabic. When he joined the mistaarvim unit in 1947, just as the Jewish-Arab war over Palestine was beginning, his Arabic was better than his Hebrew, but in his case that was seen as an advantage. He was sent in November of that year to reconnoiter in Jaffa. Another Baghdadi joined him on the mission—Gideon Ben-David, who had also been in a Zionist training network in Iraq, being prepared to settle at a kibbutz. In Jaffa, these men were suspected of being Jewish spies. They were taken for interrogation to the headquarters of the Arab forces, and then executed. Their bodies were interred to the city's east and were identified only in 1975 by the IDF unit that seeks soldiers lost in action.[114] A member of Kibbutz Palmahim, where Shemesh had lived, wrote about him in the kibbutz newsletter:

> I still remember David's arrival among us and the conversation in which he proposed himself as a candidate for membership in the training program [at the kibbutz]. I still remember the first time he took part in an assembly of the members—how strange and incomprehensible he was for us. His very life experience, his different way of talking, sometimes raised a smile among us, when we heard him trying to take part in the conversation.
>
> But in time we learned to see him in a different light. And it was the people who worked and trained with him who learned this in particular. Nevertheless, until the moment that we learned of the mission he was going on, we thought of him as [a little dense] . . . a man who doesn't understand social nuances . . . and that really was his personality.[115]

That was what Shemesh experienced: alienation in the land of his forefathers, in the promised homeland.

THE SHRINE OF THE SHOOTERS AND WEEPERS

Yet the Mizrahim who joined the Palmach benefited from the fact that when they killed Arabs, their acts were seen by the Zionist mainstream as legitimate. They were not branded terrorists, as was the case with members of Etzel. Yakuba Cohen, one of the Palmach's most prominent mistaarvim, underwent the process of affiliation with the labor movement as a teenager. Like a handful of young Mizrahi residents of Jerusalem's Nahla'ot neighborhood, Cohen joined the Working Youth movement, went for agricultural and military training at Kvutzat Kinneret, and enlisted in the Palmach's Arab Platoon. He later served in the Intelligence Corps, the Mossad, and the Israel Security Agency (ISA, better known as the Shin Bet or Shabak). In the Palmach, he and his platoon were taught the principle of the purity of arms, writes Zvika Dror, offering the example of an instance in which Cohen stabbed and killed an Arab passerby so as to avoid detection. "Decades thereafter, Yakuba says of this: the case in which I stabbed the Arab tortured me for a long time. On the radio they announced that the man had been found near the bridge and that he was mortally wounded and that his chances of surviving were nil. I was hugely tormented. When it comes down to it, the man was not part of the matter . . . perhaps I could have silenced him in another way, with a blow with a stick."[116]

What distinguished the two political tendencies—labor movement versus Revisionist Right—was not the killing itself. Both sides killed. But on the labor side, killing was seen as an unfortunate necessity. Bewailing and agonizing over it signified that its perpetrators understood that they had committed a moral offense, though one they could not avoid. This moralistic attitude was a source of pride in the labor movement. For the Revisionists, killing was an act of heroism to be proud of and to glorify. But the stories of Shemesh and Cohen and many others remind us that Mizrahim—mistaarvim or not, politically affiliated or not—took part in the 1948 war, though not exactly as Jamal Zahalka imagined. PLO Chairman Shukeiri was aware of this.

SHUKEIRI, THE MIZRAHIM, AND THE NAKBA

"Days and nights went by," Shukeiri continued with the story of Cohen, the Jew of Tiberias who feared Arab revenge if the Germans were to win, "and the year 1948 arrived. And the Jews in Tiberias began to attack the Muslims and Christians, who were unarmed; the members of the Tabari family fled, leaving their magnificent houses to be looted and their fertile land to be stolen by the Jews. At the head of the armed Jewish bands stood Tiberias's longtime Jews, the Arab Jews, Cohen and those like him."[117]

Shukeiri was an involved writer, not an impartial observer. He stressed what was important to him. This, apparently, is why he did not mention the massacre of Jews in Tiberias's Kiryat Shmuel neighborhood by Arab rebels in the autumn of 1938. Nineteen Jews were murdered that night, among them eleven children. The slaughter was etched in the memories of the city's Jews. Shukeiri focused here on another message: the betrayal by Mizrahi Jews.

THE NAKBA IN TIBERIAS: MIZRAHIM AND THE PALMACH

Yosef Nahmani, who came to Palestine from Russia in 1907 as part of the Second Aliyah, was a member of Hashomer, a leading figure in the Jewish National Fund, a purchaser of Arab land for Jewish settlement, a member of the Tiberias City Council, and a man closely acquainted with the lives of the city's Arabs. He was fifty-seven years old at the time of the 1948 war, a man who had lived a long life and achieved a great deal (he would achieve more after the establishment of Israel). In his diary about the war in Tiberias, he addressed the conduct of the Mizrahim. According to his account, he and Arab public figures tried time and again to restore order in the city. His sense was that the city's Arabs wanted peace. He noticed that small incidents in which members of Edot Hamizrah were involved had fanned the flames of conflict. The Haganah commanders in Tiberias, he wrote, lacked experience "and suffer from a feeling of bogus honor. They will not prevent the rowdy Sephardi boys from provoking the Arabs." At the same time, he noted that it was actually the members of Hashomer Hatzair and the Palmach who were the most brutal.[118]

QAWUQJI THE PRESERVER OF THE FANTASY

Fawzi al-Qawuqji was the commander of the Rescue Army, a militia sent by the Arab Legion to assist the Arabs of Palestine following the UN decision to partition the country. His force was made up of volunteers from Arab countries, serving alongside Palestinian Arabs. Qawuqji, a native of Tripoli in Lebanon, began his military career as an officer in the Ottoman army during World War I. He attended Iraq's military academy and commanded a group of volunteers who had come to the aid of Palestinian Arabs during the Arab Revolt in 1936. At the beginning of 1948, he was placed in command of the Rescue Army. His explicit mission was to prevent the establishment of a Jewish state. In practice, because of the balance of forces, he carried out harassment operations. His forces blocked the roads to Jewish settlements and attacked convoys and incidental targets. His aspiration was to conquer at least one Jewish settlement; he led attacks against a few but failed each time. In his memoir, he distinguished between Mizrahi Jews and others, voicing the old and naïve Arab belief that the Edot Hamizrah wanted to live in peace with the Arabs and that they were also willing to live under Arab protection:

> In the wake of our victory in the battle of Zara'ah [Kibbutz Tirat Zvi], which I will discuss later, and our success in cutting off the connection between the Jewish settlements in the area under our responsibility, while the British are trying unsuccessfully to save the Jews from our force, the Jews, especially the Eastern Jews, have been persuaded about the strength of the Rescue Army and that it has sufficient military resources to destroy their settlements and annihilate their inhabitants.
>
> That being the case, the leaders of some of the settlements close to us have decided to make contact with us to look into the possibility of surrender and of receiving our protection. They sent an emissary to the commander of the Hittin battalion, Captain Madlul Abbas, who was responsible for the Tulkarm district, and proposed this to him. . . . I agreed and I decided to be present myself, with an Arab delegation, to hear myself what the Jewish delegation said. At the meeting, which took place at Nur a-Shams [west of Tulkarm], the members of the Jewish delegation, who were Eastern Jews, complained bitterly about how they were treated by the Western Jews, and expressed a strong desire to receive our protection. I accepted their request on three conditions: 1. They must hand over all weapons and ammunition in their possession. 2. [They must] cut their ties to the Haganah, the Palmach, and the other terror organizations. 3. [They must] prevent Jewish elements with whom they are not acquainted from entering their settlements.[119]

Qawuqji evinces here basic knowledge of Mizrahi-Ashkenazi relations, which the Middle East's reading public during the Mandate period knew about. But he evidently did not have a sharp nose for military intelligence. The delegation that met him was not made up of Mizrahi Jews who were seeking to surrender. In fact, he met Yehoshua Palmon, a senior Haganah and Jewish Agency intelligence official. Palmon was accompanied by his longtime Arab collaborator, Ali al-Qasem (who was murdered about six months later by the chief of IDF military intelligence). They did not arrive to propose a Jewish surrender but rather to understand Qawuqji's intentions. They did this at the behest of Yisrael Galili, the Haganah chief of staff, and David Ben-Gurion.

According to Palmon's report about the encounter, the commander of the Rescue Army spoke with respect about the Jews he knew from Syria and Iraq, and said he sought a life of cooperation and peace. He regretted that the

Jews of Palestine had been induced to accept Zionism, "a movement that has its source in hubris and a lack of wisdom," as he put it. "There is no logic and justification for the Zionist aspiration for control and rule over the Arabs of Palestine and afterward the Arabs of the Arab lands," he maintained. Palmon tried to explain to him that in Palestine there was no distinction between Jews and Zionists, and that the Zionists, as the movement of the Jewish people's national revival, did not seek to rule over foreigners. Qawuqji did not accept this claim and their dispute over the nature of Zionism was not resolved.[120] A few days later, Qawuqji attacked Kibbutz Mishmar Ha'emek. His army was defeated after a pitched battle, and the Arab villages in which his forces had deployed themselves were destroyed. That same week, the Jewish forces went on the offensive, the first stage of a battle that continued until the declaration of the establishment of the State of Israel. During this period they conquered Tiberias and Haifa, Safed and Jaffa, and other areas, and the Arabs there were uprooted from their villages and towns.

The confusing combination of a sense of power, existential fear, and expectation of redemption was, in 1948, common to Jews of all ethnic origins, even if it came in different measures and with differences in emphasis. The difference between Mizrahim (those who had not allied themselves with the Yishuv institutions) and the entire spectrum of labor movement Ashkenazim was the level of organization and willingness to adhere to the directives of the Jewish autonomous authorities. With regard to attitudes toward Arabs, there was no real difference. The conduct of Jewish soldiers during and after combat was not correlated with ethnic or political affiliation but rather with individual sensibilities and values. In other words, when it came to participation in the fighting, or involvement in massacres and looting, all political currents and the members of all ethnic groups were in the same boat, for better or worse. Nevertheless, Shukeiri, in his way, like Ben-Gurion and the Yishuv leadership, attributed acts of brutality specifically to Mizrahim, as we will see in the next chapter.

In the midst of the war, large and growing numbers of Jews began arriving in Israel. The Yishuv became a state, and the Jews in Israel were transformed from a minority under the British Mandate regime into a ruling majority. This in turn led to changes in the challenges faced by the new country's leadership, as well as in the composition of the Jewish population, the relations between its different components, and relations between the Jewish majority and the country's Arab citizens.

CHAPTER 3

Little Israel, 1949–1967

In which we will accompany the immigrants from the Islamic world to the young State of Israel and into the Palestinian cities that had been abandoned by most of their inhabitants, and in which we'll become acquainted with the cafés that the new immigrants and Arabs patronized together. We will observe the outbreaks of violence that occurred from time to time, and consider the explanations given for this violence by the establishment and the media. We'll also encounter a few false accusations. We'll try to understand how and why Mizrahim were shunted off to the social margins and when they saw fit to act in concert with Arabs and when against them. We'll see which of these immigrants found themselves in the Israeli intelligence agencies, which in the Communist Party, and which employed by the state in public-works projects. We'll also encounter a Palestinian fantasy about making common cause with the Mizrahim in the eradication of Zionism, their common enemy.

In June 1949, the leaders of the Arab inhabitants of Jaffa wrote a letter to the city's military governor, in the name of the five thousand or so Arabs who had survived the war and remained in their city (seventy thousand had lived there before the war), which read in part:

> We the undersigned, Arab inhabitants of Jaffa, respectfully submit to your excellency our complaints and protests and our regret about the attacks of government representatives and new immigrants, *especially North African and Ashkenazi immigrants* [emphasis added].

After we were compelled to open our homes to the new immigrants, the immigrants behaved brutishly and claim that all our property belongs to them. We request that you take urgent action to put an end to this, because we cannot manage with Jews of this sort.[1]

The word "Ashkenazi" is the exceptional one in this letter; we'll address it soon. First, though, a bit of background. When the United Nations decided, on November 29, 1947, to partition Palestine between the Jews and the Arabs, Arabs began to assail the Jewish neighborhoods on the Jaffa–Tel Aviv border. A Jewish offensive against the Arab neighborhoods was launched in response. It is not within this book's purview to analyze the progress of the war in Jaffa and the rest of the country. But combat continued, the Jews shelled the Arab neighborhoods, and some claim that the Jewish forces deliberately escalated the fighting.[2] This combat led to the social, economic, and military collapse of Arab Jaffa, which compelled most of its inhabitants gradually to leave the city. On May 10, 1948, the Jewish Agency, represented by Amos Ben-Gurion, David's son, rejected a British proposal for a ceasefire between Tel Aviv and Jaffa. A correspondent for *Haaretz* explained that "political circles believe that as a result of this development, the remaining clutch of Arabs remaining there will leave."[3] But that wish did not come true entirely. When the Jewish forces conquered Jaffa four days later, there were still a few thousand Arabs in the city. Their leadership signed a surrender agreement (as opposed to a ceasefire), which allowed the survivors to remain. Thousands of homes abandoned by Jaffa's refugees were handed over to the Israeli custodian for abandoned properties. David Ben-Gurion wrote in his diary that "Jaffa will be a Jewish city."[4] He hoped to solve two problems at once: that of the half-ruined city and the abandoned houses within it, and that of housing the masses of Jewish immigrants who began to flow into the country even before the war had ended. This was the genesis of Israel's so-called mixed cities—tens of thousands of new immigrants, most of them Mizrahim, were sent to live in cities that had formerly been populated largely by Arabs but in which only a small number of Palestinians remained.

The government set up a commission to draw up a register of Arab houses left uninhabited and to parcel them out to immigrants, discharged soldiers, government officials, and others. But it had only limited efficacy given the situation on the ground. In practice, Jaffa was repopulated by means of squatting and countersquatting. The unofficial rule that gained acceptance was that Jews who managed to install a bed in a room and spend the night there had staked a presumptive claim to it. Sometimes such claims were enforced at gunpoint. Sometimes Arabs who remained in their homes were ejected by Jews. Some Jews used force to eject immigrant families who had grabbed rooms first. Some of the cases came before the courts, but in many other cases the law of the jungle prevailed. When it was all over, some 45,000 Jews, mainly new immigrants, were domiciled in homes in Jaffa that had previously housed Arabs. In Haifa the number was 40,000 and in Acre 5,000. About 8,000 new immigrants found homes in Lod and a similar number in Ramla by May 1949.[5]

This was the background to the letter sent by the Arab leaders in Jaffa. They refer to cases in which Jews broke into Arab homes, attempting to seize control of them, and asked the military governor "to put an end to actions of this sort in the interest of peace between the Arab and Jewish inhabitants of the State of Israel and so that hostility will not prevail between the nations." The letter was signed by the clergymen of the city's churches, the mukhtars, and Jaffa's imam. As a vanquished minority, they used civil discourse: we are all inhabitants of the State of Israel, we all want peace. They believed—or wanted to believe—that the military governor shared their interests.

WHERE DID THE ASHKENAZIM GO?

The letter refers explicitly to the ethnicity of the aggressors: "North African and Ashkenazi immigrants." At least, that is the wording of the Hebrew translation of the Arabic original that the archives preserve. The Arabic original has not survived, and we do not know whether the translation was made by a Jew or an Arab. So we have no way of knowing whether the term used in Arabic was *Sikanaj* (the Arabized cognate of Ashkenazim), or *Moskobin* (the Arabic plural of Moskobi), or *Yahud Urobiyin* (European Jews), or some other term used by Arabs in speaking of Ashkenazim. The reference to ethnicity has two interesting aspects. First, the victims were cognizant of intra-Jewish ethnic distinctions. In general, the assailants in clashes between the two national groups are labeled by their national affiliation—Jew versus Arab—not by ethnicity within those larger groups. Second, no less important but more complex, anti-Arab violence came, over the years, to be identified with Mizrahiness. In other words, the ethnicity of Jewish assailants in Jewish-Arab clashes was specified only if they were Mizrahim. That was the case, for example, in the clashes in Lod and Bat Yam in June 2021, as I was writing this book. And that was the case in other times as well, as we saw previously and will see again later in this chapter. The establishment media noted ethnicity only when the attackers were Mizrahim. This raises some questions that will run through this chapter: did Jews from the Arab world, after 1948, behave differently toward Arabs than Ashkenazim did? If so, what were the differences, and what lay behind them? Was the violence in such cases a function of the Mizrahiness of the Jews involved, or were there other, more significant variables? And what about the sense of commonality that largely characterized Sephardi-Arab relations in Palestine prior to 1929? Or was this no longer relevant by the time Israel was founded, neither to the longtime inhabitants of the country nor to the new immigrants? And where did the Ashkenazim go in the discourse on violence? Were they not mentioned in such contexts because they were the default, generic Jews?

THE GENERIC ASHKENAZIM

If Ashkenazim were indeed the default, then the letter from Jaffa's Arab leaders is the exception to the rule in its reference to Ashkenazim in the context of Jewish-Arab relations. Also note that this letter was written not by an Israeli official but by Arabs. It contrasts notably with Israeli government documents and press reports, in which the ethnicity of Jews other than Ashkenazim is noted routinely. Recall that this was the case in the coverage of events in the Mandate period as well—when there was a violent incident, if the young people involved were right-wingers, their political affiliation was noted, and if they were from Edot Hamizrah, their ethnicity was noted as well. Ashkenazi members of Etzel, or members of the Haganah who committed similar acts—beating Arabs, overturning the stands of hawkers in the markets, breaking up demonstrations, hounding Arab peddlers, murdering civilians—were not labeled ethnically.

This lacuna suggests that Ashkenazi Zionists are considered the generic Israeli Jew, whose ethnicity goes unremarked (as opposed to, say, Moroccans, Iraqis, Ethiopians, Haredim, Bedouin, or Arabs in general). They are not seen as a subgroup; rather, they are presumed to lack ethnic or any other distinction. They are, to put it in biological terms, the type specimen of the Israeli, the standard to which all others are compared. They see themselves (and are sometimes seen by others) as the standard Israeli—in their looks, their beliefs, their way of life, and so on. Other groups are measured against them and are defined by where and how they and the groups they belong to depart from the standard, becoming Haredim or Moroccans or whatever. But the Ashkenazim are generic only from their own point of view. Other Jews see them as different and label them. Sometimes Arabs do as well.[6]

HAIFA 1952: WHAT GENERICISM LOOKS LIKE

In 1952, May 1, International Workers Day, fell on the day after Israel's Independence Day, which is celebrated according to the Hebrew calendar. Independence Day's folk dancing segued straight into May Day marches. For socialist Zionists, it was one long celebration. But that's not how it was experienced by everyone else, from supporters of the right-wing parties to Arab Communists. The former resented the May Day festivities as a manifestation of labor movement rule, while for the latter, Independence Day marked the Palestinian defeat, which turned so many Palestinian Arabs into refugees, and the military regime under which the vast majority of Israel's Arabs lived. The result was that some of the celebrations in Haifa turned into violent clashes. Right-wingers attacked members of Maki, Israel's Communist Party, and Marxist-Zionist Mapam. Local offices and chapter houses of both parties were set on fire. *Maariv* reported these incidents on its front page without taking sides and without identifying the attackers. "There are some fifty injured," it informed its readers, "among them nine severely wounded evacuated to hospitals in Haifa, [and] six [people] are under arrest, among them members of Maki; Mapam's branch office has been wrecked and Maki's chapter is half-destroyed—these are the results of eight fights that broke out on the evening of Independence Day and yesterday between Communist demonstrators, groups of young dancers, and members of Edot Hamizrah."[7]

People were seriously injured and property was damaged, but what interests us here is the epithets the newspaper applied to each group. "Communist demonstrators" is a characterization according to political affiliation, without regard to religion or community (we know from other sources that the group included both Jews and Arabs). In its reference to "groups of young dancers," the newspaper made no mention of these dancers' political, religious, national, or communal membership. But these were people doing circle dances to celebrate Independence Day, so the reader would assume that they were Zionist Jews, and would probably picture them as the sons and daughters of Zionist immigrants of the first half of the century. The third group is "members of Edot Hamizrah," the only group identified by an ethnic label. Further on in the report, the writer reported additional clashes that took place on May 1, the day after Independence Day: "Yesterday, there were five minor confrontations between Arabs from the Communist ranks who came to the city and members of Edot Hamizrah who refused to allow the Arabs to enter Haifa." In these cases, the Mizrahim were identified ethnically, the

Arabs according to national and political party affiliation, and the altercation itself was between Mizrahim and Arabs. The Mizrahim were portrayed as the guardians of Jewish nationalism in the new State of Israel.

IMMIGRATION FROM NORTH AFRICA AND SOCIAL PANIC

Maariv's report on the incidents in Haifa does not reveal the writer's opinion about them. There is no mention of who started the fights, and neither side is explicitly assigned the blame. The Mizrahim are neither lauded nor criticized, certainly no more so than the dancers. But the ethnic tag itself accorded with the stereotype that attributed violent tendencies to Mizrahim. That stereotype became even more widespread once the mass immigration of Jews from North Africa commenced after the war.

Aryeh Gelblum published a series of articles in *Haaretz* in the spring of 1949 under the headline "I Was a New Immigrant for a Month." These articles became emblematic of Ashkenazi racism toward immigrants from the Islamic world, Moroccans in particular, and are widely quoted both in scholarly studies and by Mizrahi political and social activists. Yaron Tsur analyzes them in depth in his article "The Terror of the Carnival," contrasting their approach to others in the Israeli Jewish community. Gelblum's series gained notoriety because of his blunt language and the sense of Ashkenazi superiority that was the starting point for his journalistic project. He disguised himself as a new immigrant and visited immigrant camps, where he wrote his impressions both of the system charged with absorbing the immigrants and of the different groups of immigrants that he encountered. His piece on the North African immigrants appeared on April 22. "This is the immigration of a race the likes of which we have never seen in this country," he wrote. "We have before us a people who set a record for primitivism. Their level of education borders on absolute ignorance, and even worse is their lack of aptitude for taking in anything spiritual. In general, they are barely a step above the Arabs, the negroes, and the world's barbarians. In any case, it is a lower level than we were acquainted with among the former Arabs of Palestine. . . . Many of them suffer from severe eye and skin and venereal diseases. On top of all this comes prostitution and theft. . . . These are the ways of life that the Africans are bringing to the places they settle, so there can be no surprise that the country's general crime level is at its height."[8]

The scientific formulation of Mizrahi inferiority and European superiority was offered, as we have seen, by Karl Frankenstein in 1938. The flood of immigrants from North Africa further cemented and institutionalized the stereotype of the Mizrahim as primitive, violent, and similar to Arabs in their inferiority to Ashkenazim and Europeans. As is always the case with stereotypes, it contained a kernel of truth. Some of the immigrants who arrived in this initial wave came from the less educated and indigent strata of North African Jewry.[9] But some of the European immigrants who arrived after independence also came from the social margins, where violence was part of life, and many of them had not received an education because of the world war or for other reasons. But this is where the viewpoint of white supremacy came into play. "The special tragedy of the absorption [of these immigrants]," Gelblum wrote of the Moroccan newcomers, "is that, in contrast with the bad human material from Europe, there is no hope for their children. To raise their general level up from the depths of their ethnic natures is a matter of generations."[10] He was apparently not the only one who thought in this way.

Some tried to refute the stereotype. Not only Sephardim and immigrants from the Islamic world but also native-born Israelis and immigrants who were already at home in the country enlisted in the effort. One of them was Uri Avnery. Born in Germany in 1923, Avnery's family moved to Palestine in 1933. By the summer of 1949, Avnery was a respected journalist and author and a symbol of the new Hebrew man. He began his journalistic career at right-wing newspapers, where he advocated an Israeli society based on Hebrew (rather than Jewish) culture and nationality and envisioned a united Semitic realm. In 1948 he enlisted in the Givati Brigade's commando unit Samson's Foxes. He saw frequent combat and was wounded. His war memoir *In the Fields of the Philistines* became a bestseller. He also began to write for *Haaretz*. Among the topics he addressed was the common belief that the wave of immigration from the Islamic world had led to a rise in sexual crimes. "For some 'Ashkenazim,' it 'goes without saying' that only people of the East are capable of performing such deeds," he wrote. He presented the real data, which showed that most rapes were committed by established Israelis, not new immigrants, and that rapists could be found among the Ashkenazim, Mizrahim, and Arabs as well.[11] Those who were willing to be persuaded were persuaded. That didn't include the country's leadership.

BEN-GURION, MIZRAHIM, AND ANTI-ARAB TERROR

The trope that Mizrahim were violent, especially toward Arabs, was broadly accepted across Israeli society, including among its leaders, from David Ben-Gurion downward. Its origins, as we have seen, lay in the time of the Arab Revolt of 1936–39 and the controversy over the policy of restraint. From that time onward, Ben-Gurion had a penchant for stressing the Mizrahi identities of Jews who attacked Arabs, both when the assailants really were Mizrahim and when they were not. On the eve of the 1948 war, when Etzel's operations against the British and Arabs ratcheted up, the Histadrut newspaper *Davar* termed such violence "murder for murder's sake." The news reports in the same issue referred to those who carried out such acts as "blood-maddened thugs" and "homicidal dissidents."[12] David Ben-Gurion was quoted as saying that Yemenites were responsible for Jewish terrorism, and other leading officials suggested that the way to stop such acts was to open clubs for Edot Hamizrah youth. The Council of the Sephardi Community and the Yemenite Association protested the labels and Ben-Gurion expressed his regret, saying he had been quoted inaccurately.[13] But during the 1948 war, Ben-Gurion continued to attribute acts of terror to the Mizrahi ethnicity of their perpetrators. Following the Deir Yassin massacre, he wrote that "Kurds and others, members of Etzel, glorify Deir Yassin."[14] The Haganah's chief of staff, Israel Galili, spoke in the same vein following the massacre at Dawaima in the western foothills of the Hebron highlands at the end of October 1948 (today it is the site of Amatziah, a moshav in the Lakhish salient). The soldiers of Battalion 89, which conquered the village, were socially and economically diverse. Yet despite testimony that "commanders of culture [a coded term for Ashkenazim] turned into base murderers," Galili attributed the atrocities to soldiers of French and Moroccan origin and to those who had been members of the extremist terrorist Lehi underground, all of whom had histories of ruthless behavior.[15]

This is how perceptions of the labor movement elite were structured: Moroccans and right-wingers committed atrocities because it was in their nature, part of their culture, or part of their history. They were thus tagged according to their ethnicity and political affiliation. The same deeds, when committed by left-wing Ashkenazim, were termed aberrant acts that said nothing about their perpetrators. Their ethnicity was omitted and they were termed "cultured."

At the root of this discrepancy was a sense of absolute otherness. At a cabinet meeting at the end of the war, Ben-Gurion referred to the social aspect of the mandatory conscription that the government had instituted. "This was the first time that all strata of the people have found themselves together," he declared. "And among them there was rabble. We do not know the extent to which the Yishuv's ruling echelon lacks any contact and knows nothing about the life of the people, and that applies to all strata. There are common people, people from the [underprivileged] neighborhoods, and we don't know them, we are strangers to them and they are strangers to us and we live in an atmosphere of superiority. Now, with the establishment of the army, we have encountered each other. In these strata there is filth, illiteracy, and entirely different concepts about everything."[16]

And at a gathering of the IDF's high command in 1950, Ben-Gurion had this to say about the immigrants from the Islamic world: "To teach a young person who has come from these countries to sit on a toilet like a human being, to wash himself, not to steal, not to grab an Arab girl and rape her and murder her—that comes before everything else. . . . The ingathering of the exiles has brought us rabble. Melting down this rabble and reconstituting it—human, Jewish, Israeli, and after that military reconstitution—that is the foundation of the military. To be a human being, a Jewish human being, an Israeli."[17]

The good intentions are obvious—to turn all the country's Jews into moral people, clean of body and mind, modern, with Jewish and Israeli values. The problem with it became apparent not long thereafter. What did it actually mean "to be a human being, a Jewish human being, an Israeli"? Did pushing immigrants to the social and economic margins, which was what in fact happened, help them establish themselves and turn them into citizens who contributed to society at large? How was such good will compatible with the labeling of entire populations because of the actions of a few of their individual members? And how did this generalized attribution of fundamental traits of Mizrahiness—primitiveness, violence, and hatred of Arabs—affect interethnic Jewish relations and Jewish-Arab relations in Israel?

MIZRAHIM AND HATRED OF ARABS: IDEALS AND REALITIES

The Yishuv elite's perspective on the Mizrahim changed, as already noted, during the Arab Revolt of 1936–39. They had been seen as people who were closer to the Arabs than to the Zionist immigrants from Europe, but the elite now came to see them as Arab haters (without abandoning the view that they were much like Arabs). Hannah Thon, one of the founders of the Women's International Zionist Organization, claimed, as we have seen, that the Mizrahi attitude toward the Arabs was the product of a cultural crisis. She blamed institutionalized Zionism. "We exiled these families in a ghetto that erased from their hearts the culture that they brought from the countries they had lived in in the East and we have not yet brought them into the new cultural covenant and we have not yet made them partners in the Yishuv's responsibilities," she wrote then. She maintained that this was not a matter of inborn character. The Mizrahim, she asserted, aspired to spiritual development, but were given no outlet for it in Palestine. Thon added another explanation, proposing that Mizrahi animosity toward Arabs grew out of "their harsh personal experience, acquired in Palestine or in the Oriental lands in which they lived. In most of them, this inclination derives from an instinct and feeling, not founded on evidence—perhaps the legacy of persecution from previous generations. It is the legacy of their forefathers, who lived in constant fear and on the defensive."[18]

The constantly reiterated claim that Jews were persecuted in Islamic lands brings us back to the questions we opened with—to what extent was that true? To what extent did Jews feel, before arriving in Palestine or Israel, that the Arabs among whom they lived were hostile? Another question also needs to be asked: were there people who, for political reasons, encouraged these people's hatred of Arabs? The answers to the first two questions are not unequivocally clear. With regard to the third question, the answer is yes. The IDF's official policy was to instill conscious and deliberate hatred of Arabs among Mizrahi soldiers, on the basis of claims or understandings about the Jewish past in the Islamic world.[19] This was also the tactic used by the Herut party and its leader, Menachem Begin. The goal was to flatten out and amalgamate the life experiences of Jews who came from the Islamic lands, which were rich and varied, and to exchange them for a unified view of unremitting hostility toward Muslims and Arabs. In fact, Jews had a wide range of experiences in the Islamic world. The differences were due not only to the different characters of the Islamic societies from which they came (Morocco, Egypt, or Kurdistan, for example), but also to the disparate environments in which they lived—cities, towns, and villages. And individual Jews had different personalities and interactions with non-Jews, which also played a role. In other words, even Jews of the same generation who lived in the same neighborhood did not experience their lives in Muslim society in identical ways. Some were nostalgic for their places of birth and Muslim acquaintances, while others looked back in anger, painting their erstwhile neighbors in grim colors.

AN EXAMPLE FROM THE LIFE OF ANOTHER MINORITY

This point can be illustrated by taking a look at how Arab citizens describe their lives under Israeli rule. People who are familiar with the country's Arabs know that some of them stress discrimination with regard to government budgets, alienation, land confiscation, searches at airports, the racist behavior of Jews, and so on. Others, by contrast, put the emphasis on the freedom of expression and freedom of religion they enjoy, as well as economic prosperity, the social security safety net, opportunities for professional advancement, and friendly relations with Jews. Opposing perspectives can be heard from Israeli Arabs in the same family, or even from the very same person in different circumstances.

The phenomenon has two sources. First, how a majority society treats the minorities who live among them is generally not one-dimensional. It covers a large range of arenas (political, social, religious, economic, and so on), in which some interactions are positive and some negative. To this should be added people's individual temperaments and predispositions. The personal experience of members of minorities is not shaped only by the overall picture of majority-minority relations or by national and religious perceptions. There is also the way individuals frame their experiences, which is a function of factors such as personality and political consciousness. For example, a member of the majority group might cut the checkout line at a supermarket, butting in before a member of a minority group. Some people will experience this as humiliation on national grounds ("they have contempt for us, they know that we can't resist, so they cut in front of us"). Others will experience it as a routine annoyance, something done by members of all groups.

How people give expression to these feelings depends on other variables as well—for example, the context in which they speak on a given occasion, their desire to please (or challenge) the person who hears them, and the extent to which they conform to or feel unconstrained by conventional rules of discourse. A person listening to another's account of a past event must thus attend carefully, and learn what there is to be learned from it. But he should keep in mind that he is hearing the experience of an individual, expressed at a certain moment and in a certain way, no more and no less. General conclusions thus cannot be drawn from it, but neither should it be disregarded. People's personal testimonies, just like documents, are the tesserae used to piece together historical understanding.

Furthermore, the state is also involved in the process of constructing a personal memory. It offers a collective memory and invites the individual to share in it. It also lays out the boundaries of what is worthy and unworthy of memory. In the case of the history of Jews in the Islamic world, the tendency—certainly in the IDF, which played an educational role—was to propose a relatively uniform outlook of ongoing suffering, messianic hopes, and a thirst for revenge. This took the place of a more complex view of Islam and life under it. Similarly, the Israeli state and other bodies in later years inculcated a narrative according to which the Islamic countries expelled their Jews.

THE RETROSPECTIVE VIEW: A MULTIDIMENSIONAL PERSPECTIVE

Here is an example of a multidimensional view of the past, one articulated over the years by chroniclers of Moroccan Jewry who are themselves members of the community. In 1879, Alliance Israélite Universelle asked Rabbi Avner Israël Serfaty of Fez to undertake a survey of his city, its inhabitants, and its history, with an emphasis on what impelled the city's Jews to live in the city's designated Jewish quarter, the Mellah. Serfaty wrote, "I found this written in this language: that [after] the edict of Fez al-Bali [Old Fez] the Jews went up to the Mellah in 1438, and the reason was the wine that they poured into the fountain [where Muslim worshippers ritually purify themselves before their devotions] at the house of prayer."[20]

Serfaty answered a question here that preoccupied many people—how did Fez's Jewish quarter, the Mellah, apparently the oldest such quarter in North Africa, come to be? But the answer he offered is a bit obscure. What house of prayer is he referring to? What happened there with the wine? Why did it lead to the Jews' being restricted to a single neighborhood? To understand him better, we need to turn to an important book, *The Chronicle of Fez*, based on historical writings composed by members of the Ibn Danan family, among the city's sages. It begins with the year 1438 and goes through 1724. (Members of the Ibn Danan family continued to serve as Jewish leaders in Fez and Rabat until immigrating to Israel after independence.) In 1724, Rabbi Shmuel Ibn Danan assembled what remained of the materials passed down through his family, some of which were written in Arabic and others in Hebrew, and complied them into a book.[21] The volume opens with two "edicts," that is, persecutions of the Jews. One is the incident of the wine, and the second is the event known as the Harun Edicts. From these accounts we can learn a few things about the history of the Jews of Morocco, as they told the story:

> The year 5225 [1465]: The edict that was in Fez that people call the Harun Edicts was like this: There were two brothers, one king and the other rebel. Once the city's gentiles rose up, and they sent for the other one [the rebellious brother] and crowned him and brought him in. And the other one [the original king] swore that if he returned to his kingship, he would not appoint any lord and minister [governor of Fez] except a Jewish one.

> Because of our many sins, he returned to his kingship and kept his vow and restored [as governor of] the city a Jewish officer named Harun. And the Jews grew arrogant and violated commandments and changed laws and did deeds that should not be done. Among other things, they took a married gentile woman and beat her brutally, who screamed and pleaded [for mercy], but no one listened, and they continued to beat her, until the gentiles came together and slaughtered Jews in a heavy plague of killing, to the point that they killed the males until none remained of them except those who dishonored themselves [converted to Islam] for naught. To the point that among all the murdered they also killed one woman and found her two children and took them in a wagon and brought them up to the king. And they [the king and his court] took pity on the [other] women and put out a proclamation in the city that they no longer smite the Jews.
>
> For eleven days the king gathered all the converts and told them: I know [what has happened] and know the truth that you did not dishonor yourselves [convert] of your own volition; therefore anyone who desires to return to being a Jew may do so himself. So each one put his life in his hands and cast himself on the sanctification of the holy name, blessed be his name, and said I am a Jew. And he who feared for his life remained gentile, he and his seed and the seed of his seed. . . . And this is the edict that was in the year 5225.

The passage describes a period of fraternal war in the literal sense, between two brothers who were Muslim rulers. During the conflict the deposed king promised that if he returned to power, he would appoint as minister—that is, as governor of Fez—a Jew, not a Muslim. It's not clear why he made this promise, but the story tells us that when he did indeed return to power, he kept it and appointed a Jew named Harun—the Arabic form of the Hebrew name Aharon, Aaron in English—as the local ruler. The result was that the Jews "grew arrogant" and began to attack the city's Muslims, women included. The Muslim majority responded with a massacre of all the city's Jewish men, except those who converted to Islam; they then began to murder the women but were halted in the process. In the third stage, the fury began to abate. The king informed the converted Jews that they could return to Judaism. That is not to be taken for granted, because according to Muslim religious law a person who converts to Islam and then returns to his former religion (*murtadd*) is to be put to death. But in some cases, Muslim religious sages allow converts to set aside their conversions, if they can prove that they did not commit themselves to Islam of their own free will.

Ibn Danan then related the story of the wine affair:

> And twenty-five years before this there was also in Fez an immense edict called the *Khadah* [fountain] Edict, when the Jews grew arrogant and behaved wantonly to the point of going to the Great Mosque, [where] they went and blocked the water source that wells up in the mosque and filled the marble basin where the water welled up with wine and got drunk there all night, and at dawn they left and left behind a drunken Jew who fell asleep and the gentiles came and found him there and killed all the male Jews they could find. And only those who converted were saved. And they killed women and children.

Like the previous one, this incident does not accord with the view of Jews as a demeaned minority under Muslim rule. One night, a few Fez Jews got drunk near the city's central mosque, went to the adjacent fountain, and poured wine (which is forbidden to Muslims) into the water. When the Muslims arrived for their morning prayers, they found that they could not purify themselves. And they also found a drunken Jew lying there. The result was a massacre of the city's Jewish males, except for those who converted to Islam. The remaining Jews were then moved into a separate quarter, where all Jews who settled in the city thereafter also resided.

What is of interest here is not the details of these incidents but rather two things that they tell us. First, when violence erupted between the two communities, Jews were not always victims and Muslims were not always assailants; second, the Moroccan Jewish chroniclers were honest about the crimes committed by their coreligionists. They recounted and lamented the harsh edicts and the slaughter of Jews, but they did not depict the Jews as docile victims, nor did they claim that the attacks were motivated by hatred of Jews. Neither did they see the persecution of Jews as the central feature of their lives. The Jews of Fez remembered and evoked these incidents because they played an active role in the local political and social fabric, both as a community and as individuals. The explanation that the local chroniclers give for the Jewish ingathering into their own quarter is a causal one, not an ahistorical one such as the perpetual antisemitism or the unbending rules of the Islamic religion. This does not mean that the city's Jews were not sometimes attacked simply because they were Jews—that certainly happened, including in the cases cited here, in which the entire community suffered because of the actions of a few. But this fact does not negate what Ibn Danan saw as the crimes of the Jews. To use a term coined by the Jewish American scholar Salo Baron, Ibn Danan's approach does not reflect the "lachrymose conception of Jewish history."[22]

ON DIFFERENT JEWISH RELIGIOUS APPROACHES TO ISLAM

Neither was the Jewish religious approach to Islam uniform. One source that shows this appears in a commentary on Midrash Bereshit Rabba written by Rabbi Yosef ben Shalom Ashkenazi. Ashkenazi, as his name attests, was born in the German-French lands in the thirteenth century and later migrated to Spain and from there apparently to Morocco. He held extreme anti-Islam views, like the liturgical poets discussed in the previous chapter. But he came to his position from a different direction—he maintained that both Muslims and Christians were pagans. Muslim Hajj rituals—casting stones at the devil in Mina, near Mecca, or wearing a seamless garment—were, in his view, acts of idol worship. (Maimonides took a very different view, declaring that Muslims were of unblemished faith in the unity of God.)[23] But after presenting his halachic and theological analysis, Ashkenazi went on:

> Go out and see the foolishness of the sons of our people who laud and extol the faith of the Ishmaelites, and violate what is written in the Torah, *lo tehonem* [Exod. 23:33], do not find them attractive, and as if that were not sufficient, when they [the Muslims] affirm when they gather [for prayer and declare "There is no God but Allah"], the Jews and the poor who have nothing of religion [i.e., uneducated Jews] respond and say *shema Yisrael*, etc. [as a response to the call of the muezzin from the mosque's minaret] and then shower praise on this despicable nation [Islam]. And that causes them and their children to adhere to them . . . and I am not surprised by the fools of our nation who occupy themselves with praising them, but rather with those who think that they understand the faith of Jews, and these are some of the communal leaders, and justify it by saying that they praise and declare the unity of the Blessed Name [the Jewish God].[24]

The state of affairs described here illuminates an important aspect of the Jewish past in the Islamic world: interreligious rivalry was neither total nor well defined. Alongside the points of difference were points of agreement, and alongside those who sought the differences between the two religions were those whose experience was more of the shared. The upshot was that Jews and Muslims could sit together in the souk, the marketplace, hear the muezzin's call to prayer, and respond, by murmuring their own religion's declaration of God's unity. This was an experience of the social and religious fellowship that colored the lives of the Jews in Fez and elsewhere in the Arab realms, no less than persecutions and edicts and their inferior legal status as a protected minority. Throughout the history of Jews under Muslim rule, there were religious sages, both Jewish and Muslim, who opposed such close relations. The rise of nationalism in the Middle East added a new and more fraught dimension to Muslim-Jewish interactions, which became Arab-Jewish interactions—the struggle for sovereignty. In the previous chapter, we saw how nationalism affected the relations between Jews and Arabs in Palestine, with a brief detour to how they played out in Iraq. Now we have added an example from North Africa before the mass migration of its Jews to Israel.

RELATIONS IN THE AGE OF NATIONALISM

The growing strength of the Zionist movement, on the one hand, and the xenophobic current in Arab nationalism, on the other, ratcheted up tensions between Jews and Arabs in the Maghreb. The contest between the two national movements meant that the region's Jews were suspected of dual loyalty, or worse, disloyalty, by both sides. Like members of the Second Aliyah who were concerned that, in times of stress, the Jews of the Middle East would make common cause with the Arabs, so the Arabs were apprehensive that the Jews of their countries would support the Zionists in their struggle against the Arabs. Palestine's Sephardim tried but failed to mediate between the national movements so as to resolve the problem of dual loyalty, and the conflict in Palestine escalated. Under these circumstances, the position of Jews in the Arab countries grew more tenuous.[25] There were prominent Jews who made public declarations of opposition to Zionism, but this did not prevent sweeping criticism of the Jews as a whole. Here is a statement issued by the Tunisian Committee for the Defense of Palestine in 1947, directed at the country's Jews:

> It is not natural that you live with me and stab me in the back with a knife. It is not logical, son of Zion, that your existence depends on Tunisian money, which causes your commerce to flourish, while some of you donate from our money to Palestine. We can never agree to this . . . after all, we have already warned you, the Jews, at the congress

> that our committee held in the Great Mosque of Zaytouna, to refrain from all contact with the Zionists and to keep a distance from them. What has happened since? The proofs are here: Zionist broadcasts on Radio Tunis, the collection of funds estimated in the millions, Zionist newspapers that brazenly serve the goal of Zionism with no shame or embarrassment. . . . What will be the attitude of the Jews of Tunis if tomorrow the Tunisian problem enters a decisive stage, and what part will they take in the struggle, as Tunisian nationalists? Will they reply that they are neutral and that they do not need to get involved in something that does not affect them? Will they be with us?[26]

This is a classic instance of the problem of dual loyalty. The Arab states were a party to the idea that sovereignty in the Arab space is for Arabs alone. They thus fought the Zionists in order to prevent them from carving up the Arab world and seizing control of a bit of its territory. As the Arabs saw it, support for Zionism was support for the enemy in wartime, and the Zionist activity of some Jews turned all Jews into potential enemies.

The tension found expression in more than just public statements. Some ten violent anti-Jewish riots broke out in Arab countries (Egypt, Libya, Aden, Morocco, and Syria) in the years from 1945 to 1949, in which Arabs killed some 350 Jews and wounded hundreds more (this does not include the Farhud, the pogrom against Iraq's Jews, in 1941, and other attacks on Jews in that country). This was a significant increase in the frequency and extent of anti-Jewish violence, which took place against the background of the conflict in Palestine toward the end of the Mandate.[27]

AND STILL THE PICTURE IS AMBIGUOUS

But the treatment of Jews was not uniform even after the War of 1948. Here is an example (not representative, but interesting) reported in 1963 by one of the emissaries that Israel sent to Morocco to encourage its Jews to emigrate to Israel and to make the necessary arrangements for those who did:

> At the public school in Rabat a class was given "my country" as a composition subject. A fourteen-year-old Jewish girl, sitting among the Arab pupils, wrote an essay translated here word for word:
>
> "The Land of Israel which was promised to us and trampled by all its enemies, this weary land, soaked in blood, which they have miraculously succeeded in plowing and cultivating, these arid wildernesses

> which have been watered and made fruitful thanks to the bold desire of our farmers. . . . These women soldiers are trained to throw grenades, this land replete with joy and hope despite the war and the gunfire . . . which is progressing with giant steps in the mysterious world of science, this land, my land, is Israel. I love it for all its struggles, its joy, its optimism, its songs, and its dances around the campfire, and for its happy face."[28]

The girl had clearly received a Zionist education in a youth movement. She no longer saw Morocco as her home, only Israel, and she had internalized the country's pioneering spirit. She knew that it was dangerous to divulge her feelings in a Muslim school, the emissary wrote, but this did not deter her. The emissary further reported that the composition received a high grade, and that the teacher gave it to the headmistress—who was none other than the daughter of Morocco's foreign minister, Ahmed Balafrej. "The headmistress called in the student, spoke to her fondly, patted her on the head," the emissary recounted, "but asked her not to repeat such things, lest she be removed from the school."[29]

That was not a common reaction. In general, Zionist sympathies were met with hostility. The Israeli government agents working among Jewish communities in Arab countries who arranged immigration to Israel were well aware of this. So was the political leadership, which presumed that these Jews would arrive in Israel charged up with a thirst for a revenge. But reality hit them over the head in this as well.

YIGAEL YADIN AND THE NARRATIVE OF SUFFERING AND REVENGE

Like the rest of the immigrants from the Islamic world, those who immigrated and were conscripted into the army during and after the 1948 war had different sorts of memories, emotions, and views of Jewish-Arab relations. The young IDF, for its part, was interested in fostering a narrative of hostility, believing that this would bolster the immigrants' fighting spirit. This was one of Shai Hazkani's findings in his study of the IDF education department at the time, and of the views voiced by soldiers in letters to their families (which were read by the IDF censor's office so that it could track the mood of the army's soldiers). These letters were not drenched with hatred and a desire for revenge, as the army leadership expected. On the contrary. Some of the letters expressed longing for Morocco, which these soldiers, unlike the girl who wrote the composition, saw as their real homeland. They focused on their disappointment with the abusive attitude of the Ashkenazim toward the immigrants from the Arab world. Some immigrant soldiers even returned to their countries of origin.[30] This suggests that at least some of them did not perceive life there as a constant state of danger and persecution.

The censors also reported, from time to time, on letters evincing a desire for revenge. Selections from these letters were translated from Arabic, as the immigrants still had not learned Hebrew, and were included in reports sent to IDF Chief of Staff Yigael Yadin. Here, for example, is a passage from a letter written by a soldier who had been conscripted soon after his arrival from Iraq: "Out of cognizance [of the situation] and a feeling [of seeking] revenge, I am trying hard to do everything and acquire knowledge, to every extent possible, in the learning of the profession of war. I don't care about every scrape or anything. It can be hard, because I am a Jew loyal to my Jewish identity." Another soldier wrote to a friend, "You have no idea how happy I am for the day on which we will face off against the Iraqi army in particular, and the Arab [armies] as a whole, and they will see what is a Jew defending his homeland, which is truly a homeland, and not like we were there—cowards." This is the attitude the chief of staff had wished to find, and he ordered that such emotions should be leveraged. "An attempt [should be made] to discern in all these cases the particular point for these soldiers—and to work on those. Jews who were in Iraq and were constantly humiliated, in their cases one should try to bring out that point—hatred of the Iraqi Arabs. Even in peacetime. We don't have peacetime. And, perhaps even more than that—as that soldier says—the possibility of revenge against the Iraqis. Because that is something that at this moment he will be able to understand."[31]

Yadin was aware of the problematical nature of this approach. "Of course, this is dangerous and it's not simple," he noted, but he nevertheless instructed the IDF's education officers to work in that direction. This was another example of the dichotomous attitude toward Mizrahim. One the one hand, the IDF command accused them of blind hatred; on the other hand, it sought to foster that hatred.

ANOTHER DICHOTOMY?

This dichotomy stemmed from European Zionism's fundamental approach to the Jews of the Islamic world, which was based on ambiguity. On the one hand, they declared, "You are our brothers!" and "We are one people!" and "The ingathering of the exiles!" Nor was this just lip service—the Zionist movement, and the labor movement that led it, had expended much effort and sweat and blood and money and human life on establishing the Jewish state as a safe haven for all Jews. The state invested a huge number of resources in the absorption of the Mizrahim. On the other hand, it viewed Islamic Jews as Jews of an inferior type. According to Yaron Tsur, this dichotomy was a product of the tension between the national order (the fundamental principle of which was the unity of the nation) and the colonialist order (the fundamental principle of which was the superiority of the West). I propose adding another dichotomy—between the inner and outer circles. When the reference group is the other nations of the world, a Jew is a Jew, and the state has a duty to all Jews, based on Jewish solidarity and the State of Israel's standing as a representative of the entire Jewish people. But when the reference group is the Jewish people, there is an internal hierarchy based on Westernization and modernization, in their different manifestations.

At a cabinet meeting in April 1950, Yadin put forward the thesis that the Mizrahim sought revenge because of the suffering they endured in the Arab world. He included immigrants from North Africa—in contradiction of what they wrote in their letters. "They were oppressed by the Arabs in such a way," he declared, "that their hatred of Arabs is truly unmitigated. When we take them to deal with infiltrators in the south and all that involves, they do it happily." The problem, he said, was that the immigrants made no distinction between official operations in the field and vigilante actions, which had serious consequences, including Egyptian reprisals. The chief of staff maintained that foot-dragging in the Military Prosecution Office was responsible for the delays in dealing with North African wrongdoers.

This is another example of how a stereotype was constructed.

IMAGINED MIZRAHI VIOLENCE AND REPRISALS

Most Palestinians who left or were forced out of their homes in the 1948 war took refuge in places that, after the war, lay outside the boundaries of the State of Israel. Some of them stole across the borders in an attempt to return to their former homes inside the country. Others crossed the border into Israel in order to steal, or to carry out sabotage and terror attacks. These actions became a defining feature of Israel's early years. Palestinian infiltration caused disquiet and fear all over the country and took a heavy toll in blood—some 300 Israeli civilians and 260 soldiers were killed in clashes with infiltrators, Israeli reprisal operations, and exchanges of fire with the armies of the neighboring Arab states. (It is estimated that between 2,700 and 5,000 Palestinians died in these clashes, not including soldiers from the Arab regular armies who lost their lives.)[32] The reprisal operations aimed to deter such attacks but also to punish their perpetrators, provide an outlet for anger, and raise the morale of the country's Jewish citizens. A special commando unit called Unit 101 was established in 1953 to carry out reprisals. It operated for about a year before being merged into Battalion 890 of the Paratroopers Brigade.

The deadliest reprisal was carried out in October 1953 in Qibya, a Palestinian village about three kilometers over the Green Line and ten kilometers from Israel's international airport in Lod. (The Green Line is the boundary between the State of Israel and the West Bank.) The operation was decided on after a series of murders of Jewish inhabitants of the nearby town of Yehud and other settlements around it. Ariel Sharon, then the commander of Unit 101, was placed in charge. The operational order he drafted stated that "the command's intention is the execution of severe reprisal operations. . . . This means: an attack on the village of Qibya, its conquest, and a maximal blow to human lives and property."[33] The order approved the killing of civilians. Unit 101 carried out the raid, together with Paratrooper Battalion 890. The soldiers penetrated the village, placed explosive charges next to homes, and blew them up, along with the people inside them. Sixty-nine people, most of them women and children, were killed in the action, some of them in the collapse of their homes and others by gunfire. The operation was broadly condemned by the international community and was much criticized in Israel as well. But, by and large, the Israeli press and public viewed the killing of Arab civilians beyond the country's borders as legitimate.[34] Nevertheless, in this case, the magnitude of the killing in Qibya, and more so the international condemnation, led to second thoughts.

David Ben-Gurion, trying to disentangle himself from the criticism, lied in a radio address on the Voice of Israel, "The Israeli inhabitants of the frontier, *most of whom are Jewish refugees from the Arab countries or survivors of the Nazi concentration camps*, have for years been the targets of these murderous attacks. . . . But the armed forces from Transjordan did not cease their criminal attacks *until the patience of some of the border settlements came to an end*, and after the murder of a mother and her two children in the village of Yehud this week, they attacked the village of Qibya, which was one of the principal headquarters of the murderous gangs" (emphasis added).[35]

The principal purpose of this falsehood was to absolve official Israel of responsibility for the massacre in its contacts with the armistice commission and the international community. But the decision to place the blame on specific elements in the Israeli population also served other purposes—it maintained Israel's international image as an enlightened Western democracy responsibly led by the labor movement, and it sustained the labor movement's image of itself as morally superior to "others," namely, Holocaust survivors and Jews from the Arab lands.

THE OTHERS

Ben-Gurion's coupling of "Jewish refugees from the Arab countries" and "survivors of the Nazi concentration camps" was no accident. Both these groups had experienced rejection by Israel's established population. The Holocaust survivors who were sent to kibbutzim suffered psychological difficulties, and the other members sometimes sought "to distance themselves from them a bit, so that we can live our lives."[36] But the descendants of the survivors assimilated more rapidly and easily into the absorbing society, which was, as they were, primarily Ashkenazi. For the immigrants from the Islamic world, the process was longer and harder. It was a repeat of the phenomenon we saw earlier, during the Mandate period, when indigent Ashkenazi immigrants were more readily absorbed than were Mizrahi ones. A generation later, there was no way of telling who, among the Ashkenazim, was a scion of the founding generation and who of Holocaust survivors. The postwar eastern European immigrants benefited from their cultural affinity with the earlier Zionist aliyot from that same area, preferential treatment in housing and employment, and the presumption that, despite the cultural and moral maladies of the survivors, their descendants possessed potential that could be fulfilled. Within a generation, all of these factors had eliminated the differences between the two populations. The negative stereotypes imposed on immigrants from the Islamic world instead perpetuated their inferior status.

STEREOTYPES AND THE JUSTIFICATION OF REPRISALS

The violence of the Mizrahi immigrants—imagined violence in particular—served as a justification for continuing the IDF's reprisals. "The IDF's reprisal operations enabled the Israeli authorities to hold back the residents of the border regions who were the casualties [of attacks by infiltrators] from taking the law into their own hands and carrying out private acts of revenge on the other side of the border," Ben-Gurion told the Knesset in a debate about reprisals in November 1955. "Thousands of these inhabitants came from the lands of the Orient, where the citizen was brought up on the *qom*—the custom of an eye-for-an-eye vendetta—and if they were to carry out acts of revenge, it was liable to turn into a rampage and a bloodbath against innocent civilians on both sides," he argued.[37] The vendetta is indeed an accepted custom in the East, but so it is, if in different form, in the West (the word itself is, after all, Italian). The presumption that a merchant of Marrakesh or a cobbler from Fez was more intent on revenge on the basis of the principle of *qom* than was a tailor from Białystok was largely a figment of Ben-Gurion's imagination. Ben-Gurion's divorce from reality was all the starker because the individual revenge operations that we know about (there may well be more material in still classified files)[38] were in fact carried out by Ashkenazim, although they were not labeled as such in the reports. The best-known example involves Meir Har-Zion, one of the founding members of Unit 101, and three of his friends who had served with him in Battalion 890. They set out to avenge the murder of Har-Zion's sister Shoshana and her boyfriend, Oded Wegmeister, by Bedouin assailants while on a cross-border hike. Har-Zion and his accomplices murdered five Bedouin who had no connection to the incident, one by gunshot and four by knifing. In their coverage of the arrest of the four companions, two daily newspapers, *Haaretz* and *Herut,* referred to them as *bnei meshakim,* meaning young people born and bred in kibbutzim and moshavim, or as "the young Hebrews."[39] They were released a short time later and never brought to trial, because Defense Minister Ben-Gurion refused to allow the police to interrogate IDF officers.[40]

The drive to kill Arabs was characteristic of this IDF unit. Yitzhak Hofi (later general of the Central Command and chief of the Mossad) joined the Paratrooper Brigade in 1956 as deputy commander of Battalion 890. "There I learned of a phenomenon that I had not known about before—all the commanders wanted to murder an Arab personally—personally! And anyone who didn't do that—was sacked . . . that was the spirit." He decried the practice on professional grounds. "You can't fight that way," he told the officers, "neglecting your company."[41] But unlike immigrants from the Islamic world, the *bnei meshakim* were not suspected of acting out of hatred, nor did they view themselves as so motivated. As Har-Zion put it in his diary, "Our actions were not accompanied by hatred of the Arabs or hatred of any sort. We viewed all we were required to do as a requisite for the defense of [our] existence."[42]

ONE MORE THING ABOUT HAR-ZION AND MIZRAHIM

Har-Zion was wounded in 1956 in a reprisal operation against the Rahwa police fort in the southern Hebron hill country. A year later, the elite commando unit Sayeret Matkal (General Staff Reconnaissance Unit) was founded, and Har-Zion served there as a reconnaissance instructor. Building on the precedent of the Palmach's mistaarvim unit, Hashahar, the initial recruits into the new unit were young Edot Hamizrah men, most of them Arabic speakers. One day, Har-Zion took his soldiers out for an orienteering exercise in the northern Negev. In the debriefing after the exercise, it emerged that the soldiers had gone to see a movie in Ashkelon and then reached the exercise's endpoint in a vehicle. Only Har-Zion and Yehiel Amsalem, the unit's first team leader, performed the exercise on foot, as required. Har-Zion refused to accept this as the kind of prank for which Palmach soldiers were famous. He saw it as a severe violation of discipline and told the unit commander that "it's necessary to recruit for the unit only blond guys with blue eyes from [Kibbutz] Mishmar Ha'emek."[43] That didn't happen immediately, but eventually the unit turned into a bastion of the labor settlements and would remain so for several decades.

THE STEREOTYPE OF MIZRAHI VIOLENCE AS A POLITICAL TOOL

The stereotype of violent Mizrahim was useful on the diplomatic front as well. In 1949 the Israeli government decided to "liquidate the Babylonian exile" by bringing to Israel the 120,000 Jews of Iraq. Some brief background: following the Arab defeat in the 1948 war, in which an Iraqi expeditionary force had fought, and in the face of the wave of Palestinian refugees whom the Arab countries now found themselves hosting, anti-Jewish sentiment burgeoned in Iraq. The Iraqi prime minister, Nuri al-Said, proposed to other Arab leaders that they all expel the Jews living in their countries if Israel did not agree to repatriate the refugees. In the meantime, small numbers of Jews were leaving Iraq with the help of smugglers, which further exacerbated hostility toward the Jews that remained. Israel pursued a diplomatic effort aimed at enabling the Jews to leave. It organized demonstrations in front of Iraq's embassies in the United States and Europe opposing the grant of international loans for the reconstruction of the Iraqi economy, and warned that if Iraq's Jews were harmed, it would reignite the conflict and sabotage the armistice talks then under way. Israel also sent an official communiqué to the embassies of Britain, France, and the United States in Israel warning that it expected an "outburst" among Iraqi Jews in Israel aimed at the country's Arabs, of a sort that "in practical terms there is no possibility of controlling . . . if Arabs are hurt."[44] In fact, there were a few such outbursts (discussed below), but it's not clear whether or to what extent government agents were involved. Whatever the case, another foundation layer was added to the stereotype of the vengeful Mizrahim, whose aggression against Arabs could not be controlled.

THE SECOND ISRAEL VOTES

The claim that immigrants from the Islamic world hated Arabs did not come out of nowhere. Neither did the political use to which it was put during Israel's early years. The thirst for revenge is a common emotion the world over. There were Jews (from the East and from the West) who had negative feelings about non-Jews as non-Jews, and there were Jews whose life experience elicited such hostility. The Cairo-born author Jacqueline Kahanoff critiqued the pejorative Western and Israeli use of the adjective "Levantine" and instead described the Levant to Israelis as characterized by a melding of cultures and a constant search for identity. She can help us understand something else about the desire for revenge as an emotion. Kahanoff did not advocate hatred or revenge, but her capacity for reflection and her honesty about her own feelings paint a complex picture. She portrayed the emotional world of her young bourgeois Jewish friends in Cairo under British rule, who sought meaning in the context of the multifarious nature of Egyptian life, writing, "We possessed a strange mixture of pretense and desperate honesty, a great thirst for the truth and knowledge, together with a vague desire for revenge, both against arrogant European rule and against the Muslim majority that was contemptuous of the minorities among it."[45] The desire to take revenge against both the West and the Arabs is worthy of note. Something similar can be found among the immigrants who arrived during Israel's initial years.

On the eve of the country's first municipal elections, in November 1950, the journalist Amos Elon made a visit to Safed, a city whose Arab inhabitants had been uprooted two and a half years earlier. Jewish immigrants from both the East and the West had been installed in the houses the Arabs had left behind. In an article headlined "The Second Israel Votes," Elon reported his impression that the immigrants had no conception of Israel's fundamental problems, and that they were being incited to an astounding extent. Two Moroccan Jews he met told him that they had joined the Communist Party, while other immigrants from Arab countries "evinced a certain interest in Herut because of: (1) their hatred of the Arabs; (2) religion ('the Lord of hosts will come to our aid'); (3) open hostility to Ashkenazim and a sense of being discriminated against ('they call us "blacks"')."[46]

This is another example of reflexive hostility toward Arabs and Ashkenazim, with hints as to its origins. And there will be more.

ZOOM OUT: THE CREATION OF MIZRAHINESS

The hostility toward Arabs among immigrants from the Islamic world (an emotion that was not unique to them, of course), together with the view that they were primitive, helped cast them in a specific role in the Israeli-Arab drama—as the Arab-hating, revenge-seeking Mizrahim. This stereotype served both the Israeli labor movement establishment and the right-wing opposition. Some of these immigrants took part in shaping the role and others were channeled into it, while still others rejected and came out against it. Further on, we will meet all three kinds. In any case, tagging them as Arab haters was part of a broader process of defining the social and economic role of the Mizrahim—that is, melding immigrants from different Islamic lands into a single, new Mizrahi identity.

The roots of Mizrahiness as the identity of a marginal group distant from power centers can be found, as we have already seen, in the very dawn of Zionism. The mass waves of immigration of the 1950s and 1960s sharpened the dichotomy between Ashkenaziness and Mizrahiness. In a contradiction of the melting pot ethos, there was not a single Israeli identity but rather two—one for the immigrants from the Islamic world, who were fashioned into a single Mizrahi identity despite the cultural differences between their countries of origin, and a second for the Jews whose origins lay in Europe, who were shaped into a single Ashkenazi community. (In the latter case, the differences between different countries of origin were blurred even more than they were for the Mizrahim.) In this sense, Mizrahiness is an Israeli-made identity.

The Mizrahi melting pot was a product of the similar treatment that the immigrants from the different Islamic countries received when they arrived in Israel. Basically, it took the form of disdain for the social and cultural capital they arrived with, to the point of making it worthless; cultural arrogance; and preconceptions about their allegedly limited capacities. The immediate significance of this was that the absorbing culture ignored both their needs and their abilities. The result was that they were shunted off to the geographical, political, economic, and social margins. To put it another way, the Israeli establishment created the Mizrahi conditions of life. The principal expressions of this were that the immigrants were left to live in transit camps for long periods; afterward, many of them were sent to live in immigrant moshavim on the frontier, in neighborhoods left behind by Arabs in formerly Arab cities, and later to so-called development towns—new towns with mostly Mizrahi populations in remote areas with little economic infrastructure. Their capacity for learning was discounted, so young people were funneled into vocational schools. They were thus denied access to higher education, the key to social and economic mobility. The result was the creation of an education gap between the second generation of immigrants from the Islamic world and European and North American immigrants, a gap that was larger than that which had existed among their parents.[47] They were placed in low-status service roles in the IDF on the basis of their origin and the number of siblings they had, rather than in accordance with their individual abilities, which further welded them to the bottom of Israel's social ladder.

On top of this came bias in the young state's welfare system. Immigrants from the Islamic world were categorized as unskilled and were thus directed into low-wage public-works projects. That they were employed made them ineligible for public assistance. The older among them, age forty-five and up, could not, however, sign up for these jobs, which required young and physically fit workers. They thus had to live on public-assistance grants, which were very low and insufficient to support what were often large families. Legislative initiatives to favor families with many children were blocked during the state's first decade. The consequence was that a large population of immigrants from the Islamic world, most of whom were not members of the Histadrut, was pushed down to the bottom of the socioeconomic scale. This state of affairs also reinforced the Mizrahi sense that the state system was doing nothing to help them. On the contrary—as they saw it—the system looked down on them from above and blocked their integration into society.[48]

MODERNIZATION VERSUS DEPENDENCE

It is commonly claimed that the Mizrahim were pushed to the margins because they came from undeveloped countries into a modern one. In a revealing article titled "Who Worked in What, for Whom, and in Exchange for What?," the sociologists Shlomo Swirski and Deborah Bernstein offer a different perspective. As they understand it, during Israel's first decade, the economy was still in infancy, and it could not be termed modern. In other words, industrialization and modernization were made possible in part by the immigrants from the Islamic world, who served as cheap labor for kibbutz factories and for industrialists who received state subsidies. This enabled the professional advancement of Ashkenazim, both those who had long been living in the country and new immigrants. The result was an upgrade of Israeli industry, but it consigned the Mizrahi immigrants to the lower-middle class.

The absorbing Ashkenazi generation thus climbed the socioeconomic ladder; their children and grandchildren, unlike the children of the workers they employed, received an academic education and found their place "at the tip of the economic, political, scientific, and technological system, that is, the ideological system" that shaped public discourse. This discourse included axioms about what were seen as the characteristics of the typical Mizrahi Jew—primitivity, traditional religiosity, lack of education—that were used to explain the inferior socioeconomic position of Mizrahim. But it hid the fundamental reason—the way in which they were integrated into the socioeconomic system.[49]

Established Israel's encounter with the immigrants from the Islamic world, Swirski and Bernstein maintain, was not one between "good" and "bad" guys, but neither was it an ingathering of exiles, in which the tribes of Israel came together in the land of their forefathers and settled, each in their portion under vine and fig tree. It was an encounter that took place within the conditions of the capitalist world, in which certain groups—in this case the Histadrut economy and private companies—controlled the capital and technology and were closely tied to the political apparatus, while other populations were tracked into serving as labor in the service of that capital.[50]

MODERNIZATION AS OPPOSED TO DEPENDENCE: THE GLOBAL AND LOCAL CONTEXT

The modernist explanation presumed that the gap between the Mizrahim and the Ashkenazim was a temporary one. When the Mizrahim became Westernized, the differences between Israel's ethnic groups would vanish. This view had its source in the theory of global modernization, which offered an explanation for the differences between the industrialized and developed First World and the poor and hungry Third World. The inferiority of the Third World, it claimed, was temporary, the result of its being in the first stage of the modernization process. Once the developing countries reached the level of the First World, equality would reign between all countries.

Historians and economists, especially in South America, have noted that this theory seems to be divorced from historical reality. Britain and Germany, for example, never went through the stage that Egypt and Brazil are in today. That is, they were never under the rule (direct or indirect) of a foreign overlord who exploited their resources in such a sweeping manner. That being the case, the account of the stagelike nature of the modernization process is fundamentally in error. Furthermore, the modernization of the Western countries was enabled by their appropriation of the resources of the Third World. The poverty of the Third World is thus an outcome of the modernization process, not a stage along the way. To put it another way, the First and Third Worlds underwent modernization at the same time but in radically different ways and with reversed roles—the former exploited and the latter were exploited, the former prospered and the latter sank into poverty. Critics thus proposed an alternate theory, the theory of dependence, which holds that modernization created Third World dependence on the First World, and that the persistence of that dependence prevents the Third World from developing its full potential. The mere passage of time will not necessarily bring with it socioeconomic progress, because the exploitation is continuous and persists to this day, albeit often less nakedly than in the past. The dependence theory has another important feature—it explains political and economic reality by analyzing social structures and power relations among countries, not by attributing cultural inferiority or personality failures to the members of traditional cultures.[51]

Swirski and Bernstein's analysis of the Israeli case accords with the theory of dependence. Just as the West's industrialization and modernization were made possible by the exploitation of the Third World's resources, so the industrialization and modernization of Israel's established population depended on the labor of the masses of immigrants from the Islamic world, and in this case, too, that exploitation cemented power relations. The presumption of European superiority (throughout the world) and Ashkenazi superiority (in Israel) provided the exploitation with quasi-scientific validity. Modernization theory was meant, among other things, to portray the state of exploitation as temporary.

But it's important to keep in mind the unique features of the Israeli case. Unlike relations between East and West (or between the Global North and the Global South), the State of Israel was founded on a vision of national unity. The target of the emotional antipathy displayed by the political establishment, and the Ashkenazim who were connected to it, toward the Mizrahim was not due to the birthplaces of the Mizrahim but rather to Mizrahiness (which was sometimes called Levantinism), and it derived from a desire to maintain the state's Israeli-Western identity and the establishment's leading status within it.[52] Thus Edot Hamizrah teenagers who joined pioneering youth movements during the Mandate period, shedding the markers of their traditional culture and their foreign accents, became (almost) "one of us." The same was true of the Mizrahi middle class that emerged a generation or two on.

But these Mizrahi "pioneers" were few in number during the 1950s, while the putatively backward Mizrahim (and those who had backwardness imposed on them) were many.

IMPOSED BACKWARDNESS? WHY?

The sociologist Baruch Kimmerling summed things up simply: "The Jews of Morocco, for example, some of whom managed to undergo a process of Westernization in that country and gain considerable education, found themselves located on the peripheries, in which they had no chance to make use of their expertise. Their brethren who went to France with a similar or identical level of expertise were absorbed on both the employment and the class-symbolic level into the French middle class, and even filled senior positions in the French economic and intellectual elite." Basing his work on previous studies, Kimmerling noted that most of the "French Moroccans, meaning those who attended Alliance schools or felt connected to European culture, constituting a large portion of the Jews who had lived in Morocco's cities, immigrated to Europe. There they did not experience downward mobility. Quite the opposite—some moved up. In contrast, those who immigrated to Israel experienced downward mobility."[53]

Among the marks of backwardness that Ashkenazim projected onto Mizrahim was hatred of Arabs and the desire for revenge—or, more accurately, the open expression of those emotions. Violent incidents in the mixed cities thus provided a foundation for discussing—and evidence to prove—the violent nature of the immigrants from the Islamic world.

MIZRAHI VIOLENCE: RAMLA

The violence in Haifa and Jaffa wase relatively limited. Its focal point during Israel's first decade was the town of Ramla. Ramla was conquered by the IDF in mid-July 1948. Some seventeen thousand of the town's Arab inhabitants were expelled—buses took them to the line held by the Jordanian army, near Latrun. This expulsion was one of the war's most explicit cases of organized, forced deportation of Arabs. (Yitzhak Rabin, then the commander of the Harel Brigade, wrote in his memoir that "psychologically, this was one of the most difficult actions we undertook.")[54] All that were left were a few hundred of the city's original inhabitants, who were soon joined by Arab refugee families from nearby and farther away. They—about two thousand people, all told—were concentrated in a part of the city that came to be called "the ghetto." During the year following the Israeli conquest, some eight thousand Jewish immigrants were moved into Ramla. In the three years after that, another ten thousand Jews joined them. The first immigrants to arrive were given empty Arab homes to live in. When all of those were filled, two immigrant camps were put up on the edge of the city, called Ramla Alef and Ramla Bet. They were populated mostly by immigrants from Iraq who arrived as part of Operation Ezra and Nehemiah, from May 1950 to January 1952, in which most of Iraq's Jews left for Israel.

At the end of May 1949, Palestinian refugees who crossed the border murdered two Jews, both new immigrants. In July, a Jewish guard, about eighteen years old, assisted by a friend, murdered two Arab children, about twelve years of age, and threw their bodies into a well. Both the Palestinian and the Jewish murderers were brought to trial. The latter were not from Edot Hamizrah. In 1951 and 1952 there was a wave of violence of a different sort—Jews attacked the homes and businesses of Arabs, sometimes in small groups, sometimes in mobs.[55] Violent attacks surged again, following a partial lull, in September 1956. On the eve of Rosh Hashanah, the Hebrew new year, an Arab café proprietor was stabbed to death by a band of Jews, and his brother and brother-in-law were seriously wounded. In letters and discussions, on the city's streets and in meeting rooms, the issue of the ethnicity of the Jewish assailants was raised again and again.

"Iraqi Jews raided my store and badly beat my daughters," reads a cable, one of many that Arab inhabitants of Ramla sent to the Israeli authorities in the summer of 1951.[56] In Jaffa, things were also bad. An Interior Ministry district officer, Avraham Malul, reported that "the Arabs of Jaffa have good reason to fear they will be attacked by Jews from the lands of the East, because of past experience; thus in times of tension, as a precaution, they do not leave their homes alone."[57] Unlike the attribution of reprisals to Mizrahim for propaganda purposes, the violence of immigrants from the Islamic world in the mixed towns was a real phenomenon.

DISTRICT OFFICER AVRAHAM MALUL

Avraham Malul was one of the eight sons of the journalist Nissim Malul, who appeared in chapter 1 as a prominent Sephardi Zionist spokesman at the end of the Ottoman period. Following the Young Turk Revolution, Nissim advocated fashioning a common Hebrew-Arab culture in Palestine, a position that aroused the ire of some leading European Zionists.[58] Avraham, born in 1915, grew up after the collapse of the Ottoman Empire, when European supremacy was no longer in doubt. When he finished school, he went to work for the Mandate government. While working, he studied law, completing his degree just before independence. He interned in the office of Shlomo Elkayam, who also came from a Moroccan (Mughrabi) Jewish family with a long history in the country. In the 1950s, Elkayam was appointed legal counsel for the military government. Malul took a position as a district officer for the Ministry of the Interior. This was one of the career paths open to established Edot Hamizrah professionals in the new state—it involved intermediation and oversight of the Arab population and of new immigrants. Malul received a judgeship on the Magistrate's Court bench (the first of the three levels of the Israeli court system) in 1959, and some twenty years later moved up to the Tel Aviv District Court. Elkayam also reached the bench, serving from 1965 to 1981 as president of the Be'er Sheva District Court.

Another district officer who reported on violence between Iraqis and Arabs was Ovadia Lalo, who had immigrated from Iraq during the Mandate period.[59] Lalo had been one of the Iraqi Jews who gave Arabic classes at kibbutzim all over the country in the early 1940s. He taught at Ramat Yohanan and Usha in the Zevulun Valley, to the east of Haifa, which at that time were surrounded by Arab villages. He also arranged encounters between the kibbutzniks and their Arab neighbors.[60] After 1948, he went to work for the Interior Ministry.

A DISTRICT OFFICER'S ANALYSIS: THE REASONS FOR IRAQI VIOLENCE

The Ramla district officer in the summer of 1951 was another Mughrabi Jew, Avraham Hayun, who would later hold senior posts in the Interior Ministry. Part of his job was facilitating the settlement of Iraqi immigrants in Ramla as part of Operation Ezra and Nehemiah. He also tracked outbursts of violence and spoke to the city's inhabitants about them, from which he distilled three causes of Jewish-Arab clashes: "Differences in the housing conditions of the Arabs living in Ramla, which are better than those of the Iraqi immigrants. The Iraqi ambition to seize control of commercial areas in the Arab neighborhood. The Iraqis' desire to retaliate, against the Arabs of Ramla, for what the Iraqi Arabs did to them."[61]

Hayun's analysis can be restated as follows: the Iraqi immigrants in Ramla wanted, first, decent living conditions; second, to expand their control of the commercial life of the city; third, revenge. The important differences between these causes lie in the source of the hostility. Is it the product of difficulties of absorption, as the first two causes suggest, or is it the continuation of enmity that is generations old? The absorbing establishment preferred to attribute the harsh feelings to an urge for revenge that had built up over years of exile. This explanation exempted them from responsibility. But there were also immigrants who took this position.

On one point everyone agreed—the antagonists were Iraqi Jews and the city's Arabs. The question that didn't go away was to what extent the Iraqi (or Mizrahi) identity of the Jews was linked to their violent behavior. This came up for discussion in the Knesset.

RAMLA'S VIOLENCE REACHES THE KNESSET

Rustum Bastuni, an Arab Knesset member for Mapam, filed a motion for the agenda in July 1952 under the heading "attacks on Arab inhabitants in Ramla." Bastuni detailed events from that year in which "organized groups of thugs attacked, beat, threatened, and looted in the Arab ghetto in Ramla. All signs, and the form of these attacks, provide a basis for presuming that these lawless attacks were carried out in an organized way in order to shamelessly take advantage of public resentment because of the unemployment pervasive in the city."[62]

Unlike the residents of Ramla and the district officer, Bastuni made no mention of the ethnic origin of the Jews involved, nor did he blame the Jews directly. He maintained that the violence was a product of "the policy of national separation and the oppression of the working masses." Divide and rule.

Minister of Police Bechor-Shalom Sheetrit responded in the name of the government. "As early as March . . . we received troubling information that Iraqi immigrants in Ramla were clashing with and attacking the Arabs of Ramla," he said, "not all of them but a small group of seven or eight people, a group that sometimes clashes with the Arabs of Ramla not because of ethnic or racial hatred, but for material reasons. They want to take a certain place where the Arabs sit and take it for their own." He told the plenum that a committee representing the city's Iraqi immigrants had met with the local Arab committee, and that they had all agreed that the incidents were solely of a criminal nature. The police, he said, were handing these cases and bringing the wrongdoers to justice. The Knesset resolved to delegate the discussion to the Interior Committee.

SHEETRIT AND THE SEPHARDI SEAT IN THE CABINET

Minister of Police Sheetrit was the only non-Ashkenazi member of the People's Administration (the thirteen-member body that became the Provisional

Government of Israel on May 14, 1948). He served in the same post in Israel's first government. By way of background, the State of Israel's first general election was held in January 1949. Mapai won forty-six of the Knesset's 120 seats. In the process of forming a government, Mapai's "Haveireinu" (Our Comrades) forum, consisting of the party's leading figures, discussed the composition of the coalition, including the question of Sephardi representation. Some members maintained that there was no need for a Sephardi minister, and if there was, certainly not one representing the Sephardim and Oriental Communities party that Sheetrit led. That, they warned, would be seen as an acknowledgment that only the ethnic party, not Mapai, represented the Mizrahim. Meir Argov (then Grabovsky) argued that a Sephardi minister would give Sheetrit's party too much power and turn it into a "gang." But the majority supported the idea. Yosef Sprinzak said that appointing a Sephardi minister was in both the party's and the national interest. "It would be a national catastrophe and will harm us in all countries if we don't have a Sephardi minister," he said. "We are now at the beginning of the construction of the country, and there is immigration. It will be very difficult to find jobs and to absorb the immigrants, there will be hunger. If the Sephardi is outside the cabinet, he will stand at the head of the hungry. We must take such things into account." This was what made such a move in the party's interest. As for the nation's interest, he said, "this is our first fixed cabinet, and one of its missions is to gather in the oppressed from all countries. . . . We are now convening and establishing a broad coalition for all the Jews. . . . It is vital from a historical point of view that the Sephardim have representation, and as a matter of general strategy we must bring them into the cabinet in this most tragic year. Now begins the great and dangerous prosaic [stage] of our lives, and it will be decisive for the conduct of the state."

David Remez, in contrast, offered a motif that would come up again in later years with reference to Mizrahi cabinet ministers—honor. This, he said, was all they really wanted. "A Sephardi minister cannot have great pretensions," he maintained. "He can remain as a representative, and I will give him the standing of a cabinet minister, and I attach importance to the respect he will receive as a minister, so we can give him an appropriate framework and we'll manage."[63]

The nod went to Bechor-Shalom Sheetrit, born in Tiberias in 1895. Sheetrit had begun his schooling in a traditional religious *kuttab*, analogous to the Ashkenazi heder, but then enrolled in the Alliance school that opened in his city. His father nevertheless insisted that his son gain ordination as a hakham (rabbi), which he did. When the community began to pay him a salary drawn from halukah funds, he refused to take it—so he related in the short autobiography that he sent to a foreign ministry official for the purposes of composing his curriculum vitae, to use for publicity purposes, at the end of 1948. Prior to World War I, he earned his livelihood as a teacher of French, Hebrew, and Arabic at the Alliance school. At the same time, the young Sheetrit made the acquaintance of the Second Aliyah pioneers who established the first communal labor settlements, Kinneret and Degania, not far from Tiberias. He founded a Zionist sports club in the city. Toward the end of World War I, he served as the mukhtar of the moshava Kinneret, a farming village nearby that shared a name with the kibbutz.[64]

After the British conquest, Sheetrit enlisted in the police force, completed its officers course, studied law, and served as a prosecutor and judge in the Mandate government. His final post under the British was as president of the Tel Aviv Magistrate's Court. In January 1948, while still serving as a judge, his daughter Tikva and her British boyfriend, Thomas Barry, were killed by Arab assailants in Jerusalem's German Colony neighborhood.[65] When the People's Administration was established that April to serve as a provisional government, Sheetrit was named minister for minority affairs and minister of police. He received the police portfolio because of his previous service as a police officer. And he was chosen for the minority affairs post because, as a Tiberias-born Sephardi and an Arabic speaker, as well as an officer and judge, he had wide-ranging connections in Palestinian Arab society dating back to his childhood. In testimony he provided to the Haganah Historical Archives, he spoke of the good relations between Tiberias's Jews and Arabs during the Ottoman period. In this sense, he was a symbol of how Sephardim could bridge the gap between Zionism and the Arabs.

Sheetrit brought his life experience to his post as police minister as well. The Foreign Ministry, in the brief biography of him that it published, added an Oriental flourish: "Bechor Sheetrit, with his expansive and hospitable warmth, his leisureliness and his charm, is unmistakably a personality formed by the Orient. Even those who object on principle to the political representation of 'racial' communities as such welcome the emergence into public life of so distinctive and colorful a figure."[66] He was elected to the First Knesset on the Sephardim and Oriental Communities list, along with Eliyahu Elyashar, Avraham Elmalih, and Moshe Ben-Ami. The established Sephardi leadership hoped to use this electoral slate to serve as the representatives of the new immigrants from the Islamic world. Mapai's leaders wanted the immigrants to see Mapai as their representative. From the Second Knesset onward, Sheetrit was elected on the Mapai slate.

In the Knesset debate on anti-Arab violence in Ramla, Sheetrit declared from the rostrum, "I express, from this place, my sincere regret about every attack on any Arab simply because he is an Arab. . . . I would be delighted if Knesset Member Bastuni would inform the Arabs of Ramla and the Arabs of Nazareth and the Arab citizenry that in any such case they should go to the police and they will find there a ready ear, and if they do not find a ready ear they should notify me, and I am prepared to listen to their complaints day and night."[67] He seems to have wanted to believe that the police force did not discriminate between Jews and Arabs.

THE ETHNIC MOTIVATION: WAS IT TRUE OR JUST A DREAM?

The Knesset's Interior Committee, to which the plenum referred the events in Ramla, set up a special subcommittee to investigate. The subcommittee conducted a series of meetings with Jews and Arabs. The spokesman for the Arab representatives, Ismail Nahhas, was a Ramla merchant who was reported to have sympathies with the Communist Party. He said, with regard to the ethnicity of the assailants, that "the most recent attack that was carried out not long ago on the Shahin house, which brought the general strike in its wake, occurred when some 200 Iraqi Jews gathered around the house and tried to attack it."[68]

According to Nahhas, it was the Iraqi immigrants themselves who made the connection between their ethnicity and their acts of violence. One of the ringleaders appeared at a city council meeting and "cited examples of the domineering and callous way the Arabs had treated the Jews in Iraq. The fact that this man constantly referred to such things proves that he is the driving force that fans the emotional flames."[69]

Nahhas, however, believed that this person distorted the Jewish past in Iraq for personal reasons. He emphasized that both sides shared a language and socialized together in cafés. "We always try to keep in mind that there is no hatred between the two peoples," said Nahhas, not in Iraq and not in Israel. The claim that the Muslims in Iraq had brutally abused the country's Jews was opportunistic. "Certain people," he maintained, "exploit it, for whatever reasons, for their own benefit."[70] Hayun and Sheetrit had already intimated that personal interests were involved—that a small coterie of Iraqis was trying to seize control of the property of Ramla Arabs.

The committee representing the city's Iraqi immigrants wrote to the minister of the interior in a similar vein. "These clashes between a group of Iraqi immigrants and the Arabs were never a general social and public phenomenon. The background was always personal interest," they wrote. "Such clashes [based] on a personal background often took place among the Arabs themselves, but every time something like that happens between an Iraqi immigrant Jew and an Arab, people ascribe it to race and make it into a big deal."[71] The committee stressed that "the goal is to foment conflict between the communities and to disturb the public peace" but refrained from making clear whose goal this was.

The committee added a version of the events that was not mentioned in other sources. The attacks, they wrote, took place

> against the background of an insult to the honor of an Iraqi Jewish girl by an Arab boy living in Ramla. Some of the family members of the girl who learned of the matter by chance encountered the said boy in the café belonging to Shahin, and a vehement argument started between them. The proprietor of the café, who should have mediated between the two sides and brought them to a compromise, took the side of the Arab boy, which led to the reinforcement of both sides, and had it not been for the efforts of one of the members of our committee, the consequences would have been severe and regrettable.[72]

We'll encounter claims about girls whose honor was slighted in other incidents that took place in the 1960s. In most cases, we have no knowledge of what these girls and their families thought about these incidents. That is, we don't know whether the girls thought that their honor had been insulted or whether their family members thought so. But by reading between the lines, we can learn something about life in Ramla then. Iraqi Jews and Arabs knew each other well, drank coffee together, and subscribed to the same code of behavior, according to which the café owner's job was to separate antagonists, not to take one side or the other. We also learn that the Iraqi Immigrants Association in Ramla sought to calm tempers, not to inflame them because of the harshness of life in Iraq.

A writer for the periodical *Kol Yotzei Iraq Bisrael* (The voice of Iraqi [Jews] in Israel) offered, in the summer of 1952, his own perspective on what was going on in Ramla. His tone was balanced and concerned with the general good. "Muslims and Christians also live among us in the State of Israel. We, who suffered so much in the Exile, know the feelings of minorities. We must thus be exemplary in our behavior and our relations with minorities," he stated. "Whatever the reasons, the incidents that took place in Ramla cannot be justified. This is not the way! There is justice and there is law in our country, and we must refrain from taking the law into our own hands. Doing so sullies our reputation and our honor. Each of us must preserve the honor of the people and the state. Our Torah also tells us: 'for you know the feelings of the stranger, having yourselves been strangers in the land of Egypt.'"[73]

The writer's "we" includes all the Jewish citizens of Israel. He projects a sense of confidence in the state and its legal system, unlike the Iraqi Jews in Ramla, who complained that the police were defending the Arabs and arresting Iraqis for no reason. His tone is also very different from that of the Arabs who complained that the police were ignoring their grievances. He more resembles the district officers and Mizrahim who held government or other leadership posts. This is hardly surprising, given that the periodical expressed the views of young members of the established Iraqi community in Israel. Its first issue was put out in 1946 by a group of young Iraqis who were finding their way between an Iraqi-Jewish identity, a larger Mizrahi identity, and the emerging Israeli identity. After independence, the periodical took it upon itself to assist in the social and economic absorption of the immigrants of the great wave.[74]

THE EASY WAY OUT

The Knesset members serving on the subcommittee took a broad approach. They wanted to calm tempers in Ramla, and to that end they were prepared to fudge the details. Their inclination was to disregard the ethnic question. Like the Iraqi Immigrants Association and others, they maintained that the violence had no Mizrahi origins. They had a simple reason for doing so—just as Sheetrit had maintained, and as the representatives of Ramla's Arabs understood, only a small number of the city's Iraqi immigrants had been involved in the violence, and those trying to turn down the heat were also Iraqis.

The subcommittee had another goal—to prove that the violence was not national in character. This was harder to achieve, as one of its members, Moshe Erem of Mapam, remarked. He noted that Jews had also commandeered Arab businesses and orange groves in Jaffa, using violence and threats. Given that, in such cases, property always moved from Arab hands into Jewish hands, it was hard to ignore the national factor.

Another member of the committee, Yitzhak Ben-Zvi (who at the end of the year would be elected Israel's president), did not deny that such a phenomenon might exist. "In Poland, for example, terrorists pressured Jews to hand over their businesses," he noted. "Psychologically, the hypothesis suggests itself that some Jews have the same intention." But Ben-Zvi proposed that this not be discussed. "Our purpose now is not to investigate all these cases," he said. Since those involved were criminals, he argued, a national motive should not be attributed to them. "We know that we don't love the Arabs, just as they don't love us," he said, "but we can't say that in our report." He did not mean the inhabitants of Ramla but all Israeli Jews.[75]

The ethnic issue came up in the margins of the subcommittee's discussions, at the impetus of Aryeh Altman of Herut. As a loyal disciple of Ze'ev Jabotinsky, he took a baldly negative attitude toward the people of the Orient, both Jews and Arabs. Altman laid out for his colleagues his view that the Arabs living in Israel should be transferred to the neighboring Arab countries. But as long as that had not been done, he argued, Jewish immigrants from the Islamic world and Arabs should be kept separate. Camps for Iraqi immigrants should certainly not be set up next to Arab settlements because of the danger of violence. He proposed adding a sentence to the subcommittee's report: "There are, within the Jewish population in Israel, new parts of the population who, out of old habits from their countries of origin, are used to arguing melodramatically, a thing that does not exist in the population as a whole."[76] Altman's proposal was rejected, and the ethnic and national aspects of the events were removed from the agenda. The Interior Committee limited itself to recommending increased educational and informational efforts in the city and further preventative police measures.[77]

Recall that in the case of border incidents and acts of revenge, the government had no hesitation about branding immigrants from the Islamic world as the perpetrators, even when they had no connection to the incidents. But in those Ramla incidents in which they were, in fact, involved, their ethnicity was not mentioned. The state apparently wanted to disregard both the ethnic and the national aspects of these incidents, which might have implied that Jews were carrying out pogroms against the Arab minority.

THE SEPARATION PLAN

Aryeh Altman had proposed separating Mizrahi Jews from Arabs so as to avoid friction. As it happens, there were cases in which the authorities did enforce such a separation—but to prevent the two sides from becoming too friendly. An Arab-Mizrahi alliance of the oppressed did not conform to the image of the Jewish state as its leaders saw it. One example was the evacuation of the Kfar Saba immigrant camp in the winter of 1953. The evacuation came suddenly. Army trucks appeared at the camp at night following the immigrants' involvement in a class struggle organized by Maki, the Communist Party. Security officials were concerned about contacts between the residents of the camp and Palestinians on both sides of the Green Line. Rivka Guber, who was called "the mother of the sons" after she lost her two sons in the War of Independence, was volunteering at the time in the Kastina transit camp. In her memoir, she wrote that she had received no explanation of why the inhabitants of the Kfar Saba camp had been transferred to Kastina, but she surmised that it was "because at that time the border . . . was not the most appropriate place for an Arabic-speaking population that had not yet been absorbed into Jewish society."[78] In other words, new Mizrahi immigrants had not yet adopted the idea of separation, and even challenged it in practice. Another representative case was that of the Sakaneh, Lod's Arab ghetto (recall that the term "ghetto" was also applied to the area where Ramla's remaining Arab population was concentrated after 1948). North African immigrants fed up with the living conditions at the camps left them without permission and settled, of their own volition, in abandoned Arab homes in Lod, in violation of the municipality's directives. They shared the area with the few Arabs who remained there. The Lod municipality tried for years to evict them, but with only partial success. The press depicted the Old City as rife with crime, venereal disease, and degeneracy. The government's housing division built apartments for the Jewish squatters in an effort to get them out of the Sakaneh. When the process got under way and Arabs also asked for apartments in the neighborhoods built for the evacuees, the authorities ignored them. True, the housing projects had been built to enable the relocation of Jewish residents of the dilapidated and derelict area, but another goal was to ensure that Jews and Arabs lived separately.[79]

Relations between Jews and Arabs in the ancient city of Lod are depicted differently in the sources by women and men, notes Benny Nuriel in his work on the neighborhood. Women stressed the network of mutual aid among them. "One of the nicest things was when my father went off to the war, to the Sinai War [in 1956]," one of them recounted. "It was the end of the month, the twenty-ninth of October . . . he left, there was no money, no one had any. Then Awad [Munayyer, proprietor of a neighborhood grocery store] came, I remember it as if it were today, with his bicycle, and a crate of goods . . . he said [to my mother], 'Mrs. Hananiya,' that's what he called her, 'here, I've brought you this. Take money as well, so you'll have some to buy vegetables, and when Hananiya returns, pay us back.'"

The story comes from Ora Vekart, whose mother worked as a midwife for Arab women. In an interview conducted by Nuriel, an immigrant couple from Tunis told a story about a house that served as a dance club. When Nuriel asked whether Arabs came to dance there, the wife, who throughout the conversation spoke of the close relations she had with her Arab women neighbors, replied, "Of course!" Her husband, in contrast, responded "Ah . . . no-o-o, there were no Arabs, what do you think Lod was . . . the Israeli flag." Later in the conversation the husband remarked that the Arabs feared them, the Jewish immigrants, and ran away when they saw Jews. His wife interrupted him: "No, no, no running away. They were respectful." And she related that mothers had helped one another.[80]

The disparate portrayals of Arab-Jewish relations by men and women can be attributed to several factors. First, men and women experienced these encounters differently because they took place in different arenas—in public spaces for the men and in private for the women. Second, men and women followed different paths of absorption into Israeli society—many of the men served in the army, but fewer women did. Third, different levels of social regulation applied to women and men, as we will see further on. At the same time, Mizrahi men and women all shared the experience of tension between alienation and familiarity. Arabs were alien on the national and religious levels, but familiar from lives lived in close proximity and a shared culture. When such familiarity triggered anxiety—about a loss of control or a loss of identity—some turned to violence as a way of reinforcing boundaries of identity. It is not at all surprising that observers' accounts of violent altercations, and of those who participated in them, mention the good relations that generally prevailed between the two sides.

In addition, the response to the tension between alienation and familiarity was not identical everywhere. For example, Lod did not experience, during these years, the same level of violence as the neighboring city of Ramla did. It is not always big issues that set off rounds of violence. In many cases, the spark comes from specific points of tension that in some cases are resolved peacefully, whereas in others people find an outlet in aggression.

And sometimes both those involved and independent observers blame incitement from outside.

INCITEMENT: VERSION NO. 1

Recall Rustum Bastuni's assertion in the Knesset debate about the assaults on Ramla's Arabs: "All signs, and the form of these attacks, provide a basis for presuming that these lawless attacks were carried out in an organized way in order to shamelessly take advantage of public resentment because of the unemployment pervasive in the city." He did not say who the organizers were, but, reading between the lines, it's clear that he meant agents of Mapai, the ruling party. Mapai, he implied, wanted to divert public attention from the government's economic failures. The Communist Hebrew newspaper *Kol Haam* made this explicit: "Mapai functionaries in Ramla have recently been involved in fomenting hatred between Jews and Arabs and are organizing attacks by thugs and retrograde elements against the city's peaceful Arab inhabitants."[81]

INCITEMENT: VERSION NO. 2

Aryeh Altman, of the Herut party, had a very different take. The incitement, he claimed, was organized by Maki and Mapam. "I sense that we have not heard complaints about this [pressure to sell their cafés] from Arabs," he said, "and we have heard them primarily from members of these two parties, a fact that leads to a conclusion that, to me, is very clear, that members of [Mapam] and Maki are engaged in digging an abyss between us and the Arabs in order to bolster themselves. . . . They are organizing strikes all over and they have organized a strike in Ramla as well. Yes, they have told us that it was a spontaneous instance, but that is not correct, because there was not even a public meeting on the Arab side."[82]

INCITEMENT: VERSION NO. 3

Gideon Giladi, who wrote for Mapam's Arabic-language newspaper *Al-Mirsad*, saw incitement coming from a different direction. He did not address Ramla specifically but rather the general anti-Arab atmosphere in Israel as a whole and in the immigrant camps in particular. He claimed that Herut loyalists spread malicious rumors about the murder of Jews by Arabs, boasted about the Deir Yassin massacre, and called for the murder of Arabs.[83] Herut activists indeed engaged in anti-Arab incitement in 1951, when Iraqi courts imposed the death penalty on two Jews accused of planting bombs in Baghdad. Some of them demanded that two Arabs be killed for every Jew executed.[84] Knesset member Shmuel Dayan of Mapai (Moshe Dayan's father) also spoke (somewhat later) about Herut's anti-Arab propaganda. "There are among them [the immigrants] [those] who came from Arab countries, and hatred of the Arab burns within them," he maintained. "We did not speak to them about this. But when Begin waved the banner of the war, the war to expel the Arabs and to take revenge on them—he took them [i.e., the immigrants became his supporters]. A small part of them, true, but that part followed them [Herut]."[85]

Dayan's claim is notable in two ways—it reveals his awareness that anti-Arab propaganda influenced only a small part of the Mizrahim, and it reflects the labor movement's self-image of being devoid of hatred. Just as Meir Har-Zion slaughtered innocent Bedouin but insisted that he did not hate Arabs, so the movement that led to the displacement of the Arabs of Palestine in 1948 stressed its lack of hatred for Arabs as the line that divided it from Begin's Herut movement.

MIZRAHIM AND THE POLITICAL RIGHT IN THE 1950S

Dayan made his statement in a Mapai Central Committee debate about a decline in its vote share in the 1955 elections. The election results set off alarm bells in the party. The level of support for Mapai in the immigrant camps plunged from 60 percent in the previous general election to just 35 percent. "And there are precincts in which the number of votes for Herut is greater than for Mapai," reported a senior Mapai official, something that had never happened in previous elections.[86]

As we have seen, the roots of the alienation between Mizrahim and the labor movement lie in the first encounter between them, during the Second Aliyah (1904–14), and it increased during the Mandate years. After independence, it increased even more. This trend has been explained in a number of ways. The first is social and religious. In this view, the Mizrahim have traditional approaches to social, religious, and family issues that differ from those of the labor movement. The second is political, and it maintains that the two sides have different approaches to the Arab question. In other words, the Mizrahim abandoned Mapai because of its moderate positions on that issue. The third is developmental. In this account, the immigrants from the Islamic world are primitive, and this inclines them to the parties of the Right. The fourth is circumstantial—the labor movement's failures on the absorption front alienated the Jews who arrived in the great postindependence waves of immigration. These explanations are not mutually exclusive and may overlap. So far, we have considered the first two explanations in this chapter. Now we'll take a quick look at the latter two, even if they are not central to our concerns in this book.

THE MIZRAHIM'S PRIMITIVITY

One of the most prominent spokesmen for this position was, as we have seen, Aryeh Gelblum. He wrote of the Mizrahim's "lack of aptitude for taking in anything spiritual," their lack of Jewish rootedness, the violence that welled up within them, and their ignorance. He proposed a reexamination of the policy of free immigration from the Islamic world. "Perhaps it is no wonder that Mr. Begin and Herut are demanding to bring all those hundreds of thousands immediately," he wrote, "because they know that these ignorant masses, primitive and poor, are good material for them, and that only such immigration can put them in power."[87]

Debates over whether to allow only Jews with certain traits or qualifications to immigrate ("selection") took place during the initial years of Zionist immigration to Palestine, and even prior to that, among the administrators of the halukah funds. During the Mandate, it was the British who restricted the number of immigrants, and the Zionist Executive and the parties represented therein preferred to grant immigration certificates to productive people, in coordination with the British. With independence, the doctrine of free immigration was put to the test. The huge influx of immigrants complicated the task of absorbing them. The state needed to produce, out of nowhere, housing and jobs, and to address economic, social, and medical distress. The fear that public services would collapse led to debates over the desirable dimensions of immigration that crossed party lines. Prominent figures on both the right and the left, and among the religious Zionists, advocated slowing down immigration, but others, across the political spectrum, rejected any such limits. David Ben-Gurion publicly sided with those who believed in free immigration. In practice, his government from the start instituted selection on health and age grounds. When immigration from North Africa turned into a flood, the selection policy became official.[88] The considerations seem to have been economic and social, not electoral. In other words, the knowledge, or possibility, that Mapai was not popular among large parts of the North African community had no impact on immigration policy.[89] From a Zionist point of view, this is an important point in the party's favor.

THE LABOR MOVEMENT'S FAILURES AND BEN-GURION'S SELF-CRITICISM

When they analyzed the results of the elections to the First Knesset, at a time when immigration from North Africa was just beginning, Mapai's leaders realized that there was a link between the immigrants from that region and the Herut movement. "The Moroccans—they go to Herut. . . . Edot Hamizrah, it turns out, is Herut's base," said the party's secretary-general, Zalman Aran. He called for improving the lives of the Mizrahim, "in atonement for the many sins of the Ashkenazi part of the Yishuv" toward them.[90] He did not say what those sins were, but the readers of the previous chapter of this book have already become acquainted with them. In the years that followed, the list of sins grew ever longer. Mapai's leaders and rank and file were well aware of this and sought ways to remedy it, but they failed again and again.

Here are a few examples of the self-criticism voiced at meetings of the party's various bodies during the 1950s, criticism that was no less fierce than that leveled by people outside the party at the time and by critical scholars years later. At the opening of Mapai's Eighth Convention in 1956, Ben-Gurion surveyed Zionist history as a whole. When he reached the 1950s, he cited the assistance that Jews outside Israel had given to Israel's economy, along with American aid and the reparations payments from Germany that were flowing into the country. "Without this help we would not have built hundreds of new settlements, tens of thousands of public housing projects, close to 400,000 rooms over seven years, hundreds of factories, we would not have been able to guarantee employment to 800,000 new immigrants or to arrange health and educational services for them," he said. Then he reached his main point, astounding his audience with his candor:

> But we must ask ourselves if all these resources truly went solely to the absorption of immigrants and new development projects—and whether the established population has not raised its standard of living on the basis of this external aid? And it is the workers' movement, with Mapai at its head, which must first ask itself this question. . . . Our standard of living has increased no little since the establishment of the state, in all circles without exception; it has not increased only on the basis of the expansion of production and the expansion of output and exports, but also at the expense of the aid from outside that we receive from different sources. I must state: other than the security danger, I see a greater danger to our standing, to our existence, and to all the moral and social values that we proclaim—from the improper use of this external aid. To the extent that we raise the standard of living on the tab of foreigners, we enlarge two dangerous gaps—the gap between imports and exports, and the gap between the established and financially secure population and the new immigrants.[91]

In short, a considerable part of the financial aid Israel received went to raising the standard of living of the established population, rather than to building housing projects so that immigrants could be moved out of the transit camps. One result was that Mizrahi immigrants spent more time in the camps, which widened and strengthened the disparities between the First Israel (the established, mostly Ashkenazi population) and the Second Israel (the new immigrants, mostly Mizrahim). As such, Ben-Gurion's analysis was radical in the extreme, and it pulled the rug out from under the claims of those who rushed to defend the labor movement throughout its history, without engaging in any self-criticism.

One delegate to the convention, Gad Ben-Meir, gave an emotional speech about the vision of the "integration of the exiles," namely, the incorporation of all Jewish communities into a single Israeli identity and culture. That vision, he said, lay in tatters.

> As long as there is a single Jewish family that does not live in an apartment fit for human habitation, there is no basis and no hope to begin to accomplish the integration of the exiles. Close to 130,000 inhabitants of the transit camps, of all types, raise their voices in a trumpet blast that breaks out from the dungeons that have been created in their lives, out of resentment that has built up within them, out of the agonies that enfold their sleeping and waking hours, out of worries about tomorrow and the shrinking from it because of the lack of work, education, and culture, of electricity and water, of medical care and hospitalization; they sound their trumpet blast that says [to the establishment]: Are you really Jews? This voice grows ever louder, comrades, the more they think of the tens [of thousands] of immigrants from eastern Europe who were their neighbors in their tents, their lean-tos, and in the British sheds and barracks, who were once there and now are not, [because they] moved into public housing projects, while these [the Mizrahim] remained to go through "a brief period" until the cornerstone for a housing project of their own was laid. And this brief period has lasted six years so far.[92]

At another meeting on the same subject, a member of the Mapai Central Committee remonstrated against his party's hypocrisy. "In our platform, and in our programs, we preach austerity, wage restraint, but not all the party's emissaries live up to these precepts themselves. We speak loftily about settlement and the Negev and the frontier, but in practice we send only immigrants there, and no one thinks that it obligates him himself." Another member of the same forum observed "a lack of attention, warm welcome, and attentiveness by thousands of members of the [labor] party who work with the public in the Histadrut institutions, health clinics, employment offices, the managements of kibbutz factories, professional organizations." For all this the party was to blame.[93] Bechor-Shalom Sheetrit chose to focus on education and culture. "It is our duty to enlarge, each year, the number of stipends for high school [tuition] that we must send to young people who have completed elementary school," he maintained, "so that they will be trained to bear on their shoulders any burden imposed on them, and so that they will be worthy to advocate the [pioneering Zionist] idea, because the uneducated cannot advocate an idea. . . . Sometimes I weep in sorrow when I see young people in prison, and there are many of those, young people hanging out on the country's streets, and they could be people of culture, but they are not simply because they are not given the possibility."[94]

These people spoke accurately and harshly. It would be wrong to dismiss their critiques as no more than lip service, even if they were offered in internal forums. The people quoted here, and many others, felt real pain about the situation. They tried to pinpoint where things were going wrong, voiced solidarity with the Mizrahi immigrants, and demanded of themselves and their associates greater action, rectitude, and commitment. They did not belittle the state's (or the party's) accomplishments—organizing the immigration, building new settlements, creating jobs—but neither did they ignore the failures.

The gap between the ideal the party proclaimed and the actual situation on the ground can be explained in a number of complementary ways. First, the sense of Western superiority and cultural alienation was stronger than the ideal of unity and also than the sense of guilt. Second, the party officials I have quoted advocated equality, but others, less so. Third, the economic structure was stronger than the abstract idea of equality. Fourth, the established Israelis who had been involved for decades in the struggle to establish the state and in the construction of its institutions, the people who fought, or whose children fought, in the 1948 war, were weary of self-sacrifice for the nation and wanted to improve their lives. Fifth, the preference given to European immigrants who had survived the Holocaust may have been due to the guilt felt by the leadership and by government officials for having left their family members—whom the survivors so much resembled—in Europe, back when they fled Europe for Palestine. Helping these European immigrants may have served as a surrogate for helping family members who had perished.

Among the officials who were responsible for the absorption, settlement, and housing of immigrants were decent people, some less and some more so, some who believed in equality and some who did not. But they all worked within a system that was on the brink of collapse because of the heavy burden of the responsibilities imposed on it. At times they felt helpless in the face of the reasonable demands of the Mizrahi immigrants that they could not fulfill; perhaps this caused them to repress their emotions. Some of them were anxious about how the character of their country seemed to be changing—its Levantization—and feared that they would become a minority. The story they told themselves about themselves was very different from the story that was told by the immigrants who arrived after independence. The officials saw themselves as pioneers who, long before the immigrants arrived, had displayed initiative, molded the national consciousness, shouldered responsibility for the people's future, blazed trails, redeemed land for Jewish settlement, and fought and defeated the people's enemies. The immigrants, from both the East and the West, were seen as lacking in national consciousness and initiative. They had come to Israel because they had no other choice, lacked ideological backbone, and were unprepared for self-sacrifice. Once in Israel, they took no responsibility, not even for their own lives.

All of this enlarged the gap within the Jewish public between the First and the Second Israel. When the Mizrahim were shunted off to Israeli society's margins, this also affected how relations between the Jews from the Islamic world and the Arabs living in the state developed.

MURDER ON ROSH HASHANAH

On the eve of Rosh Hashanah in September 1956, the Arab proprietor of a café in Ramla, Hana Zakaria Hallaq, was murdered by Jews, who also seriously injured his son and son-in-law. Once again, the Arabs of Ramla said that the assailants were Iraqi Jews "who feel blind hatred of Arabs and who pursue them constantly."[95] But the ethnicity of the assailants was not mentioned in the media, only in closed forums. "I utterly reject any attempt to sully the name of a single community, the Iraqi community, as murderers," declared Mayor Meir Melamed. "It's true that there have been more conflicts between the communities since the Iraqi immigrants arrived, but the fact that this young murderer is an immigrant from Iraq is purely accidental. It should be noted that there are actually good relations between the minority and the Iraqi immigrants, because they are closer in terms of language, and that Iraqi immigrants also frequent these cafés." To bolster his claim, he presented cases from all over the country of fights and murders among Jews of other communities. Other senior figures in Ramla also denied that the murderer had national motives. "I do not want you to see this incident that happened here as an ethnic conflict or a conflict between the majority and the minority," Deputy Mayor Pinchas Singer told members of the Knesset who had come to look into the crime. "I am convinced that it has a purely criminal background." He was seconded by another deputy mayor, Rabbi Menachem Frenkel. Moshe Gabesa, a city council member for Mapam (and later Maki), claimed that the motive was more national than criminal: "This murder was carried out in an atmosphere in which certain things are permitted to the members of one community [the Jews] and forbidden to a member of another community [the Arabs]. . . . The problem will not be solved as long as no overall solution is found, and as long as there is not full equality for all inhabitants of this country, as is written in its constitution [Declaration of Independence], without regard to race and nationality," he said. His fellow city council members attacked him vociferously. "They [the Arabs] have more rights than we do in this city," maintained Yaakov Dadoni. "Every word that comes out of Mr. Gabesa's mouth is a lie."[96]

Almost all parties to the debate agreed that the ultimate cause of the violence was the existence of pockets of poverty and criminality among the Iraqi population in Ramla. The poverty, they concurred, was the product of the difficulties of absorption and of life in the transit camps in the city.[97] A reporter from *Maariv* who visited Ramla told his readers that the key suspect had immigrated on his own at the age of thirteen. Because he was unsupervised, he took up crime. The reporter wrote about the harsh living conditions in the transit camp where the suspect lived, where sewage flowed in the streets and there was no cultural life. "The four suspects in the murder spent five of the best years of their lives in this neglected and derelict place." He wrote not a word about Mizrahim.[98] Muhammad Haddad, a Communist who was one of the representatives of the Arabs of Ramla, thought that poverty was to blame but also referred to incitement. "We see that the conditions of the Iraqi Jews in Ramla is very difficult economically. If the economic and social situation is not good, it is easy to incite [violence]. . . . We feel that the lack of work and the difficult housing conditions is what leads to a situation in which they can be incited," Haddad maintained. "The inciters claim: the Arabs have taken your jobs and they live in better houses than you do."[99] Like others, he did not maintain that Mizrahim were by nature aggressive; rather, violence grew out of their difficult situation as immigrants. Here was a situation in which Arabs sought to improve the way in which Mizrahi immigrants were being absorbed in Israel—not only in Ramla and not only to solve a specific problem there. Maki took the same position in the Knesset, where its representatives, among them Tawfik Toubi, brought up the plight of residents of the camps. When a Mapai parliamentarian tried to ridicule him, Toubi replied, "I may be an Arab, but I am certain that I am doing more for the inhabitants of the transit camps than you are. You don't want them except as cannon fodder and to bring down workers' wages—and I want them to live in peace."[100]

We can sum up the explanations for the violence in Ramla in this way: the harsh living conditions of the Iraqi immigrants produced pockets of poverty and crime. The criminals victimized both Arabs and Jews. The claim that the Mizrahi ethnicity of the criminals was the source of the violence was hardly ever raised in public, and not by the press, either. This is worthy of mention because the public discourse at this time was replete with negative labeling of immigrants from the Islamic world.

PERHAPS ALSO THANKS TO THE COMMUNISTS

As it happened, many Iraqi Jews joined Maki and Mapam, and that may have been one reason why these parties did not attribute the anti-Arab sentiment in Ramla to the ethnicity of the Jews there. It was a general Israeli phenomenon—immigrants from the transit camps (Iraqis and Bulgarians in particular) demonstrated alongside Arab citizens of Israel in Tel Aviv and attended public meetings with Arabs in Jaffa and elsewhere.[101] But in Ramla this was particularly visible because of the May Day marches that became part of city life. They were held on the city's main thoroughfare, Herzl Street, which was then part of the Tel Aviv–Jerusalem road. Both Jews and Arabs participated, bearing banners in Hebrew, Arabic, and Yiddish.[102] As in Haifa, the marches sometimes became occasions for altercations between Zionists and non-Zionists, and in time Jews and Arabs found that more separated than united them, bringing the shared events to an end. But given the profile of Mizrahi support for the different parties at that time, Mizrahim were not seen as anti-Arab in Ramla during the 1950s.

IRAQI IMMIGRANTS AND THE LEFT

As in Europe two decades earlier, at the end of the 1940s, two movements seeking to make a better world sparred for the hearts of educated young Jews in Iraq who sought a political home—the Zionist movement and the Communist Party. The ideological and practical differences between the two are evident. For the Zionists, the solution to the Jewish problem was Jewish pioneering immigration to Palestine. For the Communists, the solution to the same problem was repairing the ills of Iraqi society and Jewish integration into that society. It is estimated that the Zionist movement in Iraq numbered some two thousand members, while several hundred Jews were active members of the Communist Party (both movements also had thousands of sympathizers as well). Both groups were persecuted by the Iraqi regime. In 1947–48, following a first wave of arrests of Communists, the Iraqi party was led by two Jews, and dozens were active at its intermediate levels. The platform of the Anti-Zionist League founded by these Jewish Communists stated, "We sincerely believe that Zionism is dangerous for the Jews, just as it is dangerous for the Arabs and for their national unity. If our goal is to struggle against Zionism and bare [its real nature] in public, we dare to do so because we are Jews and also Arabs at one and the same time." But the battle against Zionism did not absolve the Communists, and the Jews among them, as far as the authorities were concerned. The government commenced another round of hunting down and executing party members. Many were forced to flee Iraq; Jewish party members accepted the help of Zionist agents, who arranged refuge for them in Israel, the establishment of which they opposed. Upon reaching Israel, most of the senior figures withdrew from public activity. Rank-and-file members, by contrast, joined Maki or Mapam.[103] They thus found themselves once again fighting for justice and equality for Arabs and Jews.

One prominent political and social activist who emerged from Mapam was Latif Dori, born in Baghdad in 1934. He joined Hashomer Hatzair, Mapam's youth movement, in 1952, a year after arriving in Israel. He coordinated the party's activities in the Sakia and Hiriya transit camps, just east of Tel Aviv. His activity was not, however, limited to immigrants in the camps. Dori established ties with the Arab villages around Kibbutz Horshim, where he lived. Decrying discrimination against Arabs and Mizrahim by Mapai and by his own party, he was among the first to reveal to the public the massacre at Kafr Qasim. He later headed Mapam's Arab Affairs Department, remaining active into the 2000s.[104] He wasn't the only such person. We've already met Gideon Giladi, who wrote for Mapam's Arabic-language newspaper, *Al-Mirsad*; other Iraqi-Jewish writers for that publication included David Cohen, Sami Rafael, and Avraham Akri. Their work in Arabic was meant for both Arabic-speaking immigrants and Israeli Arabs. Indeed, as Mustafa Kabha has shown, immigrants from Iraq and other Arabic-speaking countries played a key role in reviving the Arabic press in Israel, both newspapers that hewed to the establishment line and those that opposed it. This was an unexpected contribution to the country's Arabic-speaking society.[105]

Young Communists like Sasson Somekh, Sami Michael, David Semah, and Shimon Ballas ("the spiritual father of the Mizrahi Left")[106] arrived from Iraq with experience in underground activity in conditions of political repression, and some of them had also done journalistic work. Sami Michael relates that when he got off the plane that brought him to Israel, on which he had been the only non-Zionist, he asked an airport porter where he could sign up for the Communist Party. The next day, he went to the nearest branch and joined.[107] Not long afterward, Michael joined the staff of the party's Arabic-language newspaper, *Al-Ittihad*. His Iraqi colleagues also began to write for the party press. They covered life in the transit camps in *Al-Ittihad* for an audience of immigrants and Arab citizens, and Arab life under the military government for the party's Hebrew newspaper, *Kol Haam*, for Hebrew readers. They published their poetry and literary prose for the most part in *Al-Ittihad*'s literary supplement, *Al-Jadid*.[108] Others worked in the camps, organized campaigns for employment, and participated in the struggle against the military government, the expropriation of Arab land, and administrative detentions. For example, following the arrest of Othman Abu Ras and Mohammad Shreydi, two prominent Arab Communist activists from the Triangle region in central Israel, then under military rule, they drafted a protest petition, sent to the Knesset Presidium in June 1956. It was signed by supporters of the Communist Party throughout the country, including residents of Majdal (today's Ashkelon). "We are shocked," the petition read, "by the new wave of oppression and persecution against the Arab population of our country, one of the most brutal manifestations of which is the imprisonment of the worker activists Othman Abu Ras and Mohammad Shreydi, who have been imprisoned despite having committed no crime. We demand the immediate release of these people and also of all innocent prisoners, so as to expunge this stain on our country's good name. We demand the end of the military government! Stop the persecution of the Arab minority! The Israeli government should adhere to the Declaration of Independence."[109]

The petition has some fifty signatures. They are not all legible, but the names include Ezra Frej, Moshe Sasson, Regina Sasson, Gurfinkel (?), Gideon Nahum, Shafik Mizmortov, Yaakov Shemesh, M. Gottesman, Ze'ev Gera, Malka Hadad, Julia Babu, and Fuad Haddad. Most of the names, of both men and women, are Mizrahi. Maki also organized public meetings about the military government, some of them held in transit camps, seeking to create a covenant of Israelis who were victims of Mapai's misrule.[110]

BITON FIGHTS RACISM

One of the sanctions that the Israeli military regime imposed on Communist activists was exile far from their homes. One such case was that of Ghassan Habib, a member of the General Secretariat of the Young Communist League of Israel in Nazareth. In November 1957 Habib was exiled to Majdal, where he was hosted by Jacques Biton, a Maki activist who, before moving there, had served as secretary of the Maki branches in Safed and then in Tiberias. Biton wrote to the Knesset Presidium about Habib. "I have decided to write to you because here, in my room, sits one of the Arab exiles from Nazareth, C[omrade] Rasan [*sic*] Habib," he declared. "I emphasize 'here, in my room' simply out of pride. I am proud that I am one of many in our country who are fighting against the repressive military regime that casts shame and dishonor on all those who support it or accept it." He continued with a critique of the military government for separating Jews and Arabs, and told a bit about himself.

> I was born in France. From childhood I was educated in the spirit of the brotherhood of nations, of [resistance] to chauvinism and racism. At the age of seventeen I fought in the Resistance against the Nazi occupation, and afterward in the ranks of the regular army as a combat soldier until the end of the war. I immigrated to Israel in '48 as a member of Mahal (Overseas Volunteers) and only afterward decided to remain in Israel, even though my entire family lives to this day in France. Because I see myself as a man of political awareness and conscience, I am convinced that the repression of the Arab minority, the terror, persecution, false accusations, slanders, arrests, and exiles serve only to do great damage to the honor of our people and our country, and to Israeli-Arab peace. For our own self-respect, for the security of our country, and for Israeli-Arab peace, the repressive military regime must be ended! Return the exiles to their homes. Do away with the military government.[111]

Biton was an exceptional human being. No matter where he was, he fought for justice—both before he came to Israel and after. He took part in workers' battles all over the country and was a dedicated member of his party. Even if there were not many like him, he can tell us something about the common

Jewish-Arab ethos of resistance to the government and its policies, which attracted some Asian and North African immigrants in the 1950s.

But the egalitarian ethos Maki offered did not make the party attractive to the great majority of immigrants. As the years went by, the number of Mizrahim who supported the party declined. There were several reasons for this. The movement's non-Zionist position, which in Iraq and Egypt and other countries was key to its ideology of equal rights, relegated it to a politically and socially, and therefore economically, marginal position in Israel. Mapai's attraction, as the governing party that could offer benefits, and that of Herut, which was in opposition to Mapai but Jewish and Zionist in its identity, was stronger than Maki's. No one could label an immigrant who supported either party as disloyal, un-Jewish, or belonging to a movement whose mother party, in the Soviet Union, was oppressing Jews and supporting and arming the Arab countries against Israel. Furthermore, as the immigrants found employment, their connection with Maki slackened. And there were two factors directly tied to the Mizrahi question. There were no Mizrahi representatives on the slates that Maki put up for elections to the Knesset. Tamar Gozansky, a Communist activist and parliamentarian, has noted the party's disregard for the identity dimension of Mizrahiness.[112] Notably, when Maki issued a statement in support of the Wadi Salib uprising—the site, in 1959, of protests against police violence against Mizrahi Jews—it made the point that "in every place where Mizrahim live in poverty, Ashkenazi workers suffering from brutal exploitation can also be found." Even if that was factually correct, the Mizrahim suffered not just economic discrimination and oppression—their culture and identity were also suppressed. Their plight was not just a matter of class, and the party ignored this.[113]

WADI SALIB AND THE ARABS UNDER MILITARY RULE

In fact, ethnic discrimination was very much present in the lives of the immigrants and bolstered their ethnic identities, even among those who supported the idea of Jewish unity in Israel or civil equality for Jews and Arabs. The leaders of the Wadi Salib protests are good examples. The protests in the formerly Arab neighborhood, where many North African immigrants were housed—including many who had been moved there from transit camps—broke out in July 1959 after a policeman shot a Moroccan Jewish resident of the neighborhood. Hundreds of the neighborhood's inhabitants took to the streets that night to stage furious demonstrations that continued into the next day. The protesters attacked institutions associated with the ruling party and private property as well—the local Mapai clubhouse, the Workers Council offices, parked cars, and businesses. The protests continued, on and off, for three weeks, and spread from Haifa to other places where Moroccan immigrants lived. The protests were led by David Ben-Haroush, who a year before had founded the Union of North African Immigrants. He was detained at the end of July after he fired his pistol into the air in an effort to evade arrest.[114] David Ben-Gurion addressed the ethnic aspect of the protest in a letter to Judge Moshe Etzioni, who chaired a commission of inquiry into the protests. According to Ben-Gurion, there were "spiritually deficient criminals" among the North African immigrants, just as there were among the Ashkenazim. The difference in the North African case, he maintained, was that these elements were garnering public support because of the immigrants' inferiority complexes. "An Ashkenazi thug, thief, pimp, or murderer cannot gain the sympathy of the Ashkenazi community (if there is such an ethnic group)," Ben-Gurion claimed, "and he would not even think of such a thing, but in a primitive ethnic group, such a thing can happen."[115]

Ben-Haroush ran in the elections for the Fourth Knesset while serving a jail term, at the head of the Union of North African Immigrants slate, but the party failed to reach the threshold necessary to gain a seat. Nevertheless, the movement left an important legacy, not only as a popular struggle but also because of its platform, which demanded that the principles of equality and freedom be put into practice. There needed to be freedom for the public and the individual, freedom of the press and freedom of religion, and discrimination and favoritism had to end. With regard to Jewish-Arab relations, it advocated "fostering peace and friendship with our Arab neighbors, an appropriate solution for liquidating the military regime, with ongoing preparedness for the security of the state, equal rights for every citizen without regard to religion or sex, [and] an improvement in the standard of living for the residents of [Arab] villages."[116] These things could not be taken for granted—while they were at the bottom of the socioeconomic ladder, under attack by the ruling power and state institutions, Ben-Haroush and his colleagues did not demand rights because they were Jews but rather in the name of the principle of civil equality, which they demanded should be applied to both Jews and Arabs.

More than a decade later, when the Black Panthers in Jerusalem presented their ideas about Israeli-Palestinian cooperation, observers stressed the influence that Ashkenazi leftists wielded on this Mizrahi protest movement. Wadi Salib teaches us that Ashkenazi allies are not a necessary condition for the Mizrahi struggle for civil equality in Israel.

CIVIL EQUALITY, NATIONAL FEELING, AND DRUZE POLICEMEN

The demand for equality does not contradict national feeling, which can be expressed in unexpected ways. In his testimony in 1959 before the commission of inquiry in the Wadi Salib protests, Ben-Haroush leveled sharp criticism at law enforcement authorities. The police, he charged, had treated the Moroccans with contempt, arrested social and political activists who voice opposition to Mapai, and used excessive force with demonstrators. He also opposed the use of Druze policemen to break up the demonstrations. "In his opinion," *Herut* reported, "Druze policemen should not be intervening in such a conflict among Jews."[117]

A struggle for civil equality, it turns out, does not obviate a sense of belonging or preferences that people might have about whom they are beaten by. Asa Kasher responded to Ben-Haroush in a letter to the editor of *Haaretz*, drawing much more radical conclusions. He argued that Ben-Haroush's statement "clearly demonstrates just how hollow the charge of discrimination is. . . . The statement is characteristic of the manner of thinking of the spokespeople for 'ethnic' discrimination. As they see it, a person must play his role in the state not in accordance with his abilities, not out of consideration of his capacities and limitations and only them, but in accordance with his [ethnic] origin and religion."[118] Kasher, who would later serve as the IDF's favorite ethicist, thus closed his eyes to the claim that the establishment itself was apportioning the country's resources in accordance with people's religion and ethnicity, and that the class he belonged to was benefiting from that.

BEING ARAB AS A PROFESSION

While immigrants from the Islamic world were staging demonstrations in which they demanded bread and jobs, and sometimes equality as well, and a gang of Iraqi immigrants in Ramla were fomenting riots so that they could commandeer Arab cafés in the Old City, and while Mizrahi and Ashkenazi Communists were carrying on a common struggle, there were Mizrahi immigrants who realized—as the establishment itself had discerned—that their Mizrahiness could be an asset. This was especially true of one of its components—knowledge of the Arabic language. In this, these Mizrahim joined members of the old Sephardi and Mughrabi families we encountered at the beginning of this chapter. And while Sami Michael, who said that he had come to Israel against his will, acted within the framework of the Communist Party of Israel, his sister, Nadia, married a young man who had been born in Egypt, Eli Cohen. Unlike his Iraqi brother-in-law, Cohen was drawn into

Zionist activity while he was still a teenager in the country of his birth. He came to Israel in 1957 and worked for a while as a bookkeeper, a job he was dismissed from in 1960. Some allege that the dismissal was a means of pressuring him to enlist in the IDF Intelligence Branch's operational unit. In 1962 he was sent as a spy to Syria. He worked there for two years, making inroads at the most senior levels of government and passing up-to-date information to his operators—until he was uncovered and executed.

Other immigrants from Arab countries were sent on missions beyond Israel's borders. Some—mostly Jews from Egypt and Iraq—were assigned to make radio broadcasts, serving as propagandists, polemicists, and psychological warriors. "I was the only 'Ashkenazi' among them, but once I proved my Baghdadi origins to my colleagues with the help of a photograph of my Grandma Serah, I was accepted as one of the gang," related Ezra Danin, who was named to head the Voice of Israel's Arabic broadcasts in 1956 (his father was Ashkenazi, his mother from an Iraqi family). Among those working alongside Danin were Shaul Bar-Hayim, Yaakov Khizmeh, Tzadok Ben-Meir, Nissim Rejwan, and David Sagiv.[119] Sagiv was born in Basra in 1928 and in 1948 served as leader of the Jewish community there. He is remembered today as a lexicographer, the compiler of a Hebrew-Arabic / Arabic-Hebrew dictionary published in 2008. Some of these men also wrote for the establishment Arabic-language press (*Al-Yawm*, *Haqiqat al-Amr*, and later *Al-Anbaa*). More than fifty years after the great wave of immigration from Iraq, the Intelligence Heritage Center published a major article on the contribution made by Iraqi Jews to the Israeli intelligence services. Lieutenant Colonel Uri Ofel, who served for many years in human intelligence (Unit 504), related that "there were two main groups among the Iraqi immigrants—young people, high school graduates, who had been Zionist movement activists; and the second group of older, university-educated people, who had been involved in the running of trains, commerce, and the administration of financial systems." These immigrants found places in military intelligence (monitoring wiretaps, military communications networks, and broadcasts from the Arab world, along with instruction, translation, and analysis), or in the Shabak, the Israeli Security Agency that operates within the country, and in the Mossad, Israel's Institute for Intelligence and Special Operations, which operates outside it. The head of the Shabak's Interrogation Department estimated that, prior to 1967, more than half of the service's interrogators and coordinators were Iraqis. After 1967, these same people formulated the operating principles for controlling the territories that Israel captured that year under military rule.[120] Intelligence officers also worked in the lexicographical field. The most important of these was Avraham Sharoni (Shaashua), who was born in Baghdad in 1918 and came to Palestine in 1934. He taught Arabic in the kibbutzim of the Jordan Valley, enlisted in the Palmach, and served for many years in the Intelligence Corps, mostly in instruction. After retiring, he published an Arabic-Hebrew dictionary in three volumes.[121] Further on, we'll see what the Arab world thought of the intelligence and propaganda work done by Israelis from the Islamic world.

For the immigrants from the Mashriq (the eastern part of the Arabic-speaking world—Iraq, Syria, and Lebanon) and from Egypt, knowledge of Arabic offered a path to career advancement and to work in state institutions. The security services saw it the same way, when it came both to intelligence gathering and to the system of direct rule over the Arabs in Israel. In 1963, when the prime minister's office prepared contingency plans for conquering the West Bank and the establishment of military rule there, it included a list of Arabic-speaking Jews who worked as teachers and school principals or in the Histadrut who could fill posts in the military government.[122]

EDUCATION, HEALTH, AND WELFARE

The list of teachers and principals indicates another important point of contact between Mizrahim and Arabs—the areas of education, health, and welfare. Jewish teachers taught in Arab schools in the Triangle, Galilee, and in mixed cities and became part of the landscape in many institutions. The educator and poet Farouk Mawasi, from Baqa al-Gharbiyya in the Triangle, wrote in his memoir that most of his schoolteachers were Iraqi Jews, leading him to adopt, to a certain extent, their accent.[123] At the same time, many teachers, both Jewish and Arab, served the authorities as eyes and ears in the Arab schools. They reported dissident pronouncements about the military government and the state, and the Arabs were thus at times suspicious about the Jewish presence in their schools. Some of the Jews, though definitely not all of them, indeed saw themselves as representatives of the regime in the villages. In the 1960s, some of the Arab municipalities replaced Jewish teachers and principals with locals (for example, in Baqa al-Gharbiyya, Tira, and Tarshiha). A former Jewish principal, Uzi Doron, enumerated these cases in a letter to the Office of the Advisor on Arab Affairs. "In all such cases, the Arab villages drink a toast to taking positions from Jews. They are pushing the Jews westward toward the sea," he wrote.[124] For Doron, running an Arab school was part of the struggle for control of the country; he felt it to be a matter of life and death. Most of the principals he listed were Iraqi immigrants, as was the person to whom he addressed the letter, Eli Amir. Amir, who would later gain fame as a novelist, worked in the Office of the Advisor.

When a medical center was opened in Baqa al-Gharbiyya, deliberately and symbolically as part of the celebration of ten years of Israeli independence, it was staffed with Jews who had immigrated from the Arab countries. It was a win for all sides—the immigrants needed work, the Arabs wanted medical services, and the state wanted to make its presence felt in the Triangle. Adam Anabusi, who studied relations between the inhabitants of the village and the medical personnel, found that the village's women were aware of the resentment that some of the immigrant women voiced against the government, and of their difficult economic plight and longing for Iraq. Perhaps this was why the village women carried on with the custom of giving gifts to their midwives on the fortieth day following a birth, including to those who received salaries from the Ministry of Health. One of these midwives, Marcelle Mukamel, had been born in Basra and completed her midwife training in Iraq in 1941, immigrating to Israel a decade later. She birthed three generations in Baqa al-Gharbiyya, where many women have fond memories of her.[125]

This channel for Jewish-Arab relationships began as a government initiative meant to make Israeli rule visible in the Arab sector, but it also facilitated personal relationships. The mitigation of military rule more than a decade after its institution opened another channel for Jewish-Arab relations in Israel. The consequences were not always pleasant.

THE CONTRACTION OF MILITARY RULE AND MIZRAHI-ARAB ENCOUNTERS

The moderation of Israeli policy toward the country's Arab inhabitants led to more encounters of more different kinds between Jews and Arabs. But in its wake the number of violent incidents increased. In September 1961, Arabs in Acre organized a demonstration to protest the killing by IDF troops of five Arab youths who tried to cross the border between the Egyptian-ruled Gaza Strip into Israel. The protesters charged that the soldiers had abused the bodies. The demonstrators, mostly high school students, marched through the streets of the city shouting, "Long live Nasser!" and "Arab Palestine," according to a report in *Maariv*. The city's Jews were infuriated. A few of them apprehended three Arab women, teachers, with the intention of beating them, but the police extricated them. An Arab passerby was less lucky—he was severely beaten. Groups of Jewish demonstrators staged a raid on the Old

City and on buses carrying Arab passengers, beating some of them bloody. The next night, a large group of Jews again tried to break into the Old City, but the police blocked them. A police report noted that the assailants were "a number of Jewish immigrants from North Africa." But in this case their violence was not condemned. The Acre City Council expressed "understanding for the feelings of the city's Jewish inhabitants and their lack of restraint."[126] Why? Because, unlike in Wadi Salib, the victims in Acre were Arabs, and the Moroccans served in this case as the executors of the violence of the sovereign state.[127] In other words, the police were responsible for law enforcement and protection of Arab rights, including their right to demonstrate. The city was officially committed to equality, and the establishment thus perhaps could not constrain the Arab demonstrators as much as they might have wished. The North African immigrants did the job for them and for Israeli Jews as a whole. Perhaps this is why the ethnicity of the attackers was cited in internal reports but not in press coverage.

Concurrent with the attacks on Acre's Arabs, Tel Aviv's Hatikva neighborhood was also up in arms. "Massive Clashes with the Police Because of the Demolition of Buildings Erected Without a License," *Maariv* reported on the same page as its coverage of the violence in Acre. "Dozens Injured on Both Sides and Many Arrests."[128] It was two years after Wadi Salib, but the storm continued. Emile Habibi, a novelist and Maki parliamentarian who wrote under the pseudonym Juhayna, may have been the only person to make a connection between the two. "Now it will become clear to the Jewish masses," he wrote, referring to the working class and unemployed, without any mention of the ethnic origins of the people involved, "that Jewish-Arab fraternity is essential in the struggle against a regime that murders young Arabs" while, at the same time, "stealing the lands of the Arab fellahs and menacing the homes of the Jewish poor in the Hatikva neighborhood."[129]

This accorded with Maki's party line and the principle of Jewish-Arab brotherhood. The Communists stressed citizenship and class identity as the foundation for creating equality. But people also harbor national, ethnic, and religious feelings that are no less strong, and sometimes more so, than those of citizenship and class. Such was the case in Rishon Lezion a year later.

RISHON LEZION, 1962

In 1962, Rishon Lezion was a small town that had grown up around a moshava. Arabs from the Triangle and the Galilee, along with Bedouin from the Negev, went there to work in construction and in the orange groves. Some of them lodged overnight during the workweek in shacks on the farmland, while others rented apartments and basements as transients. In the evenings, the Arab laborers and local Jews walked the streets of the town side by side. That's the way it was on the eve of the Sukkot holiday in October 1962, when violence broke out. We have no way of reconstructing the events precisely, but Jewish observers and participants both said that the incident began when Jewish youths came to the defense of a Jewish girl who had been harassed by Arabs at the local amusement park. According to the police report, the girl was sitting on the carousel (in another version, on the Ferris wheel) when an Arab youth sitting behind her rocked her seat. The girl's friends told him to stop, but he persisted. When the ride was over, the Jews attacked the young Arab, and another group separated the fighters. A bit later, according to the police report, a friend of the wounded Arab provoked a group of Jews, and they attacked him. His friends—according to one version, he was deliberately meant to serve as a lure—drew knives and attacked the Jews, stabbing a seventeen-year-old named Shlomo Suleiman.

A few hours later, the third round commenced. At about midnight, a posse of young Jews—they had organized weeks before under the name the Punitory Company, with the object of preventing relations between Jewish women and Arabs—set out on a revenge campaign. They attacked apartments where Arabs lived, beating many of them severely.[130] *Maariv*'s headline was "Dozens Wounded in Massive Fights Between Jews and Arabs in Rishon Lezion; Clubs, Stones, and Knives Were Used in Clashes Between Local Youths and Minority Laborers; 27 Arrested." Nineteen of the men arrested were Arabs, most of them injured, the newspaper reported. The next day it offered a follow-up story from the field, about a "wave of hatred and acts of revenge" in the town. *Maariv* did not omit mentioning that there were Jews who tried to protect Arabs during the incidents.[131]

Police officers noted that the youths involved in the fights were members of the Urfali (Kurdish) community (in other places the police referred to them as Syrians). The day after the incident, "the notables of the Urfali community were summoned to the Nes Tziona station [to meet with] the district commander in the presence of the deputy district commander and were asked to keep the peace and calm tempers and they promised to do so," the Coastal Plain District reported to the National Police Headquarters.[132] Urfa, known today as Şanlıurfa, is a city in Turkish Kurdistan. Local tradition identifies it as Ur of the Chaldees, the birthplace of the patriarch Abraham. It lies to the east of the Euphrates and is home to an ancient Jewish community. Many of its Jews moved to Jerusalem in 1896, following the first Ottoman massacre of Armenians in that region. A number of these families found work in the Rishon Lezion winery. Years later, they bought land from some of the moshava's farmers and built a synagogue and small neighborhood. The Urfalis involved in the fighting were thus native-born, from families long established in the country, not new immigrants.

Yet Yoel Marcus rehashed in *Davar* the thesis that the aggression had its origin in the experience of life in the Islamic world. "This response [of the Punitory Company] was caused by prejudices, hatred that built up over generations in the hearts of people who themselves dwelt in Arab cities and were the victims of the fists of the *shabab* [Arab youth]," Marcus claimed. Like others who preceded and followed him, he likened such Mizrahi behavior toward Arabs to European antisemitism.[133]

ARABS WHO START UP WITH JEWISH GIRLS

Arabs were uppity when they started up with Jewish girls, so Marcus heard from the young men of Rishon Lezion. Dan Margalit, then writing for *Herut*, also listened to the local youth. He heard charges of Arab attacks on and threats against Jews, harassment of women, and inebriated Arab laborers who cursed the State of Israel. "Rightfully or because of unfounded fears, many of the inhabitants sense that they are under threat," Margalit concluded. "This terror zoomed to fantastical heights when a few of the [local] boys who went to hunt rabbits in the orange groves discovered the Jewish wife of one of the locals sporting with an Arab laborer employed by her husband."[134]

The anger did not derive from Jewish religious law's prohibition against intimacy with members of other religions, nor was it based on personal grievance. Separation and control, and the desire to maintain the particularity and controlling position of the Jewish people, were at stake. The fundamental assumption was that the male is in the controlling position in sexual relations. In a state of conflict or competition, as in the Israeli case, an Arab man who has sexual relations with a Jewish woman threatens Jewish rule because he overturns the proper order. Islam takes the same position, which is why it permits Muslim men to marry Jewish or Christian women but forbids exogamous marriages of Muslim women with men of those religions. There was a more practical factor as well—young Jewish women (even if only a few) were open to relations with young Arab men, while relations between Jewish males and Arab women were almost unheard of. This engendered a sense of injustice, on the one hand, and, on the other, competition between Jewish and Arab men for the hearts of Jewish women. If a Jewish man lost the contest, anger was sure to follow.

ARABS AS MIZRAHIM AND THE CHALLENGE TO IDENTITY

Margalit reported that according to the people of Rishon Lezion, there was another problem with Arab men fraternizing with Jewish women. The Arabs, they claimed, "conceal their national identities from these young women. Many of them have taken the common family name Mizrahi, and have presented themselves as Jews." The townspeople told him an anecdote. "Just a few days ago," they said, "there was a case in which an Arab laborer brought his clothes to a laundry and said that his name was Shlomo Mizrahi. When he came to receive his washing, he couldn't remember what name he had given himself, causing a great deal of trouble to the owner of the laundry. The story spread rapidly through Rishon Lezion and raised many smiles, but apparently it produced a residue of anger among the members of the Jewish Punitory Company."[135]

Here lies another important key to what happened. The idea that Arabs were passing themselves off as Jews, and their choice, for obvious reasons, of Mizrahi names, was disruptive. It made the implicit claim that Mizrahim and Arabs were much alike, and this just when most young Mizrahim were trying to rid themselves of any connection to Arabness.

ARABS AS MIZRAHIM: THE CASE OF TZAHALA

Arabs did not present themselves as Jews only in order to flirt with Jewish girls. Here's a letter written by an IDF lieutenant colonel who lived in Tzahala, a neighborhood built in the 1950s on the border between Tel Aviv and Ramat Hasharon for senior members of the defense and security forces. These officers and officials could purchase homes there on particularly easy terms. (Ariel Sharon and Moshe Dayan lived in Tzahala, and Israel's current president, Yitzhak Herzog, whose father and predecessor in that office was a senior IDF officer, grew up there and continues to live there today.) One Lieutenant Colonel Ben-Tzur wrote to the Tel Aviv police and to Shabak's Arab Department:

> Arabs in khaki dress or European dress of some sort are walking around the neighborhood offering themselves as garden workers for cheap. The women of Tzahala innocently believe that they are from "the transit camp" and that they are doing a "good deed" by hiring them for the work.

> [People] report that a number of Arabs work there several days a week, and also report on pairs of Arabs who are ostensibly seeking work but in doing so [are] scouting each yard.
>
> Most of the residents cannot even tell that these are Arabs and talk to them about "the transit camp" and "immigrant absorption" and so on. In the recent tense days, a pair of policemen were sent to [provide for] the security of the neighborhood and its "important" residents—this is an important means but it is even more important to prevent possible advance scouting by Egyptian intelligence scouts and their agents in Jaffa and the Triangle.

The women of the security elite displayed, therefore, a certain sensitivity to the new immigrants, but could not, according to the letter, tell the difference between Jewish immigrants from the Islamic world and Arabs. In this case, Arabs were coming to seek a livelihood, or at least pretending to. The senior officers, unlike the young men of Rishon Lezion and Ramla, were concerned not that the Arabs had come to seduce their women but that they might be working as Egyptian intelligence agents. The Shabak directed the police to check Arabs entering the neighborhood for permits allowing them to leave the areas under military rule, and to send the security agency their names.[136] But beyond the security issue, there was something infuriating about this blurring of boundaries.

MIZRAHIM AS ARABS

Remember that at the end of the nineteenth century, a small number of Jews in Arab countries began to define themselves as Arab Jews. Some of them belonged to the literary elites in Baghdad, Damascus, Jaffa, Haifa, and Jerusalem; others were more of the common people, Jews who lived among Arabs. European Jews saw them as unenlightened and much like Arabs, without reference to how they identified themselves. That was true of both Polish Jews who visited the Middle East and Zionists in Palestine. They were contemptuous of the Jews of the East and used the term "Arab Jews" pejoratively.[137] During the Mandate period, the inferiority of the Mizrahim and of Arab society and culture was validated in a pseudoscientific way in the writings of Karl Frankenstein and others. The War of 1948 increased animosity toward and contempt for Arabs, who were both the aggressors and the vanquished, and these feelings were also directed against the Jews who had come from Arab countries. The new immigrants felt this intensely. Moshe

Haggai, an Iraqi Jew who settled at Kibbutz Yagur, wrote in 1950 about the members of his kibbutz:

> We, the Babylonian contingent in the kibbutz [movement] as a whole and at Yagur in particular, mostly emerged from the underground in Iraq. We had taught and had been educated to build the land. We sacrificed everything to redeem ourselves as Jews. We opened roads, broke through, soared, broke the iron bars in our minds when we could expect the death sentence or life in prison. . . . We came to you with heads held high, standing erect, with pioneering enthusiasm. But we were surprised. . . . "Babylonians, Blacks, Arabs," that's what we heard here and there against us, and that hurts and insults us.[138]

This was a painful example of the rejection of Arab identity by the absorbing society, marking the process by which the term "Arab," which had not connoted any sense of inferiority for the Jews of the Arab world and had aroused no contempt, became a derisive and insulting adjective. According to Ella Shohat, European Zionism assumed that Arab and Jewish identities fundamentally contradicted each other. Jews were therefore expected to shed all markers of Arab culture. This political demand was bound up with social scorn. Many immigrants from the East, and their children and adolescents in particular, thus found themselves concealing their Arab culture. Eli Eliahu puts it this way in his poem "Under the Ground":

> *And how can I help it if for me*
> *the operation succeeded and Baghdad*
> *died, and all that is left*
> *is the music that my father*
> *used to listen to on the stations of shame*
> *while waiting in the underground parking lot*
> *to drive me to the people's army*
> *on his way to work.*
>
> *And I will never forget*
> *the sadness of his hand as it gropes*
> *for the Hebrew, to switch quickly*
> *before we leave and ascend*
> *above ground.*[139]

"Still unexpunged from our memories is the way we ran to the radio through which filtered the sounds of the *makam* [a melody type in Arab music], which vanished with a sharp turn of a knob when the steps of Ashkenazi friends were heard," Ella Shohat writes. "In this way we turned into the establishment's loyal agents, vigilantly tracking every departure from the ordained path," namely, the path to the elimination of Arab culture and identity.[140] And here were the Arabs coming to Rishon Lezion and Tzahala and everywhere else, adopting Mizrahi names and blurring the difference between Mizrahi and Arab that the young Mizrahi generation had worked so hard to underline.

AL HAMISHMAR, MAPAM'S NEWSPAPER

A senior journalist, Gabriel Stern, wrote about this problem of impersonation in Mapam's newspaper, *Al Hamishmar*. Mapam advocated equality among Jews and between Jews and Arabs. But it was an ideal that the party's members, like humanity as a whole, found difficult to live up to in practice. Stern had been born in Germany in 1913 and came to Palestine as part of the Fifth Aliyah, a wave of immigrants who fled Germany when Hitler came to power. Prior to Israel's independence, he edited a periodical put out by Ihud, a tiny political party that advocated a binational Jewish-Arab state. In the 1960s, he served as *Al Hamishmar*'s parliamentary correspondent, also covering the transit camps and Israel's Arab population. He analyzed the reasons why Arabs pretended to be Jews.

> This unfortunate phenomenon of assimilation—more precisely: desire to assimilate and attempt to assimilate—is something we know well in every society founded on discrimination and intolerance, and more than it attests to the individual, who seeks to escape the "curse" of being a disadvantaged minority, it attests to the public ridden with arrogant racist fixations. . . . In a society of truly free people, a person of a different race or nation has no need for self-denial in order to receive the place or standing he deserves. . . . By the way, it is ironic that that Arab in Rishon Lezion coveted the particular name "Mizrahi." It is, after all, no secret that no few people whose name really is Mizrahi run away from it [and find refuge in the name] Kedmi [a literary word that, like Mizrahi, also means "of the East"] or all sorts of other innovative names . . . out of the same desire to assimilate into a society that has established ridiculous privileges. And perhaps it won't be long before every Mizrahi is an Arab, and every Arab—a Mizrahi.[141]

Stern was cognizant of the discrimination that Mizrahi immigrants and Arabs suffered, and he criticized Israel's racial hierarchy. Less than two months later, he noted in one of his columns that Israel included Arab representatives—but not Mizrahim—in its official delegations to other countries, because it was politically expedient.[142] Mizrahim who lived in Rishon Lezion themselves knew very well about discrimination and the cynical use that was made of Mizrahiness.

THE FIRST MIZRAHI PUBLIC STATEMENT

The Public Committee of Rishon Lezion's Long-Standing Residents and Builders—long-standing because some of them were scions of families that had arrived from Urfa in 1896—took it upon itself to restore calm. It was led by Menashe Mizrahi and Shlomo Suleiman, the latter a relative of the Jewish youth who had been stabbed. The committee spoke out against the stereotype of Mizrahi culture as violent and that labeled Mizrahim anti-Arab:

> A certain publication has directed at the members of Edot Hamizrah from Rishon and to established and pedigreed families serious accusations of fomenting antagonism and hostility between Arabs and Jews. . . .
>
> We, the members of the initiating committee, hereby declare: it is not the members of Edot Hamizrah who are interested in aggravating relations between Arabs and Jews. We are the architects of understanding between the two nations that are part of a single family.
>
> We call on the politicians: leave your hands off Edot Hamizrah. Only they are the guarantors of the aspiration for Jewish-Arab rapprochement. [We call on] the public: Join our efforts and fortify us. Make your contribution to truth and peace.[143]

This is the classic Sephardi Zionist approach, with roots in the late Ottoman period—the Sephardim are a potential bridge between the two peoples. Only they could understand both sides. It should be noted, however, that the attribution of violence to the Urfalis was not limited to relations with Arabs. It was part and parcel of contemporary ethnic stereotypes. "Dissolute Ashkenazim, ignoramuses, fosterers of dissension, looking for trouble . . . the entire country is in their hands and all is in their hands. Well-groomed and proud Sephardim . . . sensible and cautious Persians . . . hot-blooded Urfalis, picking fights, incantation-whispering Mughrabis engaging in witchcraft," was the catalogue Haim Hazaz offered in his novel *Thou That Dwellest in the Gardens* (1944, published in English in 1956 as *Mori Sa'id*).[144]

THE ARAB AFFAIRS ADVISOR: THE MIZRAHIM AS A CAUSE OF VIOLENCE

Another wave of violent attacks by Jews on Arabs in Ramla occurred in August 1965. Dozens of young Jews invaded the city's Arab neighborhood, already accustomed to such incidents. The youths shouted, "Murder them all!" and attacked the residents.[145] The proximate trigger for the assault was the death of a Jewish moped rider (of Iraqi extraction, as the newspapers noted) in a crash with an Arab taxi driver. "Ten [to] twelve casualties, damage to a gas station and two cab stands, twenty Jewish youths arrested—that is the sum total of the riots of *young members of the Babylonian [Iraqi] community* in Ramla," *Davar* reported (emphasis added).[146] But the accident was only what set off the violence, said young Jews who spoke to journalists. "It's all because of their behavior," one claimed. "The Arabs here make themselves look like Jews, call themselves by Jewish names, wear Jewish medallions, and start up with Jewish girls. They also do it with married women." Another added, "They've gotten too much self-confidence. Some girls have gotten in trouble because of them. Some of them have even ended up as prostitutes."[147]

Five months later, at the end of January 1966, Arabs were attacked by a gang of Jews in Netanya. The families of the Jews involved had immigrated from Tripoli in Libya. According to the report written by the Arab affairs advisor's representative in the nearby Triangle region, several young Arabs had been sitting at a café in the city, chatting with a Jewish waitress. The waitress's boyfriend blew up and struck her. The Arabs tried to protect her from her boyfriend. Both sides called for help and a general fracas ensued.[148] Young Jews got together and began to search for Arabs to beat up. They headed for the cab stands, where laborers from the villages of Tayibe and Qalansawe gathered, and attacked whomever they found there.[149]

The prime minister's advisor on Arab affairs, Shmuel Toledano, was asked about the incident in an interview with *Maariv*. Toledano came from a family of Moroccan (or Mughrabi, as they were called then) origin that had settled in Tiberias in 1862. He served in the Mossad for many years and was considered an expert on the Arabs and Edot Hamizrah. The interviewer asked him whether it was true that "the relations of the members of Edot Hamizrah with the Arab population are tenser than [with] those of other communities."

> The advisor (weighing his words): The facts show that people from Edot Hamizrah were principally involved in the events in Ramla and Netanya. (With maximum emphasis) I do not accept the opinion that they did so because they suffered from the Arabs in their countries of origin, and that there is here a kind of *revanche* [revenge], and that is because these seventeen- or eighteen-year-olds were six or seven when they left their countries of origin. It is likely, of course, that they grew up in homes full of preconceptions about Arabs. The fundamental reason, in my opinion, is the especially sharp sensitivity of members of Edot Hamizrah in the area of a woman's honor, and the fact that they live in mixed cities, next to Arabs, exacerbates this problem seventyfold.[150]

Ignored, as usual, by Toledano were the Haganah squads that took action against Jewish women who went out with Arabs during the Mandate period, beating the women and attacking their Arab boyfriends. These women came from a wide range of ethnic backgrounds; the Haganah operatives who policed them were mostly Ashkenazim who nevertheless had an "especially sharp sensitivity" to the honor of Jewish women and appointed themselves guardians of their social and sexual conduct.[151] When young Mizrahim employed violence, however, it was attributed to their primitive Oriental culture.

NOT IN THE EYES OF THE ASSAILANTS, OF COURSE

An elderly Egyptian-born Jew offered an unapologetic analysis of the attacks on Arabs in Rishon Lezion to Minister of Police Sheetrit. Like others, he compared the Jewish experience in Arab countries to what was going on in Israeli cities. "I do not intend to teach a lesson in the laws of Arab hatred of Jews, since you, sir, are Mizrahi like me," he declared in a two-page handwritten letter (this is one of the earliest documented uses of the term "Mizrahi"). "You, sir, know the verse from the Quran that the Arabs intone to us: *an malahum wawladahum wanis'ahum ghnaima lana* [their property and their children and their women are ours as plunder]." He inscribed the Arabic sentence in a more expert hand than he used for his Hebrew. "In other words, they saw every Jewish woman as a sort of plunder that was permitted to them, just as they observed it in practice in Nazareth [where Arabs had attacked a Jewish woman a few weeks earlier], and which they tried to observe in Rishon Lezion. Then these [Jewish] zealots, who are now under police arrest, rose up and responded."

The text the writer quoted is not a verse from the Quran. Statements about the division of spoils, including women, in the wars that were led by the Prophet Mohammad can be found in the hadith literature, which collects sayings of the Prophet. But these were not written about Jews in particular. In any case, the letter shows that the injunction was used in Egypt to indicate Jewish inferiority. Under the circumstances, the author of the letter saw the severe Jewish response to the harassment of Jewish women as zealotry in the positive sense of the word.

"I, during my youth in Egypt," he continued, "did many such things, and now that I have matured I do not regret my actions, and if at the time of the fight I found myself in Rishon Lezion and I saw that Arabs were hassling Jewish women, I would react to it, and were you young, sir, you would not have acted differently, and who knows how many times you, sir, protected young Jewish women. From my experience in Arab affairs, I lived in Egypt in Cairo in the Jewish quarter, and the Arabs respected this quarter due to the [Jews'] firm response to any Arab offense . . . and here in sovereign Israel, if the police do not check these incited [Arabs] it will be very bad and bitter, [and] we will reach a point where a young Jewish woman cannot walk in the street."[152]

COUNTERPOINT: SHOCKED BY THE PRIMITIVE

The newspaperman Shabtai Klugman, a Holocaust survivor who immigrated at the end of 1948, wrote for *Davar* under the pen name K. Shabtai. He was shocked by the attacks. In a well-reasoned analysis, he detailed the sources of Mizrahi anti-Arab violence. The first was the national factor ("It is true that there are occasions in which Arab children say things like 'Nasser will come and finish you off' and 'the Jews should be slaughtered'"). The second was memory ("It is true that the members of Edot Hamizrah still remember very well the persecutions and hatred of the Arabs in their countries"). The third was opposition to contacts between Jewish women and Arabs ("It is true that they go out with our girls and the poor girls don't even know they're Arabs"). The fourth was the difficulty of life on the margins ("It is true that the great majority of the participants in the disturbances in Ramla were bored teenagers and seekers of an outlet [for their frustration], many of whom are on the margins of the underworld").[153]

But Klugman emphasized the cultural aspect. "And it is true as the light of day that the Jew, every Jew, is the combined product of Jewish history and Jewish culture together with the culture of the surroundings he lived in, and therefore there are, among the members of Edot Hamizrah, hot-blooded people, just like there are among the peoples with whom they lived. And it is true that the shift from life under a dictatorial regime—and almost every regime in the lands of the Orient is dictatorial—into life in a democratic regime that grants the individual a great measure of freedom, involves complications. There are some who do not know how to use the freedom that was suddenly granted to them."

Klugman also noted that immigrants from the Islamic world possessed "a huge reservoir of good will toward the state, with an overflowing reservoir of love for the land and the nation." He maintained that their turn to violence derived in part from the mismanagement of their absorption in Israel. Their instinctive aggression, he argued, was "a terrible blow to us, the Jews. . . . The essence of the Jewish people's superiority over the non-Jewish world has its source in the veins of its culture and morality. As a result of his superiority in these areas, the Jew is a person who is governed by his intellect, and he governs his instincts." Acts like those committed in Ramla "diminished our moral level, warped our intellectual stature, and transformed us into an ostensibly backward people governed by its instincts and not by its intellect."[154]

Klugman proposed comprehensive treatment—not just education or punishment but a fundamental revolution in government and administration. All citizens should receive their due from the state, whether or not they ask for it, because "we have taught our citizens, both from the East and from the West, two of the most terrible things: that they do not receive from the government's offices what they are entitled to by law and, on the other hand, that if they threaten, break the law, and violate the peace, they receive things that they do not even deserve." Complementing the thesis of cultural inferiority that he and others put forward, Klugman pointed to defective absorption and the lack of civil equality.

MIZRAHIM, ARABS, AND CITIZENSHIP

Klugman, born in Poland, described Mizrahi culture as authoritarian and violent compared to the cultures of Europe, and many others did the same. It's a strange and eerie dichotomy coming from Holocaust survivors who, just a few years earlier, had personally experienced the violence of modern Europe. But his diagnosis of the lack of civic equality is more important. Klugman seems to have felt that there were two different kinds of citizenship in Israel, along the lines proposed years later by Yoav Peled and Gershon Shafir, who argued that three concepts of citizenship operate in parallel in Israel. The first is the liberal concept of citizenship, according to which all citizens are equal. The second is ethnonationalist citizenship, according to which Jews have more rights than Arabs. The third is republican citizenship, according to which the benefits of citizenship are reserved for the founders of the state and those who devote themselves to the general good. In Israel, the last category (at least in their own eyes) consists of the labor movement and its allies, made up mostly of Ashkenazim. Since settlement in cities of mixed Jewish-Arab population, development towns, and immigrant farming villages (moshavim) was not seen as self-sacrifice in the way that settlement in kibbutzim or pre-independence moshavim was (because these places were not freely chosen by the immigrants), the Mizrahim did not receive the privileges that were accorded to those who lived in pioneering labor settlements.[155]

Many Mizrahim adopted the concept of ethnonational (Jewish) citizenship, which gave them preference over Arab citizens while at the same time putting them on the same level as the founding generation and its descendants. But the tussle between the different conceptions of citizenship that Klugman discerned in 1965 continues today. Some of the descendants of the founding generation continue to demand recognition of their seniority and preferential rights.

A COMMENT ON PRIMITIVITY AND MODERNITY

For Klugman and others, Ramla represented Oriental primitivity not only because of its violence. Alongside Jaffa and Bat Yam, a suburb just south of Jaffa that was populated mostly by new immigrants, Ramla was home to a nightclub and discotheque culture that produced bands like the Lions of Judea (its bassist was Haim Saban, later a billionaire Hollywood producer) and the Churchills (known as Jericho Jones outside Israel). These bands produced innovative and progressive hard rock with English lyrics and achieved some international success. But according to Amos Noy, "for the ruling establishment, these phenomena were bound up with moral depravity and condemned as social aberration and the products of a disturbing failure of education, and were even linked to delinquency. It was absolutely clear that Tunis-born Nissim Sarussi and his ilk represented a culture and style that were 'current' and 'Western,' but since most of the musicians involved were Mizrahim, it was labeled as retrograde."[156]

BACK TO VIOLENCE: TOO BAD THAT HITLER . . .

Menahem Talmi, a feature writer for *Maariv*, went to Netanya to cover the events there. The resulting piece was headlined "The Mouse That Gave Birth to a Mountain." His original intention had been to write about Jewish-Arab relations, but he found something else that he could not ignore.

> The owner of a store close to the place of the delinquency, who tried to dissuade the assailants from carrying out their scheme, was warned not to interfere, because otherwise not a single stone of his store would remain on another.
>
> "What could I do?" the shopkeeper shrugged. "I'm no longer young and not strong. There were a lot of them. They had murder in their eyes. I knew that they were Jews and I was ashamed that we have among our people types of that sort. They reminded me precisely of the hooligans overseas who committed pogroms against the Jews."
>
> Someone tried to convince the rioters to stop. He also tried to persuade the people around to intervene, to prevent the disgrace. "This is exactly what the Nazis did to us in Germany! Exactly this!"—this Jew shouted emotionally.
>
> Someone from within the Jewish gang approached him and spit in his face: "Shut up, soap. Too bad they didn't finish you off in the [death] camps."[157]

"Soap" was a derogatory term for Holocaust survivors, taken from the common belief that the Nazis manufactured soap from the bodies of the Jews it gassed. This wasn't the first time a survivor was told that the country would have been better off had he been murdered by the Nazis. *Kol Haam* reported such sentiments in 1959, during "ethnic tension in Beit Shemesh" over the worsening of conditions for laborers employed in public works. "There is someone who pulls the strings who is interested in diverting the minds of the workers and inhabitants from the struggle against the authorities, who are responsible for their abject circumstances, to inter-ethnic incitement," the newspaper maintained. "In Beit Shemesh there were cries such as 'we'll slaughter all the Ashkenazim' and 'too bad Hitler didn't kill all the Ashkenazim,' which befoul the atmosphere and which are intended to prevent the unification of the suffering workers of all ethnic groups to organize for a common struggle to achieve their demands."[158]

To say "it's too bad Hitler didn't finish you off" was equivalent to using nuclear weapons in war. It ostensibly broke a taboo. "Ostensibly" because it was not uncommon in the 1960s and is not uncommon today. "Inciters" can't be blamed for its currency—incitement falls on ready ears only when there is already an emotional foundation for accepting it. So what makes it possible to voice such invective? The answer might be found in letters that Moroccan immigrant soldiers sent to their families. "We saw Jews with hearts like the Germans," wrote one of them, named Shimon. "When I see friends from North Africa in the street, one without an arm, one without a leg, those who spilled their blood in the war, I ask myself whether it was worth it," another wrote. "The European Jews who suffered horribly from the Nazis see themselves as a superior race and treat the Sephardim as if they belong to an inferior race," he told his family.[159] But this situation did not automatically make all Mizrahim hate Ashkenazim. Sometimes it produced resentment, sometimes frustration, and sometimes immense sorrow.

During the incident in Netanya, the obscenity "too bad Hitler didn't kill all the Ashkenazim" was directed at a Holocaust survivor at the height of a Mizrahi attack on Arabs carried out in the name of Jewish honor. It was one more case of hostility toward both Ashkenazim and Arabs.

HITLER, KALMAN KATZENELSON, AND *THE ASHKENAZI REVOLUTION*

The use of Hitler expletives of different kinds increased in the mid-1960s, perhaps as a result of the trial of Adolf Eichmann, or perhaps because of the growing income gap between Mizrahim and Ashkenazim owing to the German reparation payments that many of the latter were receiving. Kalman Katzenelson, the author of *The Ashkenazi Revolution* (1964), analyzed the phenomenon.

Katzenelson's book caused an uproar when it was published and is probably the most vilified book in Israeli history. It was denounced by the Knesset, the media, and the attorney general's office, excoriated on the right and on the left, condemned by Ashkenazim and by Mizrahim. There were demands to put the author on trial for fomenting ethnic hatred. Most of the critics presumably did not read the entire book and based their criticism only on a few especially harsh passages. It is a multifaceted work, full of contradictions, deep and belligerent, blending sharp insight with personal slander. It offers an original survey of history along with paranoid analysis, mixing personal and collective memories with a call to action. Like Aryeh Gelblum's articles, it became for many an emblem of Ashkenazi racism.

The book can be used to mark the extreme limit of the ideology of Ashkenazi superiority. The axiom around which Katzenelson built his book was that the Jewish people, throughout its history, had never been a single entity but rather a federation of Jewish nations. He also maintained that in recent generations, the Ashkenazi nation had constituted not only the numerical majority but also the qualitative bulk of the Jewish people. And he attributed the alleged backwardness of the Mizrahim to their embrace of Islamic fatalism. It would take at least a century and a half, he argued, until these backward groups could reach the level of the Ashkenazim. "In contrast with the vibrant Zionist movement in the Ashkenazi nation and the nation of Ladino speakers," he wrote,

> no Zionist movement worthy of its name has arisen among the Afro-Asiatic Jewish peoples (the Yemenites are an exception!). These peoples by and large marched toward decline and assimilation until the Ashkenazi incursion into the Middle East put an end to this process and produced in its place the necessity of leaving the Exile and immigrating to the State of Israel. Ashkenaz seized control of the lives and fate of these Jewish peoples. It demolished the good relations between them and the Muslim population, pulled the rug out from under their chances of assimilating, and brought the Afro-Asian Jews to the State of Israel in rapid and efficient operations by sea and by air. This Ashkenazi rule over the Afro-Asiatic Jewish nations and other non-Ashkenazi nations continues in the State of Israel. Ashkenazi rule is not the product of the means and tools at its disposal but rather of its control of time. We control the time dimension of the State of Israel, . . . and as a result we also control all that is subject to that dimension, which is everything.[160]

Katzenelson was a man of the radical Right with ties to the militant Lehi and Brit Habiryonim organizations of the Mandate period. He was a party to the claim that Zionism had upended the good relations between Jews and Muslims in the Islamic world and caused these Jews to settle in Israel. But in his view, this had caused a very real problem:

> The ingathering of the Jewish peoples in the State of Israel, in the manner in which it was done, was a problematic operation from the start. It was an operation of love for the Jewish people and Jewish solidarity. . . . But at the same time it has frightening aspects of shamefulness and abuse of the non-Ashkenazi nations. These nations, which [in the distant past] maintained reputable and in some cases very great civilizations, such as those of Sefarad [Spain] and Babylonia [Iraq],

> lost, in the process of the operation of the ingathering of the exiles, all their independence and free will. They turned into human herds following the Ashkenazi savior. It was a grandiose rescue but, at the same time, also an appalling humiliation. It was humiliation for the purpose of rescue, just like surgical operations, medical situations, and sexual situations.[161]

Historical circumstances—namely, European antisemitism—made Zionism essential for the Ashkenazim, but its success put the Jews of the Islamic lands in severe jeopardy—until the Ashkenazi Zionists came to their aid. The rescue operation piled feelings of humiliation on top of the cultural, social, and technological disparities between the Israeli Ashkenazim and the Jews of other nations. "The non-Ashkenazi nations have a sense of being deformed in comparison with the giant looming over them. Their wretched diminutiveness cries out to them everywhere—in cultural capacity and wealth, in social rank, in personal abilities."

The Sephardo-Mizrahi nations, as Katzenelson called them, responded in different ways to their forced dependence on the Ashkenazim. Some wanted to become part of the hegemonic culture and thus join the Ashkenazim in the historical arena of the twentieth century. But there were also "much less pleasant" emotional responses:

> There is, first and foremost, the form of hatred for the giant, of the expectation of catastrophes and schadenfreude. This took notable form in the context of the Holocaust and the Eichmann trial. In the folklore and profanity of these nations can be found a fairly long list of expletives identifying with Hitler and Eichmann that go so far as to express regret that these two men had not been more efficient in their work. "Too bad Hitler didn't finish all of you off," or "too bad Eichmann didn't work overtime" are common invectives among the Sephardo-Mizrahim and are voiced in their workplaces, in offices, and even in schools. . . . These Sephardo-Mizrahi expletives are the most precise measure of the nature of Sephardo-Mizrahi hatred of the Ashkenazim and for locating the difference between this hatred and the parallel Ashkenazi hatred. The accepted Ashkenazi diatribe against the Sephardim, "*frenk parekh*" [Sephardi trash], expresses personal, intra-Jewish contempt, on the same level as other similar invective such as "Lithuanian pig." . . . The Sephardo-Mizrahi expletive is of an

> entirely different type. It expresses a wish, even a prayer, directed at external demonic and Satanic forces, that they strike at the Ashkenazi and make him deformed. The Sephardo-Mizrahi curse openly sides with Hitler and active participation with him—in the realm of desire and fantasy—in the murder of Ashkenazi Jewry. The attitude of the Sephardo-Mizrahi peoples toward Ashkenaz lies on the level of the psychological responses of dwarfs who were brought into a tight confrontation with a giant. What we have here are unfathomable responses, both positive and negative, and there is even leaping from one pole to the other.[162]

Katzenelson further argued that "the line of identification with the demonic foreigner that is an integral part of the Sephardi hatred of the Ashkenazi is not characteristic only of the lower strata but rather runs through all strata of the Sephardo-Mizrahi public. This hatred has found solace and satisfaction in the Holocaust, but it did not begin with the Holocaust."[163]

For some "Sephardo-Mizrahim," this was a bit too much. They simply were not like that. There were those who in letters and articles stressed the solidarity they had displayed during the Holocaust. A Moroccan immigrant, Meir Avital, wrote in a letter to the editor of *Hatzofeh*, "I remember that when I was a young boy, and we earnestly read psalms, with great weeping, in sackcloth and ashes, fasting and praying, young and old, convened and gathered together, in supplication to the Creator, to revoke the edict of the Nazi nemesis. I also remember that moving experience, when all the children in the schools of Morocco, wearing black, their eyes brimming with tears, [stood] before the sanctuary and the Torah scrolls."[164]

Others highlighted how hundreds of Moroccan Jews had come to Israel to volunteer to fight in the War of Independence, how Mizrahim lost loved ones in battle, and the Mizrahi contribution to Israel's settlement, security, and economy. They also rejected the charge that they were part of backward Arab culture.[165]

THE POSSIBLE ALLIANCE—TRANSFER FOR THE ARABS

While it seems doubtful that these declarations of Jewish fraternity persuaded Katzenelson, he believed that there might be a way to bring the different Jewish nations closer to one another (but not in order to unite them!) over the course of many generations. There was only one area in which he believed that there was room for joint Mizrahi-Ashkenazi action—the struggle against the Arabs, or, more precisely, a population transfer in which Israel's Arab citizens would be expelled.

> The first problem that will face this [Sephardo-Mizrahi] population will involve the Arab minority in the State of Israel. The masses of Arab workers in Israel will in the future constitute dangerous competition to the popular Sephardo-Mizrahi classes. There will not always be such great demand for simple labor as there is today. The time is not far off in which the evacuation of the Arab minority will become an urgent economic necessity for the Sephardo-Mizrahi masses. Ashkenaz will then take their side in full force. The evacuation of the Arabs will reinforce closeness and solidarity between the two Jewish peoples. In the more distant future, it may be necessary to annex territories to Israel to provide livelihoods for the multiplying Sephardo-Mizrahi masses. On this point Ashkenaz will also extend its hand to help.[166]

An interesting prophecy.

THE ESCAPE FROM ASHKELON'S LOCKUP AND ASHKENAZI DISAPPOINTMENT

Mordechai Tsanin, the editor of Israel's largest Yiddish newspaper, *Letste Nayes* (in the 1960s owned by Mapai), was one of the few who publicly supported Katzenelson. Like many others, Tsanin mourned the loss of the richness of Yiddish culture and viewed Yiddish speakers as the true Jews. He also hoped for an anti-Arab Ashkenazi-Mizrahi alliance, but he was disappointed. When three Palestinian Arabs escaped from jail in Ashkelon with the help of three North African youths, he concluded that the Mizrahim could not be trusted. The incident occurred in 1965. The escapees were Arab Israeli citizens who had crossed the border into the Gaza Strip, met with Egyptian intelligence officers, and returned to Israel, where they gathered intelligence in order to carry out terror operations. *Hatzofeh*, the daily newspaper of the National Religious Party, declared that the most serious aspect of the incident was that Jews had helped the culprits escape. Tsanin stressed just who these Jews were. "Had our roots not been cut off," he charged, "if we had here, in our country, the continuation of a culture based on that of eastern European Jewry, such a case could not have happened, that young Jews from Ashkelon, ten kilometers from the border, would deviously draw a Jewish policeman into their cell and beat him severely to enable three Egyptian infiltrators to flee incarceration." Jewish criminals in eastern Europe, he wrote, had Jewish morals. "But what obligates uprooted young people, who linguistically are closer to the Arab infiltrators, their soul goes out to the songs of Farid al-Atrash, for whom the nearby Arab broadcasts are closer to their hearts than those of the Voice of Israel?" he wondered.[167]

We do not know for certain what the Jewish detainees' musical preferences were, but their names and the charges against them were reported by the press at the time. Makhlouf Dahan was under arrest for stealing a guitar; Nissim Biton, Haim Cohen, and the brothers Amos and Bechor Machlouf had been arrested on Independence Day while driving a stolen jeep. They all shared a cell with the Arab detainees. The infiltrators persuaded them to escape together. There were only a few policemen at the station at the time. Biton started shouting that the Arabs were attacking him. A policeman quickly arrived and opened the cell door; the detainees jumped on him, beat him, and began running toward the exit. The duty officer and another policeman fired at them. The Jewish prisoners halted. The Palestinians continued to run and managed to escape and cross the border into the Gaza Strip.[168] The leader of the Palestinians was Hamza Younis.

HAMZA YOUNIS—A BETAR BOXER IN EGYPTIAN INTELLIGENCE

Hamza Younis, from the village of Ara in the Triangle, was, in the early 1960s, a star boxer for the Betar sports club. In 1963 he took part in a Betar delegation to a match in Athens. According to *Maariv*, "during that visit in Greece's capital, the young Arab demanded to be permitted to visit the ancient Jewish synagogue. He presented this demand to the leaders of the delegation almost as an ultimatum. He also wanted to be allowed to don a tallit, the fringed shawl that Jewish men wear during prayers, but this was not permitted him because he isn't a Jew." From that time forward, the newspaper claimed, there was a notable change in Younis's behavior, and his connection with the team faded over time, until it came to an end.

The account of the trip that Younis offers in his memoir is entirely different. His feeling was that the team's management tried to prevent him from joining the delegation, and that after he joined, they did not want to allow him to compete. But what led to his break with the team and with Israel, and to his decision to cross the border into the Gaza Strip, was an accusation that he had tried to leave a gas station without paying. He felt that racism was choking him. A few days after being charged with this crime, he traveled to Ashkelon with his cousin, crossed the border into Gaza, and was recruited by Egyptian intelligence to spy against Israel.[169] He found himself in jail in Ashkelon after making his way back into Israel in April 1964 on an intelligence mission. He was apprehended, armed with a gun, near Kibbutz Nir Am. That's how he ended up in a jail cell with Biton, Cohen, and their friends, which he escaped with their help.

After crossing back into the Gaza Strip, Younis joined the Palestine Liberation Army, which had been founded that year. He took part in combat there in the 1967 war and in operations against Israel following the war. He was wounded, captured again by Israel, and again escaped. He resumed his military activities in the framework of Fatah, the Palestinian National Liberation Movement. He was captured again by Israel in 1971 when he reached Israel's shore north of Haifa in a commando boat. The team he led was described in the media as "one of the most daring and dangerous ever uncovered."[170] He was given several life sentences. But two years later he escaped from the Ramla prison in a complex operation and went to Lebanon, where he served under Abu Jihad, Fatah's second in command. He became a mythological figure in that movement.[171]

In any case, the assistance that Younis received from the Moroccan prisoners symbolized, for *Letste Nayes*, the greatest nightmare of the Yiddish nation—an Arab-Mizrahi alliance against Ashkenazi Zionism. This same nightmare was the great hope of a tiny minority among the immigrants from the Islamic world. And it continued from time to time to make an appearance in the Palestinian political imagination, as it had at the dawn of the era of nationalism.

THE MIZRAHI-ARAB ALLIANCE

The apprehension expressed by the Yiddish newspaper was, given the nature of anxiety itself, more profound than the menace actually was. The level of Mizrahi willingness to cooperate with the Arabs of Palestine in order to smash Zionism was very low. In contrast, there were many reasons for Mizrahim to be estranged from Arabs. Despite their differences with the Israeli leadership and the failed implementation of the ingathering of the exiles, most Mizrahim saw being Jewish as their overarching identity. They gained an obvious advantage in distinguishing themselves from the Arabs in the Jewish state, and they adopted the Hebrew language as the common tongue of all Jews. This helped create a single linguistic community despite the many differences among the members of that community. Most Mizrahim also accepted that Israel's Western alignment allowed it a higher standard of living. They also internalized the perception of Arabs as enemies and Israel's military and technological superiority over the Arab world. Most Mizrahim thus emphasized their social and political dissimilarity from the Arabs, not their connection to them.

Nevertheless, on the Mizrahi margins, the spark of a desire for a political or cultural alliance with the Arabs sometimes appeared; sometimes it was simply an expression of anger. The jailed Mizrahim in Ashkelon were a non-political example. A political example could be found among Mizrahim who joined the Communist Party and among exceptional figures such as Felix Matalon, as portrayed by his daughter, the novelist Ronit Matalon. Prior to settling in Israel, Felix associated with Muslim Marxist anti-imperialists in Cairo who were supporters of Egypt's president, Gamal Abdel Nasser. "The encounter with Zionism honed and intensified his identification with these positions, just as it intensified his liking of Nasser," Ronit wrote. In Israel he had a group of friends, calling themselves the Suhba, who put out low-budget bilingual publications that featured articles on contemporary issues. They opposed David Ben-Gurion, advocated social justice, and supported strong Mizrahi-Arab ties. But "on the matter of Arab identity," Matalon recounted, "there was a boundary line that even a man like my father knew that he could not cross: the publications were written in French and Hebrew, not Arabic and Hebrew. The Mizrahi reading public would have looked askance at using Arabic. So he intimated without elaborating."[172]

ELLA SHOHAT: ARAB HATRED AS SELF-HATRED

Distancing themselves from Arab culture was a common tendency among immigrants from the Islamic world (with the exception of Mizrahim in the intelligence services, public diplomacy, and culture, whose professions required them to maintain this connection). One reason for this distancing was the scorn that met any manifestation of Arab identity or culture, which constituted the principal barrier to entry into Westernizing Israeli culture. Among a small number of these immigrants, the shedding of Arabness was accompanied by physical anti-Arab belligerence, as in the cases mentioned above. At the time, as we have seen, this was explained in several ways: (1) a settling of historical accounts, in the form of taking revenge for years of humiliation; (2) a manifestation of a patriarchal worldview, centered on sensitivity to the honor of Jewish women; (3) the Mizrahi assimilation of the violence inherent in Islamic societies because of long years of interaction with Islam; (4) class—the Mizrahi position at the bottom of the socioeconomic scale in Israel created a measure of competition between Mizrahim and the country's Arabs over resources, as well as the adoption of separatist nationalist views, which are more widespread among the lower classes.

Religious reasons for Arab hatred were almost never cited then but became more widespread in later years, following a trend toward a return to religious observance and leadership that began in the 1980s.

The cultural scholar Ella Shohat connects the anti-Arab inclinations of Mizrahim, to the extent that these existed, to the rejection of their Arab attributes by Israeli society. Mizrahim in Israel were compelled to be ashamed of the color of their skin, their throaty Arab accents, and even of their customs of hospitality, she writes. Children tried desperately to fit into the Sabra (native Israeli) European-Israeli identity, feeling ashamed of their origins. Through the classic fun-house game, the Mizrahim began to see themselves as they appeared in the distorting mirror of the West. "In fact, the hatred of Arabs, when it takes place among Mizrahim, is not generally anything more than a repressed form of self-hatred. Mizrahi hostility toward Arabs, to the extent that it exists, is in large measure 'made in Israel,'" Shohat maintains.[173] If Malcolm X was right that the white man's greatest sin was to cause Blacks to hate themselves, Shohat adds, one must hold the Israeli establishment responsible for the self-hatred internalized by Mizrahim.

ON LOVING, LIKING, AND HATING

There were those who did not want to give up their Arab identities, or whose hostility toward the Ashkenazim overwhelmed their animosity toward the Arabs. Moshe Braver, a geographer and the author of atlases, worked for many years as a journalist, largely at *Hatzofeh*, where he wrote under the pseudonym Y. Bar-Hai. In an article headlined "Who Fosters Animosity to 'Ashkenazim?'" published in November 1963, he told of an encounter:

> A few weeks ago, two Arab laborers were working in the garden of a friend of mine who lives in Ramat Gan, near Tel Aviv. Three Israeli teenagers, sixteen or seventeen years old, immigrants from one of the Arab countries, sat on the garden fence, waiting for a girl who worked as a housecleaner in one of the nearby homes. A conversation in Arabic commenced between the teenagers and the Arab laborers, which was followed by my friend, a Jerusalem native who understands Arabic, with great interest and astonishment. "Why are you working so hard?" one of the teenagers asked the laborers. "You don't need to work for these people. You make out like you're working and you take a lot of money from them." "Which people do you mean?" asked one of the Arab laborers. "The ones you're working for, the *vusvus* [a derogatory

> term for an Ashkenazi], they don't work and they have a lot of money, they in any case live off us." From this point forward there was an animated conversation during which the teenagers tried to convince the Arab laborers that the members of Edot Hamizrah and the Arabs in Israel needed to unite and act together to end "the oppressive and exploitative regime of the Ashkenazim," while the Arabs claimed that the Ashkenazim treated them well, gave them generous wages, and even served them coffee during their work hours. My friend learned from the maid for whom the teenagers were waiting that the boys were native Israelis who lived in the Hatikva neighborhood.[174]

Another example of this way of thinking appeared in another issue of *Hatzofeh*:

> In the week preceding the Six-Day War, when the country was sunk deep in an atmosphere of anxiety and tension, a veteran teacher and educator encountered two boys, sixteen or seventeen years old, trying to remove a hood ornament from his car. . . . When he reprimanded the boys and threatened to call the police, they replied with great arrogance that "in a few more days the Arabs will come here and they and we will kill all of you." So that the teacher would understand what they meant, they offered details: "We won't leave a single Ashkenazi living in Jerusalem."[175]

The mirror image of Mizrahi hatred of Arabs was thus allying with Arabs to deal a death blow to the Ashkenazim, or at least to topple their oppressive regime.

Such violent acts and extreme feelings—toward Ashkenazim and toward Arabs—mark the fringes of the camp and of the discourse. In the middle, presumably, stood most of the Mizrahim. They felt a mixture of resentment and gratitude and varying levels of frustration toward the regime that had absorbed them, but this did not turn into hatred for all Ashkenazim. Toward the Arabs they felt a mixture of fear and suspicion and cultural affinity that had something confusing about it, but only rarely did it lead to physical aggression.

RESENTMENT AND GRATITUDE—TWO POEMS

The contradictory perspectives of Jews from the Islamic world, both the immigrant generation and the ones that followed, toward Ashkenazim, continue to coexist to this day. Yosef Ozer expresses gratitude in his poem "Yes, Yes, the Ashkenazim," which includes the language:

They invented ways of life kibbutz, kibbutzim
Kevutzah, the moshavim movement. . . .
They didn't play backgammon
Einstein didn't eat mufletot.
They delved into the father of the molecule
Played with Schrödinger's cat.

They didn't make food at a Moroccan wedding
Didn't walk around in their pajamas.
They fought malaria
Wrote poetry
Planned the National Water Carrier.
They sang songs to a sprinkler.
They built an airplane, and a nation, dreamed, struggled
God told them you are beloved of me:
They sowed and planted and the trees of Zionism were joyous.[176]

There is more than gratitude here—there is also acceptance of the Ashkenazi advantage. Moiz Ben Harosh, in contrast, writes nothing about Ashkenazi achievements in science or Zionism, addressing only their attitude toward immigrants from the Islamic world:

And you shall explain to your son on that day
Remember what the Ashkenazim did unto you
When you were famished and weary and joyful at your return to Zion
Your jewelry they stole and your children they sold
And your teachers they demeaned
And they made your writers a laughingstock
And your containers they emptied
And you were naked and bare in the desert
Thirsting for water and hungry for bread
And you did not rise to destroy them and you did not rise to extinguish them
And you embraced them and they spit on you
And you gave them identifying marks, marks of the Holocaust and marks of wretchedness

And you gave them your love and they disdained you
And you gave them your books and they burned them
And you gave them your rabbis and they jeered them
Remember, child, do not hate
And do not sit in a company of the insolent
And take you the straight path
Read their books
And learn their truths
And accept the truth from those who pronounce it
But do not receive it from them, because the Torah was not handed down through them.[177]

These poems, written in the twenty-first century, represent the extremes of Mizrahi emotions toward Ashkenazi men and women, emotions that were wound up in that encounter from the dawn of Zionism and came to the fore during the great waves of immigration. The Arabs of Palestine, like the Arab world as a whole, tracked these internal Jewish voices, and the Mizrahi struggle against Ashkenazi hegemony riveted their attention.

FATAH ENTERS THE PICTURE

Fatah was founded in 1959 and commenced its armed struggle on January 1, 1965. It sought to widen the fissure between Israel's Mizrahim and Ashkenazim. Like the early members of the Palestinian national movement half a century before, Fatah also sought to set in motion a common struggle by all of those they saw as Zionism's victims against the supremacist Ashkenazi-Zionist regime. This fantasy was voiced by a Fatah activist from a refugee camp next to Nablus in an interview with a correspondent of the French-language Tunisian newspaper *Jeune Afrique* at the end of 1966. "We hope to create political problems in Israel, to compel the Arab minority to rise up," he declared. "And why not agitate the large subproletariat composed of Jews who came from the Arab countries, the Sephardim, who are the Arabs of the central European Jews, the Ashkenazim?"[178]

Fatah's strategy was to compel the Arab states to unite and go to war with Israel. Its members believed that its guerrilla operations would prompt Israeli reprisals that would force the Arab states to respond effectively and decisively, and thus to defeat Israel. The strategy led to a major escalation in 1966–67, up until the outbreak of war in June 1967 (although Fatah's operations were not the only cause of the war). But the outcome was the opposite of what

Fatah's theorists (and the Jerusalem boys stealing hood ornaments) had set their sights on. The Arab armies were defeated yet again, and the IDF conquered the Golan Heights, Sinai, the Gaza Strip, and the West Bank, including East Jerusalem. The hopes for an Arab victory were dashed, and Fatah's belief that it could enlist the Mizrahi proletariat in the Palestinian struggle was shattered—with the exception, perhaps, of a few unusual cases.

CHAPTER 4

From War to Political Upheaval, 1967–1977

In which we will follow Jews and Arabs who knew one another before the Nakba and who met again after the Six-Day War. We will see how the expansion of Israel's borders and its labor market affected the Mizrahim. We will join the Black Panthers' protests and listen in on their debates about the Palestinian question. We'll learn about the impact of Palestinian terror attacks on Kiryat Shmona and Ma'alot and Beit She'an on the Mizrahi view of the Palestinians. We'll conclude with how the ethnic fissure affected the voting patterns of Israeli citizens in 1977.

"Shehadeh!" "Ezra!" These cries emerged simultaneously from the mouths of Ezra, the beefy longtime driver from Ben-Yehuda Street, and of Shehadeh, who sat just outside the door to Za'atar's large coffeehouse not far from the Damascus gate. I had gone for a walk through the souk [the Old City of Jerusalem's open-air bazaar]. The two men, childhood friends, both born in the Old City, embraced and kissed each other. As children, they had played together in the Hakura, the traditional playground, and later they had been colleagues as drivers. . . . The two men had maintained their friendship until twenty years ago, when the screen of division had come down on the city and the country. But, so it emerges from their conversation, even thereafter each had kept the other in his thoughts, and in any case they keenly remember the names of the siblings and uncles and aunts and mutual

> friends. . . . And of course they were curious about the children who had been born since their last meeting. Shehadeh was sorry to hear that Ezra's son had just been wounded in the war . . . and Ezra was sad to hear his friend's story about what had happened to this family member and that friend, whose savings of many years had now been lost . . . without each one even mentioning all those who had died.[1]

In June 1967, just after the Six-Day War, *Al Hamishmar* reporter Gabriel Stern offered this account of one of many encounters between Jewish and Arab acquaintances who had not seen each other since Jerusalem's division in 1948. Many of the Jews in these cases were Mizrahim, although some were Ashkenazim. Stern himself met old Arab friends and, like others, swung between soaring hopes, fear, and criticism. "People's hearts are open (not all, but many, many of them) to turning over a new leaf," he wrote. Needling the sloganeers of his own movement, Hashomer Hatzair, he added, "The ordinary person is first of all a realist. . . . He, too, longs for peace, normalization, the brotherhood of nations (no, he does not use this high-sounding term, but it looks as if he is no less sincere than those for whom the expression comes easily to their lips)."

Five years before the war, as we have seen, Stern had covered the outbreaks of violence in Rishon Lezion and Ramla. He knew something about how sitting and laughing together in a café could turn sharply into violence. His own experience as a refugee from Germany also contributed to his insight that personal relations are no barrier to national violence. "No, Ezra and Shehadeh are not pacifists and professional advocates of peace, and it is certainly reasonable to assume that their national instincts were and remain potent, and if it looks to them as if their national—or personal or ethnic—honor is sullied, it will not be hard to fan the flames of their darker urges," Stern concluded. "And they—if not themselves, then their friends—would even be capable of committing forbidden acts at a time of fervor, of the kind we have heard of also during these very days. But what they share is so vast that at a time of good will it is possible to build upon it a shared and happy future."

The picture is a familiar one: close relations and friendships between Mizrahim and Arabs, the capacity for communicating, sharing celebrations, and commiserating with one another's sorrows. The affinity is possible because they share a social circle or status. Nevertheless, the affinity is fragile, conditional, and requires each to carefully respect the other's honor (which is advisable in any sort of relationship). The parties in these friendships do not forget that they belong to contending nations. Maintaining social bonds without relinquishing one's religious and national identity would become an important feature of Mizrahi-Arab relations, as would occasional outbreaks of violence.

Stern did not, in his newspaper article, explicitly note the ethnic origin of Ezra, the Jewish driver. But the average Israeli reader would have presumed that Ezra was Mizrahi. First, Ezra is a typically Mizrahi first name. Very few Ashkenazim bear it. Second, the reference to primal urges and the commission of "forbidden acts" nods to a central element in Ashkenazi discourse about the Mizrahim. Third, of course, is the statement that "what they share is so vast," from which the reader would understand that they share a language and culture.

FAMILY REUNIONS

It was not only old friends who met anew. So did the members of mixed Arab-Jewish families that had been split by the War of 1948 whose members now wanted to reunite, or at least to see one another. There were also Jewish women—the great majority of them Mizrahi women—who had married Arabs and joined the stream of refugees into the West Bank and Gaza Strip. They wanted to reestablish contact with their Israeli Jewish families and even to return to their Jewish faith. It was not long before Rabbi Hananya Deri of Jaffa, a member of the Rabbinical Council of Tel Aviv–Jaffa, launched an operation to bring Jewish women who had married Muslims back to Judaism and to their families of origin.[2]

Rafi Siton served in 1967 as commander of Unit 504, which operated Arab agents in the Jerusalem region. He also helped Jewish women who had been living in the West Bank get in touch with their Israeli families. One of the unit's Palestinian agents, whose code name was Abir 1, told Siton, "In 1945, when we were still young, I got to know a Jewish girl in Jerusalem, from a respected Sephardi family. We fell in love and moved in together like a married couple. The girl's family could not accept that she was going out with an Arab. They banished her and declared that she was dead. Neither was my family pleased with the woman I had chosen for myself, to tell the truth, although they did not take any measures against me. We did not get married, but the girl got pregnant and in 1947 gave me a son. At her request we called him Amnon. I rented her an apartment and I supported her and the child until the war broke out and the city was divided in two." In 1948, the woman remained in Israel while Abir 1 found himself in Jordanian Jerusalem. A few days after the war, the agent asked Siton to get him a permit to enter Israel so that he could meet his erstwhile lover, who, he had heard, had moved to Haifa. He managed to locate her and their son, who was by then a paratrooper who had taken part in the conquest of the Old City. A similar story comes from Bethlehem. One of that city's inhabitants approached an Israeli intelligence officer there and asked to meet the son he had fathered with his Jewish wife before the Nakba. His wife, it turned out, had since passed away. But the unit's officers helped him find his son, who was a master sergeant in an elite IDF unit.[3]

ON THE OTHER HAND

Most of the children of interreligious marriages who remained in Israel served in the IDF, and some of them, like Amnon, took part in combat in 1967. But there were children who went with their mothers to the Arab territories as refugees and joined Palestinian resistance organizations. One of Fatah's first commanders in Jerusalem following the 1967 war, William Nassar, was the son of a Jewish mother (Odette Srur, born in Lebanon). David Ronen, Shabak's coordinator in Jerusalem, thought it important to note that "according to the halacha, he is a Jew in all respects." The Ma'alabe brothers, who murdered an Israeli cab driver, Zion Abergil, had a Jewish mother, as did Kamal Nammari, who led a Palestinian armed group in Jerusalem in 1968. And they were not the only ones.[4]

Ronen and Siton were both of Sephardi origin. Ronen had been born in Jerusalem's Old City in 1929. Rafi Siton, born in Aleppo, Syria, had settled in Israel in 1949 when he was seventeen years old. He took advantage of the year before he enlisted in the IDF to make "as intensive an acquaintance as possible with the country and its inhabitants." In his memoir he recounted his autodidactic process. "I joined the Working Youth and did not miss a single trip the movement organized," he related. For some Mizrahim of his generation, youth movements, which were created and run by members of the hegemonic Ashkenazi elite, served as an entry point into the Zionist mainstream.

Because of his Syrian origin, Siton enlisted in the intelligence service and, for that purpose, maintained his Mizrahi identity even as he adopted Western culture. "At that time, I first encountered and absorbed into myself the markers of Western culture," he wrote.

> I was always proud, and remain proud today, of my Mizrahi heritage. I get great enjoyment out of every aspect of the rich Mizrahi culture that is in my blood. But I believe that my world would not have been

> complete had I not learned to know, understand, and love Western culture as well. I mean especially Western classical music, the sound of which was foreign to me until I came to Israel. . . . Attending operas and concerts became an inseparable part of my life. . . . My siblings were certain that I'd lost my mind. They could not understand how a normal person from a respectable Mizrahi family could deteriorate to the point of listening to Western music.[5]

In recounting the process he underwent, Siton contrasted his experience to a different Mizrahi perspective, one that rejected and even disdained Western culture. It must be kept in mind that the members of groups on the cultural margins do not always seek integration. Sometimes they reject the lifestyle of the hegemonic group and prefer to separate themselves from it.

The Jewish origins of leading figures in Fatah rekindled the old Arab hopes of a Mizrahi-Arab alliance against Zionism. The Egyptian journalist and thinker Lutfi al-Khuli offered such an analysis, referring to "the racial discrimination that the Arab Jews generally suffer (the Sephardim) at the hands of the European Zionists (the Ashkenazim) who rule over them politically and economically." "When armed Palestinian resistance broke out following the June [1967] war," he wrote, "it led some Arab inhabitants of Jewish origin, such as William Najib Nassar, to join Fatah contingents struggling against the Zionist conquest."[6]

Al-Khuli was wrong to think that a boy born to a Mizrahi mother who grew up among Palestinians was in any way representative of Mizrahi Jews in general, and he thus erroneously concluded that resistance to Zionism in Israeli society was on the upswing. It was another case of hope distorting reality. A parallel and common error was committed by Israelis who met Palestinians who embraced the need for peace. They jumped to the conclusion that these Palestinians accepted the Zionist thesis that Zionism—and Israeli rule—was beneficial to them, and that they would thus soon end their struggle against it.

A STATISTICAL NOTE

Emotional encounters between Jews and Arabs who knew one another before 1967 and could visit one another after the 1967 war were not unusual. Journalists liked to write about them. But it's important to keep in mind that Israel was home to 2.3 million Jews in 1967, four times the number in 1947. This means that the vast majority of Israel's Jews in 1967 had not lived in the country prior to its partition and thus had no acquaintances in the Arab territories that their country had just occupied. Indeed, few Jews who had lived in Palestine during the Mandate period had friendly relations, or even close working relationships, with Arabs. The two groups lived separately, the Jewish and Arab labor markets were largely separate, and most Jews who immigrated during the Mandate shared no common language with Arabs. The removal of the borders between the territories and the Israeli state was thus a first opportunity for many of them to become acquainted with the regions of the country familiar from the stories of the Hebrew Bible, and with their Arab inhabitants. Israeli Jews streamed into the Arab territories. Some of them were most interested in holy sites, first and foremost the Western Wall and the Temple Mount, the Tomb of the Patriarchs in Hebron, and Rachel's grave on the outskirts of Bethlehem. Others drove around out of curiosity. Some took their families to see places where they had fought in the war. Many went to look for bargains—prices in the West Bank and Gaza Strip were much lower than in Israeli markets.

For Ashkenazim, especially those who had not lived in the country before 1948, it was their first encounter with these new landscapes and an unfamiliar culture. For Mizrahim, the encounter sometimes had something more than that—they reencountered Arabness, or the Islamic culture from which they had been cut off.

BEYOND THE BORDERS OF THE ZIONIST FORTRESS

Sami Shalom Chetrit was a boy of seven in 1967. He and his family had immigrated from Morocco only four years earlier. Chetrit would later become a prominent Mizrahi activist, poet, scholar of Israeli society, and lecturer. Here he is, many years later, looking at a family album from that time:

> Place: Gaza. June 1967. Photographer: My young uncle Michael Chetrit who drove with us for a first visit to the Arab city immediately after the conquest of Gaza and Sinai in the Six-Day War. Look at the clothes! Completely Israeli. In other words, everything was done haphazardly. Sandals for everyone, short-sleeved shirts (although we still had strict rules against sleeveless for girls) and you still see the effect of the white carbohydrates [on our physiques] . . . my mother dyed [her hair] brown. My father with his Mapai-style sunglasses. The moustache was still there, but not for long. When it became clear that the moustache marked them as Arabs, my father and several of his brothers and many other relatives shaved them off. No matter that all the

leaders of Mapai proudly displayed their moustaches, like Eshkol and Sharett and Ben-Aharon and many others. But no one would mistake them for Arabs, God forbid.

Why Gaza? Because everyone around us streamed into Gaza as soon as the security forces allowed entry. We didn't go to see the graves of patriarchs or saints in Gaza, as we did in other cities, like Hebron and Jerusalem. Gaza because it was the first window into the Arab world, the souk, the fabrics (which we bought to sew into clothes), the spices, the aromas, the records. Here I was already at the end of first grade and I felt uncomfortable. I, after all, already think that I know that the Arabs there lost the war (I saw the victory albums at home) and it was clear that they hated us. I don't remember enjoying myself. We had one joy and it was a cage with a pair of parakeets and a ton of food we bought for them. But this joy was cut short when, at a roadblock, the soldiers confiscated the parakeets and gave us back an empty cage. It wasn't pleasant, but they got a string of invectives [in return].[7]

For the Chetrit family, the conquest of the Arab territories enabled them to reacquaint themselves with the Arab world. They bought record albums, spices, and cloth that could not be found in Israel. Oshra Shaib-Lerer tells a similar story about her father, Avner Yitzhak Shaib. "The war brought something else for my father; it brought him a festival of Arabic books that could be purchased in Gaza. The house filled up with books in Arabic, which we children shamefacedly shunted off to the storeroom in back, far from the eyes of guests and friends. For Abba, the books were a path back to the mother tongue he so loved, Arabic." Her father had lived through the Farhud, the pogrom staged against the Jews on the Shavuot holiday in 1941. Muslim neighbors saved him and his family, and he saw himself as an Arab Jew, according to his daughter.[8]

Bracha Serri, a poet who had been born in Yemen in 1940, wrote in the poem "Jerusalem and Sana'a":

I yearned to kiss
those strangers
like enemies

To murmur my thanks
that they are still alive

As in the days
that have eluded me
and will not return

And all of me is a floating dream
in the Old City's alleys.[9]

The strangers, ostensibly enemies, for whose existence Serri is thankful are the Palestinians she met in the Old City after 1967. They remind her of a time that has eluded her. At least that is how the literary scholar Yochai Oppenheimer reads the poem.[10] But Balfour Hakak, a poet and social activist, has an entirely different take. As he understands it, the strangers are members of Serri's own nation, the Jews, who seem like enemies to her because of the difficulties of her absorption into Israel. "But she, with her conciliatory gaze," Hakak maintains, "kisses them nevertheless, as they belong to her people." Her joy at the encounter grows out of her reencounter with her lost Jewish brethren, and the discovery that they have survived the persecution of the nation's enemies.[11] Here are two possible readings that offer two emotional dimensions: a Jewish national reading that stresses persecution by the Arabs, contrasted with one that stresses the Mizrahi-Arab connection. One views the Arabs ostensibly (but not in practice) as enemies, while in the other, the Ashkenazim are the enemy.

Serri was disconnected from Arab life when she immigrated to Israel from Yemen in 1950. The Jews of Morocco, in contrast with those of Yemen, did not arrive in a single wave. The Moroccans were the largest Jewish community in the Islamic world, numbering about a quarter of a million people at the time Israel was established. About a third of them left their homeland between 1948 and 1956, when Morocco was under French rule. Most of these went to Israel, while a minority settled in France. When Morocco gained its independence, Jewish emigration to Israel was forbidden for a time (but continued underground in much smaller numbers). Israel signed an agreement with King Hassan II of Morocco in 1961. This was followed by Operation Yachin, as part of which another approximately hundred thousand Moroccan Jews left for Israel during the years before the Six-Day War. The Chetrit family was among them.[12] About half the Moroccan Jews living in Israel at the time of the Six-Day War were thus very new immigrants. In this they differed from, for example, the immigrants from Iraq and Yemen, the great majority of whom arrived in Israel soon after the establishment of the state.

The removal of the physical borders between Israel and the Occupied Territories reinforced the inclination of many Mizrahim to mark themselves as not-Arab—for example, in the case of Chetrit's father and uncles, who shaved off their moustaches. This is the evasive dance of attraction and separation. Recall Ronit Matalon's father, who aspired to connect to his Arab roots but made a point of writing in French, not Arabic—also the Shaib children, who hid their father's Arabic books. Many also kept secret their love of Arab music. Even so, Mizrahi immigrants were often accused of actually being Arabs, a charge that marked their inferiority. Following the occupation of the territories in 1967, members of Edot Hamizrah became even more sensitive about being seen as Arabs. To be precise, they were not apprehensive about the possibility that Arabs would see them as Arabs. There was generally nothing unpleasant about that. What they feared was the external Ashkenazi gaze, which, by lumping Mizrahim together with Arabs, "demoted" them to the level of the Arabs.

THE PALESTINIAN FEAR

This same attraction-repulsion tension was evident among Palestinians as well. Their interest in making themselves resemble Jews (Mizrahim, for the most part) grew out of a combination of utilitarianism and a natural tendency to merge into the majority society. The repulsion, or avoidance, was powered by religious, national, and communal factors. This can be seen in a book by Dr. Subhi Ghosheh, an East Jerusalem physician and political activist. In his memoir he tells the story of a complicated encounter he had in Jerusalem, a few months after the Six-Day War.

> One day, as I was walking through a Jerusalem neighborhood, I spotted a young man who looked familiar. I had met him in the past, but he now looked different. He sported long sideburns, and his hair was partly shaven. His shirt was half-unbuttoned and he wore a chain on his chest. And the pants? I couldn't understand how he could have gotten his body into them. He turned to me and said: Hello, doctor. I didn't answer. The boy repeated his greeting: Hello, doctor, don't you recognize me? I'm Ribhi . . .
>
> What have you done to yourself, I asked him. Is that what we taught you?
>
> He said: Doctor, we aren't perverts, nor are we traitors to our homeland, and we haven't lost anything of the education we received from you.

> I asked him: Does working for the Zionists do you and the rest of us honor? And are these clothes that you are wearing show that you maintain our traditions and values? You should be ashamed. You should be ashamed and start acting like a human being again.
>
> Ribhi was angry but was too diffident to respond to me vehemently. He said, Doctor, the world has changed and we need to progress with it. Don't be stringent with us, let us live and work. Don't judge us now.
>
> He didn't finish what he was saying and left. I thought I saw his eyes fill with tears.[13]

Ribhi, Dr. Ghosheh realized, was one of the many Palestinians who had started working in Israel and frequented clubs in West Jerusalem. They dressed in what was then the Jerusalem Israeli—that is, Mizrahi—fashion. This included tight pants, a tight and open shirt, long sideburns, a necklace (many Jews, to maintain their separate identity, would later add a pendant in the shape of the Hebrew word *hai*, or life). They hoped to blend in, or at least not to stand out, or perhaps to feel like part of the majority. These efforts to look like Jews appalled not only many Mizrahim but also Palestinians. As the latter saw it, it was the first stage toward an unacceptable adoption of Israeli culture and identity, a loss of Palestinian Arab identity, and assimilation. In the case of Ribhi, the story took an interesting turn. "A long time passed, during which I neither heard about nor saw him," Dr. Ghosheh continued. "In fact, not until the mid-1970s."

> And when I then heard what had happened to him, I realized that I needed to think again about his story and about many other things. The news that shocked me was that Ribhi had been arrested, along with other youths from Isawiya [an East Jerusalem neighborhood] and other places in Jerusalem, because of their military activity and the attacks they had carried out. . . . It turned out that Ribhi had begun to imitate the Israeli way of dressing and had become thoroughly fluent in Hebrew so that he could go freely from place to place without arousing suspicion and get to places that others in his contingent could not get to, and many Israelis thought he was one of them. . . . In this way he was able to plant bombs in several places. . . . Ribhi was an example of the fighting national youth, a young man who was able to use his talents and abilities and the political education he had received in order to carry out actions successfully in Zionist areas. Indeed,

> whoever succeeds in mobilizing the large population of laborers who work in the Zionist entity in the name of our problems and to liberate the homeland will enable a qualitative leap forward.[14]

This is the other side of mimicry, or camouflage. Like the Palmach's Edot Hamizrah mistaarvim, and the mistaarvim in the IDF units established in the First Intifada, Palestinians also make use of the physical similarity between them and Mizrahi Jews for their national cause—both to gather intelligence and to stage attacks—even if not to the same extent. The Arab League's deputy secretary-general spoke about the Mizrahi mistaarvim in an interview with the Voice of the Arabs radio station in Cairo in 1969. "Edot Hamizrah Jews aid the Israeli security authorities in uncovering collaborators with terrorists in the Occupied Territories," *Maariv* quoted him as saying.[15] (The Hebrew translation replaced the Palestinian Arab term "fedayeen," meaning those prepared for self-sacrifice for a higher goal, with the Hebrew word for "terrorists." But the message remained clear.) Even prior to that, the Lebanese newspaper *Al-Hawadeth*, following an interview with Fatah operatives, reported that "the Jews have always been wizards at intelligence and espionage. . . . It is known that Israeli intelligence makes much use of Edot Hamizrah Jews in its war against the Arabs."[16] The writer meant people like Rafi Siton and David Ronen.

Intimated in these remarks is how hard it was for Arabs to see Jews who had come from the Islamic world adopting the role of everyday Zionist Israelis. After all, Zionism, the Arabs knew, was fundamentally an Ashkenazi European movement that discriminated against the Mizrahim. Their disappointment in Mizrahi collaboration with the Israeli security establishment, or, more precisely, in the fact that Mizrahim had become Zionists in every respect, runs through their words. The Mizrahim, of course, joined the intelligence services as Israelis, and in the understanding that this was their path into the hegemonic Israeli society and culture. For Arabs of that generation, who still remembered Jews as neighbors and friends, the Mizrahi involvement in harming them had but one meaning: the betrayal of a long tradition of neighborliness.

THE RISHON LETZIYON ALSO LET THEM DOWN

The Six-Day War produced an outpouring of emotion in the Jewish public, a kind of euphoria that also had a spiritual element. The return to the holy places that had they had been banned from visiting when the Old City and the West

Bank were under Jordanian rule stirred up repressed religious feelings. Rabbis swiftly began to offer their opinions about the territories, Jerusalem, and the Temple Mount. One of the most outspoken was Rabbi Shlomo Goren, who wanted to mark out a Jewish place of prayer on the Temple Mount but was prevented from doing so by Defense Minister Moshe Dayan. Israel's chief rabbis, Isser Yehuda Unterman and Rishon Letziyon Yitzhak Nissim, issued a halachic ruling that forbade Jews from ascending to the Temple Mount; they were joined by dozens of other Jewish legal authorities.

This was not the only halachic issue on the agenda. The future of the territories that Israel captured in the war was also discussed in rabbinic forums. Prior to the Simhat Torah holiday of October 1967, the first since the war, Rabbi Nissim issued a halachic ruling: "The Land of Israel is the inheritance of each and every person of Israel, and no individual or public, including the government of Israel, has the power to give up even a foot of its territory. This is a halacha that it is forbidden to move from, and no halachic authority may rule otherwise."[17] Two months later, Rabbi Nissim demanded the demolition of those homes in the Mughrabi Quarter, adjacent to the Western Wall, that remained standing after the razing of the neighborhood immediately following the Israeli conquest. He charged that the inhabitants of these houses were defiling and disrespecting the wall. Anwar al-Khatib, who had served as governor of Jordanian Jerusalem prior to the war, claimed that Rabbi Nissim had cried out to Israel's building contractors, "Where are you, Israeli contractors, where are your bulldozers and your demolition tools? Swiftly remove every structure that prevents the uncovering of the Western Wall to its foundations, without any fear and without any shame or hesitation. You are to drive out those who live in these houses and to continue the work of destruction from the southern end of the wall to its northern end." According to al-Khatib, this was "part of the call of the senior religious personage, the chief rabbi of the Mizrahi Jews, who lived under all the Muslim dynasties in safety and prosperity, ever since Islam liberated Jerusalem, from Andalusia to North Africa and from Baghdad to Egypt and all the Arab and Muslim countries."[18]

We have spent enough time on the varied and highly contradictory discourse on the nature of relations between Muslims and Jews under Muslim regimes. What is important in this context is the Arab view of Jews from the Islamic world as ingrates who were injuring those who in the past had treated them well. In this view, these Jews had for many years benefited from the protection of Muslim rulers, but the moment they gained a measure of power, they allied themselves with Christians and the West against Muslims so as to seize control of Palestine, which had opened its gates to them. Many Jews reject this narrative. According to Benjamin Z. Kedar, an Ashkenazi historian, this Arab account is a whining and wimpy one.[19] I think a better way of putting it is that it is a discourse of disappointment, even if it is sometimes based on a flattering self-image rather than on facts.

The discourse of disappointment continues to appear from time to time, even generations later. In March 2000, for example, David Levy (then serving for the third time as Israel's foreign minister) responded to rocket attacks on the Galilee perpetrated by Hezbollah, a Lebanese Shiite militia that supports the Palestinian cause. If the barrages continued, he declared, "Lebanon's land will burn . . . a child for a child and a soul for a soul. Jewish blood will not be spilled with impunity."[20] The media in the Arab world responded to Levy's statement. Faisal Abu Khadra, writing in the Egyptian newspaper *Al-Gomhuria*, offered a historical and psychological analysis.

> Mr. David Levy suffers from his generation's complex, and from the fact that he is an Arab and the son of Arabs who was born in an Arab country, into Arab history and the Arabic language, ate the best of that country and drank its milk and lived under its sky and took refuge in the shade of its roof, he and his father and his mother and his grandfather and his grandfather's grandfather. And when he reached maturity, the State of Israel was founded. And as he—like every Jew in the world, all of them, without exception—is first of all a Jew, he left his homeland and the dominion of his childhood and the history of his family and in a day turned into an Israeli who bears arms and kills the son of his land and his history.[21]

Abu Khadra evinces a trace of respect, perhaps even envy, at the mobilizing power of Jewish emotion. He also argues unequivocally that the Jews of the Arab lands are Arabs. For that reason, he asserts, Jews from the Islamic world should be convicted of treason in their countries of origin, just as would happen to Muslims or Christians who took up arms against their countries. "Even if we can understand that a Polish or Russian or Hungarian Jew sees himself as an enemy of the Arabs, because there is no historical tie or life connection [between them and the Arabs]," Abu Khadra maintained, "David Levy's hostility to the Arabs is incomprehensible and unforgivable."

ASHKENAZI ARROGANCE

The veteran Palestinian journalist Yusuf Hanna, a Christian, was born in Egypt but became Palestinian and served as editor of *Filastin* from 1933 to 1948. After the 1948 war, he lived alone in a hotel in the Christian Quarter of Jerusalem's Old City. He, too, was shaken and perplexed by Rabbi Nissim's pronouncement. Hanna believed in Jewish-Arab dialogue from the time of the Mandate, and immediately after the Six-Day War he reestablished contact with Israelis, among them intelligence officials and intellectuals.[22] "How is it that your prime minister declares at every opportunity that Israel aspires to peace," he asked an old friend, an American Jewish woman he had met during the Mandate period, "when your chief rabbi issues a fatwa according to which the halacha unequivocally forbids returning any conquered territory? You don't understand how to address us. You've turned into fanatics, drunk on victory." Hanna recounted his conversation with his American friend to the journalist and writer Nissim Rejwan, who immigrated to Israel during Operation Ezra and Nehemiah and edited the Histadrut Arabic-language newspaper *Al-Yawm* from 1959 to 1966. Before 1967, Hanna and Rejwan read each other's articles, and after the war they met. "Do you know what reply to my question I received from that American lady?" Hanna asked Rejwan. "'Ah,' said the lady, 'the chief rabbi, he's an ignorant commoner. He doesn't know a thing. He's an Arab from Iraq who was a merchant. You don't need to pay any attention to what he says.'"[23]

THE PROHIBITION AGAINST RETURNING TERRITORIES

At the same time that the American lady was explaining the rishon letziyon's prohibition against returning the territories as a product of his ignorance and Arab origin—that is, his inferiority—the Movement for Greater Israel had myriad supporters who thought the same. The movement was founded in the summer of 1967, immediately after the war, at a public meeting at the Habima Theatre in Tel Aviv. "Among us then were the poet Nathan Alterman; the novelist Haim Hazaz; the profound thinker Eliezer Livneh; the legendary Benny Marshak; the beloved Chaim Yahil; the first IDF chief of staff, Yaakov Dori; Yohanan Aharoni, investigator of Sinai; the accomplished Hillel Dan; and the original thinker Eri Jabotinsky," recalled one of the movement's followers, Zvi Shiloah, in a speech at an assembly commemorating its tenth anniversary. "And still living with us today is the teacher of the generation of pioneers and warriors, Yitzhak Tabenkin, who gave his blessing to the establishment of the movement. The students of Rabbi Avraham Yitzchak HaCohen Kook and the students of Yitzhak Tabenkin; veterans of the undergrounds and ghetto fighters; members of the [pre-1948] settlement [movement] and IDF generals; poets and people of action."[24] Only two Sephardi Mizrahim were among the fifty-eight who signed the movement's original manifesto—the novelist Yehuda Burla and the jurist Avner Shaki. Burla, born in Jerusalem in 1886, wrote about Jewish communities of the East but completely accepted and defended the Ashkenazi Zionist narrative.[25] He viewed the Sephardim as backward, both culturally and nationally. "The Sephardim knew nothing and heard nothing about all the national movements that originated and developed up until the Zionist movement," he maintained. He opposed ethnic politics and found a place for himself in the labor movement in the 1920s. Fifty years later, when he was in his early eighties and a member of Mapai, he joined the Movement for Greater Israel, as did many other members of that party. In contrast, Avner Shaki, born in Safed in 1926, lived and breathed Mizrahi politics. In 1959 he ran for the Knesset at the head of the National Sephardi Party that he had founded but did not meet the threshold necessary to gain Knesset representation. Later, after becoming a law professor, he served as a member of the Knesset and cabinet minister for the National Religious Party. Both men were exceptional among the members of the old elite who were active in the Movement for Greater Israel.

One conclusion that can be drawn from those men is that support for a Greater Israel—that is, an Israel that included the conquered territories, which should not be given up for any reason—was no less widespread among the old Ashkenazi elites, both religious and secular, than it was among religious Mizrahi Jews such as Rabbi Nissim and Shaki. It's worth noting that Rabbi Zvi Yehuda Kook, the son of Rabbi Avraham Yitzchak HaCohen Kook, issued a public statement opposing withdrawal from the territories weeks before the promulgation of Rabbi Nissim's halachic ruling.[26] Another conclusion is that the Mizrahim lacked public clout at the time. Only a small number had made their way into the elites, despite the fact that they made up half the country's Jewish population. In other words, their opinion was not taken into account. Perhaps their lips moved, but their voices were not heard.

What the signatories to the manifesto and their supporters shared was the absence of any sense of discomfort at the sight of the Palestinians living in the territories conquered by Israel; at the very least, they repressed any such feeling. It's likely that their sense of allegiance to the "integrity of our land—both toward the Jewish people's past and toward its futures," as their manifesto stated, kept them from seeing the inhabitants of the territories and their degradation. Perhaps they believed themselves when they wrote that "within these borders freedom and equality—the terms at the foundation of the State of Israel—will be the lot of all its inhabitants, without distinction."[27] That being the case, they presumed that the hateful gaze of the Arabs and their humiliation at their defeat would quickly dissipate. And they disregarded the fact that the state was denying these people both freedom and equality.

THE MANIFESTO OPPOSING THE OCCUPATION

A dozen opponents of Israeli rule in the territories issued a manifesto of their own soon after the war ended. "Our right to defend ourselves against annihilation does not grant us the right to oppress others," they declared to the Israeli public. "Conquest brings in its wake foreign rule. Foreign rule brings in its wake resistance. Resistance brings in its wake oppression. Oppression brings in its wake terror and counterterror."[28]

The fundamental difference between the manifestoes lay not just in the political demands they made—one group advocated annexation and the other opposed the occupation—or in the extent of support they enjoyed (the Greater Israel manifesto received an enormous amount of support, while the opponents of the occupation made only a marginal impact). It was a matter of where they set their sights. The former evoked the nation, history, and land. The latter placed human beings and the relations between them at the center. Let's now look at the signers of the anti-occupation manifesto and their ethnicity. Nine of them, it seems, were Ashkenazim, one was an Arab, and two were Mizrahim—Haim Hanegbi, the grandson of a Rabbi Haim Bajayo of Hebron who survived the 1929 massacre there, and Eli Aminov. Both were members of the revolutionary socialist Matzpen movement.

STATISTICS FOR STATISTICIANS

The number of Mizrahi signatories on these manifestoes can offer some indication of the Mizrahi presence in public discourse, but it says nothing about the inclinations of the Mizrahi public regarding the territories. Two public opinion surveys conducted in the months that followed the war sought to provide such information. One was carried out at the beginning of 1968 by an American political scientist, Martin Slann, following the Israeli annexation of East Jerusalem and its Arab population. Slann's working hypothesis was that the survey would show differences between ethnic groups in Jerusalem on the issue of the integration of East Jerusalem Arabs into the city's governance, administration, and public spaces. He thus divided the Jerusalemites he surveyed into three groups: those from Western countries (including eastern Europe), those from the Islamic world, and those born in Israel. Here are some of the questions he asked and the answers he received, by ethnic origin.

When asked if they would support the presence of Arab policemen in East Jerusalem, the native-born Israelis and those of European and American origin answered in the affirmative by a huge margin—86 and 90 percent, respectively. Only 48 percent of the Mizrahim gave this answer. And would they support the presence of Arab policemen in Jewish areas? A positive response was given by 28 percent of those born in Israel and 42 percent of American and European origin; only 15 percent of Mizrahim gave a positive answer. With regard to having Arab members of the Jerusalem City Council, support among Mizrahim was significantly lower than among Ashkenazim and the Israeli-born—40 percent, 76 percent, and 72 percent, respectively.[29]

Slann focused on political issues. He conjectured that the Mizrahim opposed the inclusion of the city's Arabs in municipal government because of their negative experiences under Arab regimes, an explanation we are familiar with from previous decades. It is one possible explanation. Another, in addition to or instead of this one, can be found in the research literature, which focuses on the encounter between immigrants from the Islamic world and Israeli culture—specifically, the negative image of Arabs pervasive in Israel. This, it is argued, impelled many Mizrahim to distance themselves from any identification with Arabs and Arab culture by adopting anti-Arab positions. The aversion to being subjected to Arab policemen recalls David Ben-Haroush's grievance against the use of Druze policemen to disperse the Wadi Salib demonstrations.

Slann surveyed only fifty people; some of his questions were answered by only a handful. Another study, conducted at the same time, was commissioned by the Jerusalem municipality and addressed cultural and social issues as well as political ones. The sample size was also larger. Prime Minister Levi Eshkol suggested to Jerusalem's mayor, Teddy Kollek, that the findings be suppressed and destroyed. "I have received your comment," Kollek replied, "and I recognize that it is correct and right. I have therefore ordered the destruction of all copies of the survey we conducted. The only two copies are in your hands and those of the foreign minister, and I leave to your discretion whether those should also be destroyed."[30] Eshkol did not destroy his copy, so we are able to peruse its findings and, at a distance of more than half a century, ponder why Israel's leaders were shaken by the survey results.

THE SUPPRESSED SURVEY

The survey's overall topic was Jews' attitudes toward Arabs. The total sample size was 273, categorized by sex, education, ethnic group (Sephardi/Ashkenazi), native-born versus foreign-born, and occupation (white collar versus blue collar). It's important to note that the level of religious observance was not one of the variables, even though it became, from the 1980s onward, a significant, perhaps even central, factor in analyzing attitudes toward Arabs and the territories. The available copy is incomplete. Our focus here is the primary differences between Sephardim and Ashkenazim (the terms used by the pollsters) that the answers to the survey questions demonstrate.

The survey asked the respondents to rate East Jerusalem Arabs on a scale from one to seven on thirteen character traits of a positive, neutral, and negative nature. The results were unequivocal. The Jews rated the Arabs, in this order, as "a people with many dissemblers," "a people who are mostly poor," "a cowardly people," "a primitive people," and "a people who do not wash." Positive traits, such as "want peace with the Jews" and "an industrious people who like to work" came out on the bottom.[31] Women more than men thought that Arabs were cowards; more Sephardim than Ashkenazim saw them as poor, cowardly, unhealthy, and primitive.

And here are the responses of Ashkenazim, as opposed to Sephardim, on questions regarding the possibility of Jewish-Arab relations. Of the Ashkenazim surveyed, 58 percent agreed to worked alongside Arabs, compared to 40 percent of the Sephardim. With regard to attending schools together in the western (Jewish) part of the city, 55 percent of the Ashkenazim were willing, as opposed to 27 percent of the Sephardim. On the question of Arabs' being allowed to live in West Jerusalem, 48 percent of the Ashkenazim agreed, in contrast to 24 percent of the Sephardim. In other words, more Ashkenazim than Sephardim declared themselves willing to have close relations with Arabs. When it came to Arab participation in municipal politics, the disparities were smaller. Among the Ashkenazim, 50 percent supported Arab participation in elections for mayor and the city council, as did 39 percent of the Sephardim. On one central question there was no significant difference between Mizrahim and Ashkenazim. Both thought that the city's unification would lead to mixed marriages between Jews and Arabs (76 and 77 percent, respectively).

Before offering possible explanations for these different attitudes toward Arabs by ethnic origin, it's important to note that even when the disparities are stark, they are not completely dichotomous. Members of both communities could be found along the entire spectrum of opinion. Turning to the differences, Sephardim were apprehensive about the ramifications of the unification of the city for their well-being and livelihoods. According to the survey, 30 percent of Ashkenazim were concerned that the annexation of East Jerusalem would cause a rise in unemployment. A full 56 percent of Sephardim shared that apprehension. Presumably, this was a result of the fact that Sephardim and Arabs made up a disproportionate share of the unskilled labor market; as such, Mizrahim were more fearful of competition. Mizrahim tended to be more in favor of the separation of Jewish and Arab areas of habitation in the city (they evinced less desire to live in East Jerusalem, and fewer of them wanted Arabs to live on the city's Jewish side). The reason, apparently, was that they feared that living in the same neighborhood as Arabs would be deleterious to their efforts to shed their Arab traits and image. Those Mizrahim who favored living with Arabs probably sought to revive the cultural milieu they had been accustomed to before coming to Israel. The small difference (39 versus 50 percent support) on Arab representation in municipal political offices may have had something to do with the Mizrahi tilt toward the right. Another possible explanation is that Mizrahim feared that Arab political power would further dilute the little political representation they had.

THE CULTURAL SPHERE

A full 70 percent of the city's Jewish inhabitants maintained that Israel had the responsibility to foster "the cultural lives of the Arabs in the eastern area," the survey found. There was a follow-up question: "Should the Arabs be allowed to use the municipal theater, the Khan?" A positive response was given by 64 percent of the survey sample. The detailed table of results is missing from the file, but the pollster commented that men, the college-educated, and Ashkenazim tended to agree (although with notable differences among them), while women, those without high school diplomas, young people, and Sephardim were largely opposed.

Why did more Mizrahim not want to see Arabs attending plays at the Khan? One possibility is that most of Jerusalem's Mizrahim immigrated after Israel's establishment. The initial arrivals were housed at high density in neighborhoods that Arabs had left or been expelled from, such as Musrara and Baka. Later Mizrahi immigrants spent years in transit camps and gradually moved into public housing projects that were built for them in Talpiot, Katamonim, Ir Ganim, Kiryat Menahem, and other neighborhoods. Most of them worked in jobs at the bottom of the income scale. Few of them, presumably, subscribed to the Khan's theater series. It may well be that the prospect that the city's Arabs, the defeated enemies, might enjoy the city's cultural life, which the Mizrahim themselves could not afford, seemed unreasonable, even offensive. In response to another question, Mizrahim tended to agree with the statement that restaurants on the west side of the city were better than those on the east. This might best be understood by means of the sociological concept of "border work," a process in which Mizrahim aimed to distinguish themselves from Arabs and position themselves on the Western side of the culture war. It may also explain why more Mizrahim than Ashkenazim said that they did not want Arab neighbors.[32] That more Sephardim called the Arabs primitive can be seen in the same light. This is a familiar pattern among groups seeking to climb the social ladder.[33]

In the years following 1967, and even more so after the Right came to power in 1977, research on Jewish-Arab relations came to occupy an important place in Israeli sociology. This included the study of the different positions of Mizrahim and Ashkenazim. Yochanan Peres, one of the most prominent figures in this field, wrote, "Relations among Jews and between Jews and Arabs are closely interconnected. For Jews of Middle Eastern origin, the Arabs are a negative reference group. The Oriental Jews' hostility and prejudice against Arabs (which were found to be more intensive that that of European Jews) seem to be an expression of their desire to be fully accepted in Israeli society."[34] This analysis is based on two assumptions, but it is difficult to determine whether the author was aware of them or whether he simply projected them onto Mizrahim. The first is that being Israeli requires holding negative attitudes toward Arabs. The second is that Mizrahim are not Israelis in the full sense of the term. The conclusion is thus that in order to become true Israelis, they need to display anti-Arab attitudes. This is a further manifestation of the views we saw among the Moskobim of the Second Aliyah at the end of the Ottoman period. The Moskobim also expected the Sephardim to stand by them and display anti-Arab attitudes. Looking back, it is clear that their expectations became reality.

After the war, Mizrahim found themselves in a sort of trap. Social ties with Arabs would paint them as non-Israeli and would block paths of advancement into mainstream Israeli society. But an overly severe attitude toward Arabs would brand them as primitive. Either way, they acted under the surveillance of a judgmental external gaze. This is true of every person and every group. For those at the bottom of the social ladder who wish to rise, the external gaze is even more powerful.

A few points of clarification: there is no necessary connection between social affinity and political position. A person can support political conciliation without being familiar with the members of the other nation, just as it is possible to maintain personal friendships with members of the other nation but at the same time oppose political compromise with that nation. Furthermore, the external gaze on their group affects individuals' choices about the nature of their social relations (in this case, of Jews with Arabs), their political positions, and their involvement in violent acts or efforts at peacemaking, but it is not the sole factor. The norms of the in-group are also a factor. It's important, however, to keep in mind that individuals are not entirely subject to either social norms or external gazes. Each individual retains a measure of personal choice—what sociologists call "agency." In other words, they can decide, consciously or otherwise, to what extent they are obligated by social norms. Further on we will encounter perceptions about "proper norms for Mizrahim" in their relations with Arabs. In any case, the Arab gaze has very little influence on the conduct of Mizrahim. We have already encountered a number of such Arab gazes through history. Here are a few more.

ARABS ON MIZRAHIM

The view of Mizrahim as primitive was not limited to the established Israeli elites (or at least a part of them). It could also be seen among Westernized Palestinian elites. These were the people who would have been happy to patronize the Khan Theatre if it presented plays on a level appropriate for them. Menahem Milson, who in 1967 was a lecturer in the Hebrew University's Department of Arabic Language and Literature and later headed the West Bank Civil Administration, tells a relevant story. Because of his interest in Arab culture, following the Six-Day War he established contacts with Palestinian intellectuals and journalists.

One of his interlocuters was Raja Al-Issa (1922–2008), the son of the legendary editor of *Filastin*, Issa Al-Issa (1878–1950). Raja traveled all around Israel after the war, visiting many communities. He discovered an Israel quite different from the image he had formed for himself prior to the war. He shared with Milson his insights into Israeli society. "I maintain," he said, "that there are indeed Israelis we could get along with. I can divide Israelis into three types. The best of you are people like you, Menahem—born in the country [Milson was born in Haifa in 1933], educated. You are like us in many ways, and we can easily get along with you. A second type are people who are not like us to the same extent, but they are also sympathetic—people who arrived from America and western Europe. They are liberals, cultured, and educated, and we can get along with them. But the third type, and these are the worst among you, are the Mizrahi Jews, especially the Jews from North Africa. They are filthier than our own fellahs."[35]

Al-Issa voiced a sentiment that had been common at the end of the Ottoman period and persisted to a lesser extent during the Mandate. Here is evidence that it survived after 1967 as well, in the form of the intercommunal fraternity of Westernizing elites. He was contemptuous of Arab fellahs and Jewish immigrants from North Africa but addressed Milson as a friend. Milson was aghast. "I am of course fond of you, you know that," Milson replied. "But you see the Mizrahi Jews as filthier than your fellahs, while I don't see either the Mizrahi Jews or the fellahs that way. We Jews are a single nation, we share mutual responsibility, and we want to build a single society. We must develop our society, and you yours. If you think that your fellahs are devoid of education and culture, you have a lot of work to do in your society."[36]

Jewish unity and mutual responsibility are the cornerstones of the Israeli founding ethos. In the previous chapter we saw the discrepancy between that ideal and the reality that immigrants from the Islamic world encountered. But even if a certain sense of superiority over the Mizrahim was common in the central Zionist current, it included nothing that impelled it into an alliance with Palestinian elites of the sort Al-Issa proposed. Furthermore, the vision Al-Issa advocated was not that attractive: the establishment of a multinational state on the Lebanese model.

ALL JEWS ARE GOOD

Here's a brief reminder of a common mindset in Israel after the war. The Palestinians who had come under Israeli rule aroused a mixture of hostility and curiosity. Israelis were awestruck by the expansion of their borders but at the same time fearful of the terror attacks perpetrated by Palestinian organizations. They hoped for peace with the peoples of the Middle East, but in tandem began establishing Jewish settlements in the West Bank and East Jerusalem. Israel's policy was to restore everyday life in the territories as soon as possible. It aimed to raise Palestinians' standard of living by integrating them into the Israeli labor market, offering agricultural assistance, improving health services, and in other ways. (This went hand in hand with a desire to minimize the number of Palestinians in the territories.) Many Israelis hoped that the inhabitants of the territories would discover that Jews were human beings and not the monsters that Arab propaganda had portrayed, and that they would accept the Jews' right to live in peace and security in their land.

It was a nebulous but concrete hope. Nebulous because it disregarded fundamental problems between Israel and the Palestinians, such as the fact that Israel was offering the Palestinians life under foreign rule. Furthermore, it ignored the fate of the refugees and the future of the Temple Mount/Al-Aqsa. Concrete because it was constantly repeated in a variety of ways throughout the entire range of the Israeli communications media. The Israeli press gave prominent play to conciliatory statements by prominent Arabs; terror attacks were attributed to terrorist organizations in Jordan that were imposing themselves on the inhabitants of the territories. There were indeed among the latter those who hoped for peace, and even more who took exception to the armed struggle. But in retrospect (although perceptive observers saw this at the time), it is clear that they did not, following the war, give up their own national dream, whether in its Palestinian, Jordanian, or pan-Arab version.

Six weeks after the war, the mayor of Hebron, Mohammed Ali al-Ja'bari, along with other senior figures from his city, paid a visit to Be'er Sheva's mayor, Eliyahu Nawi. The press coverage conveyed optimism. "Hebron's Notables Make a Visit of Peace," was the headline in *Al Hamishmar,* which reported, "In friendly talks, everyone spoke of the peace that is urgently needed by both sides." Nawi cited the connection between Be'er Sheva and Hebron, two cities where the biblical Abraham, father of Isaac and Ishmael, had been active. "The covenant of these brothers from the same father obligates us to increase friendship and peace," he declared. *Davar* quoted Ja'bari: "The Arabs of the West Bank are interested in cooperation with the Jews and are prepared for it, and it can be done if Jewish leaders know how to take advantage of the existing possibilities."[37] Ja'bari was trying at this time to establish a body that would represent Palestinians in the territories and recognize Israel. He hoped to head it.

The conversation between the hosts and guests was conducted largely in Arabic. Nawi had been born in Basra, Iraq, in 1920, and immigrated to Palestine as a small child. He attended Doresh Zion, founded in Jerusalem in 1866 as a school for both Ashkenazim and Sephardim. But it was boycotted by the Ashkenazi community and thus became a leading Sephardi institution (both Yehuda Burla and Rabbi Uziel attended). Nawi later studied education and then law; in 1948 he enlisted in the IDF and served for six years in the Druze unit and in military intelligence, reaching the rank of major. He served at Be'er Sheva's first Magistrate's Court; in 1963 he won a race for mayor. The visitors from Hebron were familiar with Nawi's voice because of another job he had, as a commentator for the Voice of Israel's Arabic station. In that capacity, he regaled his listeners in the Arab world with folktales bearing pro-Israel messages, under the pseudonym Daud al-Natur (Daud the Guard).

Nawi was one of the veteran cohort of Sephardim-Mizrahim whose expertise in Arabic served them, and their country, in promoting Israel's public image and in gathering intelligence. They used Arabic to make their way into the security establishment and become part of the hegemonic society. With the occupation of the territories, a new channel opened up before them. There was another Mizrahi angle to the meeting in Be'er Sheva. The guests from Hebron were asked their opinion about the issue that we are plumbing here, Mizrahi-Arab relations. "At first, the inhabitants of the West Bank thought that they would receive more favorable treatment from the Mizrahim in Israel," *Al Hamishmar* quoted al-Ja'bari as saying. "But reality proved that the treatment they received from all parts of the Israeli population was the same."[38]

FOUR ARAB PERSPECTIVES

There were thus four Arab perspectives on the Mizrahim following the Six-Day War of 1967: (1) a continued revolutionary aspiration, whether in a Fatah or Marxist guise, for an anti-Zionist Mizrahi-Arab alliance; (2) condescension on the part of the Arab elites and bourgeoisie; (3) an expectation of receiving better treatment from Mizrahim (a hope that was disappointed); (4) denial that Mizrahi ethnicity was a factor in Jewish-Arab relations.

THE VOICE OF ISRAEL IN ARABIC AND AL-AQSA MOSQUE

Nawi was no longer working at the Voice of Israel in Arabic in 1967, but the Mizrahi contingent there continued to broadcast, even more energetically. As had been the custom in previous years, the station marked Muslim holidays and the Ramadan fast, which that year commenced on December 3. Every evening of that month, the station broadcast the cannon shot that marked the end of the day's fast, along with the reading of a chapter (sura) of the Quran. The station made a point of stressing that this latter broadcast came from Al-Aqsa Mosque. The Beirut newspaper *Al-Kifah* responded on the third day of the holy month, writing, "The enemy claims that this broadcast transmits the call for prayer (*al-Adhan*) and the reading of the Quran from Al-Aqsa Mosque. It makes a point of referring to Al-Aqsa Mosque as 'blessed.' . . . The truth is that there is no proof that the broadcast indeed originates from Al-Aqsa Mosque itself, because the voices of the worshippers cannot be heard. . . . Is it possible that the Jewish announcer sullies the mosque with his feet, along with the rest of the Israeli officials accompanying him and the group of soldiers guarding them? It is not possible for Israel to claim that this broadcaster with the revolting voice is a Muslim, because the Arabs of the occupied land have heard this Jewish voice many times, and his identity cannot be concealed."[39]

The Muslim listeners were not wrong. The reader of the Quran on the Voice of Israel was Filfel al-Gurji, an Iraqi Jew. Al-Gurji, a well-known musician, began to work at Radio Baghdad in 1950 but, according to Zvi Ben-Dor, "his immigration to Israel cut short his musical career and he could no longer make music his principal field. . . . Filfel worked at odd jobs while his fame began to spread as a singer at celebrations. Like many other Mizrahi musicians, he found a place for himself on the Voice of Israel in Arabic, where one of his assignments was chanting chapters of the Quran." Al-Gurji died in 1983 at the age of fifty-three. A CD of his songs, *Al-Dinya Farhana* (The world is happy), was issued in 2001 with the help of the Mizrahi Israeli singer Yair Dalal. "The story of Filfel," according to Ben-Dor, "is a fine example of the cruel dilemmas that rent Mizrahi artists who created in Arabic."[40]

THE LABOR MARKET—FUNDAMENTAL CHANGES

Al-Gurji found employment at the Voice of Israel thanks to his musical talent, knowledge of Arabic, and pleasant voice (well, perhaps not for Muslims during Ramadan). The war indeed raised the demand for Arabic speakers in government agencies, and many of those who were hired were Mizrahim. But Israel's labor market underwent a sea change following the government's decision to permit Palestinians from the territories to work in Israel. The process was slow but steady. In 1969, about twelve thousand workers from the territories were permitted to work in permanent jobs, while thousands of others, also mostly with permits, worked as seasonal laborers. Shefi Gabbai, a writer for *Davar*, wrote a positive feature story, fitting the spirit of the times and of its author, portraying how the arrangement pleased both the workers and their employers. "'They are excellent workers,' said Shlomo Kahalni, foreman for the construction of Tel Aviv's Central Bus Station, with regard to his laborers from Gaza. 'In general, we try to employ them in pairs—an Arab worker and a Jewish worker. Friendship develops between the two and they invite each other to their homes.'"[41] This may well have happened from time to time, but Gabbai's feature did not reflect the big picture of Jewish-Arab relations in workplaces.

In 1970, some twenty thousand workers from the territories received permits to work in Israel. The number had grown to sixty-four thousand by

1975 and continued to rise in the years that followed. Many thousands more worked without permits. These workers were directed into agricultural, construction, and service jobs. College-educated and white-collar Palestinians were not included in Israel's employment program for the inhabitants of the territories unless they agreed to engage in manual labor. One of the justifications for not employing Palestinian professionals was the fear that they might take jobs from college-educated Israelis, who would then leave the country. There was no such concern with regard to nonprofessional laborers, meaning Mizrahim.[42]

EDUCATION AND EMPLOYMENT BEFORE 1967

In the previous chapter we looked at two principal variables that produced an employment differential between Mizrahim and Ashkenazim. The first was the level of education in Israelis' countries of origin. The second was that Mizrahim, including the more educated, were channeled into providing a labor force for the kibbutz industry and for urban manufacturing concerns that were then on the rise. Mizrahi labor powered Israeli economic development and professional advancement for Ashkenazim, both long-established ones and new immigrants. But it welded Mizrahi immigrants to the bottom of the socioeconomic ladder. We also heard David Ben-Gurion alleging that money the new state had received to assist in the absorption of the immigrants had, in practice, boosted the standard of living of the established population at the expense of the new immigrants. These were two factors that restricted the job options of immigrants from the Islamic world. Immigrants from Morocco were treated differently from those from Iraq in employment during the initial years after they immigrated. Employers, both public and private, took greater account of the education that Iraqi (and Levantine) Jews had acquired, prior to their immigration, than of the education and work experience of immigrants from Morocco (and North Africa in general). However, this educational differential closed among the children of immigrants from the Islamic world as a whole, but at a low level common to all of them. The cause was the government's policy of directing Mizrahi youth into vocational schools, which had been initiated by Minister of Education Zalman Aran, who served in that capacity from 1955 to 1960 and again from 1963 to 1969.

Aran maintained that Israel needed to create a productive working class. "Since there was no chance of changing most of the members of economically well off Ashkenazi families and making them 'productive,'" historian Tzvi Tzameret wrote, Aran "targeted Mizrahim in underprivileged urban neighborhoods and in development towns. They, he believed, were the only hope of creating productive masses in Israel." Aran believed that this would also strengthen the Mizrahim socially and economically. In fact, however, directing members of Edot Hamizrah into vocational education prevented many of them from preparing themselves for higher education and higher positions, and thus "widened social rifts and the economic disparities in the State of Israel" along ethnic lines.[43] As Yossi Yonah and Ishaq Saporta note, "Vocational education developed in the wake of a general systemic view that was in fact indifferent to the desires of its 'clients,' seeking to harness them to 'national' goals that were in practice inimical to their own interests."[44]

The harm done can be seen in the results of a study done for the cabinet committee that examined the educational level of Jews from Asia and Africa in the mid-1970s. "Only 26 percent of the [Mizrahi] cohort continued into liberal education [in high school]; only 14 percent reached twelve years of study; only 7 percent completed the *bagrut* [high school matriculation] exams (in comparison with about 35 percent of those of European and American extraction)."[45] Mizrahim thus found themselves in low-status, low-income jobs. After 1967, tens of thousands of Arabs who arrived in buses from the West Bank and Gaza Strip streamed into Israel to fill these jobs. For some Mizrahim, this presented an opportunity to upgrade their employment.

A NATION OF EMPLOYERS

The decision to employ workers from the territories in Israel was made after much soul-searching among the members of the cabinet. Minister of Defense Moshe Dayan led those in favor. He wanted economic integration (in fact, subordination of the economy of the territories to that of Israel) and feared that high unemployment among the Arabs there would lead to unrest. He also believed that Arabs from the territories who had jobs in Israel would not want to take action against the country. The opponents voiced several concerns. First, employing these Arabs would be detrimental to the effort to encourage Palestinian emigration to the Gulf states, which was a top Israeli priority. Second, it was liable to cause unemployment among Jewish workers. Third, it would put an end to the Zionist-socialist ethos of Hebrew labor. At a meeting of the ministerial committee on the territories in April 1969, Prime Minister Golda Meir put this last point in a nutshell. "We need to make a huge effort," she maintained, "not to get to the very point we fled from, that we will be the whitest of collars, with exemplary diplomats and doctors, foremen, but the black and dirty work will be done by others. As I conceive of it, Zionism began when we fled from that point, we said no to that. When we began to soil our hands digging, paving roads, and farming . . . I am afraid that we will go back to the point we fled from."[46]

This is part of the paradox of ethnic relations in Israel. In the desire to say that Israel is a productive country that depends on its own labor, and in doing so lives up to the Zionist ideal, the country's leadership wanted some Jews to be manual laborers. But most Jewish laborers in the late 1960s were Mizrahim, who did not necessarily see manual labor as their road to personal and national redemption. To put it another way, those who believed in the ideology of Hebrew labor wanted other Jews (namely, the Mizrahim), not their own children, to work those jobs.

The public debate over importing Arab laborers from the territories to work in Israel flared cyclically. At the beginning of 1973, Histadrut's secretary-general, Yitzhak Ben-Aharon, voiced his trepidation about the social and moral implications of employing workers from the territories. It would, he feared, turn Israel into a sort of colonial state that employed a subjugated population as drawers of water and hewers of wood. Shlomo Avineri, a political scientist, wrote an article for *Maariv* laying out the reasons for employing these workers. He stressed the obligation to ensure that they received social benefits and equal pay. Employing them would, he argued, have a positive effect on the ethnic gap:

> The Arab laborer from the Occupied Territories does not today shunt aside any Jewish worker. On the contrary, given the huge expansion of the Israeli economy in recent years and the impressive social mobility that pervades our society, the Arab worker fills the place of the Jewish worker, *generally a member of Edot Hamizrah* [emphasis in the original], who, thanks to economic prosperity, has been able to advance along the rungs of the social system. . . . Most of the Jewish construction workers—and again, the decisive majority of them were members of Edot Hamizrah—have during this time turned into contractors, subcontractors, and have become self-employed. Some farmworkers have turned into agricultural and commercial entrepreneurs. In other words, the largely successful social absorption of a large portion of the members of Edot Hamizrah as the economy has developed is the key to the creation of the demand for labor that has made possible the absorption of workers from the territories into the Israeli economy. Those who deplore the disappearance of Jewish labor from

> some sectors of the economy (the deplorers and not the workers who worked in those sectors) cannot at the same time congratulate themselves about the impressive increase in recent years of the standard of living of large portions of the Edot Hamizrah population in the country. . . . This does not mean that one should unequivocally welcome the situation in which the Arabs ostensibly comprise the hewers of wood and drawers of water of Israeli society. What I cannot understand is the nostalgia for those days in which Jews—generally members of Edot Hamizrah—filled these roles. The mobility of members of Edot Hamizrah and the entry of Arab workers into the Israeli economy go hand in hand.[47]

Indeed, Mizrahim, as a group, did not lose their livelihoods as the economy opened up to Palestinian workers. On the contrary, the economic boom that followed the war advanced their professional standing and allowed many of them to move from jobs as laborers to positions as salaried foremen and small entrepreneurs. By some accounts, as we will soon see, this was one of the important factors that led many Mizrahim to support the perpetuation of Israeli rule in the territories.

THE ARMED STRUGGLE: ACRE-HAIFA, 1968

Mizrahim were not the only ones to move up the employment ladder because of the employment of workers from the territories. Arab citizens from Israel did so as well.[48] But that was not the only result of the complex encounter between the Palestinians on either side of the Green Line. In the cultural and religious realms, it encouraged young Muslims from Israel to study at Islamic colleges in the West Bank.[49] In the political field, a small number of Arab citizens of Israel enlisted in the PLO's armed struggle. Among these were the members of a Fatah cell in Acre founded under the command of Fawzi Nimr in 1969. Its six members were relatively well off, most of them with families. They were recruited at the beginning of that year by contacts in Nablus. Two of them were fishermen who, while on their boats in the open sea, received shipments of explosives from Fatah ships that sailed from Syria. When they were arrested by Israeli security forces, they had dozens of detonators, sixteen hand grenades, several kilograms of explosives, and pistols. By the time they were apprehended, they had carried out a series of attacks, among them a failed attempt to blow up the Tel Aviv–Haifa train line, a more successful attempt to blow up oil pipelines in the Kishon oil terminal, the sabotage of an electric transformer in Kiryat Hayim, and the planting of bombs in the towns of Bat Shlomo and Binyamina. Their final operation, in October 1969, was the first deadly one—they placed explosive charges alongside five residential buildings in Haifa, killing two and injuring several others. The police reported that the cell had planned to attack police officers and Palestinian collaborators with Israel.[50]

Acre itself exploded after the cell was uncovered. As it happened, on the Saturday night after the arrests, the Acre City Council convened for its first official meeting after the municipal elections to choose from among its members a mayor and deputy mayor. In the wake of the terror attacks, hundreds of residents of the city assembled around the municipal building, calling on the council to bar an Arab member, Mohammad Hubeishi, from being reelected deputy mayor. The furious protests led the commander of the local police force to suggest that the council adjourn without voting for the two offices, and the members acquiesced. The demonstrators dispersed.

But the storm did not calm. The next evening, hundreds of young Jews attacked Arabs in the Old City. The chief of the northern police district, Aharon Sela, later told the Knesset's Interior Committee that a police force there managed to block the Jews from entering the Arab neighborhoods. He offered some background: "Acre has 28,000 Jewish and 9,000 Arab inhabitants. Everyday life is entirely as it should be. It should be said that we do not have any more problems in Acre than we have in any other location. . . . The youth problem is a serious one. I don't think there is enough care given to youth. . . . Furthermore, there is a large concentration of immigrants there, whose conflict with the Arabs dates way back, and it is very easy to inflame them. I am speaking about the immigrants. They are principally immigrants from North Africa, as they constitute a large percentage. What is interesting is that, between one incident and another, life returns to being entirely normal."[51]

As in 1961, and as in the later incident in 1965, the North African ethnicity of the protesters and attackers was explained with reference to their experience in their Arab countries of origin. Once again, this time in Acre, observers noted that relations between immigrants and Arabs were generally good, in part because of the culture they shared. For example, Acre was one of the first places where a band from East Jerusalem and Bethlehem performed, in the summer of 1967 (the initiative came from Nissim Rejwan, whom we met above). *Davar* reported on parties attended by both Jews and Arabs under the headline "The Stars from the West Bank Invade Israel."[52]

This affinity suggests another explanation for the explosion of anger among Acre's Jews. It was not just that Arabs and Jews sang Arab songs together and that afterward some of the Arabs took part in attacks on Jews. The members of the Acre terror cell in fact had special relations with Jews. Its leader, Fawzi Nimr, was married to Simona Pinto, a Jewish woman from a well-known Moroccan family. They had a son and a daughter together. Pinto was also arrested and interrogated. It emerged that she had been with Nimr when he set out for some of his attacks. But she had had no idea what he was doing and was in the end released. These facts received extensive media coverage. What was not reported at the time, to the press or to the Interior Committee, was that Nimr had been a Shabak collaborator who had gotten sick of his role ("The head of the Acre ring had been a Shabak collaborator and as such took advantage of the methods he had learned about setting up secret meetings and handling people," the secret report noted.)[53] One of his motives in setting up the cell was apparently the desire to atone for his betrayal of his people.

Fawzi Nimr was sentenced to life in prison. But he was released as part of the Jibril Agreement of 1985, in which Israel let 1,150 Palestinians out of its jails in exchange for the return of three Israelis captured during the First Lebanon War. He joined the PLO command in Tunis and remarried, this time with Fatima Barnawi an East Jerusalem militant who had preceded him in joining the armed struggle. She had placed a bomb (which was discovered before it went off) in the Zion Cinema in Jerusalem in September 1967. After the establishment of the Palestinian Authority in 1994, the couple moved to the Gaza Strip, where Barnawi was appointed commander of the women's police force. Nimr was put in charge of the Authority's relations with Israel's Palestinian citizens. Pinto and Nimr's children endured many vicissitudes, some of which are depicted in Nurit Kedar and Yaron Shani's 2013 film about their son, *Life Sentences*.

A SENSE OF BETRAYAL

From the dawn of Zionism, the Arabs of Palestine have expressed their disappointment in the Jews for being so ungrateful. After Israel's establishment, and all the more so after the Six-Day War, a mirror image of this discourse became pervasive among Israeli Jews. An example can be seen in Acre mayor Israel Doron's testimony before the Knesset's Interior Committee in 1969. "We need to understand their feelings and the pent-up anger on the Jewish street," he declared. "After all, it turned out that people who had lived together with them for twenty years [had turned against them].... They had been involved in social and economic life."[54]

THE SPATIAL CONTEXT: DEVELOPMENT CITY VERSUS REGIONAL COUNCIL

At the same meeting of the Interior Committee, Acre's mayor explained that one of the principal reasons for his city's backwardness was the lack of land available for construction. He later made the same point in a letter to Prime Minister Golda Meir, in which he described the state of affairs in his city. The neighborhoods that had been built for the immigrants housed in the city and for the Arab population from the surrounding region that was concentrated there, he wrote, were typified by high density and a low level of upkeep. "Clearly, this shapes the city's sociocultural character, and here change is required," he maintained. To raise the city's social and cultural level, to build cultural and tourist centers, he added, the city needed additional land. But the Ga'aton Regional Council owned land inside the city and was not prepared to transfer it or to change the boundaries between the city and the regional council's jurisdictions.

This pattern has been repeated all over the country. In later years, many scholars and activists came to realize that the phenomenon played a major role in widening economic and social disparities. The regional councils, responsible for the farming settlements within their boundaries, received large expanses of land. Some of it was cultivated, while some was used for other profit-making ventures, such as the construction of factories that paid high property taxes. At the same time, nearby development towns faced budget shortfalls and sometimes desperately needed additional land. Acre's mayor was able to use demography as a threat. Jews, he warned, would not settle in the city, and Arabs would thus gain a majority. He asked for "the establishment of an interministerial committee at a high level to [propose] a solution and assistance in the special case of Acre as a city of mixed population desperate for additional land for construction."[55] In the end, the borders were revised, but only in the most minuscule way.

THE BLACK PANTHERS

The Black Panthers, who first appeared on the scene early in 1971, were well aware that the country's leadership treated different sectors of the population in different ways, though they might not have understood the apparatus that enriched regional councils at the expense of development towns. They had personal experience of discrimination against immigrants from the Islamic world. It was true that in Acre, as in Jerusalem, Jews beat up Arabs following Palestinian terrorist attacks on Jews, but the Panthers were more focused, and they directed their wrath and their demands at the establishment. Their first manifesto stated, "We, a group of downtrodden young people, call on all those who are sick of it all: it's enough that we don't have work, it's enough that we sleep ten to a room, it's enough to look at the housing projects built for immigrants, it's enough to get beaten up every other day, we've had enough of the promises of a government that doesn't keep them, we've had enough of discrimination, we've had enough of inequity." They called a demonstration in front of the Jerusalem municipal building.[56]

The Black Panthers originated in Jerusalem's Musrara neighborhood, just behind the city offices. It had also, from 1948 to 1967, been adjacent to the single crossing point along the barbed-wire boundary that split the city into its Israeli and Jordanian sides. The neighborhood had been home to well-off Palestinians who fled or were expelled during the 1948 war. Israel settled new immigrants, mostly from North Africa, in the subdivided homes of the Arabs and in public housing projects it built there. In the years following the Six-Day War, the neighborhood's young people, most of them Moroccan Jews, felt that they were increasingly being pushed to Israeli society's margins. They had endured severely inadequate education, housing, and employment even before the war, but their situation worsened thereafter. The Mizrahi residents of two other such areas, Mamilla and Yemin Moshe, were displaced so that their homes and neighborhoods could be renovated for wealthy people. The government allocated funds to absorb a wave of immigrants from the Soviet Union and to pay for benefits for immigrants from well-off countries. All of these actions indicated that Israel intended to leave Mizrahim on the bottom rung of the socioeconomic ladder. The public acclaim for the IDF and its commanders following victory in the war may have swept up many Mizrahim, but the vast majority were well aware of a fact that sociologists analyzed years later: the prestigious IDF combat forces, service in which conferred the status of Israeli identity in every sense of the word, were an Ashkenazi army. The air force that had destroyed the enemy's planes on the ground, the armored regiments, and the elite infantry units were manned almost entirely by Ashkenazim. Alongside them served a second-class IDF army lacking any aura, service in which provided no elevated status at all. The great majority of Mizrahim were channeled into that army, for reasons that included preconceptions built into the IDF's reception and sorting apparatus.[57] While many Mizrahim fought in combat units in the war, and about a tenth of the fifty-one soldiers who received the Chief of Staff Medal of Appreciation for their valor in the war were Mizrahim, they were not the public face of the victorious army. In addition, some of the early Panthers and their sympathizers had not even been conscripted because they had criminal records. As such, they felt no part of the general celebration.

The euphoria that followed the war thus did nothing to reduce Mizrahi frustration and anger. On the contrary, it exacerbated those feelings. News from the United States about its own Black Panther movement, from France about its student rebellion, and from the underground cells organizing all over Europe inspired these young Mizrahi men and women, who, with their darker skin, were often referred to disparagingly by Ashkenazim as "blacks." The radical leftist faction Matzpen helped them organize to rise up against discrimination and repression.

A great deal has been written about the Israeli Black Panthers' activity and views.[58] To summarize, as the War of Attrition that followed the 1967 war subsided in 1970, the Black Panthers commenced a series of demonstrations, some of them quiet and some fiery. Some Panthers were arrested during these protests and placed under preventative detention. They conducted operations that received extensive coverage in the media—for example, they stole milk bottles from the doorsteps of homes in the well-off Rehavia neighborhood in Jerusalem and gave them to needy families. They disrupted the Moroccan community's Mimouna festivities, to which cabinet members and other public figures had been invited. They also fought against Meir Kahane's extremist nationalist-religious Jewish Defense League. (One leading Panther, Saadia Marciano, was arrested for attempting to set fire to the league's offices.)[59] They demanded additional money for housing and education for the needy and left Golda Meir no choice but to meet with them and address their claims. (Meir's characterization of the Panthers following the meeting became classic: "They aren't nice").[60] They also compelled government agencies to address more seriously ethnic and social poverty and its causes.

At first, the Black Panthers did not address general political issues, but the treatment of the Palestinians was a subject that was in the air, for several reasons: first, young Mizrahim had social and economic connections with Palestinians; second, radical leftist groups were involved in Panther activities, a fact that Israeli security agencies stressed in their briefings for journalists; third, the fantasy of an Arab-Mizrahi alliance was making a reappearance in the Arab media throughout the Middle East. Some of the Panthers attended events alongside members of the PLO, which reinforced their ties to the radical anti-Zionist Left.[61] The image of the hotheaded Mizrahi Jew who hated Arabs, so pervasive in the 1960s, gave way to that of the a-national Mizrahi Jew, Arab in his culture and inclinations, who was liable at any moment to side with the country's Arabs and aim his pent-up violence at Ashkenazi Jews. The Panthers' opposition to immigration from the Soviet Union, or at the very least to paying out benefits to these immigrants, served their opponents as further evidence that their ties with Arabs were more important to them than the national ethos—just as with the Sephardim in Jaffa in 1908 with whom we opened this book.[62]

THE INTERNAL DEBATE

Not all the Panthers were interested in linking up with the radical Left, or with tying the Mizrahi struggle to that of the Palestinians. They were concerned that some of the Matzpen activists who joined them were not allies attentive to Mizrahi problems but instead were trying to take control of the struggle and direct it to their own ends. Furthermore, unlike Matzpen, the Panthers did not oppose the idea of the Jewish state. Rather, they opposed the inequality that the state had created. So they did not feel entirely comfortable with the radical leftist discourse. Some, indeed, had ties to the right-wing nationalist Herut party, either personally or by way of family members. And some of them had been involved in fights with Arabs before the Black Panthers were founded. They also realized that tying themselves to Matzpen was liable to cost them considerable public support. In interviews with the press, they expressed, from time to time, dissatisfaction with the way the press linked them to Matzpen.[63] It's worth keeping in mind a public opinion poll conducted in 1968, which asked 1,860 Israelis whether the state should continue to rule the territories. A full 94 percent answered in the affirmative, 3 percent in the negative; the rest said that they "did not know the place." This made it clear that calls for Israeli-Palestinian equality or withdrawal from the territories would be detrimental to gaining public sympathy.[64]

Nevertheless, the Panthers had something of a Mizrahi-Palestinian link. "We were not scared of Arabs, not in Morocco and not here," recounted Panther leader Reuven Abergel, who was a decade older than his colleagues. "I had Arab friends even when there was the border. We would do all sorts of little deals on either side of the fences. On the sixth day of the war I already went to a friend at Herod's Gate and slept at his place. Our connection was to there, to the Nablus Gate and Arab Musrara. Not to Rehavia and Talbiya."

There was also an economic link—Abergel and other young Mizrahim opened business partnerships with Palestinians from East Jerusalem and Ramallah—watermelon stands, clubs, and pubs. Policemen and inspectors targeted these businesses and shut them down.[65] The theoretical talk about "common oppression" was, for some of them, a lived reality. Matzpen activist Nabil Saad recalled that when he was in jail in October 1969, he met Charlie Biton, Saadia Marciano, and Haim Tourjeman, who had been detained for breaking into the Maki club in Musrara. "We conducted daily 'home meetings' on the political situation and the standing of Arab-Jews in Israel, and we agreed to meet after we were released. Indeed, the meeting took place in 1970, after we were all released," he said.[66]

The Panthers thus did not assimilate—indeed, they refused to accept—the total sum of Israel's accepted truths. As part of searching for their own way, they accepted invitations to meet with radical leftist groups in Italy. Uri Avnery, a bitter opponent of Matzpen at the time (he supported a two-state solution to the Israeli-Palestinian dispute, while Matzpen advocated a single democratic state), claimed in *Haolam Hazeh*, the weekly he edited and used as a mouthpiece, "It is almost certain that the Panthers themselves did not understand the nature of the conference that invited them, that it supported the extreme *fedayun* [Palestinian guerrilla] organizations."[67] Knesset member Menachem Porush (Agudat Yisra'el), who served also as deputy mayor of Jerusalem, agreed with Avnery. "This group has been exploited by outside elements who have fitted out these young people with a political ideology entirely unfamiliar to them. It is liable to fan the flames of passion, an amalgamation of the disgruntled for deconstructive actions against the background of personal, ethnic, and other discrimination."[68] Among the Panthers themselves, there were those who opposed this view. In July 1971, Panther activist Eddy Malka notified the press that the Panthers had guns and that foreign leftist elements were appointing the delegation to the conference in Italy. The Panthers rejected the accusations, arguing that well-off Mizrahi businessmen had donated to support the delegation. They expelled Malka from the movement.[69]

Political differences, organizational and financial difficulties, and lack of experience were among the causes of the movement's internal weakness. On top of these came defamation and attacks from outside, and establishment attempts to bring central figures in the movement over to their side. It's also worth noting that despite the Panthers' high visibility in the public discourse, some favorable press coverage, and the movement's successful organization of relatively large protests, and despite Mizrahi support for their demands, the Black Panthers never became a mass movement. Some Mizrahim rejected the talk of discrimination and believed that individuals could break away from the path that the social structure had laid out for them if they simply made the necessary effort. Others rejected the alliance with the Left. Some objected to the Panthers' tactics, and others were already tied to other political parties. And a very large number did not believe that anything could be changed by means of a public struggle. The majority, as usual, was silent.

In advance of the elections to the Eighth Knesset, scheduled for October 30, 1973, and then postponed to December 31 because of the Yom Kippur War, the Panthers formed a political party to run a slate called the Black Panthers: Israeli Democrats. The expelled Eddy Malka ran on a rival slate of his own, which he called, after the Israeli national colors, Blue-White Panthers. The Black Panthers fell just short of the threshold for Knesset representation. Malka received fewer than half the needed votes.[70] One important reason for this, though not the only one, was the war and the government's failures in the lead-up to it. With the focus on the war, social issues dropped off the public agenda.

TERROR ATTACKS AND MIZRAHIM IN POLITICS

The Likud, an alliance of right-wing parties led by Menachem Begin and his Herut faction, won the next election, in 1977. The Likud won primarily thanks to the shift of Mizrahi votes from Labor (Mapai) to the Likud. The Mizrahim were attracted by Herut's long history of criticism of Mapai's handling of immigrant absorption. But there were also deeper processes and contemporary factors that caused Mapai's downfall after forty-seven years of leadership. The ruling party was rocked by a series of corruption scandals. More seriously, hubris caused the party and the security establishment to fail to prepare for war and to ignore the warning signs leading up to it in 1973. The public held the party leadership responsible for the success of the Arab offensive at the start of the war and for the bloody toll it took on IDF soldiers fighting to beat back the Egyptian and Syrian offensives. A new centrist party, the Democratic Movement for Change (DMC, or Dash in Hebrew), offered disenchanted Labor voters a way of casting a protest vote that did not involve supporting Begin. On top of all this, the period after the war was marked by deadly terror attacks by Palestinian guerillas. In 1974, Palestinian militant factions adopted a new tactic in which armed bands crossed the border and penetrated Israeli settlements, where they took hostages while killing Israelis in their paths. That year, Palestinian contingents staged such operations in the northern city of Kiryat Shmona (on April 11, in which sixteen local residents and two soldiers were killed); in Ma'alot (on May 15, where children visiting from a school in nearby Safed were captured—twenty-two of them were killed, along with four other civilians and a soldier); in Kibbutz Shamir (on June 13; three women were killed); in Nahariya (on June 25; a mother and two of her children and an IDF soldier died); and in Beit She'an (on November 19; four civilians were killed).

Photographs of these attacks, the shattered families, the wailing children, and the demonstrations that erupted against the background of the public housing projects that were so characteristic of development towns reached every home in Israel via the country's single television station. The public's heart went out to the victims and their families, especially among those who lived in similar conditions. Prime Minister Golda Meir declared that "the brutal attacks have brought to the fore once again the situation and the problems of the development towns in the Galilee." Labor member of the Knesset Rabbi Menachem Hacohen argued that it was essential to see that "the population [in the development towns] consists nearly entirely of a single type of people. It is something that must be rectified, and the solution is that [established Israelis] must move from the city to the development towns."[71]

Hacohen's call to action was futile. Hardly anyone moved from the big cities to the northern frontier, and the development towns there continued, certainly until the wave of immigration from the former Soviet Union in the 1990s, to be populated largely by North African immigrants. "In this way the bodies of Mizrahim became the state's living [border] fence," Ella Shohat wrote about the policy of population dispersal pursued by the settlement agencies in the 1950s and 1960s.[72]

But the Mizrahim were not the only ones serving as a living border fence. So were the largely Ashkenazi residents of the kibbutzim and established settlements. The latter, however, were in a much better socioeconomic position and had much better defenses. In the wake of these attacks, the Herut party's Central Committee held a comprehensive discussion on the plight of the Mizrahim in the development towns. A delegate named Dahan (the record does not give his first name) offered a lengthy survey of the Mizrahi struggle. "We shouted 'bread and work' and the police used force to break up the demonstration. . . . The young people left, anyone who had a bit of money and a chance of getting absorbed somewhere else fled as fast as they could. . . . We asked for meetings with cabinet ministers, they treated us with contempt. When we sent the prime minister a request to meet with her so that we could speak to her about our troubles, she was too busy to receive the not nice people from Ma'alot," he said, pointedly using an expression that linked the struggle of the development towns to that of the Black Panthers in Jerusalem. "We ask for a chance to live, a chance to develop, a chance to grow up and to bring up our children, to be proud that we live in Ma'alot, and a chance to be proud that we are members of Edot Hamizrah. In Morocco I fought for my right to be a Jew and here in Israel I fight for my right to be Israeli." Begin was impressed by the presentation and appointed a delegation representing the Likud leadership to visit Ma'alot to listen to the inhabitants. At this time, Herut was bringing Mizrahim into the party's institutions as part of an effort to expand its base. The Central Committee, which had sixty-seven members in 1966, expanded to more than six hundred in 1977; in 1966, only 20 percent of the body's members were Mizrahim, but on the eve of Begin's victory they held 40 percent of the seats.[73]

The infiltration of Palestinian guerillas over the border exacerbated tensions between Mizrahim and Arabs in Israel. After the attack in Kiryat Shmona, local residents demonstrated, demanding that Arab laborers be banned from working in the city. The local Mapam Histadrut coordinator explained the protest in both cultural and political terms. "The problem is that most of the population comes from Islamic countries and their mentality is that they don't believe the gentiles, and when there is a horrendous murder of this sort, it obviously intensifies hostility," he said. "Some say that they'll take revenge. There are local political forces, especially on the right, who are exploiting the situation to make political capital." Minister of Police Shlomo Hillel was attacked when he attended the funeral of the victims; the policemen escorting him had to clear a path for him through the angry crowd.[74] That Hillel himself was Mizrahi made no difference. Perhaps because he was an Iraqi rather than a North African Jew, the North Africans of Kiryat Shmona did not see him as one of them, or perhaps they were simply so angry at the Labor government that they could not stand the presence of any official representative, no matter what ethnicity. Or perhaps, as the columnist Abu Ghassan wrote in the East Jerusalem Arabic daily *Al-Sha'ab*, Hillel had entered the government to represent Edot Hamizrah but, after being appointed, "acted as if he came to Israel from Germany, France, or the United States. The Sephardim thought that he was their representative, but he turned out to be just another member of the Ashkenazi clique. He forgot where he came from."[75] It seems more likely that the anger directed at Hillel in Kiryat Shmona grew out of frustration with his failure to advocate a tougher anti-Palestinian policy, not his failure, as a Mizrahi Jew, to serve as a mediator in the cause of better understanding between Jews and Arabs, as Abu Ghassan deluded himself into thinking.

In Kiryat Shmona, the attack also brought back the old anti-Arab discourse. One of its prime spokesmen was Rabbi Tzfaniah Drori, who had studied under Rabbi Zvi Yehuda Kook at the Mercaz Harav Yeshiva. Drori had arrived in the city about six years earlier, sent by his teacher to bring Torah learning to the beleaguered development town. He declared that Druze laborers from the Golan Heights were receiving higher wages than Jewish wageworkers, that they paid less for taxi licenses, and that they set up stands on the city's market days without paying rent for them, as the city's Jews had to do. Worst of all, "there's a story about a laborer who gave a gift to the woman who owned the apartment where he was working—a dress. A person who brings a dress can also raise it. This is a thing that has caused a crisis in families," Drori maintained. "There are a lot of handsome young men among them . . . and these young men know how to succeed with our girls better than our boys know how to do." The terrorist attack clearly was not at the center of his attention. Following the attack, Drori founded a yeshiva in the city to strengthen the city spiritually and morally.[76]

The attack in Kiryat Shmona was carried out by the Popular Front–General Command faction commanded by Ahmed Jibril. It was part of the integrated Palestinian military and diplomatic offensive that the Palestinians commenced after the Yom Kippur War, in the wake of profound regional political changes. Israel responded on the military front while refusing to reexamine the fundamental assumptions on which its attitude toward the Palestinians was based.

NAYEF HAWATMEH: FROM AN INTERVIEW IN *YEDIOT AHARONOT* TO THE ATTACK IN MA'ALOT

The year 1974 was a dramatic one for the PLO. Following the Yom Kippur War and the international call for a regional peace initiative, the organization began recalibrating its strategy. Its constituent movements and leaders disagreed intensely about what should be done. Some of them advocated carrying on with the armed struggle and making no compromises, while others advocated taking part in the diplomatic process. The Democratic Front for the Liberation of Palestine, headed by Nayef Hawatmeh, led the camp that supported talks. He took the unusual step of granting an extensive interview to an American journalist writing for the mass-circulation Israeli daily *Yediot Aharonot*, in which he laid out his thinking about how peace could be achieved. The newspaper's willingness to publish the interview was itself pathbreaking, given the government's position and the public conviction that the PLO was the country's archenemy and that any contact with it was treasonous. But the Democratic Front felt that it also needed to prove that it had not abandoned the armed struggle. Both the organizations that advocated negotiation and those that opposed it sent terrorists into Israel to carry out hostage-taking operations. On the morning of May 14, 1974, the day before the anniversary of the Nakba, as observed by the Palestinians, a three-man Democratic Front contingent crossed into Israel from Lebanon with the aim of taking hostages and demanding the release of Palestinian prisoners held by Israel. As the guerrillas made their way toward one of Ma'alot's elementary schools, they murdered a driver who was on her way home and then two parents and their four-year-old son in their apartment at the edge of the city. At the school, they found dozens of students from a religious high school in Safed who had slept in the school building overnight. They took the students hostage and sent a message out with a student they freed demanding the release of twenty prisoners from Israeli jails. Among the prisoners were Fawzi Nimr, Fatima Barnawi, and the Ma'alabe brothers.

The government at the time was a transitional one. Golda Meir had announced her resignation a few weeks earlier because of the political and intelligence failures connected to the war, but she was still serving as prime minister. Unexpectedly, she supported negotiating with the hostage takers and releasing the prisoners. Ariel Sharon, a celebrated IDF commander and hero of the recent war, then serving as a member of the Likud opposition in the Knesset, took the same position. Minister of Defense Moshe Dayan opposed it. He maintained that Israel should never cave in to terror. Dayan persuaded Meir to approve a military operation to free the hostages. The elite IDF General Staff Reconnaissance Unit (better known as Sayeret Matkal) was sent in. But the mission was marred by a series of mistakes. The Israeli sniper who fired the first shot did not neutralize the terrorist who was in a lookout post. He was only slightly wounded and sprang into action. The force that stormed the school entered the wrong classroom on the wrong floor. The terrorists began shooting the students, killing twenty-two of them. Hawatmeh blamed Israel for their deaths, on the grounds that the government had refused to negotiate. Israel blamed the murderers.[77] For many Israelis, nothing was more emblematic of the pointlessness of dialogue with the Palestinians than the juxtaposition of Hawatmeh's call for peace negotiations in *Yediot Aharonot* and the horrifying massacre that his minions carried out against these high school students.

ARAFAT'S SPEECH AT THE UNITED NATIONS AND THE TERROR ATTACK IN BEIT SHE'AN

The internal Palestinian debate led the PLO to draft the hybrid program known as the Ten Point Program, approved in June 1974. The gist of it was the continuation of the armed struggle, no recognition for the State of Israel, and the willingness to establish a Palestinian national entity on a part of the territory of Palestine (meaning the West Bank and Gaza Strip) while continuing the struggle to liberate it all. It marked a change in the PLO's previous position, which had opposed any partial political settlement in the West Bank and Gaza Strip, seeing such an arrangement as shameful surrender and treason. The Popular Front for the Liberation of Palestine, a Marxist faction led by George Habash, opposed the plan, as did other elements in the PLO. The opponents claimed that it would be detrimental to the Palestinian will to continue the struggle and would put an end to hopes for the establishment of a Palestinian state that comprised all of Palestine. The provision that the struggle would continue after the establishment of a Palestinian entity in the West Bank and Gaza Strip was no more than lip service, they charged. The program's supporters denied this charge and reiterated their commitment to the armed struggle. The opponents of the compromise, among them Jibril's organization, which had carried out the attack in Kiryat Shmona, left the PLO and established the Rejectionist Front.

In October of that year, the Arab League named the PLO the only legitimate representative of the Palestinian people (thus compelling Jordan to cede its claim to represent the inhabitants of the West Bank). The decision gave the PLO international standing, and on November 13 Yasser Arafat gave a speech before the United Nations General Assembly. For the PLO and its chief, this was an unprecedented diplomatic coup, providing international recognition of the justice of the Palestinian struggle for self-determination and recognition of the PLO as the representative of the Palestinian nation as a whole. Arafat rose to speak wearing a pistol on his hip. "Today I have come bearing an olive branch and a freedom-fighter's gun," he concluded. "Do not let the olive branch fall from my hand."

In his speech, Arafat reiterated the traditional Palestinian claim that Zionism is a colonial movement. He also referred to the Mizrahim. "The enemy we face has a long record of hostility even towards the Jews themselves, for there is within the Zionist entity a built-in racism against Oriental Jews," he maintained.[78] He saw these Jews as Arabs. In a different speech, he asserted that 1.5 million Arabs lived in Israel—half a million Muslim and Christian Arabs and a million Arab Jews. His vision, he said, was a single democratic state in which Jews, Muslims, and Christians would live in peace and fraternity.[79] Keep in mind that the idea of two states was, for the PLO mainstream, a real concession, never the ideal.

Five days after Arafat's UN speech, a Democratic Front detachment entered Beit She'an and seized the home of the Bibas family, killing in the process two neighbors and the parents of the family, after they had succeeded in helping their children flee. The Democratic Front was, as noted, a leader of that stream in the PLO that advocated negotiation. But, again, it wanted to prove that it would not abandon the armed struggle until Israel shed its Zionist character and allowed the establishment of a single democratic state between the Jordan River and the Mediterranean Sea.

The members of the detachment spent several hours in the Bibas family's apartment. Residents of neighboring apartments fled their homes by leaping from their windows. Other city inhabitants watched the events from a safe distance or helped evacuate the neighbors. Television crews from Israel and around the world filmed the action. Some hours later, IDF forces, assisted by local residents, stormed the apartment and killed the assailants. In the immediate aftermath, the town's inhabitants voiced their frustration. A few entered the apartment, abused the bodies of the dead terrorists (and also the body of one of the dead Jews, which they mistook for that of one of the Arabs), threw them out of the apartment's window, and burned them in the street in front of the cameras. Public figures, among them city leaders such as David Levy, a Likud member of the Knesset, and Beit She'an's mayor, Yitzhak Kenan, condemned the act and noted that it had been carried out by a small number of delinquents.[80]

In 1974 as in 1929, Palestinian politicians evoked Palestinian-Mizrahi brotherhood, but the Jewish blood that was spilled was almost all Mizrahi blood. The Palestinians claimed that the bloodshed was due to Zionist obstinacy. Israel claimed that it was due to the Palestinian thirst for blood. With few exceptions, Israelis of all ethnic origins accepted the official Zionist version and were unified in their opposition to negotiations with the PLO. They were inclined to disregard the fact that, during this same period, Israel had killed many times more Palestinians, including civilians, in refugee camps in Lebanon.[81] We are acquainted with this rule—each side counts only its own dead and mourns only its own.

THE PALESTINIAN POLITICAL MESSAGE

The Popular Front–General Command terrorists who carried out the attack in Kiryat Shmona left a manifesto. Prime Minister Golda Meir read it before a special session of the Knesset. "We regret that we have addressed you in the language of the gun," it stated,

> because we have not yet found an attentive ear for our just demands for the liberation of our country from the Zionist conquerors. . . . We, the Popular Front Supreme [*sic*] Command, have not come to kill for the sake of killing, but to defend ourselves and to liberate our land from the yoke of Zionist racism that serves imperialism and which leads you to the edge of an abyss. . . . We in the Popular Front General Command have resolved to carry on our armed struggle against the Zionist state until its liquidation, and to establish in its place a democratic Palestinian state in which Jews and Arabs will live without regard to religion, race, and nationality.

Geula Cohen, a member of the Knesset for Herut, interrupted Meir's reading, crying out, "What's your purpose in reading that?" Meir replied, "I am reading it so that everyone will know," adding, "This is not a liberation movement. It is a murder movement."[82]

Cohen's interjection expressed her fear that some Israelis listening might be persuaded by the manifesto. But she had no real reason to worry. Opposition to talks with the PLO spanned ethnic and political boundaries. Take, for example, Amnon Rubinstein, then a legal scholar and later a liberal Ashkenazi member of the Knesset. "Those who were killed savagely and in cold blood . . . were refugees," he declared in the immediate wake of the attack. "They are those who escaped and fled to a land of refuge. They are the ones who were forced to leave the countries in which they were born—including the 'democratic secular Arab' states'—to find sanctuary in their own country. Their murderers are not refugees. They are people who come from countries that have everything—living space, wealth, power, friends, security, strength. Their victims are the true refugees."[83]

THE TRUE REFUGEES

It was a debate that continued to blaze. Were the immigrants from the Islamic world still refugees even though they had put down roots, as Rubinstein put it, "in their own country"? Did Rubinstein really believe that Palestinians uprooted from their villages, living in camps in Lebanon, were not refugees? Was he not aware of how the Palestinian refugees in Lebanon lived? Or did he know but resort to fiery rhetoric because of the pain he felt over the Israelis killed in the attacks, or perhaps to amass political capital? We can only guess at the answers to such questions. But his language shows how utterly unacceptable the Palestinian claims—and not just the murders—were to the average Israeli.

Only a tiny number of Israelis listened to the manifesto with an open mind. They were prepared to test the proposition that the Palestinians were indeed not interested in killing Jews but actually sought a democratic and egalitarian state. In their view, the automatic and bellicose Israeli response was harming both Jews and Arabs. One of them, Dani Sa'il, was a Black Panther. What set him apart even more from his associates was that he not only thought independently and spoke his mind but also took action.

THE MYSTERIOUS DISAPPEARANCE OF DANI SA'IL

Dani Sa'il was a prominent Panther activist, involved in the organization's activities in Jerusalem even though he lived outside the city. He was arrested several times—for example, after the Panthers' disruption of the Mimouna festivities in 1970. That operation was meant to show that it was the Panthers, not political functionaries with ties to the establishment, who represented Israeli Mizrahim. Sa'il lived in Ramla, a city with long experience of Jewish-Arab tensions, including of close relations and friendship between the two peoples. He was among those who had friends on the other side. On both the social and the political fronts he felt close to the Palestinians he met as part of his activity in overseas gatherings in which the Panthers participated. At the end of 1972, he and Charlie Biton attended a meeting of radical leftist organizations. Angela Davis was there, as were members of the Red Army Faction (Baader-Meinhof Group) of Germany, the Japanese Red Army, the Irish Republican Army, and the PLO. When they returned, Sa'il was detained by the Shabak for interrogation for several days. At the time, he headed the Tel Aviv branch of the Black Panthers. But after the Yom Kippur War, he left the organization, as did another Iraqi Panther, Kochavi Shemesh of Jerusalem. Together, they founded an organization called the Black Revolutionary Force.[84]

Two years later, Sa'il began to fashion operational ties to the Popular Front for the Liberation of Palestine, without telling Shemesh. A Popular Front activist, Abd al-Alim Da'na, of Hebron, later clearly recalled the Israeli who assisted Palestinian combat activity, an unprecedented phenomenon in many respects. "The Ashkenazim controlled the country and the Mizrahim lived in shameful conditions," Da'na said about the background to what happened. "The Black Panthers were fighting against that situation. I met with Panther leader Daniel Eliayhu Sasson Sa'il, who told me that he opposed the Zionist movement and was prepared to struggle against it by all means, including the armed struggle against the racist state and the racist Zionist movement, which he saw as anti-Jewish. He was a practical man and advocated in principle less talk and more action. I felt that he was a cultured Mizrahi and connected more to the East than to the West."[85]

In the early summer of 1975, an IDF spokesman announced the capture of a Palestinian terrorist contingent that had purchased stolen IDF weapons through Sa'il. The Palestinians confessed that they had received from Sa'il explosives valued at 12,000 Israeli pounds (about $1,900 in 1975 dollars).[86] Da'na was one of the members of the contingent. Sa'il, who was in Europe at the time and feared arrest, did not return to Israel. In a phone call with Kochavi Shemesh, he denied the allegations.[87] For two decades no one knew where he was, including his family and close friends. It was the Israeli director-producer David Fisher who discovered, while working on his documentary *Buried Alive* (1996), that Sa'il was buried in Baghdad, so Sa'il's wife, Mazal, got rabbinical permission to remarry.

Sa'il was an exception among Black Panthers who believed that, to a certain extent, Palestinians and Mizrahim had suffered the same fate. Sa'il seems to have shown that the established European Zionist nightmare of a Mizrahi-Arab alliance against Zionism was not a total fantasy. But he was actually the exception that proved the rule—his friends did not join in his actions and did not defend them.

POLITICAL CONTACTS AND DIFFERENCES OF OPINION

In March 1975, Panthers Reuven Abergel, Charlie Biton, and Mony Yakim flew to Paris to seek support for their struggle and to meet with a PLO representative. They wanted to boost the organization's pragmatic stream and presumed that it would be easier for them, as Mizrahim, to engage in talks with the Palestinians than it would be for Ashkenazi Israelis. From Paris they also issued a call to Syria's president, Hafez al-Assad, to treat Syrian Jews humanely. Like the old Sephardi leadership at the beginning of the British Mandate, they believed that, as Mizrahim, they could engage in dialogue with the Arab world. But some members of the movement opposed contact with the PLO. "We protest the criminal use of funds donated for poor children that are being wasted for improper purposes such as overseas trips aimed at establishing contacts with terrorist organizations," these opponents wrote.[88]

This was more than an attempt to sully the names of the travelers by accusing them of misusing movement funds. There were real differences of opinion among the Black Panthers over whether the movement ought to offer a Mizrahi alternative to Israel's tough policy toward the Palestinians. The Panthers' first national convention, convened in September 1975, made a step in that direction. In its concluding resolutions, it declared that "to hold on to the territories is a barren and dangerous dream that led to the Yom Kippur War. . . . The Black Panther movement states that without a solution to the Palestinian problem there can be no peace in the Middle East." At the same time, the Panthers rejected the solution proposed by the Palestinians. "Peace will not be achieved by the liquidation of the State of Israel and the establishment of a secular democratic state, as the Palestinians today demand," the convention resolved. "A just peace can only be achieved on the basis of mutual recognition between Israel and the Palestinians, because Israel can be the common homeland of the two nations."[89]

TWO NATIONS

These are the most important two words in the resolution. The mainstream Palestinian view was that Judaism is a religion, not a nation. The Palestinian left-wing front maintained that no Jewish-Israeli nation had come into existence in Israel, and that therefore there was no basis for speaking about two nations or a binational solution. The Panthers, in contrast, asserted that there was a Jewish nation and that it had a right of self-determination. In this, they adhered to the general Jewish-Israeli view. That was also Matzpen's position. Even though Matzpen viewed Zionism as a colonial project that had developed artificially at the expense of the Palestinians, its members maintained that the Jewish political entity that had established itself in Israel was of a manifestly national character (it had a territory, culture, and common language). This meant that the Jewish-Israeli nation had come into being and had a right of self-determination (as opposed to the "Jewish people," who had no such right). The Palestinian Left rejected this stance. "It's a fantastic intellectual compromise," said the Popular Front's ideologue and spokesman Ghassan Kanafani (who was assassinated by the Mossad in July 1972). "It means that every group of colonialists that conquers an area and lives in it for a certain time can justify its presence there by claiming that it has developed into a nation."[90]

The decision that all of Palestine/Israel is the common homeland of two nations—the doctrine that Sephardi thinkers had championed at the beginning of the Mandate—was accepted at the Black Panther convention by a vote of twenty-seven to twenty, revealing a very real split on the Palestinian question. In advance of the elections to the Ninth Knesset in 1977, the rift took on a partisan character, as members of the movement chose to run for office on different slates, in part in accordance with their stand on the Palestinian issue. Charlie Biton and Kochavi Shemesh ran on the Arab-Jewish Hadash slate, dominated by Rakah, the New Communist List; Saadia Marciano joined the Zionist Left, running on the Sheli slate; and Shalom Cohen joined the Democratic Movement for Change, led by former IDF Chief of Staff Yigael Yadin.[91] Many Mizrahi voters, for their part, voted for the Right, ending the rule of Mapai, which dated to two decades before the establishment of the state and which had endured for twenty-nine years thereafter.

Hadash, including Charlie Biton, won some sixty-four thousand Arab votes and ten thousand Jewish votes. "In Jerusalem, in the Katamonim neighborhood and in the Musrara neighborhood, which is Charlie Biton's 'stronghold,'" *Maariv* reported, "only 700 people voted for Rakah."[92] Even after 1967, the few activists who supported a Mizrahi-Arab alliance failed to gain the support of the masses.

CHAPTER 5

From Political Realignment to Political Assassination, 1977–1995

In which we will consider how the PLO addressed the Israeli political realignment and why, in its wake, and following the First Lebanon War, Jewish ethnicity grew increasingly aligned with political outlook. We will examine the attitudes of the three major social movements—Gush Emunim, the Sephardi teshuva movement, and Peace Now—and how these in turn led to the hardening of Israel's ethnopolitical map. This will lead us to reflect on different public attitudes toward acts of revenge committed by Mizrahim and Ashkenazim against Arabs. Yitzhak Rabin's victory in the election of 1992 also requires our attention. We will delve into the role that the Sephardi spiritual and political leader Rabbi Ovadia Yosef played in the peace process, and we will share his profound grief over Rabin's assassination.

THE POLITICAL REALIGNMENT AND THE MIZRAHIM: MAHMOUD ABBAS'S ANALYSIS

Mahmoud Abbas, also known as Abu Mazen, who serves today as the chairman of the PLO and the president of the Palestinian Authority, was a member of the PLO's Executive Committee in 1977. He was the PLO's resident Israeli affairs expert. After Israel's political upheaval of 1977, he provided a sociopolitical analysis of the election in an interview in a PLO periodical. He was extremely optimistic. The interest the Arab world was taking in the election results was a new phenomenon, he said, and it meant that the region was entering an era of peace. "Anyone who says that the Israeli people voted against peace is mistaken," he maintained. "The election results are the product of internal social issues." After all, he noted, the Likud's positions on the Palestinian question were very similar to those of the hawks in the Alignment (the Labor-Mapam slate). He then went on to analyze the ethnic issue in Israel:

> Zionism never made inroads among the Arab Jews. There was no antisemitism in the Arab world, and the proof of that is that [the Arab Jews] did not immigrate to Palestine, only after the establishment of the State of Israel, and they did not take part in founding it. That despite the fact that they lived near the "Promised Land." The Arab Jews lived lives of dignity and participated in Arab public life, and we know that the Jews of Baghdad were the first to fight against the Zionist office in Baghdad in the years 1921–1922. After the establishment of Israel, the Arab-Zionist-British collusion began . . . to expel the Jews through a deal with the reactionary Arab regimes.

In Israel, Abbas continued, the Mizrahim suffered from racial discrimination, because Zionism was racist not only toward Arabs but also toward Arab Jews. They were the victims of bias in employment, housing, and education, and were kept out of high public positions. The unfortunate thing was that their oppression at the hands of the European Zionists had made them hard-hearted toward the Arabs.

The solution? "They have no way out other than to return to the Arab countries," Abbas maintained. "There are two reasons that compel us to demand that the Arab Jews be allowed to return to their original countries: (1) so as to help them extricate themselves from exploitation and discrimination against them; (2) to remedy the historical injustice committed by several Arab regimes [that pushed them out]." Not every Jew was a Zionist, Abbas stressed. "Many Jews stand against Zionism, which they see as having created a Jewish problem, not as having solved one, as the Zionists claim."[1]

ALL WRONG, ABU MAZEN, ALL WRONG

Abbas was right about one thing but wrong about many others. He was correct in maintaining that Mizrahim did not necessarily support the Likud just because they agreed with its positions on the conflict. A study performed after the 1977 elections found that a bit more than half of the Mizrahim of dovish persuasions (they were categorized as doves if they opposed further

Jewish settlement in the West Bank and Gaza Strip) voted for the Likud. These votes derived from their socioeconomic position and their ethnic origin, not from support for the Likud's positions on foreign policy and the Israel-Arab conflict.[2]

Beyond that, Abbas echoed the classic Arab historical analysis, but not the actual experience of Jews in the Islamic world. His understanding of the fissures in Israeli society was deficient, and his presumption that many Israelis would want to return to the Arab states from which they came was simply baseless. Perhaps he thought that Matzpen and the Black Panthers represented broader currents than they actually did (if so, he also was mistaken in thinking that they advocated that Mizrahi Jews return to the Arab countries). It may well be that his hope for a united Mizrahi-Palestinian front of Zionism's victims blinded him to a number of fundamental truths. The first of these was that, despite what divided them, and despite discrimination and their differences of opinion, Jews from both Europe and the Islamic world saw themselves as members of a single Jewish nation. Unlike the PLO, they did not claim that no such nation existed. Second, the mobilizing spirit of Jewish nationalism was a no less powerful influence on Jews from the Islamic world than it was on Ashkenazim. Third, the vast majority of Mizrahi Jews had no interest in returning to the countries of their birth, most of which were ruled by repressive regimes and offered a much lower standard of living than Israel did. Fourth, most of those who did leave Israel sought their fortunes in the prosperous West, not in the countries of their birth (just like many Muslims and Christians who left those same countries for Europe and North America). Only a handful, before, during, and after the 1970s, returned whither they had come. Fifth, as much as Israelis yearned for peace at the time of Abbas's interview, they were focused on Egypt, not the Palestinians.

When Menachem Begin entered the prime minister's office, he carried on the previous Labor governments' efforts to achieve a separate peace with Egypt. Two years earlier, in the summer of 1975, during the debate over the conclusion of an interim agreement in the Sinai Peninsula, Begin had fiercely attacked Prime Minister Yitzhak Rabin. Herut's young guard, along with Gush Emunim and other groups, had staged noisy demonstrations in Jerusalem's streets against the agreements, blocking roads and crying, "Rabin's a motherfucker!"[3] Seventeen months after entering office, Begin brought the efforts to a successful conclusion by signing a historic agreement. That same month, in November 1979, demonstrators in Jerusalem chanted, "Begin's a motherfucker!" It was an unusual catcall, one that neither before nor since has resonated in Israeli ears the same way that calling Rabin or his defense minister, Shimon Peres, a motherfucker did. But the background was not politics—it was ethnicity and class.

"BEGIN IS A MOTHERFUCKER"

During the decade prior to winning the election, Begin had avoided explicitly identifying himself with the Mizrahi struggle. He distanced himself in particular from the Black Panther movement. This was the opposite of the tactics of the activists from the Jerusalem branch of his Herut party, who helped the Panthers organize their demonstrations. This does not mean that Begin disregarded the Mizrahi plight. As we have seen, he was very much aware of the harsh realities in the underprivileged neighborhoods and development towns inhabited primarily by Mizrahim. He brought Mizrahim into the Likud's Central Committee and was attentive to the inhabitants of the periphery. But at that point he preferred a discourse of unity and care for the downtrodden to an explicitly ethnic message. His detachment with regard to the Panthers had several causes. Begin wanted to fashion himself as a respectable defender of democracy (quite different from the image he projected in the 1950s), and that led him to take a step back from the Panthers and their image as delinquents. Furthermore, his Herut party's traditional leadership (the so-called fighting family and its "princes," the sons and daughters of this founding generation) were part of the middle class that the Panthers attacked, as were the members of the Liberal Party, with which Herut had allied in the Likud. Furthermore, Begin supported immigration from the Soviet Union and believed that an influx of Soviet immigrants would make it possible for Israel to maintain its rule over all of the historic Land of Israel. He was also appalled by the Panthers who were talking with the PLO.[4] Nevertheless, for a variety of reasons, he gained support from a wide swathe of Mizrahim. These included his respectful attitude toward Jewish religion and tradition, his consistent critique of Mapai, his likening of the exclusion of the Mizrahim from mainstream Israeli society to that suffered also by Herut's partisans, his opening of the Likud Central Committee to Mizrahim, and the affection he had displayed toward Edot Hamizrah since his days as the commander of Etzel. Indeed, one of his government's first initiatives was to launch a program to rehabilitate the country's public housing projects in underprivileged neighborhoods. While that program ran into difficulties and complications, Mizrahim gave him credit for it. In fact, his government's free-market economic program caused prices to rise, hitting the weakest parts of Israeli society, which were primarily Mizrahi. In response, the hard core of activists from the underprivileged neighborhoods, especially the Panthers and other protest movements not allied with the Likud, staged a series of demonstrations against the government's policies.

"What began with three demonstrations at three different points in the city quickly took on the character of a general riot, spreading like a fire in a bramble field through every neighborhood in the city," *Maariv* reported in November 1979.

> Fourteen policemen, among them Southern District Police Commander Arie Ibtzen, were wounded in the disturbances. The rioters overturned a police car at the Shmuel Hanavi–Bar-Ilan intersection, smashed its windows, and set it on fire as the demonstrators cheered. . . . At the gas station intersection in Katamon, dozens of demonstrators overturned a car of the police's Special Branch, and stole weapons and a portable radio set, which were later found and returned to the police. After that, the mob stormed a branch of the Discount Bank and smashed all its windows. . . . In Shmuel Hanavi they burned the national flag, crying, "Begin is a motherfucker."

Panther leaders Charlie Biton and Saadia Marciano were among the organizers, alongside Yaakov Yonah, a leader of another protest group that had emerged out of Jerusalem's underprivileged neighborhoods, the Ohalim (Tents) movement. The street fighting continued for many long hours. Even "in the area of the Damascus Gate [of the Old City], a group of young Arabs organized and began throwing stones at passing cars," *Maariv* reported. It was a rare moment of Mizrahi-Arab anti-establishment solidarity, in which Begin was a motherfucker in the eyes of both Jewish demonstrators from the underprivileged neighborhoods and Arabs.[5] The same month, the Panthers staged a large demonstration at the West Bank settlement of Elazar, south of Jerusalem. Four buses directed by Biton and Marciano arrived there and protested the government's allotment of funds to the settlements at the expense of the poor neighborhoods. IDF forces commanded by Bethlehem's military governor arrived, and the governor ordered the Panthers to leave. They refused but said they would not resist the soldiers, who dragged them one by one onto the buses.

"The Panthers cursed [our] religion and God, called [the minister of the interior and police and leader of the National Religious Party] Yosef

Burg a 'pig son of a pig' and rampaged," *Maariv* quoted Yehuda Shekel, an Elazar settler, as saying. "There was real racist hatred in their behavior. They shouted 'vuzvuzim' [a derogatory term for Ashkenazim] at us and inflamed [the protesters] against us." During the event, the settlement's security officer fired his gun over the heads of the demonstrators. (He later claimed that he had received an alert from the military government that a terror attack was imminent.) Gush Emunim issued a statement: "The time has come for the government to decide who are its best citizens—Peace Now, the Panthers, [Nablus mayor] Bassam Shakaa—or the people of the settlements." It called on all those interested in solving their housing problems to come live in Judea and Samaria (the official Israeli term for the West Bank).[6]

Many responded to that call, but not necessarily because they had become enamored of Gush Emunim's "Greater Israel" ideology. It presumably had a lot to do with the benefits that Likud governments offered to Israelis who settled in the territories. In 1983, Mizrahim made up at least 30 percent of all such settlers; Ashkenazim made up 36 percent. (The Central Bureau of Statistics did not provide data for the rest because they were native-born Israelis.) So, while the Gush Emunim elite remained largely Ashkenazi and religious, that was not the profile of many of the settlers over the Green Line, especially—but not only—those who lived in urban settlements. In the years that followed, Mizrahim who grew up in development towns and underprivileged city neighborhoods would play an increasingly important role in populating urban and community settlements in the Sinai Peninsula's Gush Katif salient and in Judea and Samaria.[7]

THE FIRST TO NOTICE

The first observer to predict that Mizrahim would be settled in the territories was the Egyptian newspaper *Akhbar al-Yom*, which reported in February 1969 that the Israeli government was beginning to implement the Allon Plan, including the establishment of settlements in the Jordan Valley and other sparsely populated parts of the West Bank. According to the newspaper, Druze and Mizrahim would be sent to these areas.[8] The reference to the Druze is another example of how hard it is for societies in conflict to understand one another. And, unconnected to that, two years after that article's appearance, a group of Moroccan Jews from Kiryat Malakhi organized to settle in Sinai. Toward the end of 1971, they founded a moshav called Di-Zahav at Dahab, on the peninsula's southeastern coast. "I've heard from the Alliance of Moroccans in Israel," Shefi Gabbai wrote in *Davar*, "that the group seeks to prove that in Israel it is possible to find challenges other than demonstrations and joining the Black Panthers." The Dahab settlement was, Gabbai wrote, the first pioneering act by young people from development towns.[9] Settlement in the territories could thus serve the Mizrahim as a path into the pioneering ethos. Even more, it offered a solution to the housing shortages and high population density in the underprivileged neighborhoods.

Both Israeli institutions and many Mizrahim grasped this, which is why the putatively joint Jewish-Arab demonstration in Jerusalem and the demonstration in Gush Etzion did not rouse any real concern about a Mizrahi-Arab alliance against the establishment or the settlements. The peace process with Egypt, by contrast, reawakened an old anxiety—that of an Israel swamped by the Levant.

THE ANXIETIES COMMITTEE

In 1978, the Ministry of Labor and Welfare set up a commission composed of scholars and public figures and headed by the political scientist Raphaella Bilski to study the implications of peace for the State of Israel, including possible negative impacts. "Opening the borders with Egypt will bring Israeli society into a close encounter with Egyptian society," the members of the commission feared. "Some argue that such an encounter will necessarily lead to the Levanization of Israeli society, given that Israel has yet to consolidate a clear Jewish culture, and given that half of Israel's Jewish population originated in Islamic countries. Therefore, in the absence of a uniting purpose—an external enemy—Israeli society will find itself in an exposed state, exacerbating the trend toward the disintegration of Israeli society as a unique Jewish society." They also suggested that the split between Mizrahim and Ashkenazim would grow and that interreligious marriages would multiply.[10] The novelist Amos Kenan argued, at a point when the peace talks were in crisis, that Edot Hamizrah support for the negotiations terrified the Begin government. "There was a scary moment," he wrote sarcastically.

> During [Egyptian president Anwar] Sadat's visit [to Jerusalem], it was scary to see the enthusiasm that overwhelmed the members of Edot Hamizrah. They suddenly raised their heads erect. Edot Hamizrah, who were trained to hate the Arabs more than the Ashkenazim, so as to see themselves as living up to the standards set by the Ashkenazim—suddenly sensed the possibility that the standards could change. They suddenly began to see themselves as equal partners, if not more than that, in the peace process. Oh, that's scary. Oh, how

> scary. To see how Israeli superiority over the Arab, of the Ashkenazi over Edot Hamizrah, was slipping away.[11]

Perhaps there was a measure of apprehension, but not real fright. It was addressed by Israel's president, Yitzhak Navon, the scion of a Sephardi family from Jerusalem.

It is customary for Israel's president to grant interviews to the media prior to the Jewish new year, Rosh Hashanah. In Navon's 1978 interview with *Davar*, the newspaper's editor, Hannah Semer, asked him, "Following Sadat's visit to Jerusalem, when groups of Israelis spent time in Cairo, some of them received the impression that Edot Hamizrah Israelis might possibly, after peace arrives, see themselves as 'Arab Jews' and have a stronger relationship with Arab culture than to the culture taking form in our country, thus deepening the fissure between the communities. Do you not see such a danger?" Navon rejected the conjecture. "Jews maintained their cultural independence when they lived in the Arab lands," he said. "There is no reason for them to blur it while living in Israel." He focused on the positive consequences peace would have for relations between ethnic groups in Israel. "It may well be that the special capacities of the members of Edot Hamizrah will be able to find greater expression after peace than before it. Their knowledge of Arabic language and Arab culture will provide them with a broader theater of action. They will be in demand, and that will give them a good feeling," he said.[12]

Those involved in the talks with Egypt assumed that a peace agreement would inevitably affect ethnic relations in Israel. If Israelis ceased to see Arabs as enemies, and if Arab culture in all its glory were revealed to them, those who had been nurtured by that culture would no longer be seen as inferior. The old idea of the Mizrahim as a bridge to peace also made a comeback. "The cohort of European extraction in Israel failed on two scores," maintained former Knesset member Shlomo Cohen-Tsiddon. "It did not succeed in bringing a massive immigration of their communities of origin (Europe and America) to this land, just as they did not succeed in finding a formula for a modus vivendi with the Arabs. If the Sephardi-Mizrahi tribe succeeded with mass immigration, perhaps it will succeed in its efforts to achieve the long-awaited bond between Jews and Arabs in the Middle East."[13]

THE LONG-AWAITED BOND

In some areas, the Mizrahim indeed took upon themselves the mission of bringing Jews and Arabs together. One such area was health, in which an exceptional figure stood out—Ilana Basri, a newscaster on the Voice of Israel in Arabic. Together with senior physicians at several Israeli hospitals, Basri initiated the program "Doctor Behind the Microphone," which, like all the station's programs, reached listeners all over the Middle East. The program received thousands of inquiries from people in the Arab world, who also sent their medical files. Basri passed the files on to the doctors, who studied them on a volunteer basis. More than a thousand of the patients were invited to undergo treatment in Israel. Basri told a reporter for *Davar*, "Before the patient's arrival, I would send him a message, provide him with a telephone number and, when he arrived in Israel, he called me, showed up in the office, and I would accompany him to the doctors and hospitals and then visit him during his stay in the hospital." Ada Ushpiz's documentary about her evokes Basri's hope that deeds such as hers would bring Israel and Arab countries together.[14]

Mizrahim did not, as a group, mobilize in support of peace with Egypt and relations with the Palestinians, or for (or against) a peace agreement. The exception was the short-lived Panther initiative, mentioned above, and Rabbi Ovadia Yosef's support for the Israel-Egypt compact. Yosef's support stood out against the opposition of his co-chief rabbi, Shlomo Goren. In the public arena, two movements, the right-wing Gush Emunim and the left-wing Peace Now (Shalom Achshav), grappled with each other. In the words of anthropologist Michael Feige, both movements "enlisted supporters largely from the educated Ashkenazi population of the middle and upper classes." Despite the rightward tilt of most Mizrahim, Feige noted, Gush Emunim failed in its attempts to mobilize Mizrahim from the development towns and underprivileged neighborhoods.[15] The most important social movement among the Mizrahim at that time was one of an entirely different nature—the Mizrahi *teshuva* movement, which was active in the underprivileged Mizrahi communities and led to a significant revival of religious observance and Jewish spiritual discourse.

MEANTIME, IN THE NEIGHBORHOOD SYNAGOGUE

Gush Emunim and the teshuva movement emerged in the wake of the crisis of the Yom Kippur War in 1973; the fervor of religious faith fired supporters of both movements. Both believed that they were bringing Israelis closer to their father in heaven, that they were saving Israeli society from ruin. But they operated in two parallel universes. Gush Emunim grew out of Israel's bourgeois religious Zionist society. Its members sought to lead the people and to further the settlement of the entire Land of Israel. The Mizrahi teshuva movement was the initiative of ultra-Orthodox members of Edot Hamizrah, whose goal was to extricate young Mizrahim from the world of drugs and crime and provide them with meaningful lives by connecting them to tradition and the world of the Torah. From the perspective of several decades, it seems that both movements achieved their goals, if not fully. The Mizrahi teshuva movement, which formed the base of Rabbi Yosef's Shas party, profoundly altered the lives and consciousness of the inhabitants of Mizrahi neighborhoods, sweeping up, among others, many supporters of the Black Panthers. And while it did not explicitly address Jewish-Arab relations, it profoundly influenced, and continues to influence, that issue as well. Gush Emunim, together with other forces and with the support of Israeli governments of all stripes, pushed Israeli settlement in the Occupied Territories into high gear, and in doing so set in stone Israel's relations with the Palestinians and the settlement map. The two movements advanced largely in parallel, while Peace Now, founded a bit later, placed itself in contrast to both: it explicitly declared itself Gush Emunim's rival, and implicitly opposed the teshuva movement.

In December 1976, a short-lived newspaper called *Zeh Koreh* published an article under the headline "The Magician Rabbi," with the subhead "A Neighborhood Rabbi in Jerusalem Managed to Sweep into His Yeshiva Tens and Hundreds of Young Criminals and Street Kids and Is Trying to Put Them on the Straight Path with the Help of Religion and Bible Stories; Mizrahi Music with a Beat and Charisma with a Kapote Mesmerizes Believing Youths and Makes Them Religious" (*hozrim bitshuva*, literally "returning in repentance" is the Hebrew term for these youths). The article portrayed synagogues full of young men (and young women, in the women's section) raptly listening to the sermons of Rabbi Reuven Elbaz, singing Mizrahi songs, and listening to Torah lessons peppered with street talk. Today these are common phenomena, just a click away on YouTube. In the 1970s, such a style was relatively rare and at first did not draw a big audience. Rabbi Elbaz's students and audiences told the reporter about the difficult lives they led in institutions for juvenile delinquents and about their criminal pasts in burglary and drugs. "The institutions are full because they give our youth a vacuous culture rather than a Jewish culture," Rabbi Elbaz shouted. "Into what pit of iniquity are they leading our young people?"[16]

These were the first portents of the Mizrahi teshuva movement, which looked at young Mizrahim at eye level, felt their pain, and found a path into their hearts. By 1980, many thousands of them, all over Israel, had joined it. At the end of that year, *Davar* reported an evening event in Ashdod attended by a thousand newly religious Mizrahim, most of them students at three yeshivot that had opened in that city. Rabbi Elbaz was the guest of honor. The reporter stressed, over and over again, the criminal backgrounds of some of the participants and lamented that they had been cut off from Zionism. "These evenings of those returning in repentance that are anti-Zionist events," the reporter fumed, "can blossom only where Zionism does not exist, even in the city that the secular Zionist Ben-Gurion decided to found and which is itself a Zionist success."[17] Note that the term "anti-Zionist" served, in *Davar*, to designate an opponent of the labor movement, or of secular nationalism, not an opponent of the Jewish people's return to its land or of Jewish sovereignty.

1949 VERSUS 1980

The *Davar* report exemplified the mutual alienation between the labor movement and Jews from the Islamic world, a division that had its roots way back in the Ottoman era. Recall that this alienation grew at the time of the great waves of immigration that followed independence. Despite the establishment's awareness of this—which must be given its proper weight—state institutions, under Mapai governments, continued to bring to Israel people who were its opponents, for two reasons: a sense of Jewish national solidarity, and the need for Jewish immigrants who would put the state on firm demographic ground and settle along its borders. But the alienation simmered in the background all this time. Participants in a meeting of Ben-Gurion and his advisors in 1949 voiced their fear of an immigrant uprising. David Horowitz (born in Galicia in 1899, a member of the Labor Battalion and Hashomer Hatzair, in 1949 secretary-general of the Finance Ministry and later a founder and the first governor of the Bank of Israel) offered an analysis of the internal state of the country. "Today there are 51,000 people in the [immigrant] camps," he remarked. "The population in the camps and in the conquered areas [the parts of Palestine not assigned to the Jewish state by the UN partition plan but that the IDF controlled at the end of the 1948 war] constitute what amounts to a separate nation. It is a rebellious nation that sees us as plutocrats. That is material that is likely to catch fire, excellent material for Herut and the Communists. It's dynamite."[18]

As I've already noted, no one even broached the possibility of limiting immigration for this reason. The participants moved on to analyze other issues. But at the end of the 1970s, the trend was entirely clear: the immigrants from the Islamic world had not gone over to the Communists (even those who arrived in Israel with a left-wing orientation did not always do so). Most aligned with Herut. That party's antagonism toward the established elites, its emphasis on a tradition-based Jewish identity as opposed to the labor movement's declared secularism, and the immigrants' understanding that emphasizing their Jewish identity would allow them upward social mobility encouraged a turn to the right rather than to the left. The political realignment of 1977 resulted from this general trend. In the following election, in 1981, the Mizrahi move to the right was even starker. In 1977 the Likud had won thirty-two seats on the strength of Mizrahi votes, among the total of forty-three that it received. In 1981 the Likud won a full forty-eight seats, with four of the five additional seats due to Mizrahi votes.[19] It was the first election in which the norm in the Mizrahi community "mandated" a vote for the Right.

FROM FOUR COMES ONE: THE DECISIVE DECADE

As we have seen, four different attitudes toward Arabs coexisted among members of Edot Hamizrah over the years, by which I mean positions that grew out of the Mizrahiness of those who proposed and held them, not the full range of positions that could be found among Mizrahim. The first proposed a Mizrahi-Arab alliance against Zionism, on the basis of both groups' being Zionism's victims. This approach fired the imaginations of Palestinians but found few Jewish supporters. The second was the view that the Mizrahim could serve as a bridge for peace on the basis of their familiarity with Arabs, as Zionist Jews of Arab culture. This school also had its roots in the Ottoman era but never gained real influence. According to the third attitude, the Mizrahim believed that they understood Arabs and as such demanded a tough policy against them. The fourth Mizrahi attitude was one of hatred of Arabs and firm opposition to conciliation with them. Members of this group occasionally lynched Arabs in the name of the Jewish people.

The boundary between the third and fourth approaches was blurry at times, but it's important to distinguish between them. The former presumes provisional hostility between Jews and Arabs deriving from the Arab hope of defeating Israel. If the Arabs understand that there is no basis for such hope, the two nations will be able to develop close relations. The advocates of this approach do not reject such close relations in principle. The fourth approach rejects in principle close relations with non-Jews, especially Arabs, and renounces the idea of equality between Jews and non-Jews in the Jewish state. It bases itself on religious, sometimes kabbalistic ideas, and on national religious ideas; its most extreme spokesman at the time was Rabbi Meir Kahane, an Ashkenazi who received considerable sympathy in underprivileged Mizrahi circles.

All of these views coexisted over the years; the first was largely marginal, while the other three competed for support. The decade between the Likud's rise to power and the First Intifada, which began at the end of 1987, was the one in which the third and fourth options took the lead. The view of unending religious hostility gained momentum. It saw the solidification of a norm that had previously been one commonly accepted option, but one not seen as a fundamental element of Mizrahi identity, according to which Mizrahim are right-wingers. Alongside anti-Arab sentiment, Israel's fourth decade also saw the rise of anti-Left feelings.

This was the decade in which inflation soared, widening economic disparities, and in which the initial deal to erase billions of shekels of kibbutz debts was approved. It was the decade of Kahane, who preached that the left-wing elite had cast off traditional Jewish values, shunted the Mizrahim to the margins, allied with the Arabs instead, and allowed the latter to prosper and win over Jewish girls.[20] It was also the decade in which elections pivoted on the ethnic issue, when the political Right first unambiguously branded the Left as Ashkenazi, elitist, cold, and alienated from the people. In contrast, the Right identified itself with traditionalism and love for the Jewish people. On the other side, the Left associated the Right with ignorance, Mizrahiness, and Arab hatred, while portraying itself as enlightened and peace-loving. It was the decade in which a popular comedian and actor, Dudu Topaz, speaking at an election rally for the Alignment, used a derogatory term for Mizrahim, *chahchahim*, to refer to Likud supporters. Begin responded with a speech replete with love for the entire Jewish people ("Feinstein, Barazani; Ashkenazi, Sephardi; brothers"). He also noted the parallels between the Etzel underground of the Mandate years and the Mizrahim of the 1980s—two groups rejected and vilified by the labor Zionist establishment. This was the election cycle in which Likud supporters pelted Labor leader Shimon Peres with tomatoes at an Alignment rally, in response to which Peres punned that the Likud was "an indecent Mizrahi movement" (in colloquial Hebrew, the phrase also means "giving the finger," and Peres was associating the rude gesture specifically with Mizrahim)—all this during the 1981 election campaign. In the campaign that followed, in 1984, Motta Gur, a former IDF chief of staff and by this point a Labor Knesset member, equated the Mizrahim with Arabs, even as he explicitly articulated his party's usually implicit view of Ashkenazi supremacy. "We'll fuck you just like we fucked the Arabs," he shouted at Likud supporters who prevented him from speaking at a rally. It was also a decade of Palestinian terror attacks against Jews and Jewish terror attacks against Arabs. It was the decade of the First Lebanon War, and the one in which interethnic alienation morphed, among a segment of the public, into open hostility. It was also the acme of Peace Now, the decade in which one of its activists, Emil Grunzweig, was murdered when Yona Avrushmi lobbed a hand grenade at a group of demonstrators protesting the Lebanon War. Avrushmi later referred to the murder as a "Mizrahi act."

THE MURDER OF LEFTISTS AS A MIZRAHI ACT

The murder occurred on the night of February 10, 1983, when Peace Now staged a demonstration outside the prime minister's office in Jerusalem to demand that Begin dismiss Ariel Sharon, the architect of the invasion of Lebanon, from his position as minister of defense, as a commission of inquiry into the war had mandated. Right-wingers showed up to stage a counter-demonstration, Avrushmi, who had armed himself with a grenade, among them. In addition to killing Grunzweig, Avrushmi's grenade wounded nine other Peace Now protesters. "It was a Mizrahi act," he said in an interview with *Maariv* after his release from prison in 2011. "Notice that there aren't any Mizrahi leftists. I thought about it for a long time in advance. I didn't like the leftists, I thought they were collaborators and traitors."[21] But the media had already put the ethnic issue front and center in real time. Two days after the murder, the popular columnist Amnon Dankner published an op-ed headlined "I Have No Sister." It opened with the sentence: "It won't be a war between brothers, not because there won't be a war, but because it will not take place between brothers." He went on to portray the huge cultural disparity between Ashkenazim ("We had Heine and Freud and Einstein and all the wonderful synthesis between Judaism and Western culture") and the Mizrahim, with their "kissing their fathers' hands and their wonderful hospitality and their longing for Zion and naïve messianism."

> Now I want to tell you that I'm sick of commiserating and understanding. I know all those stories about discrimination and disparities and the feelings of frustration and the DDT [with which immigrants were sprayed on arrival, to kill lice] and the transit camps and Wadi Salib and Musrara and the poverty and the humiliation . . . and I also recognize

> that injustices were done. But if it means that I need to bare my neck to the killers, to offer my cheeks to the thrashers and the spitters—then no. . . . It needs to be said that a large, noisy, and violent part of the Likud's supporters sees its political activity also as an expression of ethnic hatred.[22]

Like Avrushmi, Dankner linked the grenade to the assailant's Mizrahi ethnicity and equated violence with Mizrahiness. Further on in his op-ed, Dankner compared the Mizrahim to the PLO and presented himself as the responsible adult. "Just as I am not prepared to talk to the PLO without harshly condemning its terrorist acts," he declared, "neither am I prepared to speak with the Likud's street gangs without condemning their terrorist acts. . . . You, ladies and gentlemen of the Likud Phalangists, are much more similar to the PLO than to us."

Dankner wrote this a few hours after the grenade had been cast, marking the acme of a long series of violent attacks on Peace Now demonstrations in which the ethnic dimension was on prominent display. The brothers Herzl and Balfour Hakak submitted a formal complaint about the article to the Israel Press Council, charging Dankner with ethnic incitement. A committee of inquiry established by the council, chaired by retired general Yitzhak Hofi, found that one paragraph of the article constituted an unacceptable generalization. The committee also stated that "the members of Edot Hamizrah do not oppose an exemplary humanistic advanced society" (whatever that means). But the storm continued to rage.[23] (Years later, Dankner would join the Mizrahi struggle, voicing his support for Aryeh Deri, leader of the Shas party, when he was jailed following a bribery and fraud conviction. Dankner then declared that "in an earlier period I did not understand them [the Mizrahim] and I did not display empathy for their plight. . . . The Left treats them with disrespect and arrogance.")[24]

ON COMPARING MIZRAHIM TO ARABS

Like Motta Gur two years earlier and many opinion writers over the years, Dankner stressed not only Mizrahi hostility toward Arabs but also the similarities between the two populations. He looked down on both. He profited doubly by comparing Mizrahim to Arabs. First, he reinforced the self-image of those drawing this equivalence as enlightened and European, thus declaring Ashkenazi superiority. Second, he reiterated the failure of the Mizrahi effort to detach themselves from Arabness. This "leftist" statement unintentionally revealed the assumption that both the PLO and the Mizrahim were acting on the basis of primal urges rather than political logic.

A MIZRAHI ACT: ON TRACKING AND THE SHAPING OF "MOROCCAN" NORMS

Avrushmi acted on his own. In the interview he granted after his release, he said that the murder he had committed had made him welcome and beloved everywhere. In fact, public support for him was limited. But he was hardly alone in his view that an essential element of Mizrahiness was a tough political stance. Two years earlier, Shlomo Bohbot, the mayor of Ma'alot-Tarshiha, had offered his view of Moroccan political norms. In a letter he sent to Knesset member Charlie Biton after Biton had met with PLO chairman Yasser Arafat in 1980, Bohbot declared, "You have ceased to represent our community and the weak strata and you have begun to represent the enemies of the state.... The very fact that you shook the blood-soaked hand of this mass murderer has removed you from the community and from the Jewish people as a whole." The meeting, Bohbot charged, had sullied the image of "a wonderful community."[25] A Moroccan's duty, as he saw it, was not only to the Jewish people but to the Moroccan community, and that included opposition to negotiations with the PLO.

Bohbot had been elected mayor on the Labor Party ticket. Later, from 1992 to 1996, he also served as member of the Knesset for the party. The municipality he headed was the only one in the country to unite Jewish and Arab towns. He warmly portrayed the good relations between the Jewish and Arab citizens there in an interview he gave in 1990. "How do you explain this tolerance?" the interviewer, Ron Cahlili, asked him. "Moroccans, my friend, Moroccans," Bohbot responded. "That explains everything. They say that North African Jewry is extremist, but that's not true at all. They lived together with the Arabs in Morocco and they know exactly what an Arab is."[26] This is an example of how to offer a stringent political position while maintaining proper personal relations. It's also a use of memory (true or imagined) in the service of conciliation between the two nations.

A similar position was voiced by Meir Sheetrit, a young Moroccan who joined the Likud. (He was elected mayor of Yavneh in 1973 on the Likud ticket, as a member of the Knesset in 1981, and from 1999 onward headed several ministries.) In 1988, during the First Intifada, he revived the claim that the Mizrahim were a bridge to peace.

MIZRAHIM OF THE LIKUD AS A BRIDGE

Sheetrit recalled how he had presented his position in an interview with the *New York Times*. "The interviewer asked if it was correct that the Sephardim vote for the Likud because they hate Arabs. I told him that in my opinion that's a fairytale, an image that has come into being. On the contrary, the opposite is the case. Many members of Edot Hamizrah take a moderate line. In the Likud I am a moderate, and Moshe Katsav and David Levy are not extremists. The fighting family are more extreme and Kahane is an Ashkenazi." He offered the bridge alternative: "It's actually the members of Edot Hamizrah, who know the Arab mentality, who can be a bridge for peace. As of today, they have not yet been brought into the negotiations with the Arabs. They did not invent extremism. No Sephardi established an extreme line because none were ever part of the political game. The Sephardim would like to conduct the negotiations from a position of strength and would not give in because of threats or fear." "And the Ashkenazim?" the interviewer asked. "Maybe. Some, yes," Sheetrit replied.[27] Here was a new trope—Ashkenazi appeasement.

A RESPITE: ASHKENAZI APPEASEMENT?

This is part of the sea change in the Ashkenazi-Mizrahi-Arab triangle. In Zionism's dawn, the Moskobim accused the Sephardim of appeasement and indifference to the national question. Now the roles were reversed. From this point onward, the Mizrahim would accuse the Ashkenazim of weakness. The ethnic makeup of Peace Now and its political positions were the main reason for this. In the decades prior to the political upset of 1977, it was impossible to claim that David Ben-Gurion and his associates—the leaders who led Israel to victory in 1948 and emptied the country of 80 percent of its Arab population—and the government of Golda Meir and her colleagues, who refused to recognize the existence of a Palestinian people and spurned an Egyptian peace proposal before the 1973 war, had concluded a compact with the Arabs over the heads of the Mizrahim. Following the political upheaval of 1977, the Israeli discourse about the settlements and negotiations with the PLO took on an entirely different color. A growing number of Israelis, many of them from the Ashkenazi elite, began advocating a compromise with the Palestinians much more vocally than they had while in power. The political debate took on an ethnic tinge. The IDF's imbroglio in Lebanon and the demonstrations against the war deepened the political divide, and with it the ethnic identity of the two camps, and not only in Israel. Here is an example from Egypt and another from the United States.

AL-AHRAM AND THE STATE DEPARTMENT: MIZRAHIM AND CULTURAL BACKWARDNESS

The common wisdom that Mizrahim as a whole and Moroccans in particular strongly tilted to the right became, in the 1980s, a cornerstone of the analysis of Israeli society. Both Israelis and outside observers believed it incontrovertible. One of the latter was the former US undersecretary of state, George Ball. He was concerned that with the entry of Mizrahim, who now constituted a majority in Israel, into Israel's political life, control of Israel's political reins would never return to the more moderate Ashkenazi elements who brought with them the humanitarian traditions of the West, he wrote to Morris Abram, the former national president of the American Jewish Committee.[28] So also *Al-Ahram*, Egypt's largest daily newspaper and the mouthpiece of its government. "Begin's power base is the Mizrahi Jews, who now constitute 60 percent of Israel's population," it told its readers, quoting an article by Patrick Seale. "Begin knows better than any other Israeli politician how to flatter them and enter their hearts, relying on their cultural backwardness and their religious fanaticism that hates [the members of] all other religions."[29] Once again, we see Arab elites condescending to Israel's Mizrahi masses. In both cases, the community's right-wing sentiments are attributed to the essence of Mizrahiness—Mizrahim are culturally backward and religiously extreme (*Al-Ahram*), and they have not subscribed to Western humanism (Ball).

In an effort to disprove that thesis, the sociologist Shlomo Swirski invoked Eliyahu Elyashar, the Sephardi leader who called, in the 1970s, for negotiations with the PLO. Elyashar's position was consistent with his advocacy of a compact with the Arabs during the Mandate period. Elyashar, Swirski maintained, refuted the claim that there was an inevitable link between Mizrahim and the hatred of Arabs. He attributed the rightward turn of the Mizrahim to government policy, which sent Mizrahim to live in areas of friction between Jews and Arabs and put Arab and Mizrahi laborers in competition for work.[30]

THE WORKFORCE: A CLARIFICATION

The entry of Arab laborers from the Occupied Territories into the Israeli workforce contributed, as we have seen, to Mizrahi socioeconomic advancement. But Palestinian workers can serve as an engine of Mizrahi upward mobility only in periods of growth. At times of economic crisis, such as after the Yom Kippur War and during the first half of the 1980s, when employers are compelled to contract their operations and lay off workers, the competition between untenured workers increases. The closure of small businesses can push those who rose on the ladder during prosperous times back down the rungs.

UNFORGETTABLE MEMORIES OF ARROGANCE

The right-wing Mizrahi position was put in a nutshell in a letter that a resident of Tel Aviv wrote to Israel's president, Yitzhak Navon, just prior to the 1981 election, when some Labor supporters were touting Navon, who was Sephardi, to head the party. This letter exemplified a widespread way of thinking and offered a comprehensive account of the connection between resentment caused by ongoing discrimination and abhorrence of what its writer perceived as the hypocrisy of the Left and its political positions.

> I do not know if you read the letters of members of Edot Hamizrah, the great majority of whom are people of the Right and the Likud. What I know is that you read and respond (through your secretary) only to letters from people who are "cultured," leftists, or supporters of Peace Now. You don't reply to, or you don't bother to read, letters from *chahchahim* or the rabble or the uncultured, as your party the [Labor] Alignment calls them. . . . Like all the people of the Alignment, you live on another planet and you don't know what is going on among us, among those who will determine and who determined five years ago and onward who will rule in this country, you don't know what we think about you. If you would head the party, or Rabin or Peres or [dovish Labor Knesset member] Yossi Sarid or Victor Shem-Tov [of Mapam], it will make no difference for you, we hate this party, the "Labor" Party, and no one who heads it will cleanse it of racism, hypocrisy, and of the exploitation and ridicule of us for so many years and especially during the years of its rule in this country. We were brought up by our parents, who suffered from discrimination and racism, to hate the Alignment and the Left, and we suffered further on. You should know that today, when our condition has improved, especially in recent years, against the will of the well-heeled people of the Alignment who milked us and divided up money between them at the expense of our tribulations, [we still hate you]; and now that the government in the time of the Likud has closed the spigot—that's what provokes your hatred and rage at us. . . . As I said, ever since our situation has improved we gather in the home of my mother and father, the sons and daughters and grandchildren, may they multiply, and then

> we with my parents tell the stories and debate about the penury and poverty and ridicule and derision of the people of the Labor Party at us over thirty years, from '51 when we came from Iraq. And how my father stood in the [employment] office to get work to support us, his five tiny children, and how they would tell him that there was no work, and the Alignment man after him with one child would receive work without even hiding it from my father . . . and how we were barred from getting a college education and so on and so forth, and there is no space here to describe all the favoritism and discrimination of a party that pretends to represent the oppressed workers. So even if you head the Alignment, it won't help. That party, which is tainted and loves the PLO and loves Wagner's classical music and hates us and our magnificent heritage which we are now teaching once again.[31]

The Israel State Archives preserves hundreds of files containing letters to the country's prime ministers and presidents. The writers come from all walks of life, but the great majority are those whose voices were not heard in the public square. People who could place an article in *Yediot Aharonot* or *Haaretz,* and certainly those who could get meetings, were senior and elected officials and had no need of such a channel of communication. The letters contain the entire range of the public's political opinions and emotions. The letter above expresses, in every respect, a widespread Mizrahi attitude.

AN INTRA-MIZRAHI NOTE

The author of this letter was an Iraqi. The Iraqis were more amenable to the parties of the labor movement in their different incarnations than were immigrants from North Africa. Iraqi immigrants such as Shlomo Hillel, Mordechai Ben-Porat, Shoshana Arbeli-Almozlino, Nuzhat Katzav, Moshe Shahal, and Ran Cohen were all elected to the Knesset on these parties' slates, and some of them served as cabinet ministers in Labor-led governments in the 1970s and 1980s. "It was not the emigrants from Babylonia [Iraqi Jews] who put Begin in power," declared Shevah Weiss, a political scientist and Labor member of the Knesset. He estimated that two-thirds of the country's Iraqi population voted for the Alignment in the 1981 elections.[32] That was an exaggeration. A survey conducted in Be'er Sheva showed that a significantly larger portion of Moroccan Jews than of Iraqis voted for the Likud. Among those who voted for one of the two large parties, 73 percent of the Moroccans voted for Likud and 27 percent for Labor. The figures for Iraqi Jews were 57 percent for Likud and 43 percent for Labor. In other words, the Likud was the choice of most Iraqis, but not at as high a rate as among Moroccans.[33] Rancor against the absorbing establishment and its discrimination, as seen in the letter to President Navon, the desire for change, and the identification of the Left with alienation from national values were shared by many members of the public who were, at this time, being transformed from "Edot Hamizrah" to "Mizrahim." The Left's antiwar demonstrations took place against the background of these internal Israeli divisions.

THE DRAMATIC EFFECTS OF THE LEFT'S PROTESTS

The hand grenade that Yona Avrushmi threw at Peace Now demonstrators was a sign of just how much anger the Left's protest rallies elicited on the Israeli right. These protests were an unprecedented phenomenon in Israel—the radical Left began holding demonstrations against the war in Lebanon a short time after the fighting began. Peace Now joined a bit later. Together, they questioned whether the war was justified. The demonstrations continued, with varying levels of attendance, for several long months. The massacre of Palestinians committed by Lebanese Christian Phalangists in the Sabra and Shatila refugee camps in Beirut in mid-September 1982, with logistical aid from the IDF, sparked a massive demonstration in Malchei Yisrael Square in Tel Aviv, as it was then called, bringing out a multitude of Israelis who had not opposed the war at the start. The protesters demanded an investigation of the IDF's complicity in abetting the massacre. Beyond that, it was a display of the Left's strength. But a show of force invites a show of counterforce. The Right saw the demonstration as a subversive act against the elected government by the political opposition that had lost the election. Even worse, it was providing succor to the enemy in wartime. The Right maintained that the members of Peace Now—including those, like Emil Grunzweig, who had taken part in combat in the war—were a band of traitors.[34] The result was violent counterdemonstrations, leading to Grunzweig's murder, which further widened the fissure between the rival political camps. The novelist Amos Oz, a spiritual leader of the Zionist Left, visited the development town of Beit Shemesh during this fraught time and wrote a book, *In the Land of Israel*, offering his impressions. Mizrahi Likud supporters told him, "Your whole problem is that you still don't recognize that Begin is prime minister. For you, he's trash, not prime minister. There's nothing similar to that in any other country. You've been going wild five years already, the whole country can burn down, you don't care, the main thing is to return to power. Is this the behavior of an opposition, is it? To inform on us to the whole world? To trash us? To support the enemy?"[35]

HIGH MORALS OR CONTEMPTIBLE TREASON?

The demonstrations against the Lebanon War were interpreted in two ways. The people of the Left who took part in them believed that they were acting to repair Israeli society and politics, acting out of a sense of fundamental human duty. They certainly believed themselves to be morally superior to the war's supporters. Those of them who fought in the war as enlisted soldiers and reservists believed that their service had given them the right to protest. Their opponents saw the demonstrations as sanctimoniousness that had its source in frustration at having been thrown out of government in favor of the part of the population that it considered inferior. It took a great deal of effort for those subscribing to either of these views to understand the other side.

Oz and the people he spoke to in his book, much like Avrushmi, stressed the ethnic aspect of the division. "With this crowd, the people of the barren remote cities that suddenly discovered a reason for life in opportunistic pogroms, we will never have a dialogue," wrote the poet Dahlia Ravikovitch. "Perhaps it is incumbent on us to take heart and to clasp limp hands and speak (without exaggeration) in praise of ourselves, because we have been left very much alone."[36] The harsh attacks, distance from power, and political defeat had led to despair, but also to a measure of arrogance and detachment.

A NO LESS DRAMATIC EFFECT

The sense of loneliness on the left during the war, given that the Israeli mainstream supported it, was intensified by the effect the antiwar demonstrations had on Palestinian politics. During the weeks following the Sabra and Shatila massacre, the French journalist Eric Rouleau conducted a series of interviews with senior PLO figures with whom he had close relations, mostly in Damascus. His interviewees were impressed by the fact that the largest demonstration against the massacre took place in Tel Aviv—it was much larger than any of the protests in the capital cities of Arab countries. "The fact that hundreds of thousands of people were able to express their opposition to the Begin government in Tel Aviv without fear of reprisal roused envy and appreciation among population groups that do not enjoy such freedoms," he wrote. "The intensity of the protest in Israel has already led to the fact that one no longer hears declarations of hatred or revenge against Israel and the Jews. The small Jewish community in Damascus carries on its life as usual. . . . Personal friendships have not been affected by events in Lebanon." He quoted Abu Saleh, a member of Fatah's Revolutionary Council: "I see that the Israelis are innocent of the crimes being committed in their name." And the chairman of the PLO's Political Department, Farouk al-Kaddoumi, told Rouleau, "We hope that the opposition in Israel will be able to bring about a withdrawal not only from Lebanon but also from the other conquered Arab territories, and that we will be able to establish coexistence between our peoples on the basis of the Palestinian right to self-determination and an independent state in the West Bank and Gaza." Nayef Hawatmeh, chairman of the Democratic Front, spoke in the same vein.[37] The demonstration notably strengthened the hand of that Palestinian current that supported an accord with Israel. For Israeli advocates of accommodation and withdrawal from the territories, this was good news. Not so for those who opposed withdrawal for religious or national reasons, or those who suspected that it was a Palestinian trick to establish an entity in the territories as a bridgehead toward seizing the entire country. These opponents all saw the Israeli peace camp's rapprochement with the PLO compromise camp as an act of treason.

AN ACT OF TREASON: A GEOPOLITICAL VIEW

The Israeli invasion of Lebanon was meant to ensure the security of the Galilee, Israel's northern region, by ending periodic bombardments of the region with Katyusha rockets fired by PLO forces in southern Lebanon (the government's official designation was Operation Peace for the Galilee). But that end had already been achieved through indirect negotiations between Israel and the PLO mediated by the United States prior to Israel's invasion in June 1982, and a more comprehensive proposal to resolve the problem was on the table. The strategic goal was to reshape Israel's relations with the region's state actors and with the Palestinians and to create a new Middle East. The new order would be based on smashing the PLO, removing its bases from the border with Israel, and rendering null and void its demand for the establishment of a Palestinian state in the West Bank and Gaza under PLO rule. Furthermore, Israel would install a friendly regime in Lebanon; foster alternative, pro-Israeli Palestinian leadership in the West Bank and Gaza Strip that would accede to the expansion of Israeli settlements there; and make Jordan the place in which the Palestinians would realize their aspiration for national self-determination. As Israeli Foreign Minister Yitzhak Shamir put it, "The Palestinian Arab people is not a stateless people and is not a homeless people. They already have their state . . . it is called now Jordan. Jordan is a Palestinian Arab state; its population is of Palestinian origin, its culture, language, and its mentality are all Palestinian."[38]

The Israeli scheme enjoyed only limited success. It is true that the PLO's forces, which had virtually taken over southern Lebanon, were defeated militarily. But the Lebanese Christian leader who was elected the country's president with Israeli support, Bachir Gemayel, was assassinated in mid-September (triggering the Sabra and Shatila massacre). This eliminated the keystone of the Israeli plan to turn its northern neighbor from enemy to ally. The Village Leagues that Israel had promoted as an alternative and more amenable Palestinian leadership never gained significant popular support, and Jordan adamantly refused to transform itself into a Palestinian nation-state. Israel succeeded in ejecting PLO forces from Lebanon, but the organization was able to revive itself and maneuver the politics of the Arab states to maintain its standing as the designated sole representative of the Palestinian people on the international stage. That put paid to the rest of Israel's strategy. As these events unfolded, the Left's opposition to the war, its promotion of a peaceful resolution to the conflict with the Palestinians, and the beginnings of contact with the PLO by some figures on the left infuriated many Israelis. While all of Israel's Right shared this anger and resentment, it also had a specifically Mizrahi dimension.

THE MIZRAHI DIMENSION

Apt here, too, are the sentiments that Amos Oz heard in Beit Shemesh. "Why did they bring our parents to Israel? I'll tell you why," one of the town's inhabitants told him.

> Not to do the dirty work? Then [prior to 1967] you didn't have Arabs. You needed our parents to be cleaners and servants and hard laborers. Policemen also. You brought our parents to be your Arabs. Today I'm already a foreman, he's a contractor, self-employed. And he has a moving business, he's also got his own business. A small business, lives off the crumbs left behind by Solel Boneh [an Israeli construction company established in 1924 by the Labor parties]. But what? If you give the territories back, the Arabs will stop coming to work, and on the spot you'll send us back to the dirty work like before. Even if that were the only thing, we would not let you return the territories. And that's not including the rights we have from the Torah, and not including security. Look, my daughter today works in a bank and there's an

> Arab who comes in the evening to clean the place. All you want is to see her thrown out of the bank to work at some textile machine or that she'll go back to mopping floors instead of the Arab, just like my mother who worked as a cleaning woman for you.[39]

The back cover of Oz's book states that it "is not only journalistic, literary, documentary, and not only political commentary and ideological, but rather a melding of all these." As such, there is no way of knowing whether Oz precisely and literally quoted the people he spoke with, or whether passages like the one above are composite paraphrases of what he heard from different people, or whether he produced a literary combination of fact, analysis, and art.

The Lebanon War was in the background, as was the ongoing Palestinian struggle against Israel. There were also the Jewish terror operations that had begun before the war and multiplied in number and scope thereafter. We'll soon examine and contrast Ashkenazi versus Mizrahi terror, but first we need a few words on innovations and unexpected developments in Palestinian terror following the First Lebanon War.

THE ATTACK ON THE 18 BUS, DECEMBER 1983: THE MOMENT OF TRUTH?

"Terror" is a fluid term, of course, and much depends on the eye of the beholder. The official Israeli stance is that any act of armed resistance, whether against civilians or soldiers, is an act of terror. (Today, even political resistance is termed "political terror.") The Palestinian position, as stated by Yasser Arafat in his speech to the United Nations in 1974, is that it is not the nature of the act that makes it terror but rather its purpose. Operations carried out as part of a just goal, such as national liberation, are not terror, while violent acts aimed at rule over and oppression of another nation are terror.[40] Thus while Fatah's official stance was that it opposed attacks on civilians, it did not refrain from carrying out such attacks.

The attack on the 18 bus in Jerusalem on December 3, 1983, put Fatah to the test. It took place at a time when different PLO factions were fighting one another in Lebanon during the "Camps War." Opponents of Fatah, aided by Syria, besieged Arafat and his supporters in Tripoli in northern Lebanon. The attack occurred two weeks after a prisoner deal between Israel and Fatah in which the latter released six captured Israeli soldiers in exchange for forty-seven hundred Palestinian and Lebanese prisoners whom Israel was holding in the Ansar prison camp in southern Lebanon and some sixty prisoners held in Israeli prisons. The bus bombing killed six people, including two young sisters, Nurit and Esther Polak-Mizrahi. Fatah claimed responsibility for the attack. A number of figures in the PLO leadership of the Occupied Territories who had been in contact with Israeli peace activists issued a sharp condemnation of the attack. This was unprecedented, both the condemnation itself and because they did not consult with the PLO leadership before issuing it. The Israeli, Palestinian, and international media gave the statement prominent play. Immediately afterward, Arafat's spokesman retracted Fatah's claim and announced that Fatah's position against harming civilians remained unchanged. This revision had more factual basis than did the original claim of responsibility, because the bombing had been carried out not by Fatah agents but by a group associated with the Rejectionist Front.[41]

On the political front, the condemnation demonstrated the rising strength of those in Fatah who opposed attacks on Israeli civilians, and the effect of that dialogue with the Israeli peace camp on the PLO's willingness to refrain from such attacks. But it had no effect on the personal level. The brother of the two murdered sisters, Tiran Polak, then sixteen years old, joined Meir Kahane's Kach party, becoming one of its leading activists. Other Israelis were also overwhelmed by a thirst for revenge.

ASHKENAZI TERROR, MIZRAHI TERROR

The surge in Jewish terror attacks on Palestinians during the first half of the 1980s came in the wake of a series of developments. First came Israel's withdrawal from the Sinai Peninsula as part of its peace treaty with Egypt. In another provision of that treaty, the Begin government recognized the Palestinian right of self-determination. Then came the PLO's increasing strength, the polar opposite of what many Israelis expected to be the outcome of the war in Lebanon. And Palestinian attacks on Israelis continued.

The Jewish terror attacks started before the Lebanon War. In 1980, members of the Jewish Underground (Makhteret—West Bank settlers, tied to Gush Emunim) planted bombs that injured the mayors of the West Bank cities of Ramallah, Al-Bireh, and Nablus. The group resumed its activities after the Lebanon War and in tandem with the PLO's increasing willingness to negotiate with Israel. In 1983, the group placed explosive charges near a mosque in Hebron and next to a house that settlers wanted to seize control of.[42] In the summer of 1983, three of the Underground's members (Menachem Livni, Uzi

Sharbaf, and Shaul Nir) opened fire at the Islamic Shari'a College at Hebron University, murdering three students.

In the meantime, other Jewish attacks on Arabs took place. In March 1984, a Jewish assailant threw a grenade at a bus carrying workers and students near the West Bank village of Silwad. Grenades were planted in different places in Hebron and attacks against Palestinians and Christian religious buildings in Jerusalem were carried out with high frequency by a group that called itself TNT, a Hebrew acronym for "Terror Against Terror," which operated in Jerusalem and its environs. Four members of TNT were apprehended in April 1984. They were Amram and Avi Deri and their cousin David Deri and Uri Ben Ayun, all of whom lived in Jerusalem's Ein Karem neighborhood and had become religious as part of the Mizrahi teshuva movement. They exemplified the possible connection between newly religious Mizrahim and anti-Arab violence.[43] At the end of the same month, members of the Jewish Underground were also arrested. Other Jewish terror attacks that year included one by an IDF soldier, David Ben-Shimol, on leave, who cast a phosphorus grenade and bomb at an Arab café in Jerusalem's Old City; a short time later, he fired an LAW antitank rocket at an Arab bus leaving East Jerusalem on its way to Hebron, killing one person. In 1985, three young people, whom the Israeli media described as being from good families, murdered Khamis Tutanji, an Arab cab driver from Jerusalem.[44]

The motives for these actions were varied and complementary: revenge for the murder of Jews, a desire to create deterrence, or an attempt to signal to the government that it needed to act with more determination against Palestinians. Other motives were xenophobia and the desire to avert an agreement with the Palestinians that might lead to an Israeli withdrawal from the territories. Some were carried out by individuals and others by groups from different sectors of the population—settlers, Mizrahim, and people "from good families." Ben-Shimol was a Mizrahi lone wolf. In a manifesto he left at the site of his bus attack, he wrote that he was avenging the murder of two Jews near the Cremisan Monastery just south of Jerusalem, because "for every Jew murdered, we will kill two." A letter on the attack that he sent to the attorney-general provides its ethnic context:

> I grew up in the Katamon neighborhood in Jerusalem, and all my friends and family were from North Africa. We lived for generations among the Arabs, we were friendly with them, we suffered from them, and we know them. It's clear to all of us, and that's the general

> atmosphere in the neighborhood, that you need to use force against the Arabs. . . . [The Arab] does not value morality and humanity. He interprets that as weakness. The Arabs are not considerate and are not merciful. They kill old people, women, and children, even in their own families, and they certainly have no compunction about killing us. . . . Our government does not know how to treat the Arabs. There are people [in the government] . . . some of whom bear within them the fear of the Jew in exile, and some have adopted humanistic ideas from the West that are entirely unsuitable here.[45]

The claim that Jews from the Islamic world know Arabs better than other Jews is familiar but not always persuasive. It's not clear to what extent, if any, the way of life in Morocco or Iraq is relevant to life in Israel. How similar are the Arabs and Berbers of Morocco to the Arabs of Palestine? To what extent is their attitude toward Jews based on the same foundation? After all, Muslims in Morocco viewed Jews as a religious minority, whereas the Arabs of Palestine view Jews as foreigners who settled on their land. Can someone born in Israel, Ben-Shimol, for example, claim familiarity with Arab culture and society? Whatever the case, there is in this claim a sort of connection to Arabness, and it calls on Israelis to conduct themselves according to the mores of the Arab East, without being led astray by Western human values.

Recall that the young men of Edot Hamizrah whom Yehuda Leib Magnes encountered in 1938 claimed that their Mizrahiness left them unshackled by Western morality, which they told him was foreign and irrelevant to Palestine.

There's some truth in that claim. Ben-Shimol portrayed the sociocultural milieu in which he was raised, which was a consequence of Israel's class and ethnic structure. That set the contours of the way those born into it lived. A large portion of the Mizrahi population agreed with Ben-Shimol's position. This was why the Knesset members for Shas, the new Sephardi political movement whose spiritual leader was Rabbi Ovadia Yosef, hosted Ben-Shimol in the Knesset building and supported his plea for a commutation of his sentence. Ben-Shimol benefited from Shas's embrace but did not overlook the fact that he was being discriminated against by the mainstream. "Why have the punishments of the prisoners from the [Jewish] Underground been reduced and not mine?" he asked. His lawyer, Michael Paran, added, "The Mizrahim don't have anyone who looks out for them. He disturbs them. He's not one of them. They [the members of the Jewish Underground] are good-looking, Ashkenazi, and educated. He's a poor kid from the Katamonim. That's why they won't free him." Members of his family also spoke up: "There is ethnic discrimination . . . they free Ashkenazim and the ones who look good and the Sephardim remain in jail. . . . They also acted for the sake of the homeland." The head of the Shabak's Jewish Department, Carmi Gillon, later summed things up. "He knew what he was talking about," Gillon said. "The huge lobby that operated for the Jewish Underground [and brought about their early release] did not do a thing for Ben-Shimol."[46]

"WE WERE FRIENDLY WITH THEM, WE SUFFERED FROM THEM"

The friendly but fraught interactions with Arabs to which Ben-Shimol referred were not unique to Morocco. They were a salient feature of Mizrahi-Palestinian relations in Israel at that time as well. Alongside economic competition and political hostility, there were also close and warm relations at work and in adjacent residential areas. This can be heard in the words of the inhabitants of Acre, Jaffa, and Ramla, as well as in the Katamonim where Ben-Shimol lived. It was especially true in the adjacent Pat neighborhood. A field study of Jewish-Arab relations in Jerusalem conducted in the 1980s compared relations between the mostly Mizrahi Jews of Pat and the Arabs of the adjacent Beit Safafa neighborhood with those of Jews and Arabs who lived in another Jerusalem neighborhood, Abu Tor. The principal relational mode identified in both places was that of mutual nonfraternization—minimal dealings when necessary, but no more than that. Nevertheless, in Pat the study found several common social circles to which Jewish teenagers and twenty-somethings, both men and women, belonged. Arabs (only men) from Beit Safafa were also involved. These groups encompassed several dozen youths. They generally met in the small neighborhood strip mall in Pat or the nearby open field. They bought drinks, smoked, and talked. Sometimes they went to one of the homes in Pat; sometimes they smoked hashish, and a few engaged in petty theft. Hebrew served as their common language, and in a few cases close friendships and romantic attachments developed, some between Jewish boys and girls, others between Arab boys and Jewish girls. The close relations sometimes led to conflict, especially when the romantic attachments were discovered by family members or friends who opposed them.[47]

In Abu Tor, by contrast, the investigators discerned a different sort of contact. It took place between left-wing Israelis in that neighborhood—some of them university graduates or artists—and their neighbors on the Arab side of the neighborhood. The former sought social ties with Arabs for ideological reasons, and for that reason sometimes preferred to make purchases at Arab-owned neighborhood grocery stores. "This is conduct that is not just instrumental but which also has symbolic value—it constitutes a personal declaration of the possibility of Jewish-Arab cooperation," the researchers suggested. But such intentions ran into difficult realities—political power differentials and the language barrier. "Unlike Jews of Mizrahi origin, these [the academics and bohemians] do not speak fluent Arabic and cannot conduct a real conversation [in that language]," they reported. Furthermore, they felt uncomfortable with the fact that their Arab neighbors treated them as representatives of the establishment or Israeli society, despite their leftist opinions. The upshot was that these relations never developed into real friendships.[48]

Students at Shuvu Banim ("Return, Wayward Children," also known as Birkat Avraham), a yeshiva in the Old City of Jerusalem's Muslim Quarter associated with the Breslov Hasidic community, never developed neighborly relations with the local Arabs—quite the contrary, despite the fact that many of them were Mizrahi.

RETURN, WAYWARD CHILDREN

The wave of terror of the mid-1980s did not pass over the yeshivot—seminaries for religious studies—that were established at that time in the Old City's Muslim Quarter. Here, an important distinction needs to be made: religious Zionist organizations also opened yeshivot in the Muslim Quarter, as part of their principle of resettling Jews in buildings and areas where Jews had lived before 1948 and beyond. These institutions—Atara Leyoshna and Ateret Cohanim—promoted neighborly relations with the local Arabs, if only for utilitarian reasons. The opposite was true of Shuvu Banim. The great majority of its students were *hozrim bitshuva,* many of them Mizrahim; some had criminal records. The yeshiva is located on Maale Khalidiya Street in the Muslim Quarter, in the Hayei Olam Courtyard. The courtyard had come under Jewish ownership at the end of the nineteenth century. "When the Shuvu Banim people occupied the courtyard," journalist and author Nadav Shragai recounted, "four Arab families remained there [with protected tenant status] and the Breslovers did everything they could to eject them. The families' lives turned into a continuous nightmare. The yeshiva students hounded them, cursed at them, and threw stones at their homes. . . . For months the yeshiva's sewage system leaked human waste into the neighbors' apartments. A few of the Arabs remaining in the courtyard were beaten severely."[49] Jerusalem's mayor, Teddy Kollek, reported the students' transgressions to Israel's chief rabbis, Mordechai Eliyahu and Avraham Shapira. The rabbis condemned the violence and promised to tell the institution's main donor, Avraham Dweck, to halt his contributions if the attacks did not cease. Dweck did not stop giving, and the tension continued. In December 1983, Jerusalem's police commander personally arrested Dweck because of his refusal to halt illegal construction in the yeshiva's courtyard, and Mayor Kollek asked the head of the IDF's Central Command to use his emergency powers to evict the yeshiva. The general did not reply. Kollek nevertheless believed that he would be able to eject the yeshiva ("In the end we will get them out," he told the journalist Arie Dayan. "Not because they are yeshiva students, but because they are simply not human beings"). He turned out to be wrong. The yeshiva remains there to this day.[50]

In 2021, the head of the yeshiva, Rabbi Eliezer Berland, was arrested on suspicion of involvement in the murders of two Jews during the 1980s, allegedly by the yeshiva's "modesty patrol." The murders had remained unsolved for decades. Berland was interrogated but then released. Another murder, that of Shuvu Banim student Eliyahu Amedi in November 1986, was quickly solved. It was perpetrated by a contingent of the Popular Front. The events following that murder offer a window into Jewish-Arab, Left-Right, and Mizrahi-Ashkenazi relations in Jerusalem, and all of Israel, prior to the First Intifada.

THE MURDER OF ELIYAHU AMEDI

Eliyahu Amedi, a student at Shuvu Banim, was stabbed to death not far from the yeshiva on November 15, 1986. The perpetrators were three young members of the Popular Front from the Jenin region in the northern West Bank. At the time, keep in mind, Fatah's adherents in the territories opposed attacks on Israeli civilians. Indeed, following the stabbing of another Jew in the Old City, the Fatah leadership in the territories, including Faisal al-Husseini, the leading PLO figure in East Jerusalem, severely condemned such knifings, and Fatah held a joint gathering with Peace Now at which both movements called for an end to the occupation and an end to violence.[51] Amedi's murder was followed by no such condemnation, for two reasons. First, the perpetrators belonged to the Popular Front, which did not accept Fatah's new policy. Furthermore, the yeshiva students' long series of attacks on Arabs in the Muslim Quarter made them legitimate targets as far as many Palestinians were concerned, including those who opposed attacks on civilians.

NOT JUST IN PALESTINIAN EYES

Neturei Karta, the extreme anti-Zionist Haredi faction, issued its response to Amedi's murder soon after it occurred. "This act of murder is the product of ongoing provocation for having evicted the Arab residents and having settled in their place."[52] The members of Neturei Karta understand the concept of Jewish solidarity not simply as a cover for Jewish crimes but also as an obligation to denounce the public for its crimes. The demand for repentance implied in its condemnation contains a demand to treat the Palestinians humanely.

REBUKING THE POLICE

Amedi's funeral procession set out at 3:30 in the morning from Shuvu Banim to the Jewish cemetery on the Mount of Olives. About two hundred mourners participated under heavy police guard. "The mourners laid the dead man on the street and began to take their anger out on private homes, cars belonging to Arabs, and on the gas station next to the Rockefeller Museum," Jerusalem police chief Yosef Yehudai told a reporter for *Maariv*. "We struggled with the rioters. They beat us and we beat them. With great effort we succeeded in stopping the disturbances and we let the funeral procession proceed to the Mount of Olives." To achieve this, a senior officer had to shoot in the air. The anti-Arab violence continued in the days that followed in the Old City and in Shmuel Hanavi, the neighborhood where Amedi had lived. Among other things, demonstrators threw Molotov cocktails at Arab homes in the Muslim Quarter and beat to a pulp Arabs they chanced on. The police worked hard to rescue the latter. According to Yehudai, "It was savage behavior. It hurts me to see people losing their judgment and acting on their most repulsive urges." The police presumed that "the Kach movement has played a large part in inciting the mob." In the days that followed, "groups of incited young people in the Shmuel Hanavi neighborhood . . . set fire to garbage bins, blocked main transportation arteries, and attacked policemen and Arabs." Twelve participants were arrested, among them Tiran Polak, the brother of the two Polak-Mizrahi sisters who had been killed in the 18 bus terror attack three years earlier.[53]

RECONCILIATION AND REVENGE

Demonstrations and attacks on Arabs and their property continued even after the police identified and apprehended Amedi's killers. At the end of the week of mourning for Amedi, a mourning procession that turned into a mass protest left the home of Amedi's family in Shmuel Hanavi en route to his grave on the Mount of Olives and from there to the yeshiva in the Old City. The participants banged on doors and broke windows. Rabbi Berland declared, "The blood that burns within us is not blood that has calmed. This blood cannot be covered up. . . . Now the Arabs know that they can stick a knife in every Jew. They know that all Jews are fair game. . . . But we will redeem that blood even if it costs us our souls, even if it costs us our bodies."[54] Yet Berland reversed himself when, ten days later, he took part in a *sulha,* a traditional Arab reconciliation ceremony, between the yeshiva and its Arab neighbors. The ceremony was organized by three Arab members of the Knesset who represented Zionist parties—Zeidan Atashi (Shinui), Muhammed Wattad (Mapam), and Abdulwahab Darawshe (Labor). Berland told the Arabs, "We are brothers and must live together. From this day on nothing bad will be done to you." Then, at a memorial ceremony marking the thirtieth day after the murder, he again proclaimed that Amedi's killing should be avenged.[55]

A number of Berland's students took his last statement to heart. A friend of Amedi's, Binyamin Shriki, was arrested in possession of ammunition stolen from the IDF. He was accused of purchasing it in order to avenge the murder.[56] Another student at the yeshiva, Aryeh Wolfowitz, had earlier been sought by the police for some two months on suspicion of casting Molotov cocktails at Arab homes in the Old City, in revenge for Amedi's murder.[57] Here were two students at the yeshiva who sought revenge. One was Mizrahi and one Ashkenazi, and they took personal risks to achieve their goal.

There were rabbis who called for revenge and those who called for moderation, but the dividing line between them was not ethnic. Rabbi Moshe Levinger and Rabbi Meir Kahane, both Ashkenazim, called for revenge, as did the Mizrahi rabbi Reuven Elbaz. Rabbi Ovadia Yosef called for restraint.[58] The same was true of those who consoled, beat up, and defended. Ran Cohen, a Knesset member for the left-wing Citizens Rights Movement (Ratz), went to Shmuel Hanavi with Avraham Gal, his party's legal counsel, to console the mourning family—not as a fellow Mizrahi Jew but as a public figure. Cohen was attacked and badly beaten. The assailants, as well as those who tried to protect him, were all Mizrahim. When Cohen gave his account of what happened, he did not label his attackers as Mizrahim. Instead, he characterized them along the religious spectrum. They were, he said, Haredim, who surrounded him "like black ants."[59] His companion on that visit, Avraham Gal, fought religious coercion and was anti-Haredi. Gal recounted that "before we came here, friends and journalists warned us not to enter Shmuel Hanavi this week. We decided that Ran and I would go anyway, to console the family of the murdered man. It would be wrong to leave the field to the Kahanists and the Haredi vampires." *Hadashot* reported that when the two men seated themselves in a public park in the neighborhood to chat with the members of the neighborhood committee and other residents, they were attacked by a large group of Amedi's friends. Cohen was hit in the head by a rock or a spiked club. He was cared for in a nearby apartment. When the two men went out to their car, "the Haredim began to attack the car, shattered the windows, and threw a large rock on Cohen's chest. Gal's hands, which sat on the steering wheel, were cut by slivers of glass. The Haredim tried to turn the car over. They rocked it for several long minutes as they screamed, 'Death to the Nazis. We won't let them out.'"[60]

This reminds us of a central question in the study of Israeli society.

ETHNICITY, CLASS, RELIGION

The central question that we've been circling is whether there are behaviors, perceptions, actions, or positions about Arabs that can be characterized as specifically Mizrahi. That is, can they be said to derive from the Mizrahi background and culture of those who commit or hold them. To answer this question, it is not sufficient to examine actions conducted by Mizrahim, because members of all ethnic groups in Israel have done similar things. We need to examine which sorts of actions or opinions were defined, by those responsible for them or by observers, as engendered by Mizrahiness. For example, Ben-Shimol and Avrushmi explained the murders they committed as corollaries of their being Mizrahi. The same is true of Eliyahu Elyashar and Ilana Basri, not to mention the Black Panthers, who claimed that their positive relations with Palestinians were founded on their Mizrahi identities. And here's an interesting fact: at the end of the 1980s, in a complete reversal of the discourse of the previous decades, the mainstream Israeli communications media as a rule ceased to point to the Mizrahiness of those involved in lynchings or attacks or other violent actions (the Ashkenazi background of such people had never been remarked on, as noted in previous chapters). In the cases of the attacks on Arabs in Netanya, Ramla, and Acre in the 1960s and 1970s, the press noted the Tripolitan, Iraqi, and Moroccan (respectively) ethnicities of the Jews involved. And in the mid-1980s, Avrushmi and Ben-Shimol themselves emphasized their Mizrahi or Moroccan backgrounds. But in the period leading up to the First Intifada, and during that conflict, such tagging diminished in the mainstream media with regard to acts of violence—in notable contrast to the involvement of Mizrahim in peace initiatives, as we will see below. Several conjectures about why this happened come to mind. First, perhaps journalists and pundits wanted to turn down the heat on the discourse about violence and ethnicity, which had reached new heights at the beginning of that decade. Second, there may have been a feeling that the ethnic tagging of violent acts legitimized them among some parts of the public; some Mizrahim took them as a focal point of their identities rather than being prompted to examine their actions. Third, the prominence of American Kahanists and Haredim (especially the young dropouts from Ashkenazi yeshivot) at violent events blurred ethnic lines. Fourth, by this time, Mizrahim were much less the Other of Israeli society, and therefore no longer had to be specially designated. Fifth, the Intifada brought with it the involvement of Israeli soldiers of all ethnicities in violent acts against Arabs.

THE INTIFADA

The broad-based Palestinian popular uprising in the West Bank and Gaza Strip that began in December 1987 took both Israel's defense agencies and its public by surprise. It took the PLO leadership by surprise, too. Palestinian crowds began demonstrating around IDF outposts in the Jabalia refugee camp in the Gaza Strip following an automobile accident in which four of the camp's inhabitants died. The demonstrations were fiercer than usual and spread all over the Gaza Strip and the West Bank. What set them apart was mass participation and their persistence. Both features were made possible by the political and social networks established by the Palestinian organizations (first by the Communist Party and left-wing factions, and in the early 1980s also by Fatah and the Muslim Brotherhood) in all parts of the territories and in East Jerusalem. It was the first time since the Israeli conquest—indeed, since the Palestinian Arab Revolt of 1936—that opposition to foreign rule encompassed all strata of the public. This was true even of the members of the Muslim Brotherhood, who up to that point had refrained from taking part in the armed struggle against Israel (their view was that spiritual work and a return to Islam came first). They changed their approach, establishing the Hamas movement, which took part in the demonstrations and in the subsequent armed struggle, and sought to lead them.

Israel responded forcefully, seeking to disperse the protesters, and carried out large-scale arrests to decimate the local Intifada committees, the Unified National Command that led the Intifada, and the Islamic movements that took part in it. Large IDF forces, first made up of the standing army and later of reservists, were sent into the territories by the national unity government led by Prime Minister Yitzhak Shamir of the Likud and Defense Minister Yitzhak Rabin of Labor. As the Palestinians had hoped, the uprising became an international issue and provoked, for the first time, a real split in mainstream Israeli society. But the Intifada reinforced the belief of many opponents of accommodation that the Arabs' goal was to destroy Israel and that an even harsher response was needed. At the same time, it buttressed the belief of the advocates of accommodation that the persistence of the occupation was undermining the moral foundations of Israeli society and causing it damage both internally and internationally.[61] The result was an even deeper political divide.

In the meantime, IDF soldiers perpetrated brutal acts of gratuitous violence against Palestinians. Nofar Yishai-Karin, then serving as an IDF welfare NCO, took part in a research project with psychologist Yoel Elitzur in which they interviewed soldiers from armored infantry units who had been through long tours of duty in the Gaza Strip. They divided the soldiers into five groups in accordance with their conduct during the Intifada. They called the first group "tough impulsives" (their fellow soldiers labeled them "psychopaths"), who cast aside all inhibitions and happily engaged in excessive violence. The second group were "ideologists," who supported violent conduct in principle but did not necessarily take part in it. Then there were the "conformists," who were swept along by their comrades to take part in violent acts, without enthusiasm and feeling uncomfortable about what they did. The fourth group consisted of the "reserved," who drew red lines for themselves but did not take action to avert injustices. The fifth group were the "conscientious," who were distressed by the violence and tried to mitigate it, if only for operational reasons.

Here's a sample testimony:

> After two months in Rafah [in the southern Gaza Strip], a commander arrived . . . so we went out for a first patrol with him. Six in the morning. Rafah is under curfew. Not even a dog is in the streets. Only a little four-year-old boy playing in the sand. He was building a sort of tower in the yard of his house. He [the commander] suddenly began running, and all of us ran with him. He grabbed the boy. Nofar, I'm a rat if I'm not telling you the truth. Broke his hand here, at the wrist. Broke his arm at the elbow. Broke his leg here. And began stamping on his stomach, three times, and then he left. We were all with our mouths gaping. Look at him in shock. . . . The next day I went out with him on another patrol and the soldiers already began doing the same. . . . You get it, when the commander does it, it becomes legitimate.[62]

VIOLENCE, ASHKENAZINESS, AND MIZRAHINESS

We don't know what ethnic group this violent officer belonged to, or the ethnicity of the soldier who was interviewed. We do know that soldiers from a wide variety of backgrounds, in all IDF units, took part in violent acts that violated official IDF orders. Most of these acts of violence are etched only in the memories of those who took part in them (and their victims); only a small number reached the press and, on occasion, the courts. Here's an early example: in January 1988, officers and soldiers from the weapons company of the Nahal Brigade's 50th Battalion brutally beat some twenty young Palestinian men from Hawara and Beita. They were under the command of Colonel Yehuda Meir, who was commander of the sector. (Meir said he acted in the spirit of Defense Minister Rabin's injunction "to break their arms and legs.") The young Palestinians, according to the court judgment in Meir's case, "were rounded up in the villages according to a list of names prepared by the Shabak, put on a bus, and driven out of the village, where they were taken off the bus in small groups and beaten. The beatings were carried out with clubs, some of which broke in the process, and sometimes they were kicked. The blows were generally directed at the lower extremities, but also at the upper limbs. During the beatings the locals' hands were bound and sometimes their feet as well. Their eyes were blindfolded with cloth and in a number of cases they were gagged as well."[63]

Another case that became public was that of four soldiers from the Duchifat Battalion who were filmed by a CBS television cameraman, Moshe Alpert, using large rocks to beat two Palestinian boys near Nablus. The footage—after censorship—was broadcast in Israel and around the world and caused an outcry. The solders involved were arrested, tried, and given suspended sentences. The four of them, like the unit as a whole, were from different ethnic backgrounds, as can be learned from their names: two of them were Mizrahi names (Iraqi, probably), one Ashkenazi, and one Hebraicization of an Ashkenazi name. The last had grown up in a kibbutz, while the others came from the center of the country.[64]

There were, of course, soldiers who felt uncomfortable with the orders they were given. Interviews with soldiers of left-wing orientation described how they overcame their inhibitions. Some cast off their dovish images of themselves and joined the wave of brutality, while others negotiated with their commanders over specific orders. Some tried to protest politically and were threatened with imprisonment. In the end, as one soldier said, "Soldiers talk, soldiers express their opinions on this side and that—there are soldiers who . . . who expressed contradictory, ah . . . opinions—but in the end, the bottom line was that, under the circumst— . . . working in the field, everyone, ah . . . did what they had to, exactly according to orders, in a way that was . . . above and beyond—what I said before. Unequivocally above and beyond . . . because that's why there is an army, that's why soldiers are soldiers. We're soldiers."[65]

BETWEEN "DEATH TO THE ARABS" AND "SHOOTING AND CRYING"

Attacks on Arabs carried out in violation of the law—whether, for example, the demonstrations in Ramla or Ben-Shimol's rocket—were sometimes explained by their perpetrators or by others as exemplifying Mizrahiness. This was not the case with violence carried out by the army, which was done in the name of the people as a whole and for their sake. It was therefore explained ambiguously, or attributed to instructions from above (Rabin said to break their arms and legs), or as necessary, even if excruciating. The constitutive ethos of these two types of violence was expressed in two opposing popular phrases: "death to the Arabs" and "shooting and crying." So it was up until and during the First Intifada. It changed later, as the character of the warriors in field units changed, when the army was transformed from an army of the people to an army of the peripheries, as political scientist Yagil Levy put it. In its new form, part of the army brought the "death to the Arabs" ethos to the fore.[66]

LEFT-WING PROTEST AND THE ETHNIC DEMON

The ethnic demon may have bowed its head in the discourse on IDF activity in the territories, but in the civilian realm the talk of ethnicity intensified. The principal reason was the Israeli Left's protests against the IDF's conduct in the territories. As during the Lebanon War, this protest was interpreted in opposite ways in the two political camps. On the right, the protest activity was seen as detrimental to the effort to suppress the uprising, which was essential for the survival of the country and its Jewish inhabitants. The Left, for its part, saw it as a sincere effort to maintain Israeli society's humanity in the face of the surge in Palestinian violence. The future of Israeli rule in the territories was also, as in the past, perceived in contradictory ways. For the Left, it was an immoral, anti-Jewish thirst for domination that was dooming Israel to infamy. For the Right, it was imperative for Israel's survival and, for many, a religious and national obligation.

The protest was manifold and diverse. At first, some of the news media criticized the IDF's conduct in the territories and uncovered some of the brutalities it was committing. On top of this, human rights organizations petitioned Israel's Supreme Court to compel the IDF to court-martial offending commanders and soldiers. Inhabitants of Beita and Hawara, with the help of the Association for Civil Rights in Israel (ACRI), succeeded in getting Colonel Yehuda Meir put on trial (in court, not just in a disciplinary proceeding). The military court did not sentence him to imprisonment but demoted him to the rank of private.

At the beginning of the Intifada, ACRI was virtually the only organization addressing civil rights in the territories. But the severe violations of rights during the Intifada led to the establishment, over the course of the uprising, of additional human rights associations, among them the Center for the Defense of the Individual (1988), Physicians for Human Rights–Israel (1988), Rabbis for Human Rights (1988), B'Tselem, the Israeli Information Center for Human Rights in the Occupied Territories (1989), the Public Committee Against Torture in Israel (1990), and Social Workers for Peace and Welfare (1991). Some focused on documentation and the dissemination of information, some offered assistance to individuals, and most worked in close coordination with Palestinian organizations. During the Intifada, Israel's main peace organization, Peace Now, strengthened its connections with the mainstream in Fatah, and smaller movements, such as Year 21 (founded on the eve of the Intifada), worked at high intensity and with a sense of urgency. Feminist peace movements also arose at this time: Women in Black, Bat Shalom, and Shani (Israeli Women Against the Occupation). Despite, or rather because of, the disorientation and distress that the Intifada caused, it led to a flowering of left-wing activity.

And this activity was colored white.

THE WHITENESS OF WOMEN IN BLACK

> A perusal of the common profile of a "Woman in Black" shows that they are women of considerable resources who share a similar ethnic-class background, such that they can be assigned to the sociocultural elite in Israel. The woman in black is non-religious (90 percent), of Ashkenazi origin (99 percent), with Israeli citizenship (93.9 percent), educated (85.7 percent with higher education, most of them in the humanities), relatively old (the median age is 47), and works to support herself (85 percent, of which 64.8 percent are wage earners, the rest in independent professions). Fifty-five percent of the women live without a partner (for a variety of reasons), and 25 percent of them have no children. In her younger years, the woman in black belonged to a youth movement (72 percent), and she is politically involved at a high level.

The quotation comes from a study of the movement, its characteristics, and its influences, produced by two of its members, Sara Helman and Tamar Rapoport. Women in Black was unusual in that its members did just one thing: they held protest signs at a silent vigil at central Jerusalem intersections each Friday. The group has been active for many years and remains so today. The title Helman and Rapoport gave to their article quotes slurs shouted by their opponents, who referred to their social profile and added further insults: "They Are Just Ashkenazi Women, Whores of Arabs, Don't Believe in God and Don't Love the Land of Israel."[67]

The social (and economic and ethnic) profile of Women in Black was much like that of the other protest organizations at that time (the same remains true, although less so, today), and the authors note that the same is true of social movements in the Western world as a whole. "Being of considerable resources, they are aware of their power to structure new social identities," Helman and Rapoport write. They viewed themselves as an elite ("We are the best of women," one of them said), and as standing above the people who observed them, in their perseverance, determination, inner integrity, and morality.[68]

The motivation of the members of Women in Black was ethical—they wanted to prevent attacks on Palestinians and a moral decline in Israeli society. Their critics stressed the fact that they were women and unleashed sexist invective on them every week, along with insults about their ethnicity and social class. These opponents took an alternative moral position—what, they asked, could be more ethical than to make the physical security of fellow Jews the overriding priority and be faithful to that people's tradition? That's not a new question. Is a person bound first by the moral values she believes in, or should her first commitment be to the prevailing values of the society in which she lives? But right-wing demonstrators had a hard time accepting that the Women in Black and their male allies were indeed motivated by lofty values. If they were really concerned about justice and equality, then why were they so blind to inequality in Israel, the fruits of which they had enjoyed for so many years? It's a simple fact that a privileged elite wrapping itself in an aura of moral superiority will have a lot of trouble gaining the sympathy of members of society who have long endured the arrogance and impositions of that same elite. On the other hand, people and groups who reject the principles of universal justice and equality will have trouble gaining the sympathy and support of people who believe in those principles.

According to Helman and Rapoport's study, only 1 percent of the Women in Black were of Mizrahi background. They would, of course, have welcomed more Mizrahi women into their ranks. They were certainly pleased by the gesture of one Mizrahi man who showed up at the vigil in Jerusalem week after week to hand out red roses to them. The man was Ezra Nawi, then an unknown plumber who did not accept the prevailing social and political norms. Twenty years later, he would emerge as a leader of joint Israeli-Palestinian action in the Hebron Hills in the southern West Bank.[69]

The need to open the peace movement to a wider range of Israeli society was a subject much discussed by its activists. But there was a gap between intention and action. During the Intifada's first year and in the years that followed, Mizrahi men and women with left-wing views complained that they got the cold shoulder, encountering even suspicion and mistrust, when they sought to take part in these groups' activities—all the more so when they sought staff positions with left-wing organizations.[70] The background was an unstated presumption that left-wing Mizrahim, especially those who were traditionally observant, could not be full participants because the Left was founded on the values of Western secular humanism and rationalism.[71] And perhaps there was an unconscious desire on the part of Ashkenazi activists, members of a social class accustomed to leading society who had lost their position of precedence, to maintain their power, at least in the arena of the peace organizations.

ASHKENAZI ACTIVISTS?

In their own eyes, as we have seen, Ashkenazim were unhyphenated Israelis, devoid of ethnic identity. But their opponents, those who shouted expletives at them, had no trouble identifying their unique class and ethnic characteristics.[72] That the Left had a specific class and ethnic profile was also the sociological viewpoint of Helman and Rapoport, except that they put the gender and political question at the center and saw Women in Black's demonstrations as a challenge to the prevailing social order. In contrast, sociologist Nissim Mizrachi, who analyzed the political and social protest two decades later, argued that the Left actually sought to maintain the existing order:

> Dissent against war, protest against the expulsion of foreign workers and their children, demands for social justice and Jewish-Arab solidarity: the issues raised at these events initially appear unconnected.

> The contexts also vary: armed conflict, social protest, and the struggle to reform government policy. Yet common to all of them is the clear and stable social profile of the two opposing camps. The demonstrators clearly belong to Israel's educated elite, the Ashkenazim or Jews of European origin. They include academics and professionals, the offspring of the country's founding fathers, or those having a clear demographic link to those elites. . . . Absent among them are immigrants from the former Soviet Union, religious nationalists, and ultra-Orthodox Jews, as well as Mizrahim.

Mizrachi compared the demonstrations to a masquerade on a timer, "with those formerly at the margins now in the center, and those formerly in the center now at the margins. Within a few hours, the police—a minority in uniform—'becomes' the state. Those dissenting from the events, who also overtly belong to the ethno-class margin, are repositioned in the center as defenders of the state. As for the demonstrators, the children of Israel's socio-economic and cultural elite, they become 'traitors' whose protests are perceived as veritable threats to the state's very existence."[73] Until the party ends.

THE ASHKENAZI-PALESTINIAN ALLIANCE

The growth of the protest and peace movements produced, argues Itamar Tubi Taharlev, "an Ashkenazi-Palestinian alliance" founded on sweeping the Mizrahi tragedy under the rug, in the form of a tacit agreement not to address the Mizrahi question.[74] This alliance benefits the Palestinians by giving them an entry ticket into the West through the Israeli Ashkenazi elite, while the Ashkenazim receive a sense of being welcome in the Middle East. In this view, the moral energies of the Israeli peace camp have been directed at the injustices committed against the Palestinians, for which the Right and the settlers can be blamed, rather than at the long-standing discrimination against Mizrahim, which was born and bred in the same circles that produced the Zionist Left. The Zionist Left benefits from the preservation of that discrimination. But it must be kept in mind that this is a very limited sort of alliance—only a few Palestinians and Ashkenazim adhere to it. Furthermore, in the years since the First Intifada, awareness of the Mizrahi question has grown, on the left as well as on the right. Furthermore, as the Mizrahi middle class has grown, so has Mizrahi representation on the left. To be politically and socially active, a person needs free time, a sense of competence, and a presumption that what you say will be heard. These are the rewards of middle-class life, no matter what one's ethnicity.

NOT ALL THE ASHKENAZIM, NOT ALL THE MIZRAHIM, NOT ALL THE TIME

The main drawback of social analyses is that generalization is built into them. Any statement about the emotional proclivities or responses of members of a social class or ethnic group, whether regarding a conviction of superiority or a sense of inferiority, a political stance, or an attitude toward an Other, of any sort, will necessarily be a generalization. Even if, both globally and locally, the West viewed the Orient as inferior, presumably there were Ashkenazim who did not feel superior to Mizrahim and those who sought to integrate into the Middle East, along with others who wanted to dismantle existing power relations. Even if many Mizrahim cast protest votes for the Likud, it's clear that some of them cast votes for the Right because they believed in the holiness of the Land of Israel. Alternatively, some of them voted for the Left or center because they viewed the people who had absorbed them into the country as beloved brothers and sisters and the difficulties of absorption as an unavoidable stage. We must thus keep in mind the role of sociology: to uncover and elucidate social structures and power relations. We must not forget psychology, the science that studies personality structures that lead individuals to act differently in similar situations. People have a measure of agency, which enables them to diverge from the path onto which social structures direct them. As a result, they have different life histories. Each human being maneuvers among a number of worlds of meaning. "My mother," writes the anthropologist Pnina Motzafi-Haller, "does not analyze and categorize imperatives as belonging to the 'traditional' or 'modern' world. The simultaneous [ostensibly contradictory] discourses of which she makes use are inexorably bound together in her life, and the decisions she makes emerge from a combination of terms and perceptions of the world that she adopts in part, as befits specific times in her life. . . . Her 'identity' is not defined and fixed, it is in constant flux and always in pieces."[75] In the same way, others, Ashkenazim and Mizrahim, change and metamorphose over time and according to context. In other words, relations among social groups—ethnic, class, gender, and so on—and the individuals who belong to them are not rigid.

But two things must be kept in mind. First, fundamental social affiliations, class or ethnic, have great weight in the conduct of individuals. This is the case for Palestinians rising up against Israel and those who collaborate with it, and it is the case for Israelis who demand that the state employ all measures needed to achieve victory and for those who demand that it act with restraint and strive to reach a compromise. The fact is that the emotional worlds of men and women, and their worlds of meaning, are by and large social constructs.[76]

Second, acting out of group affiliation does not mean that the emotions of the actors are not experienced on a personal or "authentic" level. For example, left-wing Ashkenazi demonstrators felt real anger and pain over Israel's conduct in the territories, not just a desire to maintain their self-images and social standing; Mizrahi demonstrators on the right sought to maintain their Jewish national values, and were not motivated only by alienation from the elitist Left.

NOT JUST ON THE POLITICAL LEFT

Mizrahim experienced a sense of disaffection not only when they took part in a protest against the occupation but also in other manifestly Ashkenazi frameworks. This was true of Mizrahim from south Tel Aviv who attended schools in the city's well-off north as part of efforts to integrate schools, and those who attended Bnei Akiva yeshivot or joined Gush Emunim settlement groups in the territories. Yehuda Yifrach, a columnist for the newspaper *Makor Rishon*, the voice of the settlement movement and the religious Right, wrote about the experience he and his Moroccan family had when they tried (and succeeded, with difficulty) to be accepted as settlers in Beit El, an Israeli settlement in the West Bank. He related that the elementary school he attended placed him on a low track in arithmetic class and that he was turned away by the local junior high school yeshiva run by the Merkaz Harav yeshiva. He was also rejected by the prestigious Bnei Akiva Netiv Meir high school yeshiva in Jerusalem because there were quotas for Mizrahim. He and his family suffered other indignities. He offered his own definition of the difference between being Ashkenazi and being Sephardi. Religious Zionist Ashkenazim, he argued, saw time as fundamentally directional, expressed in the teleological and ideological pursuit of goals, progress, and achievement. Mizrahi society, by contrast, saw time as cyclical, always returning to where it began, and this was expressed in its acceptance of people as they are, a way of life based on human connection and variation.[77]

Yifrach accepted the axiom that there are profound differences between Mizrahim (he calls them "Sephardim") and Ashkenazim, unlike those who see those differences as fleeting and superficial. He located these differences in the spiritual realm and accepted the utility of both viewpoints, and the connection between them. Gush Emunim leader Benny Katzover summed up the prevailing view of Mizrahim from the religious Zionist perspective. "I must say that I feel best when I come into contact with people of Edot Hamizrah," he declared. "This public has the healthiest sense with regard to the

Land of Israel. When you tell this public, 'this is how it is,' it understands and does not try to enter into disputations."[78] There are two sides to this statement. Seeking to commend the Mizrahim, Katzover described his positive feelings when he encountered them, and gave them high marks on the scale of love of the Land of Israel. But he also portrayed them as people whose job is to act, not think.

But there were Mizrahim who disagreed with Katzover and the Zionist political mainstream. They took the humanity of which Yifrach wrote and applied it to relations with the Palestinians as well. Following the murder of Emil Grunzweig, the literary scholar Shlomo Elbaz, the philosopher Asher Idan, and the poet and psychoanalyst Shelley Elkayam were among the founders of the East for Peace. Its principles were social justice, Israel as part of the Middle East, and pursuit of a just peace, including recognition of Palestinian nationalism.[79] Mapam activist Latif Dori, along with Elbaz and the actor Yosef Shiloach, founded the Committee for Israeli-Palestinian Dialogue in 1986, one of the first Israeli organizations to recognize the PLO.[80] During the First Intifada, the profile of the members of Mizrahi peace groups broadened to a certain extent, and their contacts with the PLO and Palestinians from the territories intensified.

The climactic moments of these contacts came at an encounter in Toledo, Spain, in July 1989, initiated by the French-Moroccan filmmaker Simone Bitton, under the sponsorship of Perspectives Judeo-Arabes. The meeting brought Mizrahi activists from Israel, Morocco, France, and elsewhere together with senior PLO figures. Tikva Levi, a Mizrahi feminist education activist from Ashkelon who was involved in Jewish-Palestinian activity in Jerusalem, offered an overview of the comprehensive vision of the Mizrahi Left that had emerged at the time (in which feminist women were prominent), and sought to offer an alternative to the nationalist discourse that had spread among the Mizrahi public.

THE TOLEDO ENCOUNTER—THE GREAT HOPE

The PLO-Mizrahi encounter took place at a time when it was still illegal for Israelis to meet with members of the PLO. For that reason, the organizers took care not to seat the PLO representatives next to the Israelis. Nevertheless, both participants and observers sensed that the event would enter the history books as a turning point in Israeli public opinion.[81]

Levi, then twenty-nine years old, presented her vision of a Mizrahi-Palestinian alliance.

If we take a look at the platforms of all the parties of the Left, listen to the speeches of politicians and intellectuals who speak about peace, for some reason, the bottom line in the best case is: "Two states for two peoples [using] the '67 borders." Let's for a moment ascend on the wings of our Mizrahi imagination and recount to ourselves how we got into this situation. I ask: and what then? Have wishes come to an end? Have dreams come to an end? Have aspirations come to an end? My claim is that that situation is the first step on the ladder. More than that, it is the most rickety step, which is liable to cast both states into an abyss if they do not continue to the second step, which is an open border. When I say open border, I do not mean that Israelis will go shopping for bargains in Palestine and that Palestinians will come to clean up our garbage. When I say open border, I see myself sitting in a lecture hall at Bir Zeit [University] as a student enrolled there, in a course on Palestinian poetry, and Al-Hakawati Theatre being hosted by Habima Theatre in Tel Aviv.

Then we'll climb up to the third step on the ladder. That is the step where the Mizrahim enter the picture, in a big way. The Mizrahim will enter at this stage because, since their immigration from the Arab countries, they were told by the Ashkenazim that everything Arab is bad, dirty, primitive, stoned cockroaches. They're two-legged beasts with hair on their faces. And this stereotype of the Arabs is the mirror that reflects the figure of the Mizrahim, since it is clear to all of us that we the Mizrahim are Arabs! What's the story, we're Arab Jews. The moment that the figure is reflected in the mirror without the mask that the Ashkenazim have stitched, the Mizrahim will stop fearing that they might be taken for Arabs, and that will happen only when a Palestinian state comes into being and when there will be an open border. In fact, these two steps are the act that will grant legitimacy to the Mizrahim. Only then will they go back to living the way they were here, in Toledo, Spain, 900 years ago; only then will they go back to living the way my parents did in Iraq before the beginning of that story called Zionism. And, my friends, my parents were not in a Jewish ghetto, my parents lived among Arabs, and lived well! . . .

For me, the Ashkenazi Right and Left are analogous, because both of them are scared to death of the third step on the ladder, the step when Palestinians and Mizrahim will create facts on the ground of life without any artificial barriers—the reality in which the borders

> will look ridiculous, a reality in which a further step on the ladder will be imposed on them, in which there will be a single state, in which everyone will be equal citizens before a just law. Not like the current situation, in which justice is in the East and the law in the West. If we look at human history, and even if we only look at the current reality, we will understand very well who will be the principal loser in the vision of a single state in which everyone will be equal before a just law. The losers will be those who have long had a hold on power, on money, on culture. You all know the answer, who that is! And whoever thinks that that is a wild Spanish dream is welcome to it.[82]

In her comprehensive, far-reaching dream, Levi used the term "Mizrahim," which was slowly, in some circles, replacing "the members of Edot Hamizrah," or "Sephardim." Sociologist Meir Amor, one of the founders of the Kedma School in Tel Aviv and one of the leaders of the Toledo encounter, said in an interview at that time that when a person says "Mizrahi," it is the first sign that they are breaking free of Ashkenazi consciousness. He believed that the transformation would come about (if it came about) when Jews from the Islamic world began to see themselves in a political context and to understand the connection between the oppression of the Palestinians and their own oppression.[83]

SPEECH AND ACTION

Amor, a reserve infantry officer, arrived in Toledo a year after spending time in a military prison for refusing to serve in the territories at the beginning of the Intifada. The public statement he issued before going to prison was translated into Arabic and appeared in Arab media outlets. "The events in the Occupied Territories are the result of a misguided policy that presumes that it is possible to repress an entire nation and prevent it from expressing its national, cultural, and social identity," he wrote. A political solution would be attainable, he added, only by means of negotiations between free people. He stressed that the problem of the Israeli residents of development towns and underprivileged neighborhoods was inextricably tied to the Palestinian question. Refusal to perform military service, he said, was a legitimate response in the face of an incompetent leadership.[84]

Unlike in the past, the Arab media outlets that published Amor's letter did not address the Mizrahi question. Mahmoud Abbas, who attended the Toledo encounter, did so explicitly, just as he had done in his article in 1977.

"The ruling establishment in Israel, with the assistance of the highly influential Western propaganda apparatus, labeled and portrayed the Mizrahim as haters of Arabs and Palestinians," he declared there. "Your very presence with us, as representatives of important parts of Israeli public opinion, proves the invalidity of this allegation against you. Thus, our welcome to you is based on your profound awareness of the advantages of a just peace under which we may all live."[85]

For a moment, it looked as if the Mizrahi-Palestinian alliance was actually taking form.

FROM THE PINNACLE OF HOPE TO THE ABYSS OF REALITY

On July 6, 1989, the day before the Israeli delegation to Toledo returned to Israel, Abd al-Hadi Ghanim, from Gaza, pounced on the driver of a number 405 bus from Tel Aviv to Jerusalem and managed to steer the bus off the highway and over a cliff. The bus flipped over and burst into flames. Sixteen passengers were killed and dozens injured. It was the worst attack on Jews of the First Intifada. Up to that point, nine Jews and 517 Palestinians had died in the conflict, according to figures provided by the IDF spokesman. Now the number of Jews killed had risen to twenty-five.[86]

The disparity between the numbers of Jews and Palestinians killed throughout all stages of the Israeli-Palestinian conflict has had, and continues to have, a huge impact on Palestinian public opinion and on how Palestinians see Israel. This is something that the Israeli public, counting and mourning its own dead, does not see. This gaze that looks only inward explains why Israelis believe their army to be the most moral army in the world, while the Palestinians, grieving again and again for their dead killed by the IDF, find that claim unconvincing.

But that is not what concerns us here. What's important for the matter at hand is the popular—including the Mizrahi—response to this bus attack in Israel. "Wave of Acts of Revenge Following the Bloody Terror Attack: Arab Driver Murdered in the South," blared a banner headline in the daily newspaper *Hadashot*. "Jamal Nassir (31) of Gaza was killed yesterday when he was hit by a rock thrown at his car, close to Moshav Shibolim in the Negev. . . . In Jerusalem on Saturday, hundreds of young people rioted, throwing rocks at Arab vehicles at the intersection of Shmuel Hanavi and Bar-Ilan Streets. Guards were deployed around the home of a left-wing member of the Knesset, Dedi Zucker, after dozens of violent rioters threw rocks at the house. Five were arrested. During the funeral of Miriam Tzerafi-Zargari, may her memory be a blessing, the day before yesterday in Jerusalem, Vice Prime Minister Shimon Peres was attacked by an angry mob that shouted at him: 'Hey Peres, hey vermin, why do you come only to funerals? The Arabs are slaughtering us one by one. Wake up, all of you, wake up.'"[87] Miriam Tzerafi was the elder sister of the well-known singer Ruhama Raz, who wrote a song, "Instead of Parting," in her memory.

By this time, the press was no longer noting the ethnic affiliation of the assailants. Neither were politicians. "Jews who throw stones at Arab passersby are primitive and hotheaded," said Minister of Police Haim Bar-Lev, making no explicit reference to ethnicity.[88] An exceptional insinuation about the Mizrahi ethnicity of the Jewish assailants (within Israel proper; in the territories the aggression was led by Ashkenazi settlers) came from *Hadashot* correspondent Zvi Gilat. When, after their return from Toledo, Meir Amor and David Hamo spoke to him about the temperate Mizrahi approach, he shared with his readers his own surprise. "Can it be?" he wrote. "After all, the polls show how much support Kahane received in underprivileged Mizrahi neighborhoods. The mob and the stone-throwers at the Ashdod junction are not particularly pale-faced. The claim that 'the Arabs only understand force' doesn't come from Galicia."[89]

Really? The phrase "the Arabs only understand force" may not have been coined in Galicia. But some of the Second Aliyah pioneers who came from Greater Russia (the Moskobim)—those who belonged to Hashomer, and later to the Haganah and Etzel—held precisely this view. This contrasted with the thinking of the Sephardi leadership, which at that time believed in dialogue.[90] But in the 1980s it was possible to argue, within the internal Israeli Zionist discourse, that it was immigrants from the Islamic world who had always led and continued to lead the use of force against Palestinians. This was in part because of the Right's accession to government and the fact that most of the human rights organizations were founded by Ashkenazim of the Left, and in part because the role Sephardim played in early Zionist history was being repressed.

"THE ARABS ARE SLAUGHTERING US ONE BY ONE"

The cry "the Arabs are slaughtering us one by one," directed at Peres at Miriam Tzerafi-Zargari's funeral, was not a statement of statistical fact but rather of pain at the death of every Jew killed by Palestinian terrorists. Prior to the 405 bus attack, the ratio of Israeli to Palestinian deaths during the First Intifada was 1:50; after the attack, it was 1:25. The mass killings of Palestinians by

Israelis compelled the Palestinians to take up arms. By the end of the Intifada in September 1993, following three years of knifings and gunfire, the number of Israeli dead reached 160, as compared to the 1,149 Palestinians killed by IDF soldiers and Israeli civilians, a ratio of 1:7.[91] (The Palestinians refrained from using firearms during the first stages of the conflict, when they hoped that a popular uprising using cold weapons would be sufficient to achieve political results.)

As knifings became more frequent, criticism of the national unity government—and the Left—grew more vocal. The government, critics maintained, was not permitting the security forces to act more aggressively against Palestinian violence. When a border policeman, Charlie (Shalom) Shlush, was killed in a stabbing attack on October 21, 1990, the feeling that the IDF was not being allowed to use all its might intensified. The attack took place about two weeks after police entered the Temple Mount to stop Palestinians who were casting rocks down on Jewish worshippers at the Western Wall. They killed seventeen Palestinians in the process. (The stone throwing followed a ceremony in which the Temple Mount Faithful, an extreme right-wing organization that sought to reclaim that site for the Jews, laid a cornerstone there for a new Jewish Temple.) Shlush, a master sergeant in the Border Police's counterterrorism unit, was on leave at his home in Jerusalem's Baka neighborhood when he heard screams on the street. He grabbed his rifle, ran outside, and saw that an attacker had already stabbed to death two of his neighbors, Eli Altaretz and Iris Azulai. He shot the assailant in the legs and then put him in a clinch to neutralize him. The two men grappled on the ground, and the attacker, Omar Abu Sirhan, managed to stab Shlush to death with the knife he still held in his hand. It was alleged that Shlush had refrained from shooting to kill because the IDF's rules of engagement did not permit it. This was seen as solid proof—for any who sought proof—that the Left and its views on human rights were causing Jewish deaths.

Baka, the neighborhood where the murders occurred, was a Peace Now stronghold in Jerusalem. But, unlike other such neighborhoods, it had a diverse population consisting of both working-class Mizrahim living in housing projects and middle-class Ashkenazi academics and professionals who moved in as the neighborhood gentrified. Relations between the two populations were largely good, but even before the Intifada there were some signs of political tension. Avishai Margalit, a Hebrew University philosopher and Peace Now activist, recounted a conversation that echoed a familiar claim. "Of course you want to finish off this thing with the Arabs," a neighbor of

Margalit's told him. "You want to give them a state, everything, because you want to put me back to working as a plasterer. You want to put us, the Frenkim [a derogatory term for Mizrahim], back to working as plasterers. You don't feel good about the fact that for us it's a little better."[92] And Tzali Reshef, one of Peace Now's leaders, devoted a chapter in his book about the movement to the murder, which begins: "The stone that was thrown from the street hit the closed shutter and shook the window behind it. Someone outside shouted 'Peace Now—a knife in the back,' and I saw Yisraela unconsciously put her head down in anticipation of the next stone, which followed immediately." He noted the neighborhood's ethnic mix: "It's one of Jerusalem's most serene neighborhoods, where two populations live side by side—the old residents, mostly Mizrahi, who were settled in the homes of Arabs who fled when the state was established, and relatively new inhabitants, largely college-educated Ashkenazim, who began buying and remodeling apartments there starting in the mid-1970s."[93] Reshef's paragraph is seeded, incidentally, with incongruities and paradoxes. He writes of Peace Now activists living in homes abandoned by Arabs in 1948, even as they call for the evacuation of Israeli settlements in the territories, and he suggests that Arabs "fled" from the neighborhood, rather than being expelled, during the 1948 war. He also neglects to remind his readers that the neighborhood was neglected and decrepit before the educated Ashkenazim arrived, which led many of the Mizrahim to leave it to buy new homes in outlying neighborhoods just then under construction. After the Ashkenazim moved in, the municipality upgraded the neighborhood's infrastructure until it became one of the city's most expensive and best-tended neighborhoods.

REVENGE

About two months after Charlie Shlush's death, his brother, Aryeh, then a soldier performing his mandatory service, set out to avenge his brother's death. Aryeh Shlush was serving then with the Combat Engineering Corps in Gush Etzion. On the night of December 27, Shlush left his base with his Galil rifle and two magazines and took up a position alongside the Gush intersection. When a car passed with a license plate indicating that it belonged to an Arab from the territories, he emptied a magazine at it and returned to his base. A Hebron physician, Dr. Faisal Amru, was mortally wounded, but his life was saved by Dr. Baruch Goldstein, who three years later would murder twenty-nine Palestinian Muslims in the Cave of the Patriarchs. Amru's sister and her daughter suffered moderate wounds. Shlush was arrested a few days later. When police detectives first encountered him, he immediately confessed to the crime. "After Charlie was murdered, I wept all the time," he told the officers who came to arrest him. "I felt horrible pain." The pain intensified, he said, when he heard about an attempt by Palestinians to stab soldiers in Gaza. He was tried and sentenced to seven years' imprisonment; his appeal was rejected.[94] Dov Goldstein, a journalist for *Maariv*, wrote of a conversation he had with "a senior government minister's driver" following Shlush's revenge attack. "What is it you want from that poor soldier, Aryeh Shlush?" asked the driver, who, from his social position, identified the media with the government and saw them as a single entity. "He suddenly had an urge to shoot at Arabs?" the driver went on. "After all, just two and a half months previously an Arab murdered his brother, policeman Charlie Shlush, in Baka in Jerusalem. Okay, I understand that no private individual is allowed to take the law into his own hands, but the judge who judges Aryeh Shlush can understand that, no?"

Goldstein noted:

> It's a conversation between equals. You need to say over and over to yourself that this young man, a model citizen, excellent worker, well-mannered and easygoing, is entitled to his own opinion. . . .
>
> I ask him if understanding motives . . . works in the opposite direction, too; after all, Arabs are getting killed almost every day. Sometimes young people, sometimes children. . . . No, he says, but I hear a tinge of uncertainty in his voice, it's not the same thing. The thing is that the Arabs always start it and the Jews always respond, as an act of revenge. So how can you say that they should get equal punishments? I try to break through with another inference—Charlie's murderer was apprehended. The police have him. He will be brought to trial and if he's found guilty, he'll be punished. The doctor, his sister, and her baby daughter are innocent of any crime. Why should they bear responsibility for the murderer's acts?
>
> They really shouldn't—the young man gives me a brief moment of gratification—and I, if God forbid a horrible thing happened to me like it did to Aryeh Shlush, I wouldn't go take revenge and attack just any innocent Arabs. That's really not just. But the punishment Shlush received, doesn't it need to take into account that he went to avenge the murder of his brother Charlie?[95]

Goldstein, representing, in his own eyes, the so-called enlightened public, found himself in a quandary. On the one hand, he admitted, he would have preferred that the driver not form an independent opinion but rather adopt his, Goldstein's, opinion, the opinion of the establishment. But he realized that this was a problematic attitude, so he struggled against it. The only recourse he had was thus to debate with the driver without really listening to him. But in debating the driver, he concealed (perhaps also from himself) a basic fact that contradicted his claim—that official Israel also treated with understanding Jews who murdered Arabs for national reasons. In January 1991 he could not have known that Shlush would have his sentence commuted by Israel's president and end up serving only two and a half years of his prison sentence, thanks precisely to the very sort of sympathy that the driver sought for him. But he certainly would have known that there were plentiful precedents for such early releases. A case in point is that of the men convicted of the Kafr Qasim massacre of 1956. Shmuel Malinki, who had been sentenced to fourteen years in prison, was released after serving forty months. And the platoon commander who was the most active force in the massacre itself, Gabriel Dahan, was sentenced to ten years but was released after about three years. He returned to his hometown of Ramla and was appointed, over the protests of the city's Arab inhabitants, to head the city's civil defense.[96]

But Goldstein was under the spell of the image that Israel marketed about itself, and he disregarded the traditional disparity between what the country declared to outsiders and its actual actions. This enabled him to maintain his sense of being a progressive in his conversation with the outraged driver.

KNIFINGS, ACTS OF REVENGE, RESCUES

In mid-1990, the Intifada metamorphosed. The Unified National Command lost control, Hamas gained strength, and individual Palestinian assailants and terrorist bands expanded their operations within Israeli proper. Popular outrage intensified in Israel's streets. Two Jerusalem teenagers, Lior Toubul and Ronen Karamani, went out on a Friday night, were forced into a Palestinian car, and were murdered. In response, "thousands of Jews went out to attack Jerusalem Arabs; they injured dozens, some of them seriously," *Hadashot* reported. After the boys' funerals, hundreds of residents of Pat surged into the neighboring Arab village of Beit Safafa (recall the fraternization of young Jews and Arabs from these two neighborhoods at the beginning of this same decade), smashed windows, and wrecked houses. "For these two who were killed we'll kill two hundred!" they shouted. Ronen Karamani's father pleaded to no avail, "I don't want anyone to take the law into his hands. There are innocent families, we live adjacent to an Arab neighborhood, Beit Safafa, and we don't want to harm them and they won't harm us. . . . We don't want to kill people, nor to go to war with our neighbors."[97] Although he apparently represented many other Mizrahim, his voice went unheard.

That's how it is in moments of anger. In the end, the disposition that sought to avoid unnecessary bloodshed and to mollify the heated passions brought on by terror attacks tilted the scales in the Knesset elections of 1992 and made Yitzhak Rabin prime minister. But, in the meantime, stabbings and revenge attacks continued. In December 1990, Iris Asraf and Moshe Ivan were stabbed to death at the aluminum factory in Jaffa where they worked; the murderers, laborers from Gaza who worked in the plant, then killed Yehoshua Hakmaz, a neighbor who had heard the victims' screams and ran to help them. A journalist, Igal Sarna, went to the scene soon thereafter. He wrote later:

> In Jaffa, across from the home of the murdered girl Iris Asraf, three Israeli Arab construction workers stand on top of the skeleton of an unfinished building doing sealing. A crowd assembles for the funeral. "There are Arabs over there," one of the mourners shouts. "Death to the Arabs!" The workers make out a group splitting off from the mourning crowd, approaching the construction site, and arming itself with boards. One of the workers descends to call for help. He hears a Jewish plasterer tell the rioters: "There are two more above," and he sees about forty people with sticks and boards running after him.
>
> A neighbor from a nearby home arrives with her two children as Rafik, the worker, is looking for cover. She sees an Arab running and thinks: a knifer. Her daughter screams "Help!" and runs to the stairwell and begins to bang on doors to ask for assistance. Two other girls who come by run with her. The light in the stairwell goes out and they hear the Arab panting near them. When a neighbor opens her door, the three girls and the Arab enter to take shelter. When Rafik puts his hand in his pocket, the neighbor is certain that he's drawing a knife. He wants to show her his Israeli I.D. card.

"I pushed him out," the neighbor tells Sarna. "He goes out without resistance and she locks the door. The rioters catch him on the stairs. They beat him until he escapes into the apartment [across the landing] whose door has opened, and locks the security door behind him. The rioters bang on the steel door, making dents and almost bending it out of shape. The neighbor from across the way, watching through the peephole in her door, sees the Arab enter the apartment and is certain that he is murdering the entire family inside. . . . Rafik calls the police, and when the policemen arrive he opens the door for them and they push him to the wall and search him. At that same moment the rioters enter through the open door and thrash Rafik and two policemen who try to call in reinforcements. 'Poor Arab,' the neighbor tells me. 'If he hadn't gone into Kadosh's apartment and locked it, they would have finished him off.'"[98]

Rafik's life was saved by the Kadosh family. Readers familiar with Hebrew family names will know that the family was Moroccan. Ilanit Ohana and Abd al-Karim Abd al-Ghani were not as lucky. In March of the same year, 1990, a knife-wielding Gazan pounced on Ohana, an eighteen-year-old girl, on Eilat Street in Jaffa. She fled toward al-Ghani's garage, and he tried to defend her and repel the assailant, but to no avail. The attacker stabbed and killed him, and then finished off Ohana as well.[99] Gan Hashnayim Park in Jaffa (also known as the Gazans' Park) is dedicated to their memory.

THE MURDER OF HELENA RAPP: EXPLICIT AND IMPLICIT

The violence in the streets continued. According to one newspaper report:

> A police officer was beaten and incurred moderate injuries. An Arab was stabbed and incurred moderate injuries. A Border Police company was sent to Bat Yam and an army contingent to the Rishon intersection to overpower the rioters. Some 120 Arabs were placed in "preventative detention" and some 20 Jewish rioters were arrested. . . . Dozens of people attacked the many police cruisers that extricated laborers from the mob, throwing stones and boards at the policemen. A police detective, Chief Inspector Albert Ohayon, was beaten over the head with an enormous iron rod and incurred moderate injuries when he tried to prevent the lynching of Arab construction workers.[100]

The unrest came in response to the murder of Helena Rapp, a fifteen-year-old girl who was killed on her way to school in May 1992. The violence went on for several days. On the third day, *Yediot Aharonot* reported that the shouts of "Death to the Arabs!" had been replaced by cries of "Death to the police!" According to that newspaper, "Thousands raged and traded blows with the police. More than a hundred were arrested."[101] The mainstream media attributed the calls of "Death to the Arabs" at the games of the Betar Jerusalem soccer team to low-status right-wing Mizrahim. "But the killing itself, in contrast, when it is carried out in an institutionalized way, endows the operation with prestige, and for many years such activity was reserved for social elites generally identified with the Left," wrote Anat Rimon Or.[102] Yet sometimes a person who shouts "Death to the Arabs" also tries to kill them. In Bat Yam, policemen, Arabs, and even high school students who were suspected of being Peace Now supporters were beaten.[103] What can we learn from that?

WHAT CAN WE LEARN?

Mainly that the anger ran very deep. It was linked to a sense of existential fear, national struggle, economic insecurity, and the sense that everyone is against us. But who is the "us" who "everyone" is against? Who makes up the mobs that go out into the street to smash windows and beat people up? In this case as well, the major media outlets did not refer to the Mizrahi ethnicity of the attackers. But they were mostly Mizrahim, and there were readers who discerned, in the language of the press, intimations that they were attributing the violence to Mizrahim.[104]

The demonstrations were turbulent and swept up masses of people, but from a broader perspective there were signs of confusion and rupture in the Israeli—and within that the Mizrahi—response to the Intifada. The family of Moshe Ivan, who was murdered in the aluminum factory in Jaffa, grieved for him. His wife, Yehudit, told a reporter, "That Arab doesn't deserve to live. I hope that he won't get the benefit of being sent to jail, where they'll feed him for years. I think that the time has come to find a proper political solution. Until then, we need to stop letting them into the country."[105] Profound loathing for the Arab who killed her husband (despite what she said were good relations between the two men) and a desire to prevent other murders by means of a temporary closure of the borders with the territories came together with a hope for a fair political solution to the Israeli-Palestinian conflict. Such confusion could also be seen in Rabbi Baruch Abuhatzeira (Baba Baruch). He came out in support of negotiations with the PLO, but when he was castigated for doing so, he said: talks, yes, giving up Judea and Samaria, no.[106] The inconsistency was a sign of what would come in the 1992 elections.

RABIN, KING OF ISRAEL

The main issue in the 1992 elections was the personal security of Israel's citizens. Yitzhak Rabin, who won the primary for the Labor Party leadership against his rival, Shimon Peres, did not hesitate to visit places that, since the Mandate period, had been traditional right-wing strongholds. In Tel Aviv's Hatikva neighborhood, with its large Mizrahi and Yemenite population, one of the inhabitants told him, "I am named after David Raziel [a founder of the Etzel underground] and I have a son named Arik and a girl named Sharon [named after the hawkish general turned Likud politician Ariel Sharon], but with Rabin it sounds as if there is a chance. With Rabin the hand no longer trembles when you ask others to vote for him." A journalist who accompanied Rabin as he canvassed underprivileged neighborhoods wrote prior to the election that "an upset [is in the making]. With Rabin, but especially in the [underprivileged Mizrahi] neighborhoods. The Likud has vanished from the field, has lost its stronghold and its certainty. . . . [For] those who were once Likud [voters] . . . Rabin is the new wall to wail at. . . . They believe that he might reconnect them to the electric grid and water system, which were cut off because of the burden of their debts." In May, Prime Minister Yitzhak Shamir held an election rally in Be'er Sheva and encountered hundreds of demonstrators who booed him and sang, "Rabin, king of Israel." Shamir asked the police to intervene and called the demonstrators "terrorists."[107] In doing so, he carried on the Israeli political tradition of the previous decade: Mizrahim who demonstrate in your favor are brothers. Those who demonstrate against you are Arabs or terrorists.

When the votes were counted, the Labor Party under Rabin had won forty-four seats in the Knesset, while Shamir's Likud had won thirty-two, a decline of eight seats for the Likud. Giora Goldberg, a political scientist who investigated the election, found that in Mizrahi towns such as Ofakim and Yokneam Illit, the Likud lost votes mostly to Labor, but that in Ashkenazi locations, such as Ramat Efal and Raanana, the Likud lost votes mostly to Tzomet, a secular nationalist party led by a former IDF chief of staff, Rafael Eitan.[108] While the voters who returned to Labor from the Likud weren't in possession of that data, they knew very well what was going on. The Likud government had not improved their lives enough. In 1991, about 40 percent of Ashkenazim had a postsecondary education, but only 14 percent of Mizrahim did. Furthermore, the Israeli-born children of Ashkenazim were better educated than their parents' generation was, while the educational profile of Israeli-born Mizrahim remained just like that of their parents.[109] Rabin's message centered on security but also offered hope—Israeli separation from the Palestinians in an effort to achieve accommodation without neglecting social issues.[110]

Rabin formed a coalition with the left-wing Meretz party and the Mizrahi Haredi Shas party. In his speech to the Knesset marking the establishment of his government, on July 13, 1992, Rabin declared that he would work to ensure Israel's security and to achieve peace with the Palestinians and Arab states. He would follow, he said, in the footsteps of Menachem Begin, who had signed the peace agreements with Egypt. Those agreements, he noted, provided for Palestinian autonomy that included the establishment of a Palestinian Authority with a strong police force. "The new government proposes to the Palestinians in the territories that they give peace a chance and cease all violent and terrorist activity during the period of negotiations over autonomy," he said.[111] Fourteen months later, he signed a declaration of principles on the White House lawn, which included recognition of the PLO and agreement to the establishment of a self-governing Palestinian Authority.

RABBI OVADIA, SHAS, AND THE OSLO ACCORDS

When they were placed before the cabinet, the Oslo agreements put Shas in a precarious position. Rabbi Ovadia Yosef had long been interested in furthering a peace process with the Arabs. Following Egyptian president Anwar Sadat's visit to Jerusalem in 1977, he had voiced his opinion that "when peace can prevent the shedding of Jewish blood, the aspiration for peace is a commandment," and "it is inconceivable to forsake Jewish souls for any patch of land." In a widely read halachic ruling, he asserted that it was the country's military and political leaders who should make the determination about whether a diplomatic agreement contributed to Israel's security.[112] But between Camp David in the late 1970s and Oslo in the 1990s, the public arena had changed. The ethnic divide had aligned much more starkly with the political divide, which itself had not been as stark at the time of the agreement with Egypt. Furthermore, Sinai differed from Judea and Samaria on the halachic, security, and historical levels. There was also the fact that the Oslo agreements were concluded by a Labor rather than, as in the case of the peace treaty with Egypt, a Likud government.

The widely varying approaches of Sephardi rabbis to matters of peace and the Arabs were already evident at the funeral of Eliyahu Amedi, a year before the Intifada. Rabbi Ovadia had called for accommodation, while Rabbi Elbaz had called for revenge. The revenge camp grew stronger during the initial years of the Intifada. Some of the members of that camp, who had previously voted for Rabbi Kahane, switched to Shas after Kahane was blocked from running again. In the face of the Oslo agreements, Shas had to decide its position on the issue.

Rabbi Ovadia, who had ruled that his party should join the Rabin government, also supported its peace initiatives. "We are of the same opinion as Rabin," he said in an interview with *Maariv* in 1992. "We need to move toward peace even at the price of painful concessions, so as to avert bloodshed," he declared. "The public knew that we were striving for peace and it supported us."[113]

Despite the rabbi's support for the peace process, many in Shas opposed the agreements. The Oslo Accords were approved by the cabinet without opposition (two ministers, Shimon Shetreet of Labor and Aryeh Deri of Shas, abstained) and then placed before the Knesset. Prior to the Knesset vote, Deri proposed that the Shas faction occupy a middle ground by abstaining; Rabbi Yosef accepted his advice. In the end, sixty-one members of the Knesset voted in favor and fifty opposed, with six members of Shas abstaining. Deri explained, "Our abstention is not because we oppose the agreement, but because we do not have anyone in the government who will oversee its implementation." (Deri had been forced to resign his cabinet post just before the vote because he had been indicted on bribery and breach-of-trust charges.) "As far as Rabbi [Ovadia] sees it," he maintained, "this is passive support for the peace agreement."[114] Another person close to the rabbi, Shas's lawyer David Glass, cited another important point after the Shas leader's death. Rabbi Ovadia's halachic ruling, he said, "is not the result of love of Ishmael [the Arabs] but rather of love of Israel. The rabbi did not love Arabs, to put it mildly. We spoke about this subject a great deal and while my views came from the humanitarian side—not to be a nation of conquerors—for Rabbi Ovadia that was not in any way a consideration." The principle was saving Jewish lives.[115]

In the months following the vote, the opponents of the agreement, both Israeli and Palestinian, did all they could to prevent its implementation. In February 1994, Baruch Goldstein slaughtered Muslim worshippers at the Cave of the Patriarchs in Hebron; in response, the Hamas leadership sent suicide bombers to attack civilians inside Israel. Once again, Israel's streets flowed with blood; in the seven years between the signing of the Oslo Accords and the outbreak of the Second Intifada (known also as the Al-Aqsa Intifada), the number of Jews killed overtook the number killed during the First Intifada, while the number of Palestinians killed declined considerably. But a new wave of attacks caused public support for the Oslo process to wane. When the Oslo II Accord was brought before the Knesset on October 5, 1995, about seven months after Goldstein's massacre, Rabin succeeded in rounding up a bare parliamentary majority, sixty-one votes, in its favor, but the number of opponents rose to fifty-nine. The Shas faction revised its position and voted against instead of abstaining. A month later, a mass demonstration in support of Rabin and the agreement was held in Kings of Israel Square in central Tel Aviv. At the end of the demonstration, Rabin was assassinated by Yigal Amir.

RABIN'S ASSASSIN, RELIGIOUS AND MIZRAHI

Following the assassination, Kings of Israel Square was renamed Rabin Square. The memorial plaque placed there shortly afterward initially read: "murdered by a kippah-wearing Jew." The presumption was that Amir's religious beliefs provided the central motive for the killing.[116] The wording was criticized and the plaque was removed. Another of Amir's identity traits was that he was Yemenite, or, in a broader sense, Mizrahi. According to anthropologist Michael Feige, the mainstream media and academic research rarely mentioned Amir's ethnic background, despite the fact that his ethnicity played a large role in the processes that led him to kill Rabin. Feige noted that Amir's family was located on the fringes of the religious Zionist community. He also pointed to Amir's individualism, and the rejection that he experienced in religious Zionist circles because of his ethnic background. Together, Feige wrote, these "created an explosive connection." His Mizrahiness led to his social and romantic ostracism (pressured by her parents, his Ashkenazi girlfriend left him), and this, combined with his individualism and his understanding of halacha, led to his decision to shoot Rabin.[117]

Like the Zionist movement as a whole, religious Zionism declared then and declares today its belief in intra-Jewish equality. But in practice it has been led by an Ashkenazi elite and has created a closed-off subculture that could be frustrating for outsiders who wanted to join it. Like the Zionist movement, religious Zionism explicitly opposed violence, except for that employed by official Jewish and Israeli bodies. But the way religious Zionists spoke about the Oslo Accords was violent and aggressive. Religious Zionists who adhered to its internal rules understood that this was no more than rhetoric and refrained from extreme acts of violence. But that was not true of the people on the community's ethnic margins, who read these violent messages and the rulings of some rabbis as saying that the halachic category of the "law of the pursuer" (*din rodef*) applied to Rabin. This meant that it was a religious imperative to kill him.

EREZ BITON: THE MIZRAHI MURDERER

The poet Erez Biton (born in 1942 in Algeria to Moroccan parents) underlined Amir's Mizrahi ethnicity in an article he published two days after the assassination under the headline "The Murderer Is a Mizrahi." But in the body of his piece, Biton argued that Amir did not represent Mizrahiness because he had been incited to commit his crime by "right-wing frameworks."

> The fact that Rabin's murderer is Yemenite [supposedly] confirms the endlessly repeated claim that Mizrahim hate Arabs and oppose peace. Such an inference is horrifying and puts paid to the diligent work, over the last few years, of Mizrahi intellectuals to become trailblazers for peace. The facts are facts. The murderer comes from a large family in a poor neighborhood in Herzliya. All the usual components of a Mizrahi traditional family. But what we have come to refer to as a "moderate traditional family," with natural values of humaneness and lack of violence, turns out to be a family that conceived and gave birth to one of the most extreme and violent [people] ever known in Israel. . . . There is no doubt that right-wing frameworks also find the children of Mizrahi families to be easy prey, [despite such families'] being fundamentally moderate and far from violence and hatred of others. The truth must also be told: not all Mizrahim like Arabs. The experience of Jews in the Islamic lands was at times harsh and bitter (with the exception of Morocco, where relations were generally positive, with mutual respect). But most of the [Israeli] nation, Mizrahim included, have opened up to new winds that are blowing with regard to the peace process, and there is a willingness to try a new way. . . . Nevertheless, the cynical use that right-wing organizations make of religion for political purposes finds the religious Mizrahim, who are ensconced in certain educational frameworks, to be easy victims of incitement. . . . I myself was witness, in the Rosh Hashanah prayers in a synagogue made up of mostly Mizrahim, that people recited a prayer for the soul of Baruch Goldstein. It's not unusual for preachers to go from one synagogue to another and to pound into [the worshippers] teachings of extremism and hatred of the government. . . . Unfortunately and painfully, the murder of Yitzhak Rabin also happened against a background of religious-national extremism. Unfortunately, that terrible link between religion and fanatical nationalism exists among us as well. The exploitation of the underprivileged for such purposes borders on the despicable and on sickening cynicism.
>
> The facts need to be stated precisely. The great majority of Mizrahim, and at the top Mizrahi intellectuals, support the peace process.[118]

That's what Biton believed, or hoped. It's difficult to say how well-founded that belief was. The assumption that the Mizrahi public (or any other public) as a whole is led by intellectuals doesn't pass the reality test. But even if there is truth in Biton's claim about Mizrahi support for peace (and there's certainly some measure of truth in it), it is no less manifestly true that Mizrahim were prominent in noninstitutional anti-Arab violence (as opposed to the violence wielded by Israel's security forces, which is transethnic and encompasses Israel as a whole) in the years that followed.

RABBI OVADIA

Rabbi Ovadia learned of Rabin's assassination when one of his close associates whispered the news into his ear while he was in the middle of the weekly Saturday night lecture he gave in his yeshiva, which was broadcast by satellite all over the world. "We have just heard a very horrible thing, due to our great sins . . . there has been an assassination attempt on the prime minister and they say he is injured, so we will now recite a prayer for his recovery," the rabbi said to the large crowd sitting before him. He began to recite the traditional prayer for the recovery of a wounded person, concluding it with an additional line directed at Rabin: "And peace will quickly come by his hand." The crowd responded "Amen."[119] When Eitan Haber, Rabin's chief of staff, announced that Rabin had died, Rabbi Ovadia wept. "To do such a deed is an abominable crime," he said. "This man, aside from the horrible and grave transgression, condemned us to ignominy. Because of him, the divine presence is liable to forsake the land." When he was interviewed on the Voice of Israel the next day, he added, "The education of the National Religious Party leads young people who learn there to do horrible things." (The reference was to the religious Zionist party that had founded the state religious school system and the network of boarding schools and yeshivot that became part of the normative life path for a large portion of the religious public, including Mizrahim; the party, once pluralist with regard to the Israeli-Arab conflict, had, by the 1980s, largely been taken over by right-wing religious nationalists.) Rabbi Ovadia viewed the assassination as the rotten fruit of religious Zionist education. "The man who was so bold as to carry out this criminal and abominable act of bloodshed has removed himself from the Jewish people, and has added sin to his crime by justifying his action with the halacha," he admonished.[120]

Rabbi Ovadia did not see the murder as a "Mizrahi act." In the past, he had, like other Sephardi public figures, proposed that Edot Hamizrah could serve as a bridge to peace. He rejected the claim "to the effect that the Sephardi Jews in Israel reject the peace process across the board." Not only that, he declared, but "had the Sephardim had a role in the peace process, it is likely that the road to peace would have been shorter."[121] That's the world of what might have been. In the real world, a young Yemenite murdered Prime Minister Rabin, perhaps because he was a Yemenite, or because of his personal religious views, or because he was an acolyte of the radical nationalist wing of religious Zionism.

After the murder, Israel continued to tighten its military rule over the territories and to constrict the Palestinians' living space. Palestinian opponents of accommodation stepped up their terror attacks. Israelis and Palestinians disagreed over fundamental questions about resolving the conflict—the establishment of a Palestinian state, borders, Israeli settlements, Palestinian refugees, Jerusalem and its holy places. At the end of 2000, violence surged to unprecedented heights. The peace process, and with it the Israeli peace camp, collapsed.

Five prime ministers have led Israel during the quarter century following Rabin's assassination, all of them Ashkenazim. Among them, Binyamin Netanyahu has served the longest. His first three-year tenure lasted from 1996 to 1999. He was reelected to that post in 2009 and served for twelve straight years, until 2021. He positioned himself as the leader of the Second Israel and its mobilizing symbol, and political, ethnic, and religious identities further aligned. Opinion polls conducted throughout this time show that among religious and traditional Mizrahim, support for Netanyahu has increased considerably, at the same time that his support among secular Ashkenazim has decreased notably.

It was not attitudes toward the Palestinians themselves that shaped attitudes toward Netanyahu. It was rather social and class affiliation.[122] But the dispute was formulated as touching on the State of Israel's very identity, on whether Israel should prioritize its Jewish or its democratic nature when the two collided, whether it should be more cosmopolitan or more set apart, more Western and liberal or more traditional. As a result, one of the arenas in which those contrasts were starkest, and sometimes most violent, was that of Israelis' encounters with Palestinians. If, at the dawn of Zionism, Mizrahiness offered the possibility of close relations with the Arabs of Palestine, by the end of this period Mizrahi identity had become, for many, an identity that coalesced (and very significantly) around intractable anti-Arab feelings.

Conclusion

Then and Now

A large group of youths massed in Bat Yam on May 12, 2021, and divided into bands that set out to attack Arab-owned workplaces on and near the city's seaside promenade. They shattered restaurant windows, smashed the furniture inside, and looted the property. A young man from Ramla, Said Musa, got caught in his car on the street and found himself trapped by the rioters. They saw that he was an Arab, dragged him out of his car, and beat him with their fists and iron rods. Throwing him on the ground, they kicked him and stamped on him until his face was a bloody pulp and he lost consciousness. The assailants continued to pummel him even then. The police presence was inadequate; the few civilians who tried to save Musa were pushed back. The entire incident took place in front of television cameras that broadcast some of it in real time. Most of the assailants made no effort to conceal what they were doing. Some of them proudly waved Israeli flags. But the presence of the cameras led to a result they had not expected. Immediately thereafter, the police began arresting the attackers, using the camera footage to identify them.[1]

The lynching in Bat Yam was part of a broader Israeli-Palestinian confrontation. Tensions between Jews and Arabs in Jerusalem escalated when Israeli courts ruled that Palestinians should be evicted from homes in the city's Sheikh Jarrah / Shimon Hatzadik neighborhood, and because of incidents of police violence at the Damascus Gate to the Old City and on the Temple Mount. Hamas, which ruled the Gaza Strip, joined the struggle and issued Israel an ultimatum. First, it must cancel the Dance of Flags parade organized each year on Jerusalem Day by religious Zionist young people, who marched through the Muslim Quarter bearing Israeli flags. Second, it must withdraw the Israeli police presence at Al-Aqsa Mosque. If it did not, the movement would launch a rocket attack against Israel. Hamas issued its demands on Jerusalem Day 2021—May 10—the twenty-eighth day of the month of Ramadan in the Muslim year 1442. When Israel did not comply, Hamas began its bombardment in an operation it called Saif al-Quds, Operation Sword of Jerusalem. Israel responded with a major bombing operation in the Gaza Strip called Shomer Hahomot, Operation Guardian of the Walls. And Jews and Arabs clashed in the mixed cities and public spaces they shared.

Internal Israeli factors also played a role in these events. They took place after an election campaign replete with demonstrations and counterdemonstrations. The campaign centered more on Binyamin Netanyahu and his personality than on political and economic issues. Nevertheless, the ethnic issue was a principal component. Many Israelis viewed Netanyahu as the representative of the so-called Second Israel, a concept that refers to the Mizrahi underprivileged stratum and that reappeared in public discourse after years over which its use had faded away. His supporters portrayed his opponents as representatives of the old Mapai hegemony.[2] Netanyahu's Likud won more Knesset seats than any other party in the election, but, short of a majority, he needed allies in order to form a coalition government. He was unable to get as many as he needed before his time ran out, and just five days before Jerusalem Day, the president asked Yair Lapid, leader of the opposition Yesh Atid party, to form a government. Lapid commenced consultations with potential coalition parties; in the meantime, Netanyahu remained in place as prime minister and leader of a caretaker government.

Back in Bat Yam in May 2021, the Channel 13 television station documented the events of May 12 in a film called *Halayla hashahor shel bat yam* (The black night of Bat Yam). It showed the attacks, the rescue attempts, and the beating of Said Musa. It also screened stills of the twelve suspects put on trial for the attack and the charges against each of them. The narrator asked, "Can we find something in common among all of them?" He answered his own question, noting that most of them were young men in their twenties living in or around Bat Yam. Almost all of them had previous run-ins with the police, earned modest salaries, and lived alongside Arabs. But he made no mention of another common denominator, one that was central and glaring for many other Israelis. He disregarded the fact that the suspects were all Mizrahim, from what is called the Second Israel. In other words, he abided by the tacit rule largely observed in the mainstream Israeli media since the

1980s—the ethnic affiliations of Jewish rioters, whether in the territories or in Israel, were not to be mentioned.

The suspects arrested in the case also made no reference to their ethnic origins. For them, their ethnicity went without saying; there was no need to refer to it explicitly. They took different approaches to claiming their innocence of the crimes of which they were accused. The father of the suspect Itzik Guetta maintained that "Itzik is not a kid who is racist. He is a boy most of whose friends I think are Arabs." Mor Atiyah, who represented two of the charged men, claimed that her clients had acted in self-defense, thinking that a terrorist attack was in progress. One of the defendants, Itzik Saban, issued the following statement: "Israel's founders would turn over in their graves if they thought that a day would come when a Jew defending his home would be called a terrorist by other Jews."[3] *Dear media, dear prosecutors,* Saban was in fact saying, *I am following in the path of the country's founders, the people of the old and good Land of Israel.* Zionism is based on violence against Arabs, which is defined as self-defense even when it is not actually so. So why this hypocrisy? Saban had not read the book you are now reading (which I only began writing at the time of the attack on Said Musa), and he probably knew nothing about the clash in Jaffa in 1908, not far from the lynching of 2021 with which this book begins, but his historical consciousness was firm enough to understand that he was carrying on a long Zionist tradition.

It's understandable that the suspects and those speaking in their name would not want to mention their ethnic origin—identifying as Mizrahi is not a good way to persuade an Israeli court to be lenient.[4] The mainstream media's omission of this information was, as we have seen, consistent with a norm that emerged in the 1980s. But in our time the mainstream media are but a pale reflection of the public discourse. Most of the action takes place on social media and in talk-backs on news websites; there, ethnic identity is a central issue. "What's amazing is that all those people who come out against the Arabs almost always look like Arabs," wrote one reader of *Haaretz* in response to a survey of anti-Arab violence in Bat Yam. "[The attackers are] Arabs in every possible way, and apparently it's not just the way they look," added another. A third added a quasi-scientific diagnosis: "[They are] Arab Jews (in other words, they come from Arab countries)."[5] Sure enough, the authors of these comments were not themselves Mizrahim but rather were Ashkenazim rehashing the stereotypes of many decades—condescension toward both Mizrahim and Arabs and identifying them with each other. In this account, this sort of violence is "Arab," and has nothing to do with "real

Jews." In this, of course, they dismissed and accepted the violence perpetrated by the Israeli state during the very same days of Operation Shomer Hahomot (the Israeli bombings of Gaza at this time killed 128 civilians, including sixty-six children, while the Arab attacks on Jews in cities of mixed population killed three Jews; another twelve Jews were killed in the Hamas bombardments, among them two children; and a single Arab was shot dead by a Jewish civilian).[6]

A more complex debate took place surrounding the trial of Elor Azaria, who was charged with killing Abdel Fattah al-Sharif. Al-Sharif was shot by IDF soldiers when he tried to stab them near the Tel Rumeida neighborhood in Hebron in March 2016. Azaria arrived on the scene after the initial incident, approached the wounded al-Sharif, who was sprawled on the ground, and shot him in the head at close range, killing him. A B'tselem volunteer cameraman filmed the shooting and the clip was disseminated by the media. The IDF chief of staff decided to bring Azaria before a military court, setting off a public controversy.

The central issue was whether a soldier is permitted to finish off a wounded terrorist who has already been subdued and presents no immediate danger. The law forbids it, but it seems logical and proper to many Israelis. But Mizrahi activists, both those who opposed Israeli rule over the Palestinians in the territories and those who supported it, said that something else was at stake. Azaria had been put on trial, they claimed, not only because of what he did but because of his social position. "Let's tell it like it is," wrote Mizrahi activists Adi Mazor and Tom Mehager. "There are Ashkenazi soldiers who go to the right units, where liquidation is a heroic act, and there are Mizrahi soldiers who do the dirtiest work of military rule in the Occupied Territories."[7] Ophir Toubul, a founder of the Tor Hazahav: Now It's Our Turn movement, who went with some of his colleagues to visit the Azaria family, put it this way: "Elor Azaria's opening position, from the very start, was his automatic identification with the mob. He and his family fit the role of the scapegoat like a glove: a Mizrahi family from Ramla, a warrior with venom in his eyes, a fan of the Beitar Jerusalem soccer team, and from there one can very quickly jump to the conclusion that he committed his action with an animal instinct of Arab hatred."[8]

This claim is consistent with a pattern that runs through this book, and which has its origin in the Mandate period. It spotlights Mizrahi violence, real or imagined, while covering up Ashkenazi violence. Azaria's defense attorneys made this same argument. What Azaria did is, in fact, an accepted norm in the IDF, for which soldiers are not brought to trial. Azaria's indictment thus constituted selective enforcement, entitling him to a defense based on abuse of process. But the court did not permit his lawyers to submit a list of cases in which IDF soldiers had killed Arabs in similar circumstances but had not been brought to trial, blocking the abuse-of-process claim.[9]

In other words, several issues were being debated at the same time, merging with one another. First, had Azaria been justified in killing al-Sharif? Second, was it proper to charge him with a crime even if his action was wrong? Third, did his Mizrahi ethnicity play a role in the decision to charge him? And there was another debate, centered on the popular movement that formed to support Azaria. Larry Derfner, a journalist who had immigrated to Israel from the United States and the author of the book *No Country for Jewish Liberals*, pointed, as other observers did as well, to the fact that Azaria's supporters were mostly what he called Mizrahim of little education. This population, he maintained, was vital to the maintenance of right-wing rule and as a reservoir of manpower for Jewish racism and fascism in Israel. And, he added, it was a wellspring of hatred of Arabs and leftists.[10] Furthermore, Derfner asserted, the pervasiveness of fascist views among Mizrahim with little education, who constituted the majority in underprivileged and lower middle-class neighborhoods, testified to something very sick in this Israeli subculture. The subculture was to blame for this disease.

Derfner's final claim deserves examination, not only because it ignores state violence and awards it liberal sanction but also because it raises the question of tracking versus choice and social structures versus people's control over their lives (agency). In the present case, the question is whether people who live in underprivileged neighborhoods are poor by choice. More precisely, did Mizrahim choose to join the lower classes? Is the state responsible for the creation and preservation of a violent subculture in certain places? Perhaps there are parts of government that have an interest in that? To analyze and understand the existence of such a subculture, we must attend to the social, historical, and political-systemic causes involved in its creation.

The long-range view we have taken, extending back to the time of labor movement ascendancy, points to trends in society and consciousness that created not only the Mizrahi periphery but also structured it as Arab-hating, both in the eyes of outsiders and as a self-definition (if with much more complexity). Under Mapai rule, a sociopolitical infrastructure came into being that serves as a foundation for the identities and loyalties of Israeli society to this day, despite its undergoing some changes. But it seems that in the three decades since the signing of the Oslo Accords, the Mizrahi lower class has increasingly adopted nationalistic views, and that these have become part of the way many Mizrahim define themselves. During these same decades, especially under Binyamin Netanyahu's governments, there have been moves aimed at bolstering this element of Mizrahi identity. These governments have also had a political interest in exacerbating such hatred. Three familiar statements illustrate this fact. The first was Netanyahu's statement, in October 1997, that Israelis of the Left had forgotten what it was to be Jewish and wanted to place Israeli security in Arab hands. In this he linked the Left and the Arabs, framing both as dangers to Jews.[11] The second was a statement Netanyahu allegedly made to his Mizrahi finance minister, Moshe Kahlon, in 2016. (It was reported by Nahum Barnea in *Yediot Aharonot*; Kahlon issued a denial, but Netanyahu did not.) "You'll never get the votes of the Mizrahim," Netanyahu reportedly told him. "Only I can get them. I know who they hate—they hate the Arabs. And I also know how to bring them the goods."[12] The third was what Netanyahu's chief of staff, Nathan Eshel, said as he celebrated the success of the campaign to make the Mizrahi Right hate Arabs and leftists. What unites the right wing is hatred, he said in February 2020. "They hate everyone," he went on, describing the "non-Ashkenazi" public, as he put it. "We've managed to drive them crazy . . . this hatred is what unites . . . our camp."[13] In other words, it was much like the situation in Israel's early days, when top IDF officers talked about how to amplify hatred of Arabs among Mizrahi soldiers. The same thing has happened in recent decades, but for internal political reasons.

People in positions of political power and the mass media wield considerable power over how Israelis form their attitudes toward the Palestinians. Intra-Jewish relations also have had a real impact on shaping the different manifestations of anti-Arab attitudes among Israelis, according to ethnicity and class. The parameters were street violence versus institutional violence; the routine violence in the IDF units that policed the territories—the Kfir Brigade and the Border Police—versus the very selective violence used by special forces; physical violence versus symbolic and administrative violence; and the contempt that grows out of persistent interaction rather than that born of distance. But once again, as in 1929, as in the terror attacks of the 1970s, the most fundamental determinant of the Jewish attitude toward Palestinians was blood—to be precise, the amount of Jewish blood spilled. And even though Palestinians' anger and despair also had its underlying causes, as did their terror attacks, Israeli Jews were not willing to listen to them in the face of the blood of their compatriots. The failure of the Oslo peace process, the outbreak of the Al-Aqsa Intifada, and the suicide attacks that characterized that uprising created one of those moments in which Israeli Jews could only see their side of the story. As such, it was a moment that reshaped Israeli views of the Palestinians. Its effect was decisive precisely because it came in response to a failed effort to find peace, and led many who had hoped for accommodation with the Palestinians to suspect that the Palestinians had no interest in peace and in fact wanted the armed struggle to continue. It's important to note that this was not just a Mizrahi or right-wing phenomenon. It encompassed all of Israel, and it had precedents in previous eras. Following the PLO's declaration of support for Iraq during Saddam Hussein's missile attacks against Israel during the Gulf War, one of Israel's most prominent peace advocates, Yossi Sarid, declared that he was no longer available to the Palestinians.[14] The left-wing Meretz party consistently came out against Israeli soldiers who refused to serve in the territories and supported IDF air force bombings of military targets in the Gaza Strip in response to Hamas barrages against Israel.[15] When blood flowed, the advocates of accommodation fell silent.

But, since our subject is Mizrahi approaches to the conflict, here are examples of how two iconic Mizrahi figures who sought accommodation reacted to the Palestinian violence of the Al-Aqsa Intifada. The first is Vicki Shiran, a Mizrahi feminist leader (we met Shiran in chapter 2, in the context of her lawsuit against the broadcast of the documentary *Pillar of Fire* on the grounds that it disregarded Jews from the Islamic world). Her feminist position was not limited to demanding formal equality between men and women and between Ashkenazim and Mizrahim. She advocated the structural and ethical metamorphosis of social relations as a whole. It would not be possible to create a new and healthy society, she maintained, while ruling over another nation. She stuck to this position after the outbreak of the Second Intifada.[16] But a series of events soon thereafter shook her. In October 2000, Palestinian citizens of Israel took to the streets to stage mass demonstrations, during which Israeli security forces killed twelve protesters and a Jew was killed from a stone thrown at his car. As Shiran experienced it, Israel's Arab citizens were joining the Palestinian armed struggle. "I am not prepared to endorse the positions of the traditional Left and am not prepared to accept that we are the only bad people in the story," she said then. "My feeling was that we were going to build a civic state, but what happened with the Israeli Arabs is a very problematic and new situation for a person of left-wing views like me, who wants to maintain a Jewish state here."[17]

The issue here is not whether a Jewish civil state based on equality is possible, or whether the concept is self-contradictory. That depends on how one defines "Jewish state," which is not what this book is about. It's the emotional and political reactions to the Palestinian terror attacks that followed the Oslo agreements that are relevant. Rabbi Ovadia's response to these attacks was much harsher than Shiran's. "These Arabs and these Ishmaelites, all of them are accursed evil people, they all hate the Jews," he said in August 2000, when the Camp David talks failed and the wave of terror surged. "Do they have faith, those people? Can you believe them? People say peace, peace—what peace? How can you make peace with those people? You go and hand over parts of the land to them. [Prime Minister Ehud] Barak wants to give Jerusalem to those people? Barak is also going to give them part of the Old City, so they'll be the neighbors of the Jews. That way they'll be able to kill us, he's running after them like a madman. What are you doing, putting them next to us? Why are you putting serpents next to us?" He explained the difference between this position and his ruling that it was permissible to trade parts of the Land of Israel for peace: "There is no connection with that ruling when handing over those parts endangers life."[18]

Eight months later, perhaps in the wake of threats on his life by Palestinians and Arabs, the rabbi issued a clarification. "I was not speaking of and did not intend to mean all Arabs, only the murderous terrorists who kill innocent men, women, and children without distinction." A few more months passed and then, in an interview he granted to the Saudi-funded newspaper *Al-sharq al-Awsat* and the Kuwaiti newspaper *Al-Watan,* he reiterated his clarification and quoted biblical verses about peace and accommodation. One of them was "Have we not all one Father? Did not one God create us? Why do we break faith with one another?" (Mal. 2:10). It was a verse that Rishon Letziyon Uziel often quoted during the Mandate period. In the interview, Rabbi Ovadia repeated his claim that "naturally, the members of Edot Hamizrah, from the Arab world, can make an important contribution to the dialogue between us because of their close acquaintance with the Arab world. We have a common and magnificent history of living as good neighbors, in mutual tolerance and respect."[19]

Generalized declarations that reject accommodation when blood is boiling should not surprise us, nor should a reversion to a more accommodating position, or a view of the Mizrahim as a bridge for peace—when emotions subside. The ostensibly contradictory statements by Rabbi Ovadia serve to remind us of the two fundamental points that we have discerned over the course of this book. First, in sacred texts (in our case, Jewish ones, but not only those), it's possible to find justifications for intensifying enmity and hatred between peoples, but also for close fraternal relations. Second, the history of Jews in the Islamic world can be narrated in different ways, and it is often narrated in different ways in accordance with the political purposes of the speaker at a given time, speaking to a specific audience. In his original sermon, Rabbi Ovadia spoke before Jews about the enmity of their Arab neighbors toward them as Jews. In the later interview, speaking to an Arab audience, he put the emphasis on neighborliness and tolerance.

Rabbi Ovadia contained within him all these contrasts—Ishmael's traditional hatred of the Jews and a desire for accommodation, intense pain at the death of Jews and a willingness to engage in dialogue, a desire for separation from the Arabs along with an affinity for Arab culture. Furthermore, Rabbi Ovadia was a man of words. And words, even the harshest ones, can always be interpreted in multiple ways. That is not always the case with actions, in particular not with murder, in which there is no going back. Yosef Haim Ben-David and two Mizrahi Haredi accomplices tortured and murdered a young Palestinian boy, Mohammed Abu Khdeir, in the summer of 2014, following the kidnapping and murder of three Jewish teenagers in Gush Etzion. The three murderers connected only to the aspect of hatred and revenge in Jewish texts. They committed a deed from which there was no turning back. They acted with exceptional brutality, but the emotions that motivated them were shared by many others. As such, a look at their life paths can assist us in understanding why they did what they did.

Ben-David, defendant number one in murder case 34700/14 heard before the Jerusalem District Court, was born in Jerusalem in July 1984. The Eleventh Knesset was elected the same month. This marked the first time that the Kach party, led by Rabbi Meir Kahane, and Rabbi Ovadia's Shas party won representation in the Knesset. It was a time of unprecedented political and social tension. Ben-David was nine years old when the Oslo Accords were signed. Some Israelis hoped that they would lead to peace for the Palestinians, while others saw them as an existential threat, one that impinged on their identities. Ben-David was twelve years old at the time of the terrifying suicide attacks that rocked Jerusalem in February and March 1996, and eighteen when the wave of suicide attacks that shredded the hearts of Jerusalem's Jews occurred during the Al-Aqsa Intifada. Many members of the public subsequently repressed these events and went on with their lives. For Ben-David, like many of his generation, they were life-defining events. And they churned within him when he heard of the kidnapping and murder of the three boys—Gilad Shaar, Naftali Fraenkel, and Eyal Yifrach.

Palestinians who support the armed struggle interpret it in different ways. Those who play an active role in it see it as a moral obligation. They maintain that it is a fundamental right to fight for personal and national freedom, even as they disagree over what means are legitimate in that struggle. For Israeli Jews, the armed struggle is an intolerable challenge. Already in 1940, Moshe Sharett said that "Arab resistance places Zionism in terrible emotional stress. It disturbs our rest and confronts us constantly with a tragic question mark about our future."[20] The common Jewish religious view—both Mizrahi and Ashkenazi, and especially among those influenced by the mysticism of Kabbalah—utterly rejects any Palestinian right to independence in the Land of Israel. "The attempts at peace are useless chatter," is how Rabbi Shlomo Ben Hamo put it, "because the sublime will [God] desires the subjugation of Ishmael to his master Isaac. And as long as there is no such subjugation, there is ongoing hatred against us and against our country."[21] Believers who hold this view can pursue different ways of bringing about redemption. Many settle through the length and breadth of the Holy Land, or study Torah because they believe that it will bring salvation. There are those who organize in political frameworks or take part in demonstrations and protests. Very few take part in acts of violence, and even then, these people generally display a measure of self-restraint. They know that unlawful and unpermitted actions against Palestinians are acts committed not only against the Palestinians and for the Jewish nation but also against the state and its authority. But those whose animosity is directed also, for historical, social, or ideological reasons, against state institutions will engage in violence without institutional sanction, out of cold calculation, hot blood, or on the basis of mystical or messianic calculations.

Violent anti-Arab demonstrations, like those in Acre (1961), Ramla (1965), Shmuel Hanavi in Jerusalem (1986), Pat in Jerusalem (1990), Bat Yam following the murder of Helena Rapp (1992), or in 2021, serve for many of their participants as a way of expressing their animosity not only toward Arabs but also against the establishment. They hold the country's veteran leadership responsible for treating the Arabs too softly and for creating the disadvantaged classes to which most of the angry demonstrators belong. This explains why the violence is also often directed at the police, and why slogans and curses are directed against state institutions and the country's elites. These mass events offer an opportunity to cry out against injustice, to gain a sense of meaning, and to represent the Jewish collective and what it wants.

People driven to commit extreme acts of revenge, or to take action meant to bring about the end of days, also come from the margins. But they tend to be of a special type. They are often individuals who have a lofty sense of mission, as in the case of the Mizrahi delinquents who murdered Abu Khdeir. Socially, they are on the very edge of the fringe, Mizrahim of a standing lower than that of the majority of their demographic. Such delinquents have been ejected from the two paths of mobility in Mizrahi society—jumping on the Mizrahi middle-class wagon careening into Israeli capitalism, or pursuing personal growth as religious scholars. That was the profile of defendant number two in the case, a minor who had been rejected by the prestigious Ashkenazi yeshiva he had aspired to attend.

Such marginal people at times see themselves, if only for a moment, as representatives of the entire nation. They cast themselves in that role out of a sense of Jewish superiority and a belief that revenge will deliver redemption. That moment may arrive because their hatred of the old elites and of the Arabs is fanned by politicians, and because of their personalities, enabling them to cast themselves as standard-bearers for the Jewish people. From the margins and from their awareness of their social inferiority grows their confidence in their role as purifiers and redeemers. They see themselves as devout Israeli Jews who are better than the Israelis of today and the Jews of the past. They know that a sense of Jewish superiority pervades Israel, and that the IDF's bombings in the Gaza Strip, in which hundreds of Palestinian children were killed, were supported by some 90 percent of the country's Jewish population.[22] They are very much aware that they are not alone in aspiring to revenge and in their desire to boost Jewish honor. Like the members of the Jewish Underground—but with a sense of inferiority that needs to be overcome—they see themselves simultaneously as representatives of the public and as people who cast aside social mores and inhibitions in order to propel the people forward. Sometimes they also suffer from ethical blindness (who doesn't, sometimes?), and sometimes they are guilty of wanton cruelty. Like some Palestinians who murdered Jews in Hebron in 1929, they place their blatant brutality at the service of the nation and the faith, not for their own sake but for ours.

"On the night between July 1, 2014, and July 2, 2014, three figures materialized out of a dark tunnel of racism, ignorance, illiteracy, and hatred—the three appellants before us, an adult and two minors aged sixteen and seventeen," wrote Supreme Court Justice Yitzhak Amit in his decision to reject the three murderers' appeal of their convictions.[23] Amit was a graduate of

Tel Aviv's elitist Zeitlin High School, served as an officer in the IDF's prestigious intelligence Unit 8200, and graduated with distinction from Hebrew University's law school. He did not go into the appellants' ethnic or religious backgrounds, nor did he address the political and social forces that created the tunnel of racism and ignorance. Instead, he focused on the issues of criminal liability and the role played by the three young men in the murder.

Nevertheless, Justice Amit's statement serves as a reminder that Israel's social structure creates tunnels of different types. Some lead to the abyss of racism, ignorance, and hatred, while others lead upward to the pinnacles of the so-called enlightened elites, whose hatred and ignorance is harder to measure. To a certain extent, hatred of Arabs is part of the way Jews and Zionists live, even if not every Jew and Zionist hates Arabs, and even if those who do don't feel that way all the time. Furthermore, the manifestations of this hatred are varied and in flux. It has religious roots and national motivations, and it is nourished also by Arab hatred of Jews (which it itself nourishes). Bloody conflict also has a role in shaping how it appears. In recent decades, the Mizrahim—in particular, religious and traditional working-class Mizrahim—are, as Ron Cahlili put it in his television documentary series *Hate*, the poster children of this emotion. Unlike other Israelis, they are not ashamed of this and are sometimes happy to state it publicly. To be precise, however, it is not Mizrahiness as an ethnic background that motivates them but rather a combination of religious viewpoint and class. As elsewhere in the world, attacks on minorities in the streets of Israel are, in fact, a matter of class. But in Israel, the correlation between class and Mizrahi ethnicity has been strong enough that in the public mind Mizrahim are identified with extralegal violence. The same is true of violence that grows out of the daily interactions of soldiers or Border Police with Palestinians in the territories. Some of this violence is carried out in the name of the law and military orders, while some of it is criminal.

For example, there was the case of a group of Border Police who abused Palestinians at the Meitar checkpoint, where Palestinians from the Hebron Hills cross into Israel proper to reach the Be'er Sheva area. The culprits systematically stole money from the Palestinians—and filmed themselves doing so. Haim Rivlin investigated the case for Channel 13's *Hamakor* program in November 2020. The report made no direct reference to the Mizrahi ethnicity of the soldiers involved, nor did the coverage of the case in the right-wing *Makor Rishon*. "It is hard to see young warriors, in uniform, behaving in such a brutal, criminal, cruel way, for their own personal benefit, in order to pocket a few hundred miserable shekels. . . . It is severe moral and ethical devastation. This is not the standard of the Israel Defense Forces," Avigayil Zayit wrote in that newspaper.[24] Not everyone agreed with her, nor did everyone disregard the Mizrahi ethnicity of these soldiers—not necessarily from the vantage point of Ashkenazi cultural superiority, like the commenters who responded to the violence in Bat Yam, but out of contrite identification. Mizrahi activist and scholar Lihi Yona wrote that the case was

> truly a classic demonstration of the daily experience of the occupation for Palestinians, and the violence that is truly routine, as horrifying as it is, in the encounter between IDF soldiers and the Palestinians. . . . Beyond this, and from my position (as a Mizrahi Jewish woman), there is something terrifying in grasping the levels of moral corruption of Mizrahi youth in the Border Police and similar units. . . . Tom Mehager has written time and again on how it is impossible to speak about justice for Mizrahim without speaking of the end of the occupation. . . . Yesterday's investigative piece was, as I see it, the most concrete proof possible of the deep flaw at the heart of the Mizrahi Right. Not just in the utter imperviousness to Palestinian suffering under the cover of the occupation, which in my opinion demands a level of callousness that is hard [for me] to accept and live with in peace, but also in the profound lack of fairness in relation to young Mizrahim, for most of whom the Border Police is a means of social mobility. You send their souls to be shredded under the rubric of romantic rhetoric on traditionalism. How can one breathe when faced with that?[25]

This is a long-standing Mizrahi political and cultural stance. It demands equality and justice for Mizrahim while also seeing the Palestinians. Either the cake needs to be divided equally among everyone, or there won't be any cake, as the Panthers said. And it also bemoans the transformation of the Mizrahim into the contractors of Israeli violence, and the fact that there are Mizrahi public figures who support maintaining rule over the Palestinians. They, too, are guilty of shredding the souls of young recruits. In a larger perspective, it is a reminder that, throughout the period covered by this book, there have been Mizrahi approaches (offered by those who explicitly speak in the name of Mizrahiness, or are seen from the outside as doing so, as I specified in my introduction) that seek to promote equality both among Jewish ethnic communities and between Israelis and Palestinians.

The concept of equality opposes the view of Jewish superiority, in its different interpretations, that are perceived to be part of Jewish tradition. This view is based in part on a verse in Deuteronomy (26:19): "He will set you, in fame and renown and glory, high above all the nations that He has made; and that you shall be, as He promised, a holy people to the Lord your God." Some maintain that this superiority and holiness require the humiliation of non-Jews. It's an approach attractive to many, among them Jews who have themselves experienced humiliation. On the streets of Jerusalem (and in other cities) it is expressed in the chant "A Jew is a soul—an Arab is a motherfucker." That's not a slogan shouted, in general, by the members of the nationalist elites. It belongs to the shabab and others on the margins. It was chanted, for example, by the youths who in the autumn of 2010 staged attacks on Arabs in Safed, soon after that city's chief rabbi, Shmuel Eliyahu—son of the previously mentioned rishon letziyon Rabbi Mordechai Eliyahu—called on Jews not to rent apartments to Arabs. It's also chanted by the boys of the extreme right-wing religious organization Lehava, who use it to rally themselves and to threaten others.[26]

As in the violent incidents of the 1960s, recounted in chapter 3, one of the arenas of the struggle for Jewish sanctity and superiority is the sexual behavior of Jewish women. It is the flagship issue of the young members of Lehava in Jerusalem, including those who set fire to the city's Hand in Hand bilingual Jewish-Arab school. It also motivated the Be'er Sheva teenager who, in early 2017, led a band of juveniles who several times attacked, with clubs, hammers, and knives, Arab men dating Jewish women. When he was brought to trial, his probation officer submitted a report on the young man, describing him as

> about twenty years old, single, living, until his arrest, in his parents' home. He spent his boyhood and teenage years with his family, which was not lacking in problems, including his parents' and one of his brother's involvement in criminal acts. This led to a lack of clear behavioral boundaries, and an atmosphere of instability. At a certain stage, after completing twelve years of schooling, the accused began attending Torah classes, grew more religious, and became a *hozer bitshuva.* He did not report for military service, apparently because he wanted to continue to study at [his] yeshiva, and when this was not arranged as the law requires, he was declared a deserter. . . . The impression is that, at the time he committed these acts, he felt illusory power and

> confidence, and believed he was "saving" these Jewish women, and felt a sense of calling in this.[27]

He came from the social margins to save the society that had banished him to the margins, and this gave him a sense not only of meaning but also of importance and power.

Nevertheless, there is a certain difference between the attackers of Arabs in the 1960s and the attackers in the 2000s, and between the so-called price-tag reprisals staged against Arabs in the West Bank by youthful settlers and Jewish aggression in Israel's cities (although, more recently, there is some overlap between them). Nissim Leon's analysis of Mizrahi Haredi society offers some help. Leon points to a central difference between the religious and Haredi nationalist streams, whose habitus is Ashkenazi and the Haredi Mizrahi community. While the former focuses on the sanctification of the Land of Israel's physical borders, and directs most of its efforts to the imposition of Jewish sovereignty throughout this territory by means of extensive settlement, the Mizrahi Haredim focus on the sanctification of the boundaries of the Jewish people, and direct their efforts to guarding the collective's borders.[28] I would add that this is the difference we can discern between the activity of the marginal youth in the two streams. While the national religious public's marginal youths turn to the hills of Samaria and Judea and attack Palestinians as part of a struggle over territory, marginal Mizrahi youth, under the influence of the Mizrahi Haredi stream, attack Palestinians because of their relations with Jewish women.

The court sentenced the assailant in the Be'er Sheva case to five and a half years in prison, but neither the incident nor the trial received any significant media coverage. An online news report on the judgment received only four comments. One of the commentors condemned the court, two praised the assailant ("the men of the Jewish nation"; "Way to go—you've got awesome merits below and above"). The fourth voiced another attitude we have already seen, which packages Mizrahi and Arab violence together: "He looks like an Arab himself, and acts like an Arab. Why do you think he's not an Arab."[29]

Recall that the connection between anti-Arab violence and Mizrahim is highlighted by Ashkenazim who feel a sense of superiority and Mizrahim who aspire to reform from within. Both groups are aware that class is a factor in the violence, but the former disregard that. Mizrahi activists are divided between those who place all the responsibility on the "Ashkenazi establishment" and refrain from any self-criticism, and those who maintain that it is unreasonable to continue to place all the responsibility on the old establishment—because, for years, there have been Mizrahim in senior positions in government and society. "In this bad system, our [the Mizrahim's] role as oppressors [of Palestinians] derives not only from our being a victim of the Ashkenazi establishment, but also from the many dividends we receive as part of that project of repression," Orly Noy wrote in an article about the television series *Hate*.[30] And Moran Habaz has called for a reformulation of Mizrahi identity, to make it cognizant of "the danger of blindly adopting hateful and racist slogans, with no exemptions and no Zahalkist concept."[31] By this Habaz means ceasing to cling to the view offered by Jamal Zahalka, who charged that the Ashkenazim created the conflict and that thus they, and not Mizrahim, are the Arabs' real rivals. In this account, Mizrahi racism can be forgiven. But Habaz argues that this account of the situation is no longer relevant, because the Mizrahim have joined the oppressors who killed Palestinians.

In his decision to deny the appeal of the young men who murdered Mohammed Abu Khdeir, Justice Amit wrote:

> But there's one thought that continues to bother me. What is the spring from which these three drew this profusion of hatred and racism, which have struck them blind, to the point that their eyes are blocked from seeing that they are strangling, smashing in the head, and burning a human being created in the divine image? And how have they forgotten that fundamental principle of Judaism, the first section that opens the Book of Books, "for in his image did God make man" (Gen. 9:6) and thus "Beloved is man, who was created in the [divine] image" (Rabbi Akiva in Tractate Avot 3:14)? What have they learned, and recited, and internalized that undermines in one blow the stations during the years of their education and their adolescence, that brought them to take the life of a young Arab so unbearably easily? . . . The murder requires incisive soul-searching in Israeli society with regard to grappling with the phenomena of racism and their metastases, putting our house in order from the foundation to the top, in the form of knowing the paths of racism, see its evil ways and remove the evil from within you.

The historical, social, and political analysis I have offered here is a contribution to that task. It shows that the tunnels of racism were dug by human beings. Among these were social groups that labeled other groups on the basis of their origins and directed them to the margins so that they themselves would remain in the center, and other elements who offered redemption by means of Jewish superiority. Racism also grows out of the human need for meaning beyond that offered by life on the margins. It reminds us that, beyond the responsibility that individuals have for their actions, there is social responsibility. This book also presents the varied voices that can be found in Mizrahi discourse over the years—voices of hatred and violence, but also voices of affinity and partnership. Some aspire to divest themselves of Arab culture, while others want to connect with it. There is also love of the Jewish people out of a sense of superiority, as opposed to love of the Jewish people and of every human being. Some Mizrahim have also proposed to mediate between Zionists and Arabs, while others have proposed an Arab-Jewish alliance on the basis of equality that would excise from Zionism its impulse for expansion and control and release the Zionists from their worst fears.

This book may have reached its end, but it remains incomplete. Many matters worthy of inclusion have been omitted, especially events of the past two decades that offer new horizons, or that can be helpful in discerning the persistence of older patterns of thought and behavior. In these final pages I have focused on violent attacks, but I do not intend to claim that violence is the central feature of Mizrahi-Arab relations. As the name of the book intimates, the fabric connecting the two communities is much more complex. I have focused on the attacks because violence has a potently attractive force, for me and for many others (especially, but not only, males). When our adrenaline rises, it casts a spell and empowers us. In moments of retrospection, violence appears before us in both its attractive and its repulsive aspects. Even as we bemoan its consequences, we cannot be certain that at the next opportunity we will remember the lessons of the past. It is hardly surprising that violence is a most stable phenomenon in human history.

A second reason for this chapter's focus on violence is that it shapes our consciousness more than anything else. It engenders fear in the human heart, and in doing so traces out people's physical boundaries—where they may go and where they will avoid going. It also draws the lines of people's emotional worlds—whom they trust and whom they suspect, whom they hate and whom they love. This applies to any type of violence, but physical violence, especially bloodshed, is the most powerful and influential type. The third reason to focus on violence is that I wrote this chapter under the influence of the violent events of the year of its composition. This is another reminder of the fact that history is the presentation of the past from the point of view of the present.

Nevertheless, I want to note briefly a few subjects that I would have liked to expand on had space permitted, simply to offer a taste of what is missing. When Said Musa was attacked by an angry mob in Bat Yam in 2021, a number of people tried to defend him. And while the assailants were all Mizrahim, there were both Mizrahim and Ashkenazim among his rescuers. Here's another example from the same time period. Two people were killed in Lod in the unrest of May 2021—Yigal Yehoshua, a Mizrahi Jewish electrician who worked in both Arab and Jewish homes, and Musa Hasuna, a tractor-trailer driver from one of Lod's oldest Arab families. About a month after the murders, Effi Yehoshua, Yigal's brother, met with Malek Hasuna, Musa's father, in order that they might console each other. The encounter was arranged in part by Nissim Dahan, a longtime resident of Lod. "I am going to meet him, you know, with a full heart," Effi Yehoshua said. "I think that the fact that he is willing to meet with us, that [shows] the fortitude of the man's soul."[32] The pursuit of accommodation and neighborliness are traditional values for both Arabs and Mizrahim.

From a completely different angle, there is Binyamin (Fouad) Ben-Eliezer, who served as minister of defense at the beginning of the Al-Aqsa Intifada. He came to Israel from Iraq on his own as a boy of fourteen and enlisted in the IDF in 1954. Many of the positions he held in the army involved working with the Arab and Palestinian population—he served as commander of the Gaza Strip, military governor and coordinator of activities in the West Bank, and first commanding officer in southern Lebanon. After entering politics, he maintained a close relationship with Egyptian president Hosni Mubarak (and offered him political asylum in Eilat during the Egyptian revolution of 2011). In his memoir, Mubarak related that Fouad served as his advisor on Jewish and Israeli affairs and received a monthly fee for his services, a claim that Fouad denied.[33] Whatever the case, Fouad placed his Mizrahi identity at the service of Zionism, in which he believed. But Zionism also served as a means of advancing his military and political career. While serving as defense minister, he visited and spoke with imprisoned Hamas terrorists who had been apprehended before carrying out suicide attacks. As a person who shared their Arab culture, he thought that he would be able to understand them better than Ashkenazim could.[34]

And there were other Mizrahi men and women who at that time sought to understand the motives of the suicide bombers. One of them was a young Mizrahi woman from Kiryat Gat who moved to Tel Aviv after completing her military service, to work and save up money to study law.

> The [suicide] attacks began and my life changed. . . . Suddenly [military] forces were all over the place, suddenly there were security guards everywhere. . . . I began to watch more television . . . and then, during this period when I was taking an interest, there was a [suicide] attack . . . and I suddenly asked myself: Hey? Who is that kid? What's his name? How is it that such a young kid does something like that? Who is his family? That was the initial moment of the transformation I underwent. It was the place that I began to ask questions that up until then I had not asked.

The speaker was Tali Fahima. "I continued to read a lot, I began to seek out Palestinians, but I couldn't really find any. It turned out that there were no Palestinians in my vicinity, at that time. . . . I began to be exposed to information that tore me to pieces emotionally, but at that stage I still found a million excuses to justify the checkpoints, the Occupation. It was simply an emotional process that dismembered me." Then she recounted her first telephone conversation with Zakaria Zubeidi, a Fatah military commander from the Jenin refugee camp. "The first conversation with him was scary. I was scared to death. . . . I was speaking to a terrorist. And Zakaria, being who he is, began talking and laughing. Right away I told him who I was, I told him that I was right-wing, and that I didn't believe in [the right of] Palestinians to live in the State of Israel. I immediately told him about the place I came from. I said to him, 'I'm not from the Left. I simply want to understand and to know.'" At some stage the Shabak identified Fahima as a threat. "I did not fit their profile. I wasn't from the Left, I wasn't Ashkenazi, I didn't have a university degree, I came from the periphery. I came from the most oppressed place [in Israeli society]. I came from the place that most menaced the existence of the State of Israel. Within two weeks came the first arrest."[35]

This was a very rare example of an alliance of the oppressed, of a Mizrahi woman connecting to her Arab side in a profound way and with a willingness to take action. Her repeated insistence that she was not a leftist was not just talk. For her, like many others, "Left" did not mean holding a system of views and opinions. It was a social signifier that referred to the veteran elites that, as David Ben-Gurion said in a quotation I used above, benefited from the money that flowed into the country to help with immigrant absorption, while the immigrants for whom the money was intended remained in transit camps. Neither did Fahima receive her analysis of relations with the Palestinians from a political framework—she arrived at it on her own. As part of that process, she developed a sense of mission and imagined herself as part of a story of rescue and redemption. "I said to myself that I was going to defend Zakaria with my body, because Zakaria, as far as I was concerned, was the Palestinian story. There were millions of Palestinian Zakaria Zubeidis, and if I could save this man, that would be as if I had saved them all."[36] In 2004 she visited the Jenin refugee camp a couple of times, where she helped the residents bring their voices into the Israeli media. She declared that in case of an Israeli attack on the camp, she would serve as a human shield for Zubeidi, who was targeted by Israel's security agencies.

Fahima was exceptional. It's much more common for Mizrahim who seek to connect with their Arab sides to seek out their distant cousins (Muslims in Morocco) than to approach their close neighbors (the Palestinians who live under Israeli rule). In some cases, they do so in the hope that it will also affect Jewish-Arab relations in Israel-Palestine; in other cases, they do so because they want to overlook what is happening at home. There's no room to go into that, either. I'll no more than mention the Abraham Accords of 2020 and the debate (including the Mizrahi debate) about them, and the treaty between Israel and Morocco that set off a momentary polemic about the nature of Jewish-Arab relations in that country, with Mizrahim lining up on either side. On one side, for example, was Meir Buzaglo, who teaches philosophy and chairs the Tikun Movement for the Renewal of Society and Culture in Israel. "The Moroccans are the only nation that loves Jews. Correct me if I'm wrong. Of all the world's nations, throughout human history, no people has loved the Jews like the Arabs of Morocco. And the love is mutual," he wrote on his Facebook page. Israel's minister of the interior, Aryeh Deri, also cited the neighborly relations between Arabs and Jews in Morocco and welcomed the treaty with a verse from the Psalms (118:24), "This is the day that the Lord has made—let us exult and rejoice in it." Dissenters, among them friends of Buzaglo's, responded immediately, claiming that presenting a complex web of relations that included pogroms and humiliations as love was original and unusual, but also false. "History is not to be falsified. The Jews also suffered a great deal in Morocco," Gabi Butbul, also a Jew of Moroccan origin, wrote in *Makor Rishon*. "What neighborliness are you talking about?" He went on to detail the difficulties of the lives led by Jews in Morocco.[37]

There are many more subjects that are worthy of touching on, but space does not allow it. The Mizrahi politicians in the Labor Party—for example, Amir Peretz, Nissim Zvili, and Eli Dayan—took, during the First Intifada, a Mizrahi position that advocated dialogue (as did their colleagues in the

Likud). What happened to them and their social and political views is worthy of consideration. There's also the golden age that Aryeh Deri had with Arab mayors from the Islamic Movement. Other interesting phenomena are the joint Mizrahi-Arab cultural scene, and the connections that Israelis of Iraqi origin made with Arabs who remained in the country of their birth. Another subject I have been unable to explore is the dynamics of relations in restaurants, supermarkets, and other places where young Jews and Arabs work together (here, too, ethnic origin is a factor). But the writing of this book has come to an end, and I cannot say all there is to say. The book has come to an end, but events continue, and as these final lines are being written, the Land of Israel, Palestine, continues to be covered with blood. Not only Palestinian blood, which is spilled as a matter of course, but also Jewish blood. March 2022 saw a terror attack in Be'er Sheva followed by a another one in Hadera and then a further one in Bnei Brak. In response came revenge attacks by settlers in the territories and IDF operations in Jenin and anti-Arab demonstrations in Israeli cities. All this happened in a state of inequality, that of a ruling nation and a ruled nation, of intense national-religious struggle, of mutual fear, of internal divisions and fissures in both communities. The book has been completed, and, while it cannot offer comfort, perhaps it can propose a slow gaze, one of many voices, and the knowledge that we have before us more than one way of understanding the world and acting in it, on each side of the Mizrahi-Arab-Ashkenazi triangle, and in the triangle as a whole.

NOTES

ABBREVIATIONS

CZA Central Zionist Archives, Jerusalem
ISA Israel State Archives, Jerusalem
LPA Labor Party Archives, Beit Berl

PREFACE

1. Landau, "Netanyahu's Blind Faith in Force."

2. Bergman and Kingsley, "Protests over Netanyahu's Judiciary."

3. *Divrei Haknesset*, Twenty-Fifth Knesset, 136th session, January 15, 2024, 16.

4. Quoted in Moran, "Sof Haolam Yamina," 27.

INTRODUCTION

1. See, for example, Toubul, "Brit hametunim mishnei hatzdadim"; Distal-Atbaryan, "Mi heziz et halabaneh sheli?"

2. On the perception of Mizrahim as a group that suffers from discrimination, and for data on the configuration of this discrimination and the legal position that rejects the recognition of Mizrahim as a distinct group, see Bitton, "Mizrahim bamishpat," especially the first part.

3. Feierberg, "Hevrah ironit bemashber"; Razi, *Yaldei hahefker*.

CHAPTER 1

1. Eliav, "Meoraot yafo befurim TRS"H." Unless otherwise indicated, all the information about the incident in Jaffa is based on this article.

2. Menachem Sheinkin to the Zionist Center in Vilna, 5 Nisan (April 6) 1908, CZA, Z4/694.

3. Noy, *Edim o mumhim*, 13.

4. David Ben-Gurion, Eighth Party Convention, August 1956, session 1, 14, LPA, 37a-1956-21-2; Aharon Yadlin, response to motion for the agenda 1258, "Failure to include the history of North African Jewry in textbooks," *Divrei haknesset*, Eighth Knesset, 261st session, February 4, 1976, 1555–56.

5. Tsur, "Hahistoriografiyah hayisraelit vehabeayah haadatit," 56–57.

6. Toubul, *Kol hator*, 21–23.

7. Eliav, "Meoraot yafo befurim TRS"H."

8. Elkayam, *Yafo-neveh tzedek*, 175–77.

9. Sakhnini, *Tabariyya*, 368; al-Askari, *Qisat madinah*; al-Rajabi, *Al-jaliyah al-Yahudiyah*; al-Khatib, *Tadhakkurat*.

10. *Hatzfirah*, "Yediot mieretz yisrael," 2–3.

11. Eliav, "Yahasim bein-adatiyim bayishuv," 120.

12. The discrepancy between the concept of the nation then and the concepts common today is evident in the revised lyrics recently proposed by Dr. Walid al-Kasab (born in Syria in 1949), in which he changes the line "And no religion will make distinctions among us" to "All the Muslims are brothers."

13. Hanioğlu, *Brief History*, 74–75; Gribetz, *Defining Neighbors*, 20–21.

14. *Mahzikei Hadat*, "Hadashot leveit Yisrael," 5.

15. *Hashkafah*, "Hag Herut haotmanit birushalayim," 2.

16. *Hashkafah*, "Hag Herut haotmanit birushalayim," 2.

17. On the dilemma and the different approaches to it, see Campos, *Ottoman Brothers*, 197.

18. Aharonovich, "Mizmor le'asaf," 24.

19. Quoted in Druyanow and Laskov, *Ketavim letoldot hibat tzion*, 4:144–45.

20. Pinsker, *Auto-Emancipation*. The English translation is by D. S. Blondheim, which I have revised slightly.

21. Y. L. Pinsker, *Auto-Emancipation*.

22. See, for example, *Hamelitz*, "London: Mikhtav galui," 6; *Havatzelet*, "A"d [al devar] haisur," 1.

23. Yusuf Zia Khalidi to Theodor Herzl, March 3, 1899, Herzl Archive, Jerusalem, H III D 13 (Hebrew translation of the French original). See also Mandel, *Arabs and Zionism*, 47–48.

24. Khalidi, *From Haven to Conquest*, 92.

25. Quoted in Mandel, *Arabs and Zionism*, 52.

26. Yahuda, "Yahaso shel Herzl liveayah." For an extensive analysis, see Evri, *Hashivah laandalus*, 102–48.

27. A Hebrew translation of Khalidi's letter was published under the heading "Hadashot shonot" in *Hamagid*, September 1, 1875, 5.

28. For the 2017 Hamas charter, see *Middle East Eye*, "Hamas in 2017"; Popular Front for the Liberation of Palestine, *Strategy for the Liberation*, 110–11. The English quotations from the Palestinian National Covenant are taken, with amendments based on the original Arabic text, from Yale University Law School's Avalon Project at https://avalon.law.yale.edu/20th_century/plocov.asp (Palestinian National Charter), and https://avalon.law.yale.edu/20th_century/hamas.asp (Hamas Covenant 1988).

29. On the different arenas of opposition to Zionism, see Avni and Shimoni, *Hatziyonut umitnagdeha baam hayehudi*. Opposition to Zionism in the lands of the East is addressed in one of the articles in that volume: Kazzaz, "Tziyonim vekomunistim beirak."

30. These quotations are from Bezalel, *Noladtem tziyonim*, 370–86.

31. On *Haherut* and this approach, see Jacobson, "Sephardim, Ashkenazim."

32. Klein, *Keshurim*, 58.

33. Hakham bashi to the governor of Jerusalem, Yaakov Shaul Elyashar Archive, National Library of Israel, Jerusalem, ARC. 4* 1271.

34. Several years' worth of news reports attest to this, e.g., Weiss and Rofe, "Karagil"; Rofa-Opir, "HC Zakkur"; *Walla*, "Beyom Kippur"; Shapira, "7 yehudim."

35. *Hatzfirah*, "Po, iha"k yerushalayim," 4.

36. *Hatzfirah*, "Yerushalayim," 3.

37. *Haivri*, "Yerushalayim ir hakodesh," 3.

38. See *Bokra*, "Video."

39. There were also clashes between Jews, Arabs, security forces, and others. See Hasson and Khouri, "Imutim partzu."

40. *Der Yud*, August 12, 1909, quoting a report in the Egyptian newspaper *Al-Mintaq*, cited in Hart, "Tel Aviv bamar'ah," 94.

41. *Filastin*, "Yafa," 1. The talk about the Moroccans and Afghans lasted a few years. See *Haherut*, "Hed haitonut haaravit," 2.

42. For more on the phenomenon and on *Filastin*'s coverage of it, see Dierauff, *Translating Late Ottoman Modernity*, 166–73.

43. Camhi, *Hevron beyalduti*, 74–75.

44. Ben-Ezer, *Parashim al hayarkon*.

45. Halperin, "Trading Secrets."

46. Ben-Shabbat, "Haod nahrish," 1.

47. Antebi-Hefer, *Keforahat altah nitzah*, chap. 6.

48. The passage was written by Mordechai Kushnir (Snir), who as a boy settled in Palestine with his parents during the Second Aliyah. Quoted in Kafkafi, "Hearah al hahistoriyah shel," 192.

49. Nadav, *Zikhronot ish hashomer*, 2–7.

50. Nadav, *Zikhronot ish hashomer*, 19, 26.

51. Barnai, "Maamadah shel 'harabanut hakolelet.'"

52. Eliav, "Yahasim bein-adatiyim bayishuv"; Bartal, "Al demutah." The latter also tells of the decline of the Sephardi community's and hakham bashi's influence because of the capitulations, which placed Jews from different places in the diaspora under the protection of the consuls of the countries from which they came. On other communities that gained independence from the authority of the Sephardi community, see Sharabi, "Hitbadlut edot hamizrah mihaedah."

53. Quoted in Efrati, *Haedah hasfaradit birushalayim*, 66–67.

54. Efrati, *Haedah hasfardit birushalayim*, 66–67.

55. Lavie, "'Kimat keein nasi,'" 21.

56. Leon, *Hamitznefet vehadegel*, 73.

57. *Hamagid*, "Nigei levavenu," 1–2.

58. *Hatzfirah*, "Ben-Yehuda beveit haasurim," 2.

59. *Hatzfirah*, "Zeh leumat zeh," 2.

60. *Hatzfirah*, "Zeh leumat zeh," 2.

61. *Hamagid*, "Hadashot shonot," 11.

62. Jonas, "Hannukah," 1.

63. Quoted in Druyanow and Laskov, *Ketavim letoldot hibat tzion*, 1:380–81.

64. Szekely, "Parashah alumah mipeiluto hatziburit." The biographical information is taken from this article. See also Eldaoudi, *Hatoeh bisvakh hehayim*.

65. Tivoni, *Kerem haya leyedidi*, 168–71; see also Jacobson and Naor, *Benei haaretz vehamizrah*, 145.

66. Abbadi, "Nisuei taarovet bein aravim," 99.

67. Forum Eretz moledet, 21 Iyar 5771 (May 25, 2011), https://www.inn.co.il/Forum/Forum.aspx/t361364#4387280.

68. Szekely, "Parashah alumah mipeiluto hatziburit," 147n32.

69. Bartal, "Al demutah," 117.

70. Ben Zion, "Moshav yisrael beyafo."

71. Shilo, "Mitfisat 'moshavtit.'"

72. Ezrah [pseud.], "Mikhtavim mihayfah," 14.

73. Channel One, *Tekumah* (1998), episode 12, "Yisrael hashniyah," https://www.kan.org.il/content/kan/kan-11/p-13871/114722/ (minute 53).

74. See https://www.facebook.com/photo/?fbid=3458395630888128&set=a.591747104219676 (August 12, 2020).

75. Cohen, "Hayav umoto shel hayehudi-haaravi."

76. Abitbol, "Hapeilut hatziyonit bitzfon afrikah," 75–76.

77. Leven, *Hamishim shenot historiyah*, 115–16.

78. Quoted in Ro'i, "Nisyonotehem shel hamosdot hatziyoniyim," 209n34.

79. Khazzoom, "Tarbut maaravit."

80. For more on this process, see Bartal, "Al demutah."

81. Osherov, "Beayat falastin."

82. The *Filastin* piece on the stalks of grain appeared on October 2, 1912, 3–4; for more on *Filastin*'s treatment of the inferiority of the East, see Dierauff, *Translating Late Ottoman Modernity*, 88–93.

83. For a concise article on these relationships, see Lev Tov, "Shekhenim nokhehim."

84. [Rokach], "Lemoed moadim," 5.

85. *Hamelitz*, "Beiha"k," 5.

86. Mani, "Edot hamizrah betel aviv," 62 (Wissotzky quotation).

87. Yizrael, "Tyutah shel kol kore," 194.

88. Chelouche, *Parshat hayai*, chap. 3.

89. Quoted in Bezalel, "Halevantinim," 77.

90. Elmalih, "Yahas haaravim layehudim bishnat," 3.

91. *Haherut*, "Od meorah," 1.

92. Bezalel, "Halevantinim." See also Evri, *Hashivah laandalus*; Jacobson and Naor, *Benei haaretz vehamizrah*.

93. Moyal, "Hitorerut," 3.

94. Tamer, "Al'isti'mar alsuhyuni."

95. On his election, see *Haherut*, "Yafo" (August, 14, 1911), 3; budget proposal, n.d., CZA, L2/69.

96. Rabbi Uziel to Rabbi Nahum, undated draft, CZA, L2/69.

97. *Haherut*, "Haraha"g Haim Nahum birushalayim," 1–3.

98. Ben-Gurion, "Medabrana deumateh."

99. Benbassa, *Haim Nahum*; see esp. 27–29 and his letters.

100. Rabbi Uziel to the Palestine Office, 2 Iyar 5672 (April 19, 1912), CZA, L2/69.

101. Elmalih, "Yahas haaravim shebesuriya," 150–54.

102. A. A., "Hatnuah haaravit besuriyah," 14–15.

103. Quoted in *Haherut*, "Yafo" (March 27, 1912).

104. Cohen, *Hokhmah mikedem*, 211.

105. Don-Yehiya, *Harav Ben-Zion Meir Hai Uziel*, 229.

CHAPTER 2

1. Zionist Commission to the military governor, September 5, 1919, CZA, L3/36; *Haaretz*, "Birushalayim," 4; *Haaretz*, "Yehudi Marocco," 3.

2. Simons, *Historical Survey of Proposals*; Masalha, *Expulsion of the Palestinians*.

3. All translations from the Bible are taken from the New Jewish Publication Society translation, sometimes amended to fit the context, unless otherwise indicated.

4. Cohen, "'Garesh ninei ben haamah.'"

5. Ben-Ya'akov, *Otzar hashirim*, 63; see also the poem "Legaresh eved vaamah / miheikhal bat melekh tamah" (74).

6. Eliyahu, *Kol Yaakov Hashalem*, 762–63.

7. Yehoshua-Raz, "Ahavat tziyon vatziyonut."

8. Mazuz, "She'elot vetshuvot beinyanei simhat torah."

9. Avi Hatzeira, Avi Hatzeira, and Hafuta, *Yagel yaakov*, 359. For the complete Hebrew text with commentary, see the National Library of Israel's Piyyut and Prayer website, https://www.nli.org.il/he/piyut/Piyut1song_010422800000005171/NLI#2,20,7848,9.

10. See Avitan, "Piskei Halakha beinyan yom haatzmaut."

11. "Jamal Zahalka in the Documentary 'Ashkenaz,'" https://www.youtube.com/watch?v=UAw4r6_RE_s&t=203s; *Divrei haknesset*, Twentieth Knesset, 46th session, September 7, 2015, 135, https://main.knesset.gov.il/activity/plenum/pages/sessionitem.aspx?itemid=568982.

12. Tawiow, *Otzar hashirah vehamelitzah*, 206.

13. Capsali, *Seder Eliyahu Zuta*, 1:141, 218–19, 272–73; Sambari, *Sefer divrei yosef*, 248, 252–53, despite his emphasis on Israel's enslavement to Ishmael.

14. Levinson, "Aliyah le"y al-manat lashuv."

15. On the Kedma-Mizraha association and the discussions it held, see Hattis, *Bi-National Idea in Palestine*, 209–82.

16. For the draft, with Rabbi Uziel's annotations, see ISA, file 894/11; see also CZA, S44/706.

17. ISA, file 894/11.

18. The Zionist Commission to the military governor, September 5, 1919, CZA, L3/36.

19. Quoted in Picard, "Reishitah shel haaliyah," 339n5.

20. Emphasis added. Ze'ev Jabotinsky, letter 183, March 7, 1918, quoted in Man, "Meah shanim."

21. Ben-Kiki, "Al sheelat hasheelot beyishuv Haaretz"; and see Evri, *Hashivah laandalus*, 210–15; Cohen and Evri, "Moledet meshutefet o bayit leumi."

22. Cohen and Evri, "Moledet meshutefet o bayit leumi."

23. On these processes, see the detailed account in Efrati, *Mimashber letikva*.

24. Haim, *Yihud vehishtalvut*.

25. Klibenski, "Tsfat," 17–18.

26. Klibenski, "Tsfat," 17–18.

27. *Filastin*, "Al-yahud al-sefaradim," 2.

28. HCJ 1/81, *Shiran v. Israeli Broadcasting Authority* (1981), IsrSC 35 (3) P.D. 365.

29. Quoted in Leibowitz-Dar, "Leyahadut hamizrah."

30. Elmalih, "Hartzaah al nesiati baari suryah."

31. Elmalih, "Tafkideinu bitnuat-hathiyyah," 1.

32. Elmalih, "Tafkideinu bitnuat-hathiyyah," 1. On the theory of decline, see Frenkel, "Ketivat hahistoriyah."

33. Testimony of Yekutiel Shevah, Haganah Historical Archives, testimony 103/23.

34. Jabotinsky, "Hamizrah," 91.

35. Quoted in Evri, *Hashivah laandalus*, 235.

36. Jacobson and Naor, *Benei haaretz vehamizrah*, 25.

37. Yosef Sprinzak to Halutzei Hamizrah, March 15, 1923, CZA, S9/1768.

38. Rosenstein, *Toldot tenuat hapoalim*, 1:35.

39. Boord, "Hahalutzim vehamahaneh," 80–81.

40. Jerusalem Workers Council, letter to the editor, *Doar Hayom*, February 24, 1928, 4.

41. Segev, *Medinah bekhol mahir*, 201.

42. Tzarum, "Teshuvah lemoetzet poalei yerushalayim," 3.

43. World Sephardi Federation, Jerusalem, to Zionist Executive, London, April 1, 1929, CZA, S30/2361.

44. Jacobson and Naor, *Benei haaretz vehamizrah*, 132–33.

45. Quoted in *Doar Hayom*, "Hasephardim vehamosdot hatziyonim," 2.

46. Quoted in *Doar Hayom*, "Hasephardim vehamosdot hatziyonim (sof)," 3.

47. See Hakeshet hademokratit hamizrahit's Facebook page, https://www.facebook.com/hakeshet/posts/1250413064976844 (June 6, 2016).

48. Sasson, "Bayna alsefaradim walashkenazim."

49. Assaf, "Dilatoriyah benusah sefarad," 2.

50. The sections that follow are based on information that appears in Cohen, *Year Zero*.

51. *Doar Hayom*, "Yerushalayim"; *Davar*, "Hameoraot birushalayim," 4.

52. *Doar Hayom*, "Arabaat asirei meah shearim yats'u zakai'm."

53. See Cohen, *Year Zero*, e.g., 28–29, 114, 186; Slutsky, *Sefer Toldot Hahagana*, 2:327.

54. Testimony of A. H. Cohen, Haganah Historical Archives, testimony 27.16.

55. Cohen, "Avi, Aharon Haim Cohen," 108.

56. Testimony of Rabbi Weingarten, Haganah Historical Archives, testimony 115.34.

57. *Haaretz*, "Meoraot Akko."

58. Cohen, "Hayav umoto shel hayehudi-haaravi."

59. Elmalih, "Meoraot umaasim," 62–63. I am indebted to Amos Noy for bringing this text to my attention.

60. National Council of the Jews of the Land of Israel, "Mar Birman mihair haatikah metalpen," September 25, 1929, CZA, J1/149.

61. Segev, *State at Any Cost*, 222.

62. Shavit, "Hairgun hapoliti vehatziburi," 9:180.

63. Quoted in Rosenstein, *Toldot tenuat hapoalim*, 1:84.

64. Quoted in Rosenstein, *Toldot tenuat hapoalim*, 1:84–85.

65. Eisenstadt, *Hahevrah hayisraelit*, 44–45.

66. Fischer, "Shenei defusim shel modernizatziyah."

67. Arlosoroff, "Milhemet hamaamadot."

68. Quoted at the Mapai Convention, December 3, 1932, LPA, 2-21-1932-16.

69. Razi, *Yaldei hahefker*, 39.

70. Arlosoroff, "Milhemet hamaamadot."

71. Slutsky, *Sefer Toldot Hahaganah*, 2:479.

72. Bein, *Aliyah vehityashvut bimdinat yisrael*, 30.

73. Razi, *Yaldei hahefker*, 34, chap. 1, and 104–5.

74. Halpern, "Jewish Social Workers."

75. David Moyal et al., memorandum to the Jewish Agency, October 31, 1937, CZA, S30/2361.

76. Adut, "Poalim ufkidim," 35.

77. Minutes of Mapai Central Committee meeting, October 6, 1937, LPA, 2-23-1937-17b, 23.

78. Chechik report, CZA, S44/508.

79. *Davar*, "Dvar hayom," 1.

80. Quoted in Slutsky, *Sefer Toldot Hahaganah*, 2:632.

81. Aderet, "Haintifadah shekadmah lekum hamedinah."

82. *Davar*, "Dvar hayom," 1.

83. *Al-Liwaa*, "Halat Yafa," 1.

84. Lapidot, *Balahav hamered*, 22.

85. *Mir'at al-Sharq*, "Mawqif alyahud alwataniyyin," 1, 7.

86. Etzel broadside, August 1938, quoted in Lapidot, *Leidatah shek mahteret*, 145.

87. Quoted in Habas, *Meoraot TRTza"V*, 544.

88. Lapidot, *Balahav hamered*, 25.

89. Quoted in Lapidot, *Leidatah shek mahteret*, 88.

90. For a broader treatment, see Jacobson and Naor, *Benei haaretz vehamizrah*, chap. 5.

91. Jacobson and Naor, *Benei haaretz vehamizrah*, chap. 5.

92. "Lo Tirzah," a declaration signed by dozens and printed in Binyamin and Peterzil, *Neged hateror*, 5.

93. Magnes, "Sihah," 53–54.

94. Thon, "Hinukh edot hamizrah," 48. On Thon and her views, see Radai, "Yotzei artzot haislam."

95. See *Sefer Toldot Hahaganah*, 2:803, 815, 831, and also Shadmi's memoir, *Kav yashar bamaagal hahayim*, 121–22.

96. Shadmi, *Kav yashar bamaagal hahayim*, 122, including the Katznelson quotation from *Davar*.

97. Frankenstein, "Hinukh hanoar miedot hamizrah," 3–4.

98. Frankenstein, "Hinukh hanoar miedot hamizrah," 4.

99. Dahan Kalev, "Kamah sheat yafah," which also contains quotations from Frankenstein's books and articles.

100. Mizrahi Democratic Rainbow—New Discourse, Mizrahi Education Project, 2016, https://tinyurl.com/2fsjvvuc.

101. Ben Gurion Archive, general files (*takak*), 1938, document 105135. For more on the Jews of Iraq during the Arab Revolt, see Bashkin, *New Babylonians*, 34–37, 102–7.

102. CZA, kkl5/5330–72.

103. This is a translation of the statement as it appears in a Haganah report from Haifa, "Hatifat shenei hatzeirim," December 28, 1938, CZA, S25/4405.

104. See previous note.

105. Ben-Zaken, *Komunizm keimperiyalizm tarbuti*; Nissan, "Hamiflagah hakomunistit hafalastinait."

106. Nissan, "Hamiflagah hakomunistit hafalastinait," 44.

107. Shukeiri, *Arba'un aaman fi al-hayah*, 198.

108. The account comes from a placard signed "the Yemenite working public," September 8, 1941, CZA, J1/2697.

109. *Hapoel Hatzair*, "Rehovot."

110. Assaf, "Kinus Tarbuti halutzi," 2. On the Arabic teachers in the kibbutzim, see Rotbart, "Tokhnit horaat aravit bakibutzhim."

111. Quoted in Zohar, "Haapalah vealiyah," 59.

112. Zohar, "Haapalah vealiyah," 61–62.

113. Fishman, *Ayanot*, 81–82.

114. On Shemesh and Ben-David, see Dror, *Hamistaarvim shel hapalma"h*, 211–17; Cohen, *Leor hayom uvamahshakh*.

115. Quoted in Dror, *Hamistaarvim shel hapalma"h*, 211.

116. Dror, *Hamistaarvim shel hapalma"h*, 109.

117. Shukeiri, *Arba'un aaman fi al-hayah*, 198.

118. Quoted in Morris, "Mabat hadash al mismakhim," 129–31.

119. Al-Qawuqji, "Memoirs, 1948 (Part 1)," 35.

120. "Meeting with Fawzi Qawuqji at Nir Shemesh—April 1, 1948," Haganah Historical Archives, file 50/25.

CHAPTER 3

1. IDF Archive, 1860/50–3.

2. Radai, *Bein shetei arim*, 188.
3. *Haaretz*, "Yafo," 4.
4. Quoted in Segev, *1949*, 88.
5. Segev, *1949*, 89–91.
6. Sasson-Levy, "'Ani ashkenazi.'"
7. *Maariv*, "Petzuim, atzurim," 1.
8. Gelblum, "Aliyat teiman uveayat afrikah," 2. For an analysis of the article that contrasts it with other positions, see Tsur, "Eimat hakarnival."
9. Tsur, "Eimat hakarnival," 133–34.
10. Gelblum, "Aliyat teiman uveayat afrikah."
11. Avnery, "Gal hapeshaim haminiim," 2.
12. *Davar*, "Nidhata hatzaa britit letavekh," 1; see also on this subject Jacobson and Naor, *Benei haaretz vehamizrah*, chap. 5.
13. Eliyahu Elyashar to David Ben-Gurion, May 1, 1947, CZA, S25/5654.
14. Quoted in Segev, *Medinah bekhol mahir*, 442.
15. Morris, *Leidatah shel beayat haplitim*, 296–97.
16. Minutes of the thirteenth meeting of the first cabinet, May 6, 1949, 2, ISA-PMO-GovernmentMeeting-0002eea.
17. Quoted in Hazkani, "Sipuro shel hadoh hahatrani." This paragraph was omitted from the printed version of the lecture in Ben-Gurion, *Tzava uvitahon*.
18. Thon, "Hinukh edot hamizrah," 47. On Thon and her views, see Radai, "Yotzei artzot haislam," 216–44.
19. Hazkani, *Dear Palestine*.
20. Avner Israël Serfaty, "Yahas Fes" (Fez, 1879), typescript copy, National Library of Israel, Jerusalem, MS 37875F, 10.
21. Benayahu, *Divrei hayamim shel Fes*.
22. The phrase "the lachrymose conception of Jewish history" was coined by Salo Baron (1895–1989). See his article "Newer Emphases in Jewish History."
23. Maimonides wrote this in his letter to Ovadiah the Convert. See Schlossberg, "Yahaso shel harambam el haislam."
24. Halamish, *Peirush kabali*, 249–50.
25. Behar, "Parshanut lahistoriyah."
26. Quoted in Saadon, "'Hamarkiv hafalastini,'" 86.
27. Saadon, "'Hamarkiv hafalastini.'"
28. Bulletin no. 79, March 14, 1963, ISA, file ג 2976/10.
29. See previous note.
30. See Hazkani, *Dear Palestine*. See also a letter from an emissary named Shoshana, sent from Casablanca to the Mapai Central Committee, July 8, 1949, LPA, 2-101-949-82. On the return of the Iranian Kurds, see Magnarella, "Aspects of Social Life."
31. Soldiers' letters reported by Yigael Yadin, and his own comments, at a meeting of education officers, in the pamphlet *Hinukh umoral betzahal*, IDF General Staff, Chief Education Officer, Information Branch (n.d.), IDF Archive, 206/385/1963, 21. I am indebted to Shai Hazkani for making the file available to me. See also Hazkani, *Dear Palestine*, 4, 89.
32. Morris, *Milhamot hagvul shel yisrael*, 114, 156.
33. Quoted in Morris, *Milhamot hagvul shel yisrael*, 276.
34. Sheffer Raviv, "Mioyev leohev."
35. For the transcript of the speech, see Morris, *Milhamot hagvul shel yisrael*, 286.
36. Segev, *Hamilyon hashvii*, 160; see that entire chapter on the absorption difficulties the survivors experienced and their treatment by established Israelis.
37. Quoted in Morris, *Milhamot hagvul shel yisrael*, 207.
38. On revenge operations by the residents of Mevo Beitar, a moshav on the Green Line southwest of Jerusalem, see *Davar*, "Yisrael gunta al retsah mevo'ot Beitar," which offers an Israeli version of events that denies wrongdoing; see also Morris, *Milhamot hagvul shel yisrael*, 600n51. There are probably other examples that I failed to locate.
39. *Herut*, "Arabaat hatseirim yeshuhraru bekarov?"; *Haaretz*, "Shoklim efsharut sgirat hatik neged."
40. Minister of defense to minister of justice, April 1955, ISA, file 7242/6; for more on the incident, see Zakbach, "Peulat hanakam shel Meir Har-Zion."
41. Hofi made this statement in a panel discussion titled "Peulot hatagmul bigvul yarden," collected in Bar-On and Shiran, *Lenokhah gevulot oyenim*, 222–43 (quotation on 241).
42. Quoted in Morris, *Milhamot hagvul shel yisrael*, 207.
43. Quoted in Zonder, *Sayeret matka"l*, 23.
44. Hillel, *Ruah kadim*, 251–55; Segev, *1949*, 164. See also Shenhav, *Hayehudim haaravim*.

45. Kahanoff, *Mimizrah shemesh*, 18.

46. Elon, "Yisrael hashniyah boheret," 2.

47. Nahon, *Defusei hitrahavut*; Amit, "Tekefut hahalukah."

48. Amor, "Hahistoriyah hailemet shel haseruv hahevrati"; Lerer, *Hakod haetni*; Maruoma-Marom, "Meafyanei mediniyut."

49. Swirski and Bernstein, "Mi avad bemah," 142.

50. Swirski and Bernstein, "Mi avad bemah," 142.

51. Lockman, *Contending Visions of the Middle East*, 154–58.

52. Khazzoom, *Shifting Ethnic Boundaries*, 126.

53. Kimmerling, *Mehagrim, mityashvim, yalidim*, 293.

54. Quoted in Shipler, "Israel Bars Rabin."

55. For a selection of letters and telegrams, see ISA, file ג 2215/22.

56. Telegram to the interior minister, August 22, 1951 (the date appears in an accompanying letter), ISA, file ג 2215/22.

57. Avraham Malul, report of the regional officer for Jafra, Ramla, and Lod, June 1951, ISA, file גל 17115/23.

58. Evri, *Hashivah laandalus*, 189–91.

59. See Lalo's district officer report, July 1952, ISA, file גל 17115/23.

60. *Davar*, "Lehidush yahasei shekhenim," 2.

61. Ramla-Lod district officer to the Tel Aviv district supervisor, September 16, 1951, ISA, file ג 2215/22.

62. *Divrei haknesset*, Second Knesset, 105th session, July 9, 1952, 2598–600.

63. Minutes of Mapai Bureau meeting with Haveireinu, February 21, 1949, LPA, 2-25-1949-12.

64. Ministry of Foreign Affairs, Information Department, "Bechor-Shalom Shitreet [*sic*]: Brief Biography (Draft)," December 16, 1948, ISA, unit 49, file ג 300/80. For more on Sheetrit and the Ministry of Minority Affairs, see Peled, "Other Side of 1948."

65. *Haaretz*, "Shenayim nirtzehu birushalayim," 6.

66. Ministry of Foreign Affairs, Information Department, "Bechor-Shalom Shitreet [*sic*]: Brief Biography (Draft)," December 16, 1948, ISA, unit 49, file ג 300/80.

67. *Divrei haknesset*, Second Knesset, 115th session, July 9, 1952, 2598–600.

68. Subcommittee on Ramla Affairs, meeting minutes, August 11, 1952, ISA, file כ 83/2.

69. Subcommittee on Ramla Affairs, meeting minutes, August 11, 1952, ISA, file כ 83/2, 4.

70. Subcommittee on Ramla Affairs, meeting minutes, August 11, 1952, ISA, file כ 83/2, 4.

71. The Iraqi Immigrants Association in Ramla to the minister of the interior, July 10, 1952, ISA, file 2268/15.

72. The Iraqi Immigrants Association in Ramla to the minister of the interior, July 10, 1952, ISA, file 2268/15.

73. Sofer, "Orot utzlalim."

74. Motzafi-Haller, "Siah intelektualim mizrahim."

75. Subcommittee on Ramla Affairs, minutes of first meeting, August 4, 1952, ISA, כ 89/15.

76. Subcommittee on Ramla Affairs, minutes of first meeting, August 4, 1952, ISA, כ 89/15.

77. "Maskanot vaadat hapnim bekesher lemeoraot ramla," August 19, 1952, ISA, file פ 1980/47.

78. Guber, *El mesuot lakhish*, 43.

79. Nurieli, "Zarim bamerhav leumi," esp. 30–31.

80. Nurieli, "Zarim bamerhav leumi," quotations on 22.

81. *Kol Haam*, "Askanei mapam beramle meorerim," 4.

82. Subcommittee on Ramla Affairs, minutes of first meeting, August 4, 1952, 1–2.

83. Gideon Giladi, "Asatir utahrid," *Al-Mirsad*, March 12, 1953, quoted in Roby, *Mizrahi Era of Rebellion*, 74–75.

84. Bashkin, *Impossible Exodus*, 149.

85. Mapai Central Committee, meeting minutes, August 22, 1955, LPA, 2-23-1955-66, 399.

86. Mapai Central Committee, meeting minutes, August 8, 1955, LPA, 2-23-1955-66, 235.

87. Gelblum, "Aliyat teiman uveayat afrikah," 2.

88. Picard, "Reishitah shel haaliyah haselektivit."

89. See the emissary reports, LPA, 2-101-949-82. On the different currents in Moroccan communities, Casablanca in particular, see Tsur, *Kehilah kruyah*, 186–217.

90. Mapai Bureau, meeting minutes, February 24, 1949, LPA, 2-25-1949-12; see also Segev, *1949*, 171.

91. David Ben-Gurion's remarks, Eighth Party Convention, August 26, 1956, session 1, LPA, 2-21-1956-37a, 14.

92. Gad Ben-Meir's remarks, Eighth Party Convention, August 28, 1956, session 5, LPA, 2-21-1956-37a, 1.

93. Mapai Central Committee, meeting minutes, August 8, 1955, LPA, 2-23-1955-66.

94. Mapai Central Committee, meeting minutes, September 6, 1955, LPA, 2-23-1955-66.

95. Report of the head of the Central District to the Department of Minority Affairs, Ministry of the Interior, September 23, 1956, ISA, file ג 2215/22 (based on conversations with the Arab inhabitants).

96. Subcommittee of the Interior Committee, report on visit to Ramla, November 22, 1956, ISA, file ג 2215/22, 8–11.

97. Subcommittee of the Interior Committee, report on visit to Ramla, November 22, 1956, ISA, file ג 2215/22, 4.

98. Goldstein, "Kan hayu hahashudim befarashat haretzah."

99. Subcommittee of the Interior Committee, report on visit to Ramla, November 22, 1956, ISA, file ג 2215/22, 5.

100. Quoted in Algazi, "Hitargnut nokhakh kfifut," 92–93n50.

101. See Algazi, "Hitargnut nokhakh kfifut."

102. Piroyansky, *Ramle Remade*, 149–54.

103. Meir-Glitzenstein, "Manhigut tziyonit," 7, 10, 11–13.

104. Bashkin, *Impossible Exodus*, 122.

105. Kabha, "Yehudim Mizrahim baitonut haaravit bisrael."

106. Shenhav, "Shimon balas," 1.

107. Meir-Glitzenstein, "Manhigut tziyonit vekomunistit," 21–22.

108. Shenhav-Shaharabani, "Mifgash mukdam."

109. Petition received by the Knesset Presidium, June 11, 1956, ISA, file כ 591–13.

110. *Kol Haam*, "Batnuah," 3.

111. Jacques Biton to the Knesset Presidium, November 26, 1957, ISA, file כ 591/13.

112. Gozansky, *Komunistim mizrahim*, 87–88.

113. Bashkin, *Impossible Exodus*, 130; Gozansky, *Komunistim mizrahim*, 95.

114. For more, see Chetrit, *Hamaavak hamizrahi bisrael*, 99–111; Weiss, *Wadi Salib*.

115. David Ben-Gurion to Judge Moshe Etzioni, August 3, 1959, Ben-Gurion Archive, Sde Boker, correspondence, August 1959, old sequence 1040.

116. Algazi, "Kol min heavar."

117. Nir, "Zu haytah," 4.

118. Asa Kasher, letter to the editor, *Haaretz*, July 30, 1959, 2.

119. Danin, *Tziyoni bekhol tenai*, 373–75.

120. Erlich, "Migdal bavel," 10–14.

121. Sharoni, *Kor hahitukh*.

122. ISA, documents and various notes, 1963, file לג 17068/10.

123. Mawasi, *Arcs from My Autobiography*.

124. Uzi Doron to Eli Amir, Office of the Advisor on Arab Affairs, April 7, 1967, ISA, file לג 17037/15.

125. Anabusi, "Sherutei habriut," 63, 1.

126. *Maariv*, "Beako hayu hitnagshuyot," 2; Acre District Headquarters to the commander of the Northern District, Israel Police, "Doh mesakem: Eruim beako vekfarei haaizor," October 3, 1961, ISA, file ל 200/36.

127. "Executors" was the term used in Yona and Mann, "Hamotziim lapoal."

128. Vinitzky, "Shekhunat hatikvah saarah bamehumot."

129. Juhayna [Habibi], "'Afn akkhitam."

130. Report to Minister of Police Bechor-Shalom Sheetrit, n.d., ISA, file ג 6839/44; see also Margalit, "Dam batzel hatapuzim," 2; Marcus, "Tzahorei hayom berishon letziyon," 3.

131. *Maariv*, "Asarot niftseu betigrot hamoniot"; *Maariv*, "3 Aravim niftseu behitnagshut halayla."

132. Report to Minister of Police Bechor-Shalom Sheetrit, n.d., ISA, file ג 6839/44.

133. Marcus, "Tzahorei hayom berishon letziyon," 3.

134. Margalit, "Dam batzel hatapuzim," 2.

135. Margalit, "Aklim stavi bishkhunat avivah," 2.

136. Shabak to the Israel Police, November 7, 1955; National Police Headquarters to the Tel Aviv District Headquarters, November 4, 1955, both in ISA, file ל 2311/14.

137. Kozłowska, "East Sees East."

138. Quoted in Glitzenstein, "Manhigut tziyonit vekomunistit," 19.

139. Eliahu, *Ani velo malakh*; English translation by the poet at https://www.poetryinternational.com/en/poets-poems/poems/poem/103-27669_under-the-ground/.

140. Shohat quoted in Oppenheimer, "Od hozer hanigun baorkeikhem," 390.

141. Stern, "Kasheh lihiyot . . . adam," 2.

142. Stern, "Hayitzug hanakhon," 2.

143. Public Committee of Rishon Lezion's Long-Standing Residents and Builders, "Vahaemet vehashalom ehevu," ISA, file ג 6839/44.

144. Bahat, "Laikarei shitat hashinuim."

145. *Maariv*, "'Lirtzoah et kulam' zaaku porim."

146. *Davar*, "Hamtihut beramle adayin lo shakhekha."

147. Quoted in *Lamerhav*, "Invey hazaam shel ramle," 3.

148. Joseph Ginat and Meir Jarrah, "Hatakrit benetanyah," internal report, n.d., ISA, file גל 17007/2.

149. Talmi, "Takrit netanyah."

150. Shmuel Toledano, interview by Raphael Bashan, *Maariv*, March 4, 1966.

151. Cohen, *Tarpa"t*, 328–31.

152. Letter to Minister Sheetrit (the name of the writer has been blotted out by the archive), October 18, 1962, ISA, file ג 6839/44.

153. Shabtai [Klugman], "Hamapalah beramla."

154. Shabtai [Klugman], "Hamapalah beramla."

155. Peled and Shafir, *Mihu yisraeli*.

156. Noy, "Keshemizrahim hayu moderna," 140.

157. Talmi, "Takrit netanyah," 7.

158. *Kol Haam*, "Metihut adatit," 4.

159. Quoted in Hazkani, *Dear Palestine*, 191.

160. Katzenelson, *Hamahapekhah haashkenazit*, 153.

161. Katzenelson, *Hamahapekhah haashkenazit*, 155.

162. Katzenelson, *Hamahapekhah haashkenazit*, 157–58.

163. Katzenelson, *Hamahapekhah haashkenazit*, 161.

164. Meir Avital, letter to the editor, *Hatzofeh*, April 13, 1964.

165. See "General Testimony" file in the Prime Minister's Office, ISA, file ג 6397/10.

166. Katzenelson, *Hamahapekhah haashkenazit*, 191.

167. Mordechai Tsanin, editorial, *Letste Nayes*, April 24, 1964, quoted in *Yediot Aharonot*, "Hamahapekhah haashkenazit matzah," 2.

168. *Hatzofeh*, "Kakh barhu shloshet," 2; *Maariv*, "Hayehudim shazru lamistanenim livroakh," 1.

169. *Maariv*, "Neetzra huliyat mehablim berahuto," 4.

170. *Maariv*, "Neetzra huliyat mehablim berahuto," 4.

171. Younis, *Al-hurub min sijn ramle*.

172. Matalon, "Shetei perspektivot," 30–31, 32.

173. Shohat, "Invention of the Mizrahim," 15–16.

174. Bar-Hai, "Mi metapeah eivah leashkenazim," 3.

175. *Hatzofeh*, "Ma Merits."

176. Ben, "Hashira kiskoop."

177. Ben Harosh, "Zakhor et asher asu lekha haashkenazim."

178. Quoted in *Davar*, "Lekomem hatoshavim haaravim," 1.

CHAPTER 4

1. Stern, "Ezra ushihada mehadshim yedidut." The quotations in the following two paragraphs are from this article.

2. Deri's efforts were widely reported in the press.

3. Siton and Shoshan, *Anshei hasod vehaseter*, 288–92 (quotation on 288).

4. Ronen, *Shenat shaba"k*, 202–18.

5. Siton and Shoshan, *Anshei hasod vehaseter*, 57–58.

6. Al-Khuli, "Nahwa jabha 'alimiyya."

7. From Sami Shalom Chetrit's Facebook page, https://www.facebook.com/samichetrit/posts/10159299505858150 (August 27, 2021).

8. Shaib-Lerer, "Hafarhud kefi shesiper li avi."

9. Serri, *Shiv'im shirei shotetut*, 144–45.

10. Oppenheimer, "Ani palit aravi."

11. Hakak, "Bracha Serri."

12. Saadon, *Morocco*, 80, 126–27; Jewish Agency, *Aliyat yehudei moroko*, chap. 2.

13. Ghosheh, *Al-shams min al-nafidha al-aliya*, 184–86.

14. Ghosheh, *Al-shams min al-nafidha al-aliya*, 184–86.

15. Halamish, "Meever lagvul," 7.

16. Quoted in Ben-Moshe, "Irgunei hateror veha 'falestinaim,'" 3.

17. Quoted in *Maariv*, "Asur levater al af shaal," 2.

18. Al-Khatib al-Tamimi, *Ma salah a-din fi alquds*, 139–40.

19. Kedar, *Im Nurit*, 163.

20. *Divrei haknesset*, Fifteenth Knesset, 90th session, February 28, 2000, 6041–45.

21. Abu Khadra, "Sarah david levi batel."

22. Osherov, “Beayat falastin,” 150–51, 220–21.

23. Rejwan, *Israel's Years of Bogus Grandeur*, 93.

24. Speech by Zvi Shiloah, clipping from the newspaper *Zot Haaretz*, ISA, file פ 2079/4.

25. Behar, “Miyehuda halevi leyehuda burla.”

26. A pamphlet on this was published by R. Kook on September 19, 1967; see https://www.yeshiva.org.il/midrash/3896.

27. Original wording of the manifesto, ISA, file פ 2731/13. The manifesto was printed in most of the daily newspapers on September 22, 1967.

28. This was published as an advertisement in *Haaretz* on September 22, 1967.

29. Slann, “Jewish Ethnicity.”

30. Teddy Kollek to Levi Eshkol, March 11, 1968, ISA, file א 7920/8.

31. Report and findings, ISA, file א 7920/8. The findings are derived from the incomplete report in this file.

32. Peres, “Ethnic Relations in Israel,” 1021.

33. Khazzoom, *Shifting Ethnic Boundaries*, 55.

34. Peres, “Ethnic Relations in Israel,” 1021 (quoted from the abstract).

35. Milson, “Pgishot bilti rishmiot im falastinim,” 118–19.

36. Milson, “Pgishot bilti rishmiot im falastinim,” 119.

37. *Al Hamishmar*, “Nikhbdei hevron,” 8; *Davar*, “Rosh iriyat hevron,” 7.

38. *Al Hamishmar*, “Nikhbdei hevron,” 8.

39. Yaakov Khizmeh reporting on the article in *Al-Kifah* to the Arab Broadcast Committee, December 13, 1967, ISA, file לג 17036/14.

40. Ben-Dor, “‘Eib, hshuma, infajrat Qunbula,” 35.

41. Gabbai, “Kelitat poalim mihashtahim.”

42. Sheffer Raviv, “Reshitah vehitgabshutah,” 155–56.

43. Tzameret, “Zalman Aran,” 324.

44. Yonah and Saporta, “Hahinukh hakdam-miktzoi,” 70.

45. Office of the Prime Minister, Public Commission on Welfare, “Education Team” [November 1976], ISA, file לג 13894/6. It is not clear from the document whether the data cover national figures on the class that graduated the previous year or consisted of a broader set.

46. Quoted in Sheffer Raviv, “Reshitah vehitgabshutah,” 145–46.

47. Avineri, “Al avodah ivrit ugvulot mediniyim,” 32.

48. Lewin-Epstein and Semyonov, “Ethnic Group Mobility.”

49. Al-Haj, “Megamot bamifgash.”

50. Proceedings of the Interior Committee of the Knesset, December 16, 1969, ISA, file לג 17007/24; Israel Police, “Modiin meyuhad” (n.d.), ISA, file ל 226/5; *Maariv*, “5 toshavim,” 2; *Maariv*, “Maasar olam lesisha aravim yisraelim,” 2.

51. Proceedings of the Interior Committee of the Knesset, December 16, 1969, ISA, file לג 17007/24.

52. *Davar*, “Kokhvei hagada polshim leyisrael,” 6.

53. Proceedings of the Interior Committee of the Knesset, December 16, 1969, ISA, file לג 17007/24.

54. Proceedings of the Interior Committee of the Knesset, December 16, 1969, ISA, file לג 17007/24.

55. Mayor Israel Doron to Prime Minister Golda Meir, February 17, 1970, ISA file לג17081/11.

56. Quoted in Chetrit, *Hamaavak hamizrahi bisrael*, 144; see also Bernstein, “Hapanterim hashhorim.”

57. Amor, “Hahistoriyah hailemet shel haseruv hahevrati”; Smooha, “Adatiyut vetzava bisrael.” See also the studies by Yagil Levy, quoted in Bloom, “Hashikhpul shel hamodel ‘mizrahi,’” 84–86; Lerer, *Hakod haetni*.

58. I base the following summary largely on Chetrit, *Hamaavak hamizrahi bisrael*, chap. 3; Bernstein, “Hapanterim hashhorim”; Lev and Shenhav, “Al tikri poel ela panter.”

59. *Al Hamishmar*, “‘Hapanterim’ huashmu benisayon”; *Hapanter Hashahor*, “Suhreru martsiano vebiton,” 14.

60. See film clip of Meir at https://www.facebook.com/watch/?v=512350639832310.

61. Bernstein, “Hapanterim hashhorim,” 76; Lev and Shenhav, “Al tikri poel ela panter.”

62. *Al Hamishmar*, “Yehudei rusya go home,” 3; for a later example, see *Maariv*, “Kochavi Shemesh sheyatza,” 10.

63. Cohen, “Shulhan meruba im hapanterim,” 3–6, 59; Shabi Amedi, who was involved in the Panthers' activity from the start as a community worker, conversation with author, October 5, 2021; Abergel, “Haideologiyah shelanu hi hakeev.”

64. "Haseker hashotef al beayot hatzibbur vedaat hakahal 1968," Viterbi Family Center for Public Opinion and Policy Research of the Israel Democracy Institute, https://dataisrael.idi.org.il.

65. Reuven Abergel, interview by author, September 29, 2021, Jerusalem.

66. "Against the Arrest of Nabil Saad," press release, Matzpen, October 11, 1969 (with a comment by Saad dated December 6, 2021), https://tinyurl.com/55w46n89.

67. Avnery, "Hapanterim huzmeny," 2. On Avnery's attitude toward the link between Matzpen and the Panthers, see also Avnery, "Panterim vekalenterizm."

68. Quoted in Lev and Shenhav, "Kinuno shel haoyev mibifnim," 138.

69. *Yediot Aharonot*, "Mimun mishlahat hapanterim," 48.

70. Chetrit, *Hamaavak hamizrahi bisrael*, 74.

71. *Divrei haknesset*, Eighth Knesset, 47th session, May 20, 1974, 1337.

72. Shohat, "Hamizrahim bisrael," 173.

73. Cohen and Leon, *Merkaz tenuat haherut vehamizrahim*, 160–62, 173.

74. Benkler, Zamir, and Galili, "Kirya koevet umetuskelet," 5; *Haaretz*, "Revavot livu lemenuhot halelei kiryat shemonah," 3.

75. Quoted in Rubinstein, "Boker tov," 51.

76. *Davar*, "Kiryah koevet," 2.

77. Bergman, *Rise and Kill First*, chap. 12; *Yediot Aharonot*, "Hawatmeh menamek," 2; for Sharon's statement in favor of freeing prisoners, see *Divrei haknesset*, Eighth Knesset, 47th session, May 20, 1974, 1337–38.

78. For an English translation of Arafat's speech, see https://al-bab.com/documents-section/speech-yasser-arafat-1974.

79. Rubinstein, "Dat umdinah bamatkonet falastinait."

80. Waksman, "David Levy," 13; Mazori, "Shum hablan," 17.

81. Chomsky, "International Terrorism."

82. *Divrei haknesset*, Eighth Knesset, 37th session, April 11, 1974, 1119.

83. Rubinstein, "Laahar sheloshah yamim," 9.

84. Yishai, "Mihu dani sail?"

85. Abd al-Alim Da'na, quoted in a filmed interview with Ahmad Jaradat and Serhio Yahni of the Alternative News Center, available at https://www.facebook.com/watch/?v=939050802817396.

86. *Maariv*, "Dani Sail hashud shekibel," 21.

87. *Davar*, "Dani Sail makkhish," 3.

88. *Maariv*, "Mishlahat shel hapanterim," 2; *Maariv*, "Hapanterim mehakim leashaf," 2.

89. Giv'on, "Hapanterim," 4.

90. Quoted in Behar, "Competing Marxisms," 230.

91. Bernstein, "Hapanterim hashhorim."

92. *Maariv*, "Meir vilner vecharli bitton," 6.

CHAPTER 5

1. Abbas, "Hiwar m'a Mahmoud Abbas," 79, 82.

2. Peres and Shemer, "Hagorem haadati babhirot laknesset haasirit," 327; Ayalon, Ben-Rafael, and Sharot, "Adatiyut vepolitikah."

3. On the demonstrations, see *Maariv*, "Asrot atsurim," 1–2; I'm also recalling my own childhood memories.

4. Goldstein, "Menachem Begin"; Shabi Amedi, conversation with author, October 5, 2021, Jerusalem.

5. Zinger, "Medurot anak huvaru."

6. *Maariv*, "Hapanterim hit'u hamishtara," 3.

7. Gillis, "Haetniyut. ken. otzeret bamahsom."

8. This was according to *Hatzofeh*, "Akhbar alyawm," 1–2.

9. Gabbai, "Gar'in yotsei maroko hekim moshav," 5.

10. This is how the committee's conclusions were presented in the media. The report itself was worded more carefully. See *Maariv*, "Nehira efsharit," 1; *JTA Daily News Bulletin*, "Research Group Warns of Problems," 2.

11. Kenan, "Madua ulean boreah hashalom," 17.

12. Navon, "Nasi uven adam."

13. Cohen-Tsiddon, "Lasfaradim Mizrahim ein yitzug."

14. *Davar*, "Yisrael mekabelet," 3; see also Ada Ushpiz's film *Gesher Belavan* (Bridge of white) (1978), https://www.youtube.com/watch?v=UoOqLyOd8Xw.

15. Feige, *Shetei mapot lagadah*, 20.

16. *Zeh Koreh*, "Harav hakosem," December 1976, copy in the Rabbi Goren file, ISA, file פ 5055/6.

17. Tzadkoni, "Mesibat hahozrim bitshuvah," 17.

18. David Horowitz at a consultation meeting on peace negotiations with the Arab states, April 12, 1949, ISA, file חצ 2447/3, 14.

19. Chetrit, *Hamaavak hamizrahi bisrael*, 198.

20. Sprinzak, *Ascendance of Israel's Radical Right*, 242.

21. Quoted in Leibowitz-Dar, "Yonah Avrushmi."

22. Dankner, "Ein li akhot."

23. *Davar*, "'Bnei edot hamizrah,'" 6.

24. Quoted in Levy, "Leidato shel baba dankner."

25. Quoted in *Maariv*, "Marokai mitbayesh bemarokai," 17.

26. Cahlili, "Marokaim, habibi marokaim," 25.

27. *Maariv*, "Meir Sheetrit," 19.

28. *Maariv*, "Ashkenazim kitsonim," 18.

29. Sil, "Hal yanjah uthaqifu," 5.

30. Swirski, "Mizrahim ufalastinim."

31. M. B. to President Navon, May 13, 1981, ISA, file 317/2.

32. Quoted in Tzedaka, "Az ma 'haavodah' hazot lakhem," 19.

33. Ayalon, Ben-Rafael, and Sharot, "Adatiyut vepolitikah."

34. Feige, *Shetei mapot lagadah*, 167, 198.

35. See Oz, "Po vesham beertz yisrael, stav 1982." Oz expanded this article into the book *Po vesham beertz yisrael bastav 1982*.

36. Quoted in Feige, *Shetei mapot lagadah*, 208.

37. Rouleau and Hawatmeh, "PLO Shifting Currents," 192.

38. Interview with the foreign minister on the Voice of Israel in English, October 24, 1981, disseminated by the Ministry of Foreign Affairs' Information Department, ISA, file חצ 6898/6; for more background, see Anziska, *Preventing Palestine*; Sayigh, *Armed Struggle and the Search for State*, 421, 466, 513.

39. Oz, *Po vesham beertz yisrael bastav 1982*, chap. 2, 131–40.

40. Gabbay, *Hatzaharot vehahlatot banose hafalastini*, 100–109.

41. For the condemnation statement, see *Davar*, "Ishim bagada meganim hahatkafa"; the Israeli television news program *Mabat Lahadashot*, December 8, 1983; and *Al-Fajr*, "Istinkar"; and condemnations on *Voice of Palestine* radio, December 7, 1983, quoted in US Foreign Broadcast Information Service, *Daily Report: Middle East and North Africa* (Springfield, VA: National Technical Information Service, 1983), 1.

42. *Divrei haknesset*, Tenth Knesset, 216th session, July 13, 1983, 2982.

43. *Maariv*, "Shisha aravim"; *Maariv*, "Avi Deri." Further details can be found in Da'awar, *Al-mustawtanun*, 162–64.

44. A brief survey of Jewish terror operations, including those mentioned here, can be found in a publication of the Knesset's Research and Information Center; see Levy and Erlich, "Alimut politit mitzad yehudim bisrael."

45. See https://drive.google.com/file/d/1NTwlboYKrIV4CqhzScMBVHs9avPqKwBT. For a more extensive treatment, see Jerusalem District Court, case 418/84, and Israeli Supreme Court, Criminal Appeal 410/85.

46. *Hadashot*, "Oreakh bemishkan hakneset," 7; *Maariv*, "H"K hizmin"; Gillon, *Shabak bein hakraim*, 97.

47. Romann and Weingrod, *Living Together Separately*, 92–94.

48. Romann and Weingrod, *Living Together Separately*, 78.

49. Shragai, *Har hamerivah*, 198.

50. See, all in *Davar*, "Meymim lisgor," 2; "Haslama beyahasei," 3; and "Mefaked mishteret yerushalayim," 2; and Dayan, "Kollek," 14.

51. Flyer by the Palestinian leadership, Orient House Archive, Jerusalem, statements file, document 1873; on the condemnation and the joint gathering, see the daily newspapers *Al-Fajr* and *Al-Sha'ab*, December 5, 1986.

52. Quoted in Zevuluni, "Neturei Karta," 2.

53. *Maariv*, "Koakh mishtara gadol," 1, 9; *Maariv*, "Yehudim zoamin," 1, 9.

54. Quoted in *Maariv*, "'Mavet laaravim,'" 1, 9.

55. *Maariv*, "Anu ahim utsrikhim," 2.

56. *Maariv*, "Talmid yeshiva," 8.

57. *Maariv*, "Hashud behashlakhat bakbukei," 5.

58. Levi and Fidel, "Ran Cohen niftza berosho," 3.

59. *Maariv*, "Im aravim," 3.

60. Levi and Fidel, "Ran Cohen niftza berosho."

61. Tessler, "Intifada and Political Discourse."

62. Elitzur and Yishai-Karin, "'Keitzad yakhol likrot matzav,'" 48.

63. HCJ 425/89, *Jamal Abed al Kader Mahmoud Zofan et al. v. Military Advocate General* (December 27, 1989), 43(4).

64. Fogelman, "Yaldei kafot."

65. Liebes and Bloom-Kulka, "'Yorim uvokhim,'" 94.

66. Levy, *Mitzva haam litzva haperiferiyot.*

67. Helman and Rapoport, "'Elah nashim ashkenaziyot levad,'" 177.

68. Helman and Rapoport, "'Elah nashim ashkenaziyot levad,'" 177.

69. For Nawi's obituary, see Hass, "Ezra nawi hifria laseder."

70. On the Mizrahi experience in left-wing movements, see the extensive survey by Hazan, "Ana yahudi." See also Shuster-Eliassi, "'Hetzi-hetzi.'"

71. See, for example, Feige, *Shetei mapot lagadah*, 170–73.

72. For an extensive treatment of Ashkenazi self-identification, see Sasson-Levy, "'Ani ashkenazi.'"

73. Mizrachi, "Sociology in the Garden," 40.

74. Tubi Taharlev first used this term in a blog post; see https://haemori.wordpress.com/2013/05/06/alliance.

75. Motzafi-Haller, *Shehordiniyot*, 129.

76. See Tubi Taharlev, "Mihahathalah ani sholel et zeh barosh."

77. Yifrach, "Lasim sof laashkenaziyut."

78. Quoted in Gillis, "Haetniyut. ken. otzeret bamahsom," 46.

79. Mahlev, "Ner zikaron ledoktor shlomo elbaz."

80. Horowitz, "Hatzadik hakafri," 24–27, 59.

81. Saragusti, "Arbaah yamim betoledo."

82. Quoted in Behar, "Lahlom et heatid."

83. Quoted in Gilat, "Kavim lamahapekhah," 11.

84. The English translation is from the Arabic version translated by Lutfi al-Khuli from the Hebrew original, in *Al-intifadah wal-dawla al-falastiniyya*, 292.

85. Quoted in Chetrit, *Hamaavak hamizrahi bisrael*, 273–74.

86. *Maariv*, "Yoman maariv, 'hamumei moah,'" 14.

87. *Hadashot*, "Gal peulot nakam," 1.

88. Quoted in *Maariv*, "Yoman maariv, 'hamumei moah.'"

89. Gilat, "Kavim lamahapekhah."

90. For more on Hashomer, see Alroey, "Meshartei hamoshavah."

91. The figures come from B'Tselem, https://www.btselem.org/hebrew/statistics/first_intifada_tables.

92. Litani in conversation with Margalit, "Lo hayu li regaim," 46.

93. Reshef, *Shalom Akhshav*, 184–85.

94. Levy, "Aryeh Shlush lehokrav," 19; Israeli Supreme Court, Criminal Appeal 1836/91.

95. Goldstein, "Ahrayut filosofit," 10.

96. On Shlush's early release, see Leibowitz-Dar, "'Ani ashem baretsah bakfar duma'"; on the opposition to Dahan's appointment, see *Kol Haam*, "Toshvei ramle haaravim tov'im piturei G. Dahan," 4.

97. Quoted in Meiri, "Banu lepoh laharog aravim," 2; *Hadashot*, "Aviv shel Ronen Karamani," 3.

98. Sarna, *Ed medinah*, 107–8.

99. See "Abd al karim ovadiah abd al gani," on the National Insurance Institute of the State of Israel's "Hostile Actions Memorial Website," https://laad.btl.gov.il.

100. Naeh and Cohen, "Hahamonim histaaru," 4.

101. *Yediot Aharonot*, "Hakriot 'Mavet laaravim' hithalfu be'mavet lashotrim."

102. Rimon Or, "Mimot haaravi ad 'mavet laaravim,'" 23.

103. *Hadashot*, "Tseirim hishtolelu berashla"ts," 9.

104. Lefkowitz, "Constructing Affective Responses"; *Hadashot*, "Tseirim hishtolelu berashla"ts," 9.

105. Quoted in *Maariv*, "Hamon niz'am," 4.

106. Quoted in Yerushalmi, "Baba Matsia," 29–30.

107. Goldberg, *Haboher hayisraeli 1992*, 151–52.

108. Goldberg, *Haboher hayisraeli 1992*, 182.

109. Smooha, "Shesaim maamadiyim."

110. Goldberg, *Haboher hayisraeli*, 163–64.

111. Rabin, *Rodef shalom*, 15–17.

112. Quoted in Alush and Elituv, *Ben-porat yosef*, 93–94.

113. Quoted in Alush and Elituv, *Ben-porat yosef*, 257–59.

114. Quoted in Chen and Pfeffer, *Maran*, 323–25.

115. Quoted in Mandel, "Harabi amar lehahzir shetahim."

116. Etzioni-Halevy, *Eretz shesua*, 12.

117. Feige, "Retzah rabin vehashulayim," 48.

118. Biton, "Harotzeah hamizrahi," 20.

119. "Maran Harav Ovadia Yosef barga'im le'ahar retzah Rabin," https://www.youtube.com/watch?v=8lqv-KZgWEw.

120. Quoted in Alush and Elituv, *Ben-porat yosef*, 267.
121. Quoted in Alush and Elituv, *Ben-porat yosef*, 98.
122. Sorek and Ceobanu, "Benjamin Netanyahu as a Mobilizing Symbol."

CONCLUSION

1. *Hamakor, Halaylah hashahor shel bat yam.*
2. Kan Hadashot, "Hayom ani holekh lirtzoah," https://www.youtube.com/watch?v=K-_4i9ZazVc.
3. *Hamakor, Halaylah hashahor shel bat yam*, minute 49:40 (Guetta), minute 51:30 (Saban).
4. Bitton and Kricheli Katz, "Disparities on the Basis of Nationality."
5. See the reader responses to Shimoni, "Beit knesset a"sh kahane."
6. Associated Press, "Irgun Human Rights Watch."
7. Mazor and Mehager, "Hereg hamehabel behevron."
8. Toubul, "Haasafsuf meshalem."
9. Yona and Mann, "Hamotziim lapoal."
10. Derfner, "Who Are in the Mobs."
11. Kan Hadashot, "Netaniahu larav Keddurie," https://www.youtube.com/watch?v=N_5rVMDUI18, minute 1:16.
12. *Marker*, "Ma hoshvim Binyamin."
13. *Marker*, "Nathan Eshel."
14. Antler, "Yossi Sarid Hutkaf bemeretz," 4.
15. *Haaretz*, "Ein sibah lehatzbia meretz."
16. Shiran, "Lefaaneah et hakoah."
17. Quoted in Krief, *Hamizrahit*, 210.
18. Quoted in Alush and Elituv, *Ben-porat yosef*, 372–74.
19. Quoted in Alush and Elituv, *Ben-porat yosef*, 377–78.
20. Moshe Sharett, "Mavo lasheelah haaravit," lecture given in Jerusalem, May 6, 1940, CZA, S25/22201.
21. Ben Hamo, "Hakriah leshalom leor hahalakhah," 25.
22. Ben-Meir, "Hebetim politiyim vedaat hakahal."
23. Israeli Supreme Court, Criminal Appeals 2067/16, 2277/16, and 4713/16.
24. Zayit, "Lo darkenu."
25. Lihi Yona on Twitter, November 24, 2020, https://twitter.com/lihiy/status/1331220652783755264.
26. On the attorney general's decision not to open a criminal investigation against Rabbi Shmuel Eliyahu, see Zarhin, "Nisgar hatik neged"; on the chants in Safed, see Krayot Magistrate's Court, 61366-10-10, *State of Israel v. Ben Tzion (detainee) et al.*
27. Be'er Sheva District Court, felony case 35048-04-17.
28. Leon, "Harediyut mizrahit."
29. Curiel, "5.5 shnot ma'asar."
30. Noy, "Al hasidrah 'sinat mavet.'"
31. Habaz, "Hanearim."
32. Oded Zinger, televised news report, Kan evening news, June 9, 2020, https://www.youtube.com/watch?v=icuRgw1Cw_A.
33. *Globes*, "Mubarak."
34. Fouad's interviews with the imprisoned Hamas operatives were published in *Haaretz*'s weekend supplement on June 26, 2002.
35. Fahima, "Korim li tali fahima," 37–38.
36. Fahima, "Korim li tali fahima," 37.
37. Butbul, "Asur lesalef."

BIBLIOGRAPHY

A. A. "Hatnuah haaravit besuriyah, haahdutiyim vehayehudim." *Hapoel Hatzair* (Jaffa), May 2, 1912.

Abbadi, Nasser. "Nisuei taarovet bein aravim layehudim bisrael." Master's thesis, Tel Aviv University, 1991.

Abbas, Mahmoud. "Hiwar m'a Mahmoud Abbas." *Shu'un Filastiniyya* 68–69 (August 1977): 78–92.

Abergel, Reuven. "Haideologiyah shelanu hi hakeev: Defusim tziyoniim shetzarikh lishbor kedai lehakim smol atzmai." In *Hasmol haatzmai bisrael, 1967–1993: Asufah lezikhro shel noam kaminer*, edited by Matan Kaminer, 77–87. Mevaseret Zion: November Books, 2019.

Abitbol, Michael. "Hapeilut hatziyonit bitzfon afrikah ad sof milhemet haolam harishonah." *Pe'amim* 2 (1979): 65–91.

Abu Khadra, Faisal. "Sarah david levi batel." *Al-Gomhuria* (Cairo), March 18, 2000.

Aderet, Ofer. "Haintifadah shekadmah lekum hamedinah." *Haaretz* (Tel Aviv), April 16, 2016.

Adut, Rami. "Poalim ufkidim: Halukat haavodah hamaamadit-etnit birushalayim bishnot haarbaim vehahamishim." Master's thesis, Tel Aviv University, 2005.

Aharonovich, Yosef. "Mizmor le'asaf." *Hapoel Hatzair* (Jaffa), n.d., 1908.

Al-Fajr (Jerusalem). "Istinkar." December 8, 1983.

Algazi, Gadi. "The First Act in the Struggle of the *Ma'abarot*, 1951–1952: Contestation amid Subjection." In *Entangled Histories in Palestine/Israel: Historical and Anthropological Perspectives*, edited by Dafna Hirsch, 152–88. New York: Routledge, 2024.

———. "Hitargnut nokhakh kfifut: Maavak hamaabarot 1951–2." *Zmanim* 149 (2024): 76–95.

———. "Kol min heavar: Mered vadi salib." *Hagadah Hasmalit* (Tel Aviv), December 2, 2008. https://tinyurl.com/3eu2j5py.

Al Hamishmar (Tel Aviv). "'Hapanterim' huashmu benisayon lehatzit misradei haligah lehaganah." June 25, 1972.

———. "Nikhbdei hevron arkhu bikur shalom biveer sheva." July 23, 1967.

———. "Yehudei rusya go home." March 22, 1972.

Al-Liwaa (Jerusalem). "Halat Yafa." April 22, 1936.

Alroey, Gur. "Meshartei hamoshavah o rodanim gasei ruah: Meah shanah laagudat hashomer." *Cathedra* 120 (2005/6): 77–104.

Alush, Zvi, and Yossi Elituv. *Ben-porat yosef: Hayav, mishnato, umehalakhav hapolitiyim shel harav ovadiah yosef.* Or Yehuda: Kinneret, 2004.

Amit, Karin. "Tekefut hahalukah haetnit lemizrahim uleashkenazim bekerev mehagrim vetzeetzaeihem bashuk haavodah hayisraelit." *Megamot* 44 (2005): 3–28.

Amor, Meir. "Hahistoriyah hailemet shel haseruv hahevrati." *Sedek: A Journal on the Ongoing Nakba* 5 (2010): 32–41.

Anabusi, Adam. "Sherutei habriut bameshulash tahat hamimshal hatzvai: Merkaz habriut bebaka al-gharbiyya kemikreh bohan." Master's thesis, Hebrew University of Jerusalem, 2020.

Antebi-Hefer, Elioz. *Keforahat altah nitzah: Korotav hamuflaim shel mishpahat Antebi.* Tel Aviv: World Center for Aleppo Jews Traditional Culture, 2011.

Antler, Datit. "Yossi Sarid Hutkaf bemeretz." *Hadashot* (Tel Aviv), August 17, 1990.

Anziska, Seth. *Preventing Palestine: A Political History from Camp David to Oslo.* Princeton: Princeton University Press, 2018.

Arlosoroff, Haim. "Milhemet hamaamadot bemetziut haeretz-yisraeli." 1926. Ben-Yehuda Project. https://benyehuda.org/read/2068.

Askari, Yasir al-. *Qisat madinah: Safad*. Cairo [?]: Palestine Liberation Organization, 1989.

Assaf, Michael. "Dilatoriyah benusah sefarad." *Davar* (Tel Aviv), January 25, 1928.

———. "Kinus Tarbuti halutzi." *Davar* (Tel Aviv), November 14, 1940.

Associated Press. "Irgun Human Rights Watch ma'ashim et hamas befish'ei milhama." *Haaretz* (Tel Aviv), August 12, 2021.

Avi Hatzeira, Yaakov, Shimon Avi Hatzeira, and Avraham Hafuta. *Yagel yaakov: Sefer piyyutim vetokhahot leadmo"r rabeinu yaakov abuhatzeira*. Jerusalem: Ner Yitzhak, 1994/95.

Avineri, Shlomo. "Al avodah ivrit ugvulot mediniyim." *Maariv* (Tel Aviv), February 16, 1973.

Avitan, Meir. "Piskei Halakha beinyan yom haatzmaut." Archived from meir-avitan.co.il at https://drive.google.com/file/d/1-hl4iXEwdMYqNQsmRRYGoT2ruFH3-6Xf.

Avnery, Uri. "Gal hapeshaim haminiim." *Haaretz* (Tel Aviv), August 26, 1949.

———. "Hapanterim huzmeny a"y" irgunim maoistiyim." *Haolam Hazeh* (Tel Aviv), October 6, 1971.

———. "Panterim vekalenterizm." *Haolam Hazeh* (Tel Aviv), May 19, 1971.

Avni, Haim, and Gideon Shimoni, eds. *Hatziyonut umitnagdeha baam hayehudi*. Jerusalem: Hasifriya Hatzionit, 1990.

Ayalon, Hanna, Eliezer Ben-Rafael, and Stephen Sharot. "Adatiyut vepolitikah: Hebetim nishkahim." *Megamot* 30 (1987): 332–48.

Bahat, Yaacov. "Laikarei shitat hashinuim bein mahadurah kama lemahadurah batra bitzirat haim hazaz." *Tarbitz* 39 (1970): 390–414.

Bar-Hai, Y. [Moshe Braver]. "Mi metapeah eivah leashkenazim." *Hatzofeh* (Tel Aviv), November 8, 1963.

Barnai, Jacob. "Maamadah shel 'harabanut hakolelet' birushalayim bitkufat haotomanit." *Cathedra* 13 (1979): 47–69.

Bar-On, Mordechai, and Osnat Shiran, eds. *Lenokhah gevulot oyenim*. Re'ut: Effi Meltzer, 2017.

Baron, Salo. "Newer Emphases in Jewish History." *Jewish Social Studies* 25, no. 4 (1963): 245–58.

Bartal, Israel. "Al demutah harav adatit shel hahevrah hayehudit birushalayim bameah ha-19." *Pe'amim* 57 (1994): 114–24.

Bashkin, Orit. *Impossible Exodus: Iraqi Jews in Israel*. Stanford: Stanford University Press, 2017.

———. *New Babylonians: A History of Jews in Modern Iraq*. Stanford: Stanford University Press, 2012.

Batrik sil. "Hal yanjah muthaqifu isra'il fi fardalsalam 'ala bighin." *Al-Ahram* (Cairo), January 24, 1983.

Behar, Almog. "Miyehuda halevi leyehuda burla." In *Hapiyut katzohar tarbuti*, edited by Haviva Pedaya, 223–65. Tel Aviv: Hakibbutz Hameuhad, 2013.

Behar, Moshe. "Competing Marxisms: Creation of (Settler) Colonialism and the One-State Solution in Israel-Palestine." In *The Arab and Jewish Questions: Geographies of Engagement in Palestine and Beyond*, edited by Bashir Bashir and Leila Farsakh, 220–49. New York: Columbia University Press, 2020.

———. "Parshanut lahistoriyah hasotzio-politi ha'kedam yisraelit' veha'pnim yisraelit' shel yehudei arav." *Politika* 14 (2004/5): 109–29.

Behar, Shiko [Moshe]. "Lahlom et heatid." *Haokets* (Tel Aviv), August 4, 2012. https://www.tinyurl.com/3hkz5fyr.

Bein, Alexander. *Aliyah vehityashvut bimdinat yisrael*. Jerusalem: Am Oved and Hasifriya Hatziyonit, 1982.

Ben, Menachem. "Hashira kiskoop: Hamshorer sheoneh leamnon levi." *Makor Rishon* online, August 23, 2018. https://www.makorrishon.co.il/nrg/online/47/ART2/501/697.html.

Benayahu, Meir, ed. *Divrei hayamim shel Fes: Gezerot umeoraot yahudei maroko kefi sherashmum benei misphahat ibn danan ledoroteihem*. Tel Aviv: Tel Aviv University, 1992/93.

Benbassa, Esther, ed. *Haim Nahum: Rav rashi sephardi bapolitikah, 1892–1923*. Jerusalem: Dinur Center, 1998/99.

Ben-Dor, Zvi. "'Eib, hshuma, infajrat Qunbula: Likrat historiyah shel hamizrahim vehaaravit." In *Hazut mizrahit*, edited by Yigal Nizri, 29–44. Tel Aviv: Bavel, 2004.

Ben-Ezer, Ehud. *Parashim al hayarkon.* Electronic edition, Ben-Yehuda Project. https://benyehuda.org/read/18922.

Ben-Gurion, David. "Medabrana deumteh o pakid dati." *Haahdut* (Jerusalem), July 8, 1910. https://benyehuda.org/read/6750.

———. *Tzava uvitahon.* Tel Aviv: IDF, Maarachot, 1955.

Ben Hamo, Shlomo. "Hakriah leshalom leor hahalakhah." In *Leket maamarim, eduyot utmunot bimlot hamishim shanah lamoraot tarpat behevron,* edited by Hannah Barnes, 14–25. Kiryat Arba: n.p., 1978/79.

Ben Harosh, Moiz. "Zakhor et asher asu lekha haashkenazim." *Haaretz* (Tel Aviv), December 15, 2021.

Ben-Kiki, Hayyim. "Al sheelat hasheelot beyishuv Haaret." *Doar Hayom* (Jerusalem), August 30, 1921.

Benkler, Raffel, Israel Zamir, and Yosef Galili. "Kirya koevet umetuskelet." *Al Hamishmar* (Tel Aviv), April 19, 1974.

Ben-Meir, Yehuda. "Hebetim politiyim vedaat hakahal." *Adken Astrategi* 11, no. 4 (2009): 25–29. Institute of National Security Studies, Tel Aviv University. https://www.inss.org.il/he/wp-content/uploads/sites/2/2022/12/f-1151684224.pdf.

Ben-Moshe, Eliezer. "Irgunei hateror veha 'falestinaim.'" *Lamerhav* (Tel Aviv), March 25, 1968.

Ben-Shabbat, Shmuel. "Haod nahrish." *Haherut* (Jerusalem), July 19, 1911.

Ben-Ya'akov, Avraham. *Otzar hashirim, hahiburim vehadrashot shel harav yosef hayim.* Jerusalem: Machon Haktav, 1994.

Ben-Zaken, Avner. *Komunizm keimperiyalizm tarbuti.* Tel Aviv: Resling, 2006.

Ben Zion, Simha. "Moshav yisrael beyafo." *Yediot Iriyat Tel Aviv,* May 1949, 22–24.

Bergman, Ronen. *Rise and Kill First: The Secret History of Israel's Targeted Assassinations.* New York: Random House, 2018.

Bergman, Ronen, and Patrick Kingsley. "Protests over Netanyahu's Judiciary Overhaul Spread to Israel's Military." *New York Times,* March 6, 2023.

Bernstein, Deborah. "Hapanterim hashhorim: Konflikt umehaah bahevrah hayisraelit." *Megamot* 25 (1979): 65–80.

Bezalel, Itzhak. "Halevantinim harishonim biyishuv haothomani: Zehutam hatziyonit veyahasam laArabness." *Pe'amim* 125–27 (2010/11): 75–98.

———. *Noladtem tziyonim: Hasfardim beeretz yisrael batziyonut uvathiyah haivrit bitkufat haothomanit.* Jerusalem: Yad Ben-Zvi, 2007.

Binyamin, R. [Yehoshua Radler-Feldman], and Yaacov Peterzil, eds. *Neged hateror.* Jerusalem: n.p., 1939.

Biton, Erez. "Harotzeah hamizrahi." *Yediot Aharonot* (Tel Aviv) ("Yitzhak Rabin, 1922–1995, Memorial Supplement"), November 6, 1995.

Bitton, Yifat. "Mizrahim bamishpat: Haein' kayesh.'" *Mishpatim* 41 (2022): 456–516.

Bitton, Yifat, and Tamar Kricheli Katz. "Disparities on the Basis of Nationality, Ethnicity, and Gender in Road Accident Compensation in Israel." *Journal of Law and Courts* (2002): 1–17.

Bloom, Etan. "Hashikhpul shel hamodel 'mizrahi' bisdeh hahevrati hayisraeli." Master's thesis, Tel Aviv University, 2003.

Bokra. "Video: Wadi Joz tushayi' juthman shahadat al'unf Maryam al-Takruri." April 18, 2021. https://bokra.net/Article-1461368.

Boord, Matan. "Hahalutzim vehamahaneh: Yahasam shel halutzei emek hayarden layehudei tiveriyah bishnei haasorhim harishonim lehityashvut haovedet." *Israel* 21 (2013): 61–86.

Butbul, Gabi. "Asur lesalef." *Makor Rishon* (Jerusalem), December 20, 2020. https://www.makorrishon.co.il/opinion/293839.

Cahlili, Ron. "Marokaim, habibi marokaim." *Hadashot* (Tel Aviv), November 19, 1990.

Camhi, Ovadiah. *Hevron beyalduti: Hevron lifnei horbanah.* Jerusalem: Ogdan, 1966.

Campos, Michelle. *Ottoman Brothers: Muslims, Christians, and Jews in Early Twentieth-Century Palestine.* Stanford: Stanford University Press, 2011.

Capsali, Elijah. *Seder Eliyahu Zuta.* Edited by Aryeh Shmuelevitz, Shlomo Simonsohn, and Meir Benayahu. 3 vols. Jerusalem: Ben-Zvi Institute, 1975/76–1982/83.

Chelouche, Yosef Eliyahu. *Parshat hayai.* Tel Aviv: Bavel, 2005.

Chen, Nitzan, and Anshel Pfeffer. *Maran: Ovadiah yosef, habiografyah.* Jerusalem: Keter, 2004.

Chetrit, Sami Shalom. *Hamaavak hamizrahi bisrael*. Tel Aviv: Am Oved, 2006.

Chomsky, Noam. "International Terrorism: Image and Reality." *Crime and Social Justice* 27–28 (1987): 172–200.

Cohen, Doron B. "Avi, Aharon Haim Cohen." *Pe'amim* 113 (2008): 99–150.

Cohen, Geula. "Shulhan meruba im hapanterim." *Maariv, Mussaf Shevui* (Tel Aviv), June 25, 1971.

Cohen, Hezi. *Hokhmah mikedem: Sipurei hakhamim mikehilot hasefardiot veedot hamizrah*. Rishon Lezion: Yediot Aharonot, 2016.

Cohen, Hillel. "'Garesh ninei ben haamah, Adonai ish milhamah': Hayahas lamuslimim bapiyut hayehudi ledorotav." *Jama'a* 25 (2021): 133–52.

———. "Hayav umoto shel hayehudi-haaravi, beeretz yisrael umehutzah lah." *Iyunim Bitkumat Yisrael* 9 (2016): 171–200.

———. *Tarpa"t: Shenat haefes basikhsukh hayehudi–aravi*. Jerusalem: Keter and Ivrit, 2013.

———. *Year Zero of the Arab-Israeli Conflict: 1929*. Translated by Haim Watzman. Waltham: Brandeis University Press, 2015.

Cohen, Hillel, and Yuval Evri. "Moledet meshutefet o bayit leumi: Bnei haaretz, hatzharat Balfour, vehasheelah haaravit." *Teoriah Uvikoret* 49 (2017): 291–304.

Cohen, Uri, and Nissim Leon. *Merkaz tenuat haherut vehamizrahim, 1965–1977*. Jerusalem: Israel Democracy Institute, 2011.

Cohen, Yeruham. *Leor hayom uvamahshakh*. Tel Aviv: Amikam, 1968/69.

Cohen-Tsiddon, Shlomo. "Lasfaradim Mizrahim ein yitzug." *Davar* (Tel Aviv), February 27, 1978.

Curiel, Ilana. "5.5 shnot ma'asar leyhudi shetakaf aravim." *Ynet* (Tel Aviv), November 5, 2018. https://www.ynet.co.il/article/5389453.

Da'awar, Ghassan. *Al-mustawtanun al-sahaina fi al-dafa al-gharbiyyah*. Beirut: Markaz al-Zeituna, 2012.

Dahan Kalev, Henriette. "Kamah sheat yafah, lo roim sheat morokait." Mizrahi Democratic Rainbow—New Discourse. http://tinyurl.com/y274jrxs.

Danin, Ezra. *Tziyoni bekhol tenai*. Jerusalem: Kidum, 1987.

Dankner, Amnon. "Ein li akhot." Op-ed. *Haaretz* (Tel Aviv), February 18, 1983.

Davar (Tel Aviv). "'Bnei edot hamizrah einam nogdim hevrat mofet humanistit mitkademet.'" May 8, 1983.

———. "Dani Sail makkhish et hashamot negdo." May 26, 1975.

———. "Dvar hayom." Editorial. April 19, 1936.

———. "Hameoraot birushalayim." August 18, 1929.

———. "Hamtihut beramle adayin lo shakhekha." August 24, 1965.

———. "Haslama beyahasei yeshivat birkat Avraham birushalayim ushkheneha haaravim." December 5, 1983.

———. "Ishim bagada meganim hahatkafa." December 8, 1983.

———. "Kiryah koevet." April 17, 1974.

———. "Kokhvei hagada polshim leyisrael." September 8, 1968.

———. "Lehidush yahasei shekhenim." December 5, 1940.

———. "Lekomem hatoshavim haaravim vahasfaradim." December 13, 1966.

———. "Meaymim lisgor et yeshivat birkat Avraham." April 11, 1983.

———. "Mefaked mishteret yerushalayim atsar ishit et rosh yeshivat birkat Avraham." December 14, 1983.

———. "Nidhata hatzaa britit letavekh beinyan shvitat neshek T"A-Yafo." April 27, 1947.

———. "Rosh iriyat hevron mekave leshalom bein yisrael laaravim." July 23, 1967.

———. "Yisrael gunta al retsah mevo'ot Beitar." June 24, 1954.

———. "Yisrael mekabelet holim mikoa artsot arav." August 24, 1976.

Dayan, Arie. "Kollek: Hem lo benei adam." *Koteret Rashit* (Tel Aviv), December 14, 1983.

Derfner, Larry. "Who Are in the Mobs Behind Israeli Army Sgt. Elor Azaria?" April 23, 2016. http://www.larryderfner.com/2016/05/07/who-are-in-the-mobs-behind-israeli-army-sgt-elor-azaria.

Dierauff, Evelin. *Translating Late Ottoman Modernity*. Gottingen: V&R Unipress, 2019.

Distal-Atbaryan, Galit. "Mi heziz et halabaneh sheli?" *Israel Hayom* (Tel Aviv), December 28, 2020.

Doar Hayom (Jerusalem). "Arabaat asirei meah shearim yats'u zakai'm." March 26, 1930.
———. "Hasephardim vehamosdot hatziyonim." July 6, 1928.
———. "Hasephardim vehamosdot hatziyonim (sof)." July 8, 1928.
———. "Yerushalayim." August 18, 1929.
Don-Yehiya, Shabtai. *Harav Ben-Zion Meir Hai Uziel*. Jerusalem: Zionist Organization, 1954/55.
Dror, Zvika. *Hamistaarvim shel hapalma"h*. Tel Aviv: Hakibbutz Hameuhad, 1986.
Druyanow, Alter, and Shulamit Laskov, comps. and eds. *Ketavim letoldot hibat tzion veyishuv eretz yisrael*. 4 vols. Tel Aviv: Tel Aviv University, 1982–93.
Efrati, Nathan. *Haedah hasfardit birushalayim, 1840–1917*. Jerusalem: Bialik Institute, 1999/2000.
———. *Mimashber letikva: Hayishuv hayehudi beeretz yisrael bemilhemet haolam harishonah*. Jerusalem: Yad Ben-Zvi, 1991.
Eisenstadt, Shmuel Noah. *Hahevrah hayisraelit*. Jerusalem: Magnes, 1982/83.
Eldaoudi, Salim. *Hatoeh bisvakh hehayim*. Edited by Yaffa Szekely. Jerusalem: Yuvalim, 2001.
Eliahu, Eli. *Ani velo malakh*. Tel Aviv: Helicon, 2008.
Eliav, Mordechai. "Meoraot yafo befurim TRS"H (1908)." *Hatziyonut* 3 (1973): 152–97.
———. "Yahasim bein-adatiyim bayishuv hayehudi beeretz yisrael bameah ha-19." *Pe'amim* 11 (1982): 118–34.
Elitzur, Yoel, and Nofar Yishai-Karin. "'Keitzad yakhol likrot matzav?' Mehkar narativi al maasei avlah shel hayalei tzahal baintifadah." In *Ketem shel ananah kalah: Hayalim, hevrah, vetzava baintifadah*, edited by Yoel Elitzur, 39–76. Tel Aviv: Hakibbutz Hameuhad, 2012.
Eliyahu, Shmuel, ed. *Kol Yaakov Hashalem*. Jerusalem: Darkei Horaah Larabanim, 1996/97.
Elkayam, Mordechai. *Yafo-neveh tzedek: Reshitah shel tel aviv*. Tel Aviv: Ministry of Defense, 1990.
Elmalih, Avraham. "Hartzaah al nesiati baari suryah." Manuscript. Av 5679 [Summer 1919], CZA, L3/728.
———. "Meoraot umaasim." *Mizrah Umaarav* 4, nos. 13–18 (1929/30): 61–63.
———. "Tafkideinu bitnuat-hathiyyah." *Doar Hayom* (Jerusalem), August 15, 1919.
———. "Yahas haaravim layehudim bishnat 5671 [1911–12]." *Doar Hayom* (Jerusalem), October 31, 1926.
———. "Yahas haaravim shebesuriya el hamilhamah." *Hapoel Hatzair* (Jaffa), December 6, 1912.
Elon, Amos. "Yisrael hashniyah boheret." *Haaretz* (Tel Aviv), November 19, 1950.
Erlich, Yochi. "Migdal bavel: Rav siah al terumatam hanikhbadah shel yotzei irak labinyan hamodiin hayisraeli." *Mabat Malam* 53 (April 2009): 10–14.
Etzioni-Halevy, Eva. *Eretz shesua*. Tel Aviv: Nir, 2000.
Evri, Yuval. *Hashivah laandalus: Mahlokot al tarbut vezehut yehudit-sefaradit bein arviyut laivrityut*. Jerusalem: Magnes, 2020.
Eyal Kafkafi, "Hearah al hahistoriyah shel hashomer vehahaganah." *Cathedra* 73 (1994): 189–93.
Ezrah [pseud.]. "Mikhtavim mihayfah." *Hapoel Hatzair* (Jaffa), September 9, 1910.
Fahima, Tali. "Korim li tali fahima vaani lo peilat smol." *Pithon Peh* 3 (2007): 27–45.
Feierberg, Haim. "Hevrah ironit bemashber: 'Habeayah hamizrahit' bamerhav Tel Aviv veyafo baet meoraot trtz"u." *Sugiyot hevratiyot bisrael* 1 (2006): 171–207.
Feige, Michael. "Retzah rabin vehashulayim haetniyim shel hatzionut hadatit." *Teoria Uvikoret* 45 (Winter 2015): 31–56.
———. *Shetei mapot lagadah: Gush emunim, shalom akhshav vaitzuv hamerhav bisrael*. Jerusalem: Magnes, 2002.
Filastin (Jaffa). "Al-yahud al-sefaradim." Editorial. September 3, 1921.
———. "Yafa." October 18, 1913.
Fischer, Shlomo. "Shenei defusim shel modernizatziyah: Al nituah habeayah haadatit bisrael." *Teoria Uvikoret* 1 (Summer 1991): 1–22.
Fishman, Ada. *Ayanot: Darkah shel bat yisrael el hahaklaut*. Jerusalem: Zionist Organization, 1945/46.
Fogelman, Shai. "Yaldei kafot." *Haaretz* (Tel Aviv), December 30, 2010.
Frankenstein, Karl. "Hinukh hanoar miedot hamizrah." *Davar* (Tel Aviv), June 9, 1938.

Frenkel, Miriam. "Ketivat hahistoriyah shel yehudei artzot haislam biymai habeinayim." *Pe'amim* 92 (2001/2): 23–61.

Gabbai, Shefi. "Gar'in yotsei maroko hekim moshav bedahab shebemifrats eilat." *Davar* (Tel Aviv), September 15, 1971.

———. "Kelitat poalim mihashtahim: Mivtza gadol shehitzliah." *Davar* (Tel Aviv), November 11, 1969.

Gabbay, Moshe ed. *Hatzaharot vehahlatot banose hafalastini*. Efal: Yad Tabenkin, 1990. English translation at https://al-bab.com/documents-section/speech-yasser-arafat-1974.

Gelblum, Aryeh. "Aliyat teiman uveayat afrikah." *Haaretz* (Tel Aviv), April 22, 1949.

Ghosheh, Subhi. *Al-shams min al-nafidha al-aliya*. Beirut: Mu'assasat al-Abhath al-Arabiyya, 1988.

Gilat, Zvi. "Kavim lamahapekhah hamizrahit hamitkarevet." *Hadashot* (Tel Aviv), August 4, 1989.

Gillis, Rivi. "Haetniyut. ken. otzeret bamahsom: Lasheelat hazehut haetnit bahitnahluyot." *Teoria Uvikoret* 47 (Winter 2016): 41–63.

Gillon, Carmi. *Shabak bein hakraim*. Tel Aviv: Miskal and Yediot, 2000.

Giv'on, Shlomo. "Hapanterim: Yesh lahtor ledu kiyum im hafalastinim." *Maariv* (Tel Aviv), September 25, 1975.

Globes (Ramat Gan). "Mubarak: Shilamti le-Fuad Ben Eliezer sakhar hodshi." March 14, 2012. https://www.globes.co.il/news/article.aspx?did=1000733166.

Goldberg, Giora. *Haboher hayisraeli 1992*. Jerusalem: Magnes, 1992.

Goldstein, Amir. "Menachem Begin, tenuat herut vehamehaah hamizrahit." *Israel* 12 (2007): 1–28.

Goldstein, Dov. "Ahrayut filosofit." *Maariv* (Tel Aviv), January 3, 1991.

———. "Kan hayu hahashudim befarashat haretzah." *Maariv* (Tel Aviv), September 13, 1956.

Gozansky, Tamar. *Komunistim mizrahim: Hamaarakhah neged aflayah adatit ulemaan hazkhut lediyur*. Haifa: Pardes, 2018.

Gribetz, Jonathan. *Defining Neighbors: Religion, Race, and the Early Zionist-Arab Encounter*. Princeton: Princeton University Press, 2014.

Guber, Rivka. *El mesuot lakhish*. Tel Aviv: Davar, 1961.

Haaretz (Tel Aviv). "Birushalayim." September 10, 1919.

———. "Ein sibah lehatzbia meretz." February 5, 2009.

———. "Meoraot Akko." September 8, 1929.

———. "Revavot livu lemenuhot halelei kiryat shemonah." April 14, 1974.

———. "Shenayim nirtzehu birushalayim." January 15, 1948.

———. "Shoklim efsharut sgirat hatik neged 4 hatseirim bnei hameshakim." March 28, 1955.

———. "Yafo." May 10, 1948.

———. "Yehudi Marocco." September 14, 1919.

Habas, Bracha. *Meoraot TRTza"V*. Tel Aviv: Davar, 1936/37.

Habaz, Moran. "Hanearim: Lahashov mehadash al activism mizrah." *Haokets* online (Tel Aviv), October 3, 2019.

Hadashot (Tel Aviv). "Aviv shel Ronen Karmani." August 8, 1990.

———. "Gal peulot nakam beikvot pigua hadamim." July 9, 1989.

———. "Oreakh bemishkan hakneset." July 13, 1989.

———. "Tseirim hishtolelu berashla"ts." May 26, 1992.

Haherut (Jerusalem). "Haraha"g Haim Nahum birushalayim." June 15, 1910.

———. "Hed haitonut haaravit." June 30, 1911.

———. "Od meorah shel antishemiyut behayfah." June 19, 1911.

———. "Yafo." August 14, 1911.

———. "Yafo." March 27, 1912.

Haim, Abraham. *Yihud vehishtalvut: Hanagat hasfaradim birushalyaim bitkufat hashilton habriti, 5678–5708*. Jerusalem: Carmel, 2000.

Haivri (New York). "Yerushalayim ir hakodesh." April 23, 1893.

Haj, Majid al-. "Megamot bamifgash uvaoryentatziyah bein hafalastinim bisrael levein hafalastinim bashtahim." *Medinah Vahevrah* 4, no. 1 (2004): 825–44.

Hakak, Balfour. "Bracha Serri: Yerushalayim vesanaa." e-mago, November 21, 2010. https://benyehuda.org/read/32721.

Halamish, Moshe, ed. "Meever lagvul." *Maariv* (Tel Aviv), May 7, 1969.

———. *Peirush kabali livreshit raba ler' yosef ben shalom haarokh ashkenazi*. Jerusalem: Magnes, 1984.

Halperin, Liora R. "Trading Secrets: Constructions and Contexts of Two Middle Eastern Jewish Guards in the Early Petah Tikva Agricultural Colony." *International Journal of Middle Eastern Studies* 51, no. 1 (2019): 65–86.

Halpern, Ayana. "Jewish Social Workers in Mandatory Palestine: Between Submission and Subversion Under Male Leadership." *Nashim: A Journal of Jewish Women's Studies and Gender Issues* 35 (Fall 2019): 75–96.

Hamagid (Krakow). "Hadashot shonot." March 15, 1894.

———. "Nigei levavenu." January 4, 1894.

Hamakor. Halaylah hashahor shel bat yam. https://13tv.co.il/item/news/hamakor/season-20/episodes/isnmt-902621850/.

Hamelitz (St. Petersburg). "Beiha"k." August 10, 1885.

———. "London: Mikhtav galui." May 30, 1882.

Hanioğlu, Şükrü. *A Brief History of the Late Ottoman Empire*. Princeton: Princeton University Press, 2008.

Hapanter Hashahor (Jerusalem). "Suhreru martsiano vebiton." August 11, 1972.

Hapoel Hatzair (Jaffa). "Rehovot." January 10, 1913.

Hart, Rachel. "Tel Aviv bamarah hakfulah shel haitonut haaravit bashanim 1881–1930." *Kesher* 39 (Fall 2009), 92–101.

Hashkafah (Jerusalem). "Hag Herut haotmanit birushalayim." August 10, 1908.

Hass, Amira. "Ezra nawi hifria laseder shel haelyonut hayehudit." *Haaretz* (Tel Aviv), January 21, 2021.

Hasson, Nir, and Jack Khouri. "Imutim partzu leyad sh'ar shkhem." *Haaretz* (Tel Aviv), April 17, 2021.

Hattis, Susan Lee. *The Bi-National Idea in Palestine During Mandatory Times*. Haifa: Shikmona, 1970.

Hatzfirah (Warsaw). "Ben-Yehuda beveit haasurim." January 14, 1894.

———. "Po, iha"k yerushalayim." October 31, 1877.

———. "Yediot mieretz yisrael." April 24, 1894.

———. "Yerushalayim." May 23, 1889.

———. "Zeh leumat zeh." December 27, 1893.

Hatzofeh (Tel Aviv). "Akhbar alyawm: Yisrael mevatsaat tokhnit alon." February 16, 1969.

———. "Kakh barhu shloshet hamistanenim mikele Ashkelon." April 20, 1964.

———. "Ma Merits." September 3, 1971.

Havatzelet (Jerusalem). "A"d [al devar] haisur leheahez bah"k [beeretz hakodesh]." July 4, 1884.

Hazan, Netta. "Ana yahudi: Kinun zehut mizrahit bemifgashim im falastinim." Master's thesis, Hebrew University of Jerusalem, 2014.

Hazkani, Shai. *Dear Palestine: A Social History of the 1948 War*. Stanford: Stanford University Press, 2021.

———. "Sipuro shel hadoh hahatrani al 'beayat hamizrahim' betzahal." *Musaf Haaretz* (Tel Aviv), August 12, 2015. https://www.haaretz.co.il/magazine/2015-08-12/ty-article/.premium/0000017f-e499-d568-ad7f-f7fb34600000.

Helman, Sara, and Tamar Rapoport. "'Elah nashim ashkenaziyot levad, zonot shel aravim, lo maaminot baelohim velo ohavot et eretz yisrael': Nashim beshahor vaetgar haseder hahevrati." *Teoria Uvikoret* 10 (Summer 1997): 175–92.

Herut (Tel Aviv). "Arabaat hatseirim yeshuhraru bekarov?" March 24, 1955.

Hillel, Shlomo. *Ruah kadim: Beshlihut mahtartit leartzot arav*. Tel Aviv: Yediot Aharonot and Ministry of Defense, 1985.

Horowitz, Moshe. "Hatzadik hakafri." *Koteret Rashit* (Tel Aviv), July 2, 1988.

Hroub, Khaled. "A Newer Hamas? The Revised Charter." *Journal of Palestine Studies* 46, no. 4 (2017): 6–27.

Jabotinsky, Ze'ev. "Hamizrah." In *Ekronot manhim livayot hashaah*, edited by Yosef Nedava, 90–96. Tel Aviv: Jabotinsky Institute, 1981.

Jacobson, Abigail. "Sephardim, Ashkenazim, and the Arab Question in Pre–First World War Palestine: A Reading of Three Zionist Newspapers." *Middle Eastern Studies* 39, no. 2 (2003): 105–30.

Jacobson, Abigail, and Moshe Naor. *Benei haaretz vehamizrah: Yehudim vaaravim bitkufat hamandat habriti*. Jerusalem: Van Leer, 2020.

Jewish Agency, Aliyah Department. *Aliyat yehudei moroko, 1962–1971*. Jerusalem: Jewish Agency, 1972.

Jonas, Shlomo. "Hannukah." *Hatzvi* (Jerusalem), December 18, 1908.

JTA Daily News Bulletin. "Research Group Warns of Problems Resulting from Peace with Arabs." November 10, 1978.

Juhayna [Emile Habibi]. "'Afn akkhitam." *Al-Ittihad* (Haifa), September 29, 1961.

Kabha, Mustafa. "Yehudim Mizrahim baitonut haaravit bisrael, 1948–1967." *Iyunim Bitkumat Yisra'el* 16 (2006): 445–61.

Kahanoff, Jacqueline. *Mimizrah shemesh*. Tel Aviv: Yariv and Hadar, 1978.

Katzenelson, K[alman]. *Hamahapekhah haashkenazit*. Tel Aviv: Anakh, 1964.

Kazzaz, Nissim. "Tziyonim vekomunistim beirak, 1941–1950." In *Hatziyonut umitnagdeha baam hayehudi*, edited by Haim Avni and Gideon Shimoni, 205–23. Jerusalem: Hasifriya Hatzionit, 1990.

Kedar, B. Z. *Im Nurit*. Jerusalem: Carmel, 2019.

Kenan, Amos. "Madua ulean boreah hashalom." *Yediot Aharonot* (Tel Aviv), February 24, 1978.

Khalidi, Walid. *From Haven to Conquest: Readings in Zionism and the Palestine Problem Until 1948*. Beirut: Institute for Palestine Studies, 1971.

Khatib, Amin al-. *Tadhakkurat*. Bir Zeit: n.p., 1992.

Khatib al-Tamimi, Anwar al-. *Ma salah a-din fi alquds*. Jerusalem: n.p., 1989.

Khazzoom, Aziza. *Shifting Ethnic Boundaries and Inequality in Israel: Or, How a Polish Peddler Became a German Intellectual*. Stanford: Stanford University Press, 2008.

———. "Tarbut maaravit, tiyug etni usgirut hevratit: Hareka lei-hashivyon haetni beyisrael." *Sotziologiyah Yisraelit* A, no. 2 (1999): 385–428.

Khuli, Lutfi al-. *Al-intifadah wal-dawla al-falastiniyya*. Cairo: Markaz al-Ahram, 1988.

———. "Nahwa jabha 'alimiyya." *Al-Ahram* (Cairo), June 14, 1968.

Kimmerling, Baruch. *Mehagrim, mityashvim, yalidim*. Tel Aviv: Alma and Am Oved, 2004.

Klein, Menachem. *Keshurim: Hasipur shel benei ha'aretz*. Tel Aviv: Hakibbutz Hameuhad, 2015.

Klibenski, Y. "Tsfat: Politikah aravit." *Hapoel Hatzair* (Jaffa), June 30, 1921.

Kol Haam (Tel Aviv). "Askanei mapam beramle meorerim hitnagshuyot." July 1, 1952.

———. "Batnuah." June 25, 1958.

———. "Metihut adatit gam beveit shemesh." July 21, 1959.

———. "Toshvei ramle haaravim tov'im piturei G. Dahan." October 31, 1960.

Kozłowska, Magdalena. "East Sees East: The Image of Jews from Islamic Countries in the Jewish Discourse of Interwar Poland." *Middle Eastern Studies* 54, no. 1 (2018): 114–27.

Krief, Moshe. *Hamizrahit: Sipurah shel hakeshet hademokratit vehamaavak hahevrati bisrael 1995–2005*. Rishon Lezion: Globes, 2005.

Lamerhav. (Tel Aviv). "Invey hazaam shel ramle." August 27, 1965.

Landau, Noa. "Netanyahu's Blind Faith in Force." *Haaretz* online, October 17, 2022. https://www.haaretz.com/opinion/2022-10-17/ty-article-opinion/.premium/netanyahus-blind-faith-in-force/00000183-e74d-d0ac-adc3-e7cdd7750000.

Lapidot, Yehuda. *Balahav hamered*. Jerusalem: self-published, 1936/37.

———. *Leidatah shek mahteret: Haetzel bishnot hashloshim*. Jerusalem: self-published, 2014.

Laskov, Shulamit, ed. *Ketavim letoldot hibat tziyon veyishuv eretz yisrael*. Vol. 1. Tel Aviv: Tel Aviv University, 1982.

Lavie, David. "'Kimat keein nasi': Hehakham bashi kidmut leumit baitonei Eliezer Ben-Yehuda." *Israel* 26 (2020): 21–46.

Lefkowitz, Daniel. "Constructing Affective Responses to Nationalistic Violence in Israel." *PoLAR: Political and Legal Anthropology Review* 18, no. 2 (1995): 105–18.

Leibowitz-Dar, Sara. "'Ani ashem baretsah bakfar duma': Hozrim lateroristim hayhudim." *Maariv* (Tel Aviv), August 14, 2015.

———. "Leyahadut hamizrah lo hayah tafkid behakamat hamedinah." *Makor Rishon* (Jerusalem), October 10, 2011. https://

www.makorrishon.co.il/nrg/online/47/ART2/294/414.html.

———. "Yonah Avrushmi: Bizkhuti hasmol hayisraeli neelam." *Maariv Sofshavua* (Tel Aviv), July 29, 2011.

Leon, Nissim. *Hamitznefet vehadegel: Leumiyut shekebeged baharadiyut hamizrahit*. Jerusalem: Van Leer, 2011/12.

———. "Harediyut mizrahit vehanativ hateo-etnokrati bisrael." In *Dat veleumiyut: Hanhagah vehagut yehudit basheelah haaravit*, edited by Ephraim Lavie, 259–82. Jerusalem: Carmel, 2016.

Lerer, Zeev. *Hakod haetni: Kab"a, mizrahim, ashkenazim*. Jerusalem: Van Leer, 2021.

Lev, Tali, and Yehouda Shenhav. "Al tikri poel ela panter: Hapanterim hashhorim vapolitikat hazehuyot bereshit shenot hashivim." *Teoria Uvikoret* 35 (Autumn 2009): 141–64.

———. "Kinuno shel haoyev mibifnim." *Sotsyologia Yisraelit* 12 (2010): 135–58.

Leven, Narcisse. *Hamishim shenot historiyah: KY"H*. Translated by Avraham Elmalih. Jerusalem: Alliance Israélite Universelle, 1921/22.

Levi, Ran, and Yair Fidel. "Ran Cohen niftza berosho." *Hadashot* (Tel Aviv), November 21, 1986.

Levinson, Rabbi Yaakov. "Aliyah le"y al-manat lashuv." *Ohr Hamizrach* 1, no. 1 (1963/64): 4–5.

Lev Tov, Boaz. "Shekhenim nokhehim: Kesharim tarbutiyim bein yehudim laaravim beeretz yisrael beshilhei hatkufaah haothomanit." *Zmanim* 110 (Spring 2010): 42–54.

Levy, Assaf. "Leidato shel baba dankner." *Walla*, September 8, 2000. https://news.walla.co.il/item/19422.

Levy, Shelly, and Jonathan Erlich. "Alimut politit mitzad yehudim bisrael." Jerusalem: Knesset Research and Information Center, August 17, 2005.

Levy, Yagil. *Mitzva haam litzva haperiferiyot*. Jerusalem: Carmel, 2007.

Levy, Yossi. "Aryeh Shlush lehokrav." *Maariv* (Tel Aviv), January 2, 1991.

Lewin-Epstein, Noah, and Moshe Semyonov. "Ethnic Group Mobility in the Israeli Labor Market." *American Sociological Review* 51, no. 3 (1986): 342–52.

Liebes, Tamar, and Shoshana Bloom-Kulka. "'Yorim uvokhim?' Al hahitmodedut im dilemot musariyot basherut hatzvai bashtahim." In *Hamilhamah hashviit: Hashpaot haintifadah al hahevrah bisrael*, edited by Reuven Gal, 85–105. Tel Aviv: Hakibbutz Hameuhad, 1990.

Litani, Yehuda, in conversation with Avishai Margalit. "Lo hayu li regaim shel 'laazazel haaravim haeleh.'" *Hadashot* (Tel Aviv), January 30, 1987.

Lockman, Zachary. *Contending Visions of the Middle East: The History and Politics of Orientalism*. Cambridge: Cambridge University Press, 2004.

Maariv (Tel Aviv). "Anu ahim utsrikhim lihyot yahad." November 26, 1986.

———. "Asarot niftzeu betigrot alimot bein yehudim vearavim berishon lesion." October 15, 1962.

———. "Ashkenazim kitsonim vesfaradim metunim." October 1, 1982.

———. "Asrot atsurim, hafganot lelo takdim." August 22, 1975.

———. "Asur levater al af shaal meadmata shel eretz Yisrael." October 27, 1967.

———. "Avi Deri yihye ed medina neged ahiv." April 10, 1984.

———. "Beako hayu hitnagshuyot bein yehudim learavim." September 24, 1961.

———. "Dani Sail hashud shekibel 12 elef l"i mehuliyat hamehablim behevron." June 9, 1975.

———. "Gal sinah umaasei nakam." October 16, 1962.

———. "5 toshavim meako hashudim besiyua le-6 hamehablim." December 3, 1969.

———. "Hamon niz'am beyafo takaf mekhoniyot." December 16, 1990.

———. "Hapanterim hit'u hamishtara vehashomrim." November 12, 1979.

———. "Hapanterim mehakim leashaf." March 25, 1975.

———. "Hashud behashlakhat bakbukei tavera al batei aravim hisgir et atsmo." February 6, 1987.

———. "Hayehudim shazru lamistanenim livroakh." April 20, 1964.

———. "H"K hizmin et Ben Shimol lamishkan." July 13, 1989.

———. "Im aravim lo yukhnesu liskhunat shmuel hanavi mi yenake otah?" November 24, 1986.

———. "Koakh mishtara gadol meavteakh et haravim." November 17, 1986.

———. "Kochavi Shemesh sheyatza be-1991 lemoskva lehabia hitnagduto lealiyah mirusya." January 8, 1991.

———. "'Lirtzoah et kulam' zaaku porim ahehitnaplu al toshavim aravim beramle." August 23, 1965.

———. "Maasar olam lesisha aravim yisraelim havrey huliyat hamehablim meako." June 1, 1970.

———. "Marokai mitbayesh bemarokai." October 28, 1980.

———. "'Mavet laaravim' shaagu yehudim." November 24, 1986.

———. "Meir Sheetrit: Hamishpaha halohemet hem hakitsoniyim yoter." July 29, 1988.

———. "Meir vilner vecharli bitton nivharu a"h hakol haaravi." May 25, 1977.

———. "Mishlahat shel hapanterim beparis menasa lehipagesh im netsig ashaf." March 19, 1975.

———. "Neetzra huliyat mehablim berahuto shel mitagref mitztayen lesheavar bebeitar." October 25, 1971.

———. "Nehira efsharit shel poalim mimitsraim vehashtahim leatarei bniya banegev tesaken et ayarot hapituah." April 9, 1979.

———. "Petzuim, atzurim, umoadon harus." May 2, 1952.

———. "3 Aravim niftseu behitnagshut halayla." October 16, 1962.

———. "Shisha aravim niftseu beotobus shehutkaf biriot." March 5, 1984.

———. "Talmid yeshiva neesham beahzakat homrei habala." September 22, 1987.

———. "Yehudim zoamin takfu shotrim vearavim." November 18, 1986.

———. "Yoman maariv, 'hamumei moah.'" July 10, 1989.

Magnarella, Paul A. "A Note on Aspects of Social Life Among the Jewish Kurds of Sandandaj, Iran." *Jewish Journal of Sociology* 11, no. 1 (1968): 51–58.

Magnes, Y[ehuda] L[eib]. "Sihah." In *Neged hateror*, edited by R. Binyamin and Yaacov Peterzil, 53–54. Jerusalem: n.p., 1939.

Mahlev, Dudi. "Ner zikaron ledoktor shlomo elbaz, mori verabi." *Haokets* online (Tel Aviv), September 9, 2003.

Mahzikei Hadat (Lvov). "Hadashot leveit Yisrael." September 11, 1908.

Man, Nir. "Meah shanim lelo yad vezekher." *Alei Zayit Vaherev* 14 (2003/4): 24–25.

Mandel, Neville J. *The Arabs and Zionism Before World War I*. Berkeley: University of California Press, 1976.

Mandel, Roy. "Harabi amar lehahzir shetahim." *Ynet* (Tel Aviv), October 11, 2013. https://www.ynet.co.il/articles/0,7340,L-4439266,00.html.

Mani, Menashe. "Edot hamizrah betel aviv." *Yediot Iriyat Tel Aviv*, September–October 1947, 22.

Marcus, Yoel. "Tzahorei hayom berishon letziyon." *Davar* (Tel Aviv), October 17, 1962.

Margalit, Dan. "Aklim stavi bishkhunat avivah." *Herut* (Tel Aviv), October 18, 1962.

———. "Dam batzel hatapuzim." *Herut* (Tel Aviv), October 17, 1962.

Marker (Tel Aviv). "Ma hoshvim Binyamin vesara Netanyahu al Mizrahim?" February 13, 2016.

———. "Nathan Eshel: Hatzibur halo Ashkenazi sone hakol." February 29, 2020.

Maruoma-Marom, Shoshana. "Meafyanei mediniyut harevahah biyisrael bishnot hahamishim vehashisim vehithavut shikhvot hametzukah hamizrahiyot." *Teoria Uvikoret* 26 (Spring 2010): 113–36.

Masalha, Nur. *Expulsion of the Palestinians: The Concept of "Transfer" in Zionist Political Thought*. Washington, DC: Institute for Palestine Studies, 2012.

Matalon, Ronit. "Shetei perspektivot: Kolot matrimim." In *Kolot Mizrahim: Likrat siah mizrahi hadash al hahevrah vehatarbut hayisraelit*, edited by Guy Abutbul, Lev Grinberg, and Pnina Motzafi-Haller, 28–35. Tel Aviv: Masada, 2005.

Mawasi, Farouk. *Arcs from My Autobiography*. June 27, 2021. https://alantologia.com/blogs/45874.

Mazor, Adi, and Tom Mehager. "Hereg hamehabel behevron: Tismonet hashin gimmel hamizrahi." *Haokets* (Tel Aviv), March 28, 2016. https://tinyurl.com/54jtr6e6.

Mazori, Dalia. "Shum hablan veshum katyusha lo yazizu otanu." *Maariv* (Tel Aviv), November 22, 1974.

Mazuz, Meir. "She'elot vetshuvot beinyanei simhat torah." JDN.co, October 20, 2016. https://www.jdn.co.il/beit_hamidrash/754248.

Meir-Glitzenstein, Esther. "Manhigut tziyonit vekomunistit bamivhan klitat olei irak bisrael." *Pe'amim* 101 (2014/15): 5–38.

Meiri, Doron. "Banu lepoh laharog aravim." *Hadashot* (Tel Aviv), August 8, 1990.

Middle East Eye. "Hamas in 2017: The Document in Full." May 2, 2017. https://www.middleeasteye.net/news/hamas-2017-document-full.

Milson, Menahem. "Pgishot bilti rishmiot im falastinim." *Kivunim Hadashim* 22 (June 2010): 112–23.

Mir'at al-Sharq (Jaffa). "Mawqif alyahud alwataniyyin." November 21, 1936.

Mizrachi, Nissim. "Sociology in the Garden: Beyond the Liberal Grammar of Contemporary Sociology." *Israel Studies Review* 31, no. 1 (2016): 36–65.

Moran, Meirav. "Sof Haolam Yamina." *Musaf Haaretz* (Tel Aviv), February 16, 2024.

Morris, Benny. *Leidatah shel beayat haplitim hafalastinim*. Tel Aviv: Am Oved, 1991.

———. "Mabat hadash al mismakhim tziyoniim merkaziim." In *Tikun taut*, 104–40. Tel Aviv: Am Oved, 2000.

———. *Milhamot hagvul shel yisrael, 1956–1959*. Tel Aviv: Am Oved, 1996.

Motzafi-Haller, Pnina. *Shehordiniyot*. Tel Aviv: Bavel, 2023.

———. "Siah intelektualim mizrahim: Hamaavak lekinun zehut, 1946–1950." In *Kolot Mizrahim: Likrat siah mizrahi hadash al hahevrah vehatarbut hayisraelit*, edited by Guy Abutbul, Lev Grinberg, and Pnina Motzafi-Haller, 70–78. Tel Aviv: Masada, 2005.

Moyal, Shimon. "Hitorerut." *Haherut* (Jerusalem), February 2, 1912.

Nadav, Yitzhak. *Zikhronot ish hashomer*. Recorded by Avraham Ovadiah. Edited by Yosef Tubi. Tel Aviv: Ministry of Defense, 1986.

Naeh, Buki, and Matti Cohen. "Hahamonim histaaru." *Hadashot* (Tel Aviv), May 25, 1992.

Nahon, Yaakov. *Defusei hitrahavut hahaskalah umivneh hizdamnuyot hataasukah: Hameimad haadati*. Jerusalem: Jerusalem Institute for Israel Studies, 1987.

Navon, Yitzhak. "Nasi uven adam." Interview by Hannah Semer. *Davar* (Tel Aviv), September 29, 1978, 17.

Nir, Yoel. "Zu haytah hafganah shel anashim shedarshu tzedek." *Herut* (Tel Aviv), July 28, 1959.

Nissan, Shai. "Hamiflagah hakomunistit hafalastinait 1936–1939." Master's thesis, Hebrew University of Jerusalem, 2014.

Noy, Amos. *Edim o mumhim: Yehudim maskilim benei yerushalayim vehamizrah bithilat hameah ha-20*. Tel Aviv: Resling, 2017.

———. "Keshemizrahim hayu moderna: Yitzugim lo oriyentalistim shel Mizrahim bisrael bishnot hahamishim vehashishim." In *Hahistoriyah haarukah shel hamizrahim: Kivunim hadashim baheker yehudei artzot haislam*, edited by Aviad Moreno, Noah Gerber, Esther Meir-Glitzenstein and Ofer Schiff, 127–44. Sde Boker: Ben-Gurion University of the Negev, 2021.

Noy, Orly. "Al hasidrah 'sinat mavet' shel ron Cahlili, sihah mekomit." *Local Conversation*, August 31, 2019. https://tinyurl.com/2p8s9xdh.

Nurieli, Benny. "Zarim bamerhav leumi: Hayehudim haaravim bageto belod, 1950–1959." *Teoria Uvikoret* 26 (Spring 2006): 13–42.

Oppenheimer, Yochai. "Ani palit aravi: Shirah politit mizrahit." In *Kol kore beoz: Politikah veshirah bisrael*, edited by Asaf Medani and Nadir Tzur, 85–107. Jerusalem: Israel Political Science Association, 2012.

———. "Od hozer hanigun baorkeikhem." *Pe'amim* 125–27 (2011): 377–407.

Osherov, Eli. "Beayat falastin, hasheelah hayehudit ufitronot politiyim nishkakhim: Nekudat hamabat haaravit, 1908–1948." PhD diss., Hebrew University of Jerusalem, 2021.

Oz, Amos. *Po vesham beertz yisrael bastav 1982*. Tel Aviv: Am Oved, 1983.

———. "Po vesham beertz yisrael, stav 1982." *Davar* (Tel Aviv), November 26, 1982.

Ozer, Yosef. *Emek yizrael yerushalayim*. Ramat Gan: Ilmur, 2013.

Peled, Alisa Rubin. "The Other Side of 1948: The Forgotten Benevolence of Bechor Shalom Shitrit and the Ministry of Foreign Affairs." *Israel Affairs* 8, no. 3 (2002): 84–103.

Peled, Yoav, and Gershon Shafir. *Mihu yisraeli: Hadinamikah shel ezrahut murkevet*. Tel Aviv: Tel Aviv University, 2005.

Peres, Yochanan. "Ethnic Relations in Israel." *American Journal of Sociology* 76, no. 6 (1971): 1021–47.

Peres, Yochanan, and Sara Shemer. "Hagorem haadati babhirot laknesset haasirit." *Megamot* 25 (1984): 316–31.

Picard, Avi. "Reishitah shel haaliyah haselektivit bishnot hahamishim." *Iyunim Bitkumat Yisra'el* 9 (1999): 338–94.

Pinsker, Y. L. *Auto-Emancipation*. English translation by D. S. Blondheim. New York: Federation of American Zionists, 1916. Available at https://www.jewishvirtuallibrary.org/quot-auto-emancipation-quot-leon-pinsker.

Piroyansky, Danna. *Ramle Remade: The Israelisation of an Arab Town, 1948–1967*. Haifa: Pardes, 2014.

Popular Front for the Liberation of Palestine. *Strategy for the Liberation of Palestine*. Utrecht: Foreign Language Press, 2017.

Qawuqji, Fawzi al-. "Memoirs, 1948 (Part 1)." *Journal of Palestine Studies* 1, no. 4 (1972): 27–58.

Rabin, Yitzhak. *Rodef shalom: Neumei hashalom shel yitzhak rabin*. Tel Aviv: Zmora Bitan, 1995.

Radai, Itamar. *Bein shetei arim: Haaravim hafalastinim biyrushlayim veyafo, 1947–1948*. Tel Aviv: Tel Aviv University, 2015.

———. "Yotzei artzot haislam—dimuim vetfisot bahevrah hayishuvit: Hamikreh shel Hannah Helena Thon." *Iyyunim* 32 (2019): 216–44.

Rajabi, Shehada al-. "Al-jaliyah al-Yahudiyah fi al-Khalil, 1917–1936: The Jewish Community in Hebron, 1917–1936." Master's thesis, An-Najah University, 2000.

Razi, Tammy. *Yaldei hahefker: Hehatzer haahorit shel Tel Aviv hamandatorit*. Tel Aviv: Am Oved and Sapir, 2009.

Rejwan, Nissim. *Israel's Years of Bogus Grandeur: From the Six-Day War to the First Intifada*. Austin: University of Texas Press, 2006.

Reshef, Tzali. *Shalom Akhshav*. Jerusalem: Keter, 1996.

Rimon Or, Anat. "Mimot haaravi ad 'mavet laaravim': Hayehudi hamoderni mul haaravi hahai betokho." *Teoria Uvikoret* 4 (Spring 2002): 23–57.

Roby, Bryan K. *The Mizrahi Era of Rebellion: Israel's Forgotten Civil Rights Struggle, 1948–1966*. Syracuse: Syracuse University Press, 2015.

Rofa-Opir, Sharon. "HC Zakkur: Lishmor al ha'aravim meavanim beyom kippur." *Ynet* (Tel Aviv), October 7, 2008. https://www.ynet.co.il/articles/0,7340,L-3606391,00.html.

Ro'i, Yaacov. "Nisyonotehem shel hamosdot hatziyoniyim lehashpiyah al haitonut haaravit beeretz yisrael bashanim 1908–1914." *Zion* 32 (1967): 201–27.

[Rokach, Eliezer]. "Lemoed moadim." *Havatzelet* (Jerusalem), September 23, 1885.

Romann, Michael, and Alex Weingrod. *Living Together Separately: Arabs and Jews in Contemporary Jerusalem*. Princeton: Princeton University Press, 1991.

Ronen, David. *Shenat shaba"k: Hahearkhut bihudah veshomron, shanah rishonah*. Tel Aviv: Ministry of Defense, 1989.

Rosenstein, Tzvi. *Toldot tenuat hapoalim beeretz yisrael*. 3 vols. Tel Aviv: Am Oved, 1955–66.

Rotbart, Lee. "Tokhnit horaat aravit bakibutzhim, 1939–1945." Manuscript.

Rouleau, Eric, and Nayef Hawatmeh. "PLO Shifting Currents." *Journal of Palestine Studies* 12, no. 2 (1983): 192–94.

Rubinstein, Amnon. "Laahar sheloshah yamim." *Haaretz* (Tel Aviv), April 14, 1974.

Rubinstein, Danny. "Boker tov." *Davar* (Tel Aviv), September 13, 1974.

———. "Dat umdinah bamatkonet falastinait." *Davar* (Tel Aviv), January 11, 1977.

Saadon, Haim. "'Hamarkiv hafalastini' behitpartzuyot alimot bein yehudim levein Muslimim baartzot haislam." *Pe'amim* 63 (1994/95): 86–131.

———. *Morocco*. Jerusalem: Ben-Zvi Institute, 2003.

Sakhnini, Issam. *Tabariyya: Taarikh mawsu'i.* Beirut: Arab Institute for Research and Publishing, 2009.

Sambari, Yosef. *Sefer divrei yosef: Elef umeah shenot toladah yehudit batzel Haislam.* Jerusalem: Ben-Zvi Institute, 1993/94.

Saragusti, Anat. "Arbaah yamim betoledo." *Haolam Hazeh* (Tel Aviv), July 12, 1989.

Sarna, Igal. *Ed medinah.* Tel Aviv: Am Oved, Xargol, 1992.

Sasson, Eliyahu. "Bayna alsefaradim walashkenazim." Op-ed. *Al-'Alam al-Isra'ili* (Beirut), December 22, 1927.

Sasson-Levy, Orna. "'Ani ashkenazi, hahorim sheli lo roim et atzmam kekaeleh': Hevdelim bein doriim bitfisot shel ashkenaziyut." In *Marei makom: Zehuyot mishtanot umikumim hevratiyim bisrael,* edited by Zeev Shavit, Orna Sasson-Levy, and Guy Porat, 149–78. Jerusalem: Van Leer, 2013.

Sayigh, Yezid. *Armed Struggle and the Search for State: The Palestinian National Movement, 1949–1993.* Oxford: Clarendon Press, 1997.

Schlossberg, Eliezer. "Yahaso shel harambam el haislam." *Pe'amim* 42 (1990): 38–60.

Segev, Tom. *1949: Hayisraelim harishonim.* Jerusalem: Domino, 1984.

———. *Hamilyon hashvii: Yisraelim vehashoah.* Jerusalem: Keter, 1991.

———. *Medinah bekhol mahir: Sippur hayav shel David Ben-Gurion.* Ben Shemen: Keter, 2018.

———. *A State at Any Cost: The Life of David Ben-Gurion.* Translated by Haim Watzman. New York: Farrar, Straus and Giroux, 2019.

Serri, Bracha. *Shivi'im shirei shotetut.* Jerusalem: self-published, 1983.

Shabtai, K. [Shabtai Klugman]. "Hamapalah beramla." *Davar* (Tel Aviv), August 27, 1965.

Shadmi, Nahum. *Kav yashar bamaagal hahayim.* Tel Aviv: Ministry of Defense, 1995.

Shaib-Lerer, Oshra. "Hafarhud kefi shesiper li avi." Mizrahi Democratic Rainbow. December 17, 2020. https://www.facebook.com/hakeshet/posts/pfbid02y95vWHVurpnBdZHgyqiruonbPm9Lvun7ptDcxgaRdRssfqxDpiwcevgHK3Mdero7l.

Shapira, Avraham. "7 yehudim neetzru beta'ana sheyidu avanim." *Hakol Hayehudi* (Jerusalem), September 24, 2015. https://tinyurl.com/fkb9da2d.

Sharabi, Rachel. "Hitbadlut edot hamizrah mihaedah hasefaradit." *Pe'amim* 21 (1984): 31–49.

Sharoni, Avraham. *Kor hahitukh: Yomano haneelam shel Avraham Sharoni.* Edited by Nahem Ilan. Jerusalem: Carmel, 2020.

Shavit, Yaacov. "Hairgun hapoliti vehatziburi shel hayishuv hayehudi." In *Hahistoriyah shel eretz yisrael,* edited by Yehoshua Porath and Yaacov Shavit, 9:174–93. Jerusalem: Keter and Yad Ben Zvi, 1982.

Sheffer Raviv, Omri. "Mioyev leohev: Hadiyun hatziburi bisrael beasher lashimush bekoah tzvaei neged ukhlusiyat hagadah hamaaravit, 1965–1969." *Cathedra* 163 (2016/17): 105–30.

———. "Reshitah vehitgabshutah shel hashlitah hayisraelit al haukhlusiyah hafalastinit bagadah hamaaravit uvertzuat azah, 1967–1969." PhD diss., Hebrew University of Jerusalem, 2019.

Shenhav, Yehouda. *Hayehudim haaravim: Leumiyut, dam, vaetniyut.* Tel Aviv: Am Oved, 2004.

———. "Shimon balas haya haav haruhani shel hasmol hamizrahi." *Haaretz Tarbut Vesifrut* (Tel Aviv), October 3, 2019.

Shenhav-Shaharabani, Yehouda. "Mifgash mukdam umeuhar im haav haruhani shel hasmol hamizrahi." *Haaretz Tarbut Vesifrut,* October 3, 2019.

Shilo, Margalit. "Mitfisat 'moshavtit' litfisah yishuvit klalit." *Zion* 57 (1992): 73–74.

Shimoni, Ran. "Beit knesset a"sh kahane, 10 neeshamim bitkifat aravim ushkhunat Meriva ahat." *Haaretz* (Tel Aviv), February 14, 2022.

Shipler, David K. "Israel Bars Rabin from Relating '48 Eviction of Arabs." *New York Times,* October 23, 1979.

Shiran, Vicki. "Lefaaneah et hakoah—Livro olam hadash." In *Laahoti: Politikah feministit mizrahit,* edited by Shlomit Lir, 25–39. Rishon Lezion: Globes, 2005.

Shohat, Ella. "Hamizrahim bisrael: Hatziyonut minkudat mabatam shel korbanoteha hayehudim." In *Zikhronot asurim,* 140–205. Tel Aviv: Kedem, 2001.

———. "The Invention of the Mizrahim." *Journal of Palestine Studies* 29, no. 1 (1999): 5–20.

Shragai, Nadav. *Har hamerivah*. Jerusalem: Keter, 1995.

Shukeiri, Ahmad. *Arba'un aaman fi al-hayah al-'arabiyyah wa'al-dawliyyah*. Beirut: Dar al-Nahar, 1973.

Shuster-Eliassi, Noam. "'Hetzi-hetzi': Barukh asani homah." *Haokets* (Tel Aviv), July 15, 2016.

Sil, Batrik. "Hal yanjah uthaqifu isra'il fi fard alsalam 'ala bighin." *Al-Ahram* (Cairo), January 24, 1983.

Simons, Chaim. *A Historical Survey of Proposals to Transfer Arabs from Palestine, 1895–1947*. Kiryat Arba: self-published, 2004.

Siton, Rafi, and Yitzhak Shoshan. *Anshei hasod vehaseter*. Tel Aviv: Yediot Aharonot, 1990.

Slann, Martin. "Jewish Ethnicity and the Integration of an Arab Minority in Israel: A Study of the Jerusalem Incorporation." *Human Relations* 26, no. 3 (1973): 359–70.

Slutsky, Yehuda. *Sefer Toldot Hahaganah*. Vol. 2. Tel Aviv: Ma'arachot, 1963.

Smooha, Sammy. "Adatiyut vetzava bisrael: Teizot lemehkar vediyun." *Medinah, Mimshal, Vayahasim Beinleumiim* 22 (1984): 5–32.

———. "Shesaim maamadiyim, adatiyim, veleumiyim vedemodratiyah bisrael." In *Hahevrah hayisraelit: Hebetim bikortiyim*, edited by Uri Ram, 171–202. Tel Aviv: Brerot, 1993.

Sofer, Moshe. "Orot utzlalim." *Kol Yotzei Iraq Bisrael* 28 (September 1952): 3.

Sorek, Tamir, and Alin M. Ceobanu. "Benjamin Netanyahu as a Mobilizing Symbol in Ethno-Class Divisions Among Jewish Israelis, 2009–2021." *Ethnic and Racial Studies* 45, no. 10 (2021): 1961–82.

Sprinzak, Ehud. *The Ascendance of Israel's Radical Right*. New York: Oxford University Press, 1991.

Stern, Gabriel. "Ezra ushihada mehadshim yedidut." *Al Hamishmar* (Tel Aviv), June 23, 1967.

———. "Hayitzug hanakhon." *Al Hamishmar* (Tel Aviv), December 4, 1962.

———. "Kasheh lihiyot . . . adam." *Al Hamishmar* (Tel Aviv), October 22, 1962.

Swirski, Shlomo. "Mizrahim ufalastinim." In *Al shivyion veal milhama*, edited by Shlomo Swirski and Asher Idan, 6–8. Haifa: Yated, 1984.

Swirski, Shlomo, and Deborah Bernstein. "Mi avad bemah, avur mi utmurat mah? Hapituah hakakali shel yisrael vehithavum halukat haavodah haadatit." *Mahbarot Lemehkar Velabikoret* 4 (1980): 5–66.

Szekely, Yaffa. "Parashah alumah mipeiluto hatziburit shel harav Maklouf Eldaoudi, hakham bashi shel ako vehayfah: Teudah mueret." *Cathedra* 109 (September 2003): 139–60.

Talmi, Menahem. "Takrit netanyah: Akhbar sheholid har." *Maariv* (Tel Aviv), February 4, 1966.

Tamer, Mustafa Effendi. "Al'isti'mar alsuhyuni." *Filastin* (Jaffa), July 22, 1911.

Tawiow, Israel Haim. *Otzar hashirah vehamelitzah*. Tel Aviv: Dvir, 1929.

Tessler, Mark. "The Intifada and Political Discourse in Israel." *Journal of Palestine Studies* 19 (1990): 43–61.

Thon, Hannah. "Hinukh edot hamizrah." In *Neged hateror*, edited by R. Binyamin and Yaacov Peterzil, 46–49. Jerusalem: n.p., 1939.

Tivoni, Shlomo. *Kerem haya leyedidi: Musah alful*. Tel Aviv: Hakibbutz Hameuhad, 1977/78.

Toubul, Ophir. "Brit hametunim mishnei hatzdadim." *Israel Hayom* (Tel Aviv), November 10, 2020.

———. "Haasafsuf meshalem: Elor azariah, korban haneorut." *Makor Rishon* (Jerusalem), January 5, 2017. https://www.makorrishon.co.il/nrg/online/1/ART2/855/556.html.

———, ed. *Kol hator: Tziyonut masortit-sepharadit*. Tel Aviv: Miskal, 2021.

Tsur, Yaron. "Eimat hakarnival: 'Hamorokanim' vehatmurah babeayah haadatit bisrael hatzeirah." *Alpayim* 19 (2000): 126–64.

———. "Hahistoriografiyah hayisraelit vehabeayah haadatit." *Pe'amim* 94–95 (2002–3): 7–57.

———. *Kehilah kruyah: Yehudei moroko vehaleumiyut, 1943–1954*. Tel Aviv: Tel Aviv University and Am Oved, 2001.

Tubi Taharlev, Itamar. "Mihahathalah ani sholel et zeh barosh: Haslalah rigshit shel

Mizrahim baperiferiyah hayisraelit." *Teoria Uvikoret* 54 (Summer 2021): 149–61.

Tzadkoni, Dani. "Mesibat hahozrim bitshuvah." *Davar* (Tel Aviv), September 18, 1980.

Tzameret, Tzvi. "Zalman Aran vehaproduktivizatziyah shel benei 'edot hamizrah.'" In *Hevrah vakalkalah bisrael: Mabat histori veakhshavi*, edited by Avi Bareli, Daniel Gutwein, and Tuvia Friling, 295–326. Jerusalem: Yad Ben-Zvi, 2005.

Tzarum, Nahman. "Teshuvah lemoetzet poalei yerushalayim." *Doar Hayom* (Jerusalem), March 4, 1928.

Tzedaka, Shaul. "Az ma 'haavodah' hazot lakhem." *Davar* (Tel Aviv), April 22, 1983.

Vinitzky, Moshe. "Shekhunat hatikvah saarah bamehumot." *Maariv* (Tel Aviv), September 24, 1961.

Waksman, Yosef. "David Levy: Hakol soldim min hamaaseh hamevish." *Maariv* (Tel Aviv), November 21, 1974.

Walla. "Beyom Kippur: Yiduyei avanim birushalayim." September 26, 2012. https://news.walla.co.il/item/2570642.

Weiss, Efrat, and Sharon Rofe. "Karagil: Teunot ve-yiduyei Avanim beyom kippur." *Ynet* (Tel Aviv), September 27, 2001. https://www.ynet.co.il/articles/0,7340,L-1154089,00.html.

Weiss, Yfaat. *Wadi Salib: Hanokhah vehanifkad*. Tel Aviv: Hakibbutz Hameuhad, 2007.

Yahuda, A. Sh. "Yahaso shel Herzl labeaya haaravit." *Hed Hamizrah: Biton Hayahadut Hasefaradit* (Jerusalem), October 7, 1949.

Yediot Aharonot (Tel Aviv). "Hakriot 'Mavet laaravim' hithalfu be' mavet lashotrim." May 28, 1992.

———. "Hamahapekhah haashkenazit matzah et mekadmeiha." June 5, 1964.

———. "Hawatmeh menamek." May 19, 1974.

———. "Mimun mishlahat hapanterim al ydei tnuot smolaniot." July 14, 1971.

Yehoshua-Raz, Ben Zion. "Ahavat tziyon vatziyonut bekerev yehudei afganistan." In *Yuvalei ahavah: Kovetz zikaron leyuval heiman hy"d*, edited by Yosef Yuval Tubi, Shmue Glick, and Rina Levine Melamed, 4. Jerusalem: Heiman Family, 2007.

Yerushalmi, Shalom. "Baba Matsia." *Kol Hair* (Jerusalem), January 26, 1990.

Yifrach, Yehuda. "Lasim sof laashkenaziyut haelitistit batziyonut hadatit." *Makor Rishon* (Jerusalem), November 30, 2014. https://www.makorrishon.co.il/nrg/online/11/ART2/651/724.html.

Yishai, Sarit. "Mihu dani sail?" *Haolam Hazeh* (Tel Aviv), May 28, 1975, 22–24.

Yizrael, Rami. "Tyutah shel kol kore meet yoel moshe Solomon." *Cathedra* 10 (1979): 177–94.

Yona, Lihi, and Itamar Mann. "Hamotziim lapoal: Mizrahim vaalimut ribonit bisrael." *Mishpat Uminhal* 23 (2020/21): 59–110. https://law.haifa.ac.il/wp-content/uploads/2021/11/LYIM.pdf.

Yonah, Yossi, and Ishaq Saporta. "Hahinukh hakdam-miktzoi vitzirat maamad hapoalim bisrael." In *Mizrahim bisrael: Iyun bikorti mehudash*, edited by Hanan Hever, Yehouda Shenhav, and Pnina Motzafi-Haller, 68–104. Jerusalem: Van Leer, 2002.

Younis, Hamza. *Al-hurub min sijn ramle*. N.p.: n.p., 1999.

Zakbach, Efrat. "Peulat hanakam shel Meir Har-Zion: Metziyut vazikaron." *Israel* 21 (2003): 37–59.

Zarhin, Tomer. "Nisgar hatik neged harav shekara limnoa mekhirat dirot laaravim." *Haaretz* (Tel Aviv), July 8, 2012.

Zayit, Avigayil. "Lo darkenu." *Makor Rishon* (Jerusalem), November 25, 2020. https://www.makorrishon.co.il/opinion/286043/.

Zevuluni, Noah. "Neturei Karta: Haretsah hino pri hitgarut." *Davar* (Tel Aviv), November 17, 1986.

Zinger, Tzvi. "Medurot anak huvaru." *Maariv* (Tel Aviv), November 21, 1979.

Zohar, Zvi. "Haapalah vealiyah b' misuryah bishnot haarbaim: Tovanot vehirhurim." *Pe'amim* 66 (1996): 43–69.

Zonder, Moshe. *Sayeret matka"l*. Jerusalem: Keter, 2000.

INDEX

Notes
Arabic surnames prefixed by *al* or *el* (the) are alphabetized under the element following the particle (e.g. Khatib, Amin al-). Hebrew names might appear in different English transliterations, based on the way their holders write them in English (e.g., Biton and Bitton).